1855 FIRST KINDERGARTEN IN THE UNITED STATES ORGANIZED AT WATERTOWN, WISCONSIN

1857 NATIONAL TEACHERS ASSOCIATION FORMED, LATER BECOMING THE NATIONAL EDUCATION ASSOCIATION

1862 MORRILL ACT, CREATING FEDERALLY SUPPORTED LAND-GRANT COLLEGES, SIGNED BY PRESIDENT LINCOLN

1867 NATIONAL DEPARTMENT OF EDUCATION CREATED BY CONGRESS, LATER BECOMING THE U.S. OFFICE OF EDUCATION

1873 FIRST PERMANENT PUBLIC KINDERGARTEN ESTABLISHED AS PART OF THE ST. LOUIS PUBLIC SCHOOL SYSTEM

1874 TAXATION FOR SECONDARY SCHOOLS UPHELD BY THE MICHIGAN SUPREME COURT IN THE KALAMAZOO CASE

1876 FIRST GRADUATE WORK BEGUN AT JOHNS HOPKINS UNIVERSITY

1898 NATIONAL CONGRESS OF MOTHERS (NOW NATIONAL CONGRESS OF PARENTS AND TEACHERS) ORGANIZED

1900 ASSOCIATION OF AMERICAN UNIVERSITIES ORGANIZED

1902 FIRST PUBLIC JUNIOR COLLEGE ORGANIZED AT JOLIET, ILLINOIS

1910 FIRST PUBLIC JUNIOR HIGH SCHOOLS OPENED IN BERKELEY, CALIFORNIA, AND COLUMBUS, OHIO

1916 MEASUREMENT OF INTELLIGENCE BEGUN BY LEWIS TERMAN

1916 AMERICAN FEDERATION OF TEACHERS ORGANIZED AS AFFILIATE OF THE AMERICAN FEDERATION OF LABOR

1917 FEDERAL ASSISTANCE FOR VOCATIONAL EDUCATION PROVIDED THROUGH SMITH-HUGHES ACT

1917 AMERICAN ASSOCIATION OF TEACHERS COLLEGES ORGANIZED, LATER MERGED IN THE AMERICAN ASSOCIATION OF COLLEGES FOR TEACHER EDUCATION

1918 COMPULSORY EDUCATION MADE EFFECTIVE LEGALLY IN ALL STATES

1918 PROGRESSIVE EDUCATION ASSOCIATION FORMED AS AN OUTGROWTH OF THE PROGRESSIVE MOVEMENT IN AMERICAN EDUCATION

1919 FIRST PERMANENT NURSERY SCHOOL OPENED

1920 FEDERAL-STATE COOPERATION IN VOCATIONAL REHABILITATION EDUCATION INITIATED BY SMITH-BANKHEAD ACT

1923 WORLD FEDERATION OF EDUCATION ASSOCIATIONS, FORERUNNER OF WORLD CONFEDERATION OF ORGANIZATIONS OF THE TEACHING PROFESSION, ORGANIZED

1925 OREGON DECISION RENDERED BY THE U.S. SUPREME COURT, STATING THAT CHILDREN OF COMPULSORY SCHOOL AGE CANNOT BE REQUIRED TO ATTEND PUBLIC SCHOOLS

1936 SCHOOL LUNCH PROGRAM AND OTHER EMERGENCY GRANTS INITIATED BY THE CONGRESS DURING THE DEPRESSION

1941 EIGHT-YEAR STUDY PUBLISHED, DOCUMENTING EFFECTIVENESS OF PROGRESSIVE EDUCATION

1944 FIRST GI BILL FOR VETERANS' EDUCATION PASSED BY CONGRESS

1946 MEMBERSHIP OF UNITED STATES IN UNITED NATIONS EDUCATIONAL, SCIENTIFIC AND CULTURAL ORGANIZATION (UNESCO) APPROVED BY CONGRESS

1946 FULBRIGHT PROGRAM FOR INTERNATIONAL EXCHANGES APPROVED BY CONGRESS

1948 SMITH-MUNDT ACT FOR GLOBAL PROGRAM "IN INFORMATION AND EDUCATIONAL EXCHANGES" APPROVED BY CONGRESS

1948, 1949 McCOLLUM AND ZORACH DECISIONS OF U.S. SUPREME COURT RENDERED ON RELIGIOUS INSTRUCTION IN PUBLIC SCHOOLS

1950 NATIONAL SCIENCE FOUNDATION CREATED BY CONGRESS "FOR THE PROMOTION OF BASIC RESEARCH AND EDUCATION IN THE SCIENCES"

This calendar of Historical Highlights of American Education is continued on the inside of the back cover.

American Education

American Education

Eighth Edition

Richard Wynn
University of Pittsburgh

Chris A. De Young
(deceased)
Illinois State University

Joanne Lindsay Wynn
Formerly, University of Pittsburgh

McGraw-Hill Book Company

New York St. Louis San Francisco Auckland Bogotá
Düsseldorf Johannesburg London Madrid Mexico
Montreal New Delhi Panama Paris São Paulo
Singapore Sydney Tokyo Toronto

AMERICAN EDUCATION

3 4 5 6 7 8 9 0 DODO 7 8 3 2 1 0 9 8

Library of Congress Cataloging in Publication Data

Wynn, Dale Richard, date
    American Education.

    First–3d editions by C. A. De Young, published under title: Introduction to American public education; 4th–7th editions by C. A. De Young and R. Wynn, under title: American education.
    Includes bibliographies and index.
    1. Education—United States. I. Wynn, Joanne Lindsay, joint author. II. De Young, Chris Anthony, date   Introduction to American public education. III. Title.
LA210.D45 1977   370′.973   76-23390
ISBN 0-07-072208-0

This book was set in Helvetica by Textbook Services, Inc.
The editors were Stephen D. Dragin, Cheryl Mehalik, and Phyllis T. Dulan;
the cover was designed by Ben Kann;
the production supervisor was Joe Campanella.
New drawings were done by B. Handelman Associates, Inc.
R. R. Donnelley & Sons Company was printer and binder.

CREDITS FOR PHOTOGRAPHS

to

Sherry and Gibby

Lee Anne and Jeff

Rachel

Contents

Preface

Educating people of all ages both in and out of school is the major enterprise of most civilizations. In the United States, education is the major occupation of approximately 60 million people and more than three of every ten people are directly involved in educational work. Approximately $100 billion is spent annually on educational enterprises.

Because education pervades so much of American life, perhaps the surest way to understand its people—their aspirations, dilemmas, and values—is to study their educational endeavor. This book is addressed to all who would seek deeper understanding of American education—undergraduate and graduate students, teachers, supervisors, administrators, school board members, other educators and citizens.

Originally created in 1942 by our deceased coauthor, Chris De Young, this book, we believe, has remained in print continuously over a longer period of time than any other book on the subject. This eighth edition is the culmination of more than a third of a century of intensive evaluation of the book in colleges and universities across the land and in many countries abroad.

This edition is a thorough revision of the book. The pace of change in educational thought and practice is so rapid that it could not be otherwise. The historical, philosophical, social, and psychological foundations of each chapter have been brought up to date. Contemporary developments in educational programs and practices have been added. More attention has been given to the future of educational development because of the compelling necessity to look ahead in a world so beleaguered by fateful problems and perplexing choices. As Galsworthy warned, "If you do not think about the future, you cannot have one." Figures, tables, pictures, and other illustrative material have been updated to reveal the current educational scene.

The book's revision has been shaped by the authors' own experience in several decades of teaching and administrative experience at all levels of education, the considered judgment of countless other educators who have participated in surveys of the book's utility conducted by the publisher, and the critical comment of expert reviewers, particularly David Engel, Samuel Francis, Paul Masoner, Leslie Marietta, Maxine Roberts, Warren Shepler, Seth Spaulding, Godfrey Stevens, and John Trump. The entire list of people who have helped to improve the book is far too long for reproduction here. Nevertheless we are deeply indebted to them all, although we must accept full responsibility for the opinions and any errors in the pages which follow.

It is entirely appropriate that our deceased coauthor's name, Chris De Young, appear on the cover and title page. Although it has been revised extensively since the last edition which he helped to write, this book reflects much of his rare insight and rich philosophy. Moreover, he was a dear friend and professional partner whose inspiration still permeates our endeavor as it does thousands of his other colleagues and students around the world. He undertook the authorship of this book, as he did all of his work, with rare diligence, scholarship, and literary style. He had a love affair with all humanity, and we loved him dearly. He was truly a world citizen, fluent in many languages and a teacher of teachers in many lands. We are proud that his name is still associated with ours in this work.

If this new edition enriches the reader's understanding of American education and helps him or her to contribute to the improvement of the human condition through education, then our labors will have been well expended and Chris De Young's rich legacy reinvested.

Suggestions to the reader

Each chapter of this book begins with a section titled "You will have mastered this chapter when you can. . . ." This is intended to help you focus on the most important concepts in each chapter. They can serve as checklists to help you review each chapter. Examinations may emphasize your mastery of these objectives. Generous use has been made of footnotes and bibliographies to guide your further study of materials that may be of interest to you. The suggested activities at the end of each chapter may help prompt your study of matters of interest to you. You should also be aware of the Glossary at the end of the book, which defines many concepts that may not be familiar. It will be a helpful source of review for examinations. The many headings throughout the chapters will help you locate major themes and will be helpful in your review. We have prepared a very extensive index to help you locate easily any material within the broad scope of the book.

We hope that the study of this book will be a bracing and rewarding educational adventure.

Richard Wynn
Joanne Lindsay Wynn

American Education

Chapter 1
Criticism and issues in education

Criticism and educational progress: an uneasy alliance

It is instructive to begin a discussion of American education with an examination of some fateful issues and criticisms buffeting our schools. Criticism is the lifeblood of free societies and the best antidote for dogmatism and complacency. Macaulay, the great English historian, observed that people are "never so likely to settle a question rightly, as when they discuss it freely." Criticism is so essential to our democratic society that its preservation is guaranteed by the First Amendment to the Constitution.

Criticism, if honest and responsible, causes open-minded people to reexamine assumptions, reconsider goals, gather and evaluate evidence, consider alternatives, and view problems anew. Through these processes of rational inquiry, educational policies and practices are reassessed and often improved.

Criticism of education has become almost a national pastime. Few, if any, institutions of American life are subject to as careful scrutiny and intensive criticism as the schools. Some of this criticism is justified; however, we later shall argue that much of it is quixotic, contradictory, exaggerated, impressionistic, and without intellectual foundation. Such criticism contributes little to educational progress and, in the minds of many, exacerbates the malaise in our educational enterprise. As former U.S. Commissioner of Education Sidney Marland has warned, "We have reached that point in time when further nonconstructive criticism of our educational system is no longer in any sense, or for any purpose, useful."

THE NATURE OF CRITICISM OF EDUCATION

Education becomes the target of intense public criticism for three compelling reasons. First, schools serve society's most vital legacy, its children. Second, education is regarded as a critical force in improving the human condition. Third, education is very expensive, representing by far the largest single public expenditure in most communities. Let us examine briefly the nature of current criticism of education.

Some criticism is justified; some is quixotic and contradictory. Almost any allegation against the schools can be demonstrated somewhere. There are students who cannot read, curriculums that are irrelevant to the needs of students, teachers who cannot teach, and schools that are poorly administered. The gap between what is and what could be in our schools is great. Reasonable people easily disagree about the dimension of this gap. They also disagree about what should be. Like most public institutions, schools have been slow to respond to social change. Many schools have neither formulated their goals nor measured their progress very carefully.

Americans reverse priorities in education with bewildering frequency. The dramatic appearance of Sputnik in 1957 nearly triggered national hysteria that we were faltering dangerously in our defense posture. Incredibly, Rickover, Conant, and others concluded that our schools were to blame.[1] (Curiously, when our space effort later surpassed the Soviet Union's, no one insisted that the schools take the credit.) The critics argued that schools must concentrate rigorously on cognitive learning—particularly in mathematics, science, and foreign languages—to strengthen our defense posture. In 1949, Conant, in his book *Education in a Divided World,* had expressed the worry that we might educate too many scientists and engineers. But a decade later, after Sputnik, he was covering the country trying to find out why we were not turning out more.

The tough curriculum that Conant prescribed in the late 1950s, which many schools adopted, became an almost perfect target for much that later romantic critics—Goodman, Friedenberg, Kozol, and others—despised in the 1960s. The civil rights movement, the Great Society, our concern for the poor and for minority groups, and the courts' insistence on equal rights all changed our educational priorities from elitism to egalitarianism. Yet Conant

was strangely silent. The schools, we were told, must become pleasant, not difficult; humane, not rigorous; child-centered, not subject-centered; and affective, rather than exclusively cognitive. The romantic critics argued that undue emphasis on subject matter and academic rigor destroys the intrinsic adventure of learning by crippling natural interest and curiosity in learners. These new critics rediscovered Rousseau and Dewey, who had been denounced by proponents of the tough curriculum. Thus the pendulum of reform reverses itself inexorably. Few reforms are given the time to be achieved or are adequately evaluated. The schools are asked to change direction suddenly and completely and then are excoriated for having moved in another direction in the first place.

Then, too, many critics contradict the fundamental interests of the populace, who pay the bills and supply the clientele. For example, many critics—among them Holt, Silberman, Kozol, Dennison, Goodman, Friedenberg—were calling for a relaxation of the regimen of the schools and for granting more freedom to learners in the open schools they advocated. But a Gallup poll of public opinion revealed that the most important problem in schools, in the minds of the general public, was not lack of freedom but its opposite—discipline. While the romantic critics were insisting that schools were dreary and unhappy places for students, the students' views, as documented in Chapter 3, were diametrically opposed. Although their comments are quixotic and contradict the public mood, the critics come and go undaunted.

Some criticism is exaggerated; some is impressionistic. Critics of education are often gifted in hyperbole. Consider the titles of some recent books and articles: *Murder in the Classroom; Our Children Are Dying; They Die So Young; Death at an Early Age; Requiem for Urban Schools; American Education: A National Failure.* Some accused the schools of "the annihilation of the human spirit," "the processing of juveniles for the military-industrial complex," and "the deliberate frustration of real learning." Sometimes the hyperbole was tempered with the gratuitous confession that some few schools were exceptions.

This almost endemic exaggeration of the shortcomings of schools, which characterizes the writings of so many popular critics (and certainly helps to sell their books), is mentioned here not to

---

[1]See, for example, Hyman G. Rickover, *American Education: A National Failure,* Dutton, New York, 1963.

disparage the legitimacy of well-reasoned criticism, but to protest journalistic overkill. Conant *(The American High School Today)* and Silberman *(Crisis in the Classroom)* drew conclusions about education from visits to schools across the nation, but their data were largely impressionistic and soft. And Illich *(Deschooling Society)* gathered impressions of American schooling from his office in Mexico. Such conclusions and impressions are often inaccurate and therefore, hazardous.

Over the years, butchers, bakers, and submarine makers have written and spoken freely about the failure of our schools. Yet, our students' achievement—in comparison with the achievement of students in other highly advanced cultures—has been exemplary, as noted later. Criticism without intellectual roots borders on charlatanism. This may explain in part why criticism of education has diverged so often from the attitudes of teachers, parents, and students. Other critics, however—notably Holt, Kozol, and Herndon—were practicing teachers, and their observations merit attention.[2]

Much criticism is negativistic. Many critics are more expansive about what they detest in schools than about what they would treasure. Gross,[3] for example, summarizes ten principles on which the radical reformers stand. Seven of them specify arrangements that must be "abolished," "thrown out," or "broken"; only three suggest positive alternatives. Illich[4] argues that schools are beyond redemption and that society must be "deschooled," a proposal which, predictably, has not been taken seriously. Wilson Riles, Superintendent of Public Instruction in California, sounded the appropriate rejoinder for the polemics of the negativists when he said: "We've had plenty of criticism. We recognize the enormous problems; now we need help. The next writer of a book criticizing education will be invited to come to my office with a workable plan, and to go into the classroom and demonstrate it."

[2]See John Holt, *How Children Fail,* Pitman, New York, 1964; Jonathan Kozol, *Death at an Early Age,* Houghton Mifflin, Boston, 1967; and James Herndon, *The Way It Spozed to Be,* Simon & Schuster, New York, 1965.

[3]Ronald Gross, "From Innovation to Alternatives: A Decade of Change in Education," *Phi Delta Kappan,* September 1971, pp. 22–24.

[4]Ivan Illich, *Deschooling Society,* Harper & Row, New York, 1971.

Criticism as self-fulfilling prophecy. As we emphasized earlier, criticism is the lifeblood of reform in a free society. But unreasoned or exaggerated criticism can be dysfunctional. If students are told often enough that their schools are failures, they can lose all expectation of success in learning. The prophecy of failure then becomes preordained, and reform becomes more difficult. Bayard Rustin, Executive Director of the A. Philip Randolph Institute, noted that much radical reformers' criticism is counterproductive:

I find many of the arguments superficial, unconvincing, and, in many cases, profoundly reactionary. To insist, as some have, that the schools have totally failed the black child is more than simply inaccurate; it makes attainment of true reform that much more difficult. . . . From our point of view, we may soon find that it is not the schools but their misguided critics who are irrelevant.[5]

Educational reformers truly interested in improving schools would do well to practice the physician's first imperative: First, do no harm.

The major issues and problems. It is impossible within one chapter—indeed, within one volume—to deal fully with the many issues in education. We have chosen for discussion in this chapter several more important and pervasive ones. The following chapters will treat many more particularized issues. Figure 1-1 reveals the major problems confronting the schools according to a recent public opinion poll.

Education for what purpose?

It is futile to debate about many issues in education until the question of purpose is resolved, if, indeed, it ever can be—or should be—in a free and pluralistic society. One might begin with the question: What is education? This question has been debated at least since the time of Plato. We prefer, however to deal with the more specific question: What is the purpose of education? A report submitted to the President's Commission on School Finance noted that our greatest failure has been our reluctance to think seriously about the purpose of

[5]Bayard Rustin, "Irrelevant Schools or Irrelevant Critics," *New York Times,* Dec. 31, 1972, p. 5.

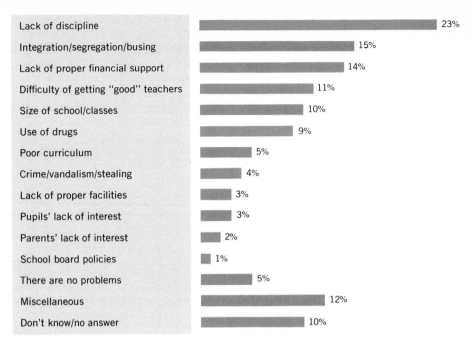

Lack of discipline	23%
Integration/segregation/busing	15%
Lack of proper financial support	14%
Difficulty of getting "good" teachers	11%
Size of school/classes	10%
Use of drugs	9%
Poor curriculum	5%
Crime/vandalism/stealing	4%
Lack of proper facilities	3%
Pupils' lack of interest	3%
Parents' lack of interest	2%
School board policies	1%
There are no problems	5%
Miscellaneous	12%
Don't know/no answer	10%

Figure 1-1 Opinion poll on the question: "What do you think are the biggest problems with which the public schools in this community must deal?" These responses are not very compatible with the criticisms of schools expressed by popular writers. (Adapted from the Seventh Annual Gallup Poll of Public Attitudes toward Education, *Phi Delta Kappan*, December 1975, p. 236. Totals add to more than 100 percent because of multiple answers.)

our schools. We agree. Are schools failing? This question cannot be answered until we have agreed upon evaluative criteria that are purpose related. We shall tackle the critical question of purpose by drawing attention to the major educational philosophies of our time. Each attempts, in its own way, to resolve the question of purpose.

PROGRESSIVISM

Progressive education has its roots in the pragmatic philosophy of William James, but the great educational philosopher John Dewey brought it into sharpest focus and made its practice exemplary. Kilpatrick, Counts, Rugg, and others also added to its intellectual base. Dewey believed that the school is primarily a social institution and that education is a social process. He saw education as the process of living, not as preparation for future living. Dewey contended that it is impossible to prepare children for any precise set of conditions. The only way to prepare learners for future life is to give them command of themselves. Dewey regarded children's individual needs, interests,

and social activities—rather than the subject-oriented structure of knowledge—as the true basis of learning. Progressive educators view students and the curriculum as two aspects of a single process in which children relate what they already know to what is unknown in the world about them. The truly progressive approach calls for "recreating the curriculum" to develop new subject matter from human experience. The school is seen as a forum of community life. Although Dewey regarded education as a fundamental method of social progress and reform, he did not feel that schools should be used to remake the social order.

Dewey defined education as the continuous reconstruction of experience. This view has been translated into curriculum theory through the concept of the "experience-centered curriculum," or learning by doing. Learning by doing emphasizes intelligent reflection upon what is done and what can be learned from the doing experience. Progressive educators regard this as the essence of reasoning, and they value it highly. Dewey insisted that the process of education and the goal of education are one and the same thing. Although

Dewey regarded education as a social process, he valued both cognitive and affective development and insisted that neither could be nurtured fully without the other. Thus, progressive educators emphasize the total development of the whole child. They stress that learning should be derived from students' interests and needs. In a child-centered school, the children assume more responsibility for their own learning. In truly progressive education the school is not isolated from the children's lives. In sum, progressive education is a bold and revolutionary effort to humanize our schools.

Progressive education reached its zenith in the late 1930s, culminating in the famed Eight Year Study, which documented rather well the success of this approach when properly applied. It showed that progressive schools outperformed traditional schools in both cognitive and affective gains. Although never practiced widely, progressive education has influenced educators over the years, particularly in helping us view learners and learning from a new and more humane perspective. Open education, described in Chapter 9, is a modern manifestation of neoprogressivism that borrows somewhat from Dewey but lacks the well-reasoned rationale so characteristic of his thought.

EXISTENTIALISM

Existentialists believe that a person *is* what he or she *does* and that existence is shaped by behavior. One comes to know oneself through one's choices in life; one becomes what one decides to be. We are free, according to existentialists, to place whatever value or meaning we wish upon our milieu or environment. Some religiously oriented existentialists, such as Kierkegaard and Tillich, believe in an ultimate resolution of the human predicament through some form of transcendent being. On the other hand, atheistically oriented existentialists, such as Sartre, believe that our being and meaning have no justification beyond our own choices and that the certainty of death negates all meaning. Regardless of these differences over the possibility of transcendent being, existentialists agree on the primacy of our human freedom to choose for ourselves without benefit of authority beyond ourselves.

Existentialist educators believe that the purpose of education is not simply to help learners cope with existence but to help them fully *experience* their existence. Existentialists would measure education not merely by what learners know but, more importantly, by what they are *capable of knowing and experiencing*. Existentialism places heavy emphasis upon affective learning—the development of feelings, values, and tastes—because these determine decisions and direct subsequent learning. Education for choice is emphasized, and the most basic educational issue is that of selecting the appropriate knowledge for mastery. Existentialists believe that we have no fixed nature but that we shape our being by our choices. Thus, it is more important that learners be able to make rational choices for themselves than that they accept indoctrination about the current "right" choices in society. Morality is very important to existentialists, but in their view, it cannot be *taught* didactically; it must be *caught* through self-discovery.

The existentialist view of education has enjoyed wide currency among the more activist youth culture, as well as among the romantic critics of education. Many of the alternative schools and free schools described in Chapters 6 and 7 are built upon the existentialist view. Many free schools also support the goal of liberating students in the learning process as well as reconstructionists' views on radical social change, discussed next.

RECONSTRUCTIONISM

Reconstructionists have much in common with both progressives and existentialists. Reconstructionists, however, are social reformers primarily,

Learning by doing emphasizes intelligent reflection upon what is done and what can be learned from the doing experience.

and they are committed to the renaissance of modern civilization. According to the reconstructionist view, we are in the midst of a revolutionary era, and education must serve to help people toward utopia through control of the industrial system, public services, and the cultural and natural resources essential to a life of decency, peace, justice, and security. This view places more emphasis upon the common social good than does the more idiosyncratic existentialist view. Reconstructionist educators see education and social reform as much the same process. They see the curriculum as problem-centered, and they regard education as a critical means of intervention in world affairs. Reconstructionists would answer in the affirmative to Counts' classic question: "Dare the schools build a new social order?" Unless schools do, reconstructionists contend, neither they nor society are likely to survive. In this view schools should be held accountable for the elimination of poverty or injustice, and they should reconstruct any society that permits poverty and injustice to flourish. Others, such as the noted philosopher Sidney Hook, are troubled by this view and contend that schools should educate students to learn to their maximum so that they, not their schools, may decide what is to be changed and how. When the schools determine what is to be changed, says Hook, there is serious danger of indoctrination, which is anathema to many educational philosophers.

LIFE-ADJUSTMENT EDUCATION

During the 1950s the concept of life-adjustment education came into prominence. Concerns of everyday living—keeping well, understanding self and others, making a living, adjusting to the natural environment, dealing with social and political structures and forces—were seen as the focal points in curriculum structure. More recent additions to the list might be career education, consumer education, safety education, sex education, and drug-abuse education. Life-adjustment proponents differ from reconstructionists in that they emphasize the healthy adjustment of youths to the existing social, political, and physical milieu, while the latter stress the reconstruction of that milieu and environment to reduce the pressures for adjustment. Supporters of life-adjustment education contend that their approach helps to prepare all young people for useful and satisfying lives as citizens and homemakers and that it is a powerful force in retaining a large number of youths who otherwise would drop out of school. They contend that life-adjustment education is the logical response to the problems raised by universal education and compulsory schooling and that it serves all youths, even those of modest ability and aspiration. This view of education provides the philosophical basis for a number of antipoverty educational programs, such as the National Youth Corps.

EDUCATION AS PERSONAL PSYCHOLOGICAL DEVELOPMENT

Some educators believe that sound psychological development is the essence of all growth and development and the key to satisfying, productive living. They believe that schools should help children to develop healthy attitudes of self-acceptance. The process of self-discovery is used to find personal significance in everything that is learned. The critical focus is on the questions: Who am I? What does it mean? What difference does it make? This point of view has been articulated by educational psychologist Arthur Jersild, among others. Education for personal development is also compatible with the expectations of the so-called "turned on" generation, youths who are interested in mind- and soul-expanding experiences such as transcendental meditation, encounter groups, communal living, behavior modification, values clarification, Eastern mysticism, and astrology. All these efforts are pointed toward deeper introspection and understanding of self and others. This philosophical approach concentrates largely on affective development and holds cognitive development as valuable only to the extent that it aids clarification and understanding of values and feelings. Opponents of this view claim that it substitutes passion for reason, feelings for thought, means for ends, and relevance for significance.

ESSENTIALISM

Essentialist, or basic education, places almost exclusive emphasis upon learners' cognitive development. Indeed, many essentialists disdain the affective and contend that too much attention to tastes, feelings, and values distracts students and interferes with cognitive learning. They see the basic-skill subjects and the classic academic disciplines—language, history, physical sciences—as being of transcending worth. Conant, Bestor, Hutchins, Rafferty, and Koerner, along with the Council for Basic Education, defend basic education on the grounds that, once mastered, these basic subjects have "generative power" which provides learners with the fundamental modes of inquiry. Students then are able on their own initiative, throughout life, to master more complex inquiry into the basic subjects themselves or, if one wishes, into the more "trivial" fields of the arts and vocational education.

Essentialist educators are more interested in determining what should be taught than in finding out what students wish to learn. They are more interested in training the mind than in reconstructing either society or individuals. Essentialists tend to be more elitist than egalitarian in their social views. They would measure school quality in terms of students' achievement on standardized tests. To them, knowledge for its own sake is perfectly defensible. They defend arbitrary and high standards for all learners; rigid marking, promotion, and retardation practices; rigorous intellectual discipline; and academic competition. The essentialist definition of education and the curriculum is narrow. This view is more popular with academicians than with educational psychologists. The most persuasive criticism of basic education is twofold: First, there is evidence that most learners cannot succeed with cognitive learning if their affective development is in disarray; second, strictly basic education cannot well serve the needs of a society committed to mass education of all students on all levels of ability, need, and interest. Essentialism, although largely out of fashion during the past decade, is currently enjoying some renaissance, not so much from ideological conviction, perhaps, but as a result of budgetary pressures for the elimination of all "nonbasics" in school.

SUPERNATURALISM

Supernaturalism is a philosophy of education that emphasizes moral, ethical, and spiritual development based upon revealed truth of a Supernatural Being. This point of view is commonly invoked to support church-affiliated schools as well as the inclusion of religious education, prayer, and moral

Essentialist, or basic education, places almost exclusive emphasis upon the learners' cognitive development through classic academic disciplines, such as the physical sciences.

values in public school classrooms. This approach to education emphasizes intellectual commitment to Christian or other religious doctrines. It regards moral growth as the essence of all learning and holds that knowledge unattuned to morality is of little worth and even dangerous. This point of view contends that ultimate truth is revealed by the Scriptures or other sacred writings, not by individual or group discovery. Proponents of this view believe that morality can be taught didactically and that there is little room for independent thought in morality.

EDUCATION FOR NATIONAL AND GLOBAL SURVIVAL

This view of education emphasizes that schools are no exception to the principle that all institutions of our national life must address the compelling problem of survival. Education, according to this view, must be an instrument of national defense and foreign policy. It must contribute to our strength as a nation. Education is seen as an instrument of power upon which our survival depends—especially in a world divided between free and communist nations. This view of education is widely held by patriotic organizations and has served as justification for the passage of the National Defense Education Act.

Some educators disparage the chauvinism implicit in education for national survival and argue instead for a global view of survival. They stress not superpatriotism but international understanding and cooperation, along with other concerns expressed in Chapter 15. Harold Taylor, among others, stresses this larger view of global survival and emphasizes the critical need for schools to face the problems of war, pollution, environmental contamination, population growth, cross-cultural conflict, depletion of the world's resources, and ethnocentricity.[6]

Are the schools failing?

Ivan Illich, in *Deschooling Society,* contends that schools have failed or, at least, have outlived their usefulness. He and others feel we should abandon our schools or no longer require compulsory attendance. Let us examine this serious charge.

Illich supports his argument by noting that children learn to walk and talk without schooling; but he fails to note that most people remain illiterate in countries where schooling is not compulsory. In *Must We Educate?* Carl Bereiter contends that substantial numbers of children have failed to learn rudimentary skills adequately and that governmentally controlled schooling robs children and parents of essential freedom in determining their own lives. Evidently, few people take such observations seriously.

Surely one of the most pragmatic and reliable tests of schools' alleged failure is the degree of consumers' satisfaction. When parents were asked in a recent Gallup poll whether they felt that their children were learning what they should in school, an overwhelming 82 percent felt that they were. When asked if their children want to go to school, 83 percent reported that they did.[7] These re-

sponses should put to rest the popular myth that schools are failures and prisonlike monstrosities, regardless of the school-is-doomed literature that says otherwise.

EDUCATION AND THE EQUALITY OF EDUCATIONAL OPPORTUNITY

Several critics have taken support from the Coleman study, *Inequality: A Reassessment of the Effect of Family and Schooling in America,* which reported that schools have little impact on eliminating poverty or equalizing economic prosperity of our citizens. But to conclude that schools are failures (as Coleman does not) is as senseless as concluding that hospitals must be abandoned because they fail to equalize healthful living among people or because some people die in them. If income equalization, commonly regarded as socialism, is our goal, then the means must be political and economic, not educational. Many people have construed Coleman's findings to mean that schools make little difference in students' educational attainment. However, Guthrie notes that other researchers have demonstrated from Coleman's data that schools can have a significant impact upon students.[8]

THE NATURE OF THE DIALOGUE

Harry Broudy, in his trenchant analysis of educational criticisms in *The Real World of the Public Schools,* laments the oversimplification, distortion, hasty generalization, and rampant utopianism that permeate the dialogue about school failure. Philip Jackson, another distinguished educator, objects to the demagogic style, hysterical tone, propagandistic aims, scanty evidence, flaws in logic, deficiencies in historical perspective, unbalanced judgments, and negativistic stance of the school-is-dead literature. Jackson concludes:

Our schools are neither dead nor dying, but neither, unfortunately, are they marked by a degree of vitality and energy that befits the grandeur of their mission. Paradoxically, and even ironically, the writings of those who

---

[6]For further discussion of the various philosophical views outlined above and their influence upon criticism of education, see James J. Shields, *The Crisis in Education Is Outside the Classroom,* Phi Delta Kappa, Bloomington, Ind., 1973 and R. Freeman Butts, "The Search for Purpose in American Education," *Today's Education,* March-April 1976, pp. 77–85.

[7]Stanley Elam (ed.), *The Gallup Poll of Attitudes toward Education, 1969–1973,* Phi Delta Kappa, Bloomington, Ind., 1973, pp. 162–163.

[8]James W. Guthrie, "What the Coleman Reanalysis Didn't Tell Us," *Saturday Review,* July 22, 1972, p. 45.

would bury us may well stimulate such an infusion of new life.[9]

Many radical critics reacted to the unrest among students during the early 1970s by concluding that the students were rebelling against prisonlike conditions in the schools and that, therefore, the schools were failures. In 1970, for example, Goodman predicted dire consequences for the schools:

The disorders will increase. A certain number of schools, especially high schools—and perhaps in rich suburban neighborhoods—will be burned down. It seems likely that in the next few years the children in junior high school are going to play truant in droves. . . . In this emergency, some other people will begin to say what I am saying now.[10]

Goodman could not have been more wrong. Within a few years of his ominous prediction, disorders among students had practically disappeared, and the vast majority of secondary students—as documented in Chapter 6—were expressing satisfaction with their schools. Fortunately, most educators and the general public did not take Goodman seriously and did not see schools as being beyond repair and ripe for abandonment.

THE ACHIEVEMENT OF AMERICAN SCHOOLING IN COMPARISON WITH OTHER LANDS

Tanner warns that when academicians declare that schools make no difference in the lives of other people's children, and demand the very best schools for their own children, they are acting to destroy our democratic ideals. He cites evidence that American schools are accomplishing what few other countries have attempted: to provide secondary education for virtually all young people and higher education for most. He reasons that American schools, with all their faults, have accomplished more than any of our other social institutions in generating the expectancy of opportunity for all people.[11]

The prophets of doom for our schools would do well to read Jean-Francois Revel's *Without Marx or Jesus.* Like de Tocqueville, an earlier French observer of American culture, Revel finds a quiet but effective social revolution already underway in the United States. Revel sees the United States as the only place where this could happen. He attributes much of the successful thrust of this latter-day American revolution to the ability of our schools to engage youths in reflective thought and problem-solving as well as to the information revolution that has provided people with abundant knowledge through the mass media.

Those seeking hard evidence about the academic achievement of our schools should examine the report of a massive $6 million study comparing achievement of 250,000 secondary school students in twenty-two countries, including the United States. Conducted by the International Association for the Evaluation of Educational Research, this study revealed that the top students in the United States are performing as well as or better than the top students in most other countries in most subjects. United States students ranked higher than those in any other country in reading comprehension and literature. Only the performance of top students could be judged fairly, because the United States retains more than 75 percent of its students through the terminal year of secondary education, as compared with 45 percent in Sweden, 29 percent in France, 20 percent in England, and 13 percent in the Netherlands, for example. Our remarkably higher retention rate is in itself a noteworthy measure of the accomplishment of our schools. This study also revealed that the performance of our more able students is not hindered when masses of students are given access to comprehensive schooling.[12] Coleman commented that these data from the international study of students' achievement "suggest to me somewhat more hopefulness about schooling than we had in the past."

We do not believe that our schools are failing. We see no evidence to support such a sweeping generalization. But we do believe that schools could be better than they now are, and we point out

[9]Philip W. Jackson, "Deschooling? No!" *Today's Education,* November 1972, p. 22.

[10]Paul Goodman, *New Reformation: Notes of a Neolithic Conservative,* Random House, New York, 1970, p. 124.

[11]Daniel Tanner, "The Retreat from Education—for Other People's Children," *Intellect,* January 1974, p. 23.

[12]See Joseph Featherstone, "Measuring What Schools Achieve," *Phi Delta Kappan,* March 1974, pp. 448–450, for a summary of the findings of this study.

the direction of that improvement in the following chapters.

Should public schools be compulsory and monopolistic?

A number of school reformers, building on the schools-are-failing argument, suggest that the public schools should be divested of their compulsory and monopolistic nature. Some critics call for the repeal of compulsory attendance laws. (The term "compulsory education," which is sometimes used, is inappropriate. Society may be able to compel school attendance, but it cannot compel learning.) Some would wipe out the laws entirely and make attendance a voluntary matter at all ages, an idea that is objectionable to most people, according to opinion polls. Others, such as the National Commission for the Reform of Secondary Education, simply would reduce the upper limit of required attendance to 14 years of age. Compulsory education, it is argued, is not consistent with a free society; violates the religious beliefs of some people; is not effectively enforced beyond age 14; requires a level of education beyond what is needed for many jobs; keeps youths in school who don't want to be there and who may harm the schools; requires higher costs; and is not necessary, since youths with basic skills can acquire further education on their own from the mass media.[13] Some critics have compared school attendance with a twelve-year prison sentence, an analogy that probably would astonish most convicts. (There was a time when those who could attend school were considered privileged; but now, in the minds of some, they are oppressed.)

Arguments favoring compulsory attendance laws through age 18 emphasize that the rights and needs of children and society are not beyond regulation in the public interest, that youths freed from compulsory school attendance will be exploited by employers, that schooling becomes even more important as the influence of the family declines, that the gap between the poor and the rest of society would be widened by disparity in levels of schooling, and that education through high school is necessary to provide the enlightened citizenry upon which a free and democratic society depends. Some also argue that many school truants are not heroes rebelling against the regimen of the school but criminal rascals who shake down other students to support drug habits.

The authors agree with Robert Hutchins that compulsory attendance is necessary so that every child may be given the chance to become the kind of citizen that our Constitution requires. This obligation is too important to be left to the whims and resources of parents. We do, however, favor revision of attendance laws to permit exceptions for students who refuse to be educated or who are incorrigible troublemakers and for students with genuine educational alternatives such as on-the-job training programs. These exceptions should be reviewed carefully by a team of parents, counselors, teachers, employers, and community agencies. We would like to see schools and communities experiment with a wide variety of alternative educational and vocational experiences for those youths who are turned off by conventional schools. We are intrigued by the proposal of a California study commission which recommends that fourteen years of tuition-free schooling be available to all, that only the first eight years be compulsory, and that the remaining six years be available anytime throughout life.

Some reformers argue that the monopoly of conventional schools be broken through a wider choice of competitive alternative educational experiences. Presumably, this competition would be good for all schools. Many have proposed that a voucher, perhaps equal to the cost of public schooling, be given to parents to use in any school of their choice. This plan has generated considerable skepticism and is discussed in Chapter 11. With or without vouchers, alternative schools have proliferated across the land, and we favor that. These alternative schools, discussed in later chapters, manifest a significant but quiet revolution in educational reform, and they seem to offer important options to students who do not succeed in conventional schools. Broudy points out that alternative schools may be defended or attacked on logical or empirical evidence, or both; therefore, he is skeptical of the evidence.

---

[13]For further discussion of this issue, see Howard M. Johnson, "Are Compulsory Attendance Laws Obsolete?" *Phi Delta Kappan*, December 1973, pp. 226–232; or William F. Rickenbacker (ed.), *The Twelve Year Sentence*, Open Court, La Salle, Ill., 1974.

Although we applaud the proliferation of alternative schools, particularly within public school systems, we do not support the voucher system. We believe that education is far too important a governmental concern to be committed safely to private families shopping around for it. We think it is impossible for parents alone to make intelligent choices when highly skilled professionals cannot evaluate schools with consistency.

Accountability: Why? For what? By whom? How?

"Accountability" is surely one of the most fashionable terms in educational parlance these days. Now every state either is operating some kind of accountability or assessment program or is about to do so. Accountability is an old but complex concept with a great variety of meanings. We think accountability means that persons with responsibility should be held answerable for their share of effectiveness in achieving the organization's goals at costs commensurate with their productivity. One can hardly quarrel with the concept in principle, but, as we shall see, it presents feasibility problems that boggle the mind.

WHY?

Several powerful thrusts lie behind the accountability movement in education. Many people are dissatisfied over the rapidly rising costs of schools and are demanding that further costs be justified by evidence of a commensurate increase in the quality of service. Much of the opposition to accountability comes from teachers who see it as blame-inducing and punitive, as indeed it is in some quarters. Their typical response is, "Pay us more money, reduce our load, increase our independence, and accept on faith that better results will follow"—a point of view that is not very reassuring to most parents or school board members.

In its best sense, accountability efforts should be addressed to these purposes:

- Measuring educational progress toward established goals
- Publicizing the results of the measurement
- Identifying and correcting weaknesses

- Redirecting expenditures into more productive programs
- Improving education for the disadvantaged
- Generating information necessary for educational planning and decision making

FOR WHAT?

Accountability begs the "for what" question, since it is an unremitting goal-seeking concept. No accountability system can work and no educator can accept an accountability system unless the school's purposes or objectives are made explicit. As noted earlier in this chapter, the goals of education are ambiguous and conflicting. One great benefit of the accountability movement is that it forces attention upon the need to clarify purpose in education. Every state and many local school systems have begun to assess needs in the realization that this is an essential prelude to accountability systems.

BY WHOM?

The Coleman study, mentioned earlier, suggested that what happens in the home and in the community has greater impact upon what a child achieves than anything that happens in school. If a child comes to school unloved, hungry, emotionally disturbed, with bad attitudes about school and learning, then how do we sort out the share of accountability that belongs with the home and the share that belongs with the school? If a school board puts so many students in a classroom that the teacher is unable to try all known alternatives to teach each to read, then how do we sort out the teacher's accountability from the board's? This kind of problem occurs in trying to measure the accountability of all those involved with education. It includes legislators, courts, administrators, counselors, and even society at large.

HOW?

Accountability has certain feasibility problems. All accountability systems require some type of measurement and evaluation. Although the technology for measuring cognitive growth has been around for years, measurement of affective development is much more difficult. But even measurement of cognitive growth is not without difficulty. Comparison of local scores on standardized achievement tests with norms based on national data is tricky business and subject to misinterpretation. Trying to allow for variations in students' intelligence is also hazardous. Even apart from their stigmatizing effect on children, intelligence tests can be criticized for cultural bias, illogic, irrelevancies, and errors. Authorities are more and more questioning the validity of both achievement tests and intelligence tests and whether they may have an unwholesome effect upon children and schools.[14]

Various other kinds of evaluation systems include measures of teachers' performances in terms of their behavior, their interaction with students, their classroom climate, and other factors. The evaluation of teachers is discussed in Chapter 2.

The demand for accountability has accelerated the development and refinement of evaluation technology in education, a worthwhile byproduct of the movement. Yet, all accountability systems depend upon communication of the aggregate results of the evaluation, and this also has feasibility problems. A variety of structural arrangements can produce accountability, including state assessment programs (discussed in Chapter 13) and cost-effectiveness analysis; program, planning, and budgeting systems; voucher plans; and performance contracting. These various arrangements are discussed in Chapter 11.

All accountability systems should include (1) specification of purposes or goals, (2) specification of criteria upon which evaluation of performance is based, and (3) communication of the results of the evaluation. Some accountability systems also contain elements of competition. The major criticism of accountability efforts derives from their alleged pejorative nature, their alleged displacement of humane concerns by cost-benefit concerns, and their possible damaging effects upon teachers and students.[15]

We believe that such criticisms are not necessarily indigenous to accountability efforts but may

arise from unwise implementation. The thrust for accountability in education is powerful and irreversible. Nor should it be reversed, because the principle is defensible; it is our responsibility as educators to invent ways of accounting for our effectiveness. If we cannot or will not stand accountable, then we are unworthy of professional status. Accountability systems, well-reasoned and sensibly applied, help to reduce the credibility gap between teachers and the public, particularly exasperated taxpayers. Without accountability systems, we have little defense against irresponsible criticism.

Education in a pluralistic society

The United States, more so than most countries, is populated by a heterogeneous people of diverse racial and ethnic subcultures. This diversity of our people contributes to the richness of our heritage, but it also poses a number of critical educational problems that we shall explore now.

THE EDUCATION OF MINORITY GROUPS

We begin our consideration of education in a pluralistic culture by getting an important historical perspective on the education of our largest minority groups—blacks, American Indians, Hispanics, and Asians and Pacific Islanders.

Blacks. Blacks constitute more than 11 percent of our population and reside in virtually all parts of the nation, but especially in the Southeastern states and in large cities. Long-time victims of discrimination and disadvantage in employment, housing, and education, black Americans are understandably insistent in demanding more equal opportunity. A deep faith in the power of education forces much attention upon the schools.

The history of how blacks have been disadvantaged is long and sordid. General public support for the education of blacks began in New Jersey in 1777, where public funds were made available for the support of schools for blacks. Other Northern states and a few cities in the South also provided funds for a few schools. But these were the exceptions rather than the rule. More typical was the ex-

[14]For an excellent series of articles on the subject, see Sheldon H. White and others, "The Myth of Measurability," *The National Elementary Principal*, March/April 1975, pp. 2–81.

[15]For further study of the accountability issue, see Don T. Martin, George E. Overholt, and Wayne J. Urban, *Accountability in American Education: A Critique*, Princeton Book Co., Princeton, N.J., 1976.

perience of Reverend David Alexander Payne, the great minister of the African Methodist Episcopal Church and the first black president of Wilberforce University. At the age of 18, the Reverend Mr. Payne opened a school for free blacks in Charleston. In 1835 the state of South Carolina, alarmed by this enterprise, forbade any person to operate a school for blacks. The few schools for blacks that did remain in the South were forced to operate underground. Some whites risked fines and imprisonment by secretly teaching eager blacks.

After the War between the States, the Freedmen's Bureau, supported by federal funds, helped to establish over four thousand schools for blacks in the South. Various missionary societies joined the effort. Many schools for blacks grew out of the determined efforts of a remarkable band of hardy ex-slaves who saw in education the prime hope for the rise of their people. The little-known but nevertheless admirable work of the great black educators of the late nineteenth and early twentieth centuries in establishing schools and colleges for blacks is discussed in detail in Chapter 7. The stories of the rise of great Negro colleges, such as Bethune College, Tuskegee Institute, Fisk University, Howard University, Morehouse College, Wilberforce University, and the Normal and Theological Institution of Kentucky, parallel in many respects the biographies of their distinguished black presidents, Mary McLeod Bethune, Booker T. Washington, Charles S. Johnson, Mordecai Johnson, Benjamin Mays, William Scarborough, and William Simmons, respectively. Federal lands were appropriated to Tuskegee Institute. Howard University, located in the nation's capital, is one of the few private universities that receives most of its annual appropriations from the federal government for operating purposes.[16]

Booker T. Washington, along with other blacks and many whites, made spirited pleas for better educational opportunity for blacks. Charles T. Walker, a black pastor from New York City, made an impassioned appeal before the 1903 convention of the National Education Association for the educational needs of blacks, arguing that good schooling for blacks could become a vital force in the economic regeneration of the South. These

pleas went largely unheeded for half a century, resulting in the greatest anachronism in our history as a nation.

The vast majority of Americans—black and white —would hope to see Dr. Martin Luther King's great dream realized, as he described it in his address at the March on Washington in 1963:

I have a dream that one day . . . little black boys and black girls will be able to join hands with little white boys and white girls and walk together as sisters and brothers. . . . This will be the day when all of God's children will be able to sing with new meaning "My country 'tis of thee, sweet land of liberty, of thee I sing. Land where my fathers died, land of the Pilgrims' pride, from every mountainside, let freedom ring."

The problem of equalizing educational opportunity for black Americans is so important and so pervasive that various facets of it are dealt with

"I have a dream that one day little black boys and black girls will be able to join hands with little white boys and little white girls and walk together as brothers and sisters." *Dr. Martin Luther King*

[16]For a more detailed discussion of the history of black education, see Charles H. Wesley, "The Education of Black Americans," *Ebony*, August 1975, pp. 143–147.

throughout this book, particularly in Chapters 3, 7, 12, and 14.[17]

American Indians. The education of American Indians, or native Americans as many of them prefer to be called, has been handicapped by a tragic historical relationship between Indians and whites. Except for two great Indian nations that operated their own schools with marvelous success, the Choctaws and Cherokees, most of the relatively few other Indians who were educated in the nineteenth century attended schools operated badly by the federal government and by religious denominations. Eventually, most of the other private schools for Indians were taken over by the federal government with disastrous results. Indian children were removed long distances from their homes, sometimes forcibly, to attend schools in converted old army forts, and their native languages, religions, and cultures were suppressed in a drive to "civilize the natives." As one observer noted, at best this was a prescription to open doors of opportunity to Indians for success in the white world; at worst it was an instrument of cultural genocide. This tragic circumstance was mitigated by two forces: The schools were too few to reach most Indian children, and many who were enrolled ran away to return to the reservations. Under the Indian Reorganization Act of 1934 many schools for Indians were built on reservations, but control of these schools remained with white society, which still was intent on "Americanizing" the Indians.

Today most elementary schools for Indians are located on reservations, while most secondary schools are boarding schools away from the reservations. Only 25 percent of Indian children and youths now attend schools run by the Bureau of Indian Affairs, 8 percent attend private schools run by missionaires, and the remainder attend public schools on or near their reservations.

Enrollment of Indians in school is increasing rapidly. It is stimulated by the Indians' recent commitment to universal education beyond the elementary level as well as by the increase in the Indian population, which is growing faster than the general population. For example, a generation ago, only one Navajo child in four was in school;

today 90 percent of the Navajo children are in school. For other tribes, the picture is less bright. Dropout rates are still twice the national average, and the turnover of teachers in Indian schools is excessive. Many entering students have no background in English. The goals of education for the Indians are not well defined. With few exceptions, the schools are not well adapted to Indian culture, and the climate of the traditional American classroom is not very compatible with the learning style of the Indians. However, Indian children, while materially impoverished, are not culturally deprived and do not suffer the psychological deprivation associated with the broken families of the urban poor. Indian family life is traditionally strong and supportive.

Several recent analyses of Indian education have yielded a number of proposed reforms, including: the establishment of a National Indian Board on Indian Education; Indian control of local schools serving Indians; better funding of Indian schools; development of curriculum materials that better reflect the history, culture, and values of these noble people; the preparation of more Indian teachers for service in their schools; more support for college rather than vocational education for Indian high school graduates; and the strengthening of public schools serving the reservations.

Several exemplary Indian schools are beginning to emerge, a number of them under the financial support of the Indian Education Act of 1972. The Institute of American Indian Arts in Santa Fe is doing a remarkable job of transforming the brightest and some of the most rebellious young Indians into outstanding leaders by helping them find self-direction and self-respect through a "return to Indianness" and escape from dependence on white culture. Another exciting departure is the experimental school at Rough Rock, Arizona, which is controlled by an all-Navajo school board; the curriculum is bicultural, and the instruction is bilingual. A new Indian college, the Navajo Community College at Tsaile Lake, Arizona, and the older Haskell Indian Junior College in Lawrence, Kansas, have become forerunners for other Indian colleges that are appearing increasingly, organized and controlled by the Indians themselves. Self-determination has become the watchword in Indian education, as manifested in the Indian Self-determination and Educational Assistance Act.

[17]For further discussion of the issues regarding equal educational opportunity for blacks, see Thomas Sowell, *Black Education: Myths and Tragedies*, McKay, New York, 1972.

This legislation is helping local tribes take over educational responsibilities formerly held by the Bureau of Indian Affairs. It is hoped that our nation someday will redress the shameful racism which has demeaned and impoverished these first Americans and reward them for their fierce loyalty to this country, their pride in their culture, and their hope for the future.[18]

Hispanic. Our population includes over ten million people of Hispanic origin. Approximately six million are Mexican-Americans (or Chicanos), two million are of Puerto Rican origin, one million are of Cuban origin, and the remaining one million come from Central or South America or other Spanish-speaking cultures regardless of race. The Mexican-Americans reside in largest numbers in the Southwestern states, the Puerto Ricans in the New England and Middle Atlantic states, and the Cubans in Florida and the New York metropolitan area.

Some Hispanics are migrant crop workers whose squalid residences shift with the harvests, but most are city dwellers who live in "barrios." With large families and limited education, they suffer severely from unemployment and poverty. The children of migrant families are further handicapped educationally by frequent transfers among schools. Many of them do not speak English well upon entry into school. Too many schools have discouraged their use of Spanish in the classroom and have failed to help them acquire a sense of dignity and self-confidence. According to a report by the U.S. Civil Rights Commission, many Mexican-Americans attend schools predominantly isolated from American students. Nearly two-thirds of them are reading below grade level, and more than half of the Mexican-Americans drop out of school before completing high school. The commission recommended that Hispanic persons be encouraged to become teachers and counselors and that in-service programs be aimed toward helping all teachers appreciate and sustain the culture and expectations of these people. Certainly they can learn well and live with dignity and purpose. Bilingual and bicultural education, dis-

cussed in Chapter 9, is considered to be the prime medium for making this goal a reality.[19]

Asians and Pacific Islanders. Some 1½ million people in our population are predominantly Japanese, Chinese, Filipino, Korean, Vietnamese, Malaysian, or Polynesian or have other Asian or Pacific Island origins. The largest number are Japanese, Chinese, and Filipino, in that order. These people are concentrated in the larger cities of the West Coast states and Hawaii. They manifest a diversity of native languages, cultures, religions, and biological traits. Although they make up only about 1 percent of the population, they merit consideration in this land of immigrants. Earlier immigrants discriminated badly against them in terms of social, economic, and educational opportunities, even though they commonly display strong family life, industriousness, pride in their cultures, and loyalty to the United States. The American public is slowly coming to realize that the rich cultural backgrounds of such minority groups add a vital ethnic contribution to our pluralistic society. Again, bilingual and multicultural educational programs are the prime means for enriching their opportunity in our land and for enriching our land by their presence.[20]

EDUCATION AND UPWARD MOBILITY

America was settled by the greatest migration in human history—a migration of poor and oppressed people, discontented with the tyranny and inequality of opportunity abroad. Immigrants came to our shores with vastly different languages, religions, cultures, political faiths, racial and national backgrounds, and social and economic status. To the public school fell the task of making 30 million new American citizens. No other nation ever assimilated such a heterogeneous population as rapidly and as completely. These people came to America in search of a classless society where there would be equal opportunity. Throughout our history, visi-

[18]For further discussion of the problems and progress of American Indians' education, see Estelle Fuchs and Robert Havighurst, *To Live on This Earth: American Indian Education,* Doubleday, New York, 1972.

[19]For further discussion of the problems of educating the largest group of Hispanic people, see Manuel H. Guerra, "Educating Chicano Children and Youths," *Phi Delta Kappan,* January 1972, pp. 313–314.

[20]For further discussion of the education of these people, see Seymour Fersh, "Orientals and Orientation," *Phi Delta Kappan,* January 1972, pp. 315–318.

tors from other lands have been struck by the general equality of conditions achieved by our people.

The United States, more than any other major nation, makes educational opportunity available to its citizens. For example, more than twice as many children from blue-collar families reach the final year of secondary school in the United States than in most Western European countries. No other major nation retains 75 percent of its young people through high school, as does this country. Neither does any other nation provide higher education for as large a percentage of its youth as does the United States.

Free public education has unlocked the door of opportunity for millions. Great scientists, diplomats, athletes, artists, teachers, businesspeople, physicians. lawyers, and individuals in other fields have risen in America despite diversity of race, religion, national origin, or social or economic position of family. The census records an increase of over 122 percent in black professional and technical workers since 1950. Today a larger percentage of American blacks attend college than do people of all colors in virtually all other lands. In

We can be grateful that minority groups have resisted homogenization into the Anglo-dominated culture of our schools and society.

perhaps no other country is it possible for people of modest origin to rise so far and so fast. In no other country have the common people achieved such a large measure of political power, social status, and economic prosperity. The success of America is the story of faith in the common people.

END OF THE MELTING-POT MYTH

Although our schools helped assimilate (some would say forced) 30 million immigrants—most of them from Europe—into our Anglo-dominated culture, another 30 million or more black Americans, native Americans, Hispanics, Asians, and Pacific Islanders have not been assimilated fully. Why not? Although some of these minority groups have been here for generations, they share certain characteristics that put them at a disadvantage. First, they are physically different from the dominant group. Because of physical traits, many of them cannot blend well into the larger society; therefore, they became visible targets of discrimination. Second, the cultures of each of these groups differed significantly from the white, Anglo-Saxon, Protestant norms, making their assimilation difficult. Because they were not assimilated easily into an alien culture and were discriminated against, each group—in the interests of self-preservation and ethnic pride—fiercely maintained close group ties that further segregated them from the larger society.

In retrospect, we can be grateful that minority groups have resisted homogenization into the Anglo-dominated culture of our schools and society. The schools, of course, were to be the vehicle for this chauvinistic goal. The schools taught immigrant children contempt for their language and culture and imposed on them a shame, self-alienation, and self-rejection from which we are just now beginning to emerge. Small wonder that ethnic minorities found the schools, like the larger society, alien, hostile, and self-defeating. Many subcultures in our society—the Amish, Black Muslims, and American Indians are noteworthy examples—rejected the melting-pot ideal and resisted the press toward integration in school and society. They saw this movement wiping out cultures that were dear to them. They saw also the injustice to young people who had difficulty competing in schools and in society, which measured success in terms of white, Anglo-Saxon, Protestant norms. For some ethnic groups the handicap was exacerbated by instruction carried on in the English language, which was not spoken in their homes. Within the past quarter century particularly, these people helped us all gain a new appreciation of cultural pluralism.

CULTURAL PLURALISM THE NEW IDEAL

We are coming slowly to the conviction that cultural pluralism permits the retention of rich and diverse cultural heritages that contribute to richness and variety of our larger society. (Who, for example, would argue that Chinese, Mexican, Italian, French, and Greek restaurants should be integrated into a single American cuisine?) We are slowly reducing our ethnocentrism and realizing that cultural pluralism permits peaceful coexistence of groups with different subcultures.

When we begin to welcome ethnic differences as an opportunity rather than a misfortune, then, as Teilhard de Chardin put it, we can begin to "live pluralistically in many worlds and cultures simultaneously." Havighurst, who has devoted much of his life to the study of cultural pluralism, believes that this concept includes four crucial elements:

● Mutual appreciation and understanding of the various cultures in the society
● Cooperation of the various groups in the civic and economic institutions of society
● Peaceful coexistence of diverse lifestyles, folkways, manners, language patterns, religious beliefs, and family structures
● Autonomy for each subcultural group to work out its own social future, so long as it does not interfere with the same right for other groups.[21]

Several black educators have stated the challenge poignantly. Professor Hugh Scott believes that

the integrity and viability of this democratic, pluralistic society depends in large measure on the effectiveness of our schools as agents of social consciousness and reform. . . . The schools must vigorously work toward actualizing our constitutional principles and giving substance to the American dream. If the schools are

relegated to the role of passive observers of social injustice, they cease to serve the interests of all Americans.[22]

We finally have come to realize that the melting-pot syndrome is not only impossible but undesirable. Rather than the melting pot, someone has suggested the analogy of the "salad bowl," in which each ingredient preserves its identity and is respected for what it is while at the same time blending into a harmonious whole that is enriched by the diverse elements.

THE DILEMMA OF UNITY AMID PLURALISM

The tolerances of cultural pluralism are not infinite. When cultural pluralism is interpreted to permit extreme separatism or segregation in school and society, then it becomes difficult to develop that cultural unity which is essential to some degree in any nation. If minority or majority groups are educated separately or are instructed only by persons of their own group, they are unlikely to develop the intercultural understanding and skills needed to prosper in society. For example, black studies designed for black students exclusively may strengthen black pride, but they contribute little to blacks' appreciation of, say, Oriental cultures or to other groups' appreciation of black cultures. Although the schools should accommodate and cherish cultural differences, they also must teach respect and commitment to the common cultural values that bind our people together. Cultural diversities should not be exaggerated at the expense of cultural unity, symbolized by *E pluribus unum*—one people from many. As James Banks has put it, "The schools should foster those differences which maximize opportunities for democratic living but vigorously oppose those which do not."[23]

The schools often are caught in the dilemma between maximizing understanding and respect for cultural differences and at the same time trying to build common cultural values. The golden mean

[22]Hugh J. Scott, "Reflections on Issues and Conditions Related to Public Education of Black Students," *Journal of Negro Education,* Summer 1973, p. 418.

[23]James A. Banks, "Cultural Pluralism," *Educational Leadership,* December 1974, p. 166. See also Gwendolyn C. Baker, "Cultural Diversity: Strength of the Nation," *Educational Leadership,* January 1976, pp. 257–260.

[21]Robert G. Havighurst, "The American Indian: From Assimilation to Cultural Pluralism," *Educational Leadership,* April 1974, p. 587.

Schools should accommodate and cherish cultural differences but also teach respect and commitment to the common cultural values that bind our people together.

between these two sometimes polarized goals is difficult to attain. It is small wonder, then, that the schools' role in a culturally pluralistic society is difficult to define, for society itself is ambiguous in its tolerances.

The school desegregation and integration controversy

Without doubt, the most agonizing and perplexing educational problem in our 200 years as a nation has been that of school desegregation and integration. No school problem has caused so much bitterness and bloodshed.

HISTORICAL, LEGAL, AND SOCIAL PERSPECTIVES

Before 1954 Southern communities traditionally maintained dual school systems—one for blacks and one for whites. Then, in the historic case of

Brown v. Board of Education of Topeka, the U.S. Supreme Court ruled: "In the field of public education, the doctrine of 'separate but equal' has no place. Separate facilities are inherently unequal." The Court also held that racial discrimination in public education was unconstitutional and that schools must strive to end racial discrimination "with all deliberate speed." Too many recalcitrant officials interpreted the latter phrase to mean "as slowly as possible." The decision did not bring immediate redress to racial injustice in education but did precipitate a long bitter struggle that was fought in the courts, in the legislative chambers, and sometimes in the streets. In the two decades that followed the decision, many school districts engaged in ingenious delay and outright resistance to the decision. Many districts adopted the "freedom of choice" policy, by which students were presumably free to enroll in any school of their choice in the district. But many black students were harassed in their attempts to enter predominantly white schools. Sometimes minor changes were made in school-attendance areas to permit a few blacks to attend white schools while maintaining in effect the old dual school system. These and other efforts created traces of desegregation, or "tokenism," but failed to measure up to the spirit of the Court's decision. To enforce the ruling, Congress passed the Civil Rights Act of 1964, forbidding discrimination in schools and withholding federal funds from segregated school districts.

De jure segregation (deliberate discrimination by race in assigning students to schools) has been unconstitutional since 1954. The term "desegregation" refers to the undoing through legal remedy of previous *de jure* segregation. The term "integration," on the other hand, refers to the process of mixing students of different races in schools for either legal or moral reasons to overcome *de facto* segregation, which we will consider next.

In the North, particularly in the cities, white and black students also were segregated in schools, not always as a matter of policy but circumstantially, as an artifact of segregated housing patterns. Such *de facto* segregation began to accelerate in the North after the Civil Rights Act of 1964. In many urban communities the flight of whites from public schools became a mass exodus when black enrollment reached 30 percent. Many white families either moved to the suburbs or sent their children to private schools. "Segregation academies" sprang up throughout the South and in some Northern communities. In some communities there are more white children in private schools than there are children in the entire public school system. Virtually none of the segregation academies are accredited, and most offer an education that is separate from but inferior to that in the public schools. In many Southern districts the public schools became predominantly black while the private schools became predominantly white; in effect, a dual segregated system was recreated. In Atlanta, for example, when the school enrollment went from 70 percent white to 90 percent black between 1958 and 1976, the courts held that massive busing to achieve racial balance was neither feasible nor reasonable and would only hasten departure of the remaining whites. Thus the superintendent of Atlanta concluded, as did many other school officials in urban school systems, that from now on the goal had to be not integration, but quality education for all children. Many observers felt that court-ordered desegregation had gone about as far as it could go in the big cities of the South.

In the early 1970s there was some hope that predominantly black urban school districts and white suburban school districts might be merged into one metropolitan district to achieve integration in both. A few districts went in that direction voluntarily. Elsewhere, plaintiffs asked the courts to mandate busing between city and suburban schools to achieve racial balance. A landmark case in Detroit, *Milliken v. Bradley,* affected other cities as well, when the U.S. Supreme Court ruled that busing was not required unless there was evidence of discrimination in establishing school districts' boundaries, as was not the case in Detroit. While busing foes hailed this as a victory, Justice Thurgood Marshall, voting with the minority in the 5-4 decision, called it "a giant step backward." Many civil rights leaders agreed. However, this decision did not affect court-ordered plans for desegregation, including busing if necessary, to overcome intracity segregation in the schools of Denver, Boston, and other cities. In Denver, desegregation has been accomplished smoothly and effectively, while in Boston it has encountered enormous resistance. Denver lacks the key ingredient that seems to generate the fiercest resistance to school integration—many low-income whites. The courts are inclined to require intracity busing to achieve better racial balance only if *de facto* segregation appears intentional.

Litigants sought to have *de facto* segregation declared unconstitutional because they felt that equal educational opportunity required the creation of racial balance (integration) within schools of a school district or even across school districts. Although some successes were attained in this litigation in lower courts, the argument was lost in appeals to higher courts. Presently, the legal weapon for integration is not strong in bringing about racial balance in cases of *de facto* segregation.

THE BUSING CONTROVERSY

A study by the U.S. Commission on Civil Rights revealed that although two-thirds of the people say they support integration, most people generally are opposed to busing, which is the only way of achieving integration in many communities. (Blacks are divided almost evenly in their positions on busing.) The report stated that the public seriously misunderstands the facts of the busing controversy, that those who do understand the facts are more supportive of busing, and that most people who express an opinion are willing to support limited busing when there is no other way to achieve integration. A Gallup poll concluded that "opposition to busing should not be linked with racial animosity."[24]

On the other hand, a fair degree of racial balance has been achieved in many school districts across the country, particularly in districts without major concentrations of black students or too many low-income whites. With the help of citizens' groups, both black and white, many school boards and administrators have moved forth courageously and wisely with plans for school integration. Sacramento and Berkeley, California; Evanston, Illinois; Rochester and White Plains, New York; Hart-

ford, Connecticut; and Seattle, Washington, are especially noteworthy for the diplomacy of their superintendents and boards of education in working toward the integration of their schools. Even in Jackson, Mississippi, long a bastion of die-hard white supremacy, a plan to desegregate the schools through busing had the support of the Chamber of Commerce and was implemented rather smoothly.

PROGRESS AND RETROGRESSION

As illustrated in Figure 1-2, progress has been made in the education of minority groups. College enrollment of blacks has increased by nearly 100 percent in the past decade. Approximately 20 percent of college-age blacks are enrolled in college, compared with 25 percent of the white population. Approximately 72 percent of black youths complete high school, compared with 85 percent of white youths. Approximately 3 million blacks are enrolled in schools with white majorities, an increase of more than 2 million since 1968. The percentage of black students in predominantly white schools is highest in the Southern states. where it is approximately 50 percent, compared with the national figure of 36 percent. In the South, only 9 percent of blacks attend all-black schools, compared with 10 percent for the nation. In the North, 71 percent of black students attend predominantly black schools.

Thus integration remains an elusive goal in many communities, and the press in that direction is subsiding. Massachusetts, the first state to legislate the withholding of state funds from districts with predominantly black schools, recently repealed the act. The New York Board of Regents disavowed its former commitment to establish quotas for racial balance and is concentrating instead on enforcing efforts to promote equal opportunity for all races. The federal government, during the Nixon and Ford administrations, left the battle to the courts.

A factor in the retreat from integration has been the conclusion—based on a number of studies—that the home, not the school, makes the greater difference in the educational and economic destiny of people. Although this conclusion has been debated widely, many people, especially legislators, lost their zeal for promoting equal op-

[24]For further discussion of the complex issues of busing, see Joseph T. Durham, "Sense and Nonsense about Busing," *Journal of Negro Education*, Spring 1973, pp. 322–330; Nicolaus Mills (ed.), *The School Bus Controversy*, Teachers College, New York, 1974, and Robert L. Green and Thomas F. Pettigrew, "Urban Desegregation and White Flight," *Phi Delta Kappan*, February 1976, pp. 399–402.

Figure 1-2 Level of school completed by persons 25 years old and older, by racial group, 1940–1975. (U.S. Bureau of the Census.)

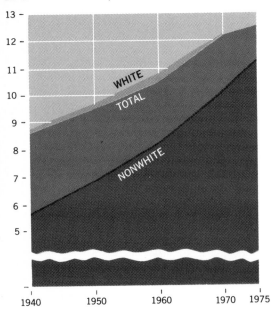

portunity for minorities through school integration. Many blacks have begun to reject integration as a desirable goal and see it, instead—as do many whites—as the loss of neighborhood schools. For example, Coleman Young, Detroit's black mayor, says that he "sheds no tears for cross-district busing" and favors, instead, increased financing of schools to improve educational opportunity for all.

The retreat from integration rests on ideological as well as political grounds. In earlier times it was agreed that black children would achieve better in integrated schools and that children of all races would acquire better attitudes toward each other if integrated. Both common sense and research results, including the Coleman report, seemed to document that. More recently, Coleman, although still favoring integration, concludes that mandatory busing inadvertantly creates a new kind of segregation, more insidious than that of the past. He believes that white flight from the cities results from many causes in addition to bigotry, including crime and violence in the schools, the movement of industry to the suburbs, urban blight, congestion, and a decline in the quality of urban schools. After reviewing research on the relationship between school desegregation and school achievement of blacks, two writers concluded that low achievement and racial tensions will not disappear through racial balance in the schools. They urge educators to free themselves of the notion that there is something magical in whiteness—that, without it, black or red or brown children cannot learn.[25] Professor Hugh Scott of Howard University expresses the same view, that black children do not need to attend the same schools as white children in order to learn. Such a premise, he argues, denies blacks their humanity.[26]

SCHOOL DESEGREGATION AND SCHOOL ACHIEVEMENT

Nancy St. John has synthesized the massive research on the relationship between school integration and student achievement. Although some evidence is ambiguous and inconclusive, the weight of evidence from these studies suggests the following:

- There is no significant difference in the cognitive development of students in segregated or desegregated schools.
- The self-concepts and aspirations of black students tend to be stronger in segregated schools.
- Racial attitudes and behavior may be either improved or damaged through desegregation.[27]

St. John's is probably the best reference for serious students interested in hard research evidence on the pros and cons of school desegregation and the conditions necessary to make it effective. Daniel Levine would add the conclusion that integration of schools on a socioeconomic basis appears more beneficial to academic achievement than integration on the basis of race, but he concedes that political reasons make this difficult to accomplish.[28]

A number of black leaders have taken the position that two things are necessary to raise the educational opportunity for blacks: quality schools for black students and a commitment by the black community to recommit black children to the traditional ethic of pride in work and excellence. The latter is well expressed by our first black four-star general, Gen. Daniel James:

I believe in what my mother called the power of excellence, your own individual excellence. She said don't get so busy practicing your right to dissent that you forget your responsibility to contribute and you will prosper as you contribute to the welfare of this country.[29]

WHAT OF THE FUTURE?

Like the majority of Americans, we share Dr. Martin Luther King's dream of black and white children walking hand in hand to school and of "brotherhood from sea to shining sea." We join noted black leaders Roy Wilkins, Executive Director of the National Association for the Advancement of Colored People, and Bayard Rustin, Executive Di-

[25]Beloine W. Young and Grace B. Bress, "A New Educational Decision: Is Detroit the End of the School Bus Line?" *Phi Delta Kappan*, April 1975, p. 519.

[26]Hugh J. Scott, op. cit., pp. 414–426.

[27]Nancy H. St. John, *School Desegregation: Outcomes for Children*, Wiley, New York, 1975.

[28]Daniel U. Levine, "Integration in Metropolitan Schools: Issues and Prospects," *Phi Delta Kappan*, June 1973, pp. 651–657.

[29]As quoted in *The Pittsburgh Press*, Aug. 24, 1975. p. A-30.

rector of the A. Philip Randolph Institute, in rejecting the separatism of the races in school and society. Rustin contends that black militants' drive for black power, never a significant force in the black people's struggle, has left our nation polarized and has immobilized that broad base of interracial cooperation which reached its zenith in the 1963 March on Washington. Wilkins inveighs against separatism and sees it as exacerbating racial hatred, violence, and discrimination. Similarly, distinguished black educator Thomas Sowell, in his trenchant book *Black Education: Myths and Tragedies,* finds no promise in black studies, discrimination that favors blacks, or separatism in schools and society.

Our consciences accept no ultimate alternatives to an integrated society and school system. We think it is easy to underestimate the degree of integration that has been achieved and will continue to occur as the educational and socioeconomic differences between blacks and whites are reduced. As Nathan Glazer points out, black ghettos are getting smaller, and housing and employment are becoming increasingly integrated. Discrimination against racial minorities, especially in education, is receding rapidly, although integration proceeds slowly and even retrogresses in urban districts.

Where do we go from here? We have neither the wisdom nor the space to answer this complex question fully, but here is our position in brief. First, there must be no retreat from our commitment to racial equality in education. Second, while it will take time to overcome *de facto* segregation, we can and must eradicate *de jure* segregation in schools wherever it remains. Third, we must commit massive financial resources, largely from federal funds, to improving educational opportunity for all children who need it. This requires preferential funding of schools heavily populated by children from poor families of all races, since most school segregation is based more on socioeconomic factors than racial ones. Fourth, whites must be sympathetic and supportive of blacks' insistence upon controlling predominantly black schools. This is a reasonable expectation, given the failure of whites to control these schools. Fifth, we are inclined to agree, reluctantly, that forced integration of schools is, for the present at least, coun-

terproductive in many urban areas. This is not necessarily the case elsewhere. Sixth, people of all races must work together patiently and courageously to foster voluntary plans of school desegregation wherever possible, a stratagem that has been fairly successful in many communities. Finally, we must hold firm to the long-range ideal of integration in education. We recognize that this goal awaits much progress in interracial relations and attitudes—surely one of the most compelling obligations for all educators. One day, then, the prophecy of the great educator Ernest Melby may come true: "The Negro is going to save American civilization, because he is going to force you and me to face up to our heritage."

The dilemma of quality versus equality

MORAL AND LEGAL PERSPECTIVES

The dilemma between elitism and egalitarianism in our culture goes back at least as far as the Hamiltonian-Jeffersonian discourses on the matter. Generally speaking, we are committed to an egalitarian society in principle but not always in reality. Alexis de Tocqueville, in his brilliant book *Democracy in America,* written in 1835, commented in his opening paragraph on the striking equality of our people:

Amongst the novel objects that attracted my attention . . . in the United States, nothing struck me more forcibly than the general equality of the condition among the people. . . . The more I advanced in the study of American society, the more I perceived that this equality of conditions is the fundamental fact from which all others seemed to be derived [30]

De Tocqueville attributed much of the strength of our civilization, which he admired greatly, to this equality among the people. To be sure, it was and is a level of equality not found in most other nations. But equality is a relative thing, and Americans are increasingly sensitive to the inequalities that persist, all the more so because of the equal

---

[30]Alexis de Tocqueville, *Democracy in America,* New American Library, New York, 1956, p. 26.

protection guaranteed by the Fourteenth Amendment. Although we proclaimed two centuries ago that all people are created equal, it was not until 1954 that separate schools for blacks and whites were ruled inherently unequal just by reason of their separation. It was another two decades before the principle of equal educational opportunity was applied to rich and poor students. Although many states had adopted "equalization formulas" for the allocation of state funds to schools, these formulas guaranteed only a minimum or foundation level so low that wealthy districts exceeded it, thereby creating unequal opportunity.

The California Supreme Court, in *Serrano v. Priest* (1971), rendered a decision that triggered national trauma over public school financing patterns. The court held that California's system of school financing violated the equal-protection clause of the Constitution, because allocations of state funds for education were inequitable. They were based upon the unequal wealth of districts as measured by local property tax revenues. The court held that "the quality of a child's schooling should not be a function of wealth other than the wealth of the state as a whole." Within a few years of the *Serrano* decision, similar cases were tried in two-thirds of the states.[31] The U.S. Supreme Court in 1973, in a similar case, *San Antonio Independent School District v. Rodriguez,* in a 5-4 decision, said that education, although extremely important, is not a fundamental right and is not entitled to strict constitutional protection. The Court found the Texas school finance system, which relied heavily on local property taxes, "chaotic and unjust" and agreed that the inequities should be eliminated. However it insisted that this was a responsibility of the state, not the Court.

Although the U.S. Supreme Court did not regard equal educational opportunity as an inherent constitutional right, a number of state courts held otherwise under the equal-protection guarantees of their state constitutions. The pressures from these state court decisions triggered the creation of study commissions in all the states. Their recommendations are summarized in Chapter 11.

FINANCIAL PERSPECTIVE

These study commissions awakened public concern over inequality in education, and their recommendations led to reform of the school finance structure in some states, a process that has yet to run its course and that is contested bitterly in many states. If educational opportunity in financial terms is "leveled up" to the ninetieth percentile, it would require an extra $6 billion annually, which is not politically feasible in these times. Equalization through "leveling down," on the other hand, is anathema to well-financed districts that resist sharing local tax revenues with other districts at the cost of sacrificing quality in their own schools. To equalize educational opportunity at a level that states are willing to afford would reduce drastically the quality of many fine school systems. So the dilemma of equality versus quality is most poignant in financial terms.[32] Even if educational expenditures could be equalized *within* the states, the question of inequality *among* the states remains, as illustrated in Figure 1-3. There is also the question of whether inequalities in spending among schools in the same district violate the equal-protection principle. The implications of applying the equal-protection principle to higher education boggles the mind.

Many have asked, reasonably, whether equality of educational opportunity must be defined in terms of expenditures per pupil. Coleman, in his *Equality of Educational Opportunity,* reported that per pupil expenditure had virtually no relationship to students' achievement in school. But Guthrie and his associates reviewed other research and concluded the opposite in their book *Schools and Inequality.*[33] In one of the most controversial books in recent years, *Inequality: A Reassessment of the Effects of Family and Schooling,* Christopher Jencks and associates unleashed several bombshells on the educational scene: (1) that racial

---

[31]For further discussion of this case and similar cases, see Robert J. Wynkoop, "Trends in School Finance Reform," *Phi Delta Kappan,* April 1975, pp. 542–546.

[32]For more detailed discussion of this issue, see Charles W. Fowler, "Should We Take Care Lest We 'Equalize' Our Schools into Mediocrity?" *The American School Board Journal,* June 1975, pp. 47–50.

[33]For discussion of Coleman's and Guthrie's conclusions, see Robert Hassenger, "The Equal Educational Opportunity Debate," *The National Elementary Principal,* November/December 1974, pp. 21–33.

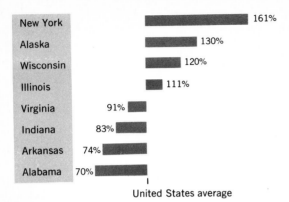

New York	161%
Alaska	130%
Wisconsin	120%
Illinois	111%
Virginia	91%
Indiana	83%
Arkansas	74%
Alabama	70%

United States average

Figure 1-3 Current expenditures per pupil in average daily attendance in public elementary and secondary schools in selected states as percent of national average, 1974–1975. (National Education Association, *Financial Status of the Public Schools, 1975*, p. 36. Copyright © 1975 by the National Education Association. All rights reserved.)

desegregation would eliminate only about 20 percent of the difference between black and white students' achievement as measured by achievement tests; (2) that the resources of the schools do not affect achievement test outcomes appreciably; and (3) that schools have few long-term effects upon the later financial success of those who attend them. The last conclusion was especially hard to believe, because Americans typically had accepted on faith the premise that equality in educational opportunity is essential to equality in economic opportunity, although education does not guarantee economic success, of course. Neither Coleman nor Jencks recommended segregation or reduction in school expenditures; neither contended even that schools *could* not make a difference, but only that schools *do* not now make a difference. Many critics attacked both the methodology of the Coleman and Jencks studies and their conclusions.

THE IQ DEBATE

Shortly after the Jencks report, still another bombshell appeared. Arthur Jensen, a leading educational psychologist, in his book *Genetics and Education*, contended that intelligence is largely a function of heredity and that changes in environment affect intelligence in only a few unusual cases. Jensen stated that blacks were about fifteen points lower than whites in the standard distribution of IQ throughout the population, although he noted that "the full range of human talents is represented in all the major races . . . ." He argued that no amount of compensatory education could improve intelligence, since it is a matter of nature rather than nurture. Needless to say, many have criticized Jensen's work. Some attacks are based on methodological grounds, others are based on ideological grounds. One main thrust of the rebuttals is that intelligence tests are biased culturally against blacks.[34] The conclusions drawn by Coleman, Jencks, and Jensen were reported widely in the mass media, while the rebuttals were confined largely to professional journals of narrower circulation. The original conclusions of these three authors also were subject to popular distortion and misunderstanding.

On the basis of the Coleman, Jencks, and Jensen works, school boards, legislators, governors, the Congress, courts, and presidents came to question whether education could diminish poverty, whether better financing of schools made any difference, whether the financing of schools need be equalized, and whether desegregation was necessary or effective in redressing economic or educational inequities among the races. The Jencks report was cited in the U.S. Supreme Court's decision in the *Rodriguez* case as justification for the position that unequal expenditures among the schools did not in itself contravene the equal protection of the Constitution.

THE COST-QUALITY RELATIONSHIP IN SCHOOLING

The Coleman, Jencks, and Jensen studies did raise the serious question of whether it is possible to achieve equality through education. If not, then the goal of equal educational opportunity becomes far less important in the minds of many. But a flaw in reasoning is evident to others. If we really

[34]For a synthesis of this debate, see H. I. Eysenck, *The IQ Argument*, Open Court, LaSalle, Ill., 1971.

believe that expenditure level has no consequence, then wealthy districts have no reason to resist sharing their revenues with poorer neighbors. As John Coons, a prominent advocate of reforming school finance, put it, "If money is inadequate to improve education, the residents of poor districts should at least have equal opportunity to be disappointed." The issue hinges on the relationship, if any, between the cost and the quality of education and whether the quality of education can be measured properly in terms of cost per pupil. The staff of the National Educational Finance Project, after reviewing the massive research on the matter concluded that the "per pupil expenditure does not tell the whole story, but it is a significant index of differences among the schools."[35]

THE IDEOLOGICAL DEBATE

The dilemma of quality versus equality may be debated in ideological as well as financial terms. In the years immediately following Sputnik, when the essentialist view and the view of education for national survival were in their ascendancy, the forces of elitism surfaced anew. Critics of education spoke more of excellence than of equality. Many assumed that our schools could not be both good and equal. Some argued that the absence of tough academic standards in elementary and secondary schools, while accommodating the many, diminished the achievement of the gifted. Open-door admissions to higher education, it was argued, diluted the quality of higher education. Rickover compared American academic standards with the more elitist European systems but did not allow for the more highly selective admissions standards of the latter. He concluded that American schools were "a national failure." Although the civil rights drive, the Great Society, and court decisions reversed the argument, some still would opt for elitism in our educational system. These people find no comfort in the results of the comparative study mentioned earlier of top American secondary school students' achievement in relation to students in more elitist schools abroad. The study demonstrated that education for all does not lead

necessarily to mediocrity. We believe that quality and equality can be attained simultaneously.

CAN WE AFFORD TO EDUCATE EVERYONE WELL?

We come now to an important issue related to the cost-quality question. Some feel that the costs of education are outrunning our fiscal means. Whether or not that is so depends on our values. As a nation we spend approximately as much money on recreation as we spend on public elementary and secondary schools. We spend about as much on alcoholic beverages as we spend on public higher education. It becomes a question of whether we may wish to spend less on liquor in order to have more available for higher education. Taxes in the United States constitute about 30 percent of our gross national product, a smaller percentage than that of most Western European nations. Compared with these countries, we evidently value public services less in proportion to our wealth than we value other goods and services.

In Chapter 11 we take the position that education is viewed properly not as a burden to society but as an income-producing, high-yield investment. We conclude that the issue is not whether we can afford to support our educational system as we ought to, but whether our failure to do so constitutes an economic burden we cannot afford to bear.

The dilemma of freedom versus structure

THE PRESS FOR FREEDOM IN SCHOOLS

A critical debate rages over the relative value of structure and control in schools, on the one hand, and freedom, on the other. Romantic critics are, like Pollyanna, blindly optimistic in their demand for the elimination of constraints on behavior in schools. They stress the importance of freedom in the learning environment. In fact, they make freedom the watchword for current reform in education, as manifested in the titles of the literature of roman-

[35]*Future Directions of School Finance,* National Educational Finance Project, Gainsville, Fla., 1971, p. 6.

tic criticism: *Freedom and Beyond* (John Holt), *Free Schools* (Jonathan Kozol), *Free to Learn* (Martin and Harrison). They argue for freedom from political control of schools, from regimentation, from arbitrary standards of performance, from graded school organization, from structured curriculum, from competition among students, from corporal punishment, from suspension of students, from compulsory attendance, from predetermined or teacher-imposed learning objectives—the list goes on and on. Kozol believes that the problem of educational reform is the problem of somehow getting much more freedom into our schools. In short, romantic critics argue that if we remove the shackles that now oppress and depress students and liberate their natural curiosity, intelligence, and desire, they will learn effectively and naturally.

Teachers, too, are demanding increased freedom for themselves—freedom to bargain, to strike, to ignore court injunctions; freedom from super-

vision; freedom from accountability for their performance. And the courts have expanded the limits of student freedoms as well, granting freedom from expulsion from school without due process, freedom of access to formerly confidential records, freedom to exercise the constitutional rights afforded adults, and freedom from the schools' former role *in loco parentis.*

Generally speaking, we applaud the movement toward greater freedom in schools. With its ideological roots in Rousseau, this movement is essentially humane and wholesome. It undoubtedly has contributed much to the growing sense of satisfaction that students are finding in school. However, it poses some substantial questions that courts and romanticists may ignore but that school administrators may not.

First, let us examine the freedom to learn what one chooses. As Broudy points out, we may grant each cultural group the right to learn what is

Some school critics argue that if we remove the shackles that oppress students and thereby liberate their natural curiosity they will learn effectively and naturally.

"beautiful" to them with the right not to learn anything else. But if students are really free, they should not be subject to the demands and values of their own ethnic group, either.[36] Moreover, can students be free to succeed in a multicultural society when they fail to understand that society or fail to master the skills necessary for success within it?

Then there is the question of whether untrammeled exercise of freedom will begin to invade the rights and well-being of others. Former United States Commissioner of Education Marland asks:

Would the present phenomenon of student rebellion, defiance of authority, hostility, vandalism, obscenity and other forms of unacceptable behavior in many of our schools have occurred if large numbers of teachers had not, themselves, first broken the laws, defied the courts, and coerced students to support strikes by absenting themselves from school illegally?[37]

THE PRESS TOWARD MORE CONTROL

Elsewhere in this book we draw attention to the frightening rise of violence and vandalism in schools, which costs $500 million annually, an amount equal to the annual expenditure for textbooks. In 1973 there were 70,000 physical assaults on teachers and hundreds of thousands of assaults on students. More than 100 students were murdered on school grounds. In many urban schools, we are told, teachers carry guns for self-protection, and students are afraid to use school rest rooms. Extortion among students is not uncommon.[38]

There are different views on how to cope with such problems, and they relate to the dilemma of freedom versus structure. Silberman, for example, sees discipline problems as the result of mindless school administration and argues for greater freedom. Dobson, a pediatrician, in his book *Dare to Discipline*, takes the opposite view. He contends

that we have raised a generation of young people on the concept of permissiveness and that it has become a disaster. He believes that school authorities maintain too little control over students, that self-control cannot develop in an environment which places no obligation on children, and that self-discipline never results from self-indulgence. He argues that the essential ingredient of every successful football team, orchestra, or business is discipline, which schools are failing to develop.

Rightly or wrongly, the public's sympathies are overwhelmingly in favor of greater control. In the annual Gallup poll on attitudes toward education, discipline is identified as the primary problem. Only 3 percent of the people feel that discipline is too strict; 48 percent feel that it is too lax; 33 percent think it is about right; and the remainder have no opinion. In most districts, administrators are under intense pressure to intensify disciplinary practices.

We generally favor humane schools with the least amount of regimen and the greatest opportunity for students to participate reasonably in their own regulation. However, we also agonize over the bloodshed of those who fall victim to the small minority of troublemakers. Since this minority cannot and should not be denied educational opportunity, and since their presence in schools constitutes a hazard to others, we favor the establishment of separate alternative schools for them, as described in later chapters.[39] Nevertheless, the perplexing dilemma of finding the golden mean between freedom and structure in schools will continue to perplex educators and citizens.

Religion and public interest

Church and state interests sometimes collide because both seek to guide the conduct of people. In the countries from which they came, our ancestors saw the entanglement of church and state and the consequences detrimental to both. They were persuaded that it must not happen here and, through the First Amendment, sought to build

[36]Harry S. Broudy, *The Real World of the Public Schools*, Harcourt, Brace, Jovanovich, New York, 1972, pp. 81–82.

[37]"Marland Appointment Stirs Controversy," *Phi Delta Kappan*, November 1970, p. 140.

[38]See *Discipline: Crisis in Schools—The Problems, Causes, and Searches for Solutions.* National School Public Relations Association, Arlington, Va., 1973, for an alarming documentation of the dimensions of this problem.

[39]For other solutions, see "Violence in the Schools," *The American School Board Journal*, January 1975, pp. 27–37.

what the courts have called a "wall of separation" between church and state. The application of this intent has been contested ever since. In Chapter 14 we will discuss the more important Supreme Court decisions on this issue.[40] These decisions have protected the religious freedom of people by sustaining the right of persons to send their children to church-affiliated schools; by excusing on religious grounds children of Amish families from compulsory school attendance; and by excusing from the flag salute those children whose religious beliefs would thereby be offended. The courts have permitted students to be released from public school attendance under certain conditions for religious instruction. Although devotional use of the Bible is forbidden in public schools by the U.S. Supreme Court, the Bible may be studied for its literary and historical qualities. Comparative religions and the role of religion in history also may be studied. Contrary to popular belief, not all prayer is forbidden in public schools—only prayer that is compulsory or prescribed.

The population disagrees sharply about whether public funds should be used to subsidize church-affiliated elementary and secondary schools. Gradually, the U.S. Supreme Court has whittled away at these subsidies for purposes other than school transportation, school lunches, and textbooks. It permits but does not require such subsidies. President Ford lamented the Court's decision in wiping out tax credits and state tuition payments for families whose children attend church-affiliated schools. He expressed hope that some constitutional means of aiding parochial schools might be found. Pennsylvania persists in trying to find ways of aiding parochial schools at the state level, undaunted by the fact that it probably holds the record for previous unconstitutional attempts. Nor is the issue dead in other states.

Advocates of public aid for private schools contend that these schools render a public service and should not be denied public support. They insist that parents should not be impeded in their constitutional right to send their children to private schools. If parents must pay taxes for the support of public schools, in addition to fees for the support of the private schools, they are, according to the argument, subject to "double taxation" and are discriminated against.

On the other hand, many people contend that public funds should not be given to private schools, over which the public has no control. They contend that the constitutional right of citizens to send their children to private schools does not oblige the government to help pay the costs any more than the guarantee of the right to bear arms obliges the government to subsidize citizens' purchases of guns. They believe that private school attendance is a voluntary choice and that the contention of discrimination is therefore not relevant.

Proposals have been advanced for amending the Constitution to permit public financial support of church-related schools and to permit voluntary prayer, Bible reading, and religious exercises in the public schools. Opponents believe that tampering with the Bill of Rights to ordain certain exceptions to the separation of church and state poses serious hazards. No doubt debate will continue about how much separation should exist between church and state in the field of education. We discuss other issues relating to religion and public education later in this book.[41]

Who controls the schools? Who should control them?

Few questions set off more debate and controversy than these two. Teachers' organizations claim that boards and administrators have too much power, while boards and administrators claim that teachers have usurped too much of their power already. And at the national and state levels, teachers' organizations claim that legislators are unsympathetic with school needs. About the only thing that everyone might agree upon is that the students have little power to influence schools at any level of government. Small wonder that the public is confused

---

[40]For more detailed discussion of these decisions, see Robert L. Jackson, "The Supreme Court Says 'No,'" *Compact,* September/October 1973, pp. 10–13.

[41]For further reading on these issues, see Lawrence Byrnes, *Religion and Public Education,* Harper & Row, New York, 1975.

by the debate and finds it difficult to sort fact from the propaganda that is spread generously in the struggle for power over education. The propaganda from each sector carries much the same theme: Give us more power and be assured that education will be improved greatly.

THE LURE OF POWER OVER SCHOOLS

Power over education is an alluring goal for several reasons. Education is a critical factor in gaining ideological advantage on the great issues of our time. Education is also big business and offers political patronage and profits for many vested interests. Then, too, education affects our most precious and formative resource—children. We are not suggesting that all efforts to gain power over education are nefarious. Regardless of their disagreements, most school board members, teachers, administrators, students, citizens, minority groups, and others are genuinely persuaded that education could be improved if each had more influence upon decisions affecting it. All these groups claim an important equity in schools, and nobody seems to like being governed by others these days.

The controversy is exacerbated by the diverse expectations of each group involved with the schools. To overgeneralize merely for purposes of illustration, many citizens are interested primarily in results and costs. Administrators are interested in neat, orderly methods of dispensing education. Boards are interested in retaining and strengthening powers of governance. Teachers are interested in making schools profitable and satisfying places of employment. Teachers' organizations are interested in building their memberships and gaining advantage in competing with other groups. Politicians are interested in whatever position will support their reelection, especially if it ensures that school expenditures are cost-beneficial.

THE CHANGING BALANCE OF POWER

Schools have always been controlled by a balance of power among (1) various levels of government—federal, state, local, and recently community; (2) employers and employees; and (3) professional and lay interests. Several developments have altered this balance of power drastically. Reorganization of school districts, consolidation of schools, and population growth (discussed in Chapter 12) have increased the size of school districts vastly while decreasing their number. This has widened the gap between board members and individual citizens and resulted in some decline in the power of the constituency. The rise of collective bargaining by teachers has greatly increased their power—and, inadvertently, the power of superintendents—at the expense of school boards' power. Certain federal legislation (see Chapters 11 and 14) has increased the federal bureaucracy's power over schools. The trend toward full state funding of public education (discussed in Chapters 11 and 13) has increased the power of the state over education at the expense of local powers. Students, alas, can point to very little increase in their powers, although court decisions and concern for students' rights have strengthened the protections of due process.

Many observers feel that the schools are already out of control and that all of society must suffer from the raw struggle for power which is taking place. We are dismayed not so much by the competition for power over schools—even when that struggle is self-serving, as it so often is—but by the lack of effective mechanisms for resolving these diverse expectations without resorting to displays of power. The competition for power is multilateral, but many problem-solving mechanisms—collective bargaining is a good example—are bilateral. Our present means are ineffective in harmonizing these interests. We must devise better governance structures that allow greater participation by all but that have mechanisms to forestall any single group from running away with the power. We now shall consider, more briefly than we would wish, several thrusts for power.

TEACHERS' POWER

Teachers claim two bases for the legitimation of their power over schools. First, they are employees, and society has progressively recognized the rights of employees to help shape the destiny of their organizations, particularly in terms of wages, hours, and conditions of employment. Second, teachers are professionals and thereby claim privileged insight and competence in dealing with the decisions necessary to improve schools. The spread of collective bargaining rights to include public employees is a logical response to the first claim but, in the minds of many, an inappropriate response to the second claim. Many states now have collective bargaining laws that grant teachers and other public employees the right to organize and to bargain, along with provisions for resolving impasses. The National Education Association (NEA) and the American Federation of Teachers (AFT) are pressing for a federal law, similar to the National Labor Relations Act, that would extend these rights to teachers nationwide.[42]

Collective bargaining in education. Many states now have laws requiring school boards to bargain with teachers and other employees. Some states have laws that permit bargaining but do not mandate it. Other states have no laws on this matter. Bills have been introduced in Congress to authorize bargaining by teachers on a national basis. At present, no such bill has been enacted.[43]

Collective bargaining has been effective in many districts in resolving personnel problems bilaterally instead of unilaterally. It has produced higher salaries, fringe benefits, and improved conditions of employment for teachers. It has helped to reduce turnover of teachers and has been a factor in increasing the supply of teachers. Communication among teachers, boards, and administrators has improved, and grievance procedures have helped reduce unfair treatment of teachers.

Teachers' organizations have sought to extend the scope of bargaining to include everything of interest to them, including curriculum matters, the selection of principals, and a wide array of other traditional management prerogatives. Although we believe that teachers should participate widely in virtually all important decision making affecting schools, we think their participation should come

through faculty groups rather than through negotiators at the bargaining table.

In many districts collective bargaining has polarized teachers against school boards, parents, and students. Edward Shils, consultant and specialist in industrial and school negotiations, feels that collective bargaining in education may be destroying our schools. He accuses teachers of acting selfishly and of not considering the best interests of students. Teachers deny this and invoke the slogan that what is good for teachers is good for students, a position that many parents regard as sophistry.

Strikes by teachers. Another controversial issue is whether teachers should strike. Most teachers' organizations insist that collective bargaining cannot be effective without the right to strike. They declare that this right, if recognized by law, acts to deter strikes. However, in recent years there have been far more strikes in Pennsylvania, where strikes by public employees are permitted by law under certain conditions, than in any other state. Yet, teachers have fared no better at the bargaining table in Pennsylvania than they have in New York, where teachers' strikes are forbidden by law and where tough penalties are available when the provision is violated.

The courts have held consistently that strikes by public employees are illegal unless permitted by the statutes of the states, as they are in a few states. These decisions are based on the opinion that public services, such as teaching, are for the benefit of the public and not for the benefit of any group and that every government employee is enjoined not to interrupt these essential governmental services. Nevertheless, teacher strikes continue throughout the country, in violation of the law in most states. The National Commission on the Causes and Prevention of Violence has warned:

Is each group to be free to disregard due process and to violate laws considered objectionable? If personal or group selectivity of laws to be obeyed is to be the yardstick, we shall face nationwide disobedience of many laws and thus anarchy. . . . Every time a court order is disobeyed, each time an injunction is violated, each occasion on which a court decision is flouted, the effectiveness of our judicial system is eroded. How much erosion can it tolerate?

---

[42]For further discussion of the pros and cons of this issue, see Myron Lieberman, "Confusion and Controversy: Brace Yourself for Plenty if Congress Passes the Collective Bargaining Law for Teachers," *The American School Board Journal*, April 1975, pp. 41–43.

[43]For an analysis of state collective bargaining laws and the prospects for a federal law, see Thomas James, "Seeking the Limits of Bargaining," *Compact*, June 1975, pp. 13–16.

The growing power of teachers' unions. Powerful teachers' unions are competing for control not only of the teaching profession and its conditions but also of education itself. Along with other unions for public employees, teachers' unions are competing for dominant interest in representing *all* public employees, of which teachers make up the largest group. A single union of public employees could easily become the largest and most powerful union in the land, powerful even beyond its membership numbers because of its ability to shut down essential government service.

Both the NEA and the AFT are determined to ensure the election of school board members and state and federal legislators who support their cause. Both have demonstrated some success toward that goal in recent years. Consider this warning from Helen Wise, former president of the NEA:

In 1972, teachers helped elect about one-third of the House of Representatives and more than one-third of the 33 candidates elected to the Senate. That was just for openers. . . . And let me sound the warning once again: 2 million school teachers are a political force to be reckoned with. Be it a President, a senator, a state legislator, or a school board member—it cannot and will not ever again be politically "safe" to ignore the needs of 46 million children.

Clearly the NEA means business. It has established a Political Action Committee with funds of $1.5 million to elect its friends to office. The issue may be whether our schools and other public enterprise will be governed by their employees or by the will of the people.

There is enormous power to be gained; the stakes are almost beyond comprehension. The struggle will be bitter, and children and society may suffer. The chief rivals in this struggle are the teachers' unions, the associations of school boards, and citizens' organizations.

At issue also is the vital question of whether teachers' unions eventually will merge into a single, all-powerful union, or whether the enormous prize will discourage the tradeoffs necessary for a merger. So far, except in a few states and localities, rival unions have been more determined to protect their organizations' autonomy and power than to unite as a single voice for teachers.

Major issues. The substantive issues at the bargaining table in years past have been salary and conditions of employment. The issues over the next fifteen years will include these two as well as job security and related matters— tenure, dismissal, retirement, the use of instructional technology and paraprofessionals—and the control of schools. (These issues are discussed at length in later chapters.) The decline in enrollments, the rise in unit costs, the tight economic pressures, and the disappointment of many people with their schools will intensify public interest in accountability of teachers. There will be pressure from the public to evaluate teachers more rigorously and to fire or furlough teachers on the basis of performance; pressure to weaken or abolish tenure protections; and pressure to differentiate salaries on the basis of the quality of teachers' work. Teachers' organizations, though not necessarily their rank and file, will vigorously oppose all these pressures. The position of the teachers' unions will continue as it has been: Pay us more money, reduce our workload, free us from evaluation and accountability, let us control the schools, and accept on faith that better teaching will follow.

Tenure laws and tenure quotas—job security based on seniority rather than on competence —will polarize many young teachers and professors who are shut out and older teachers and professors who are protected. Seniority considerations will be disadvantageous to members of minority groups and to women in higher education, making them the last to be hired and the first to be fired. This polarization will tend to radicalize young teachers, those in minority groups, and females, particularly those in higher education and those seeking administrative career positions in public schools. Teachers' unions will respond with pressure for more liberalized retirement benefits and turnover through earlier retirement, rather than through dismissal or furlough. This maximizes the unions' income from dues and reduces internal friction, but at an enormous cost to the public.

The continued high cost of education, particularly when the economy is depressed, will bring even greater public pressure for economical operation of schools and colleges. Caught in the pressures from both sides, school boards and administrators will be forced to make greater use of instructional technology and paraprofessionals.

Teaching, the last of the great labor-intensive enterprises, probably will be accomplished more by technology or semiautomated systems than by human systems of instruction sometime after 1985, when the costs of these alternatives may become competitive. The question of whether the cost-benefit advantage will favor technological systems may be ignored because decisions probably will be based on political and economic considerations rather than on pedagogical considerations. Critical factors in this fateful choice will be whether the teachers' unions are successful at negotiating job-security provisions by 1985 and whether they merge into a single national union powerful enough to shut down schools across the land.

We view the vast majority of individual teachers favorably because of their sense of professional responsibility, their concern for the greater public good, and their desire to render an honest day's work for a fair day's pay. The rise of the National Association of Professional Educators is some evidence of individual teachers' good faith. This organization is opposed to a federal collective bargaining law, compulsory union membership, closed shops, agency shops, strikes, and lockouts. It is opposed to the erosion of the decision-making powers of elected boards. Educators who hold such views will have an opportunity to make the teaching profession something other than a "conspiracy against the laity," as George Bernard Shaw characterized all professions. Certainly the remainder of this century will be a bracing and exciting era for everyone concerned with education.

CITIZENS' POWER

The conventional wisdom has been that the ultimate control of schools rests with the people. It is true that citizens entrust day-to-day governance of the schools to their local school boards and to state and federal legislatures. Through their franchise they can replace their representatives and, in many states, can vote on referendums affecting capital outlay, school budgets, and tax levies for school purposes.

The alleged decline in citizens' control. A study by James Guthrie, reported in *Public Control of Public Schools: Can We Get It Back?* revealed that public control of schools has been declining since World War II and is now virtually lost. Guthrie regards school board members as a "miniscule group" that wields little political influence. He attributes the decline of public control to two major factors: (1) powerful teachers' unions that have won for teachers economic gains far above the growth of the gross national product as well as the political power to veto school board policy making; and (2) a new professional bureaucracy of professional school managers. Guthrie cites other contributing factors—principally urbanization, population growth, and the consolidation of school districts—all of which have contributed to the growth of school districts and the erosion of public control.

A two-year nationwide survey for ways to improve schools conducted by the U.S. Office of Education produced agreement that improvement is needed but disagreement on how to do it. The study noted, as we have, that everybody wants more control for themselves—state agencies, local districts, teachers, and citizens. Agreeing with Guthrie, the report found "private enclaves" of top educators had seized control of education, and the report concluded that they must give it up. Curiously, administrators were at the same time lamenting a decline in their control and were prescribing means for reclaiming it.[44]

The drive toward reclaiming citizens' control. The National Committee for Citizens in Education (NCCE) proclaimed itself ready to recapture citizens' control of education. It, too, conducted inquiries into school governance and concluded that public education is "out of control" but that no single group has emerged supreme, although teachers' organizations are seen as the strongest and most effective single source of power. Without adequate citizen influence, it warned, teachers' power might become unlimited. The NCCE pledged itself to the task of "mobilizing citizen action around high impact issues," such as the selection of instructional materials, budgetary decisions, and protection of students' rights. The NCCE is a nonprofit organization supported by individual

---

[44]See, for example, Thomas E. Williams, "Governance Is the Real Issue: A Management Manifesto," *Phi Delta Kappan*, April 1975, pp. 561–562.

membership fees and a subsidy from the Ford Foundation. It regards itself as a sort of "Common Cause" for public education.[45]

A number of books appeared in the mid-1970s calling for a mobilization of citizens' power to recapture control of the schools from professional educators. Harvey Scribner, former chancellor of the New York City school system and coauthor with Leonard Stevens of *Make Your Schools Work*, claimed that "public control of schools is close to a fantasy" and urged parents to battle with professional educators because they "display an uncommon capacity to resist fundamental reform." Martin Busken, in his book *Parent Power*, likewise urged parents to confront the "bureaucratic school jungle," which, he claims, opposes the interests of children and parents. Carol Kimmel national PTA president, in addressing the National Association of State Boards of Education in 1975, stated that taxpayers and parents "may rise in wrath against the schools" and that "parents are now seeking and may soon demand a way to be heard, as they watch local control of 'their' schools continuing to erode."

It is too early to forecast the success of various efforts by citizens to recover whatever control they may have lost, but it appears likely that we are headed for a major confrontation between citizens and professional educators over control of schools. If citizens can become effectively mobilized—and that is a very big "if"—we have no doubt that they could ultimately prevail in this struggle.[46]

The need for power equalization. We would like to see a more effective multilateral approach by those who have legitimate concern for the schools—teachers, students, school boards, legislators, and citizens—with careful definition of the roles of each in goal setting, decision making, governing, and evaluating. We regard this multilat-

eral approach as the only effective check and balance against runaway power grabs by self-serving interest groups. Lord Acton's classic admonition is germane: "Power tends to corrupt; absolute power corrupts absolutely."

The dilemmas of community control. One special aspect of citizens' control deserves further mention. Chapters 12, 13, and 14 discuss the division of control over schools among federal, state, and local levels of government. Here we will look at a recent subdivision—community or neighborhood control of schools. The movement toward community control of schools has had its greatest thrust in poor neighborhoods of large urban school systems where citizens feel that the established, centralized bureaucracy is not responsive to their educational needs. Many large districts have moved toward decentralization of power and toward greater community control of local schools. By now, second thoughts are beginning to emerge. It has been pointed out that community control has simply transformed power from a central body that lacked sufficient funds, facilities, and insights to many neighborhood groups that lack the same. Others suggest that the movement toward community control has not come to grips with the essence of the urban school problem: how to overcome the disadvantages of poverty that underlie the learning difficulties of children in inner-city school systems. One study showed that reading scores of students in New York City were lower after community control went into effect. Some have concluded that community control simply recreates separate but sometimes unequal schools and leads to racism and anarchy. Kenneth Clark, once an advocate of this movement and a member of the New York Board of Regents, has changed his mind. He now speaks of the decentralization of schools in New York City as a "disastrous experiment" and deplores the manner in which selfish groups used the movement to advance their own political ends to the detriment of the real mission, teaching children.[47] Perhaps it is too early to abandon hope for community control of schools. Perhaps we have not yet found or refined sufficiently the proper

[45]For further description of this new organization, see Phillip G. Jones, "An Uncommonly Earnest Citizen Group Is Trying Hard to Become the Common Cause of Education," *The American School Board Journal*, March 1975, pp. 41–45.

[46]For further analysis of public control, see Mortimer Smith, "Can Control of Public Schools Be Returned to Citizens?" *Council for Basic Education Bulletin*, September 1974, pp. 1–3 and Carol Kimmel, "Putting the Public Back in Public Schools," *The National Elementary Principal*, March-April 1976, pp. 33–35.

[47]For further reading on the New York failure, see Martin Schiff, "The Educational Failure of Community Control in Inner-city New York," *Phi Delta Kappan*, February 1976, pp. 375–378.

means for accomplishing it, as its defenders suggest.

The impossible dream

Much criticism of education is born of an impossible dream. The schools have become victims of what Adlai Stevenson called the "revolution of rising expectations." Simply stated, we have expected our schools to reform society—but very often society does not wish to be reformed outside the schools. To criticize the schools' failure at social reform is, we think, grossly misleading and unfair. The schools have been expected to do more than they possibly could.

The schools have been called upon to arrest drug abuse, reduce highway fatalities, combat venereal disease, overcome racial injustice, reduce unemployment, entertain the public with sports extravaganzas, produce wise consumers, conduct charitable drives, and perform a host of other tasks. Almost any problem in society is viewed almost immediately as "an educational problem," and people turn to the schools expecting instant success. Thus the schools become both the scapegoat for the ills of society and the source of hope for their cure.

The schools can cure social problems only to the extent they cause them. We expect the schools to inculcate in young people the most idealistic moral, social, and economic principles, while the larger society commonly sets a poor example. The schools are asked to desegregate even while community housing patterns remain stubbornly segregated. During the era of the Great Society, particularly, the schools were expected to eliminate poverty, while tax loopholes were maintained for the rich. Later, the schools were expected to indoctrinate students with respect for law and order, while our highest public official violated the law and was pardoned promptly without trial. The schools were expected to teach good citizenship and intercultural relations, while our government bolstered dictatorships abroad. Schools were expected to dissuade young people from acts of violence, while government agencies plotted the assassination of heads of state abroad. The schools were asked to quicken instruction in environmental

protection, while powerful business interests sacrificed the environment for profit, often with governmental acquiescence.

We expect schools to provide safe places for our young but we show them an average of 1,300 murders on television between the ages of 5 and 15. Parents insist upon stricter control of troublemakers in schools, while courts insist such students remain in school and romantic critics call for relaxed regimen and control. Finally, teachers engage in unlawful strikes and disdain court injunctions while railing against the disobedience of students.

After we integrate a society that doesn't want to be integrated, we may succeed in integrating the schools. *After* the larger society lives by the Bill of Rights and the golden rule, we can hold students responsible for the same. *After* society comes to value things of the mind over material things, we can expect children and youths to cherish similar priorities. Henry Steele Commager pointed out the problem in a brilliant article:

If our educational enterprise is in disarray, it is in part because we have asked it to perform a miracle—to teach the young to understand the world they live in and the one they are to live in in the future when we ourselves show little awareness of our fiduciary obligation to that future. . . . Nothing that is fundamental and lasting can be achieved without a change in the standards, the values, the objectives—moral as well as social—of society.[48]

It is folly to expect that this hypocrisy goes undetected among our students. Clearly a society that is unwilling or unable to manifest its idealism can hardly expect the schools to make up the difference. To importune or indict our schools for the failures of the larger society is sheer hypocrisy.

Our children are educated by the larger society throughout their lifetime, but they are *schooled* for only a brief period. Education is not something we can hand over to schools. Commager points out that only in the last two centuries have we thought of schools as the sole or even primary formal agency for dispensing the whole of education. Only quite recently have we expected schools to

[48]Henry Steele Commager, "Public Responsibility and the Educational Enterprise," *The National Elementary Principal,* May/June, 1975, pp. 11, 15. Copyright 1975, National Association of Elementary School Principals. All rights reserved.

accommodate everyone. Commager notes too that nineteenth-century romanticists had faith in education and in infinite human perfectibility, while today we are disillusioned with education, if not with ourselves.

Is the outlook for education as dreary as many critics would have us believe? We think not. Clearly we need realistic and attainable goals for our schools, and fortunately new management technology is producing them. There is also greatly increased awareness—especially among young people—of the injustices endemic to our society, injustices that repudiate the observations of de Tocqueville and the vision of Jefferson. In addition, the next generation of adults is more determined to repair the schools than to inveigh against them. Indeed, as noted later, young people do not share the critics' views that the schools are failures. We earlier noted Revel's conviction that a revolution against injustices and inequities is well underway here and that our country, more than any other, provides the milieu for its success. Daniel Moynihan concludes that most of the events which tore American society apart are now behind us, never to occur again. They grew out of a population explosion that created a new social class of youths segregated from the larger culture and alienated by it. Moynihan finds that the youth culture is being integrated rapidly into the larger culture. He predicts a more stable society in decades ahead, with a stability and conservatism characteristic of societies whose population growth has plateaued. He also believes that our institutions finally are becoming more open and more able to cope with change and conflict. He thinks we have come out of our time of trouble and are back to a time of peace.[49] Perhaps the impossible dream is becoming possible.

This chapter discussed the most pervasive criticisms of education and outlined the important issues facing educators. Readers will encounter many more specific issues in the chapters that follow. It is fitting to end the chapter with a challenge from one of our favorite educators,

California's Superintendent of Public Instruction, Wilson Riles:

If we are to halt that self-defeating downward spiral of loss of faith and loss of hope, it is up to us in the classrooms of America to give the lie to the critics who say schools make no difference. A most critical element in restoration of faith in America and its institutions is not the exhortations of some political pollyannas in Washington, but the actions of millions of classroom teachers all across America. It is through your dedication to the individual child, your commitment to excellence, and your willingness to involve the parent and the community in the educational process that we will not only restore public confidence in education as a foundation for a better life, but we will also restore society's faith in itself.[50]

Suggested activities

1. Consider your own schooling, or segments of it, and analyze it in relation to the philosophical bases of education explained in this chapter.
2. State your views about compulsory education and how you think the laws should be amended, if at all.
3. Describe the reforms in education that you consider to be most crucial in equalizing educational opportunity for members of minority groups.
4. State your position on the dilemma of quality versus equality in education.
5. Interview several superintendents of schools and several presidents of local teachers' unions to discover what each considers to be the most critical issues in education and compare the results.
6. Consider the various proposals advanced to strengthen the accountability of schools. Select those which you consider most sound and explain why you think so.
7. Review the philosophical bases of education stated in this chapter. Decide which one you prefer and prepare an essay defending it.
8. Select a popular magazine and make a list of the educational issues it has considered during the past year. Compare the results with your own list of most critical issues.
9. State your position on the question of whether public funds should be provided for private education.
10. Prepare a critical review of one of the books listed in the bibliography that interests you.

[49]"Moynigan Spreads Optimism," *Phi Delta Kappan,* November 1973, p. 219.

[50]Wilson Riles, "The First Eight Years," *The American Teacher,* May 1975, p. 6.

Bibliography

Bailey, Stephen: *The Purposes of Education*, Phi Delta Kappa, Bloomington, Ind., 1976. Description of developments that appear to be reshaping purpose in education toward the pursuit of happiness.

Blanshard, Brand: *The Uses of a Liberal Education*, Open Court, La Salle, Ill., 1973. Delightful, witty, and sensible treatment of the purposes of education.

Bowles, Samuel, and Herbert Gintis: *Schooling in Capitalist America*, Basic Books, New York, 1976. Argument that schools promote inequality and cannot do otherwise without a socialist economic system.

Broudy, Harry S.: *The Real World of the Public Schools*, Harcourt, Brace, Jovanovich, New York, 1972. Strong rebuttal of the criticisms of schools advanced by romantic and radical critics.

Byrnes, Lawrence: *Religion and Public Education*, Harper & Row, New York, 1975. Helpful to teachers in clarifying the legal, psychological, and pedagogical aspects of teaching about religion in the public schools.

Elam, Stanley (ed.): *The Gallup Poll of Attitudes toward Education, 1969–1973*, Phi Delta Kappa, Bloomington, Ind., 1973. Analysis of data gathered on the public's attitudes toward a wide variety of educational issues.

Eysenck, H. I: *The IQ Argument*, Open Court, La Salle, Ind., 1971. Balanced treatment of the issues regarding the IQ debate with respect to race and environmental variables.

Fantini, Mario D.: *What's Best for Children?* Doubleday, New York, 1974. Discussion of the collision between teachers' power and parents' demands for accountability and the need for alternatives to the public schools.

Glasser, William: *Schools without Failure,* Harper & Row, New York, 1969. Classic work on the causes of students' failures in schools and the cures through increased involvement of students in their learning activities.

Goodlad, John I., M. Frances Klein, and associates: *Behind the Classroom Door*, Jones, Worthington, Ohio, 1971. Case material from observations in many schools illuminates the issues in educational change.

Haskens, Jim (ed.): *Black Manifesto for Education*, Morrow, New York, 1973. Collection of ten essays by important black educators suggesting remedies for the failure of schools to serve the needs of black students.

Heckinger, Fred M., and Grace Heckinger: *Growing Up in America,* McGraw-Hill, New York, 1975. Historical account of reform and politics in education, including the controversies and struggles between elitist and egalitarian forces.

Hook, Sidney: *Education and the Taming of Power,* Open Court, La Salle, Ill., 1973. Well-known educational philosopher contends that radical critics tend to corrupt education; a defense of Dewey's philosophy of progressive education.

Illich, Ivan: *Deschooling Society,* Harper & Row, New York, 1971. Powerful criticism of schools and a radical remedy—abolish them.

Jones, J. William: *Discipline Crisis in the Schools,* National School Public Relations Association, Arlington, Va., 1973. Discussion of the problems, causes, and possible solutions to the problem that citizens consider the most critical of all school problems—discipline.

Kimbrough, Ralph B., and Michael Nunnery: *Educational Administration*, Macmillan, New York, 1976, chapters 11 and 14. Analysis of the social and political influences upon the control and administration of schools.

Lerner, Max: *Values in Education,* Phi Delta Kappa, Bloomington, Ind., 1976. Examination of current direction of values in education in relation to many of the issues discussed in this chapter.

Lucas, Christopher J.: *Challenge and Choice in Contemporary Education*, Macmillan, Riverside, N.J., 1976. Explanation of six major ideological perspectives on the purposes of education.

Martin, Don T., George E. Overholt, and Wayne J. Urban: *Accountability in American Education*, Princeton Book Co., Princeton, N.J., 1976. A critique of the accountability movement in education.

Mills, Nicolaus (ed.): *The School Bus Controversy,* Teachers College, New York, 1974. Series of articles on the problems and means of achieving better racial balances in schools through busing.

National Committee for Citizens in Education: *Public Testimony on Public Schools,* McCutchan, Berkeley, Calif., 1975. Report of public testimony and recommendations for solving problems of school governance and policy making and of power imbalance between teachers' organizations and the public interest.

Postman, Neil, and Charles Weingartner: *The School Book,* Delacorte, Dell, New York, 1973. A no-nonsense discussion of what schools are, why they exist, what makes them good or bad, and issues of concern.

St. John, Nancy H.: *School Desegregation, Outcomes for Children,* Wiley, New York, 1975. Excellent review of the evidence from research on the effects of school segregation on children and young people.

Sexton, Patricia: *Women in Education,* Phi Delta Kappa, Bloomington, Ind., 1976. Review of progress toward changing roles of women in education with consideration of barriers to further improvement.

Shields, James J., Jr.: *The Crisis in Education Is Outside the Classroom,* Phi Delta Kappa, Bloomington, Ind., 1973. Synthesis of the various philosophical views of the purposes of education and their influence upon criticism of schools.

Sowell, Thomas: *Black Education: Myths and Tragedies,* McKay, New York, 1972. Trenchant analysis of the problems in the education of blacks and the mistakes that are being made in trying to solve them.

Stent, Madelon D., William R. C. Hazard, and **Harry N. Rivlin:** *Cultural Pluralism in Education,* Appleton Century Crofts, New York, 1973. Practical examination of the myths of a melting-pot society and the way in which schools can make cultural pluralism work.

Tresconi, Charles A., Jr., and **Emanual Horwitz, Jr.** (eds.): *Education for Whom?* Dodd, Mead, New York, 1974. Readings on basic research, concepts, and ideas relative to achieving more equal educational opportunity; discusses the philosophical, sociological, economic, and legal problems involved.

Wasserman, Miriam (ed.): *Demystifying School,* Praeger, New York, 1974. Anthology of writings analyzing a cross-section of contemporary educational issues.

Chapter 2
Teachers and other personnel

YOU WILL HAVE MASTERED THIS CHAPTER WHEN YOU CAN

Define

- performance-based teacher education and evaluation
- accreditation
- affirmative action
- differentiated staffing

Describe

- the components of teacher education and trends
- the problems and trends in staff development
- teacher centers

Analyze

- evaluation of teachers and teaching
- arguments regarding tenure
- the rivalry and issues among teachers' organizations
- the impact of accountability on the teaching profession

Shall I teach?

We all want to do the things that seem important to us, and we develop our own sets of values out of our experience; but each occupation, too, tends to impose a set of inherent values upon its workers. When these occupational values are compatible with our own values, we experience a sense of satisfaction and worthwhileness in our work. Through purposeful employment, then, we progress toward our most valued goals in life, for work provides a major means to their realization. In searching for a career, then, one must ask: "What values and goals do I seek in life? What do I hope to achieve in life? In what occupation can I pursue my aspirations most effectively?" Let us consider some of the unique aspirations that can be realized through teaching.

Teaching offers singular opportunities for the realization of many important, intrinsic values in life. It enables—indeed requires—teachers to engage in a never-ending pursuit of knowledge. The world of the teacher is a world of learning. The opportunity for self-education for those of insatiable intellectual curiosity is unmatched in any other profession. It is in the education of others that teachers find the secret of their own education. The teacher's role in educating others is becoming increasingly profound. We have traditionally thought of teachers as the dispensers of information. Today they must be conceived as something far more than that. The knowledge explosion has forced upon us, fortunately, a new concept of the teacher. It is no longer possible to dispense during the school years all the knowledge that students will need in their lives, and so we have come to stress "learning how to learn" as the essence of modern education. Thus the new role of teachers becomes that of stimulating learners' curiosity, sharpening their powers of independent intellectual discovery, and strengthening their ability to organize and use knowledge on their own initiative—in short, helping learners acquire lifelong powers of self-education.

The modern teacher has often been spoken of as an exemplar of fine scholarship, a model scholar whom students may emulate, the very embodiment of his or her discipline. This new role of the teacher as exemplar, far more profound than the role as mere dispenser of information, extends the impact of teachers on the modes of thought and methods of study of students throughout their lives. Thus teachers are sustained by the challenge of implanting this important intellectual vestige of themselves in others. To help in guiding another generation's chance to grow is perhaps the noblest form of human expression. This is immortality beyond compare and is as near to having a share in eternity as one can come in this earthly setting. This is indeed a difficult task.

Many teachers are attracted by the intellectual challenge of the task. Others choose to become teachers because of their fondness for working with people in a very personal manner. This close interpersonal relationship is manifested in both heartaches and joys. The heartaches include the discouragement of trying to teach students who will not or cannot learn well, the futility of trying to overcome the deep scars that society has imposed upon some children, and the heavy toll on one's conscience imposed by this awesome responsibility for so many young lives.

People wish to be engaged in socially useful work. Throughout this book, we have stressed the paramount importance of teaching. There are people who believe that teaching is surpassed in importance by no other occupation. Table 2-1 lists the behaviors of teachers that are effective. You may wish to compare yourself with the elements of this table.

The World Confederation of Organizations of the Teaching Profession has summarized well the most essential qualities of the effective teacher:

The teacher must possess high personal qualities of an intellectual and ethical character. The teacher in his personal life as well as professional life must always be aware that he is a model for the pupils. The love of children, faith in his vocation, personal devotion and commitment are equally indispensable, as is courage in all difficult situations. Patience, intellectual curiosity, critical thinking and tolerance are also essential because the teacher must in his work respect the child in his charge and help him to develop his individuality. These qualities must be supported by good physical and mental balance, a sense of humor, and enthusiasm which will develop in the class a relaxed and peaceful climate of learning among the students.

To our minds, the most preeminent hallmark of the ideal teacher is a spirit of reverence for children and youths.

Teacher education

Every profession is measured in part by the level and quality of its members' professional preparation. We now shall consider the accreditation of

To help in guiding another generation's chance to grow is perhaps the noblest form of human expression.

Table 2-1 Generalized descriptions of critical behaviors of teachers

Effective behaviors	Ineffective behaviors
Is alert, appears enthusiastic	Is apathetic, dull; appears bored
Appears interested in students and classroom activities	Appears uninterested in pupils and classroom activities
Is cheerful, optimistic	Is depressed, pessimistic; appears unhappy
Is self-controlled, not easily upset	Loses temper easily, is easily upset
Likes fun, has a sense of humor	Is overly serious, too occupied for humor
Recognizes and admits own mistakes	Is unaware of, or fails to admit, own mistakes
Is fair, impartial, and objective in treatment of students	Is unfair or partial in dealing with students
Is patient	Is impatient
Shows understanding and sympathy in working with students	Is short with students, uses sarcastic remarks, or in other ways shows lack of sympathy with students
Is friendly and courteous in relations with students	Is aloof and removed in relations with students
Helps students with personal as well as educational problems	Seems unaware of students' personal needs and problems
Commends effort and gives praise for work well done	Does not commend students; is disapproving, hypercritical
Accepts students' efforts as sincere	Is suspicious of students' motives
Anticipates reactions of others in social situations	Does not anticipate reactions of others in social situations
Encourages students to try to do their best	Makes no effort to encourage students to try to do their best
Classroom procedure is planned and well organized	Procedure is without plan, disorganized
Classroom procedure is flexible within overall plan	Shows extreme rigidity of procedure, inability to depart from plan
Anticipates individual needs	Fails to provide for individual differences and needs of students
Stimulates students through interesting and original materials and techniques	Uninteresting materials and teaching techniques used
Gives clear, practical demonstrations and explanations	Demonstrations and explanations are not clear and are poorly conducted
Is clear and thorough in giving directions	Directions are incomplete, vague
Encourages students to work through their own problems and evaluate their accomplishments	Fails to give students opportunity to work out their own problems or evaluate their own work
Disciplines in quiet, dignified, and positive manner	Reprimands at length, ridicules, resorts to cruel or meaningless forms of correction
Gives help willingly	Fails to give help or gives it grudgingly
Foresees and attempts to resolve potential difficulties	Is unable to foresee and resolve potential difficulties

SOURCE: David G. Ryans, *Characteristics of Teachers*, American Council on Education, Washington, 1960, p. 82.

these programs, the components of teacher education common among the institutions engaged in this work, the problems and trends in teacher education, and the current level of education of teachers.[1]

[1]Readers interested in the historical development of teacher education and descriptions of various types of programs are referred to Martin Haberman and T. M. Stinnett, *Teacher Education and the New Profession of Teaching*, McCutchan, Berkeley, Calif., 1973, chaps. 2–5. See also the historical calendar at the end of this chapter.

ACCREDITATION OF PROGRAMS

Accreditation, in the context of our discussion, is the recognition or approval of a college or university program of preparation in a professional field, such as teaching, granted by a voluntary, nongovernmental agency according to specified criteria and standards of quality. Controversy over these criteria and standards is not uncommon, abetted particularly by persons who regard the criteria or standards as too arbitrary or restricting. Accreditation serves a number of purposes: to improve teacher education; to help students, employers, and state certification bodies identify institutions of established quality; to stimulate the evaluation of teacher education; and to quicken the exchange of good practice among institutions responsible for teacher education. The National Council for the Accreditation of Teacher Education, organized in 1954, was recognized in 1956 by the National Commission on Accrediting as "the sole national agency for accreditation of teacher education." The council (NCATE) is autonomous with regard to the policies and procedures it follows.[2]

NCATE has no legal basis for its function, since accreditation of teacher-education institutions is not required by law. However, NCATE does accredit approximately 40 percent of the 1,300 teacher-education institutions that produce approximately 80 percent of the nation's teachers. NCATE is governed by representatives of the American Association of Colleges for Teacher Education, the National Education Association, the Council of Chief State School Officers, the National Association of State Directors of Teacher Education and Certification, the National School Boards Association, and representatives of various learned societies. NCATE suffers from inadequate financing. Its accreditation teams, consisting of unpaid volunteers, visit approximately one hundred campuses a year. NCATE has been the center of a political tug-of-war between the teachers of the NEA and the professors of education in the teacher-training institutions for greater control over the teacher-education function. Some observers speculate that one reason for the NEA's struggle for more control over accreditation is to decrease the number of teachers being prepared as a means of strengthening the profession's bargaining stance. State departments of education, seeking to retain controls over professional standards and to counteract the increasingly aggressive posture of the teachers' unions, are increasing their constraints over teacher-education curriculums. Teacher-training institutions object to the constraints imposed by both the state departments and the teachers' organizations. This conflict is becoming increasingly politicized in many states.

[2]Readers interested in the standards that NCATE applies to the accreditation of teacher-education programs are referred to Haberman and Stinnett, op. cit., chap. 13.

MAJOR CURRICULUM BELIEFS

NCATE prepared a working statement entitled "The Teacher Education Curriculum." It contains the following major beliefs regarding in-college preparation for teachers: "The curriculum for teacher education should be attractive to capable students who seek a good basic education for themselves and adequate preparation for a professional career."

The statement also includes the following major convictions:

- All teachers should be well-educated persons.
- The curriculum should produce an area of subject-matter concentration for each teacher.
- Teachers should have specific preparation for their specific responsibilities.
- The curriculum should include a well-organized program of professional work, including laboratory experiences.

COMPONENTS OF TEACHER EDUCATION

These curriculum beliefs usually are implemented through programs in four areas: general or liberal education, specialized education in subjects or grade levels, professional education, and supervised practice in teaching. These components are illustrated in a model design of teacher education in Figure 2-1.

General or liberal education. Fundamentally, liberal education includes the social sciences, the natural and physical sciences, and the humanities. Teachers work in a broad profession, not a narrow trade. They are responsible for the general education of young Americans—the workers and citizens of tomorrow. Therefore, teachers are expected to have a rich cultural background.

Specialized education in subjects or levels. Prospective teachers should complement a broad cultural and general education with specialization in the subjects, fields, or levels in which they expect to teach. For teachers in elementary school, the preparation is usually in terms of grade levels, although academic specialization by elementary school teachers is becoming much more common and is required in some states.

Professional education. Usually, the require-

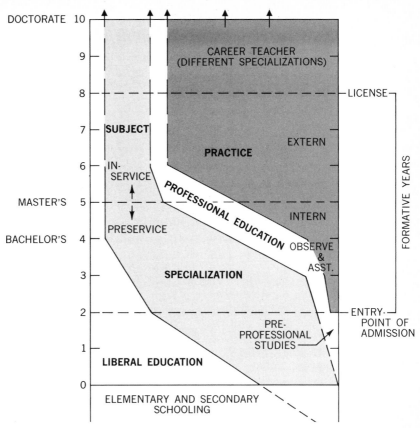

Figure 2-1 A design for teacher education. This design shows the ideal mix of liberal education, specialization, professional education, and practice through an eight-year program extending from entry into college until licensure. The second year of college becomes a common point of formal entry. Practice begins immediately and is broadened after preservice study, which is merged into in-service education. Liberal education is extended through the entire career. (Reprinted from National Commission on Teacher Education and Professional Standards, *The Real World of the Beginning Teacher,* National Education Association, Washington, 1966, p. 13. Copyrighted by the National Education Association, 1966.)

ments in specific professional education are stated in terms of semester hours. The median requirement is 24 semester hours for elementary teachers and 18 semester hours for secondary school teachers. Most teacher-education institutions go beyond the legal minimum. In some colleges this professional work is concentrated in the last year or two, but in the majority it is spread over the upper three years. For some it is concentrated in a fifth year or a sixth year, as will be indicated later. For some it is diffused over several years.

Directed observations, case studies of students, and activities in preparation for student teaching are essential phases of professional education because they include actual experience with children. As has been repeatedly stated, the verb "to teach" has two accusatives—the student and the subject. Some knowledge of students can be acquired through observation, practicums, and direct student teaching.

Supervised practice in teaching. One of the most important aspects of preservice education is experience as a student teacher. "Student teaching," or "practice teaching" as it may be termed, gradually inducts prospective teachers into the full responsibility of the teaching-learning activities under the skillful guidance of a supervising, or helping, teacher and the college's director of student teaching along with faculty colleagues.

A higher level of experience for future teachers is provided through internships comparable to those in medicine. Internship vitally integrates the theoretical and practical aspects of the student's education and has many other significant values. It gives the beginning teacher a chance to spend the first year in a superior school under conditions conducive to growth, it provides guidance and supervision at the time they are most needed, it makes possible a gradual transition from student to teacher, and it serves as a period of testing and probation. These values and others are derived from internship plans now conducted jointly by many institutions of teacher education and cooperating schools. These internships are often found in curricular patterns such as the five-year programs. Half-time graduate study is often combined with a half-time paid internship, terminating in a master's degree.

Nearly all teacher-education institutions provide facilities for students to experience actual teaching in the campus laboratory school, in teaching centers described later, or in other off-campus schools. Many teacher-education institutions provide opportunity for students as early as their sophomore year to visit schools to observe and analyze teaching methods and to observe learners. The Association for Student Teaching, organized in 1920, has helped to strengthen the supervision of student teaching.

CURRICULAR PATTERNS IN TEACHER EDUCATION

Three elements of teacher education—general or liberal education, specialization in subjects or fields in which the student expects to teach, and professional work, including student teaching —are organized in various patterns. There is considerable disagreement over the merits of each. Actually, this disagreement is part of a larger quarrel over the proper balance among these three areas in the total preparation program. However, there is great diversity in both the format and the quality of teacher education among the 1,300 institutions that prepare teachers. This great diversity, and the controversy that accompanies it, is understandable in view of the equally great divergence over what constitutes effective teaching. The criti-

cal relationship between the desirable educational experiences of children and the preparation of teachers is illustrated in this poignant parable:

Greeting his pupils, the master asked:
"What would you learn of me?"
And the reply came:
"How shall we care for our bodies?
"How shall we rear our children?
"How shall we work together?
"How shall we live with our fellowman?
"How shall we play?
"For what ends shall we live? . . ."
And the teacher pondered these words, and sorrow was in his heart, for his own learning touched not these things.[3]

WEAKNESSES IN TEACHER-EDUCATION PROGRAMS

George Denemark, former president of the American Association of Colleges for Teacher Education, has identified ten weaknesses of teacher education that demand reform:

1. Inadequacies and irrelevance of much that presently constitutes the general or liberal education component
2. The hostile academic atmosphere in which teacher education is conducted
3. Lack of conceptual framework for teacher education
4. Simplistic views of teaching and teacher education
5. Inadequate interlacing of theory and practice
6. Continued acceptance of the single model, "omnicapable" teacher
7. Low standards for selection and retention of students in teacher education
8. Schedule rigidities and cumbersome procedures for curriculum change
9. Absence of student opportunities for exploration and inquiry
10. Schizophrenic role expectations for teacher-education departments

PROBLEMS OF TEACHER EDUCATION

The problems confronting teacher education are legion, and space permits brief mention of only a few. Teacher education is generally underfinanced. Most colleges and universities have

---

[3] J. Crosby Chapman and George S. Counts, *Principles of Education*, Houghton Mifflin, Boston, 1924, frontispiece.

badly shortchanged their schools or departments of education in comparison with other professional schools.

Perhaps the greatest shortcoming of teacher education has been its general inability to prepare teachers who are capable of providing effective instruction for children from economically depressed neighborhoods. These children need superb teaching most. They are not incapable of learning, but it takes more professional skill to reach them. Undernourished, underprepared, and often hostile to conventional schooling, they require patient and imaginative teaching. Many of them are members of minority groups and have difficulty responding to teachers who belong to the majority culture and who are inexperienced in relations with minority groups. Teacher Corps trainees are the shining exception to this generalization. These sensitive young people complete teacher education addressed specifically to educating children of poverty. Their success in slum schools derives from their capacity for love, openness, and a sense of humanity. But there are not enough of them. The preparation of more and better teachers for educationally and economically disadvantaged students is surely a prime educational challenge of our time. Just as we arrange for the best surgeons to perform the most difficult surgery, so we must arrange for the most skillful teachers to guide the education of children whose learning is most difficult. We have not done that before now. Too many slum schools have been staffed in large part by teachers who remain after the more attractive schools have made their choices, although some city school systems are attempting to reverse this situation.

Another problem of teacher education is the ambivalence between the education courses and the real world of classroom teaching. Preservice preparation and in-service education usually are not articulated well.

TRENDS IN TEACHER EDUCATION

Teacher education, like all education, is constantly adapting to changing needs and circumstances.

MAT programs. During the 1950s and 1960s, many colleges and universities began Master of Arts in Teaching (MAT) programs in which graduates of liberal arts colleges undertook a fifth year of postbaccalaureate study in education and in a teaching field leading to the master of arts degree. This advanced study was related closely to a teaching internship in a school system in cooperation with the college or university. Many of the MAT programs were subsidized by the Ford Foundation and were intended to accelerate the recruitment of liberal arts graduates into education during the decades of the great shortage of teachers. Another not so incidental intention was to reduce the emphasis on education courses and increase the emphasis on liberal arts education, a plan that fit the biases of the Ford Foundation. Many MAT programs are still in existence.

The MAT programs, along with other efforts, did help to develop more effective cooperation between professors of education and professors in the liberal arts fields in the teacher-education enterprise. This led to a more interdisciplinary approach to research and program development affecting the preparation of teachers.

Microteaching. In the 1960s, educational technology—particularly kinescopes and closed-circuit television—was used increasingly to provide clinical analysis of teachers' behavior in classrooms. This mode of instruction, known as "microteaching" or "clinical experience," was borrowed from medical education and has been applied increasingly to teacher education as a means of diagnosing and improving the performance of teachers.

Teaching centers. The trend toward the use of teaching centers in strengthening the student teaching experience is especially noteworthy. In earlier years student teachers were scattered almost indiscriminately among many school districts, most of which operated traditional instructional programs unattuned to newer curricular and instructional developments. More recently many schools of education are placing all their student teachers and especially teaching interns in a few carefully selected school districts that are in the forefront of contemporary educational practice. This arrangement not only permits more intensive college and public school interaction and cooperation in the student teacher's field work but also provides a more supportive environment for exploring modern pedagogical methods under expert supervision.

Performance-based teacher education. A new

trend is the movement toward performance-based teacher education (PBTE) and competency-based teacher education (CBTE). We shall use the former term, although many writers use the terms synonymously. Elam has identified several essential elements inherent in PBTE:

● Competencies (knowledge, skills, behavior) to be demonstrated by student teachers are derived from explicit conceptions of teachers' roles, made public, and are used as the basis for assessing student teachers' behavior

● Criteria to be used in assessing competence are based upon these competencies, which made public, and are stated explicitly in terms of expected levels of mastery under specified conditions

● The student's competency is based on objective assessment of performance and knowledge relevant to planning for, analyzing, interpreting, and evaluating situations or behavior

● The student's rate of progress is determined by demonstrated competency rather than by time or course completion

● The instructional program is intended to facilitate the development and evaluation of the student's achievement of competencies specified.[4]

Considerable support for PBTE has come from NCATE, from the state departments of education, and from a number of state legislatures that have made it a mandatory basis for certification, as well as from the federal government, which has invested $15 million in its development. Many claim that PBTE will force teacher-education institutions to become more accountable by fixing attention on students' mastery of essential competencies, thereby making them more effective. In addition, PBTE leads to a rethinking of the certification of teachers, basing it on competency rather than on the accumulation of course credits.

Although the objectives and characteristics of PBTE are largely laudatory, the movement is beset by a number of problems. We think it is unsound as well as infeasible. It lends itself better to the *science* of teaching than to the *art* of teaching, which is difficult to break down into specific, modular competencies. We rejected this fragmented approach (called "elementalist psychology") to teaching

children years ago, and we think it is equally inappropriate to the teaching of teachers. Some argue that PBTE is too mechanistic and behavioralistic and is insufficiently humane. Others point out that educators have always been unable to agree upon what constitutes good teaching and that PBTE cannot overcome that ambiguity. Some critics point out that almost all attempts to identify competencies have been derived from brainstorming among educators of teachers rather than from a solid theoretical base or from educational research findings. Other problems arise from the difficulty of assessing many of the teaching competencies. To our minds, both PBTE and CBTE so far lack sound theoretical basis. Many educators feel that PBTE has been oversold.[5]

Other problems affecting PBTE are the rather strong opposition of the American Federation of Teachers and the wait-and-see attitude of the National Education Association. One of the most telling criticisms of PBTE is that too many states and institutions have moved too quickly without sufficient developmental work, which has resulted in premature crystallization of programs. At present, PBTE is in its infancy; whether or not it will improve children's reading levels and make them run joyfully to school cannot be determined until we have much more experience and research evidence. However, it is clear that the movement has considerable thrust, and it may change teacher education substantially in many institutions.

Other trends. Teacher Corps, VISTA, and other federally funded projects were directed toward better preparation of teachers for the inner-city schools where improved teaching effectiveness is most imperative. Other federally financed programs, such as the Education Professions Development Act, were designed to prepare more and better teachers for educationally and physically disadvantaged children and youths.

Many scholars have devoted their energies to the improvement of teacher-learner interaction. For example, Flanders and others developed interaction analysis, a systematic means of analyzing the

[4]Adapted from Stanley Elam, *Performance-based Teacher Education: What Is the State of the Art?* American Association of Colleges for Teacher Education, Washington, 1971, p. 67.

[5]For further reading on the pros and cons of PBTE, see Clifford D. Foster, "Analyzing the PBTE Approach," *Educational Leadership,* January 1974, pp. 306–309; and Gordon Lawrence, "Delineating and Measuring Professional Competence," *Educational Leadership,* January 1974, pp. 298–302.

interaction between the teacher and the class, which is helpful in improving teaching techniques. Some institutions are incorporating sensitivity training into teacher-education programs. Sensitivity training is a laboratory approach toward deepening the student teacher's awareness and understanding of self and students and the interaction between the two. Increased emphasis has also been placed on helping teachers to individualize instruction, sometimes in conjunction with individually prescribed instruction, which is discussed in Chapter 9.

LEVEL OF TEACHER EDUCATION

There is substantial evidence of a dramatic improvement in the American teacher's professional qualifications. Between 1950 and 1976 the proportions of elementary school teachers with four years of college preparation rose phenomenally from 50 to almost 99 percent. At the secondary school level, less than 1 percent of the teachers have had less than four years of college-level education. The public school teacher without a college degree is rapidly disappearing. Nearly all states now require the bachelor's degree for certification. One-third of all public elementary and 40 percent of the secondary school teachers hold the master's degree, and the proportion is constantly rising. Some districts now require the master's degree for initial employment. This steady improvement of the nation's teaching force, even during periods of rapid growth in school enrollments (and resulting personnel shortages), is clearly one of the most heartening signs of wholesomeness in our educational system.

Certification of teachers

The certificate of a teacher serves to give status; to protect its holder against unfair competition with unqualified teachers; to control the granting of licenses; to provide a means for the improvement of instruction; to yield information on which a continuous inventory of teachers and their qualifications may be based; to authorize the payment of salaries; and, most important, to protect society from inadequately prepared teachers.

A license, certificate, or permit to teach in the elementary and secondary schools is required in all states, each of which develops its own certification procedures and standards. Certification requirements vary widely among the states, and future teachers should not assume that meeting the requirements in one state grants automatic certification in all others, although many states do have reciprocity agreements. Four years of college-level preparation is required by virtually all states for certification of teachers. Approximately half the states require an oath of allegiance and a certificate of good health. Most states require a statement of recommendation by the candidate's college or employing officer. Although a few states require certification for teachers in junior colleges, other college teachers generally are not required to hold certification. Many states are moving toward improved certification practices, such as:

Elimination of substandard or emergency certificates

Four years of approved teacher education with a bachelor's degree as a minimum and with a fifth year as soon as possible

A minimum of 15 semester hours of professional work including student teaching

A probationary period of not less than three years under professional guidance

Discontinuance of permanent or life certificates

Centralization of general certification in a state agency

Reciprocity among states in certifying qualified teachers

Use of equivalency exams to permit candidates to "test out" of certain requirements

Certification based upon demonstrated mastery of essential competencies rather than upon the accumulation of credits

Greater emphasis on qualitative competencies and professional growth

Increasing responsibility for teacher-education institutions through an approved program approach to accreditation and certification

More simplicity and less specificity in certification requirements

Increase in the number of state professional practices acts in which teachers exercise more responsibility for setting certification standards

Requiring teachers to continue formal professional study beyond the baccalaureate degree in order to qualify for permanent certification

Many state affiliates of the NEA have lobbied

successfully for the establishment of state commissions made up of teachers to appraise professional practices. This tends to give the organized teaching profession more control over the standards of preparation and certification and over entry into the profession—a hallmark far better established in the other learned professions such as medicine and law.[6]

Supply and demand of teachers

For the first time since World War II the supply of teachers began to equal the demand in the early 1970s, and by the late 1970s a substantial surplus of teachers had accumulated. The shortage of elementary and secondary school teachers was especially severe during the first two decades following World War II. Shortages of teachers persist in certain sectors of the educational scene—particularly in early-childhood education, special education, vocational and technical education, and in secondary school mathematics and science. In recent years approximately half the graduates of teacher-education institutions have been unable to find employment in education. The U.S. Office of Education has estimated that the nation will have a surplus of more than a million teachers in 1977. In view of this mounting surplus, many teacher-education institutions are cutting back admissions of students, some by as much as 50 percent. The oversupply of teachers prevails at the college and university level as well. Some estimates reveal that college and university faculties are almost set for the remainder of the twentieth century, with the normal attrition of faculty members being roughly equal to the reduction necessary to balance reduced enrollments. Although a number of vacancies will have to be filled, the outlook for young holders of doctorate degrees in higher education is exceedingly grim. Many colleges and universities are responding to financial stringencies and declining enrollments by the imposition of hiring

freezes, by the adoption of tenure quotas, and, on some campuses, by the abolition of tenure.

In a recent survey it was discovered that 36 percent of the public school systems surveyed were furloughing teachers. Most states with tenure laws are bound by criteria governing the selection of teachers for dismissal or furlough. These criteria include seniority of teachers in subject fields or grade levels where cutbacks are necessary and merit ratings of the teachers' performance or combinations of the two. The tenure laws commonly provide that furloughed teachers have first option on later vacancies which may arise in their teaching fields or grade levels. Under these circumstances, job security is a crucial concern, and many teachers' associations and unions are attempting to negotiate guarantees of continued employment for all teachers desiring to continue. These associations commonly argue that the surplus of teachers and declining enrollments should be viewed as an opportunity to retain current staffing levels by reducing class size, by extending early-childhood and adult education programs, and by enriching and extending the regular curriculum. However, it is difficult to persuade taxpayers and legislatures that a sharp reduction in students should not be accompanied by a reduction of teachers.

During periods of surplus, spurious factors sometimes intrude on the selection of teachers when vacancies do occur. Some boards are tempted to give preference to local candidates out of a sense of altruism toward hometown residents. Although this thoughtfulness is understandable, the practice is nevertheless lamentable. The school system exists not as a charitable institution to provide jobs for favored persons but as the means to provide the best possible education for students. This principle dictates that the choice always should be made in favor of the best candidate available.

Recruitment, selection, placement, and appointment of teachers

RECRUITMENT

During the period of shortage of teachers, efforts were made to attract more and better persons to the profession. The Education Professions Devel-

---

[6]Prospective teachers should examine the certification requirements in any states in which they may wish to teach by consulting National Education Association, *A Manual on Certification Requirements for School Personnel in the United States*, Washington, 1976, or by inquiring from the department of education in their state.

opment Act (EPDA) of 1967, discussed more fully in Chapter 14, added a substantial measure of federal funding for the recruitment, preparation, and continuing professional development of teachers and other educators.

A recent Gallup poll shows that teaching is a top career choice of college students today. The Student Action for Education (formerly the Future Teachers of America), under the auspices of the National Education Association, enrolls high school students in local chapters to help them become more familiar with career opportunities in teaching and learn how to enter the profession.

Within the past decade, the proportion of teachers who are married, the proportion under 30 years of age, and the proportion of male teachers have grown substantially. Thus dies the stereotype of the old-maid schoolmarm.

The Negro population is another sector of the labor force that is being attracted to teaching in far greater numbers. Blacks have been tragically underutilized in all the learned professions. A 1973 study by the American Council on Education showed that the proportion of black college faculty members (3 percent of the total) and female faculty members (20 percent) is increasing very slowly, even though there are affirmative action programs on most campuses.

SELECTION

The selection of teachers takes place at many points: when students are selected for admission to teacher-education programs and, later, when some are selected to be graduated and certificated to teach; when candidates are selected for teaching positions; and when probationary teachers are selected to continue into tenure positions.

Selection of teachers is difficult because the evidence regarding those characteristics demonstrably related to success in teaching is not as decisive as one might like. Teaching ability is a complex constellation of talents that are not easily sorted out, defined, and measured. National associations of school administrators, classroom teachers, and school boards combined their efforts to review the research findings on indicators of successful teaching and published their conclusions in an excellent publication by the American Association of School Administrators entitled *Who's a Good Teacher?* In brief, this study reports the following conclusions:

There is only slight relationship between intelligence and rated success as a teacher although a minimum level of intelligence is certainly important.

Mastery of subject matter, although important, is not a major factor in teaching performance.

Good grades in college are consistently related to effective teaching.

Teachers with the most professional knowledge tend to be the more effective teachers.

Teachers who have had professional preparation are generally more effective than those who have not.

Teachers' rated effectiveness at first increases rather rapidly with experience, levels off at five years and beyond, and shows little change for the next 15 or 20 years, after which it tends to decline.

Teacher effectiveness is not significantly related to the socio-economic status of the teacher.

Differences in sex account for little of the difference in success among teachers.

Differences in marital status account for very little difference in teaching effectiveness.

Differences in aptitudes are of little value in predicting success in teaching.

Differences in attitudes account for little of the variation in effectiveness among teachers.

By far, the most significant development in the selection of teachers and other educators has been the impact of affirmative action considerations. School districts have discriminated notoriously against females in administrative positions and against members of minority groups in all positions in education. The evolution of legal protection against discrimination in hiring practices began with the Civil Rights Act of 1964, which was limited to race and national origin. President Johnson in 1965 signed an executive order prohibiting discrimination against any employee or applicant for employment because of race, religion, color, or national origin. One year later another executive order added sex discrimination to the list. In 1971 Title 41 of the Code of Federal Regulations extended equal rights protection further by requiring certain categories of employers, such as schools and universities, to file affirmative action plans. These plans are "a set of specific results-oriented procedures to which a contractor commits himself to the objective of providing equal employment opportunity." The Rehabilitation Act of 1973 extended fair employment protections to handicapped persons as well. Many state and local human relations commissions have been established to monitor fair employment procedures.

At first many employers felt obliged to set quotas for members of minority groups and females, and some extended preferential consideration to these people even over better-qualified whites or males. This led to charges of "reverse discrimination" and precipitated intense controversy and some litigation. Federal guidelines relative to affirmative action plans were later revised to require that goals be sought by means of "every good faith effort" rather than using quotas to be guaranteed through hiring. The guidelines do require that vacancies be advertised widely and that determined effort be made to recruit female candidates and those from minority groups. They also require employers to analyze their work forces to determine whether females and members of minority groups are employed in the same or greater proportion as in the available pool of the labor market by job category. The revised guidelines make it clear that employers are not required to hire unqualified people nor even to favor minority groups or females over better-qualified candidates of any race or sex.

Affirmative action plans have generated controversy. Some critics contend that they go too far; others hold that they are not stringent enough. And there are difficulties involved in defining what a minority group is. The term commonly includes blacks, Hispanics, American Indians, and Asians and Pacific Islanders. Some ask why fair employment protections should not be extended to include Armenian-Americans, Jews, sightless persons, homosexuals, and many others. But progress is being made—seldom as fast as justice would require—but certainly in a direction that would have pleased the noted suffragist Susan B. Anthony. In 1852 she demanded the floor at the convention of the New York State Teachers Association and deplored discrimination against women in education. Unfortunately, declining school enrollments at all levels are cutting back vacancies at the very time that legal support for fair employment practices is consummated. Moreover, when teachers are furloughed on the basis of seniority, affirmative action progress can be nullified. The first to be fired are often the last ones hired—women and members of minority groups.

PLACEMENT

School administrators look to four possible sources for the identification of candidates for positions in their schools: (1) noncommercial teacher-placement agencies, (2) commercial teacher-placement agencies, (3) recommendations of candidates by acquaintances of the superintendent, and (4) unsolicited applications by candidates.

Teacher-education institutions maintain the most important noncommercial agencies for placing their graduates and alumni. Many beginning teachers find their first position through college or university teacher-placement offices. Many school systems arrange appointments for interviews with candidates through these offices and regularly interview student teachers. Most teacher-education institutions offer placement services to their students and alumni. Some charge a service fee to handle the processing of credentials. College placement offices are in a good position to render effective service for several reasons: They usually have a personal interest in, and acquaintance with, their students; they have ready access to their students' records, professors, and cooperating teachers; because they are nonprofit, their interest in the quantity of their placements need not interfere with the quality of their services; they usually maintain close contact with the school systems they serve and can offer valuable information to candidates about the quality of these schools and their personnel practices; and they can offer valuable career counseling service to their clients.

Candidates should prepare credentials carefully and file them with the placement office early in their senior year. They should become personally acquainted with the placement director or a member of the staff. They should state clearly the kinds of positions they will accept and identify any undesired geographic areas. Many beginning teachers lack adequate understanding of the whole employment process and the ability to assess their own potential realistically. Their professors can be helpful in solving such problems. The Association for School, College, and University Staffing (ASCUS) enrolls most of the placement offices of teacher-education institutions and attempts to promote greater effectiveness in helping teachers find employment.

In 1967 the formidable powers of computers

were brought to bear on the teacher-recruitment efforts through nationwide centralized clearinghouses for referrals. For example, NEA-SEARCH is a central computerized staffing service sponsored by the National Education Association; it matches candidates with vacancies in educational institutions at home and abroad. Teachers interested in obtaining a new position supply information about their qualifications, minimum salary requirements, range of geographic availability, and other relevant matters, and this information is stored in the computer. The computer quickly matches candidates and vacancies and prints out a list of names and addresses of suitable candidates for each vacancy. The subsequent processes of checking, evaluation, and negotiating are undertaken by employees and employers. A small registration fee is required of NEA-SEARCH candidate-registrants, and another small fee for each candidate's name is charged to the employer. Students can obtain further information about NEA-SEARCH from their college placement offices.[7]

A small percentage of school systems utilize the services of commercial placement agencies. The smaller the school system, the more likely it is to recruit candidates through commercial teacher-placement agencies. These private agencies typically charge 5 or 6 percent of the candidate's first-year salary for their services, in addition to a small registration fee. Many commercial placement agencies subscribe to the standards and ethical practices established by their parent organization, the National Association of Teachers' Agencies, to which the better ones belong. Addresses of commercial teachers' agencies are given in their advertisements, which appear frequently in the journals of the National Education Association, the American Federation of Teachers, and various state education associations.[8]

Nearly all school systems welcome unsolicited applications from candidates interested in positions in the particular district. Thus, in most school systems, it is appropriate for a candidate to submit a letter of application for a teaching position

without knowing of a particular vacancy. Many teachers are self-recruited in this manner and receive their first appointment without reference by a placement office. The larger the school system, the easier it is for a candidate to locate a position in this manner. The importance of genuine care and thoroughness on the part of both candidate and employer in the appointment process can hardly be overstated.[9]

APPOINTMENT AND DEPLOYMENT

The appointment of teachers—a power that should be carefully exercised—is usually made upon the basis of credentials, records in college, participation in extracurricular activities, personality, personal interviews, and experience.

The best practice in the employment of personnel is, first of all, for the board of education to adopt a set of sound personnel policies, recommended by the superintendent and staff. In consonance with written and accepted policies, good boards of education will appoint only teachers recommended by the superintendent. Teachers are commonly elected by the board as professional employees and are assigned to positions as needed. Teachers may be assigned to the same group of students for all or most of the school day, as in the self-contained classroom most commonly found in the elementary school, or to several classes in the same subject-matter field or group of fields, as in the departmentalized organization typically found in high schools and in a number of elementary schools. Both of these patterns of organization and their variations are described in other chapters.

Although the term "team teaching" is often used loosely to identify a wide variety of collaborative activity, essentially it means that several teachers—usually three to seven—are combined in an instructional team under the general direction of a team leader. The team may be organized vertically to include various subjects on one or two grade levels. The form is a flexible one, and it permits

---

[7]NEA-SEARCH, Department 80, 1201 16th St., N.W., Washington, D.C. 20036.

[8]Readers interested in using the services of any of the twenty-eight commercial teacher-placement offices affiliated with NATA can obtain a directory of these agencies and other information by writing to the association at 1825 K Street, N.W., S-706, Washington, D.C. 10006.

[9]Readers interested in finding teaching positions will find the following publications helpful: *Teaching Opportunities for You,* Association of School College and University Staffing, Madison, Wis., 1975; *Careers in Education,* National Education Association, Washington, 1976; *Guide to Applying for Educational Employment,* National Education Association, Washington, 1974; and *Teaching as a Career,* Government Printing Office, Washington, 1971.

Teaching specialists work with classroom teachers through team teaching and differentiated staffing to capitalize on unique talents more effectively.

teaching teams to vary widely. Team teaching represents an effort to use teachers' time and talents more effectively. The group arrangement permits each member of the team to specialize in some particular aspect of instruction and to give more time to planning, preparation, and evaluation. No longer isolated in the traditional classroom, teachers in teaching teams have more opportunity to see their colleagues at work and to improve their own skills in the process. During some of the school day one teacher may lecture to several combined classes, permitting other teachers to give more time to planning, study, counseling, remedial work, and other tasks.

Another pattern of collaborative teaching effort, differentiated staffing, has attracted considerable attention in recent years and promises to become an exciting trend. Figure 2-2 illustrates one model of differentiated staffing. This plan differentiates the assignment, responsibility, status, and salary of teachers on the basis of variations in their preparation, competence, experience, and interest in some

form of collaborative group-teaching enterprise. It also commonly utilizes subprofessionals and nonprofessionals, such as teaching interns and teacher aides. These distinctions in assignment are usually accompanied by differentiation in rank, such as master teacher, senior teacher, staff teacher, associate teacher, teacher aide, resource-center aide, and lab assistant, as in the Temple City, California, prototype. Each position has a different salary range and educational requirements.

The advantages claimed for differentiated staffing include (1) more effective utilization of teaching talent; (2) differentiation of pay on the basis of responsibility and talent rather than on lockstep advancement through years of experience; (3) encouragement of good teaching techniques, such as flexible scheduling, better match-up of learning resources with learners' needs, and better individualization of instruction; (4) more incentive for the advancement of good teachers within the ranks of teaching through much higher salaries and professional challenge for talented teachers.

Continuing professional development

The knowledge explosion has encompassed the world of classroom teaching just as it has all learned endeavors. Educators whose professional knowledge and skills are not up to date become not only increasingly obsolete but downright dangerous to society. Teachers never "complete" their education. As the saying goes, "Who dares to teach must never cease to learn." Throughout their careers, teachers are in pursuit of fuller knowledge—general education, specialized education in subject-matter fields, and professional education. This continuing professional development is sometimes spoken of as "in-service education." We prefer the broader terms "continuing professional development" or "staff development."

This stimulation toward fuller knowledge, unsurpassed in any other occupation, represents one of the great satisfactions and attractions of teaching. It is known that many people with vigorous intellec-

tual curiosity are attracted to teaching because of its incitement to constant inquiry.

PRINCIPLES OF STAFF DEVELOPMENT PROGRAMS

One study of teachers' attitudes toward in-service education revealed that nine of ten teachers agreed with the following principles:

- In-service programs must include activities that allow for the different interests which exist among individual teachers.
- In-service programs should include special orientation activities for new classroom teachers.
- The real test of an in-service program is whether it helps teachers to cope with professional tasks more successfully.
- Teachers need to be involved in the development of purposes, activities, and methods of evaluation for in-service programs.
- One important measure of the effectiveness of an in-

Figure 2-2 Model of differentiated staffing. (From Fenwick W. English, "Differentiated Staffing: Refinement, Reform, or Revolution?" *ISR Journal*, vol. 1, Fall 1969, p. 229.)

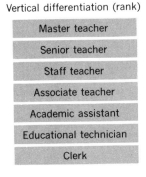

Vertical differentiation (rank)

Master teacher

Senior teacher

Staff teacher

Associate teacher

Academic assistant

Educational technician

Clerk

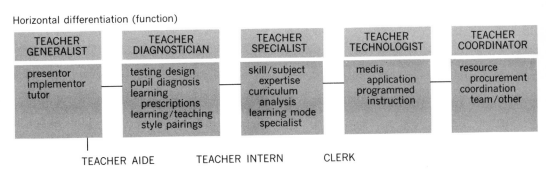

Horizontal differentiation (function)

TEACHER GENERALIST	TEACHER DIAGNOSTICIAN	TEACHER SPECIALIST	TEACHER TECHNOLOGIST	TEACHER COORDINATOR
presentor implementor tutor	testing design pupil diagnosis learning prescriptions learning/teaching style pairings	skill/subject expertise curriculum analysis learning mode specialist	media application programmed instruction	resource procurement coordination team/other

TEACHER AIDE   TEACHER INTERN   CLERK

Many people with vigorous intellectual curiousity are attracted to teaching because of its incitement to constant inquiry and professional development.

service program is whether teachers use the results of their training in the classroom.

● The primary purpose of in-service programs is to upgrade teachers' classroom performance.

● Teachers should have an opportunity to select the kind of in-service activities that they feel will strengthen their professional competence.

● One of the most motivating in-service activities is an opportunity to become acquainted with new teaching practices of innovative programs.

● Teachers should receive some release time for in-service education activities.[10]

Unfortunately, many teachers are not enthusiastic about in-service programs. The principles

[10]Adapted from Jack L. Brimm and Daniel J. Tollett, "How Do Teachers Feel about In-service Education?" *Educational Leadership,* March 1974, p. 522.

stated above are not consistently applied. Many programs are not evaluated carefully, and such evidence as we have seems to show that they have little benefit. There are exceptions, of course. As school finances tighten and economies are sought, staff development programs may be curtailed by reduced funding or may be eliminated altogether. The NEA is seeking control of staff development programs for teachers as one element of a national system of NEA control of the profession. In many districts, teachers are using collective bargaining to achieve greater input into the planning of staff development programs.

TRENDS IN CONTINUING PROFESSIONAL DEVELOPMENT

A 1975 publication of the National School Public Relations Association, *Inservice Education,* noted the following recent trends in professional development:

● Less dependence upon formal graduate courses
● More responsibility for programs among local school districts
● More programs cooperatively planned and managed by teachers' associations in local districts
● Growth in the office of staff development in local districts
● More participation of teachers in assessing needs to determine topics of programs
● More state certification credit granted for local programs
● More professional development activities provided on "company time"
● Court-ordered staff development programs to remedy racial discrimination

TEACHER CENTERS

A promising development in the continued professional development of teachers is the rise of approximately 5,000 teacher centers across the nation. These centers combine a conference room, a professional library including curriculum materials, and a workroom where school faculties may gather to work individually or collectively with the resources they need to solve teaching problems. Teacher centers originated with outstanding success in Great Britain. Although there are now almost as many models as there are centers, the better ones in this country appear to have some common attributes. They are designed:

- To improve the effectiveness of teachers by facilitating their acquaintance with new educational developments, by intensifying informal exchanges among teachers on how to solve common problems, and by developing new homemade curriculum materials and courses of study
- To help teachers, administrators, and others learn in a collegial mode, thereby facilitating change
- To help educators learn by doing rather than by listening
- To focus upon teachers' needs rather than upon institutional concerns

Teacher centers are customarily established by local school districts, or by teacher-education institutions, or by both jointly. They may be housed in an empty classroom and include a conference room, a library of curriculum materials, and audiovisual equipment.

Teacher centers are popular among teachers and teachers' organizations because teachers must control the centers for them to be successful. Teachers see them as a welcome departure from traditional in-service programs that have too long been controlled by supervisors or administrators, research and development centers, college professors, textbook publishers, or others. At least one-third of the states now have administrative regulations or guidelines governing the teacher centers. Some receive outside funding from the federal government, foundations, and teachers' organizations. Teacher centers are evidently on the threshold of wide expansion and popularity. They are based on the sound belief that improvement in educational practice is most likely when teachers hold the initiative for their own professional development.[11]

SUPERVISION OF TEACHING

Today supervision is thought of as the means by which teachers receive organized help in order to stimulate their continuous professional develop-

[11]For further description of teacher centers, see Allen Schmeider and Sam Yeager, *Teacher Centers*, American Association of Colleges for Teacher Education, Washington, 1975.

ment. This was not always the case. In its earliest form, supervision was conceived as a means of controlling the quality of teaching through classroom inspection and arbitrary prescriptions for improved practice. Although this approach may have been appropriate in the days when teachers were not well prepared, it makes far less sense today, although, alas, it is still far too common in traditional school systems. In better schools today, supervision is seen as enlightened professional leadership in improving the total teaching-learning situation. It seeks to stimulate self-analysis and guide teachers' self-direction. Its strategy is not to inspect and control, but rather to release and coordinate the creative abilities of teachers. In many schools, the title of "supervisor" is being displaced by "helping teacher." The mood of this modern concept of supervision is cooperative, nondirective, supportive, flexible, and problem-centered. Although it may include classroom visitation, its emphasis is upon cooperative analysis and evaluation of teachers' behavior and collaborative efforts to find means of improving teaching. Its strategy is that of studying and improving curriculum and instruction broadly.

The methodology of supervision today has also been broadened. It includes individual and group study of the day-to-day problems of teachers, often through action research. Workshops focusing upon the real problems of teachers frequently make use of outside consultants who are expert in dealing with the problems under consideration. Curriculum development projects provide opportunity for teachers to learn more about learning and teaching as a by-product of program development. Many schools grant released time to teachers to observe master teachers at work as a means of acquiring better methods for themselves. Never before has there been such intensive effort on so many fronts toward the improvement of the teaching art. Opportunities for continued professional development for teachers are truly exciting.

EVALUATION OF TEACHERS

Rising public discontent over education has generated interest on the part of administrators, boards of education, state legislatures, and state departments of education in the task of evaluating teachers. The drive toward greater accountability in education implies that we must find effective ways to evaluate the work of educators, both individually and collectively. Accountability stresses the importance of evidence necessary for determining who is doing the job well and who is not. The close relationship between evaluation and factors such as salary differentiation, promotion, tenure, and dismissal is not lost by either teachers or their employers. Consequently, evaluation schemes tend to produce anxiety and generate controversy.

"Evaluation" may be defined as the gathering of evidence regarding the quality of teaching or educational practices in the light of objectives, criteria, and standards as the basis for decision making. For many years evaluation of teachers was based upon primitive rating scales that used criteria which were poorly related to effective teaching. Such scales were used by principals and sometimes supervisors who often were incapable of delivering reliable and valid judgments. In recent years more careful distinction is being made between formative evaluation and summative evaluation, with greater emphasis upon the former. Formative evaluation is continuous, diagnostic, remedial in nature, bilateral, and individualized; and it aims toward the continuous improvement of teaching and learning. Summative evaluation tends to be terminal, unilateral, adversarial, and uniform; it aims toward quality control and administrative decisions bearing on tenure, dismissal, and salaries. In formative evaluation, particularly, emphasis has shifted away from traits of teachers or students' achievement toward combinations of teachers' behavior, teacher-student interaction, and students' learning behavior.

The term "performance evaluation" is gaining currency as a means of involving teachers and administrators cooperatively in a systematic sequence of tasks that aim:

- To set instructional objectives
- To establish criteria and standards for evaluation in terms of teachers' performance levels and/or students' achievement levels
- To select or develop the instruments necessary for gathering data
- To analyze and interpret the data for evaluative purposes

- To inject feedback of conclusions into a recycling process of refining or modifying the goals, criteria, instruments, and evaluation of the future

These tasks involve close cooperation among administrators and teachers to get at the critical questions: What are we trying to do? What evidence to we need? How well are we doing? How can we improve?

Thus performance evaluation brings teachers themselves into the process and capitalizes upon the formidable advantages of self-evaluation. There is a growing trend toward the involvement of students in the upper grades in evaluating teachers. Evidence supports the belief that students can make valid and reliable assessment of teachers' performance. Some districts use evaluation teams that include teachers, but this practice is expensive.

The major trends in evaluation of teachers include:

- Increased involvement of teachers in the development of evaluation programs and procedures
- Greater linkage among educational objectives or goals and teachers' behavior and students' achievement
- Displacement of rating scales by qualitative descriptions of teachers' behavior, students' achievement, and teacher-student interaction
- More attempts to combine processes with input
- Increased emphasis on formative evaluation and less on summative evaluation
- Increased use of students and teams of persons in the evaluation
- More careful attention to considerations of due process regarding teachers' rights of appeal, hearings, and reviews of evaluations

We believe that all these trends move in the right direction. We recognize that evaluation of teachers is still difficult and imprecise, notwithstanding the large volume of research. We regret the American Federation of Teachers' traditional hostility toward evaluation of teachers. The National Education Association, on the other hand, has sustained an active interest in evaluation and has properly insisted that teachers have input into the design and operation of evaluation procedures. Approximately 40 percent of the states have made some kind of official requirement for the formal evaluation of teachers, usually requiring local districts to do the job without specifying how. Problems of evaluating teachers are increasingly becoming the subject of bargaining between teachers and school boards, and many negotiated contracts now make provisions for it.[12]

Welfare of teachers and conditions of employment

The destiny of any profession is determined in large measure by conditions of employment. If adequate provisions are made for employees' welfare, then more able people are attracted to the profession, and they are more inclined to remain in it. Under ideal conditions of employment, teachers are likely not only to find greater job satisfaction but also to be more productive. Collective bargaining has brought keener awareness to the importance of conditions of employment and has forced unilateral decision making in this regard to become bilateral.

INDUCTION

The orientation and induction of new teachers are not well managed in most schools, judging from the severe drop in morale among first-year teachers.

Why do so many become disenchanted almost as soon as they begin? Many beginning teachers are assigned to subject-matter fields or grade levels for which they are not prepared. Often beginning teachers are assigned to the least desirable classes or schools or are given the most unattractive club sponsorships, which veteran teachers can escape because of their seniority. In many cases their collegiate preparation has been too abstract and their student teaching has taken place in the bracing environment of the better-financed and better-administered school systems

in middle-class communities. Small wonder that they are quickly frustrated and disappointed when they find themselves, a year later, teaching in run-down schools with poor materials and equipment and being neglected by administrators and supervisors. Many teachers are ill-prepared to cope with the problems of instruction and discipline that are thrust upon them. Often they are unfamiliar with school regulations and routines. Most beginning teachers have not yet become familiar with their instructional materials and have not developed a backlog of lesson plans from which they can draw. Everything is new to them, and they have not had time to develop confidence and security in their teaching style. Many of them work in self-contained classrooms in isolation from more experienced colleagues who could help them. When these conditions prevail, it is not surprising that many young teachers lose heart.

Enlightened school systems are searching for ways to help beginning teachers. Some districts begin a systematic program of orientation as soon as new teachers are hired. They are given copies of their textbooks, courses of study, and other instructional materials in early summer so that they may become familiar with them before the opening of school. Orientation meetings are held to introduce them to their superiors and colleagues, to familiarize them with the buildings in which they will work, and to acquaint them with the resources that they may call upon when they encounter difficulty. School procedures are explained to them, and they are given help in preparing for the opening of school. Orientation is viewed as a continuing process that lasts at least throughout the first year of teaching. Group and individual conferences are held with new teachers during the year to provide clinical help with their problems as they see them. Good schools reverse the traditional practice by giving beginning teachers lighter and easier assignments than normal until they have had an opportunity to gain experience and confidence.

Despite these enlightened practices, which appear increasingly in better schools, many new teachers will continue to work in less fortunate circumstances. We can offer only this assurance: Be patient and persevering. Although a great many inexperienced teachers become disconsolate after a year or two, many eventually overcome their in-

---

[12]For further discussion of teachers' evaluation, see Robert Olds, "Performance Evaluation Rates a Closer Look," *Compact*, May/June 1974, pp. 13–16.

securities and disappointments and find teaching a satisfying occupation.

TEACHERS' SALARIES

Clearly one of the most important hallmarks of any profession is the adequacy of its salaries. Society has a way of judging the eminence of an occupation by the salaries it pays. On this criterion, teaching in this country did not fare well until recently. It was not until 1961 that the average salary of teachers exceeded the average salary of employees in manufacturing, most of whom are nonprofessionals. The average salaries of federal government employees were substantially higher than the average salaries of elementary and secondary school teachers until the 1970s. Nevertheless, over the past decade the average annual salaries of the instructional staffs in public elementary and secondary schools have increased rather sharply. Research shows little correlation between teachers' salaries and students' achievement.[13]

There are, of course, great variations in salaries scheduled and paid to teachers across the nation, although these differences are gradually being reduced. For example, the average teacher's sala-

[13]U.S. Office of Education, *Do Teachers Make a Difference?* Department of Health, Education, and Welfare, Washington, 1970, p. 4.

Table 2-2 Example of part* of teachers' salary schedule, *Pittsburgh, Pa., Public School Teachers' Salary Schedule, 1978*

Step	Bachelor's degree	Master's degree	Master's degree plus 30 credits
1	$10,500	$11,600	$12,200
2	11,400	12,100	12,700
3	12,000	12,600	13,200
4	12,600	13,200	13,800
5	13,100	13,800	14,400
6	13,600	14,500	15,100
7	14,300	15,200	15,800
8	14,800	15,900	16,500
9	15,400	16,900	17,500
10	18,600	20,300	20,900

*Additional salaries are scheduled for other levels of preparation including B.A. + 10 credits, B.A. + 20, M.A. + 10, M.A. + 20, M.A. + 50, M.A. + 60, and doctorate.

ry in Alaska is almost twice the average teacher's salary in Mississippi.

More than half the states have enacted legislation to mandate minimum salaries for teachers throughout the state. These mandated minimums tend to be lower than the minimum salaries actually paid in most local districts. Most local districts have adopted their own salary schedules, commonly after negotiation with the local teachers' organization. Table 2-2 illustrates a fairly typical teachers' salary schedule. To a large degree it determines automatically the initial base salary, the amount and number of annual increments (vertical column), the amount and number of increments paid for advanced academic preparation (horizontal column), and of course the maximum salaries to be paid teachers in each classification. The schedule illustrated in Table 2-2 is a single salary schedule, as nearly all are, since it prescribes a single schedule for both elementary and secondary teachers. An index-type schedule, which establishes an index or ratio for each horizontal and vertical classification, often relates the salaries of supervisors and other specialists with the base salary for teachers. Thus the index schedule automatically adjusts the salaries of all professional employees (administrators are commonly excepted) to any change in the base salary for teachers. These salary schedules are usually supplemented by scales prescribing extra pay for duties outside the classroom, such as supervising extracurricular activities.

Controversy surrounds the criteria for differentiating salaries among teachers. Teachers' organizations insist that differentiation be based solely on two factors: years of experience and levels of academic preparation. School boards tend to favor differentiation based on merit or performance. Some districts have used merit rating scales to differentiate teachers' salaries, but this practice is subject to many reasonable criticisms. Teachers lack confidence in the reliability of the ratings. Ratings, if imposed unilaterally, tend to impair interpersonal relations between teachers and administrators or supervisors who handle the ratings. Criteria on most rating scales are not related well to factors inherent in effective teaching.

Many teachers feel that merit rating plans depress average salaries. Some schools are moving toward differentiated staffing as a solution to differentiating teachers' compensation. As noted earlier, some districts are adopting performance-based evaluation systems that are designed to measure teaching effectiveness in terms of cooperatively set goals. Although few of these plans have yet been linked with the structure of compensation, that potential is clear for the future.

Teachers' salaries tend to be quite attractive to women in comparison with salaries paid in other comparable occupations, particularly when the nine-month work year is taken into account, although many men still find more attractive salaries in other learned occupations. In general, the greatest gains are realized in large districts. Regional differences in teachers' salaries are reduced somewhat. Some districts have started a trend toward eleven-month contracts for teachers.

Perhaps the greatest weakness in public school salary structures is the depressed level of maximum salaries in many districts. In most learned professions, the difference between beginning salaries and maximum salaries is much greater than it is in teaching. The organized teaching profession's general insistence upon lockstep salary schedules without differentiation of salary with respect to quality of performance has helped to constrain the level of maximum salaries.

Salaries of faculty members in higher education vary tremendously across the land. While the average professor's salary exceeds $30,000 on some campuses, it is less than half that on some others. On the average in the mid-1970s, faculty salaries in higher education were not keeping pace with inflation. Unlike public schools, many colleges and universities—particularly those not engaged in collective bargaining with faculty organizations—do not follow standard salary schedules and instead negotiate salaries with individual professors. This practice has permitted sharp discrepancies to arise on many campuses between male and female teachers' salaries. This condition is now being corrected under legislative mandates to eliminate sex discrimination in all aspects of education.

FRINGE BENEFITS

Perquisites of employment, referred to as "fringe benefits," are becoming increasingly common in most fields of employment, including teaching. Virtually all teachers enjoy a guaranteed annual wage. Many people are fond of calling attention to the long vacation periods that teachers enjoy, and this is, in itself, an attractive feature of teaching. However, teachers' relatively short work year serves also as a depressant on salaries, making this a mixed blessing.

Long-term leaves of absence are another fringe benefit offered to teachers by approximately half the states and by many local districts in other states. Known as "sabbatical" leaves, because they are customarily available every seventh year, these leaves are intended to permit teachers to engage in full-time advanced study, to travel, to participate in exchange teaching, to render service to professional organizations, or to seek restoration of their health, among other activities deemed in the best interests of schools. Nearly half the states have laws either permitting or mandating leaves of absence for teachers for specified reasons, such as those mentioned above. Sometimes the laws specify that partial salary must be paid to the teacher on leave; others allow this to be decided by the local district.

Most school systems provide some sort of paid sick leave for teachers. Two-thirds of the states make statutory provision for sick leave. Some school districts permit unused sick leave to be accumulated without limit. In many districts the amount of sick leave with pay that may be accumulated depends upon the length of service. Most districts permit a few days' leave with pay annually for death or serious illness in the immediate family. Some districts permit a few days' leave with pay each year for religious holidays or for personal reasons. Most districts permit unpaid leaves of absence for maternity. Courts have recently ruled that requiring teachers to begin and end maternity leaves at arbitrary times specified by the employer is unreasonable and violates the equal-protection clause of the Fourteenth Amendment. The U.S. Equal Employment Opportunity Commission makes it clear that commencement and duration of maternity leaves must be treated the same as leaves for other disabilities. Some courts also have ruled that absence resulting from pregnancy or child-birth disability will merit the same salary coverage as would be provided through health insurance or provisions regarding other illnesses or disabilities.

A few districts have installed sick-leave banks, an arrangement that we think is meritorious. Sick-leave banks are similar to blood banks. The bank accepts a few days' sick-leave equity from each member and guarantees perhaps forty-five days of paid sick leave if needed. If the balance of days in the bank falls below an acceptable minimum, members are assessed a few more days to build up the reserves. The sick-leave bank provides more flexibility than is possible in conventional plans and tends to discourage many abuses common to ordinary sick-leave plans. Some districts add unused sick-leave benefits to severance pay, which is prorated according to number of years of teaching and is paid upon retirement.

Absenteeism is becoming an expensive and frustrating problem for many districts. The cost of substitute teachers in New York City alone is more than $70 million a year. Not surprisingly, absenteeism is much higher on Mondays and Fridays. Many teachers, sad to say, exploit the sick-leave provisions by claiming illness when such is not the case. This is unethical and unprofessional behavior. Many districts are cracking down on unwarranted sick-leave absenteeism, which puts a double cost on the district—the regular teacher's pay under sick leave and the substitute teacher's pay. Moreover, students' education suffers because substitutes are less effective than regular teachers.

The larger the school district, the more likely it is to provide group life insurance, hospitalization insurance, medical-surgical insurance, liability insurance, disability insurance, and tax-sheltered annuity plans. Many school districts share in paying the premiums of various types of insurance for their employees. Most states include teachers under the provisions for workmen's compensation protection covering a wide variety of occupational disabilities.

The NEA, the AFT, the AASA, and other professional organizations for educators offer various types of low-cost group insurance policies for their members, such as life insurance, travel-accident insurance, and personal liability insurance. The sharp rise in the frequency and intensity of physical attacks on teachers is a matter of grave concern in many districts, particularly in urban areas. Many teachers have been assaulted and sometimes raped by students or outsiders. Security personnel have been added, and teachers in some districts have been issued electronic alarms that can summon help immediately to any location. Some teachers' associations are negotiating agreements that require districts to provide insur-

ance coverage for teachers who suffer disability from assaults that occur on school premises. Some districts also provide income protection that is not deductible from sick leave for absences caused by such assaults.

Fringe benefits for teachers are being extended because more and more school systems recognize the importance of these indirect emoluments in attracting and holding good teachers. The organized teaching profession has often insisted on such benefits at the bargaining table.

College faculty members typically enjoy most of the fringe benefits discussed above. Sabbatical leaves are more common and more generous on college campuses than in public school districts. Colleges also tend to be more generous in short-term personal and professional leaves for teachers. Many colleges provide tuition scholarships for spouses and children of faculty members.

TENURE

Tenure laws are enacted primarily to protect the academic freedom of learners and the public, protecting them from teachers who might be intimidated by fear of dismissal for reasons unrelated to effective teaching. Prior to the passage of tenure laws, many teachers were dismissed capriciously because of their political, religious, or other beliefs or because of unpopular personal conduct. Tenure laws also protect senior faculty members from boards that might like to replace them with people willing to work for less. Tenure laws prevent special interest groups from purging faculties of teachers whose views or values differ from theirs. Tenure laws also establish due-process safeguards to ensure justice in instances where teachers must be dismissed. Some courts recently have held that certain procedures of due process must be extended to probationary teachers as well.

Slightly more than two-thirds of the states have statewide tenure laws. All but four of the remaining states provide for tenure but make exceptions for certain districts, usually the smaller ones. Permanent tenure laws typically specify that teachers, after satisfactory probationary service of from one to five years, cannot be dismissed except for specified reasons, such as incompetence, neglect of duty, insubordination, or decline in enrollments. They usually provide for hearings and other due-process considerations.

A bitter controversy now rages in many places over the matter of tenure, both in public school systems and in higher education. Defenders of tenure, including most teachers and their associations, cite the familiar arguments stated above and have generated stormy resistance to all efforts to abolish or weaken tenure provisions. However, some nontenured teachers may oppose tenure when it blocks their opportunity for continued employment.

The issue of tenure, largely dormant during periods of rapid growth of school systems and colleges, has erupted with enormous bitterness during the current period of financial retrenchment in education. College faculty senate meetings, once attended by a few yawning professors, now fill large auditoriums to overflowing. Professors and administrators passionately debate proposals to modify tenure. Enrollment declines and fiscal stringencies have made it necessary for many school systems and colleges to reduce the size of their teaching forces. Even when faculty furloughs or firings are not at issue, debate can be hot. Boards of trustees and administrators, who have not always been enthusiastic about job security for subordinates, point out that with no growth in student bodies and under present tenure policies 80 to 90 percent of the faculty will be tenured by 1980. On many college campuses few faculty replacements will be needed for the remainder of this century. This closes the door to new hiring or, in some cases, continued employment of newcomers previously discriminated against—mainly women and members of nonwhite minority groups. This circumstance virtually eliminates the opportunity to infuse faculties with young, ambitious teachers who have new ideas and pedagogical styles. Instead, it provides a sinecure for some "academic sluggards who, once tenured, enter upon a precocious semi-retirement," as one college president put it.

Administrators and governing bodies often advocate quotas in the percent of faculty positions available for tenure protection, a proposal that is anathema to teachers' organizations. Teachers insist that tenure does permit the dismissal of incompetents, which is true; but the process is thought by administrators to be too time-consuming, difficult, and disruptive except in extreme cases. One line of reasoning contends that tenure is no longer appropriate or necessary when teachers now have adequate protection through collective bargaining, grievance procedures, and the courts. While all agree that incompetent teachers or professors are a liability to both the profession and their institutions, the issue is how competent teachers will find adequate protection from biased or inept administrators or boards if tenure laws and policies are abolished or weakened.[14]

DISMISSAL

Closely related to tenure is, of course, the matter of dismissal. Courts are becoming considerably more involved in reviewing firings by public employers, particularly in protecting the constitutional rights of both tenured and probationary teachers. In one landmark case, *Goldberg v. Kelly* in 1969, the court established these essential elements of due process:

- Timely and adequate notice detailing the reasons for the proposed termination
- Effective opportunity to defend oneself by confronting adverse witnesses
- Opportunity to cross-examine witnesses
- Adequate notice before the hearing
- Opportunity to be heard
- Assurance that the decision makers' conclusions will be based only on evidence presented during the hearing and that they will be impartial

Many cases that formerly have gone uncontested because of the costs of litigation are now going to court with the financial backing of the NEA and other teachers' organizations. However, it must not be assumed that teachers are winning all the cases. The court upheld the firing of a New Jersey teacher whose sex had been changed; the school board contended that students might suffer adverse psychological consequences by having a teacher whose sexual identity had been changed. Some courts have held that practicing homosexuals cannot be dismissed unless it can be shown that their sex habits render them incompetent or undesirable in the classroom. Other courts have held that if a homosexual teacher is convicted of a morals charge or is found guilty of promoting homosexuality, that teacher then may become an unfit model for children. One woman teacher who

[14]For an interesting series of articles about tenure, see Myron Lieberman et al., "Tenure: Status and Prognosis," *Phi Delta Kappan,* March 1975, pp. 450–465.

posed nude in a men's magazine was protected from dismissal. The court ruled that there was no evidence that the teacher was incompetent in the classroom. Courts are also adamant that equal standards be applied to both sexes. Female teachers, for example, cannot be dismissed for allegedly immoral behavior unless male teachers are dismissed for the same behavior. The general rule of the courts is that teachers cannot be fired for exercising their constitutional rights unless their behavior materially impairs their effectiveness in school and unless the same standards of conduct are applied equally to both sexes.

RETIREMENT

All states now have retirement systems for teachers; in most instances membership is compulsory. Teachers commonly contribute 5 to 6 percent of their annual salaries in most states, and that sum is matched by a contribution from the local district or from the state or, in some cases, from both. Formulas for computing retirement benefits for teachers are commonly based on a percentage of an average annual salary over the last several years times the number of years of employment in teaching. In many states the annual retirement annuity is approximately half the average annual salary in the latter years of employment. The annuity is paid until the retiree's death.

Many states mandate retirement by a certain age, usually between 60 and 70. A number of cases in litigation are challenging the constitutionality of mandatory retirement on the grounds that it discriminates against and denies due process to one age class.

Although half the states permit teachers to purchase credit in retirement programs for years of service rendered in other states, provisions for reciprocity in retirement benefits are not adequate in most states.[15] Thirty-seven of the states have integrated their retirement plans with Social Security, while in the other states these benefits are independent of each other. A few large city school systems maintain their own retirement systems.

Inflation has hit retired persons especially hard. Most retirees are forced to live on fixed incomes

[15]Readers interested in the specific provisions of retirement systems for teachers in any of the fifty states should see *Teacher Retirement Systems,* National Education Association, Washington, 1974.

from benefits that may have seemed adequate a decade ago, but costs of living have increased sharply since then. State affiliates of the NEA and the AFT are pressing for retirement plans that permit teachers to retire with full benefits after twenty-five years of service. We do not think this is in the better interests of the larger society, which simply cannot afford the luxury of paying hundreds of thousands and perhaps eventually millions of other workers not to work during almost half of their productive lives. We do approve of gradual retirement plans that permit older teachers to reduce the tempo of their work while retaining some income and a sense of personal usefulness.

College teachers have several retirement advantages over most public school employees. The Teachers Insurance and Annuity Association (TIAA) is a nationwide retirement plan available for professors on most four-year college campuses. Thus professors lose nothing in their retirement when they move from one college to another. The administrative costs of this well-administered plan are underwritten by the Carnegie Corporation, which reduces the cost to professors. The TIAA also provides optional tax-sheltered annuities, as well as some built-in protections against inflation.

PROFESSIONAL ETHICS FOR EDUCATION

A profession can rise no higher than the code of ethics it adopts and uses daily. Among the groups with whom teachers come in contact in their work are the board of education, administrators, supervisors, teachers, nonteaching staff, pupils, parents, and the community. Teachers are frequently confronted with ethical problems: Should teachers accept gifts from students? Should one discuss another teacher's weaknesses with a parent? Should teachers engage in illegal strikes or ignore court injunctions while on strike? Should teachers support a school policy that they do not believe in? Should teachers disregard their contractual obligation with a district to accept a better position two weeks before the opening of school? As guides to the ethical behavior of teachers, codes of ethics have been developed by state associations and the National Education Association. The NEA adopted in 1963, and subsequently revised, the *Code of Ethics of the Education Profession.* This code has been adopted by all state associations and is subject to extensive review every five years. We strongly urge readers to study it carefully and to use it as a guide for professional conduct. The American Federation of Teachers' *Bill of Rights for Teachers* should also be examined.

Teachers' organizations

Membership and participation in professional organizations can help educators to continue their growth. In some areas of the world—for example, Canada—membership in the professional teachers' organization is required by law. In the United States, teachers generally are free to join or not to join professional organizations.

Educational organizations may be classified by primary objective, such as the promotion of childhood education (Association of Childhood Education); by subject fields (the National Council of Teachers of Mathematics); by major function, such as the accrediting of schools (National Council for Accreditation of Teacher Education); by academic level of institutions, such as elementary schools (Los Angeles Elementary Teachers Club or American Association of University Professors); by religious affiliation (National Catholic Education Association or Association of Hebrew Teachers Colleges in America); by labor affiliation (American Federation of Teachers); or by scope, such as geographical areas (Memphis Education Association, Illinois Education Association, or National Education Association). Because of their simplicity, the geographical classifications—(1) local, (2) state, (3) national, and (4) international—are utilized here as a framework for outlining professional educational associations.

LOCAL ORGANIZATIONS

Although teachers are not organized in some small school districts, most public and private school teachers do belong to a state or a national educational organization of some sort. Most local associations, but not all, are affiliated with state components of the NEA or the AFT. A few local associations are affiliated with both. This banding together serves many purposes. The Association of Classroom Teachers of the NEA states that it is the peculiar function of local teachers' organizations to provide teachers with an opportunity to understand the problems of their respective communities and to acquaint the public with the needs of its

teachers and its schools. In the local education association is found the growing edge of the organized teaching profession. It is the unit of organization that has wielded powerful influence for improved conditions of employment through collective bargaining with local school boards.

STATE ORGANIZATIONS

Local units may be organized as parts of some larger whole, such as the county or state associations. Many of these are determined by fields, as social studies teachers; by grade levels, as elementary school teachers; or by function or personnel, as city superintendents. The main core of organized professional activity within the state, however, is the statewide, all-inclusive society, which is usually known as the state education association, state teachers' association, or state federation of teachers. The usual purpose of these organizations, as indicated in their state journals and as reflected in their activities, is to perform on a statewide basis what the local groups seek to do. There is a major emphasis on professional improvement of the members; the advancement of teacher and student welfare; service to the schools and communities in the state, particularly through lobbying for legislation; and active cooperation with the associations of other states and with national associations. Two states, Hawaii and Wisconsin, have authorized compulsory unionism for their teachers. State organizations exercise important influence on educational policy. There is a vigorous drive by these organizations in many states to gain more control over certification, teacher education, and professional standards through state professional standards commissions. In a few states, the state organizations of the NEA and the AFT have merged to present a united front for teachers' interests at the state level. In many states bitter rivalry exists between affiliates of the NEA and the AFT. This rivalry has not been in the best interests of students, schools, or even teachers.

NATIONAL ORGANIZATIONS

There are literally scores of national associations of educators. Many of them are specialized by subject fields, while some are more general. We shall describe a few important ones.

National Education Association (NEA). This national, all-inclusive education organization is also the largest teachers' association in the world. It was organized in 1857 as the National Teachers Association. The name was changed to the National Education Association in 1907, when it was incorporated under a special act of Congress. By 1976 membership in the NEA was approximately 1.8 million. In brief, its purposes are these:

The National Education Association is dedicated to the upbuilding of democratic civilization and is supported by the loyal cooperation of the leaders of the United States to advance the interests of the teaching profession, promote the welfare of children, and foster the education of all the people.

The NEA renders two kinds of services. First come those services which reach the members directly, such as *Today's Education,* which has the largest circulation of all professional journals, and other publications, as well as conventions of the association, its departments, and allied organizations. These help to promote personal growth and educational research and to build up the common mind of the profession. The growing edge of this movement is the NEA's support of the drive for collective bargaining at local, state, and national levels through its substantial staff of field workers and financial resources. The second type of service is indirect. Like the values that citizens receive from their taxes, these benefits are often overlooked. An important function of the association is to develop a high level of public understanding of education and a desire for good schools. It aims to elevate the character and advance the interests of the teaching profession and to promote the cause of education in the United States. It is not, however, an agency of the federal government.

The NEA was once an all-inclusive voluntary organization of teachers and administrators in pre-elementary, elementary, secondary, higher, and adult education. However, collective bargaining by classroom teachers intensified cleavages between teachers and administrators, resulting in the withdrawal of principals' and administrators' organizations from direct affiliation with the NEA to autonomous status. This same development has been common in many state and local organizations.

NEA policies are determined by a representative assembly that comes from all over the United States each summer to meet in an annual convention. This body consists of delegates elected by state and local organizations of teachers. The administration of the affairs of the association is handled by this representative assembly, a board of trustees, an executive committee, and a board of directors. The professional and clerical staffs, working under the direction of the executive secretary are housed in the association's building in Washington, D.C.

The NEA is an independent organization unaffiliated with labor unions. It favors collective bargaining as a means of improving the profession. It endorses strikes against school systems when negotiations are unsuccessful in obtaining better salaries and improved working conditions. It also supports proposed federal legislation that would grant all teachers collective bargaining rights including the right to strike. According to *The Congressional Quarterly,* the NEA is twelfth among the top-spending lobbying groups in Washington. Through its state affiliates the NEA is seeking vigorously to represent college professors in collective bargaining on many campuses.

American Federation of Teachers (AFT). This national organization is affiliated with the AFL-CIO but is relatively autonomous with respect to its program and policy. The AFT contends that education has traditionally had its greatest support from organized labor, and the affiliation with the AFL-CIO offers a strong power base for correcting the economic and political injustices from which education allegedly suffers. The federation has the following two main objectives:

1. To consolidate the teachers of the country into a strong group which would be able to protect its own interest.
2. To raise the standard of the teaching class by a direct attack on the conditions which, according to the federation, prevent teaching from reaching its desired status. Among these conditions are lack of academic freedom and civil liberty and the absence of self-determination of policy and of democratic control.

The official organs of the AFT are *The American Teacher* and *Changing Education.* The federation maintains standing committees on the following: academic freedom, democratic human relations, pensions and retirement, protection of teachers' rights, state federations, taxation and school finance, vocational education, working conditions, adult and workers' education, child care, and educational trends and policies. The AFT has drawn up a *Bill of Rights of Teachers.*

The federation has launched a drive to unionize college professors. Administrators are not usually permitted membership in the AFT on the grounds that they represent management rather than labor. Many AFT locals and much of its membership are found in city school systems. The United Federation of Teachers, the New York City local, was the first teachers' organization to win collective bargaining rights in a large city school system. By 1976 the membership of the AFT was less than one-third that of the NEA, although reports of membership in the AFT vary substantially.

Although the AFT and the NEA are presently locked in competitive and sometimes acrimonious rivalry for membership and support of the nation's teachers, there have been overtures toward the merger of the two organizations. The president of the AFT is Albert Shanker, a tough and effective labor organizer. Shanker helped organize and guide the merger of the New York AFT and the New York State Teachers Association, an affiliate of the NEA, into the first such merger at the state level. Shanker is a delegate from that combined body to the NEA convention, where he commonly speaks in favor of an NEA-AFT merger at the national level, a prospect which he admits is dim at the moment. Shanker is also a vice-president of the powerful AFL-CIO and a member of its board of directors.[16]

American Federation of State, County, and Municipal Employees (AFSCME). With 700,000 members this union is the fifth largest union in the AFL-CIO, almost twice as large as the AFT but half the size of the NEA. Although it is not a teachers' union, the AFSCME has added certain school supervisory personnel to its membership, much to the chagrin of the AFT. It has also joined the NEA as one of two big unions in the Coalition of Public Employes (CAPE), formed in 1973. CAPE is an effort to bring the united voice of public employees to the educational lobbying scene. President

Shanker of the AFT has been sharply critical of these moves by the AFSCME. He hates to see this large rival AFL-CIO union in a coalition with the NEA after his own unsuccessful attempt to merge the NEA with the AFT. It is believed that Shanker would like to head a national teachers' union representing all the nation's teachers and eventually a giant union of public employees within the AFL-CIO. The AFSCME is a powerful obstacle to that goal. Curiously, then, the AFSCME finds itself more often in agreement with the NEA than with the AFT.

Department of Public Employees, AFL-CIO (DPE). To darken the picture further, the AFL-CIO in 1975 established the Department of Public Employees, which covets the potential constituency of 2 million public workers including teachers, who could make up the largest group of members within it. Public employees constitute the fastest-growing sector of the labor movement in the country at present. The DPE has the enthusiastic support of the AFT, while the AFSCME—at one time the largest single unit within it—has withdrawn after a power struggle between Shanker and AFSCME's President Jerry Wurf. It will be interesting—perhaps tragic—to watch the four-way rivalry of the AFSCME, the AFT, the NEA, and the DPE unfold in the years ahead.

Council for a United Profession (CUP). In 1973 five leading educational organizations—all former components of the NEA—formed a loose coalition (a "discussion council," really) called the Council for a United Profession (CUP) to "maintain organizational unity among teachers, supervisors, and administrators." This was done, it was said, because the NEA's present course would "fracture the concept of a united profession." The groups affiliated with CUP are the National Association of Elementary School Principals, the National Association of Secondary School Principals, the American Association of School Administrators, the Association for Supervision and Curriculum Development, and the Association of Classroom Teachers.

National Association of Professional Educators (NAPE). NAPE is a national organization of teachers and other educators who are disenchanted with the political action of both the NEA and the AFT. NAPE is committed to improving the professional status and compensation of educa-

---

[16]For more information on the AFT—its goals, accomplishments, and platform—see its journal, *The American Teacher*, September 1975; for its president's views on teachers' problems, see Albert Shanker, "Why Teachers Are Angry," *The American School Board Journal,* January 1975, pp. 23–26.

tors but is opposed to national collective bargaining, compulsory union membership, closed shops, agency shops, strikes, and lockouts in educational institutions. It charges that teachers have lost freedom because unions control hiring, firing, evaluation, and transfer of teachers and because elected school boards have final decision-making authority.

Organizations of black educators. Several organizations of educators, most notably the Black American Teachers Association and the National Association for Afro-American Education, bring together educators interested in strengthening educational opportunity for blacks, improving professional opportunity for black teachers, and promoting black cultures and Afro-American studies.

National Catholic Education Association (NCEA). Educators in Catholic schools and colleges commonly hold membership in the NCEA, founded in 1904. This organization maintains four regional offices and a headquarters in Washington, D.C. Through this association, Catholic educators meet for the exchange of ideas, interpret their efforts to the public, cooperate with other organizations, conduct research, and otherwise strengthen educational practice for Catholic parochial schools and colleges. The NCEA publishes the *National Catholic Education Association Bulletin.*

Other religious organizations. Most other major religious faiths, particularly those operating church-related schools, also maintain educational associations for educators and others interested in sectarian education in their faith.

Professional fraternities and honor societies. The *Education Directory of Educational Associations,* published by the U.S. Office of Education, lists 158 national professional fraternities, honor societies, and recognition societies. The more prominent ones for educators are Kappa Delta Epsilon, Alpha Delta Kappa, Pi Lambda Theta, Phi Delta Kappa, and Phi Sigma Pi. Membership in many of these fraternities and honor societies was formerly restricted to one sex or the other; but this practice has now been discontinued in many of them.

INTERNATIONAL ORGANIZATIONS

As is indicated in Chapter 15, many organizations listed in the *Directory of Educational Associations* contain in their titles the word "World" or "International." The NEA has an active Committee on International Relations. Many countries were represented in the World Organization of the Teaching Profession, discussed in Chapter 15. It was organized in Glasgow, Scotland, in 1947 and was reorganized as the World Confederation of Organizations of the Teaching Profession in 1952. This organization has been recognized by the United Nations as an official consultative body. The International Council on Education for Teaching (ICET) is an international association of institutions and individuals interested in improving teacher education throughout the world and in the cross-cultural sharing of information about teacher education. It works closely with the WCOTP. The International Federation of Free Teachers Unions is an international trade-secretariat comprising forty-eight labor-affiliated teachers' unions in forty-three countries of the free world. It is dedicated to bringing teachers into the trade union movement.

Other professional personnel

Some common professional positions other than teaching are outlined below.

ADMINISTRATORS

Among the persons engaged in an executive capacity are superintendents, assistant superintendents, principals, department heads and administrative deans, presidents, and other administrators, including business and building officials. College administrative positions are discussed in Chapter 7.

Superintendents. Local public and private schools employ approximately 17,000 chief administrators known as superintendents of schools or, in smaller districts, as supervising principals. A recent study of the superintendency by the American Association of School Administrators revealed that 99 percent of the superintendents were males at the time of the study.[17] The AASA has launched a drive toward sexual equality in education, including equal opportunity for the employment of females in administrative positions.

The functions of administration can be classified into four general areas: administration of the educational program, administration of finance and facilities, personnel administration, and administration of school-community relations. The administration of the education program is regarded as the central and most important function of administration. School buildings, records, faculties, budgets, and all the rest of the school environment have meaning and importance only to the extent that they contribute to the quality of instruction and learning.

As school districts have increased in size, they have employed an increasing number of assistant superintendents specializing in such functions as curriculum and supervision, school finance and business management, personnel administration, and community relations.[18]

Principals. The unit of education that means the most to children, parents, and the community is the individual school, of which the principal is the head. Principals constitute by far the largest group of administrators, approximately 90,000. These positions range all the way from teaching principals in small schools to principals of immense schools. There are elementary school principals, middle school principals, high school principals, and evening school principals. In some cases, particularly when they have charge of both elementary and secondary education, they are known as "supervising principals." Many large schools employ assistant principals. A master's degree and successful teaching experience are usually required. In many private schools the head educational administrator is known as the "headmaster."

The principal is the person to whom teachers are directly accountable. The principal should be held accountable for the total educational program of

Dr. Joan Abrams, superintendent of Red Bank, N.J. schools, is one of the small but growing minority of women in top school administrative posts.

the school building. Unfortunately this is not possible in many schools because the principal has little to say about such critical matters as the selection of teachers, the formulation and administration of the budget, and other decisions which are often preempted by school boards, the central office staff, and bargaining teams. Too often a principal's accountability outruns his or her authority.[19] The school principal is often caught in the conflict between employer and employees and is expected to mediate conflicts without sufficient power base or authority. The application of systems management, particularly management by objectives, has placed new emphasis upon careful delineation of the principal's job in terms of organizational goals, allocation of authority commensurate with accountability, and specified criteria by which the principal's work is to be evaluated and redirected.

The role of the principalship was once defined primarily in terms of instructional leadership, that

[17]*The American School Superintendency.* American Association of School Administrators, Washington, 1971.

[18]Readers interested in more information about the superintendency or the assistant superintendency as career opportunities should see *Profiles of the Administrative Team,* American Association of School Administrators, Arlington, Va., 1971.

[19]For further discussion of these and other problems in the principalship, see Keith Goldhammer and associates, *Elementary School Principals and Their Schools,* Center for the Advanced Study of Educational Administration, Eugene, Ore., 1971.

is, improvement of curriculum and instruction. But the rise in curriculum and instructional specialists in the central office, the growth of team teaching and differentiated staffing, and other developments have tended to relocate some of this responsibility with teachers and office personnel. Also, the increase of discipline problems and other managerial responsibilities have diverted the principal's time and energy. The principal's role is seen increasingly as a mediator of problems and conflicts at the building level and as a coordinator and facilitator who sustains an organizational environment that permits other employees to function effectively. Many authorities regret the decline in the principal's instructional leadership role.

Virtually all principals are recruited from the ranks of teachers who have completed a master's degree with concentration in educational administration, supervision, and curriculum. Although half of high school teachers are women, only 5 percent of high school principals are women. And while 84 percent of elementary school teachers are women, only 20 percent of elementary school principals are women—down from 41 percent in 1948. Although schools are staffed largely by women, men run them just as men tend to run other governmental and business enterprises. This discrimination against female administrators is now subsiding gradually as a result of fair employment practices and affirmative action plans in schools.

Teachers turn to counselors to help with students with severe problems.

Two major organizations contributing to the in-service education of these administrative men and women are the National Association of Elementary School Principals and the National Association of Secondary School Principals.[20]

STUDENT PERSONNEL SPECIALISTS

Colleges and universities and most large school systems have developed a staff of specialists responsible for various student personnel services. In public schools, these specialists are usually under the direction of the superintendent or director of student personnel services. The outstanding qualifications for these persons are special training in guidance; a knowledge of adolescent physiology and psychology; a liking for, and sympathetic understanding of, students and their problems and possibilities; the ability to aid in the solution of individual problems; the art of inspiring confidence and respect; and plenty of patience. Usually a master's degree is required. We now shall discuss some personnel services briefly.

Counselors and guidance personnel. Many persons are employed in guidance programs. This work involves studying students' learning capacities, needs, and interests; guiding their efforts; and then seeing them through until they obtain a position or are admitted to a higher level of schooling. Guidance ought to be systematic and functional so that students will not make important educational decisions, vocational choices, and life adjustments on the basis of mere guesses, false assumptions, or meager information. Virtually all colleges, high schools, middle schools, and some elementary schools include counselors on their staffs. Teachers turn to these counselors for help with students whose problems require understanding and expertise beyond what teachers can provide.

Home and school visitors, school social workers, and community agents. Although there are distinctions among these classes of positions, they are all usually occupied by persons trained in social work. These personnel act in a liaison capacity between the school and the home and community. They are especially skilled at mobilizing the help of community agencies—such as family welfare agencies, child welfare agencies, and parole authorities—in responding more effectively to the needs of young people.

School psychologists. Many schools and colleges are employing psychologists in an effort to treat causes rather than symptoms of unusual behavior by students and to retard mental illness. The school psychologist's responsibilities include conferences with parents and teachers to promote understanding of individual students' problems, conducting psychological examinations of students with severe learning or adjustment problems, making recommendations for resolving students' problems, helping teachers to conduct child studies and interpret and use test data, and conducting in-service training programs to deepen teachers' understanding of the growth and development of children and youths. In some severe cases where solutions lie beyond the resources of the school, the psychologist makes referrals to psychiatric services available in psychiatric clinics, hospitals, or other agencies.

Ombudsmen. A few school districts and a larger number of colleges have established the position of ombudsman. An "ombudsman" is a person of either sex who has no administrative authority but who has the authority to investigate and recommend appropriate action regarding complaints or injustices to students; to establish due-process procedures and to act on grievances or alleged violations of students' rights; to suggest changes in policies or practices to relieve latent complaints and grievances; and to mediate conflicts. We would like to see this position become more common in schools and colleges.

Health personnel. The school health program is composed in whole or in part of the following services: health instruction, health examinations, medical attention, communicable-disease control, promotion of mental health, provision of healthful environment and regimen, and health supervision of teachers and employees. To perform these services well, a varied health team is needed, including a physician, a dentist, a nurse, a health educator, and a nutritionist.

Teachers usually have access to these specialists through the school nurse, who is prepared to receive students with health problems or students who become ill or injured in school. If a student requires help beyond what the nurse can offer, he or she will be referred to school physicians or the hospitals or other appropriate agencies. Nurses usually will counsel teachers on students' physical problems that require modification in their learning environment and often will help with classroom instruction in health education.

INSTRUCTIONAL SUPPORT SPECIALISTS

The extension of the school curriculum and the development of instructional technology have generated an array of specialists in curriculum, supervision, and instructional technology, often under the coordination of an assistant superintendent for curriculum and instruction. Many educators who are former master teachers are engaged in instructional supervision, as described earlier in this chapter.

Librarians and coordinators of instructional materials are prepared to help teachers instruct students in the use of libraries and centers for instructional materials, as described in Chapter 10. Upon teachers' requests they can order books and periodicals and other instructional materials needed to supplement students' textbooks. When commercial materials are unavailable or inappropriate, they can help teachers develop homemade instructional materials, such as displays or audiovisual materials. They can temporarily release to the classroom library collections of materials related to a unit of work for the convenience of students and teachers.

Some districts employ research and development specialists who are skilled in helping teachers study instructional problems, design new programs of instruction or improve existing programs, and evaluate them. They also can prepare proposals and applications for federal or private funding of new programs.

PARAPROFESSIONAL PERSONNEL

Among the "paraprofessional" personnel in education (those who work alongside the professionals) are aides or "auxiliary school personnel." They free classroom teachers from some subprofessional, routine tasks so that they have "more time to teach." Hence, a growing number of schools and colleges employ subprofessional personnel such as teacher aides, theme readers, laboratory assistants, and clerical aides. Teacher aides, often used in connection with team teaching, are sometimes also employed to relieve teachers of large classes from nonprofessional or semiprofessional tasks.

These aides perform such tasks as arranging instructional materials; reading aloud and storytelling; arranging bulletin board displays; keeping attendance and other records; supervising bus loading; helping with field trips; scoring objective tests; and supervising study halls, lunch periods, and playgrounds. Such aides often have some higher education, and often they are young persons aspiring to teaching careers. Some schools employ theme readers or lay readers to assist English teachers in the massive task of correcting students' compositions. These readers are often housewives with college majors in English who enjoy this part-time work. Similarly, college graduates with backgrounds in science are sometimes employed as laboratory assistants to science teachers. A number of schools employ secretarial and clerical aides for their faculties.

Teaching aides are used on all educational levels, from pre-elementary education, where they might serve as helpers in Head Start programs, to graduate education, where they may function as teaching assistants.[21]

VOLUNTEER PERSONNEL

Schools and colleges depend heavily on a variety of volunteer personnel, including members of the state and local boards of education (discussed in Chapters 12 and 13), college boards of trustees (discussed in Chapter 7), members of lay advisory committees and parent councils, PTA members, and educational volunteers.

School volunteers. One of the most interesting and promising recent developments is the phenomenal increase in school volunteers across the nation. Begun by the Public Education Association in New York City in 1956 and conceived by its director, Frederick McLaughlin, this movement now includes an estimated 2½ million volunteers in all fifty states. The movement has been accelerated also by financial support from the Ford Foundation and by the leadership of the National School Volunteers Program. Several state departments of education, notably Florida and California, have promoted school volunteer programs.

School volunteers come from all walks of life and include people of all ages and both sexes. They include high school and college students, retired persons, and businesspeople. Anyone willing to donate an hour or two a week may volunteer. Some companies release employees on salaried time to teach short courses related to their work or to tutor students in special fields. Much of the volunteers' efforts are directed toward children of the urban poor, children selected for help by their classroom teachers. Volunteers work under the direction of certified personnel. Unlike paraprofessionals, volunteers are unpaid. Thus they help to improve learning without increasing costs. Volunteer help is aimed at:

- Assisting teachers in nonteaching tasks and tutoring
- Giving teachers more time for more professional work
- Helping children acquire more positive attitudes toward school
- Providing better understanding of school problems
- Providing needed services to children
- Strengthening relations among school, community, and home

In some districts, "teacher partners" are selected from the ranks of parents and given more training and more responsibility than the typical school volunteer.

The school volunteer movement is not without

---

[21]For further description of the work of paraprofessionals, see Nan Coppock and Ian Templeton, *Paraprofessionals*, National Association of Elementary School Principals, Arlington, Va., 1974.

problems. Many volunteers function without adequate training and supervison. Often their work is not well coordinated and not evaluated. In New York and California the AFT opposes the use of school volunteers because they may perform duties for which they may not be competent and they may reduce the number of jobs for professional employees. However, if a vote were taken among classroom teachers who have worked with school volunteers, we suspect it would be overwhelmingly favorable. We feel the advantages of the school volunteer movement far outweigh its disadvantages. There is no other conclusion to be drawn from the spectacular growth of the movement.[22]

Lay advisory committees. Lay advisory committees in education are not new. The local board often appoints an advisory committee of citizens to help with school policies. These lay groups, selected by the board of education or by community groups, bring citizens back into educational partnership with the board, the superintendent of schools, and the teachers. This total team marshals lay leadership on the side of better education. Citizens may serve on short-term committees that are assigned a specific project, such as a building program, or on long-term committees that are delegated a continuing constructive challenge. The Elementary and Secondary Education Act requires that school districts establish an advisory council of parents for the entire school district as well as one for each school building to help plan, implement, and evaluate programs funded under this act. The members of the councils must have children in school and must be elected by the parents in the attendance areas.

Parent-teacher associations. Most school districts have PTAs that are affiliated with the state PTA and the National Congress of Parents and Teachers, which is discussed in Chapter 12. Parents and teachers have found the PTA an effective vehicle for sustaining children's security, well-being, and success in school. Through this organi-

zation, thousands of parents learn about the school curriculum, teaching methods, children's growth and development, and the problems and needs of their schools. Parents, teachers, and administrators learn to know each other better through this organization and to understand each other's problems and responsibilities. Through their PTAs, many parents assist in school libraries, in cafeterias, and on playgrounds; they help with field trips, health examinations, and many other tasks. Many PTAs are active in Head Start programs. Many also lobby to support legislation. They launch local fund-raising projects for their schools and mobilize community support for school budgets and referendums. Nonetheless, the PTA movement has lost much of its vigor in many districts.

The future

The most important factor in the future of the teaching profession was discussed in Chapter 1—teachers' power. Here we shall turn our attention to other matters. The supply of teachers, despite union efforts to control it, will outrun demand for the next several decades. This will tend to depress teachers' salaries and will not strengthen their stance in bargaining and lobbying. The oversupply of teachers will tend to exacerbate unrest among teachers and polarization within the profession. Unlike some forecasters, we do not think pressures for fair employment and affirmative action will recede within the next decade. The logistics of the job market will continue to depress employment opportunities for members of minority groups at all levels and for women in higher education particularly.

The proliferation of studies and experimentation in teacher education will inescapably bring fundamental improvement to the professional preparation of teachers. The artificial line between preservice education and in-service education will become obscured, partially because of the rise of teacher centers. As has so long been true in other professions, the responsibility for professional education in teaching will be shared increasingly by both teacher-education institutions and school

---

[22]For further discussion of the school volunteer movement, see Nita B. Whaley, *School Volunteers*, National School Public Relations Association, Arlington, Va., 1973.

The Development of the Teaching Profession

1794	First formal teachers' organization, Society of Associated Teachers, organized in New York City
1823	First private normal school started in Vermont
1827	First state legislation provided for training of teachers in New York
1838	First state normal schools established in Massachusetts
1843	Authority to issue state certification for teachers established in New York
1845	First state teachers' associations begun in New York and Rhode Island
1857	National Teachers Association formed, later the National Education Association (NEA)
1893	Normal school of Albany, New York, made Albany State Teachers College and empowered to grant degrees
1896	First statewide teacher retirement system adopted in New Jersey
1904	National Catholic Education Association formed
1909	First state teacher tenure law passed in New Jersey
1916	American Federation of Teachers organized as an affiliate of the American Federation of Labor
1917	American Association of Teachers Colleges formed
1930	National Survey of Teacher Education authorized by Congress
1938	National Organization of Future Teachers of America organized
1946	National Commission on Teacher Education and Professional Standards launched by the NEA
1946	World Organization of the Teaching Profession started (1952 WCOTP)
1948	Three teacher education groups merged into the American Association of Colleges for Teacher Education
1954	National Council for Accreditation of Teacher Education made operative
1958	Loans to future teachers in public elementary and secondary schools made available by the National Defense Education Act
1959	Ford Foundation grant of $9 million made to strengthen teacher education
1961	Collective-bargaining rights gained by New York City teachers, triggering similar movements across the country
1963	The Code of Ethics of the Education Profession adopted by the NEA
1963	Conant's survey of teacher education and his recommendations published in The Education of American Teachers
1965	Federal executive order given, forbidding discrimination in school and other employment
1966	Training begun for volunteers in the National Teacher Corps
1967	Education Professions Development Act approved by Congress

1972	Teacher demand in United States equalled by supply for first time in a third of a century	1975	Department of Public Employees (including AFT and AFSCME) formed within AFL-CIO
1973	Coalition of Public Employees (including NEA and AFSCME) and Council for a United Profession (including AASA, NAESP, NASSP, and ASCD) formed	1977	Teacher surplus exceeded one million

systems. The theory of the college program and the realities of the public schools will be joined in teacher preparation and continuing professional development. The colleges and universities will work in closer relationship with the school systems in easing new teachers gradually into full professional responsibility under the joint guidance of professors of education and school administrators. We do not share many educators' enthusiasm for performance-based teacher education. The concept is not sound ideologically, and the feasibility problems, we fear, are insurmountable.

The isolation of teachers from society will be reduced. As schools are called upon to serve as instruments of social purpose, the interaction between schools and communities will be quickened. This trend is evident in the antipoverty programs, in which schools are forced to cooperate more fully with community agencies. This will reduce both teachers' isolation and their autonomy. It will create frictions and dilemmas, but in the long run it should strengthen both school and community.

We see gradual but fundamental changes in the role of classroom teachers. Instructional technology and the application of systems theory to instructional programs will relieve teachers from the role of being sole dispenser of knowledge through lectures and recitations and will place heavier emphasis upon the diagnosis and evaluation of students' learning problems and the prescription of learning activities to meet their needs. We see a growing core of school specialists who will assist teachers in the diagnosis of learning problems, which will permit teachers to concentrate more directly on specific instructional tasks. This movement toward higher professionalization and specialization of teachers' work will result in fewer teachers and more paraprofessionals, along with

more instructional hardware and software, as described in Chapters 9 and 10. Broudy predicts that in the future perhaps 85 percent of didactic instruction will be delivered by paraprofessional technicians, much of it outside the school in homes and community centers.[23]

We predict greater use of differentiated staffing in schools, an arrangement that is eminently sensible and compatible with several other powerful forces in education, such as the press for salary differentiation on some basis other than ratings or seniority, the movement toward open education, and the ambiance of greater collaboration that has been hastened now by teacher centers. The pressure for evaluating teachers will intensify, and teachers will play a greater role in the development of such programs, which will tend to emphasize formative rather than summative evaluation. Summative evaluation will have its own thrust from increasing demands for teachers' accountability and sounder bases for dismissing and furloughing teachers.

With respect to salaries, we think negotiation will tend to shift from local districts to state capitals as education moves toward fuller state funding. We predict continued advancement in the fringe benefits of teaching, especially in sick-leave banks, liberalized retirement benefits, and job security. Tenure and job security particularly will become major issues in bargaining during the next decade.

While our view of the future of teaching is mixed, we rejoice in teachers' newly won sense of professional pride and destiny. Better trained, more self-confident, with stronger career commitment, and

---

[23]Harry S. Broudy, in Theodore W. Hipple, (ed.), *The Future of Education: 1975–2000,* Goodyear, Pacific Palisades, Calif., 1974, pp. 40–41.

more conscious of their professional dignity, teachers will continue to press for full professional stature.[24]

Suggested activities

1. Make a critical self-evaluation to determine whether you should enter or remain in the teaching profession.
2. Review reports of studies of first-year teachers and of teachers who have dropped out and summarize in order of importance those reasons which appear to explain teachers' disenchantment with their teaching positions.
3. Prepare a set of specifications derived from your reading of this chapter that you might use to evaluate a school system in which you are considering employment.
4. List some advantages and disadvantages of being a school principal, supervisor, or head of a department.
5. Review the research on selecting and evaluating teachers and summarize your findings.
6. Describe the best elementary or secondary school teacher you know.
7. Describe the type of educational work other than teaching which might interest you.
8. Study an NEA report about the supply and demand of teachers and report on those fields which are most undercrowded and most overcrowded.
9. Study the literature on differentiated staffing and prepare a report that summarizes its essential elements and the advantages which are claimed for it.
10. Prepare a report on "What It Takes to Teach Poor Children."

Bibliography

Allen, Dwight W., and **Eli Seifman** (eds.): *The Teacher's Handbook,* Scott, Foresman, Glenview, Ill., 1971, section 1. Almost an encyclopedia of practical information for teachers, including their education, in-service training, methods of teaching, and organizations.

Barun, Robert J.: *Teacher Power: The Story of the AFT,* Simon & Schuster, New York, 1972. Sharply critical and controversial account of the past and present of the AFT.

Castetter, William B.: *The Personnel Function in Educational Administration,* 2d ed., Macmillan, New York, 1976. Comprehensive treatment of the administration of the professional staff in school systems.

Cheers, Arlynne L., and **Lamore J. Carter**: *Teaching and Learning in the Model Classroom,* Exposition Press, New York, 1974. Pragmatic textbook for aspiring teachers that emphasizes the dynamics of teacher-learner interaction.

Donley, Marshall O.: *Power to the Teacher: How America's Educators Became Militant,* Phi Delta Kappa, Bloomington, Ind., 1976. Traces the rise of teachers' militancy, treats the issue of control of teaching, and predicts future trends.

Gerwim, Donald (ed.): *The Employment of Teachers,* Mc-Cutchan, Berkeley, Calif., 1974. Includes teaching careers, salary practices, job satisfaction, collective bargaining, and the future of the profession.

Gross, Beatrice, and **Ronald Gross** (eds.): *Will It Grow in the Classroom?* Dell, New York, 1974. Anthology of outstanding teachers' views of what teaching is about.

Haberman, Martin, and **T. M. Stinnett**: *Teacher Education and the New Profession of Teaching,* McCutchan, Berkeley, Calif., 1973. Historical backgrounds and contemporary analysis of all aspects of teacher education.

Hitt, William D.: *Education as a Human Enterprise,* Charles A. Jones, Worthington, Ohio, 1973. Interesting textbook for aspiring teachers.

Knox, Warren B.: *Eye of the Hurricane,* Oregon State University Press, Corvallis, 1973. Fifteen essays on the roles of various school administrators.

McNeil, John D., and **W. James Popham**: "The Assessment of Teacher Competence," in Robert M. W. Travers (ed.), *Second Handbook of Research on Teaching,* Rand McNally, Chicago, 1973, pp. 218–244. Review of research findings on evaluation of teaching performance.

National Education Association: *Careers in Education,* Washington, 1974. Analysis of various professional positions in education and how to prepare for them.

————: *Guidelines to Fringe Benefits for Members of the Teaching Profession,* Washingon, 1975. Analysis of fringe benefits available to teachers in various states and local districts.

————: *A Manual on Standards Affecting School Personnel in the United States,* Washington, 1976. Breakdown of certification requirements in all fifty states for teachers, administrators, and other certified positions in education.

————: *Teacher Retirement Systems,* Washington, 1971. State-by-state descriptions of retirement systems for teachers.

Rousculp, Charles G.: *Chalk Dust on My Shoulder,* Merrill, Columbus, Ohio, 1973. Warm, human, charming autobiography recalling twenty years of teaching.

Ryan, Kevin (ed.): *Teacher Education,* 74th Yearbook of the National Society for the Study of Education, University of Chicago Press, 1975, part II. Compilation of eleven scholarly chapters dealing with the general nature of teacher education, its issues, and its future.

[24]For further reading, see Frederick A. Rodgers, "The Past and Future of Teaching," *Educational Leadership,* January 1976, pp. 282–286.

Sabine, Gordon A.: *How Students Rate Their Schools and Teachers,* National Association of Secondary School Principals, Reston, Va., 1971. Poll of students' opinions and comments on what they like and dislike in teachers.

Schimmel, David, and **Louis Lisher**: *Legal Rights of Teachers,* Harper & Row, New York, 1973. Handbook for teachers detailing their legal rights and obligations.

Scobey, Mary M., and **A. John Fiorino**: *Differentiated Staffing,* Association for Supervision and Curriculum Development, Washington, 1973. Clear exposition of differentiated staffing with case descriptions of a number of leading models.

Snyder, Philip C.: *What Every Teacher Should Know about Finding a Job,* Branden Press, Boston, 1973. Valuable book for beginning teachers on how to apply for a job, size up a teaching position, and understand teachers' organizations.

Stinnett, T. M., William H. Drummond, and **Alice W. Garry**: *Introduction to Teaching,* Charles A. Jones, Worthington, Ohio, 1976. Discussion of opportunities and careers in education, the work of the teacher, teaching as a profession, legal aspects of teaching, and the personal qualities of the good teacher.

Templeton, Ian: *Paraprofessionals,* National Association of Elementary School Principals, Arlington, Va., 1974. Description of the various tasks performed by a variety of paraprofessionals and the reforms necessary to make them work.

Walter, Robert L.: *The Teacher and Collective Bargaining,* Professional Educators Publications, Lincoln, Neb., 1975. Primer for teachers on major issues and problems in collective bargaining.

Wilson, Elizabeth C.: *Needed: A New Kind of Teacher,* Phi Delta Kappa, Bloomington, Ind., 1973. Discussion of teachers' qualities and skills needed in modern education.

Chapter 3

Learners

Learners in contemporary culture

THE ERA OF THE COUNTERCULTURE

The introduction to this chapter in the previous edition, published in 1972, spoke of the youth "counterculture" of the 1960s and early 1970s. It called attention to the alienation of young people from society. Youths manifested this alienation in unconventional lifestyles, rejection of materialism and customary success goals, fascination with drugs, and protest. Suddenly we were all conscious of young people as a powerful social force. The reasons for their protest were comprehensible. They saw the hypocrisy between the professed idealism of our culture and the reality of an unpopular war in Southeast Asia, poverty in the midst of plenty, social discrimination, and despoilation of the environment.

Small wonder that youths rebelled against the establishment, particularly against that part which touched their lives directly—the schools. Many adults found significance in the youth movement. It was fundamentally humane, at least in ideology if not always in action. It was existential, and it revered naturalism—not Darwin's naturalism of the survival of the fittest, but Rousseau's naturalism that emphasized human beings' relatedness to nature and environment and the worthiness of natural behavior over artificial conduct. Although strident, radical, quixotic, self-righteous, and often anti-intellectual and self-indulgent, the campus-led youth movement prompted fundamental cultural, political, and educational reform. It helped to lower the voting age to 18, to accelerate the passage of civil rights legislation, to quicken society's concern for protection of the environment, to end our military and political intervention in Southeast Asia, to reform our political conventions and other institutions of government, and to reform our educational institutions.

THE ERA OF THE QUIET GENERATION

As the seeds of this counterculture movement were flowering in the larger culture, students abandoned—at least for the moment—their evangelism and activism. Campuses are once again serene, and polls of students' attitudes suggest the emergence of a "quiet generation" of young people. One explanation suggests that youths may be more disenchanted by past failures than exhilarated by successes. A more plausible explanation suggests that the threat of unemployment and economic pressures have diverted their energies to coping with the business of preparing to earn a livelihood. Yet another more hopeful explanation suggests that young people have found schools and society capable of responding to their more compelling demands. They are persuaded that the political and social order can be repaired within the system without revolution. A recent study[1] of the attitudes of high school students revealed their fundamental faith in the American government and little desire to alter the system drastically. Although today's high school students acknowledge corruption in government, their attitude is overwhelmingly sympathetic. They also express concern about overpopulation, environmental preservation, the health of the American economy and the labor market, and the diversion of funds to the military budget that they feel could be better spent for the country's social needs.

THE DIFFICULTIES OF ADOLESCENCE

These are difficult times for young people. Adolescence is often turbulent. It comprises the awkward transition from childhood immaturity and dependence upon adults to adulthood and personal independence and responsibility. This transition is fraught with difficulty, especially in a society that artificially prolongs it through extended schooling and isolation of youths from the work world until adulthood. All this happens when young people are maturing more rapidly.[2]

Harold Shane, in his book *The Educational Significance of the Future,* calls attention to some values that should guide our lives and work. Earlier generations, in less complicated times, could find ideals to believe in, according to Shane. He calls attention to "institutional overload," the growing inability of our institutions to deal effectively with the compelling problems of our time—rising crime, injustice, unemployment, among many others. For example, the inability of our schools to achieve the laudable goal of racial balance and equality of educational opportunity is distressing. Change in family life is another manifestation of institutional overload that has created anxiety and insecurity among many youths. It is estimated that a quarter million young people under age 18 leave home or are thrown out each year. Unable to find jobs, many of them turn to friends, relatives, or community youth centers in the cities. A frightening number turn to crime. Teenage prostitution has increased sharply. Although child abuse is not new, the alarming increase in its frequency causes a monumental problem for many youths in our culture.

Shane also notes that

the lack of a viable future-focused role image poses a task of considerable consequence to our schools as they endeavor to motivate more young learners to conceive of themselves in tomorrow's world of work—a future in which they experience dignity, respect, and other rewards in any one of many socially useful jobs rather than wistfully longing for one of the so-called prestige jobs, which require and employ only a small fraction of our manpower as professional workers, executives, owners, and entrepreneurs.[3]

The work ethic is deeply rooted in our culture. Our needs for self-respect, status, and dignity are satisfied largely through work. Unfortunately, we have come to disdain those who are unemployed or not employed in prestigious occupations. Young people have accepted this work ethic. The study of high school students' attitudes mentioned earlier

[1]*The Mood of American Youth,*National Association of Secondary School Principals, Reston, Va., 1974.

[2]For further discussion of adolescence, see James S. Coleman, *Youth: Transition to Adulthood,* Report of the Panel on Youth of the President's Science Advisory Committee, University of Chicago Press, 1974.

[3]Harold G. Shane, *The Educational Significance of the Future,* Phi Delta Kappa, Bloomington, Ind., 1973, p. 46.

reveals that they have extremely determined and ambitious career plans. Unlike many of their predecessors, they do not intend to drop out of society or avoid work. They are greatly concerned about jobs, marriage, and family obligations, and they have grand salary expectations. To them the future looks good.[4] But the reality appears to be otherwise. Automation and cybernation are hastening the time when only half the potential work force will be gainfully employed to support both themselves and the other half. The labor needs of the country and the work ethic of our young people will no longer harmonize unless such programs as the Peace Corps and VISTA can be expanded to help unemployed youths find socially useful work outside the production of goods and services. Thus the time-honored work ethic will fuel the frustration and disenchantment of young people and perhaps prompt them to doubt their worth and dignity.[5] Ideally we could accomplish what the ancient Greeks dreamed of, that Golden Age in which people would be relieved from labor to enjoy the good life. To do so, we must tackle the task of modifying the old work ethic and help young people find dignity and meaning in pursuits other than paid employment. Many ethical dilemmas, unknown to earlier generations, face the youths of our culture. Brown poses the problem in these terms:

Not only are many of man's institutions incapable of resolving the problem he now faces, but his values, inherited from the past, are inconsistent with his survival. Values which are widely held . . . are becoming threats to our future well-being. Man must evolve a new social ethic.[6]

Learners in the school culture

THE OPPRESSIVE SCHOOL MILIEU

Schools may be thought of as complex social systems of interacting components that include such aspects as the milieu of the community, the school

[4]*The Mood of American Youth*, pp. 27, 29, 33.

[5]For further discussion of this problem, see Erwin R. Smarr and Philip J. Escoll, Jr., "Humanism and the American Work Ethic," *Today's Education*, January–February 1974, pp. 83–85.

[6]Lester R. Brown, *World without Borders*, Random House, New York, 1972, p. 74.

governance system, and various subsystems within the schools. One subsystem is the school culture, which may be thought of as a syndrome of customs, values, constraints, and mandates that influence people's behavior within the social system.

Until recently, students[7] were expected to accommodate to the school, rather than the other way around. Although much has been said about the child-centered concept of schools, and although many schools have been modified in that direction, nevertheless many practices violate this doctrine. The graded school groups children by age or achievement level and assumes uniform standards of achievement for all as requisite for promotion. Promotion policies, grading systems, programs of study, graduation requirements, college entrance requirements, disciplinary procedures, and school governance in general proclaim the primacy of the schools over students. This stance, still supported by many fundamentalists, regards students as a product and the schools as factorylike bureaucracies to ensure that "production" falls within tolerable limits of achievement and deportment.

Many school boards, administrators, and teachers once cherished a tidy, efficient system and had little patience with demonstrations, grievances, or nonconforming behavior. The legal principle of *in loco parentis* proclaimed that the schools were surrogate parents. This principle stood unchallenged since the beginning of schooling and gave legal sanction to almost unilateral control of schools by authorities. Although many administrators and teachers were indeed kindly and humane, the climate of most schools was nevertheless more paternal or unilateral than transactional. The intense student unrest of the 1960s and early 1970s was in large measure a protest against the oppression of many schools and colleges.

STUDENTS' ALIENATION FROM THE SCHOOLS

A tragic consequence of this milieu was that many students learned to hate school and learning. Many reacted with bitterness and disruptive behavior and were expelled from school. Others dropped out as soon as they could; if age made attendance compulsory, they dropped out in spirit.

[7]We regard people of all ages who are acquiring knowledge as "learners." We regard people who are doing this in school as "students."

Dropout rates rose particularly in most urban schools, where one student in four quits without graduating from high school. Many of these students are not deviates or delinquents but are simply victims of schools with a restrictive culture that prevents them from finding satisfaction and meaning in education.

THE REFORMATION OF THE SCHOOLS

The emergence of students' constitutional rights. Belatedly society came to realize that denial of schooling to disaffected young people was also denial of opportunity for the pursuit of happiness. We learned that these young people made up the major sector of those who became unemployable, went on welfare, or got in trouble with the law. It became evident that it would be far less expensive and more humane to accommodate the schools to students than to sustain the high cost of caring for them later. The courts found denial of education an abrogation of students' constitutional rights. Many states enacted "right to education" laws that forbade the expulsion of students unless they were clear and present danger to other students or teachers. Many schools undertook to accommodate the schools to students and to make education more appealing. Briefly, such accommodations included differentiation of school curriculums to serve students' needs and interests, the provision of alternative schools, greater opportunity for all students to participate in critical decisions relating to the school culture, and the establishment of codes of students' rights and responsibilities.

Thus one powerful force in the revolution that transformed students' relationship with the schools has been the emergence of a new legal doctrine that students do not surrender their constitutional rights when they enter the schoolhouse. The doctrine of *in loco parentis* has died. Students' rights and responsibilities now include prohibition of discrimination on the basis of race or sex, the right to due process in decisions affecting their destiny, the right to access of school records, and the right to privacy in sensitive matters. In 1975 the U.S. Supreme Court added the right to a statement of charges, a hearing, and defense by counsel before suspension from school.

The concern for individuality. The second major force in this revolution of the school culture has been an emerging concern for the damage to the human spirit that results when schools fail to accommodate individual differences among students. We speak, for example, of the "Pygmalion effect" that occurs when students are stereotyped by their differences. They tend to accept and become whatever the school labels them. Eliza Doolittle, in *My Fair Lady,* noted that she would always be a flower girl to Henry Higgins but always a lady to Colonel Pickering because those were the self-fulfilling prophecies each man placed upon her. When schools treat students as though they are dull or delinquent or handicapped, they tend to become so. When schools strive to help students acquire positive self-images, they tend to do so and behave accordingly.[8] We are fond of Goethe's observation: "When we treat a man as he is, we make him worse than he is. When we treat him as if he already were what he potentially could be, we then make him what he should be."

The pathology of students' failure. When schools impose uniform standards of achievement upon all students, they foreclose concern for variation in students' rates and styles of learning. Many schools have altered their concepts of standards by thinking of "mastery learning." In this strategy students are expected to reach at least a minimal level of mastery of essential content or skills but with variation in the length of time required. Students are not discriminated against or stereotyped on the basis of these rates. Instead of labeling them slow learners and forcing them to repeat grades or subjects, many schools have adopted ungraded or continuous progress organization. Grade levels are abandoned, along with the concepts of failure and nonpromotion. Marking practices are changing too, moving toward more descriptive accounts of students' achievement rather than letter grades that, when low, reinforce the concept of failure. We finally have realized that the institutionalization of failure in schools causes disastrous and often irrevocable consequences in the self-concept of students.

[8]For a report of an interesting experiment that demonstrated this phenomenon, see Robert Rosenthal and Leonard Jacobson, *Pygmalion in the Classroom,* Holt, New York, 1968.

Jean Grambs, author of *Schools, Scholars, and Society,* states these consequences clearly:

School failure delivers a direct message to the child that he is not good, and this message comes across with exceptional clarity from the most powerful figure in the child's world after his parents. It is impossible for an individual, even a child, to sustain for long massive doses of self-dislike, which are engendered by being told how inadequate he is. One obvious dynamic is to turn in hatred upon those others who have succeeded, those other "good" children. With increased increments of failure, eventually the child must turn on adults and later on all of society. The relationship between school failure and delinquent behavior has been known for some time.[9]

It is small wonder that Glasser's book, *Schools without Failure,* became a best seller among educators. Glasser described a school milieu devoid of failure, in which all students are winners, respected and rewarded for what they have become in terms of goals that are meaningful and attainable. Glasser's book has had powerful impact on the transformation of the school culture into one that is responsive to and respectful of individual students, not one that sorts out and labels as failures those who cannot or will not adapt to the rigidities of the school. Perhaps we are approaching that goal which one of our nation's great educators, Ernest Melby, considered most critical:

The first thing that I want schools to do is send every child home every day liking himself better than when he came in the morning, because we don't want him to drop out. If he drops out, we can't do much for him.

The hazards of sex-role stereotyping and racial discrimination. Sex-role stereotyping is another cause for concern in the school culture. This problem cuts two ways. As noted in Chapter 10, textbooks have typically reinforced the image of males as aggressive, brave, and disposed to success in high-status occupations. Females, however, have been viewed as passive, inner-directed, inferior, and disposed toward following their male peers. Teachers and administrators, like the rest of society, have tended to reinforce these polarized role expectations, much to the disadvantage of

women. When teachers are primarily women and administrators are almost always men, sex stereotyping becomes even more vivid. High schools, colleges, and vocational schools once restricted entry into certain courses, particularly vocational courses, on the basis of sex.

On the other hand, boys in nursery schools, kindergartens, and early elementary schools face women teachers almost exclusively. Until they reach high school, boys encounter school cultures that are far more feminine than masculine. This feminine influence, some authorities claim, contrasts with the boldly masculine culture that boys encounter in their neighborhoods. Patricia Sexton of New York University suggests that the major reason girls do better than boys in school is because schools are run too much by and for females. Whether sex stereotyping is more harmful to one sex than the other is not the point; schools must strive to eliminate discrimination and stereotyping on the basis of sex and thus harm neither group.

Racial discrimination, another pernicious practice in the culture of still too many schools, is so complex and pervasive that we have treated it at length in Chapter 1.

Misbehavior and punishment. The factors outlined above account for the aberrant behavior of some young people. This behavior may be manifested in vandalism or more serious crimes, misuse of drugs, or other forms of antisocial behavior. When adults are polled on the most critical problems in schools, discipline is always near the top of the list. Educational fundamentalists tend toward a Calvinistic approach to the problem and urge tighter controls over students' behavior. They invoke the old maxim of spoiling the child by sparing the rod. Others—and the authors agree—believe that readin' and 'ritin' and 'rithmetic should not be taught to the tune of the hickory stick. Yet only a handful of states forbid corporal punishment. Four out of five large school districts sanction it, although its use is generally considered to be on the decline. In 1975, the U.S. Supreme Court affirmed a lower court's ruling that corporal punishment of students is not unconstitutional when (1) students are forewarned of the kinds of behavior that may result in spanking, (2) corporal punishment is not the "first line" of punishment, (3)

[9]Jean D. Grambs, *Schools, Scholars, and Society,* Prentice-Hall, Englewood Cliffs, N.J., 1965, p. 77.

another teacher witnesses the spanking, (4) a written explanation of the punishment is made available to parents upon request, and (5) the punishment is not excessive.

We agree with the report, prepared by a panel of educators who studied the problem and published by the National Education Association, which concluded that we should move quickly to end the practice of "inflicting pain upon students, except for purposes of restraint or protection of self (teacher) or other students." There are several good reasons for this position. First, corporal punishment does not work; psychologists agree that corporal punishment is ineffective and has undesirable consequences. In fact, any kind of punishment to halt negative behavior is less effective than positive reinforcement of desired behavior through rewards. Corporal punishment attacks the symptoms of misbehavior rather than its causes. Worse yet, it teaches students that they live in a violent world and that brute force is an acceptable means of dealing with people, a lesson that may carry over into their treatment of siblings, peers, or even their own children. Husbands may no longer beat their wives, army officers their soldiers, nor employers their employees. Why should children be the last to be liberated? We believe that physical punishment contributes to students' alienation from school and interferes with learning. Although many parents and some teachers and administrators disagree, we welcome the growing movement sponsored by the National Committee to Abolish Corporal Punishment in Schools. When punishment is necessary, we think there are better means of punishment, such as denial of privileges.[10]

Participation of students in setting standards of conduct. Many schools have moved toward giving students more opportunity to participate in setting standards of acceptable conduct, to define their rights in the school, and to specify their responsibilities. Students' participation helps generate support for acceptable behavior and peer pressure against unacceptable behavior. It tends

---

[10]For further discussion of corporal punishment and alternative approaches to discipline, see *Discipline Crisis in the Schools: The Problem, Causes, and Search for Solutions*, National School Public Relations Association, Arlington, Va., 1973; and Adah Maurer, "Corporal Punishment," *American Psychologist*, August, 1974, pp. 614–626.

to have a wholesome effect upon the school climate.

Students must understand their rights and responsibilities and have confidence that they will be treated fairly. The most effective and moral responses to students who misbehave, which humane educators have long recommended, include greater participation by students in school governance, curriculum reforms that involve students through greater relevance to contemporary life, elimination of discrimination against members of minority groups, elimination of arbitrary standards of achievement and behavior, relaxation of unreasonable rules of conduct, protection of due process to prevent punishment of the innocent, and, perhaps above all, teachers who are themselves exemplars of superb interpersonal relations and whose behavior is consistent with the golden rule.

Improving students' attitudes toward school. Many schools are moving in these directions, and results can be seen in the attitudes of high school students. In the study mentioned earlier, three-fourths of these 2,000 students praise their high school education. Most report that good student-teacher interaction exists in their schools. They feel that their high schools are challenging them to develop their abilities, and they praise their teachers' attempts to individualize instruction. They hold generally positive attitudes toward teachers, counselors, and administrators.[11]

Human growth and development

Christianity and other great religions revere the inherent worth of every human being. This doctrine holds that each person should have every opportunity for the fullest possible self-realization and for the competence needed to deal with the problems of life. Education in a democratic society holds the prime responsibility for seeing that all individuals develop to their maximum potential. Modern educational thought holds that this potential can be increased through good teaching. American education is founded on the belief that mass education does not deny respect and care for the individual,

---

[11]*The Mood of American Youth.*

that quality and quantity in education can coexist. American education seeks to arouse in all learners a profound sense of self-respect and personal integrity.

UNDERSTANDING LEARNERS

To teach students is to understand and respect them. Since our earliest recorded history, we have been engaged in the study of children and youths. The story of educational progress is, in large measure, the story of deeper understanding of learners. In recent years the behavioral sciences have yielded new knowledge of the growth and development of human beings. This understanding points the way toward better adaptation of the schools to the unique needs of students and toward more effective teaching. Recent studies in the life sciences, the physical sciences, and the social sciences have made increasingly important contributions to knowledge about the growth and development of persons.

PRINCIPLES OF HUMAN DEVELOPMENT

The understanding of children is fundamental to the task of teaching them. Complete understanding is never reached, but increased understanding comes through the expanding body of knowledge about learners' growth and development. Certain generalizations can be made from this body of knowledge:

1. Human behavior is influenced by many complex and often obscure factors. One powerful factor is the learners' home environment. Behavior is based upon past experiences, shaped by present circumstances, influenced by hopes and plans for the future, and initiated by some sort of motivation. Motivation is a powerful influence upon learning.
2. Learning is a natural but not always enjoyable process, although the capacity for learning varies widely among individuals. Learners fail to learn because some impediment impairs their learning. Frequently, faulty teaching is an impediment.
3. Each person is unique. Individuals not only differ from others but are in a constant process of change themselves. Individual differences increase as children grow older.
4. All persons have some potential for growth and development. This potential can be increased by good teaching but is influenced by learners' environments.

Each person should have every opportunity for the fullest possible self-realization and for competence needed to deal with the problems of life.

Each person is unique. Individuals not only differ from each other but are in a constant process of change themselves.

5. The entire human organism is involved in learning and development. Mental development cannot be considered in isolation from learners' physical, social, and affective status.

6. Human growth is continuous but not constant. Several developmental stages are discernible among learners, and rates of growth vary. Learning tasks must be attuned to individual learners' readiness and stages of development.

7. Learners are influenced greatly by the values of the groups to which they belong. During the early years of life, their families may be a powerful educative force. As learners become increasingly detached from family life in later years, group identity and loyalty become increasingly influential on their development.

8. Many agencies other than schools have powerful impact upon what is learned—mass media of communication, commercial and industrial establishments, the church, among others. The home and the school bear neither full burden nor full responsibility for human growth and development.

9. Classroom learning is largely the result of teachers' behavior in initiating and guiding activities, in reinforcing learners' responses, and in sustaining involvement in the learning process.

10. The social milieu of a learner's life is a crucial factor in shaping both the desire and the opportunity to learn. Therefore extending the opportunity and conditions of learning is a social, economic, and political matter, as well as a pedagogical matter.

11. Learners are influenced by their state of well-being. Poor nutrition, fatigue, and abuse of medication or drugs tend to influence learning.

We do not yet fully understand human development, although contemporary studies are rapidly adding to our knowledge of this complex process. For example, studies are being made of the medical, biological, and chemical forces impacting upon human development. The science of neurobiology, which has a long history, is revealing the physiological roots of brain disorders. It offers hope for the rehabilitation of certain types of neurological impairment. Linus Pauling has demonstrated the relationship between certain chemical imbalances in the body that result from malnutrition and faulty mental functioning. This work suggests that some mental patients may be suffering from a correctable chemical deficiency. Perhaps learning may be improved eventually through chemical intervention. James McConnell's celebrated experiments with rats suggest that memory is essentially a chemical process and that drugs can improve learning.[12]

FACETS OF GROWTH

Learners have not one but several facets of growth. The Bible, in an account of the early life of the Great Teacher, gives us an excellent description of all-round growth and development: "And Jesus increased in wisdom and stature, and in favor with God and man" (Luke 2:52). He increased in wisdom (mentally), in stature (physically), in favor with God (spiritually), and in favor with other people (socially). Teachers and parents should promote this four-dimensional growth, the facets of which are discussed in following sections.

Mental development. Mental development is really the growth of a number of specific mental abilities that include social intelligence, motor intelligence, perceptual speed, reasoning, memory, word fluency, verbal comprehension, facility with numbers, and understanding of spatial relationships. Each ability has a somewhat different growth rate, and each can be measured. The rate of mental development is a function of both genetic potential and environment. As discussed in Chapter 1, there is considerable controversy over the relative importance of genetic potential (nature) and environment (nurture) in the development of intelligence. Normal mental development is also dependent upon wholesome physical, nutritional, emotional, and social development. This important point was not recognized in early theories of psychology and is still missed by many critics who fail to appreciate the importance of the school's attention to the total development of children. Pleas for exclusive concentration on mental development—without regard for children's physical, social, and emotional well-being—are not in accord

with modern understanding of human development.

"Intelligence" may be defined as the *capacity* for learning. It is an important factor, but not the only factor, affecting learners' progress in school. Binet, a French psychologist, and his physician colleague, Simon, the pioneers of intelligence testing, believed that intelligence could be modified through training. But for a long time later the general view was that intelligence was determined by heredity and that it remained constant throughout life. Some recent investigations suggest that it is possible under certain conditions to accelerate the rate of mental growth in the capacity to learn. Some educators dispute this conclusion.

Piaget's general theory of intellectual development helped to clarify our understanding of intelligence and learning. Piaget projected a sequence of stages of learning that are related to age. He believes that the sequence of these stages holds true for all children but that the ages in which the learning stages evolve depend upon the native endowment of individuals and the quality of their environment. Piaget's construct is both a nature and a nurture theory of intelligence, a point of view now rather widely accepted.

Intelligence, as the capacity for learning, is commonly measured in terms of mental age. When mental age is divided by chronological age, the quotient, expressed as intelligence quotient (IQ), provides a measure of the rate of intellectual growth. Thus a 10-year-old child with a mental age of 12 would have an IQ of 120 (12 divided by 10 and then multiplied by 100 to avoid the inconvenience of decimals). Intelligence sometimes is regarded as a single trait, and we apply certain labels, such as bright or dull, to individuals.[13] But this is misleading, since there are a number of different components of intelligence. In Chapter 1 we called attention to the abuse of intelligence tests and the dangers of stereotyping learners on the basis of them.

Without normal maturation—that is without the changes in the characteristics of an individual resulting from intrinsic development—training may be of little or no avail. Differences in heredity appear to establish the rates of maturation, which

[12]For a review of some of these studies, see Edward A. Sullivan, "Medical, Biological, and Chemical Methods of Shaping the Mind," *Phi Delta Kappan*, April 1972, pp. 483–486; Maya Pines, *The Brain Changers: Scientists and the New Mind Control*, Harcourt, Brace, Jovanovich, New York, 1974.

[13]For a discussion of the limitations of intelligence tests in measuring mental capacity, see Sheldon H. White et al., "IQ: The Myth of Measurability," *The National Elementary Principal*, March/April 1975, pp. 2–78.

cannot be overcome by teaching in normal learners. Thus maturation determines both the rate and the limit of an individual's learning ability.

Children's academic achievement is commonly measured by standardized tests; results are expressed in terms of normal achievement for students of a given age. This measure is sometimes referred to as "educational age." By comparing a learner's educational age and mental age, it is possible to determine whether or not achievement is commensurate with capacity for learning.

Physical development. By far the most significant aspect of physical growth with respect to learning is the development of the central nervous system, since it is the mechanism for learning. It comprises the brain, spinal cord, and nerves. Very few people function anywhere near their intellectual capacity. The central nervous system, it is estimated, contains approximately thirteen billion neurons, but the ordinary person probably uses no more than one billion in a lifetime. Neurologists, pharmacologists, and biological and medical researchers are learning more about the functioning of the central nervous system. During the prenatal period the human organism develops from a single cell into a complex system capable of many activities. The spinal chord, nerves, and lower portion of the brain are relatively mature at birth, but the cerebral cortex, the locus of learning and complex behavior, continues to mature. Birth, therefore, is not really the beginning of life and growth, but rather an important change in the environment of the human organism.

After birth the infant grows very rapidly in height and weight. However, this rate of growth is vastly slower than that which occurs during the prenatal period, and the rate actually slows down progressively from birth to maturity. During infancy, legs grow more rapidly than the trunk and head. The brain also grows quite rapidly. Muscles grow fast, and many complex physical skills, such as walking and talking, are acquired during this period.

Gradually the rate of physical growth in children decelerates until about 9 to 13 years of age, when another spurt of growth continues for two or three years. For the first decade of life boys and girls grow at about the same rate. But puberty overtakes girls earlier than boys, with the result that girls from 11 to 15 are heavier and taller than most boys of the same age. At 15 or 16, girls' rate of growth

slows markedly, while boys continue to grow until about age 20. After 20 most people continue to grow in weight but not in height.

During surges of growth, children need greater energy to sustain the growth itself. During these periods they find it more difficult to study and to withstand strain. This is often a difficult period for their parents and teachers, as well as for children. Anything that disturbs children may interrupt their growth. When a child fails to grow or loses weight, something is interfering with his or her well-being and is cause for concern. On the other hand, spurts of growth occur at slightly different times for different children. If this is not understood, normal periods of slow growth may cause undue anxiety. Proper education can help to sustain sound physical growth and motor development.

Tallness and shortness are partly hereditary. Environment and nutrition also have an effect upon growth. Studies seem to indicate that each generation is slightly taller and healthier than preceding generations.

Social development. Children mature socially and emotionally as well as physically and mentally. Social and emotional maturity are related to other facets of development. For example, children and youths of advanced mental maturity tend to be more advanced socially and are larger and stronger physically as well. However, this general rule has many exceptions.

As children become members of a large and more complex group, they become more aware and responsive to others. The egocentric infant becomes a social conformer. Older children learn to be more sensitive to the feelings of others and to be more cooperative in groups. They form strong attachments to peer groups and participate more effectively in team sports, gangs, clubs, and other cooperative activities.

As normal children reach puberty, they acquire greater understanding and acceptance of themselves. They develop more confident relations with both peers and adults. Although they still need guidance and support from the family, they become less dependent upon their parents. However puberty presents a special social problem, since girls mature more rapidly than boys during this period. Boys and girls of the same age and in the same class in school have quite different attitudes toward the opposite sex. Girls at this age are quite interested in boys, who are likely to hold girls in disdain. Fortunately, this situation does not continue for long.

As adolescence is reached, boy-girl relationships become more mature. But rapid sexual maturation poses new problems. Relationships with the opposite sex pose problems for some teenagers. Adolescence is a turbulent period of development. Physical growth is rapid—sometimes too rapid from the standpoint of poise and grace.

Adolescents yearn for the independence of adulthood, but at the same time may be frightened by the prospect of it. In urban society the family has generally less impact on youths' values than it did when youths were an integral part of a productive family unit. Children and youths are no longer well integrated into patterns of adult life. Their association with adults tends to be more superficial and divested of meaning. This isolation from adult life drives young people more and more to peer groups and contributes to their alienation from adult culture.

As noted earlier, the difficulties of adolescence are exacerbated by the withholding of adult prerogatives from youths, who are maturing more rapidly than earlier generations.

The social development of children and youths can be strengthened immeasurably by the school. Both social and emotional behavior are learned. Fine schools do not leave social development to chance. They accept society's expectation that the school should guide and encourage this development. Opportunity is given children within the school program to develop wholesome understandings of and relationships with others.

Personality development. A learner's self-esteem is an important factor in maturation. From nursery school to graduate school the learner is searching for an answer to that omnipresent question: "Who am I?" Young people are in constant search of personal identity and meaning in life. They strive to find purpose in living. This search becomes increasingly difficult in a world with weapons of mass destruction, urbanization and high densities of population, unemployment, economic dislocations, lack of integrity in government, strident stimuli of the mass media, and the lure of drugs and narcotics as means of escape from distressing reality. Students may be anxious over

success in school, particularly when schools set arbitrary standards of achievement that may be unattainable or irrelevant. Schools can help to relieve this identity crisis by demonstrating that they really care about each human being, by accommodating to the individual differences of each student, by establishing viable and realistic expectations of students, by helping them deepen their understanding of themselves, and by wholeheartedly joining them in their quest for identity.[14] There are, of course, many other facets of personality development.

Moral development. Robert Havighurst has identified five stages of character development:

1. The amoral, impulsive stage during which the person follows his impulses with no sense of morality. This stage usually prevails during the first year of life.
2. The egocentric, expedient stage during which the person is still primarily interested in satisfying his own desires but modifies this selfish behavior for the sake of personal safety or making a good impression on others. This behavior is normal between the ages of 2 and 4.
3. The conforming stage, between the ages of 5 and 10 commonly, in which the person is strongly motivated to conform to the demands and expectations of the people with whom he lives.
4. The irrational conscience stage, also normal for children from 5 to 10 and beyond, in which the person strives to satisfy without criticism the moral teachings of parents and teachers. A kind of rigid and unexamined morality prevails.
5. The rational conscience stage, beginning in adolescence, in which emotional and intellectual independence is sought through one's own reasoning and acceptance of moral values.

The moral development of some persons is arrested short of the last stage, and they never reach mature moral behavior. Most persons have in their makeup some aspects of all five stages of moral character development.

Havighurst believes that schools can influence the development of morality by providing teachers of exemplary character and by providing more opportunities for reflective thinking, particularly during high school years, on social problems and his-

[14]For further discussion of this problem, see Stanley Coopersmith and Jan Silverman. "How to Enhance Pupil Self-esteem," *Today's Education*, April 1969, pp. 28–29.

torical events that hinge on moral choices.[15] Research studies suggest that schools generally have not had much impact upon the values which youths acquire in life.

Creative learners

Creative learners are those who are capable of invention, discovery, or constructive originality. It is sometimes assumed that the term "creative" is synonymous with "mentally gifted." Although it is true that for certain activities a minimum IQ is prerequisite, creativity does not appear to be a function of intelligence, nor is it measured by intelligence tests. Research suggests several capabilities that seem to characterize gifted learners. First, gifted learners are adept at "divergent thinking"; that is, they resist premature closure on a single solution to a problem but instead entertain mentally a variety of possible solutions which they weigh carefully before selecting the best. Second, creative learners are able to discern more complexity in whatever they are doing. They are challenged by complexity and seek to find order in it. Third, creative learners place greater reliance on their keen intuition and hunches and trust their nonrational mental processes.[16] Creative people generally have strong sensory perceptions and value systems that are keenly aesthetic and theoretical.

Project Talent and the Institute of Personality Assessment and Research at the University of California, along with other organizations, have directed their attention to the identification and nurture of gifted learners. This is an important enterprise because all of society gains from the efforts of a relatively few highly creative persons. It is important that schools understand the nature of creativity, identify potentially creative learners who come from all strata of society and all races, and develop the kind of stimuli and support that will help creative students to develop more fully. Many critics of education believe that schools typically

not only fail to nurture creativity but, worse yet, stifle creativity in students by rewarding conformity and stifling nonconformity. Thoreau said that the creative person "hears a different drummer. Let him step to the music which he hears, however measured or far away." Creative learners are generally more productive in independent study than in group activities, and they achieve most when they are instructed by creative teachers. The National Association for Creative Children and Adults and the Association for the Gifted, a component of the Council for Exceptional Children, are preeminent organizations for persons interested in the education of gifted learners.

Mentally gifted learners

Concern for mentally gifted learners is by no means new. Eminent educational psychologists such as Lewis Terman, L. S. Hollingsworth, Paul Witty, Jacob Getzels, and Phillip Jackson, among others, have been concerned with the education of mentally gifted learners for decades. The great intensification of interest in finding and developing top intellectual talent is one of the most significant and widespread recent trends.

WHO IS MENTALLY GIFTED?

There is no universally accepted definition of the mentally gifted—learners sometimes referred to also as "academically talented" or "superior." Perhaps the most common concept of mentally gifted learners would include those with high mental capacity having IQs exceeding 125 or 130, although intelligence alone is not an adequate measure of giftedness. These learners can be identified by standardized intelligence tests, such as the Revised Stanford-Binet or the Wechsler Intelligence Scale for Children; by their marks; and by teachers' judgments. The term "giftedness" can be applied, of course, to a variety of talents. A child may be gifted in reading but not in art. The most outstanding characteristic is high verbal ability.

Intellectually, gifted learners are, of course, capable of learning more fully and more rapidly. However, this superior capacity for learning is not automatically sustained without appropriate instruction. Indeed, one of the tragedies of life is the

---

[15]Robert J. Havighurst, "What Research Says about Developing Moral Character," *NEA Journal*, January 1962, pp. 29–30.

[16]For further discussion of the nature of creativity, see Frank Barron, "The Dream of Art and Poetry," *Psychology Today*, December 1968, pp. 19–23, 66.

failure of many gifted people to realize their full potential because of inadequate educational experience. A report by the U.S. Office of Education revealed a potentially critical waste of the talents of 2 million undiscovered gifted students in our schools, especially nonwhite students. Much of this neglect is caused by inadequate funding of educational programs for gifted learners. The report states that intellectually creative talent cannot survive educational neglect and apathy.

Mentally gifted learners possess superior ability in reasoning and generalizing. They can deal more easily with abstract ideas. They may or may not have a positive attitude toward school, depending upon the school's ability to accommodate their giftedness. They tend to be more creative and inquisitive. Gifted learners have higher vocabulary levels, superior memory, longer attention spans, and are more persevering. They have more varied interests and are more capable in independent study. They are likely to be more interested in nonfiction than in fiction, and they outgrow children's literature more quickly. They tend to read omnivorously.

PROVIDING FOR MENTALLY GIFTED LEARNERS

Good teachers and good schools have always sought ways of identifying and encouraging able students. On the other hand, many teachers have found it easy to become preoccupied with helping slow learners and have assumed that the bright students would take care of themselves. Without much effort on their own part or on the part of the teacher, these students have usually met academic standards geared to the average ability of the group. However, in too many instances they have not been challenged to the full measure of their ability. Too often they have become indifferent.

Many proposals have been advanced for caring for gifted learners in school. Most procedures can be classified into three basic patterns: grouping by ability, acceleration, and independent study.

Grouping according to academic ability was once widely practiced, but then fell into disrepute on the grounds that it fostered an educational elite, encouraged undesirable feelings of superiority or inferiority among students in the upper and lower groups, denied future leaders an opportunity to associate with their future followers, and was un-

democratic. In some cases superior students are grouped in separate classes. Since most learners are not equally gifted in all subject fields or learning tasks, some schools have developed flexible groupings. Thus a child may be in an advanced science group, an average art group, and a lower group in physical education. A student may move to a higher or lower level group at any time. Primary teachers have practiced this type of grouping for many years. Grouping makes it possible for a teacher to work with a narrower range of ability.

Acceleration is an arrangement by which gifted learners advance through school more rapidly than others. This may be accomplished by early admission to kindergarten and first grade, by going through an ungraded school in less time than others, by skipping grades, by completing high school work early and undertaking college-level work in high school, or by advanced placement in college. One argument favoring acceleration is that it permits students to complete college and undertake careers and marriage earlier in life. Since the early twenties are the most productive and creative years for many people, it is argued that entry into a career should come as early as possible. The usual argument against acceleration is that an accelerated student's social and emotional maturity may not be commensurate with that of their older classmates.

Independent study is an arrangement whereby gifted learners are neither segregated nor accelerated but rather are given extended work, usually performed on their own initiative, beyond that expected of average learners. This arrangement is less disruptive of the school organization. Also it means that the gifted learners receive a larger total amount of education than is possible under an accelerated program, since their years of schooling are not cut short. Through such independent study gifted learners may go further than the remainder of the class. They may do extra work in the same area in which the class is working, such as research or creative writing, beyond that expected of others. Or they may work at a level in advance of the rest of the class, such as studying elementary algebra in a junior high school general mathematics class, or being enrolled in advanced placement courses to earn college credit while in high school.

Many claims and counterclaims are made for

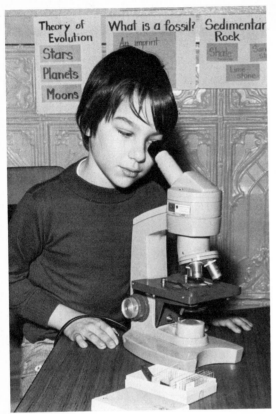

Through independent study, gifted learners perform extended work on their own initiative.

each of these patterns. The evidence indicates that all three patterns show considerable promise and that gifted learners can profit from any of the arrangements. It is important that a plan or combination of plans be suited to the individual school, its learners, and its faculty. Experience and research have identified several crucial aspects of educating gifted learners:

1. We need better means of identifying intellectually gifted learners early.
2. Much more must be learned about the nature of giftedness and about creativity, critical thinking, personality, and value concepts associated with it.
3. We need more experience with, and better evaluation of, curriculums, organizations, and methods of instruction for gifted learners.
4. Placing gifted learners with gifted teachers is beneficial.

5. We must investigate the impact of society's attitudes and values on the nurture of giftedness.[17]

Much interesting experimentation in meeting the needs of gifted learners is underway. Among the organizations supporting the study of gifted learners and developing better programs for them are the National Association for Gifted Children and the National Education Association's Project on the Academically Talented.

Learners with disabilities and handicaps

Various terminology has been used loosely to describe a variety of learners who have difficulty in learning for a number of reasons. The imprecision of the terminology has tended to stereotype children inappropriately and has created misunderstanding with respect to the school's proper response to them. Let us therefore clarify some terms. An "exceptional child" (or "atypical child") is one who deviates so markedly intellectually, physically, socially, or emotionally from what is considered normal growth and development that he or she cannot receive maximum benefit from a regular school program. Such a child requires a special class or supplementary or different instruction and services. A "handicapped child" is one who is mentally retarded, hard of hearing, deaf, speech impaired, visually handicapped, seriously disturbed emotionally, crippled, or otherwise impaired physically. Such handicaps require education in a special class or supplementary instruction or services. Handicapped children may be classified more specifically in a number of categories, such as visually handicapped or orthopedically handicapped (see Figure 3-1), discussed later.

Children suffering from learning disabilities essentially have problems of perception. Perceptual disorders cause difficulty in auditory or visual discrimination and have nothing to do with intelligence. These disorders frequently result from delayed development of the neurological system. A consequence of these disorders is a significant

[17]For further study of the education of the gifted, see Elizabeth M. Drews et al., "Special Feature on the Gifted and the Talented," *Today's Education,* January/February 1976, pp. 26–44.

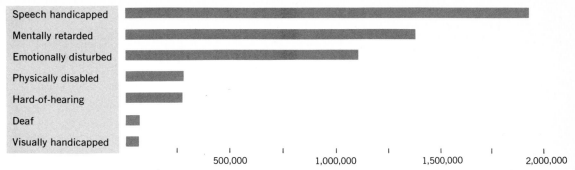

Figure 3-1 Number of handicapped children, ages 5–18, needing special education services.

discrepancy between a learner's apparent capacity for learning and his or her achievement. Other categories of learning problems are described later in this chapter and defined in the Glossary.

RIGHTS OF LEARNERS WITH DISABILITIES AND HANDICAPS

Great advances have been made in the improvement of education for children and youths with handicaps and disabilities. We now understand better the nature of the disabilities and the approaches to instruction that are most effective. Progress has been accelerated by a historic U.S. District Court decision that in 1971 ordered Pennsylvania school districts to educate all retarded learners between the ages of 4 and 21 whatever the cost. Within a few years this "right to education" concept was expanded by the courts to include mentally and emotionally handicapped learners.[18]

In 1975 the Education of All Handicapped Children Act was enacted by the federal Congress; it established a national policy of assuring "free, appropriate public education" for all the nation's 8 million handicapped children between the ages of 3 and 21. Prior to the act, 1 million of them were receiving no education, and half the remainder were probably receiving inadequate education, which indicates the neglect that led to passage of the act. The act requires all states to locate and identify all handicapped children and provide a

curriculum responsive to the needs of each. If possible, these children are to be educated alongside other children. If that is not possible, they must be educated in their homes or in hospitals or in other institutions. If local districts cannot provide the education, then the state must. The act also includes a number of due-process provisions for these learners, protections against improper placement, and parents' right of access to relevant records. The act is truly a milestone in our struggle for educational opportunity for everybody.

NEW ORIENTATION TO LEARNING DISABILITIES

This accelerated development of education for handicapped learners prompted a new orientation to the problem. In an earlier time, educators were disposed to focus upon the causes of learners' disabilities and stereotype them accordingly. The constraints imposed upon their learning by their handicaps, sometimes exaggerated, were impressed upon both students and teachers. This tended to become a self-fulfilling prophecy for many. Children with hearing difficulties, for example, were sometimes called deaf and subtly persuaded that they could not function normally. Small wonder that they succumbed. Other children with undetected brain damage that did not necessarily impair their learning seriously were labeled "mentally retarded." Teachers and parents often expected too little or too much of them. If too little was expected, the children fulfilled the expectation. If too much was expected without appropriate accommodation by the school, frustration and possible psychological damage were added to the student's handicap. If the child's disability incon-

---

[18]For further discussion of the legal struggle for better education for the handicapped, see Frederick J. Weintraub and Alan Abeson, "New Education Policies for the Handicapped: The Quiet Revolution," *Phi Delta Kappan*, April 1974, pp. 526–529.

venienced the classroom teacher, the teacher sometimes shirked the responsibility by rationalizing, "This child doesn't belong in this room." Many children were placed in special education classes where they became more handicapped through exclusion from the broader experiences of the regular classroom. Thus the disabled learner label, once applied, tended to condition the child's entire life even though the disability usually applied to only a part of his or her activity. In sum, the focus of this concept was upon causes and limitations of the disabilities and the accommodation of the child to the limitations rather than upon maximizing the student's remaining capabilities.

THE EMERGENCE OF MAINSTREAMING

Many schools failed to realize that learners with severe physical disabilities, even brain damage, were still quite able intellectually. Physical, emotional, and social disabilities, unless extreme, need not inhibit learning. With modern educational methods and materials, it is increasingly possible for children to be educated in the conventional classroom (often spoken of as "mainstreaming") by properly trained teachers, unless the student's impairment is too severe.

Birch, one of the pioneer advocates of mainstreaming, defines it as "providing high-quality special education to exceptional children while they remain in regular grades for as much of the day as possible." He lists these reasons to support mainstreaming:

- The capability to deliver special education anywhere has improved.
- Parental concerns are being expressed more directly and forcefully.
- The rejection of the labeling of children is growing.
- Court actions have accelerated changes in special education procedures.
- The fairness and accuracy of psychological testing has been questioned.
- Too many children were classified psychometrically as mentally retarded.
- Civil rights actions against segregation uncovered questionable special education placement practices.
- Nonhandicapped children are deprived if they are not allowed to associate with handicapped children.
- The effectiveness of conventional special education was questioned.

- Financial considerations foster mainstreaming.
- American philosophical foundations encourage diversity in the same educational setting.[19]

IMPORTANCE OF EARLY IDENTIFICATION OF LEARNING DISABILITIES

It has also been discovered that the identification of disabilities in early childhood and appropriate intervention in the child's environment can reduce the effects of the disability. To illustrate, when autistic children have difficulty interacting with teachers and other children, their education is impeded and their handicap in life compounded. But many autistic children have little difficulty interacting with the impersonal talking typewriter, particularly in preschool years. As a result of this happy circumstance, they often are able to learn to interact with other people, and their disability is reduced. Early identification of children with disabilities often prompts early clinical treatment of correctable conditions before the impairment accumulates and emotional problems result. Much of the educational response to the alleviation of disabilities in early-childhood education has been prompted by the Handicapped Children's Early Education Assistance Act, passed by the Congress in 1968. Head Start programs, day care centers, nursery schools, and kindergartens are doing a better job of identifying disabled learners earlier.

OTHER NEW APPROACHES

The relief of disabilities caused by physical and emotional disorders has been quickened by the merger of educational, psychological, and medical resources in the identification and treatment of these children. Many school systems are establishing clinical teams consisting of educational, medical, psychological, and other special persons and agencies closely coordinated with the

[19]Jack W. Birch, *Mainstreaming*, Council for Exceptional Children, Reston, Va., 1974. For further discussion of mainstreaming, see W. Edwin Martin, "Some Thoughts on Mainstreaming," *Exceptional Children*, November 1974, pp. 150–153; Roger Reger, "What Does 'Mainstreaming' Mean?" *Journal of Learning Disabilities*, October 1974, pp. 57–59, or Frederick Andelman and others, "Mainstreaming," *Today's Education*, March/April 1976, pp. 19–29.

classroom.[20] Many learners with severe physical problems who in earlier years would have been assigned to residential schools for learners with visual or hearing disorders are now increasingly attending regular school classrooms for part of the school day but spending the remainder of their time in special education facilities designed to help them reduce the impairment of their disability. In this new view, the medical or psychological cause of the learning impairment becomes less important, while the modification of the learners' behavior in such a way as to condition them for intellectual training becomes more important.

Instructional technology has also helped the school to accommodate more effectively to the needs of handicapped learners. For example, electronic amplification devices reduce the handicap of hard-of-hearing children. A new type of polyethylene paper permits sightless persons to communicate readily by writing and reading conventional letters and numbers rather than braille. An oversized, automatic ball-point pen or blunt pencil raises characters a few thousandths of an inch above the paper's surface so that they can be identified by touch. Programmed instruction and computers permit far greater accommodation to the individual differences of students with various learning disabilities. Innovations in school architecture and school buses permit physically handicapped students much more mobility. Many other examples could be cited.

Perhaps the most important factor is the classroom teacher. The achievement of learners with disabilities can be quite remarkable when guided by a teacher with adequate knowledge, compassion, and skill.

Despite the trend toward including in the regular classroom many children formerly assigned to special education classes, some learners have disabilities so severe that special education facilities are still necessary for them. We turn now to a consideration of four categories of handicapped children—intellectually impaired, physically handicapped, emotionally handicapped, and socially and culturally handicapped—while reemphasizing that only those learners who suffer extreme

handicaps in any of these categories are necessarily in need of education in special classrooms, although many may need special accommodation in regular classrooms.

INTELLECTUALLY IMPAIRED LEARNERS

It is very important to distinguish between two types of subaverage intellectual functioning: learners with neurological handicaps and learners who are otherwise mentally retarded. The former may be bright and capable of normal academic progress, while the latter are not. The distinction is imperative if the neurologically handicapped are not to be relegated to the same fate as the others through the neglect of the schools, as indeed a great many are.

Neurologically handicapped learners. The term "neurologically handicapped" is used with reference to persons with any impairment of the central nervous system, whether mild or severe, whether congenital or the result of accident. The term "minimal brain dysfunction" excludes the more severe neurological disorders such as cerebral palsy and epilepsy. The incidence of brain dysfunction in children is increasing, amounting to an estimated proportion of one in ten among school-age children. It is estimated that remedial facilities in schools are available for less than one in twenty of the children so affected, a tragic circumstance.

Neurological dysfunctions can result from several causes: injury to the fetus, poor prenatal care, injury or oxygen deprivation during pregnancy or birth, malnutrition, chemical or blood irregularities, genetic aberration or illness of the expectant mother. We have no idea how many children go through life unable to achieve their full potential because of prenatal or natal damage. Recognizing and responding to the tricky symptoms are more important than discovering the causes. Often the symptoms are not manifested until a child enters school. The symptoms may include such things as erratic performance in schoolwork, easy distraction of attention, swift changes in mood, and clumsy psychomotor skills. The victim may fall further and further behind in school unless appropriate special remediation is provided. Inept in play, the child may be rejected by peers. Eventually he or she may feel worthless, give up, and compound

[20]For a description of this team approach to learning disabilities, see Murray M. Kappelman, "Learning Disabilities: A Team Approach to Diagnosis and Prescription," *Educational Leadership,* May 1975, pp. 513–516.

the miseries by social and emotional maladjustment.

Many of these learners would be capable of fairly normal educational progress and social adjustment even with present knowledge. Some schools are demonstrating remarkable success in reaching these learners, but fewer than 10 percent of the teachers needed for this work have received the special preparation necessary.

Within recent years there has been a remarkable confluence of educational, medical, neurological, and psychiatric energy and expertise in dealing with children with learning disabilities.[21] This new collaboration among the professions is yielding far better understanding and remediation of the problems of learning disability. Much of this new understanding and better practice in the field of learning disability offers promise for the improvement of learning for all students.

There are several consequences of neurological impairment. The most common form is dyslexia, which affects perhaps as many as 10 percent of the early school population to one degree or another. Its cause is unknown. It is regarded as a genetic, neurological dysfunction that results in imperfect directional sense. Dyslexia is unrelated to intelligence. The dyslexic child reverses letters, words, and numbers: "b" becomes "d," "left" becomes "felt," and "42" becomes "24." Auditory perception may be similarly distorted. Without special instruction, the dyslexic child is likely to have difficulty learning to read and may suffer emotional disorganization as a result of academic frustrations. We mention dyslexia here because there is little general awareness of this particular disability.[22]

Neurological impairment is of course manifested in many other ways. The autistic, minimally brain-damaged child, for example, tends to be withdrawn, uncommunicative, and shy. These children have learning problems and appear to be intellectually retarded. Without understanding of the causes of the problem, psychiatric help is often not effective. Relief must be found instead in behavior

modification to reduce the learning problem through appropriate educational placement, individualized counseling, and tutoring.

"Hyperkinetic behavior disturbance" is the fancy medical term for the hyperactive child, whose problems may stem from brain dysfunction incurred during late pregnancy and birth. These ebullient children (the condition disappears at puberty) demonstrate all the behavior that adults dislike—enormous physical activity including yelling, fighting, running about, and generally disrupting things. Hyperactive children have short attention spans and are easily distracted; they thus are difficult to teach. The condition is difficult to diagnose and seldom is discovered before a child enters school. It affects about 3 percent of the children in elementary schools, boys more commonly than girls. Small doses of amphetamines, such as Ritalin and Dexedrine, have a sedative effect on these children which, curiously, is the opposite of their effect on adults. These drugs do not cure hyperactivity, nor do they inhibit learning. They are nonaddictive and, according to most medical opinion, are safe in small doses.

Schrag and Divoky, on the other hand, contend that the hyperactive child is a myth; that hyperactivity is not a medical entity; that Ritalin has dangerous side effects; and that schools coerce helpless children into becoming more passive.[23] However, a panel of experts appointed by the Department of Health, Education, and Welfare looked into the matter of amphetamine treatment and gave qualified approval as long as diagnosis and treatment are under proper medical attention and with parental consent.

Mentally retarded learners. The term "mental retardation" is commonly used to cover a wide diversity of below-average intellectual functioning. Mental retardation may result from a variety of causes: diseases such as German measles, poor prenatal or postnatal care, oxygen deprivation at birth, physical injury, or disordered chromosomes.

For purposes of this discussion, we will exclude

---

[21]The term "learning disability" was once confined to perceptual disorders arising from neurological impairment. Recently the term has become a catchall for almost any learning deficit.

[22]For further discussion of this disorder and what neighborhood schools can do to help students, see Benjamin H. Pearse, "Dyslexia," *American Education*, April 1969, pp. 9–13.

[23]Peter Schrag and Diane Divoky, *The Myth of the Hyperactive Child*, Pantheon, New York, 1975, condensed in Peter Schrag and Diane Divoky, "Learning Disabilities: Education's Newest Growth Industry?" *The National Elementary Principal*, March/April 1976, pp. 7–18. For discussion of how teachers can help hyperactive children, see Beverly J. Small, "The Hyperactive Child," *Today's Education*, January/February 1974, pp. 34–36.

the learners with neurological dysfunctions discussed earlier. Mental retardation is no longer regarded as a condition that is easily diagnosed. Perhaps as many as half the students now treated as mentally retarded could have developed normal intelligence if they had received treatment in early childhood.

Retarded learners' mental ages and IQs suggest the limitations of their abilities of association, comparison, comprehension, generalization, and symbolization as compared with those of normal learners. Limited vocabulary and reading skills handicap these children in learning other subjects. Attention span is short, and the children forget easily. These unfortunate children fall further and further behind the age norm for learning as they grow older. Mentally retarded students have less ability to learn from experience than normal learners. They are less capable of making social adjustments and often manifest behavior problems. Most mentally retarded learners closely resemble normal persons of corresponding age in physical appearance. The techniques of behavior modification and operant conditioning are often effective both with mental retardation and with emotional distubance.

Retarded learners tend to become frustrated by the difficult demands placed upon them by school and society. Many of their antisocial behavior patterns result from their impairments and should not be confused with deliberate negativism. However, even these shortcomings should not be considered immutable. The potentiality of most mentally retarded learners can be raised through good teaching.[24] Both physical and mental examinations should be given in most cases to be sure that the apparent mental retardation is not in reality the manifestation of some physical disability such as poor hearing.

Mentally retarded children are commonly classified into three groups: the educable, the trainable, and the custodial. While the lines of demarcation between these groups are not absolute, the educable mentally retarded (EMR) are generally regarded as those with IQs between 50 and 75, approximately 3 percent of all children. The trainable

are those few children whose IQs are below 50 but who are capable of some learning. Custodial children, extremely few in number, have IQs below 30 and are practically incapable of any learning. The Children's Bureau estimates that of each one thousand persons, thirty are mentally retarded. Of this thirty, approximately twenty-five are educable, four are trainable, and one is custodial.

Educable learners are increasingly included in regular classroom instruction rather than in special education classes as a result of recent more open and optimistic views of the potentialities of the mentally retarded. These learners have attenuated cognitive development. Some experts believe that by attacking the emotional, social, and motivational aspects of the problem, educable children can become capable of greater academic achievement than was heretofore expected. New instructional materials created especially for educable learners, along with better instructional methods, have had a significant impact upon the education of these people. Materials and content must be within the range of the educable child's capacity if they are to be meaningful. Materials should be closely related to the child's environment and experience. Assignments should be within his or her range of ability. As much as possible the educable child should be given extra help. Since slow learners have particular difficulty with verbalization and abstractions, television and other visual aids are particularly helpful.

Trainable learners are those who are unable to profit from regular classroom experience but who will not need to spend their lives in institutions. With appropriate instruction, trainable children are often capable of learning to take care of themselves, to make a reasonably adequate social adjustment, and to learn simple occupational skills. Many, however, are not able to become occupationally self-sufficient. Some trainable children are enrolled in special ungraded classrooms in public school systems. Others are provided for in residential schools for the mentally deficient.

Custodial children are so limited in intelligence that education is out of the question for them. They usually require close supervision and care at home or in a residential institution especially equipped for the care of the mentally retarded.

Many mentally retarded youngsters are further handicapped in life by parents who are unwilling or unable to understand their child's mental handi-

[24]For a good discussion of new developments in the field of mental retardation, see C. P. Gilmore, "The Strange Malady Called Learning Disability," *New York Times*, magazine section, Mar. 2, 1975, pp. 14–21.

cap. Unfortunately, some teachers are not as sympathetic to and understanding of mentally retarded youngsters as they should be. Like all handicapped children, they must be accepted for what they are and helped to achieve up to their level of ability, however modest it may be.

PHYSICALLY HANDICAPPED LEARNERS

Several types of physically handicapped learners require special consideration.

Visually handicapped learners. Visually impaired learners have the same basic educational needs as learners with normal sight. Many of the techniques which a teacher should use with visually impaired learners also enhance the learning of all.

Alert teachers are on the lookout for behavior that is symptomatic of poor vision: frequent mistakes with words or figures; inability to study without eye discomfort; complaint of headaches; peculiar head positions, squinting, or frowning; holding books too close to the eyes; ability to see objects at a distance more clearly than those at close range; inability to see objects at a distance; redness and swelling of the lids; inflamed or watery eyes.

Any symptoms of defects discovered by the teacher should be reported for further examination, diagnosis, and remedial treatment by an eye expert. It is estimated that one in every four schoolchildren needs some eye care. Medical treatment obviously is the first provision.

Partially sighted learners are those with vision of 20-70 or less after correction. Some systems maintain special classes for them. However, partially sighted youngsters should be educated in regular classrooms. It is important for teachers to be aware of such handicaps and make appropriate adjustments in classroom organization and procedure. For example, partially sighted students should be located so that their desks receive adequate light. They should be located near the front of the room so that they can see the teacher and chalkboard as easily as possible. The teacher should verbalize material on the chalkboard and state explanations and instructions clearly so that visually impaired students are not disadvantaged. It is important that partially sighted learners use their vision within reasonable limits because unused vision tends to

be lost. Teachers and other students should avoid giving too much help. Safety can be a problem, particularly in fire drills or in unseen hazards in the school or on the playground.

The teacher's physical contact with a visually impaired student can communicate the warmth that a smile or eye contacts give a child with normal sight. Realistic understanding and accommodation rather than pity should characterize the relations of the teacher and other students with visually impaired learners.[25]

New media of instruction have helped visually impaired learners to overcome their handicaps in regular classrooms. Typewriters and books with large type are also available. Voice tapes and other audio equipment help to reduce the learners' dependence upon visual communication.

Deaf and hard-of-hearing learners. The primary problem in the education of those who have never heard speech is the unavailability of the normal use of language as a vehicle of communication. Even the hard-of-hearing often have difficulty with language development, which handicaps their acquisition of the basic skills. Deaf children require education in special classes. Hard-of-hearing learners whose disability is not too great can be educated in regular classrooms if adequate accommodation is made for them. Children with severe hearing loss may develop psychological problems because of their isolation from dialogue with others.

Teachers should recognize the following possible symptoms of hearing loss: failure to respond to calling of a name, cocking of the head to one side, failure to follow directions, looking in a direction other than the source of sound, watching others and following their movements, frequent requests for repetition of a word or phrase, faulty pronunciation of common words, or speaking in an unusual voice. The easiest and surest way of identifying students with impaired hearing in one or both ears is with the use of the audiometer. Perhaps half of all hearing damage and subsequent school failure could be prevented by early detection and remediation. The hearing-impaired student needs medical care. Progressive deafness comes on so

[25]For further discussion of the classroom accommodations that the teacher may make to help visually impaired students, see Lou Alonso, "The Child with Impaired Vision," *NEA Journal*, November 1967, pp. 42–43.

gradually and so insidiously that it frequently escapes notice until it is too severe to be corrected.

Children with residual hearing are usually given auricular training by means of electronic aids, such as the radio ear, an instrument that magnifies the human voice so that the pupils can hear the words of the teacher. Every desk is equipped with a headphone and a rheostat so that pupils can adjust the intensity to their own need. A device, the captioning module, translates television sound into captions that appear on the picture and can be read by hard-of-hearing students. The Special Education Instructional Materials Center in the U.S. Office of Education is developing a variety of instructional materials to help the hard-of-hearing. Another technique, known as infracode, permits deaf children to "hear" through a network of nerve receptors in the skin that pass along to the brain vibrations which are perceived as sound. Above all, the students need to acquire confidence in their ability to live with normal people in a world of sound.[26]

Speech- and language-handicapped learners.
Children with speech impairments constitute by far the largest group of physically handicapped students in the nation's schools. Speech defect has been defined as any acoustic variation from an accepted speech standard so extreme as to be conspicuous in the speaker, confusing to the listener, or unpleasant to either or both. Among these defects are stuttering, lisping, lalling, cluttering, nasality, thick speech. baby talk, hoarseness, and defects caused by organic difficulties, such as cleft palate or cerebral palsy.

Undesirable personality traits may accompany inadequate speech. An enfeeblement of the general health or extreme nervous excitement may aggravate the condition of a stutterer. Deaf children have speech problems because they do not hear spoken language. Autistic children fail to speak because of psychological disorders. Because of speech defects children may not display normal ability and may thus be falsely rated low in mentality. Teachers should seek to identify pupils with speech difficulties and to understand the major causes of the trouble.

The classroom teacher, through daily contacts with students, is the usual avenue for locating speech defectives. Many schools employ speech therapists who make periodic surveys of all children and undertake speech-correction treatment with those having speech difficulties. However, the demand for speech therapists outruns the supply.

A very common but fallacious observation is that a child will outgrow a speech defect. Many speech problems that have no organic origin can be corrected in the primary grades through the encouragement of teachers who refuse to accept as normal the continuation of baby talk beyond the early years of childhood. Perhaps no group of physically handicapped children can be helped more completely than those having speech defects. According to many case studies, speech-correction treatment has improved the personalities of antisocial pupils.

Classroom teachers should in no way threaten or ridicule students who have a speech impairment. Teachers should encourage them to speak despite their difficulty. It is important also to enlist the help of parents and suggest ways in which they can encourage more wholesome speech development in an anxiety-free home environment.[27] Participation in creative speech classes and choral speaking can make the voice quality of both handicapped and normal children more pleasing and effective.

The human values of speech reeducation cannot be overemphasized. People are prone to make allowances for the blind, the deaf, and the crippled in limb, but not for those crippled in speech. Children who stammer, for example, may actually be punished for reciting. Even though they know their lesson, they are often a source of merriment to comrades, a torment to themselves, and an object of sympathy to their teacher.

Crippled and other health-impaired learners.
Paradoxically, modern medical science has decreased the incidence of some types of physical disabilities while increasing others. Many scourges, such as polio, have been virtually eliminated. But medical practitioners are also saving more defective babies at birth and in infancy. Congenital deformities constitute the largest single category of disabled children. Heart and circulatory defects are approximately ten times as com-

[26]For further information see Hazel Rothwell, "What the Classroom Teacher Can Do for the Child with Impaired Hearing," *NEA Journal,* November 1967, pp. 44–46.

[27]For more information, see Evelyn Y. Allen, "What the Classroom Teacher Can Do for the Child with Speech Defects," *NEA Journal,* November 1967, pp. 35–36.

mon now as they were a decade ago. Accidents are increasing the incidence of crippled learners. Many students from low-income families are the victims of malnutrition. The incidence of venereal disease is increasing among adolescents. During this decade many classroom teachers, along with the general public, have become much more knowledgeable about such disorders as cystic fibrosis, nephrosis, muscular dystrophy, anemia, hemophilia, and cerebral palsy, the principal cripplers of children.

Some crippled or health-impaired learners are so severely handicapped that they must be educated at home either through personal tutoring or through radio, television, two-way radio-telephone, and other electronic means of communication. Others are educated in special schools or special classrooms of regular schools when their physical disability is too severe to be accommodated in regular classrooms. Most states now provide special financial subsidies for the transportation of these students and for the special educational facilities and instruction which they may require. An increasing number of states are requiring ramps, door treadles, and other barrier-free facilities for children on wheelchairs. Many advances in the design of self-propelled wheelchairs, school buses, school furniture, and school buildings have given crippled children more freedom of mobility, more self-reliance, and better access to the educative experiences that normal children enjoy.[28]

Abused or neglected learners. A terrifying number of children (estimates range from 60,000 to 150,000) are the victims of beatings, sexual abuse, starvation, and even torture. In 700 cases annually death is the tragic consequence. Until recently we have failed to realize the extent of this horrible misfortune. We have simply been unable to believe that parents are capable of strangling, molesting, fracturing, starving, or torturing their children. These barbaric acts, which are reaching epidemic proportion, commonly multiply the number of children who are both physically and emotionally handicapped through no fault of their own.

The Education Commission of the States has studied child abuse and has urged the strengthening of statutes to provide more adequate protec-

tion of the young and to require all professional persons to report suspected cases. Half the states now require teachers to do this. Schools can help also by making sure that social agencies follow through appropriately. Public attention should be called to this calamity, which occurs in ghetto, middle-class, and wealthy families. Where parental reform is impossible, abused children must be relocated in foster homes. The most fundamental approach is for schools to offer better programs of parent education so that the next generation of parents is more civilized in its relations with its children. Studies suggest that many of the most abusive parents were themselves the victims of abuse as children, another reason for the elimination of corporal punishment at home and at school.

Teachers can help to identify victims of abuse by watching for these signs: contusions, sleeping in class, coming to school without breakfast or money for lunch, inadequate dress in cold weather, aggressiveness, coming to school too early and staying too late. Clearly teachers are the first line of defense. The National Center on Child Abuse and Neglect was established by the Child Abuse and Protection Act of 1974 to help reduce this problem.[29]

As is the case for most handicapped learners, the school should seek to modify its organization and regimen to accommodate these students in the regular classroom unless their disability is too severe. However, exaggerated program modifications or overprotection can deprive students of normal opportunities to adjust to the environment, to establish satisfying social relationships, to face problems and risks, and to develop self-control. The attitudes of teachers and students toward these handicapped persons are vital.

It is quite important that teachers strive to reduce the social and emotional impact of these students' condition lest secondary handicaps compound their physical disabilities and encumber their adjustment to life. New educational technology is helping to relieve physically handicapped stu-

[28]For further information, see Frances P. Connor, "What the Classroom Teacher Can Do for Crippled and Health-impaired Children," *NEA Journal*, November 1967, pp. 37–39.

[29]For further consideration of this problem, see Bert Shanas, "Child Abuse: A Killer Teachers Can Help Control," *Phi Delta Kappan*, March 1975, pp. 479–482.

dents from dependence upon conventional materials that they may find difficult.

All schoolchildren should have annual physical and dental examinations so that disorders may be identified and corrected early. Unfortunately, many school health examinations are too superficial to detect maladies, particularly in their incipient stages.

The advances in instructional technology, new insights into teaching methods appropriate for the physically handicapped, and the support of medical and psychological resources can help physically impaired learners to fill productive occupations and enjoy satisfying lives, thereby reducing their burden upon themselves and upon society. Thus the higher costs of educating these learners are returned.

EMOTIONALLY HANDICAPPED LEARNERS

According to the National Institute of Mental Health, more than ten school-age children and youths per hundred suffer some form of emotional disorder, two need psychiatric services, and less than one is getting it. More than half a million young people are brought before the courts each year for juvenile delinquency, many of them suffering from emotional disorders. The suicide rate among the school-age population has more than doubled within the past decade. Most students who commit suicide reveal warnings that teachers should recognize. Remarks like "I'm no good" and "You won't be seeing me any more" should be taken seriously. Dramatic changes in behavior, excessive use of drugs, giving away prized possessions, unusual preoccupation or boredom, or hallucinations should alert the teacher to possible danger and prompt immediate psychiatric attention.[30]

Admissions to juvenile mental hospitals are increasing about three times as fast as the total juvenile population. The number of mentally ill persons in the nation exceeds the number of patients suffering from any other malady; they occupy almost half the hospital beds. In many cases drug addiction is rooted in emotional disorder. These are indeed frightening statistics.

Frequently the causes of mental illness and emotional disorder can be traced to early child-

hood; and since many of the symptoms appear then, early identification and treatment of disturbed persons is crucial. But only 10 percent of the nation's school systems have programs and resources to help children with mental handicaps, and most of these deal with mental retardation rather than emotional disturbances. Many counties have no mental health clinics, and very few communities provide an acceptable standard of services for mentally ill children. Many disturbed children are sent to the adult wards of state mental institutions, where they stay for the rest of their lives at a cost far in excess of the psychological rehabilitation that they need. It is no wonder that the Joint Commission on Mental Health of Children concluded that this country's failure to alleviate mental disorders is creating a "quiet emergency" of growing and serious proportions.

Disturbed youngsters manifest various forms of atypical behavior. Their behavior may be aggressive, such as provoking fights, defying authority, destroying property, or disrupting class; or it may be more passive, such as withdrawal or daydreaming. Some emotionally disturbed children show a traumatic aversion to school, sometimes referred to as "school phobia." They may fear separation from parents or may have a fear of being held captive. Many school dropouts, delinquents, and criminals come from the ranks of the emotionally disturbed. These people often have normal or superior intelligence, but their emotional disturbance usually makes them so disorganized or antisocial that they cannot adapt to the expectations of the school or society. A study of dropouts from Harvard University revealed that nearly half of those who leave do so for psychiatric reasons. Many are bright students who see their identity threatened by competition with other bright students. This feeling of inadequacy causes depression and is related to the rise in drug usage. The report concludes that colleges focus primarily on the intellectual development of students and ignore their emotional development.

Ordinary classroom teachers are not prepared for the difficult task of identifying emotionally disturbed children except for those who are obviously psychotic. Neither are ordinary teachers prepared to practice therapy to correct emotional disorders. Emotionally impaired students should be referred to the school psychologist. Diagnosis and therapy of psychotic and neurotic children require the spe-

[30]See Susan A. Winicoff and H. L. Resnik, "Student Suicide," *Today's Education*, April 1971, pp. 30–32, 72.

cialized service of a clinical psychologist or psychiatrist. But in many schools the number of referrals to these specialists is far greater than they can handle, and only the most severe cases receive treatment.

Compassionate teachers can help to prevent mental illness by maintaining a classroom environment that threatens students' mental health as little as possible. A wholesome interpersonal relationship between teacher and student is the first essential. For some, school is the only place in the world where there is any chance for real security, affection, and encouragement. For such a child, having a relationship with an adult who cares is therapeutic in itself. Students must enjoy at least some measure of success if they are to be at peace with themselves and others. Rigid marking and promotion practices and arbitrary standards of achievement that are beyond their reach tend to condemn some children to failure. Repeated failure breeds mental disorder. Thus the primary goal is to encourage children to proceed at a pace that is comfortable for them in dealing with assignments that interest them and are within their capability. In this way children can be helped to gain approval and self-respect, the prime antidotes to emotional disorder.

Teachers can help children with latent emotional disorders to anticipate crises and strengthen their "stress immunity." Students can be encouraged to express negative feelings rather than to suppress

Schools can help students anticipate crises and strengthen their stress immunity.

them and find a scapegoat to attack. Role playing and other forms of sociodrama can be used to help students relieve themselves of hostility and aggression in a nonthreatening setting. In sum, teachers should strive to prevent as much emotional disturbance as possible through humane teaching methods. In any case, it is less burdensome for teachers to try to prevent emotional disturbance in the classroom than to try to deal with its aftermath.

Many of the causes of emotional disturbance, however, lie outside the classroom, and teachers usually have little control over these forces.[31] The National Mental Health Act has helped states, counties, and cities by subsidizing psychiatric services and establishing the National Institute for Mental Health. These programs have transformed many emotionally handicapped persons into self-sufficient, productive, confident citizens and have thus repaid their cost to society many times over.

SOCIALLY AND CULTURALLY UNDERPRIVILEGED LEARNERS

Our nation numbers in its midst socially and culturally disadvantaged people such as sharecroppers, migratory farm workers, immigrants, exiles, slum residents, and others. Robert Coles, a research psychiatrist, in his poignant book *Children of the Poor,* speaks of these as "the children the schools have never served" and "wanderers we would rather not see." Although socially and culturally disadvantaged people come from all races, a disproportionate number are from minority groups. Much of the literature on culturally disadvantaged students focuses on racial and ethnic minorities. But studies show that poverty, along with its related social, cultural, and psychological consequences, is the common denominator of the disadvantaged. Many socially and culturally underprivileged young people come from families that are highly mobile.[32] Changing schools can be a psychological and social prob-

[31]For further discussion of what classroom teachers can do to reduce emotional disturbances, see William C. Morse, "Disturbed Youngsters in the Classroom," *Today's Education,* April 1969, pp. 31–37.

[32]For further discussion of migratory children's schooling problems, see Jeanne Park, "Children Who Follow the Sun," and Ida B. Bragdon, "How to Help Migrant Children," both in *Today's Education,* January/February 1976, pp. 53–56 and 57–58.

lem for any student, and it is compounded when moving is frequent. Leaving friends and familiar teachers can be as wretched an experience as the loneliness of a new and unfamiliar school and community. The problem can be complicated when the new student is not properly placed academically in the new school. The complexity and congestion of urban living, often combined with discrimination in housing and employment, add to the misery of the urban poor. They often congregate in overcrowded, dreary, unsightly, and unhygienic ghettos, where schools and social agencies are grossly inadequate. These slum neighborhoods are often characterized by crime, delinquency, filth, dope addiction, alcoholism, sickness, broken homes, and violence. When children's homes are culturally deprived, their parents uneducated and apathetic about education, and their schooling unrelated to their most pressing problems, it is small wonder that they have difficulty learning.

The Coleman report, *Equality of Educational Opportunity,* concluded that children's home background is more important to their success in school than the school itself. Middle-class persons often assume that the culture of poverty or of racial minorities is largely disordered. Such is not always the case. These subcultures are often characterized by family lifestyles that are highly organized; relative freedom from strain, self-blame, and parental overprotection; abundant good humor and enjoyment of the company of others; and informality. One review of research concluded that the average self-concepts of black children and other members of minority groups do not differ significantly from the average self-concepts of their white counterparts.[33]

But under conditions of abject poverty and neglect, these young people may either withdraw from life or become aggressive. Those who withdraw sit silently in school until they can drop out. For them the conditions essential for learning are destroyed. They see only hopelessness in their lives. Learning is virtually impossible for them until hope, self-confidence, and trust have been restored. Other children react to deprivation with aggressive behavior. Since they have not yet lost hope, they attack other students, teachers, the school, or the community. They can still communicate but do so on their own terms. Since they still have hope, they seek unorthodox channels of achievement which are often incompatible with institutionalized mores because the schools do not appear to be responsive to their needs.

RESPONSE OF THE SCHOOLS AND THEIR LIMITATIONS

Recent studies indicate that these effects of early life are neither permanent nor irreversible. Until recently, academic weaknesses of disadvantaged children in school were attributed largely to the cultural deprivation theory. Although cultural deprivation is a contributing factor, more recent thought indicates that the primary factor is the limitations of the schools found in culturally deprived neighborhoods. The orientation of the school's teachers, students, and curriculum to middle-class values and products may seem unreal and meaningless to disadvantaged children from lower-class families. Many of them do not have the advantage of the "hidden curriculum" of middle-class families, where they are read to, taken on trips, talked with, and given other educative experiences. Handicapped by inadequate language development, disadvantaged children have difficulty in learning to learn at school under conventional instruction. Their crowded homes often fail to provide a quiet and convenient place for study. Often they are malnourished and lack adequate medical care. If their parents and older siblings are undereducated, they lack exemplars of school success.

Although these factors probably contribute to difficulty in learning in conventional schools, the school is responsible if it does not accommodate to the child's particular needs. Failures of the school have been categorized as (1) the failure to match teaching method with children's different learning styles, (2) the failure to use material that is related to their knowledge or background of experience, and (3) the failure to use materials and methods that engage their feelings.[34]

Schools must expand and enrich the social and cultural experiences of these children to compen-

---

[33]E. Gnanaraj Moses, Perry A. Zirkel, and John F. Greene, "Measuring the Self-concept of Minority Group Pupils," *Journal of Negro Education,* Winter 1973, pp. 93–98.

[34]Gerald Weinstein and Mario Fantini (eds.), *Toward Humanizing Education: A Curriculum of Affect,* Praeger, New York, 1970, pp. 21–22.

The curriculum must be closely attuned to the real-life interests of students if school is to have any meaning for them.

sate for the barrenness of their homes. They must be given more than the usual opportunity to assume constructive social roles within the school. The school curriculum must be closely attuned to the real-life problems and aspirations of children if school is to have any meaning for them. Above all, they need to see the relation between education and life.

Many cities have initiated programs of compensatory education for socially, economically, and culturally disadvantaged children and youths in the inner city. These compensatory programs, as their name implies, attempt to compensate for children's disadvantages by offering them special educational experiences and services. Stronger ties between the home and the school are sought to generate parental understanding and support for the child. Very often the child is incapable of learning until the more serious dysfunctions in the home are relieved. Social agencies, churches, social and civic groups, child-guidance centers, juvenile courts, the police, youth centers, and various other governmental agencies are imperatively needed to help relieve the out-of-school roots of slum children's problems. Parental education and early-childhood education programs are quite important.

The most seriously maladjusted must be removed from their own school environment and placed in correctional institutions for their own good, as well as for the welfare of other students who may actually be endangered by their presence.

However, it must not be assumed that all socially and culturally deprived children come from families that are low on the socioeconomic scale. Some children of middle and upper-class parents are also victims of homes that are socially and culturally barren—homes without fine books, music, or art or in which they are given no motivation to learn. Broken homes, brutality, parental hostility, apathy toward education, and other ills are not the exclusive legacy of poor families. Other aspects of the education of the poor and of minority groups in our society are discussed in Chapter 1.

THE CRITICAL IMPORTANCE OF THE TEACHER

The most important variable in the education of disadvantaged youngsters is the teacher, whose attitude is quite important. Kenneth Clark, an eminent social psychologist, asks to what extent underprivileged children do not learn because their teachers do not believe they can learn, do not expect them to learn, and do not help them to learn. Clark believes that children who are treated as though they are uneducable invariably become uneducable. Samuel Shepard, an early pioneer in the improvement of schools in the inner city in St. Louis, explains that teachers must be convinced that beneath the dirt, bad language, tardiness, and even recalcitrance of any student is the unique and infinitely precious human being whose inherent dignity renders him or her worthy of our most sincere respect and efforts to develop the fullest possible potential.

Teachers must be helped to meet disadvantaged children on their own ground. This does not mean that standards should be compromised or children condescended to; indeed, they should be held to high but attainable standards of work. It does mean that teachers must recognize the standards of the culture from which these students come and turn these standards to educational advantage. Effective teachers must understand the culture of poverty, must know the conditions under which their students live, and must develop teaching methods that are compatible with their students' unique styles of learning. Clearly the prime

attribute of teachers is respect for disadvantaged children because this is the key to winning their respect and cooperation.[35]

Drug-handicapped learners

Although the effects of many drugs, alcohol, and narcotics on the mind and body are not fully understood, there can be no question that prolonged use of many drugs or narcotics results in irreversible brain damage, genetic disturbance, and faulty fetal development. Aside from the physical hazards, drugs and narcotics are capable of causing psychological damage; they permit one to escape from the problems of life by taking a pill or swill or smoking a weed, and they may thereby prevent an individual from attaining full emotional, social or intellectual maturity. Many drugs are capable of disturbing mental processes and behavior sufficiently to expose the user and others to additional hazards in ordinary activities of life, such as driving a car. The incidence of drunken driving among teen-agers is frightfully high. It is estimated that half a million teen-agers are already alcoholics. Half a million young people are hooked on hard drugs. Truly, drug abuse has reached crisis proportions. However, there are some indicators that the crest of drug abuse by young people has passed.

Many drug users find themselves inadequately prepared emotionally to deal with the problems of life and look forward to the escape which tranquilizers, amphetamines, barbiturates, hallucinogens, or narcotics provide. However, this escape is temporary and illusory and often deflationary over the long run. Too often it becomes only a rigid defense against growing up.

What can schools and society do to relieve the problems caused by the abuse of drugs and narcotics? A volume would be required to answer this complex question fully, if indeed such an answer is possible. In a more general sense, schools should help to quicken students' enjoyment of life, decrease their boredom with school and reduce academic pressures to a manageable point. Schools

---

[35]For further discussion of effective stratagems in the education of ghetto children, see Gertrude Noar, *Teaching the Disadvantaged*, National Education Association, Washington, 1967.

can help students acquire a sense of self-realization and fulfillment, and find deeper meaning and excitement in life through more authentic and wholesome experiences such as music, art, athletics, and other physical, aesthetic, and social activities. In sum, schools should strive to help remove the causes of drug and narcotic abuse. Schools should provide students with more authentic information about drugs, alcohol, and narcotics. Drug-abuse education programs, described in Chapter 9, are important.

Schools should facilitate the detection and referral of victims of drug abuse as early as possible. Teachers should recognize the symptoms of drug abuse—wearing long sleeve clothes even in warm weather; use of sunglasses indoors; unusual outbreaks of temper; changes in quality of homework, attendance, speech, grades, behavior, or appearance—although these symptoms do not always indicate drug abuse. School boards should adopt well-reasoned policies and guidelines for dealing with students who use drugs. Drug pushers should be driven from the school and arrested.

Psychiatrists and psychiatric social workers are sometimes available. Schools without on-site emergency help should establish "hot-line" counseling and referral services to outside agencies that are capable of providing emergency help for students who are in danger from drugs. Unfortunately virtually all communities lack sufficient resources for the treatment of drug addiction. Certainly the rehabilitation of students addicted to hard drugs is a task well beyond the capability of schools.

Teachers, administrators, and counselors must become far more familiar with the drug and narcotic problem so that they can discuss the problem knowledgeably with students both individually and in classes. Students should be able to level with their teachers and counselors on such problems with impunity and with the assurance that they are being understood. Lines of communication should be kept open, and students should be free to confide in teachers and parents. Scare tactics should be avoided. Schools should undertake programs of adult education so that parents too may understand the phenomenon more fully and react sensibly when their children use drugs or narcotics. Finally, teachers should strive to become well-adjusted citizens, demonstrating that it is possible to lead full and satisfying lives without resort to chemicals. Young people are searching for models of human conduct and have the right to find them in school faculties. Teachers and parents who are themselves "turned on" by life without recourse to drugs or narcotics are probably the best preventatives.[36]

Pregnant learners

The number of teen-age pregnancies is increasing annually. Many unwed college, high school, and even some junior high school girls are becoming mothers. The number of illegitimate births among persons of all ages has tripled in the last quarter-century. The number of pregnant girls who have abortions is not known. Both married and unmarried pregnant learners have a high school-dropout rate. Until fairly recently it was not uncommon for schools to deny enrollment to married students and to pregnant girls. Indeed this practice was common among colleges years ago.

For many years the only formal education available to pregnant girls was instruction at home conducted by the school district or programs conducted in maternity homes by social agencies. However, more and more school districts are establishing special educational programs for pregnant girls and young mothers who have not completed their high school education. These programs may be found in regular high schools as supplemental to the conventional curriculum. Sometimes special education centers are established for these learners, but this is undesirable because it tends to stigmatize them. The better programs focus upon three major objectives: (1) to increase the chances of normal pregnancy and childbirth and to protect the health of the infant and its mother, (2) to help girls solve the personal problems which have led to or resulted from pregnancy and to help direct them toward a satisfying future, and (3) to help girls keep up with their schooling during pregnancy and thereby increase their chances of continuing their education after childbirth. Courses in prenatal care, nutrition, and

---

[36]For further information on how schools can help, see *Drug Crisis: Schools Fight Back with Innovative Programs,* National School Public Relations Association, Arlington, Va., 1971.

infant care are commonly instructed by teams of obstetricians, psychologists, nurses, and nutritionists.

The U.S. Supreme Court has decreed that pregnancy, whether in or out of wedlock, is insufficient grounds for exclusion from school except out of demonstrable concern for the well-being of the student or unborn child. In fact, some state attorneys general have held that pregnant girls within compulsory school age must attend school unless excused by medical certificate. One facet of the problem seldom dealt with is the school district's responsibility for helping the fathers of these unborn children assume their new responsibilities more effectively.

The future

As we enter our third century as a nation, we are on the verge of achieving our long-sought ideal of providing education for all learners as well as the right kind of education for each, regardless of mental, physical, emotional, or social limitations. This is resulting from the conjuction of two major forces: first, the recognition of our clear legal and moral obligation to do it and, second, our rapidly developing knowledge about *how* to do it.

The sudden burst of interest in expanding human consciousness is an exciting and fateful development. Although some facets of this thrust —yoga and spiritualism, for example—go back many years, concentrated and programmatic research directed at the human nervous system has accelerated greatly within the past decade. We will speak briefly of some of the thrusts originating from the disciplines of psychology, medicine, pharmacology, biology, chemistry, genetics, and pedagogy.

TRANSPERSONAL PSYCHOLOGY

As eminent psychologist Robert Kantor pointed out, "A revolution in psychology usually foreshadows a revolution in education and, to my mind there is a revolution in psychology." As noted earlier in this chapter, we all function far below our full potential. Transpersonal psychology seeks to raise our achievement toward our potential in all aspects of our sensory, psychic, and spiritual being. Transcendental psychology is concerned with

- Altered states of consciousness, such as hypnosis, dreams, and transcendental meditation
- Psychic phenomenon, such as extrasensory perception (ESP), psychic healing, reincarnation, and parapsychology
- Higher states of being, such as self-transcendence, spiritual growth, ecstasy, cosmic consciousness, spiritual communication, and peak experiences

We have neither the space nor the understanding to deal with all aspects of transpersonal psychology, so we will speak briefly of two that have significance for education.

Transcendental meditation (TM). Transcendental meditation is a concept of consciousness that may change our notions of the nature of education and of individual fulfillment. It originated with Maharishi Mahesh Yogi of India and has emerged as a new discipline related to the science of creative intelligence (SCI). Transcendental meditation is a way of concentrating one's attention toward subtle states of thought until one reaches the deepest sources of thought. This experience seems to be mind-expanding, producing more direct and creative thought. Major research in TM is being conducted in approximately fifty universities and institutes. This research reveals that meditators enjoy higher levels of enthusiasm, energy, creativity, self-confidence, learning ability, and self-realization. It is rather like a drugless "high." It has liberated some people from drugs and may turn out to be our best antidote for drug abuse.

Transcendental meditation may become significant for educators because it seems to reduce stress and tensions that interfere with learning, as well as to quicken learning ability, expand consciousness, accelerate creativity, and intensify knowledge of the relationship between the learner and the object of study. TM promises higher levels of performance for teachers as well as learners. SCI is being taught in junior high schools, high schools, colleges, adult education programs, industrial and military training, and in athletics.

Evidence also suggests that TM has a beneficial effect upon physical health, as reported in Herbert Brown's best seller, *The Relaxation Response.* However, we regard TM and other developments mentioned below as interesting but tentative frontiers of human development that require more careful evaluation lest they be prematurely applied in schools.[37]

Behavior modification. As the term implies, "behavior modification" is the process of changing behavior toward a more desirable direction. It draws upon Skinner's concept of operant conditioning and Pavlov's classical conditioning. Oversimplified, it seeks to reinforce desirable behavior through rewards and to discourage undesirable behavior by withholding rewards. Ideally, emphasis would be almost exclusively on the former. In schools, for example, the strategy might be to reward students for working. This reduces the time they have for loafing and thereby the necessity for punishing, or withholding rewards for loafing. Teachers, counselors, psychologists, and administrators may work together systematically to ensure that the entire school environment rewards positive behavior. The rewards may be tangible or extrinsic at the outset, as long as they are alluring to learners. The better long-range approach gradually displaces tangible rewards with more intrinsic rewards, such as social recognition and approval.

There is some evidence that behavior modification works. Self-control has been acquired by people once confined to strait jackets. Children have been relieved of autism, psychoses, and other physical and psychological disorders. Some psychotherapists contend that behavior modification may control overt manifestations of personal problems without correcting their basic causes. It nevertheless holds promise for reducing many severe behavior problems of students and, let us hope, may eventually eliminate corporal punishment and expulsion from school. Skinner's books *Waldon Two* and *Beyond Freedom and Dignity* have helped many people to a broader understanding of behavior modification.[38]

Other approaches. Besides TM, SCI, and behavior modification, the following aspects of transpersonal psychology are gaining attention:

- Biofeedback, a form of conscious, powerful control of body functions that operates on the principle of brain wave control, which has promise for relief from physical disabilities that impair learning as well as for physical education and athletics
- Body consciousness, a means of achieving high integration of mind and body as manifested in yoga, bioenergetics, rolfing, karate, and kung fu, which also have implications for health and physical education
- Psychic research, which is exploring the thesis that the mind can operate externally and perhaps independently of the body
- Neuroscience, the orthodox study of the brain and nervous system, a study in which rapid progress is being made[39]

The hope that one may draw from this multifaceted attack on understanding human consciousness is that the capacity of the human mind is infinite. All of us, unless brain-damaged, have enormous latent mental abilities. What a future this portends for education!

PSYCHOSURGERY

Psychosurgery includes the process of surgical intervention in the brain and nervous system. We spoke earlier of experiments in which animals without instruction acquire skills through the transplantation of brain tissues from animals that have mastered the skills. Much of this is still in the rudimentary stage, but it does suggest that memory and certain other forms of learning may be transplanted from one human being to another somewhere in the distant future.

CHEMOTHERAPEUTIC INTERVENTIONS

Discussed at length earlier in this chapter, biochemistry may promise improved mental, emotional, and physical activity for many. It is possible that chemicals one day may reduce many mental disorders, relieve mental retardation, and prevent

---

[37]Readers interested in learning more about TM and SCI should see Maharishi Yogi, *Transcendental Meditation,* New American Library, New York, 1968; or Paul H. Levine, "Transcendental Meditation and the Science of Creative Intelligence," *Phi Delta Kappan,* December 1972, pp. 231–235.

[38]In addition to Skinner's works, readers interested in pursuing this further should see Bertram S. Brown, "Behavior Modification," *Today's Education,* January/February 1976, pp. 67–69.

[39]For further study of these facets of transpersonal psychology, see John W. White, "The Consciousness Revolution," *Saturday Review,* Feb. 22, 1975, pp. 15–19.

or retard senility. We may come to look upon chemicals more as the cure than the cause of mental aberrations.[40]

GENETICS

Genetics is another field that offers mind-boggling possibilities. We may learn to modify all life through various interventions in the reproductive process. It is now possible to make a prenatal examination of a fetus and to abort the birth of gravely defective children. Through genetic counseling parents can learn of potentially defective genes and their probabilities of producing defective children. Through the use of sperm and ova banks, controlled reproduction may avoid the risk of using reproductive cells that appear hazardous. Genetic surgery is also a distant possibility. Eugenics is the science of producing better organisms through selective breeding. Selective human breeding generates grave ethical dilemmas. Who will decide which human characteristics are prized and worthy of reproduction and which attributes should be eliminated? Also, the controversy surrounding legalized abortion is part of the issue.[41]

PEDAGOGY

Educational systems applications, such as programmed instruction and others described in Chapters 9 and 10, are rapidly extending our understanding of the highly complex task of learning. As we understand more about learning, we understand more about teaching. Just as the limits of human consciousness are being pushed back, so is the effectiveness of teaching being improved. We predict that in the year 2000, the pedagogy of 1976 will seem primitive. Improved teaching certainly will equip future generations of learners with much greater learning capacity that we can yet imagine.

Until that time, we will need many more special-education teachers for the handicapped. In this sector of the educational work force demand still outruns supply. Many universities prepare special-education teachers, and good programs of teacher education include attention to handicapped children as part of the regular program.[42] The work of these teachers is substantially facilitated by a marvelous array of electronic instructional technology described in this chapter and in Chapter 10.

. David Krech, a University of California psychologist, sums up the future of the extension of human consciousness in the word "psychoneurobiochemeducation." The combination of these sciences may one day (probably not before the year 2000) eliminate the need for most special education as we now know it and may change the nature of intelligence. Consider the powerful impact upon society of the next generation of learners, who will operate routinely at intellectual levels that we associate today with only the honor students. Learners will be brighter, better informed, and equipped with improved powers of analysis, abstraction, and reasoning. All children who are not brain-damaged will learn to read.[43] If we can meanwhile relieve the cruelties of poverty, overpopulation, malnutrition, and disease, we can reduce not only the task of special education but also the alienation of the poor by opening more equal opportunity to them. Technically, these goals are not unrealistic. However, the necessary reeducation of teachers, administrators, and school boards may be a formidable matter.

ECSTASY OR BRAVE NEW WORLD?

One may look upon the developments described above as our final approach toward the highest levels of human consciousness and ecstasy, which

---

[40]For further discussion of this topic, see James Bosco, "Behavior Modification Drugs and the Schools," *Phi Delta Kappan*, March, 1975, pp. 489–492; and Susan D. Iversen and Leslie L. Iversen, *Behavior Pharmacology*, Oxford, New York, 1975.

[41]See Bentley Glass, "Evolution in Human Hands," *Phi Delta Kappan*, May 1969, pp. 506–510.

[42]Readers wishing to explore professional training for careers in special education should consult *Special Education Careers: Programs of Professional Training in Special Education*, available from the Bureau of Programs for the Handicapped, U.S. Office of Education, Department of Health, Education, and Welfare, Washington.

[43]For an elaboration of this point of view see Fred T. Wilhelms, "Tomorrow's Students," *National Elementary Principal*, April 1970, pp. 5 –10; and Herbert A. Otto, "New Light on the Human Potential," *Saturday Review*, Dec. 20, 1969, pp. 14–17.

have been sought since the beginning of recorded history. Many hail these thrusts as a probable quantum jump in the liberation of all people from the constraints that mental, physical, and psychological limitations have always imposed. By the twenty-first century we all will be functioning closer to our full potential.

Others are frightened by the prospects these developments may hold if misused. They see ominous possibilities of thought control that could transform us right into Aldous Huxley's *Brave New World,* George Orwell's *1984,* or Anthony Burgess' *Clockwork Orange.* Schrag and Divoky warn against the use of drugs, behavior modification, and other interventions in the lives of people. They regard them as an effort to condition learners to distrust their own instincts and to regard deviation from a narrow standard of approved norms as sickness and to rely on the institutions of the state and on technology to define and engineer (their) health.

These may be predominantly positive forces toward a rather optimistic future for learners. One may well question the more dismal forces: the ruination of a large sector of new generations of youths crippled mentally and physically by drugs and venereal disease; the physical deterioration of humanity through wars or atmospheric, environmental, and nutritional contamination; and the social breakdown of future generations along racial or religious lines through the segregation of people in school and society. These are frightening and real possibilities. Neither scenario is foreordained. Our readers, as educators, will play a strategic role—perhaps the most crucial role—in influencing the direction of that future. This must be one of the most bracing and fateful challenges that human beings have ever faced.

Suggested activities

1. Choose a book listed in the bibliography and prepare a critical review.
2. Take a position on the issue of corporal punishment in schools and establish an argument to support it.
3. After reading several articles on the topic, prepare a set of symptoms that teachers might use in identifying possible victims of child abuse in the classroom.
4. Read references in the bibliography dealing with children of poverty and analyze your own potential for teaching children from slum communities.

5. It is said that more teachers leave teaching or fail to enter teaching because they cannot—or fear they cannot—maintain discipline than for any other reason. List the considerations and strategies which you consider most important for effective classroom control of students by the teacher.
6. Explain means by which the classroom teacher may discover and nurture latent interests and unique talents of children in the regular classroom.
7. Study carefully one exceptional student, keeping a careful record of all pertinent data, and compare his or her characteristics with those associated with average pupils of the same age.
8. Suggest the most effective ways in which mentally gifted children can be nurtured in the regular classroom.
9. Describe the ways in which mentally retarded children can be helped most effectively in the regular classroom.
10. Prepare a "Guide for Classroom Teachers in Identifying Potential Dropouts and Reducing the Causes of Their Disaffection with School."

Bibliography

Birch, Jack W., and **B. Kenneth Johnstone:** *Designing Schools and Schooling for the Handicapped,* Thomas, Springfield, Ill., 1975. Guide to shaping space, instructional materials, facilities, educational objectives, and teaching methods to the needs of handicapped learners.

Brutten, Milton, Sylvia O. Richardson, and **Charles Mangel:** *Something's Wrong with My Child,* Harcourt, Brace, Jovanovich, New York, 1974. Informative and practical analysis of the nature of learning disabilities—how to identify and accommodate them.

Cohen, Daniel: *Intelligence: What Is It?* M. Evans, New York, 1974. Readable and practical analysis of the nature of intelligence, the factors that affect it, problems in measuring it, and the controversial beliefs of Jensen, Shockley, Jencks, and others.

Coleman, James S.: *Youth: Transition to Adulthood,* University of Chicago Press, Chicago, 1974. Report of the Panel on Youth of the President's Science Advisory Committee dealing with the social, psychological, and educational problems of adolescents.

Cottle, Thomas F.: *Black Children, White Dreams,* Houghton Mifflin, Boston, 1974. Sociologist's description of black children's views of themselves and their world, offering practical help for white teachers' understanding of black children and youths.

Cremin, Lawrence A.: *Public Education,* Basic Books, New York, 1976. Discussion of out-of-school educative forces, such as family and mass media, and their impact on learners and schools.

Dennison, George: *The Lives of Children,* Random House, New York, 1969. Classic and moving description of the development of children; should be read by all teachers.

Disque, Jerry: *In Between: The Adolescents' Struggle for Independence,* Phi Delta Kappa, Bloomington, Ind., 1974. Helpful explanation of adolescent growth and development and its meaning for educators.

Fine, Benjamin: *The Stranglehold of the IQ,* Doubleday, New York, 1976. Argument that children become victims of self-fulfilling prophecies when educators place too much confidence in IQ tests.

Gardner, Howard: *The Shattered Mind,* Knopf, New York, 1975. Well-written book on the nature of mental disabilities and the needs of children so affected.

Gersoni-Stavn, Diane: *Sexism and Youth,* Bowker, New York, 1974. Source book of readings on sexism in children's literature, education, games, family life, and community; helpful for educator wishing to eliminate sex stereotyping in schools.

Gordon, Ira J.: *Children's Views of Themselves,* Association for Childhood Education International, Washington, 1972. Argument that the best way to understand children is to consider how they see themselves and an explanation of how this may be done.

Haring, Norris G. (ed.): *Behavior of Exceptional Children,* Merrill, Columbus, Ohio, 1974. Introduction to special education with discussion of various types of learning disabilities.

Hilts, Philip J.: *Behavior Mod,* Harper's Magazine Press, New York, 1974. Readable treatment of behavior modification techniques—achievements, weaknesses, and promises.

Holt, John: *Freedom and Beyond,* Dutton, New York, 1972. Classic statement of the importance of freedom in the lives and the education of children.

————: *How Children Learn,* Pitman, New York, 1967. Another classic work by this celebrated educator on the nature of learning and the manner in which schools should sustain that freedom.

Ladd, Edward T.: *Students' Rights and Discipline,* National Association of Elementary School Principals, Arlington, Va., 1976. Practical help for teachers in dealing with discipline problems in schools.

Lindsey, Paul, and **Ouida Lindsey:** *Breaking the Bonds of Racism,* ETC Publications, Homewood, Ill., 1974. Describes lifestyles of blacks and their views about education and teaching.

Love, Neonore, Jacques W. Kaswan, and **Daphne B. Bugental:** *Troubled Children,* Wiley-Interscience, New York, 1974. Explores the psychological problems of children and suggests ways of helping them at school and at home.

Macht, Joel: *Teaching Our Children,* Wiley-Interscience, New York, 1975. Nontechnical discussion of practical means of dealing with undesirable behavior of children and youths.

Margolin, Edythe: *Young Children,* Macmillan, New York, 1976. Explanation of the nature of young children—how they learn and the educational experiences they need.

National School Public Relations Association, *Discipline Crisis in the Schools: The Problem, Causes, and Search for Solutions,* Arlington, Va., 1973. Analysis of the issues of strictness versus permissiveness, corporal punishment, students' rights, and others as they relate to disruptive behavior and suggestions for improvement.

————: *Dropouts: Prevention and Rehabilitation,* Arlington, Va., 1972. Discusses early detection and preventative measures for alternative ways of educating children who cannot make it in conventional classrooms.

————: *Drug Crisis: Schools Fight Back with Innovative Programs,* Arlington, Va., 1971. Discusses successful drug-abuse education and guides teachers in understanding the drug culture.

————: *Education of the Gifted and Talented,* Arlington, Va., 1972. Discusses identification of gifted learners and successful means of stimulating their educational fulfillment.

————: *Student Rights and Responsibilities,* Arlington, Va., 1972. Reviews legal foundations of students' rights, school district codes of students' rights and responsibilities, and how students should be involved.

Nichtern, Sol: *Helping the Retarded Child,* Grosset & Dunlap, New York, 1974. Expert distillation of mass of research with practical ideas on how social attitudes of retarded children can be improved through greater emotional fulfillment in their lives.

Piaget, Jean, and **Barbel Inhelder:** *The Psychology of the Child,* Basic Books, New York, 1969. Synthesizes forty years of work by experts on child development from infancy through adolescence.

Pines, Maya: *The Brain Changers: Scientists and the New Mind Control,* Harcourt, Brace, Jovanovich, New York, 1974. Critical analysis of new neurological, biochemical, medical and psychological interventions in learning and development.

Schlosser, Courtney D.: *The Person in Education,* Macmillan, Riverside, N.J., 1976. A humanistic approach to the educative process.

Schrag, Peter, and **Diane Divoky:** *The Myth of the Hyperactive Child,* Pantheon, New York, 1975. Broader than its title suggests, a serious challenge to the whole business of drugs, behavior modification, and other interventions in the lives of children.

Smith, Robert M., and **John T. Neisworth:** *The Exceptional Child: A Functional Approach,* McGraw-Hill, New York, 1975. Analysis of concepts in special education, new developments in teaching students with problems, and types of learning disabilities.

Chapter 4
Early-childhood education

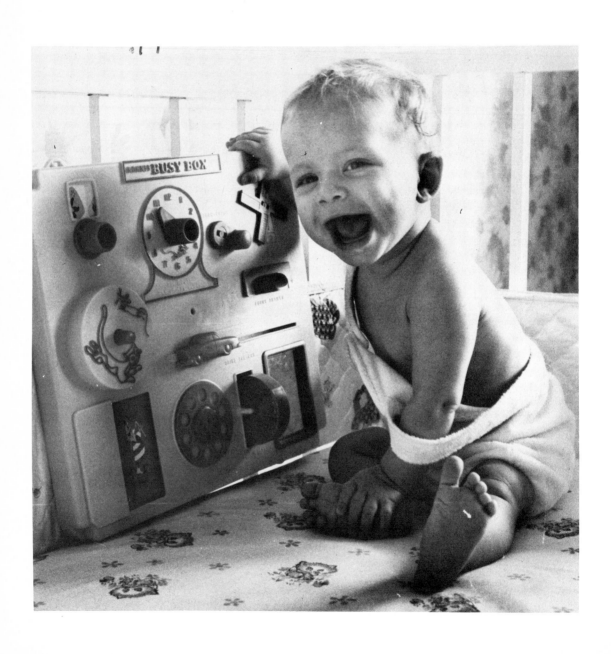

Foundations of early-childhood education

Early-childhood education is no longer all doll-houses and ring-around-the-rosy. It is rapidly becoming psychoneurobiochemeducation, massive environmental intervention, Sesame Street, and crib learning. All these fairly recent developments are discussed in this chapter. They illustrate the exciting changes that are transforming early-childhood education. Samuel Kirk, an expert on special education, was once asked, "What is the most appropriate age to introduce children to a formal educational program outside of or in collaboration with the home?" Kirk answered, "During the mother's first month of pregnancy."

It is ironic that the first years of life, the most im-portant years in human growth and development, should be the last to be included in schooling. Clearly, early-childhood education constitutes the last frontier in the development of our lifelong educational system. In the long run, it may be the most exciting. Early-childhood education covers the entire period from birth through entry into the elementary school, usually at the age of 6 or 7.

DEVELOPMENT OF EARLY-CHILDHOOD EDUCATION

Early-childhood education should be based on what is known about the growth and development of children. Many have contributed to this fund of knowledge, which has helped to establish standards for the practices of early-childhood education.

PERCENT OF
INTELLIGENCE

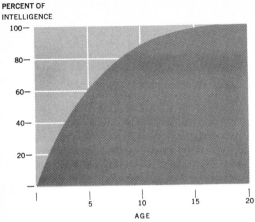

AGE

Figure 4-1 Comparison of age and percentage of mature intelligence achieved. (Adapted from Benjamin S. Bloom, *Stability and Change in Human Characteristics*, Wiley, New York, 1964, p. 136.)

Contributors to the shaping of early-childhood education. Although it is impossible to mention everyone who has had a profound effect on early-childhood education, we will discuss a few leaders who have influenced and guided educational thought in this area.[1]

G. Stanley Hall in 1883 undertook a memorable study of the "contents of children's minds upon entering school," which revealed that young children understand far less of the world about them than had been assumed. His study led to other, similar studies that provided a sounder basis for the development of learning experiences for early-childhood education.

The writings and teachings of William James and John Dewey stressed the importance of the early-childhood years in the educational and social development of children and youths. Dewey's famed University Elementary School at the University of Chicago, established in 1896, admitted 4-year-olds into an educational program that was well articulated with the entire elementary school.[2]

Arnold Gesell, formerly of the Yale University Clinic of Child Development, has added much to our understanding of children's intellectual, physical, emotional, and social growth. His classic books, *The First Five Years of Life: A Guide to the Study of the Preschool Child* and *Infant and Child in the Culture of Today: The Guidance of Development in Home and Nursery School,* had a profound impact not only on nursery school programs but also on the home and family life of generations of young children.

Benjamin Bloom in 1964 published a report of classic researches in learning under the title *Stability and Change in Human Characteristics.* This book documented what many educators had long suspected—that from conception to age 4, one develops 40 percent of mature intelligence; from age 4 to age 8, another 30 percent; and after age 8, the remaining 30 percent (Figure 4-1). More than three-fourths of a human being's total intellectual capacity is established by the third grade.[3] This finding underlined the importance of early-childhood education and helped educators understand why $1 spent to overcome learning disabilities early in life could accomplish more than $10 spent on remedial education in the upper elementary years and in high school. There is reason to believe that if children do not receive intellectual stimulation during those important early years, their capacity to learn may be severely stunted. For the children of poverty, this often means preordained failure in school and in life.

O. K. Moore, of the University of Pittsburgh, demonstrated that the years from 2 to 5 are the most creative and intellectually active period in life. He showed that children are capable of extraordinary feats of inductive reasoning if left to themselves in what Moore calls a "properly responsive environment." Moore uses such devices as the "talking typewriter," a typewriter with jumbo-size type that automatically pronounces the sounds of the letters which the child types.

---

[1]For an interesting history of early-childhood education, see Marvin Lazerson, "The Historical Antecedents of Early Childhood Education," *Early Childhood Education.* Seventy-first Yearbook of the National Society for the Study of Education, University of Chicago Press, Chicago, 1972, pp. 33–53.

[2]For an insightful look at the development of early-childhood education and the impact of Dewey and other educational leaders, see Fred M. Hechinger and Grace Hechinger, "American Childhood: The Utopian Myth," *The National Elementary Principal,* September/October 1975, pp. 10–23.

[3]Benjamin Bloom, *Stability and Change in Human Characteristics,* Wiley, New York, 1964, p. 69.

Jean Piaget, a Swiss psychologist, also influenced early-childhood education to a great extent by studying the process of developing intelligence and by stimulating research. He found that intelligence emerges from a child's sensory experience with concrete objects which the child can act upon, that language development is essential to increased powers of thinking, that repeated exposure to a thing or an idea in different contexts contributes to the clarity of comprehension, and that accelerated learning of abstract concepts without related direct experience may result in symbols without meaning. Much of contemporary thought, research, and experimentation about appropriate educational experiences for young children is being rooted in concepts of educational psychology and pedagogy advanced by Piaget and his Swiss colleagues, as well as many other psychologists.[4]

Benjamin Spock spent much of his career studying and describing young children. His popular book *The Common Sense Book of Baby and Child Care* has sold millions of copies around the world. In this and his later book *Dr. Spock Talks with Mothers,* this eminent student of young children combined his knowledge of pediatrics with rare insight into the social, emotional, and intellectual dimensions of growth in childhood. Although Spock's main contribution has been in the realm of parental education, his belief that growing and learning proceed more smoothly if permitted to occur in the child's own way and time has helped shape our concepts of early-childhood education.

Many others, some mentioned later in this chapter, have contributed to the fund of knowledge and research that helps shape the education of young children.

Beginnings of nursery education. The genesis of nursery education goes back to the beginning of families, and in some countries parents are still solely responsible for teaching their young children.

Plato was among the first to emphasize the importance of education in early childhood, incorporating a community school for very young children

into his ideal republic. Comenius is generally credited with the establishment of the first nursery school, although it was not known as such.

Jean Oberlin, a French minister and educator, established an exemplary infant school in France in 1769 for children from impoverished homes. He sought in his school to relieve poor children of the great disadvantages they would otherwise encounter in elementary schools. In this effort, he became a sort of eighteenth-century precursor of what we commonly call "compensatory education."

In England the Macmillan sisters, Margaret and Rachel, at the turn of the last century began experimenting with the education of young children in cooperation with hospitals, combining pedagogy with psychology and hospital experience in nursing under medical supervision. Hence the name "nursery school" and the beginning of its gradual spread through England. The British style of "open education," typified by the British infant schools,

The years from two to five are the most creative and intellectually active in life.

The Development of Early-Childhood Education

1826	First nursery school in the United States established
1855	First kindergarten in America founded in Watertown, Wisconsin
1868	First training school for kindergarten teachers started in Boston
1873	First permanent kindergarten established as part of the St. Louis public school system
1884	Kindergarten Department added to the National Education Association
1892	International Kindergarten Union (now Association for Childhood Education) formed
1897	National Congress of Mothers (now the National Congress of Parents and Teachers) organized
1897	Association of Day Nurseries of New York City organized
1908	Child Study Association of America organized
1912	Federal Children's Bureau established
1913	Division of Kindergarten Education created in the U.S. Office of Education
1919	First permanent nursery schools opened
1933	Nursery kindergartens started by Federal Emergency Relief Act
1936	Legislation implemented by Congress for maternal, child health, and child welfare services (Social Security Act)

1962	Earmarked funds for day-care services made available to state welfare departments (Social Security Act)
1964	Economic Opportunity Act (war on poverty) passed by Congress, containing several provisions for compensatory schooling, including pre-elementary education for the disadvantaged
1965	Project Head Start, introduced originally as part of the summer program in the war on poverty, made a year-round part of pre-elementary programs
1967	Head Start extended upward experimentally by Follow Through Project for disadvantaged pupils
1968	Handicapped Children's Early Education Assistance Act passed by Congress
1969	Office of Child Development started in U.S. Office of Education
1971	Inclusion in public school systems of pre-elementary programs for all children age 4 and beyond recommended by Education Commission of the States Task Force on Early Childhood Education
1972	Federal funds for day-care centers and child development authorized
1974	Brookline, Massachusetts, Early Education Project established as prototype for public school educational program beginning almost at birth
1975	Education for All Handicapped Children Act legislated, guaranteeing education for handicapped children beginning at age 3
1976	Record $22 million budgeted by federal government for early-childhood education

has influenced pedagogy in American programs. It has tended to make many of them more flexible, more humane, and more child-centered.

Maria Montessori, the first woman ever granted a medical degree from an Italian university, became interested in the education of mentally defective children. She developed methods and materials that permitted such children to perform as well on school tasks as normal children experiencing instruction. Later she concentrated on the education of children of normal intelligence. She established the propositions that very young children are capable of grasping rather sophisticated concepts and skills, that they like to learn under proper conditions, and that they learn most effectively through their senses. Montessori felt that a "prepared environment" is necessary; that is, special teaching materials should be provided to stimulate pupils' senses. Today there is great interest in the Montessorian method in the United States, and there are more than six hundred Montessori schools across the nation.

The first nursery school in the United States was opened by Robert D. Owen in his famous model community at New Harmony, Indiana, in 1826. In 1919, the first public nursery school in the United States was started. Most of the early nursery schools were affiliated with universities and established as laboratory schools for the preparation of childhood education leaders and for the systematic study of young children. Later a number of private nursery schools were opened. Occasionally public school systems provided nursery schools. The Great Depression of the 1930s prompted a federal program of financial support for nursery schools as a means of enriching the lives of young children from destitute families. World War II stimulated further growth of nursery schools, as an increasing number of mothers went to work in war industries, thereby creating a demand for daytime care and education of their children.

Strong impetus to the development of nursery schools was generated by the Economic Opportunity Act of 1965, with its subsequent extensions. This act provided funds for public schools and other community agencies for use in pre-elementary education programs for children of low-income families as an essential part of the war on poverty. These programs, commonly referred to as Head Start programs, once reached half a million youngsters annually. The Elementary and Secondary Education Act also stimulated the development of early-childhood education for children of poverty. By 1976 about one-third of all of the 3- to 4-year-olds were enrolled in preprimary education—a figure that has more than tripled since the introduction of Head Start. Head Start led in 1967 to the initiation of pilot programs in Follow Through—a project to reinforce and extend upward, into the kindergarten and lower elementary grades in public and private schools, the role of early education in the war on poverty.

Early beginnings of kindergarten education. Friedrich Froebel is generally regarded as the father of the kindergarten movement. He established the first kindergarten ("garden for children") in Blankenburg, Germany, in 1837. He felt that the educative process should be started when the child is 3 or 4 years of age. Froebel saw the importance of play, not simply as amusement, but as the natural means by which young children gather information about the world and learn to adjust to it, a classic concept which still permeates modern kindergartens.

The first kindergarten in America was established by Mrs. Carl Schurz in her home in Watertown, Wisconsin, in 1855. Four years later, Elizabeth Peabody and her sister, Mrs. Horace Mann, established a kindergarten in a house in Boston. Elizabeth Peabody is often spoken of as the "apostle of the kindergarten in the United States."

Susan Blow, an American teacher interested in Froebel's concepts of the kindergarten, opened the first continuous public school kindergarten in 1873 in St. Louis. St. Louis kindergartens became so successful that they attracted nationwide attention. Blow soon opened a training school for kindergarten teachers, who contributed to the success of the kindergarten movement across the country.

GOALS OF EARLY-CHILDHOOD EDUCATION

Early-childhood education should provide meaningful experiences so that children can develop socially, physically, intellectually, and emotionally. It should not just prepare children for kindergarten or for first grade; it should be important in itself. It should help children to live their early years richly and happily.

Goals of nursery education. A study of the primary goals of nursery schools administered by public school systems revealed the following objectives in decreasing order of frequency: growth in self-esteem, social development, emotional development, language development, growing independence, physical development, mental development, preparation for regular school years, awareness of needs and strengths, and awareness of physical needs. Considerable controversy exists concerning the relative emphasis that should be placed upon cognitive development versus affective development of children. It appears that increasing emphasis is being placed upon the former in many schools.

Goals of kindergarten education. For those who have not attended a nursery school, the kindergarten is an extension of home life; for others, it is a continuation of the work begun in the home and the nursery school. The general goal of the kindergarten, which is unhampered by requirements in subject matter and skills, is to give children abundant opportunity for enriched experiences. According to James Hymes, specialist in early-childhood education:

The joy school brings to [the child's] life, the sense of fulfillment, is the prime standard by which to judge a program. This one basic goal sets the pace for the quality of the adult-child relationship, of child-to-child relationships, of space and materials and methods and content. If these do not add up to a tingling sense of vigorous living within the youngster, a fundamental point has been lost, no matter what other gains may seem to show up on any tests.

But schools—kindergartens—are not for the individual alone. Schools are society's insurance policy. We rely on them to ensure that our world will become an ever better place. As we seek to nurture the best quality of the child's living *now,* at this moment in his life, we must simultaneously seek to build those human qualities that make the child good for all of us to live with . . . .

The second major goal of kindergarten—from the standpoint of the rest of us, from the standpoint of society—is to have the child begin to breathe in the air of the best of human society, the healthiest form of human association that a teacher's finest dreams can devise.[5]

[5]James Hymes, Jr., "The Goals of Kindergarten Education," in American Association of Elementary-Kindergarten-Nursery Educators, NEA, *Kindergarten Education,* Washington, 1968, pp. 12–13.

Home education

THE IMPORTANCE OF THE HOME IN EARLY-CHILDHOOD EDUCATION

In the early life of the child, the home is preeminently the educational and social center; it is both a school, with the parents as teachers, and a social laboratory of human relationships. Consequently, the home should be a well-designed and appropriately furnished place for living and learning. In a world of change, the child should find the home a haven of hope, love, and security, a place made increasingly secure by local, state, and national efforts in child and maternal welfare. Unfortunately, there is an appalling amount of child abuse in the United States. Often such abuse permanently damages children emotionally and mentally, as well as physically (see Chapter 3).

It is easy to overlook the tremendous amount of learning that takes place before children enter school, even before they go to nursery school. They learn to walk, dress themselves (after a fashion), and feed themselves; they acquire a conversational command of the language and a pretty fair vocabulary (unless they come from culturally disadvantaged homes). They learn to enjoy having stories read to them, to create simple stories themselves, and to draw, play, and perhaps even to read a little. Truly these are surprising accomplishments for such young minds.[6]

After years of study and practice in elementary education, the famous educator John Goodlad observed that "what the child brings to school from his home and what he encounters from others seems to add as much to learning as what the school itself puts in." There is growing evidence that learning patterns in children are fixed long before they start to school, and that these patterns are set irreversibly during the first few years. This underlines the importance of home education for very young children.

J. McVicker Hunt, director of the Psychological Development Laboratory at the University of Illinois and former head of the National Laboratory on Early Childhood Education, believes that it is possible to speed infants' development rapidly by enriching their environment through recorders that

[6]For a look at infants' capabilities, see Lewis P. Lipsitt, "Babies: They're a Lot Smarter Than They Look," *Psychology Today,* December 1971, pp. 70–72, 88–89.

produce interesting sounds and voices, mobiles that respond to babies' reactions, and a variety of simple toys for the crib. This activity is combined with increased interaction between infants and their parents. All this transforms life in the crib from boredom to joy, entertainment, quickening of perception, development of simple motor skills, and an increased zest for life at the very outset of human experience. Hunt concludes from his experiments that infancy is the time to prevent cultural retardation and that programs which begin as late as age 4 are probably already remedial education. He contends that infants in a culturally disadvantaged background could be elevated from the upper levels of mental retardation to successful college work through the enrichment of their environments in infancy.[7]

The Preschool Project at Harvard's School of Education has provided deeper insight into the early years of children's development. The project was undertaken to discover why some 3-year-olds were able to develop intellectual skills rapidly while others were not. To find the answer, the researchers looked at the first three years of the child's family life, and they found these years to be extremely important. In these early years the child has an insatiable curiosity, a grasp of language, and a zest for learning. If parents and siblings respond with fluent conversation and warm relations, the child's cognitive development is quickened. Burton L. White, director of Harvard's preschool project, says: Our research of the last eight years at the Harvard pre-school project has focused on how a minority of families from many backgrounds regularly do an outstanding job of rearing their children during the first years of life. We have become convinced that the job is best done in the home by the family.[8]

The Brookline Early Education Project (BEEP) is administered by the public schools in Brookline, a suburb of Boston, and the Harvard Graduate School of Education. BEEP is a comprehensive program of educational and diagnostic services for children from birth up to age 2. The period from 8 to 18 months is thought to be especially critical in children's development. The project is designed to watch the development of physical, intellectual, and psychological growth of children in order to encourage the development of abilities and to detect as soon as possible any handicaps. BEEP has three components: medical and psychological diagnosis, remediation, and education of parents. Parents are given instruction in ways to help children and in things to watch for in their development. Families have access to toys, equipment, and other resources and are encouraged to enroll children before they are born. BEEP is funded by the Carnegie Corporation and the Robert Wood Johnson Foundation. With additional funding, services will expand to include children up to age $4\frac{1}{2}$. There is great interest in this program, even though it is still considered experimental. Other school systems are planning similar programs.[9]

The ready availability of fine children's books, records, and toys helps children advance their interests, knowledge, and talents. Unhappily, in some homes these stimuli are missing. Toy lending libraries, which are becoming more common, are helping to ease this problem. In other homes, ambitious parents expect too much from precocious children, and the roots for later discord between parent and child, and for a poor self-concept on the child's part, are established.

TELEVISION AND HOME EDUCATION

Certainly the prevalence of television in many homes has extended young children's perceptions of their world. Indeed, "Sesame Street," the popular television series for preschool children, may prove to be one of the most revolutionary breakthroughs in early-childhood education. This hour-long daily program aims to combine delightful entertainment with education to help prepare preschool children for formal education. It is estimated that half of America's twelve million 3- to 5-year-olds have seen the program, and it is telecast in more than fifty countries. Other programs have also demonstrated the potential of television for mass education, and programs are increasingly addressing themselves to the preschool audience.

National Educational Television, with a grant

[7]For an account of Hunt's interesting work, see Patricia Pine, "Where Education Begins," *American Education,* October 1968, pp. 15–19.

[8]Burton L. White, "Preschool: Has It Worked?" *Compact,* Education Commission of the States, July–August 1973, p. 7.

[9]For more detail on this interesting program, see Maya Pines, "Head *Head* Start," *New York Times Magazine,* Oct. 26, 1975, pp. 14, 58–71.

Sesame Street, the popular TV series for young children, may prove to be one of the most revolutionary breakthroughs in early-childhood education.

from the U.S. Office of Education, is producing other educational television programs aimed at 3- to 5-year-old preschool children, as well as programs for elementary school children.

Certainly the potential for both commercial and educational television is enormous, although much of the commercial fare is probably miseducative. Today 97 percent of American families own television sets. The average preschooler has plenty of time to watch. Studies reveal that the average child will have chalked up approximately four thousand hours of television viewing before entering school. Since approximately two-thirds of a child's intellectual development occurs before the age of 6, this period in life is extraordinarily formative. Studies suggest that mass educational television is the most effective, inexpensive, and delightful way to help most children get a "head start" at home.

PARENTAL AND FAMILY-LIFE EDUCATION

There is persuasive evidence that a mother's diet and general health during the period of pregnancy affect both the physiology and the intellectual capacity of the fetus. The emotional and intellectual climate established in the early home life of the child can have profound impact upon the ability to succeed in school and in life. Indeed a child's relations with parents and siblings in infancy may ordain his or her entire future. Clearly these circum-

stances underline the importance of both early-childhood education and parent education on child care and development.

If the home is unresponsive, the child can actually be trained to be helpless. Many discoveries suggest that schools should undertake better programs of parental education to help the family educate preschoolers.

An experiment at the University of Illinois demonstrated that children whose mothers received such special training in wholesome family life gained as much as 7 points in IQ scores. Another experiment at Catholic University revealed an average rise of 17 points in IQs of 15-month-old boys in Washington who were tutored for one hour weekly. In Pacoima, California, surprisingly good results have been obtained by having fifth- and sixth-graders tutor kindergarten children from a ghetto in suburban Los Angeles.

Parental education includes such considerations as the role of mother and father and siblings in early-childhood development, conscious and unconscious motivations of parents in their relations with their children, family group dynamics, interaction between parent and child, parents' needs and expectations, and children's needs and expectations.

Many churches have established programs of home- and family-life education, often with emphasis on the role of the home in establishing moral values in early childhood. The United Presbyterian Church of the United States maintains a national office of family-life education research. Other community agencies offer courses, clinics, lectures, and study groups addressed to early-childhood education.

Some parent-teacher associations sponsor the project of enrolling expectant mothers in classes that meet with the school nurse or doctor. Many hospitals offer prenatal education courses for expectant parents. Many city, county, and state health departments distribute free literature on the care of mothers and babies. A publication of the Government Printing Office entitled *Infant Care* is often available free of charge. The U.S. Office of Education is distributing kits for parents in the inner city to help their children with reading readiness.

Many colleges are performing significant services in the fields of preparental and postparental guidance. The study of preschool children has also been advanced by numerous child institutes, such as the Department of Child Development and Family Relations at Cornell University, the Institute of Child Development and Welfare at the University of Minnesota, the Iowa Child Welfare Research Station at the University of Iowa, the Harvard Center for Research in Child Health and Development, and the Yale Clinic of Child Development. Universities commonly offer courses on children's growth and development and parental education as part of their adult education programs.

Of the various formal agencies promoting parental education, the local school—public or independent—offers the greatest possibilities for development. These established institutions give instruction in family-life education to both girls and boys. Some schools allow juniors and seniors to participate in early-childhood education classes, thus providing practical experience.[10] Some schools also conduct classes for adults who are expectant parents, hold baby clinics, provide guided observation in play groups, and organize family centers for consultation. Local schools may become the nucleus of the parental education program in the community, with the cooperation of all agencies interested in child welfare, especially the home.

The Living Room School Project is a new approach to encourage preschool education at home. The premise is that the home is a natural learning place filled with an endless supply of teaching tools. Teachers help parents to see the possibilities in using themselves and their homes as resources for teaching their children. The parents are shown how to provide educational experiences and activities and how to use simple, inexpensive items from the home as teaching tools. This project is operated by the Bureau of Cooperative Educational Services (BOCES) in Nassau County, New York, and is supported by the U.S. Office of Education, under Title III of the Elementary and Secondary Education Act. Six Nassau County school districts are operating these centers for parents and their children from $2\frac{1}{2}$ to $4\frac{1}{2}$ years of age. A number of Parent and Child Centers (PCCs) have been established with support from the federal government. Many are modeled after the prototype developed by Ira Gordon at the University of Florida. Neighborhood residents are trained to go into the homes to teach and play with babies and toddlers and to help parents, grandparents, and siblings create a model home for sound mental, physical, and social growth. These centers provide comprehensive health, educational, and social services to families. A local university is affiliated with each center. Most centers are under the supervision of Head Start. Each center serves about sixty-five families, averaging one hundred children. These home-centered programs are especially vital in rural areas where travel to preschool centers might be impossible and in communities where space for child-care centers is unavailable.

The Home Start child-care project, patterned after Head Start, involved 3- to 5-year-old children in 1,150 families in sixteen Home Start centers. Home Start mothers spent time with their children in games, conversation, and reading and writing readiness. This project provided education and health services for children. Although funds ran out for Home Start in 1975, Terrel Bell, then Commissioner of Education, had plans for a model program in early-childhood education that would make use of local schools to train parents to teach children at home. The effort would take place in fifteen large cities and selected suburban and rural communities. The schools would share their educational resources—such as toys, books, and visual aids—with the homes. Bell's book, *Your Child's Intellect: A Guide to Home-based Preschool Education*,[11] could serve as a textbook for parents. It provides practical applications of educational principles and can be used independently by parents.

A number of other publications[12] are available to help parents understand better this period of early

---

[10]See E. Dollie Wolverton, "Teaching Teen-agers about Parenthood," *Compact,* July–August 1973, pp. 29-31.

[11]T. H. Bell, *Your Child's Intellect: A Guide to Home-based Preschool Education,* Olympus Publishing, Salt Lake City, Utah, 1973.

[12]See, for example, Adele Faber and Elaine Mazlish, *Liberated Parents/Liberated Children,* Grosset & Dunlap, New York, 1974; Loren Grey, *Discipline without Fear,* Hawthorn, New York, 1974; Dorothy J. Kiester, *Who Am I?: The Development of Self-concept* (pamphlet), LINC Press, Durham, N.C., 1973; and Virginia E. Pomeranz with Dodi Schultz, *The First Five Years,* Doubleday, Garden City, N.Y., 1973.

childhood and the manner in which they can strengthen the development of their children.

Nursery education

Nursery education has gained status in recent years. Although the number of 3- to 5-year-olds has decreased, nursery school enrollments in the last decade have more than doubled. Educators and others who regarded nurseries primarily as baby-sitting agencies have begun to see them in a new light. One reason for this new interest in nursery education is the mounting research evidence stressing the importance of the first five years in stimulating intellectual growth, as well as in fostering social and emotional development. Another reason is that the women's liberation movement has increased the demand for nursery schools and day-care centers. Declining enrollments in public schools have emptied classrooms and displaced teachers. Some feel that these classrooms can be put to good use for early-childhood education and that many unemployed teachers could be retrained to teach these classes.

SCOPE OF NURSERY EDUCATION

The day nursery and the nursery school are the most common forms of organized education for very young children. The day nursery is a social-welfare institution designed to give day care to children of working mothers. Since approximately half the married women in this country are employed, the day nursery is an important educational agency. It has been projected that by 1980 there will be 6 million working mothers with children under 6. The federal government has supported day-care centers as a means of helping mothers on welfare find employment by relieving them of baby-sitting during the day. Day-care centers have been booming, a process which has been intensified by the demands of the women's liberation movement. The movement contends that mothers should not have to be withdrawn from employment any more than fathers should by the need to care for their children. The nursery school, which has characteristics of both a nursery and a school, in a sense is a downward extension of the kindergarten, enabling younger children to benefit from supervised educational and social experiences. Perhaps the most dramatic demonstration of the power of institutionalized early-childhood education is manifested in the kibbutz day-care centers in Israel. Here trained teachers offer excellent education from earliest infancy. The Soviet Union also emphasizes early-childhood education.

Many nursery schools are designed primarily as day-care centers, providing play, recreation, and custody for children of working mothers; but many also strive to develop the children's intellect. Some day-care centers have little educational value and should not be misrepresented as educational institutions if they serve only a baby-sitting function. Some schools are staffed by professionally trained educators and have abundant instructional materials. Others are less well organized, staffed, and equipped. Some accept children between the ages of 2 and 6; others limit their clientele to 4- and 5-year-olds. Some operate all day and year-round; others offer only half-day sessions during the regular school year. Some charge rather impressive tuition fees; others, usually with public subsidies, are designed to serve children of low-income families or children whose mothers work.

Many authorities advocate the extension of education to even lower age groups. In balance, this would appear to be a sound development if it were properly conceived and if the overall welfare of children were carefully protected from unreasonable pressure. There is compelling evidence that the earliest experiences of childhood can have profound and irreversible effects upon intellectual growth throughout life. One's achievement in life depends greatly upon educative experiences prior to age 6, the point at which public education still begins for many children. We believe that the implications of this important discovery challenge the old doctrine that the public has no responsibility for the education of children below the age of 5 or 6 unless they are from homes of poverty. We regard the area of early-childhood education as the last great frontier of educational development, which, if properly conceived and developed, can have profound benefit upon our entire educational system.[13]

[13]For an approach to the improvement of day care, see Sheila M. Rothman, "Liberating Day Care: A Modest Proposal," *Phi Delta Kappan*, October 1973, pp. 132–135.

CHARACTERISTICS OF NURSERY EDUCATION

General types. There are five basic types of nursery schools. Some school systems operate nursery schools that are organized within the elementary school unit. This arrangement, similar to that of most kindergartens, is considered quite acceptable. A few school systems have organized nursery schools within an administrative unit of early-childhood education that includes nursery, kindergarten, and primary levels. A few secondary schools have affiliated nursery schools, thereby providing high school homemaking and social studies classes with direct experiences with young children. A number of colleges and universities have established nursery schools to serve as laboratories for the training of nursery school teachers or for education in child care or family life, child development, and psychology. But more than half the nursery schools in America are separate from other educational units. Most are sponsored by private franchise, welfare agencies, foundations, churches, parents, or other private organizations or individuals. Head Start programs, described later in this chapter, may fall in either of the first two categories or may operate independently from other school units.

Enrollments. Although Head Start programs and other public and private nursery schools and day-care centers have more than doubled over the past decade, prekindergarten programs still serve only 13 percent of their potential population. There are approximately 7 million children under 6 whose parents work or who for other reasons would be a potential market for nursery school. Only about 1.3 million children are receiving some sort of preschool care. The percentages of white and nonwhite students enrolled in prekindergarten programs are approximately equal. Prekindergarten programs are more available to children of low-income and high-income families than to children of middle-income families. Enrollments are substantially lower in nonmetropolitan areas of the country (see Figure 4-2).

Support and control. Nursery schools are administered by many different and varied agencies. Some are publicly funded through various government agencies, such as these divisions of the

PERCENT

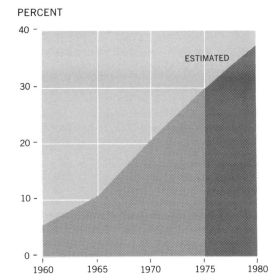

Figure 4-2 Percent of 3- and 4-year-olds enrolled in school. (U.S. Bureau of the Census; estimate by authors.)

Department of Health, Education, and Welfare (HEW): Office of Child Development, Social and Rehabilitation Service, and Office of Education. Most of these programs are funded by the Social Security Act, Elementary and Secondary Education Act, Manpower Development and Training Act, and the Economic Opportunity Act. In 1976 $22 million was budgeted for early-childhood education.

An increasing number of public employers are also now providing day-care centers for children of their employees. The U.S. Office of Education, for example, in 1971 opened a model day-care center for children of persons employed there, the first time that the Office of Education operated an educational program for children on its premises. The center is used as a workshop to demonstrate important concepts and practices in early-childhood education as part of the federal government's interest in encouraging and strengthening this movement through both public and private auspices.

Some nursery schools are run by public school systems. A few states have responded to public pressure and are planning free public education for 4-year-olds. These states include California, New York, and Massachusetts.

One of the most astonishing developments in early-childhood education in the last decade has been the remarkable rise of thousands of private nursery schools sponsored by private industry. By

1975 half the nursery schools were profit-making private schools. They bear an array of both staid and quaint names—Universal Education, American Child Centers, L'Académie Montessori, Little Shavers, Mary Moppets Day Care Schools, Romper Room Enterprises, Institute of Contemporary Education, and Playcare Centers, among others. Some large companies operate chains of child-care centers. Most large companies involved in child-care centers, however, are more interested in franchising them to local residents.

Another type, the parent-cooperative nursery school, sponsored and administered as a nonprofit enterprise by parents, has grown up in the 1970s. Its expenses are met by tuition fees. Parents and teachers together develop policies and programs, and some parents participate in the school as aides to teachers.

There is strong disagreement about whether nursery education should be administered by public schools or by private organizations. Those favoring public school administration feel that early-childhood education is so important that it should be available free to all children, not just to the rich and the poor. The public school seems to be the answer. Some also argue that many privately run schools are not providing adequate care and in some cases are even damaging children. They say these schools are inefficient and haphazardly run by amateurs who have little knowledge of educational concepts or techniques.

The American Federation of Teachers (AFT) strongly favors public school administration of early-childhood education because it feels that public schools are better equipped to provide a higher quality of education. Classrooms now vacant because of lower enrollments could be put to good use, and unemployed teachers could be put back to work.

Many favor the extension of free, universal public education downward to all 4- and 5-year-olds. Others argue that there is no evidence that children need early education or question whether children profit from it. Some people feel that the public school cannot handle early-childhood education and point to the criticisms of Kozol, Holt, and others that the public schools are dehumanizing. Many believe that alternative schools would better serve this age group, with community boards and parent advisory committees. They feel that public schools place too much emphasis on cognitive learning rather than on free, experiential, unstructured learning. Many favor vouchers so that parents may be free to make their own choice of school.[14]

Environment. The physical environment of nursery education should be safe and attractive and should stimulate learning. It should be open and free. The outdoors should be utilized as an important part of the learning environment.[15]

Organization. Nursery schools connected with public schools most commonly offer a one-year program in half-day sessions for 4-year-olds. A few public school nursery programs and many private nursery schools enroll children younger than 4, sometimes as young as 3 or even 2 years of age. The average size of classes in public nursery schools is about sixteen or seventeen. Public nursery schools are about evenly divided between those which accept all students and those which accept only disadvantaged students.

Curriculum. The curriculum of nursery education is broad in scope, for it is planned to meet all the needs of growing youngsters from 2 to 4 years of age.

Authorities agree that it is necessary to look upon children as learners from birth and to realize that the habits of learning are more important than the actual material learned. As Jerome Bruner put it, "We begin with the hypothesis that any subject can be taught effectively in some intellectually honest form to any child at any stage of development." The learning activities are of two general kinds: those which are routine in nature—that is, occur at a specific time every day—and those in which children are given a choice of activities that vary from day to day.

Staff. The quality of nursery education, like that of any school program, depends on teachers. Effective nursery school teachers have a thorough

---

[14]For a report of the role of the public schools regarding day care, a look at governmental funding, and the position of the AFT, see John Mathews, "Day Care: What Role for Public Schools?" *Compact*, June 1975, pp. 19–21.

[15]See Margaret F. Skutch and Wilfrid G. Hamlin, "Environmental Flexibility for Preschoolers," *Phi Delta Kappan*, January 1975, pp. 326–328.

background of preparation in child development, teaching method, parental education, children's literature, science, music, art, and social science. They are able to choose instructional material and equipment according to the needs of young children and to understand the importance of the physical environment in early-childhood education. Above all, they have the personal qualities important for all teachers and especially important for teachers of young children—warmth, friendliness, affection, honesty, respect for children and parents, and self-understanding. Teachers of the disadvantaged must have the capacity to accept and respect youngsters who are not always well-scrubbed, well-mannered, and able to learn easily with conventional instruction.

Great use should be made of other trained personnel in addition to teachers, including aides, health personnel, social workers, and other interested adults. A low student-adult ratio is necessary for an effective early-education program. Great importance is being placed on the role of parents and siblings in many programs. The education and involvement of parents are stressed. Goodlad and his associates feel that the early-childhood education program is more effective when coordinated with the home and family. Many feel that the involvement of parents, and even of the community, can make important contributions in the success of these programs.

EDUCATIONAL PROGRAM OF NURSERY SCHOOLS

Early-childhood school programs vary widely, and considerable disagreement arises over the virtues of various ones. Most programs conducted by the public schools have been low-pressure, permissive programs that emphasize children's socialization and emotional development. They tend to be rather unstructured, and they deliberately postpone formal instruction until kindergarten or first grade in the belief that children are not ready for formal instruction in reading and other subjects until they have acquired a mental age of 6. These programs are disputed by some authorities who believe that reading readiness can be developed much earlier and that students' intellectual growth can be seriously stunted by delaying formal instruction. Advocates of this view prefer childhood education programs, such as the Montessorian

method, that are highly structured approaches to self-instruction in which children are free to progress at their own rates through a programmed sequence of cognitive tasks.[16]

The Bereiter-Engelmann approach to early-childhood education is an even more controversial departure from traditional early-childhood education. In this program, young children are drilled vigorously in cognitive tasks that would be confronted by much older children in more conventional schooling. Some educators have sounded strong warnings against this trend, cautioning that children can be harmed emotionally by discouragement resulting from tackling tasks for which they are not ready.[17]

Recently Soviet scientists and psychologists have discovered bioplasmic forces, unified bodies of energy that are believed to keep our body organs growing and functioning. These forces are thought to be the source of human growth and maintenance of all physical, emotional, and mental activities. There are actually photographs of these forces. Earl J. Ogletree, of Chicago State University, discusses bioplasmic forces in terms of learning maturation.[18] Based on research evidence and knowledge of the bioplasmic forces, he believes:

If the child has not reached the indicated levels of maturity and is forced or persuaded to do intellectual learning, there occurs a premature use of the bioplasmic or energy forces for thinking. The physical body is robbed of the growth forces needed to develop the brain (the head) to its fullest potential for physical growth.

Ogletree further states:

Therefore the popular educational approaches of today, with their intellectual heavy-handedness, will never allow children to develop and blossom naturally. They can only do damage, making children into premature, unhappy adults.

[16]For further discussion of the Montessorian method, see Kathy Ahlfeld, "The Montessori Revival: How Far Will It Go?" *Nation's Schools*, January 1970, pp. 75–80.

[17]Carl Bereiter and Siegfried Engelmann, *Teaching Disadvantaged Children in Preschool*, Prentice-Hall, Englewood Cliffs, N.J., 1966.

[18]For an interesting account of bioplasmic forces and their effects on intellectual development, see Earl J. Ogletree, "Intellectual Growth in Children and the Theory of Bioplasmic Forces," *Phi Delta Kappan*, February 1974, pp. 407–412.

A report by Moore, Moon, and Moore for the Hewitt Research Center discusses early education and cites research suggesting that children are not ready for schooling until at least age 8 or perhaps older. Findings show that visual and auditory systems are not fully developed before then. Also, studies indicate that changes in brain patterns would place a child's ability to sustain abstract thought at between ages 7 and 11.[19] Many people feel, because of some of the research, that the answer to early-childhood education lies in teaching parents. Through parents and other members of the family, preschool children can be given the stimuli they need in the home, rather than through institutionalized learning.

Even though young children can acquire certain skills early, it is probable that they could manage the same skills with less effort and frustration later and that teaching could be more efficient if undertaken somewhat later. The problem revolves around the need to protect unready children from precocious learning while maintaining a school organization flexible enough to permit others, who are ready, to proceed.[20]

The Institute for the Development of Education Activities (I/D/E/A), an affiliate of the Charles F. Kettering Foundation, has found through research that the curriculum of many nursery schools has remained the same for twenty years; that schools lacked adequate facilities, equipment, trained staff members, and custodians; that the pay is low; that learning activities lack variety and richness; and that activities are highly structured, with two-thirds of the activities being directed by teachers.

CURRENT PRACTICES IN NURSERY EDUCATION

The scope of nursery schools is being broadened. Now they are not merely safe places to leave children; rather, they are educational centers for all-round growth. Emphasis is on emotional as well as mental, physical, and social adjustments.

The clientele is changing and enlarging. Nursery schools are no longer either a luxury for a few favored children of well-to-do families or a home for paupers. The middle economic group is beginning to reap the benefit of preschool service. Children in new housing projects and in rural areas are being included. A marked trend is the provision of nursery school education for exceptional and underprivileged children. Many handicapped boys and girls profit even more from early training than normal youngsters. Courts have mandated that early-childhood education be provided for handicapped children starting at age 3.

More storefront academies, such as the East Harlem Block Schools in New York, are providing nursery and kindergarten education as well as tutoring services for older children. These schools in ghetto-area stores are usually private or semipublic and help to bring early-childhood education closer to the community. The Department of Health, Education, and Welfare has set up what they call 4-C centers (Community Coordinated Child Care), which are responsible for health, education, and social care of children. Similar centers may eventually be set up in communities throughout the nation.

The Black Child Development Institute has in recent years worked with the Office of Child Development in identifying worthwhile programs, especially those involving blacks. Some other agencies active in helping communities receive federal funding for child care are the Bank Street Day Care Consultation Service and the Day Care and Child Development Council of America, Inc.

More attention is being devoted to nursery school learning experiences. Among the main factors considered in determining children's readiness for group experiences are their age and general maturity; their ability to give and take, to form attachments to other adults besides parents and to exchange affection and interests with peers; and their desire to come to nursery school. At the Worth Elementary School in Illinois, a program to provide a smooth transition from home to kindergarten has been successful for a number of years. Each week for twenty-two weeks, 4-year-olds attend hour-long sessions. The children receive an orientation to the building and programs of the school. This is just one of many attempts to help ease the transition to schooling. Through Project Developmental Conti-

---

[19]For research findings and suggestions by the authors based on these findings, see Raymond S. Moore, Robert D. Moon, and Dennis R. Moore, "The California Report: Early Schooling for All?" *Phi Delta Kappan*, June 1972, pp. 615–621.

[20]Maya Pines' book, *Revolution in Learning: The Years from Birth to Six*, Harper & Row, New York, 1968, presents a well-written description of the wide variety of pre-elementary school programs, with a fair analysis of their advantages and limitations.

nuity, the Office of Child Development has given $65,000 to each of fourteen communities to help them provide transition programs between the preschool and school.

In 1975 Congress passed, as part of Title XX of the Social Security Act, legislation for custodial day care, omitting the educational parts of the act. This reduced the funding, since no teachers will be needed and the approved worker-child ratio is set at 1:17.5. This was disappointing to advocates of child-care centers.

Other than the federal funds, few states provide funds for prekindergarten education. Most funding comes from local tax levies. State departments of education are taking a more active part in the guidance and supervision of nursery schools. As of 1973, fourteen states have established offices of child development. Some states are requiring higher standards of certification for teachers. The number of nursery school personnel is being increased, and better-qualified teachers are being hired. Some nursery schools have specialized workers such as recreation directors, dietitians, parental-education specialists, home counselors, and other social caseworkers. Welfare services, such as those performed by visiting housekeepers, are helping to improve conditions in the home. These traveling mothers render many services for children. The health program includes appropriate physical activities, proper food and rest, the regular services of a physician, and a daily inspection by a qualified person.

One of Missouri's interesting early-childhood programs is the Saturday School Program, funded by Title III of the Elementary and Secondary Education Act. This program provides low-cost services to 4-year-olds and their parents. School facilities and equipment are used on Saturdays, and homes are used during the week. There are twenty children in a class, and the adult-child ratio is 1:4 or 1:5. Twenty-five half-time teachers and ten other part-time personnel provide education and services to about eight hundred children. Services include hearing and vision tests, measurement of mental age, language development, and others. Study groups and counseling sessions are available for parents.[21]

Chicago's Child-Parent Center program is a compensatory program designed to promote better interpersonal relations between disadvantaged and average children, as well as to provide educational experiences. These centers offer education for children from age 3 through age 9. The project has been very successful. Administrators attribute their success to early intervention, involvement of parents, program continuity, and structured basic skills orientation.[22]

HEAD START

The Economic Opportunity Act of 1965 created a vast number of nursery-level programs commonly referred to as Head Start. When the first plans for Head Start were announced in 1965, some hailed it as the beginning of a revolution in which this important sector of education would at long last become a permanent and integral part of the regular educational system. By 1972 more than 1 million children were enrolled in federally supported early-childhood programs. Now Head Start enrolls 350,000 children each year, many on a full-year basis. The Office of Child Development was created in the U.S. Office of Education to coordinate Head Start and other federally supported early-childhood education programs. There are 9,400 Head Start centers. Head Start was born of the nation's concern for helping young children from poor homes in the metropolitan ghettos, the Appalachian hills and valleys, the Indian reservations, the Alaskan native's arctic wastes, the tropical territorial schools, and the migrant-worker camps escape the vicious cycle of poverty and despair by giving them a "head start" in school. Many middle-class families have a so-called hidden curriculum for their young children at home—travel, story reading, books, records, toys, discussions, and the ubiquitous television set—that does an effective job of preparing them for kindergarten. Most impoverished families do not. Children from such homes may never have heard a complete sentence spoken, held a pencil in their hand, seen a museum or art exhibit, visited a physician or dentist, seen themselves in a mirror, or played with

[21]For a description of the Saturday School Program, see Arthur L. Mallory, "Missouri's Approach: More of the Same Is No Answer," *Compact,* July–August 1973, pp. 15–17.

[22]For more information on the Child Parent Center Program, see A. Jackson Stenner and Siegfried G. Mueller, "A Successful Compensatory Education Model," *Phi Delta Kappan,* December 1973, pp. 246–248.

children other than their siblings; they may not even know their own names. Lacking an understanding of the language, an acceptable self-concept, robust health, and intellectual curiosity, they are destined to failure in school even before they begin. Head Start was initiated to remedy this situation.

The activities of Head Start programs are fairly similar to those which characterize good nursery schools. A typical day might include *free play*—digging in a sandbox or looking at picture books; *group activity*—singing or telling stories; *outdoor exercise*—playing with large blocks or climbing jungle gyms; *field trips*—excursions to the zoo or a boat ride; a *rest period;* and a *snack* or *meal*. Classes are usually small, limited to fifteen or twenty children. Emphasis upon intellectual achievement is increasing in many nursery schools, focusing largely upon reading and language development. Parents and lay volunteers usually help the teachers. The involvement of parents in the program is deliberate as a plan for arousing their interest in the education of their children and as a means of improving slum parents' attitudes toward school and teaching

them methods of child care. The programs tend to emphasize the personal. Children's names are displayed prominently on their desks and lockers to give them a sense of personal identity and importance. Dental and medical examinations are included to identify and attempt to correct physical disabilities that might impede learning and development.

How well are the Head Start programs succeeding? The evidence is mixed. Gains of 10 to 15 points in IQ scores are not uncommon. First-grade teachers commonly report that Head Start pupils make a much faster and better adjustment to first grade. An elementary school principal in a slum neighborhood reports that since Head Start, "school is a place that families have begun to trust for the first time." But there are problems too. The shortage of qualified nursery school teachers has forced the use of many lay people with little or no preparation for teaching. Some Head Start programs try to deal with the children as they would first-graders—teaching the alphabet, regimenting them, and assigning them tasks for which they are not yet ready. When Head Start programs are poorly conceived or poorly handled—and many

The involvement of parents in Head Start programs was planned to arouse their interest in the education of their children and to improve their attitudes toward schooling.

still are—they may help children to hate school sooner. Many programs are run by nonschool agencies that are long on good intentions but short on professional know-how. In many cases the objectives of Head Start programs are undefined or poorly defined. Frequently the programs are followed by primary units in the elementary school that fail to accommodate the unique needs, problems, and limitations of disadvantaged children. When this happens, the benefits gained from Head Start programs are soon lost.

A report for the Department of Health, Education, and Welfare by Urie Bronfenbrenner examines evaluations of intervention programs. Results of studies showed that children made substantial cognitive gains during the first year of the programs, but by the first or second year after completion of the programs, the gains declined. By the third year, the children had fallen back into the problem range.[23] Burton L. White of Harvard says:

I do not mean to say that Head Start has had no important benefits. Certainly, there have been substantial health benefits. Certainly, more families have a heightened awareness of educational issues in early childhood. There may even be benefits for the social development of Head Start children that we have not yet measured. But, as for the central goal of heading off educational underachievement, the results have been disappointing.[24]

Julian Stanley, a professor at Johns Hopkins University who has studied compensatory education for preschool and primary grades, advocates the elimination of age-grade organization and recommends team teaching for children with less than average abilities. He also stresses the importance of working with parents. Some people believe that many Head Start programs fail because they are not adequately funded. Edward Zigler, former director of the Office of Child Development and presently director of the child development program at Yale University, places the yearly cost for adequate child care at $20 billion, a sum too great for the federal government alone to provide.

In balance, many gains from Head Start are evident. At the very least, Head Start has acquainted us with the problems of educating children of poverty, stimulated research and creative practice in dealing with them, quickened parents' interest in early-childhood education and in interacting with the schools, and pushed our attention to human growth all the way back to the crib.

Kindergarten education

SCOPE OF KINDERGARTEN EDUCATION

Kindergarten education usually covers the period of schooling just before children enter first grade, whether they have had nursery school experience or not. The entrance age is generally set at approximately 4 or 5 years, although some junior kindergartens admit younger children.

Unfortunately, the size of the typical kindergarten is increasing as a result of a shortage of funds and an abundance of children. Some kindergarten programs have been eliminated for financial reasons. The typical public school kindergarten program runs one year and enrolls students for half a day, five days per week.

The separate problems of the nursery school and the kindergarten are joined in the common responsibility of providing continuous, broadening, and deepening experiences for children.

Early experience with Head Start programs revealed that gains of children in these programs were soon lost if the kindergarten and primary units followed were not addressed to the same purposes and methods introduced in Head Start. The importance of compatibility and articulation between prekindergarten and kindergarten experiences was recognized by the introduction of Follow Through programs supported by the federal government through the provisions of the Economic Opportunity Act. These programs brought to the kindergarten and primary unit the same attention to individual differences; parental cooperation and involvement; and the child's social, psychological, physical, and mental problems that characterized Head Start programs.

CHARACTERISTICS OF KINDERGARTEN EDUCATION

General types. Kindergartens may be classified according to general categories, namely, research, teacher education, home and family-life education,

---

[23]For these and other findings of this report, see Urie Bronfenbrenner, "Is Early Intervention Effective?" *Day Care and Early Intervention,* November 1974, pp. 15–18, 44.

[24]Burton L. White, "Preschool: Has It Worked?" *Compact,* Education Commission of the States, July–August 1973, p. 6.

social service, behavior problems, cooperative, summer school, nursery school and kindergarten combined, private, federally supported, and public school kindergarten. The two most common forms of affiliation are with private organizations and the public school. According to methodology of teaching, kindergartens are sometimes Froebelian, Montessorian, conservative, or child-development-oriented. Whatever the label, the prevailing type of kindergarten seeks to educate the whole child from 4 to 6 years of age by supplementing the home, the nursery school, and other educational agencies.

Enrollments. Although most kindergartens are found in systems with enrollments of 2,500 and over, the increase in consolidated elementary schools is bringing the advantages of the kindergarten to many rural communities. It is estimated that kindergartens now serve approximately two-thirds the potential kindergarten population. Approximately 2.1 million children attend public kindergartens, and about 360,000 attend private ones. The percentages of white and black 5-year-olds attending kindergartens have been approximately equal in recent years. Because of increased recognition of the importance of kindergartens, enrollments have been increasing as more states and local districts undertake the provision of kindergarten education. (See Figure 4-3 for enrollment data.)

Figure 4-3 Enrollment in kindergartens. (U.S. Office of Education, *Statistics of State School Systems*, estimates by authors.)

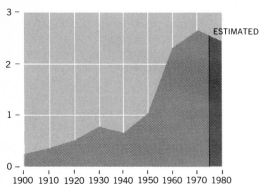

MILLIONS

PROGRAM AND PROCEDURES OF KINDERGARTENS

The kindergarten program is extremely flexible—it has no required subjects as such, but does have content. The key principle is learning by doing. In planning the curriculum, attention is given primarily to promoting physical, mental, social, and emotional growth.

Until recently, kindergarten did not provide certain formal training, such as instruction in actual reading, but it did provide experiences that helped prepare children for the elementary grades. Such experiences include bringing children into a school learning environment; enlarging their circle of friends through the addition of another adult—the teacher—and many peers; enriching their speaking vocabulary; training in speech through careful enunciation and pronunciation; creating interest in books through storytelling and looking at books; developing left-to-right eye movements through reading a story told in pictures; stimulating arithmetic concepts and simple skills through counting objects while seeing numbers and through seeing spatial relations, size, and order; and facilitating development in writing through drawing, cutting, and other forms of eye and hand coordination, including creative painting, rhythms, music, dramatic play, and science experience. The goals are implemented through a flexible schedule of activities. The kindergarten has traditionally been more concerned with children's development, including readiness for reading, than with mastery of content. More and more, however, kindergartens have been introducing content and seeking to impart some mastery of the fundamental skills, particularly reading and language development.

Other valuable experiences gained through kindergarten activity are those which strengthen social relationships, such as learning to care for possessions, developing respect for the property of others, gaining a concept of group property, taking turns and sharing, listening to the group, talking before the group, group planning, evaluating experiences, and using conventional greetings and requests. However, experimenting, problem solving, clarifying ideas, acquiring information about the environment, and participating in creative ideas are especially important.

Perhaps the most valuable gains from kindergarten experience derive from growth in self-understanding, self-realization, and self-esteem by young learners.

CURRENT PRACTICES IN KINDERGARTEN

Many changes are being forced on traditional kindergartens because of the tremendous impact of the nursery education movement. Because many nursery schools are beginning to take over the function of the typical kindergarten, the kindergarten's program is getting more complex, and more formalized learning is taking place in many instances. In some kindergartens around the country, reading is being taught to children, as are other fundamental skills.

Although the primary emphasis of kindergartens is upon the basic skills, particularly reading and language development, many other subjects are introduced at a rudimentary level. Music, fine arts, and drama, for example, are usually emphasized because of their contribution to creative self-expression. More attention is being given to developmental tasks that are set by maturation of the children, their creative self-motivation, and the demands of society.

A trend is to integrate kindergartens as part of a continuous program in early-childhood education. Kindergartens are losing their status as an isolated part of the school system and are being incorporated into a primary unit embracing the nursery school and kindergarten, plus the lower two or three grades. There is more intervisitation between nursery school, kindergarten, and first-grade teachers.

California has effected an important statewide program of early-childhood education. The program is voluntary for children from kindergarten to third grade. Eventually younger children may be included. Beginning in 1973, the program provided education for 172,000 children (14 percent) in 1,013 schools in 800 districts. The program expanded to include 22 percent in the 1974–1975 academic year, and 32 percent in 1975–1976. Each program is designed at the local level by those working with it. There is continual evaluation and modification of programs, since accountability is built into them. Plans must be flexible and must meet the needs of all children. They must include various systems for organizing students, such as multiage and nongraded. They must also include

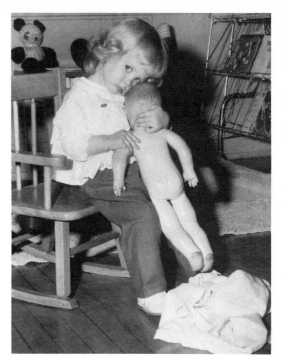

Kindergarten helps children develop wholesome feelings, attitudes, and values along with their cognitive development.

in-service programs for staff and plans for learning activities.

The California plan for early-childhood education provides for continuous progress, so that children can proceed at their own rate. Wide use is made of participation by parents and individualized instruction. The teacher's role is one of planner and manager—the leader of a team comprising parents, aides, volunteers, and students. Low adult-pupil ratios are maintained because these additional personnel are used. The role of the principal is critical, giving leadership, keeping records of students' needs and progress, and helping to develop all personnel involved with the program. Auxiliary personnel such as counselors, psychologists, and nurses are also used. According to Wilson Riles, superintendent of public instruction in California, the program is a success.[25] For ex-

[25]For a report on the progress of California's early-childhood education program after two years, see Wilson C. Riles, "ECE in California Passes Its First Tests," *Phi Delta Kappan*, September 1975, pp. 3–7.

ample, a typical child gained eleven months for every ten months of instruction in reading. Riles says:

From all of the evidence we have seen to date, early childhood education is a success. Children are more eager to learn and they are learning more. We are finally preventing failure, rather than providing too little, too late in the form of remediation.

We are finally bringing quality education to all children—ECE is not just for the rich or just for the poor, not just for the gifted or for the handicapped, but for all children.[26]

More funds must be made available if California is to meet its goal to include all 5- to 8-year-olds in all 4,500 elementary schools in the state.[27] Other states are operating early-childhood programs but California's program is on such a large scale that it is having great impact on others across the country.

The concept of full-day kindergartens is spreading. The American Association of Elementary-Kindergarten-Nursery Educators (E/K/N/E) and others who favor this feel that full-day kindergartens provide a more balanced program and extend instructional opportunities for a richer, more effective learning experience. Also, many children are already used to a full day's program from attending Head Start and day-care programs. Except for reading and number work, programs are usually unstructured. Children are usually grouped heterogeneously and housed in an elementary school building.

A public-relations program for kindergartens, including a brochure for parents, has been developed in many schools. The National School Public Relations Association has prepared a very helpful handbook for parents of pre-elementary children entitled *The First Big Step*. The National Education Association has produced a documentary film, *The Time of Their Lives,* to encourage public interest in kindergarten education.

Many multisensory aids, such as tapes, phonograph records, and films, help children to understand the world of material things. They also assist teachers in interpreting to parents and the public the role of kindergartens. Radio and television are being used increasingly, especially to educate parents. Some schools use learning centers in kindergartens. Learners are instructed to perform simple tasks through headphones and cassettes. A teacher or aide, also using headphones, monitors progress and provides help when necessary.

Many state legislatures have considered early-childhood education of sufficient importance to enact legislation providing specifically for the establishment and maintenance of kindergartens as a part of the public school system, but a fifth of the states still provide no funds for kindergartens. According to the Education Commission of the States Early Childhood Project in 1972, nine states mandate that school districts provide kindergarten education on a voluntary basis, thirty-seven states permit schools to offer it, and four states have no legislation regarding it. Forty-two states provide some state aid for kindergarten programs. Proportions vary from 9 percent in New Mexico to 75 percent in Oklahoma. Very often minimum standards for facilities, class size, and certification of kindergarten teachers are inadequate.[28]

The future

The wide diversity of programs and practices in kindergarten and nursery education will continue. Experimentation and research will greatly improve and enrich the education of young learners. Newer

[26]Wilson Riles, "The First Eight Years," *The American Teacher,* May 1975, p. 7.

[27]For interesting pro and con reading and insights into the California program of early-childhood education and its implications in the movement, these articles are recommended: Wilson Riles, "The First 8 Years Count the Most," *Compact,* July/August 1973, pp. 12–14; Raymond S. Moore, Robert D. Moon, and Dennis R. Moore, "The California Report: Early Schooling for All?" *Phi Delta Kappan,* June 1972, pp. 615–621; Elizabeth Lewis, "The Real California Report: A New Approach to Education," *Phi Delta Kappan,* April 1973, pp. 558–559; and Raymond S. Moore, "Further Comments on the California Report," *Phi Delta Kappan,* April 1973, pp. 560–561.

[28]For a picture of current funding, practices and data on kindergarten and other early-childhood programs on a state-by-state basis, see Edward H. Robinson and Sandra L. Robinson, "Early Childhood Education: Practice Outpaces Theory," *Phi Delta Kappan,* April 1975, pp. 566–568.

instructional technology, such as television, will help to strengthen learning. Emphasis upon programs for children from poor families will continue.

In nursery schools great flexibility and experimentation should be encouraged with diverse forms and practices. The organization of the schools should be relatively open, nongraded, flexibly scheduled, and enriched by television and other instructional technology. Collegial patterns of collaborative teaching with liberal use of teacher aides and parents help to maintain both easy relations between school and home and more one-to-one relations between child and adult during these important early years.

In kindergartens attention to cognitive development of all 5-year-olds will be increasingly emphasized. Permissive legislation will be replaced by the compulsory establishment of kindergartens on a voluntary attendance basis. Because retrenchment often causes public school authorities to abandon kindergartens, the interests of young children must be safeguarded through adequate legislation. The gradual acceptance of kindergartens as a legitimate and permanent part of the public school system is inevitable. They will continue their vestibule function and open doors to wider horizons.

The future presages a steady growth in the number of kindergartens and their enrollments, even though birth rates are dropping. Within the next decade, nearly 100 percent of 5-year-olds, 50 percent of 4-year-olds, and 30 percent of 3-year-olds will be enrolled in programs of early-childhood education. More state departments will add to their staff specialists in the supervision and guidance of local programs for early-childhood education.

The sharp rise in the number of day-care centers operated by private industry will probably continue in response to the need for early-childhood education for communities without public programs. In all probability, nursery schools will accommodate many more children of younger age as the importance of infancy in educational development is increasingly recognized. This recognition is being accelerated by the recommendations of many eminent persons and organizations.

Future expansion of early-childhood education is probable. Whether this expansion will be manifested in the continued conglomeration of programs run by both public and private agencies, many of them poorly conceived and badly articulated, or whether we shall see early-childhood education become largely an integral three- or four-year seamless unit incorporated in the public school system remains to be seen. We would prefer the latter, but we expect the former. Certainly early-childhood education, whatever its form, will reach downward to serve children at much earlier ages, even below the age of 2. At this level the better programs will be well integrated with programs to educate parents. There will also be greater involvement by siblings and teen-agers in Head Start and other early-childhood programs. Recent programs have demonstrated that massive intervention in the lives of young children to provide rich academic, medical, and social services can have a far more profound impact on human development than anything in later life. Some predict that this will prompt an inversion of our educational priorities in which the most money, ablest teachers, best facilities, and finest curriculums are made available to the youngest rather than the oldest students. This could indeed become a revolution in educational thought and practice. However, it will unfortunately be many years before worthwhile educational experiences become widely available at public expense to the vast majority of children.[29]

Increased use will be made of the concept of environmental mediation, through which the child's milieu during early life is deliberately structured to offer the most favorable climate for personal growth. By improving the young child's environment it is possible, according to the research of David Krech,[30] to increase the memory cells, the brain, and the cerebral hemispheres, thereby increasing the capacity to learn and raising the child's IQ. Another development, which Krech calls "psychoneurobiochemeducation," involves the application of biochemistry to the stimulation of learning through the use of drugs to alleviate

[29]See Edward Zigler, "Myths and Facts: A Guide for Policymakers," *Compact*, July–August 1973, pp. 18–21.

[30]David Krech, "Psychoneurobiochemeducation," *Phi Delta Kappan*, March 1969, pp. 370–373.

learning problems in early childhood. Exciting developments suggest that early-childhood learning will be remarkably improved in the decades ahead with profound positive impact upon the human condition generally.[31]

Suggested activities

1. Visit a private nursery school for children from well-to-do families and a Head Start program for children from low-income families and prepare a report comparing and contrasting the two programs.
2. Prepare a case study of a child under 6 years of age whom you know well.
3. Prepare a report describing the kind of home environment that is ideal for early-childhood development.
4. Visit a preschool program for children from low-income families and prepare a report on the desirable qualities of teachers for such work.
5. Prepare a report, based on your reading, predicting the nature of early-childhood education a decade or so hence.
6. Discuss the selection of books, toys, and games for preschool children.
7. Prepare a critical analysis of the Montessorian method of teaching in nursery schools and kindergartens.
8. Outline an ideal program of professional preparation for teachers at the preschool level.
9. Study Montessori's and Piaget's theories of early-childhood education and prepare a report comparing and contrasting them.
10. Read as much as you can about Head Start programs and prepare your own critical evaluation of them.

Bibliography

Almy, Millie: *The Early Childhood Educator at Work,* McGraw-Hill, New York, 1975. Examines the role of teachers in early-childhood education. Discusses problems, issues, research, and experimental programs.

Austin, Gilbert R.: *Early Childhood Education: An International Perspective,* Academic Press, New York, 1976. A description of early childhood in various cultures of the world.

---

[31]For an interesting discussion of some of these developments, see Harold G. Shane, "The Renaissance of Early Childhood Education," *Phi Delta Kappan,* March 1969, pp. 412–413.

Bell, T. H.: *Your Child's Intellect, A Guide to Home-based Preschool Education,* Olympus, Salt Lake City, Utah, 1972. Handbook for parents to use in giving children learning experiences at home. Includes both theory and application.

Fein, Greta G., and Alison Clarke-Stewart: *Day Care in Context,* Wiley-Interscience, New York, 1973. Comprehensive study of research and issues regarding day care, as well as guidelines for implementing day-care programs.

Goodlad, John, M. Frances Klein, and Jerrold M. Novotney: *Early Schooling in the United States,* McGraw-Hill, New York, 1973. Reports on a study of early-childhood education theories and practices in nine major American cities.

Hildebrand, Verna: *Introduction to Early Childhood Education,* Macmillan, Riverside, N.J., 1976. Comprehensive treatment of early childhood education programs.

Hipple, Marjorie L.: *Early Childhood Education,* Goodyear, Pacific Palisades, Calif., 1974. Presents situations that teachers face in early-childhood education, including curriculum, facilities, parents, and administration.

Hymes, James L., Jr.: *Teaching the Child Under Six,* Merrill, Columbus, Ohio, 1968. Practical treatment of teaching preschool children, focusing on specific teaching problems.

Leeper, Sarah H., Ruth J. Dales, Dora S. Skipper, and Ralph L. Witherspoon: *Good Schools for Young Children,* 3rd ed., Macmillan, Riverside, N. J., 1974. A guide for working with three-, four-, and five-year-old children.

Margolin, Edythe: *Young Children: Their Curriculum and Learning Processes,* Macmillan, Riverside, N. J., 1976. Discussion of how young children learn and the kinds of educational experiences best suited for their development.

Montessori, Maria: *The Secret of Childhood,* Ballantine, New York, 1972. Describes the nature of children and the materials, methods, and knowledge necessary to help them want to learn.

Moore, Raymond S., and Dorothy N. Moore: *Better Late Than Early: A New Approach to Your Child's Education,* Dutton, New York, 1975. Documented look at the arguments against early schooling.

National Education Association: *Kindergarten Education,* Washington, 1968. Discusses preschool children, goals of kindergartens, readiness for kindergarten, and typical programs.

National School Public Relations Association: *Early Childhood Education: Current Trends in School Policies and Programs,* Arlington, Va., 1973. Discusses the pros and cons of early schooling and describes the various types of day care.

Pines, Maya: *Revolution in Learning: The Years from Birth to Six,* Harper & Row, New York, 1967. Observations and unfavorable criticisms of preschool and early-childhood programs.

Spodek, Bernard: *Early Childhood Education,* Prentice-Hall, Englewood Cliffs, N.J., 1973. Discusses the importance of early-childhood education, including curriculum models.

Stanley, Julian: *Compensatory Education for Children Ages Two to Eight,* Johns Hopkins, Baltimore, Md., 1974. Overview of six studies representing different approaches used in dealing with compensatory education.

Steinfels, Margaret O'Brien: *Who's Minding the Children? The History and Politics of Day Care in America,* Simon & Schuster, New York, 1973. Describes day care from the nineteenth century to the present and discusses policies and attitudes concerning day care.

Weber, Lillian: *The English Infant School and Informal Education,* Prentice-Hall, Englewood Cliffs, N.J., 1971. Describes how English educators have reformulated educational practice through strengthening the human dimension of learning.

White, Burton L.: *The First Three Years of Life,* Macmillan, Riverside, N.J., 1975. Excellent, detailed guide to the intellectual and emotional development of young children, drawn from studies of infant and child development at Harvard.

Chapter 5

Elementary education

YOU WILL HAVE MASTERED THIS CHAPTER WHEN YOU CAN

Define

- **differentiated staffing**
- **open education**
- **self-contained classroom**
- **nongraded organization**

Describe

- **the multiunit school**
- **the middle school concept**
- **elementary school patterns of organization**
- **teaching techniques most often used in elementary schools today**
- **some features of elementary school programs**

Analyze

- **the relative merits of various types of vertical organization**
- **the relative merits of various types of horizontal organization**

Foundations of elementary education

Few of us understand the crucial relationship between popular enlightenment and the preservation of liberty better than a humble and unschooled New England farmer at the close of the eighteenth century. This man, William Manning, in 1798 completed a manuscript entitled *Education the Key to Libbertie*. He began with a modest disclaimer of his qualifications for the task. He was, he admitted, not a man of learning, having never had more than six months of schooling in his life; he had not traveled more than 50 miles from the place of his birth, and he was no great reader of "antiant history." Although unschooled, Manning neverthe-

less understood very well that free governments had been tried before and had always failed. He hoped desperately that this new venture in free government would find a better destiny. That was why he set out to explore the question: "The Causes why a free government has Always Failed and a Remidi aganst it." He concluded that free governments had failed because of the ignorance of the people, that "the ondly remidi is knowledge," and that therefore "Education is the Key to Libbertie."

A year later Thomas Jefferson introduced a bill in the Virginia legislature that would have provided free elementary education for all young citizens. Like Manning, Jefferson saw clearly the relationship between education and liberty. He argued

135

that "the general objectives of this law are to provide an education adapted to the years, to the capacity, and the condition of everyone, and directed to their freedom and happiness." Jefferson's bill was not enacted. Manning's manuscript was not published.

But half a century later, several states heeded Jefferson and Manning by enacting the first laws that were to establish free public common schools for all.

THE ESTABLISHMENT OF PUBLIC ELEMENTARY EDUCATION

In early America free elementary schools were organized much later than the universities. An exception occurred in New York State, where, under Dutch rule, a free tax-supported elementary school was established in Fort Amsterdam in 1633. Colonial New England, especially Massachusetts, took the first steps toward the permanent establishment of schools for the common people. The "Old Deluder Act" of 1647 required the various towns to establish and maintain schools. Numerous laws were passed in the colonies in regard to free education. But permissive rather than mandatory legislation was the usual type of school regulation. Thus the colonists permitted free public education in theory, but in practice they supported few free schools.

Elementary education in the eighteenth century was entrusted to reading and writing schools. These were followed by "dame schools," in which a woman taught her own children and others from the neighborhood in her home between household tasks. These dame schools were primarily for little children; when older pupils came to school in the winter, a man teacher was usually employed. The dame schools were followed by primary schools, which became the nonsectarian forerunners of today's elementary schools.

Public education struggled to become nonsectarian. Throughout the colonial period, elementary education had a strong religious tone. Moral and religious truths were emphasized constantly. The school was often made the servant of the church, and numerous religious denominations established their own schools. The pupils were usually taught reading, writing, arithmetic, singing of hymns, prayers, and catechism. Often parochial schools were granted aid from state funds. Grad-

ually the pendulum swung from sectarianism to secularism. The first state to adopt a constitutional provision prohibiting sectarian instruction in public schools was New Hampshire in 1792.

Elementary education in America encountered many obstacles, including the social beliefs and prejudices that the colonists carried with them from the old country. The concept of social classes or castes extant in England during the colonial period made education a matter of private rather than state support. Persons of wealth sent their children to privately supported schools or engaged tutors to teach them at home. For those unable to do this, pauper schools were established. But because of the stigma attached to being a pauper, these schools were often not patronized by them.

The struggle to make schools free to everyone and the financial responsibility of all was one of the most bitterly contested conflicts in our history. Passions ran high. Opponents held that it was "heresy to partially confiscate one man's property to educate another man's child." Some objected to public schools because they were secular. Some opposed state control of education. Some thought it improper for the children of well-to-do families to attend the same school as children from ordinary homes. Others preferred distinctions based on religion, race, or sex. A few simply did not believe in education at all. Small wonder that opposition existed. At no time or place in history was there a precedent for the concept of free, universal education.

But the supporters of the public school movement were people of determination and vision. They argued that the well-being and vitality of the nation depended upon the knowledge of all citizens, that universal suffrage could not succeed without universal education, and that public wealth must be used to save underprivileged children from ignorance and poverty. Social reformers joined the cause, hoping that free education for all in the same schools would spare the new nation from the rigid class system typical of the Old World, from which many emigrants had sought escape in America. The crusade was won in Massachusetts in 1837 under the leadership of Horace Mann, who insisted that "the general intelligence which they [the public schools] are capable of diffusing, and which can be imparted by no other human instrumentality, is indispensable to the con-

Historical Calendar

The Development of Elementary Education

1633	Elementary school established by the Dutch in New York
1642	Earliest colonial educational law passed in Massachusetts
1647	"Old Deluder Act" passed by Massachusetts, requiring towns to establish and maintain schools
1789	Massachusetts school law enacted, requiring a school in every community
1834	Free elementary education first adopted by Pennsylvania
1837	"Common-school revival" started by Horace Mann
1852	First compulsory law for part-time school attendance passed by Massachusetts
1890	First full-time compulsory school attendance law passed in Connecticut
1896	Experimental progressive school established by John Dewey at University of Chicago, starting the progressive movement in elementary education
1903	Child-centered curriculum stimulated by John Dewey's The Child and the Curriculum
1918	Compulsory education made effective in all states
1948	Basic policy for elementary education presented in Education for All American Children
1964	Prototypes of Individually Prescribed Instruction and Individually Guided Education launched to raise elementary school achievement through individualized instruction
1965	Elementary and Secondary Education Act passed by Congress, directed mostly toward students from low-income families
1968	Follow Through Project expanded nationally and extended upward into the early elementary grades
1969	Grants made by Ford Foundation to help American schools adapt applicable aspects of British primary education
1970	Right to Read, a nationwide program with accent on elementary schools, launched
1970	Elementary and Secondary Education Act, largest of all federal grants to education, extended by Congress for three-year period
1971	Daily television reading series premiered by Children's Television Workshop as "The Electric Company"
1971	Sharp decline in elementary school enrollments, ending a third of a century of growth
1976	Strong back-to-basics movement gained momentum in elementary schools
1977	Bilingual-bicultural education programs widespread in elementary schools

tinuance of a republican government." In 1834, Pennsylvania, under the leadership of Thaddeus Stevens, adopted a state program of free schools. Other states followed this example—some not until the twentieth century—and eventually elementary education, and later secondary education, was transformed from a private luxury into a public necessity.

Making elementary education compulsory involved another struggle. A hundred years ago attendance was generally optional. One may look to Massachusetts for the contribution of the compulsory elementary education law in 1852 and to Connecticut, under the leadership of its indefatigable Commissioner, Henry Barnard, for its administration and methods of enforcement. Compulsory schooling was bitterly opposed by many people who argued that it deprived the parents of their inalienable rights, that it was not necessary in order to secure attendance, that it was an uncalled-for assumption of powers by state governments, that it was inimical to the spirit of free democratic institutions, and that it was an obstacle in the employment of child labor.

Most states now demand that every normal child attend some type of school for at least eight months annually between the ages of 7 and 16, or until the eighth grade is completed. Several states have enacted laws raising the compulsory school age to 18. Today many question the constitutionality of compulsory education, as noted in Chapter 1.

GOALS OF ELEMENTARY EDUCATION

Elementary education generally is concentrated upon developing in children command of the fundamental processes or tools of learning and a general understanding of the world they live in. Although it accents the intellectual, it is broader than this, giving attention also to the development of desirable attitudes and systems of values.

The leading American educational philosopher and molder of the policies of the elementary school was John Dewey. In 1896 Dewey established an experimental school at the University of Chicago where he tried out some of his educational plans. In 1904 he joined the faculty of Teachers College, Columbia University, where he taught and influenced thousands of teachers. His book

School and Society, published in 1899, affected markedly the function of the school in society.

The Gary public school system, which modified its program in 1941, and other systems which made innovations in elementary school organization, such as the Winnetka system, were inspired by John Dewey. His emphasis upon doing and living was basic in the elementary school program. The following typify John Dewey's philosophy:

I believe that as such simplified social life, the school life should grow gradually out of the home life; that it should take up and continue the activities with which the child is already familiar in the home. . . .

I believe finally, that education must be conceived as a continuing reconstruction of experience; that the process and goal of education are one and the same thing. . . .

I believe that education is the fundamental method of social progress and reform. . . .

I believe that every teacher should realize the dignity of his calling; that he is a social servant set apart for the maintenance of proper social order and the securing of the right social growth.[1]

Some of Dewey's ideas have been misinterpreted and misapplied. Nevertheless, the progressive idealism of John Dewey and his followers has had a significant and constructive influence upon all learning levels, especially the elementary.

A publication by the Association for Supervision and Curriculum Development, entitled *The Elementary School We Need,* summarizes the major commitments of the modern elementary school:

1. **Health and physical development of children.** Elementary schools seek not only to maintain but also to improve the health status of children. Through planned programs of physical education, health education, and safety education, as well as through physical examinations, elementary schools demonstrate a major concern for health and physical development. The willingness of elementary schools to adapt their programs to provide for the physical needs of children has made it possible for many pupils who have serious physical handicaps to enter the regular school program.

2. **Mental health and personality development of children.** The importance of helping children to achieve an adequate concept of self dominates the

[1]John Dewey, "My Pedagogic Creed," *The School Journal,* Jan. 16, 1897, pp. 77–80.

activities of many elementary schools. There is concern for providing opportunities for children to experience success and a sense of achievement in what they do. Efforts to provide a setting which minimizes tension for children characterize much of the teaching in the elementary school. Teachers are aware of the needs of children to be secure and to feel that they belong as worthy human beings.

3. **Development of understanding of the social and scientific worlds.** The importance of helping children to understand their environment has led to reorganization of content materials. There is a conscious effort in many elementary schools to bring the immediate world of children into a perspective that affords them a better understanding of the remote and abstract. Fundamental skills and knowledge are presented in a more functional setting in order that these concepts may lead to further learning and more effective living in the world of today.

4. **Development of the skills of effective participation in a democratic society.** The attention that many elementary schools direct to the early participation of children in group living has altered the content of instructional activities as well as the ways in which they are organized. In seeking to help children develop responsibility, self-direction, and effective communication with others, elementary schools provide a climate as well as varied opportunities for learning and practicing the responsibilities and the skills of living in a democratic society.

5. **Development of the values consistent with democratic living.** Closely related to the skills for participating in a democratic society are the values implied in maintaining such a society. Some of these values are honesty, respect for individual personality, personal and social responsibilities, freedom of thought and of speech, and the learning and use of methods of intelligence. Elementary schools seek to help children develop a sense of commitment to these values. Social issues and concerns are a part of these classroom experiences, and there is an emphasis on intrinsic motivation to help children aspire to worthy human roles.

6. **Creative activity.** In seeking to stimulate creativity, many elementary schools strive to achieve a program that is less rigid and sterile than the programs of some schools in past decades. Creativity is perceived as an aspect of behavior that permeates all areas of the curriculum and is a characteristic of all children. Creative classrooms are stimulating and supportive places in

Through programs of physical education, health education, and safety education, elementary schools foster physical development and good health practices.

which varied approaches are used to solve problems, to express ideas, and to communicate with others.[2]

Characteristics of elementary education

ENROLLMENTS

A significant phenomenon in American education has been the marked increase during the 1950s and 1960s in the number of pupils enrolled in both public and private elementary schools, as shown in Figure 5-1. But beginning in the early 1970s the number of births feeding our school system is approaching a fairly stable figure of 4 million per year. It is estimated that public and private elementary school enrollments (kindergarten to grade 8) in 1980 will be quite a bit lower than those of 1970. At present almost 100 percent of children of elementary school age are attending school.

[2]Adapted from George Manolakes, *The Elementary School We Need,* Association for Supervision and Curriculum Development, National Education Association, Washington, 1965, pp. 20–21. Copyright 1965, Association for Supervision and Curriculum Development.

ENROLLMENT
(IN MILLIONS)

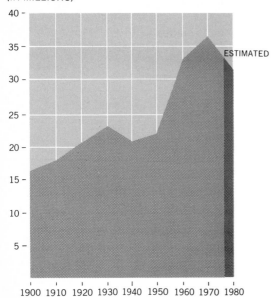

Figure 5-1 Total enrollment in public and private elementary schools, K–8. (U.S. Office of Education, *Digest of Educational Statistics.*)

About one in ten is enrolled in a private or parochial school.

SCHOOL SIZE

The simplest form of elementary organization is the small school—the one-teacher or one-room school. Here all six, seven, or eight grades are seated in one room, and a teacher may have as many as thirty classes a day, depending upon the number of students, their placement in grades, the curriculum, and the flexibility of administration.

The large schools tend to be located in large population centers. Two or more teachers may be assigned to a grade, or a departmental organization may be utilized. The average elementary school has an enrollment of slightly over four hundred. The size of the elementary school tends to increase with the size of the community.

THE NEIGHBORHOOD SCHOOL

A traditional elementary institution based primarily on its location is the neighborhood school. It is intended to serve the children of the immediate small community. This elementary school has helped to eliminate or reduce long-distance travel for children. Recently it has been brought into the political and judicial limelight because of issues in desegregation. The neighborhood school is not an effective means for promoting integration, and it is often invoked to avoid desegregation. *De facto* segregation—that caused by residence patterns—often leads to predominantly white schools in some suburbs, and a continuation of mostly black schools in urban areas. Related to the plans for desegregating neighborhood schools is the plan to bus or cross-bus pupils to secure better racial balance. Open enrollment—that is, letting students attend any school of their choice within their own school district—has been advocated by some as a remedy for racial desegregation problems. However, it has had no major impact. Unfortunately, the educational possibilities of neighborhood schools are often subordinated to emotionalism and racial conflicts. The issue of desegregation is further discussed in Chapter 1.

SUPPORT AND CONTROL

Most schools are controlled and financed by the public. These public elementary schools enroll approximately 90 percent of all students who attend the elementary school. About $3\frac{1}{2}$ million (10 percent) of all American elementary students attend private elementary schools, either parochial or other private institutions. Many private schools are closing because of fiscal problems. Some schools are especially designated as experimental or demonstration schools and may be affiliated with various universities and colleges as the training ground for student teachers or as laboratory schools for research.

In some communities, special schools are provided for exceptional students, particularly those with severe learning disabilities or physical handicaps. These schools may be either public or private. Classes in these schools are usually smaller, grade lines are often obscured, and teachers have been given special preparation. Classes for handicapped children provide special facilities and materials, and the content and method of teaching are adapted to the particular needs of students. Appropriate standards of achievement are set to match students' abilities. However, the trend in recent years has been toward "mainstreaming" more and more exceptional children into the regular school classrooms to the extent that their learning or physical disabilities will permit.

Scope and organization of elementary education

Elementary education is difficult to define because of the extreme variety of practices in its organiza-

tion, administration, and curriculums. In terms of children's ages, it is the educational institution for pupils from approximately 6 to 12 or 14 years of age. In terms of grades, elementary education generally includes grades 1 to 6. In many smaller districts, however, it generally embraces grades 1 to 8, as indicated in Figure 5-2.

The common subdivisions of elementary schools are usually grouped as follows: primary, grades 1 to 3; intermediate, grades 4 to 6; and upper, grades 7 and 8. Kindergartens may be included in the primary level, whereas junior high schools are usually considered part of secondary education.

Figure 5-2 Scope and organization of elementary education. In the first column on the left, elementary education is shown to consist of eight compartments called grades, with rigid promotion practices. In the next pattern, the number of divisions is reduced to three—primary, intermediate, and upper grades—with greater articulation and flexibility. In the middle column, kindergarten and nursery school have been added and combined into a pre-elementary unit; the upper three years have been combined into a middle-school unit, which many communities no longer regard as elementary education. In the second column from the right, the seventh and eighth grades are assigned to secondary education and the two remaining components become the upper and lower elementary school. In the pattern at right, there is one continuous six-year unit—perhaps ungraded—with kindergarten and perhaps nursery school added.

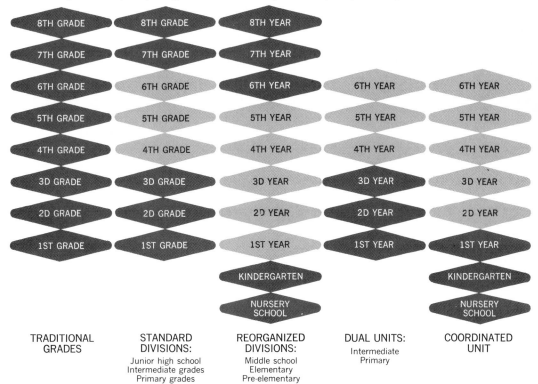

These three major areas should not be construed as disparate units, but rather as components of an organized whole, since children's growth and development are continuous rather than periodic. Some schools obliterate grade lines and organize the six or seven years as a unit, the latter embracing kindergarten, as indicated in the last column of Figure 5-2.

A number of school districts are organizing middle schools, or intermediate schools, as they are sometimes called. Middle schools may comprise grades 7 and 8, grades 6 to 8, or grades 5 to 8. In many cases the middle school is thought of as something "in the middle," between the elementary school and the secondary school and organizationally apart from both. For purposes of discussion, the middle school is included in this chapter.

INTERNAL ORGANIZATION

There are two major dimensions of school organization—vertical and horizontal. Vertical organization relates to the movements of students in time through the levels of the educational system. Graded, multigraded, and nongraded classrooms are systems of vertical organization. Horizontal organization relates to the grouping of students at the same educational levels within class groups and their assignment to teachers. Self-contained classrooms, departmentalized classrooms, and ability groupings are some of the systems of horizontal grouping. Open education, a form of organization within the classroom, is discussed in Chapter 9.

Vertical organization. The traditional pattern of vertical organization has been the graded school. Five-year-olds are accepted in kindergarten and under normal circumstances are moved along one grade each year. Teachers and textbooks are assigned by grades and are known as "third-grade teachers" or "fifth-grade geographies." A specific body of subject matter is assigned each grade level. Children who fail to meet the standards are sometimes retained for one or more years.

The graded school's major disadvantage is its unrealistic assumption that all children should cover the same material at the same rate. At the end of the year, the school decides whether slow learners will repeat all or none of the same grade, even though their progress may have been satis-

factory in part of the curriculum. In recent years there has been a trend away from having children repeat grades, because of the problems that often accompany it: poorer performance during the second year in the grade, resignation to failure, and problems of social and physical adjustment. More homogeneous classes do not result, and teachers are not freed from the task of providing for differences among students, even though graded schools sometimes create that illusion.

Growing dissatisfaction with graded schools has led several school districts to modify or depart from graded organization.[3] The best known of the earlier forerunners in this direction were the St. Louis, Pueblo, Dalton, Cambridge, and Winnetka plans, named after their cities of origin, which attempted in one way or another to permit students to progress through the school at their own rates. The Winnetka plan, executed by Carleton Washburne in the Winnetka, Illinois, public schools, was based on the concern for individual differences among children. Individuals worked at their own rate on predetermined units which they were expected to master. The curriculum also provided opportunities for developing creative talents and individual interests and abilities. Although all such plans have been discontinued or greatly modified, they were the early prototypes of the present broad-scale attack on the lockstep nature of graded schools.

Some schools have adopted multigraded organizations in which grade designations are retained but two or more grades are combined in the same classroom. Children work at several grade levels simultaneously—perhaps studying fifth-grade reading, sixth-grade science, and fourth-grade arithmetic. Some schools provide for an exchange of pupils from different grades or classrooms for part of the school day so that they can study with other children at similar levels of achievement.

A departure in vertical organization is the nongraded, or ungraded, system, in which grade lines are eliminated completely. Nongraded schools have appeared with increasing frequency, largely since 1954. John Goodlad, director of the famous University Elementary School at UCLA and profes-

---

[3]See Lyn S. Martin and Barbara N. Pavan, "Current Research on Open Space, Nongrading, Vertical Grouping, and Team Teaching," *Phi Delta Kappan*, January 1976, pp. 310–315.

sor of education, was a pioneer in nongraded organization. Many school systems are using nongraded sequences in one or more of their schools. Nongraded plans exist most commonly at the lower age levels; that is, children between the kindergarten and fourth grade are grouped in the primary unit. However, some districts have developed an entire elementary school program, and in some cases even middle school programs, using the nongraded plan.

In most nongraded schools the same educational experiences are undertaken by all, but at different rates of speed. The units are subdivided to permit children to move among the divisions, at intervals of a few weeks, to join others at their same level of achievement. Grouping is usually determined on the basis of reading achievement. Sometimes the same teacher stays with the group for three years. The nongraded school, sometimes called the "continuous-progress plan," practices the philosophy that school organization should adapt to children rather than having children adapt to the organization. It has brought corresponding changes in curriculum organization, reporting of pupil progress, development of teachers, and other aspects of teaching practice.

The multiunit school is a form of ungraded organization developed by the Wisconsin Research and Development Center for Cognitive Learning at the University of Wisconsin (see Figure 5-3). It was designed to implement Individually Guided Education (IGE), a system to raise achievement levels of elementary school children by individualized instruction. Specific learning tasks are used by students, and traditional textbooks, lockstep grades, and self-contained classrooms are discarded by teachers. Instruction is built around the individual's own rate of learning, style of learning, motivation, and starting knowledge. Children are in multiage groups called units, each unit comprising from 100 to 150 students, 3 to 4 teachers, 1 teacher aide, 1 secretary, and 1 intern. One school might have four units containing the following age groups: 4–6, 6–9, 8–11, and 10–12.

Individually Guided Education makes extensive use of team teaching. It includes models for developing instructional materials and for measuring and assessing readiness and progress. Weekly planning and evaluation sessions are held both at the building and system levels. A research program is in effect to develop meaningful ways to

enrich the curriculum. Over two thousand schools in thirty-five states have begun using the multiunit concept since IGE's inception in 1964. There is a great deal of support for IGE. State networks are being formed in twenty-three states to provide assistance and encouragement to schools, teacher-education institutions, and state education agencies. Four regional institutes also provide technical assistance and other help to schools in their region. Studies indicate that the environment of the multiunit school has improved children's performances and their attitudes toward school. Teachers also seem happier and more satisfied with the results of their work.[4]

Horizontal organization. A basic problem in any system of horizontal grouping is class size. The median size of elementary classes, about twenty-seven students, has remained fairly constant in recent years. The number tends to be smaller in the primary than in the middle and upper grades and smaller in small districts than in large ones. A poll of teachers' opinions conducted by the NEA revealed that most teachers regard an elementary class size of twenty to twenty-five as ideal. To reduce all elementary classes to this size would require the expenditure of billions of dollars for classrooms and for teachers' salaries and other services. Many innovations have been undertaken in the direction of more flexibility in class size. The use of team teaching, differentiated staffing (a system of selecting, employing, assigning, and utilizing teachers in accordance with their abilities, talents, preparation, and experience to make the greatest use of their abilities and to give them the maximum opportunity for professional fulfillment), and electronic and mechanical devices have resulted in classes of 100 or more at times, and in much smaller groups at other times, depending on the type of learning experience.

Self-contained classrooms and departmentalization are alternative horizontal organizations. A departmentalized class is instructed by more than one teacher, often by a different teacher

---

[4]See Herbert J. Klausmeier, "The Multi-unit Elementary School and Individually Guided Education," *Phi Delta Kappan*, November 1971, pp. 181–184, for more detail regarding IGE; see also John H. Proxtor and Kathryn Smith, "IGE and Open Education: Are They Compatible?" *Phi Delta Kappan*, April 1974, pp. 564–566.

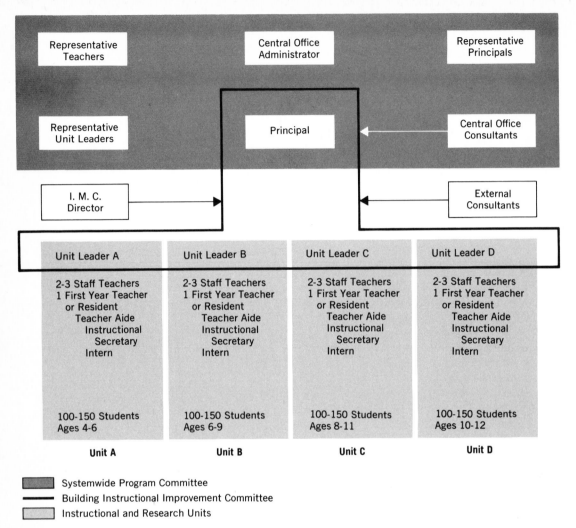

Representative Teachers	Central Office Administrator	Representative Principals
Representative Unit Leaders	Principal	Central Office Consultants

| I. M. C. Director | | External Consultants |

Unit Leader A	Unit Leader B	Unit Leader C	Unit Leader D
2-3 Staff Teachers 1 First Year Teacher or Resident Teacher Aide Instructional Secretary Intern	2-3 Staff Teachers 1 First Year Teacher or Resident Teacher Aide Instructional Secretary Intern	2-3 Staff Teachers 1 First Year Teacher or Resident Teacher Aide Instructional Secretary Intern	2-3 Staff Teachers 1 First Year Teacher or Resident Teacher Aide Instructional Secretary Intern
100-150 Students Ages 4-6	100-150 Students Ages 6-9	100-150 Students Ages 8-11	100-150 Students Ages 10-12
Unit A	**Unit B**	**Unit C**	**Unit D**

▓▓ Systemwide Program Committee
── Building Instructional Improvement Committee
░░ Instructional and Research Units

Figure 5-3 Organizational chart of a multiunit school (SOURCE: Wisconsin Research and Development Center for Cognitive Learning.)

for each subject. Platoon organization is a pattern of partial departmentalization in which the students move, but not always with the same group, from teacher to teacher for different learning activities. Departmentalization requires teachers to specialize in a single subject or a few subjects. The growing use of differentiated staffing has increased the frequency of specialization.

In the purest form, a self-contained classroom is one in which a single teacher meets with a single class for the entire school day and has complete and sole responsibility for instruction. Self-con-

tained classrooms enable a teacher to establish better understanding and rapport with students. They also facilitate integration of learning among various subject fields. In recent years, typical self-contained classrooms have done away with the concept of a single teacher who has sole responsibility for the total education of a group of students for a year. Modern self-contained classrooms tend to give the teacher the major responsibility for a group of twenty-five students; but resource teachers and specialists contribute to the students' total education by teaching specialized subjects such as art, music, and physical education and by assisting the classroom teacher in coordinating activities with the curriculum. The self-contained classroom has lasted because it is sound and flexible. It can keep its own basic structure while incorporating useful aspects of other plans of organization.

The "dual progress plan" is a semidepartmental scheme in which elementary school children are grouped according to ability for half the day to study the "cultural imperatives"—speech, vocabulary, spelling, grammar, reading, writing, literature, and social studies. The remainder of the day is spent in an ungraded vertical system studying the "cultural electives"—mathematics, science, art, music, and foreign languages. In essence this is an effort to combine the advantages of both departmentalized and self-contained classes, and of both graded and ungraded organization, with ability grouping.

Another choice in horizontal organization lies between heterogeneous and homogeneous grouping. In heterogeneous classes students are grouped by age or grade without regard for ability or achievement. Schemes of homogeneous grouping, usually referred to as "ability grouping," seek to reduce the range of abilities in a classroom by sorting pupils into classes on the basis of their intellectual capacity or academic achievement. In one type of homogeneous grouping, sometimes referred to as a "multiple-track plan," pupils are arranged according to ability. The curriculum is held constant for all groups, but the time to complete it varies according to pupils' speed of achievement. Thus bright pupils might complete the elementary program in five years, while slower learners might take eight. Like departmentalization, ability grouping was once common in elementary schools, and then it waned in popularity; but since 1954 it has been revived in a growing number of school systems.

Advocates of ability grouping claim that it enables schools to adapt the content and methods of instruction to students of different levels of ability. Teaching is supposedly simplified and improved when the range of ability in a single class is reduced. Brighter students, it is claimed, can learn more, progress more rapidly, or both, when instruction can be attuned to their superior ability. Homogeneous grouping has been criticized on the grounds that it is to some degree an illusion, since

students grouped on the basis of ability may be quite different with respect to achievement, or vice versa. Moreover, students who are grouped according to their ability or achievement in reading may vary with respect to ability or achievement in other subjects. Several studies have shown that regardless of the basis of grouping, the reduction in the range of ability is too small to permit teachers to ignore individual differences that remain. It is also argued that such grouping encourages intellectual snobbery among bright students and resignation to mediocrity among those less able.

Individually Prescribed Instruction (IPI) and other types of programmed instruction will tend to reduce some of the traditional dilemmas in the grouping of students for instruction. Programmed instruction permits the prescription of instructional tasks individually tailored to the abilities and needs of each student, thus accommodating a wide range of individual differences in abilities among a heterogeneous group of students. Individually Guided Education (IGE) and the multiunit school described earlier are good examples of how differentiated staffing can be used for more effective education. Widespread use of IGE, IPI, and other plans of differentiated staffing and programmed instruction will eventually render obsolete the debate over homogeneous versus heterogeneous grouping when the former becomes unnecessary.

So far research has failed to demonstrate the superiority of one pattern of grouping over another, even though one type may have evident face validity. The pattern of organization used in schools must coincide with the schools' basic philosophy and purposes. No organizational pattern can substitute for good teaching, although it can facilitate more effective teaching. The teacher is still the major force that motivates learning, bringing curriculum resources to learners according to their needs and capabilities.

Programs and practices in elementary education

EDUCATIONAL PROGRAMS

Educational programs are, in general, composed of broad curricular areas that together provide opportunities for a total, well-rounded education for elementary school students. These broad areas are language arts (reading, handwriting, listening, literature, spelling, speech, creative writing, second languages); social studies (history, geography, political science, economics, conservation); mathematics; science (scientific information and principles, environment education, technology, physical world); health and physical education (health concepts, physical fitness, skill development, safety, recreation); fine arts (music, art). No one subject or field of interest should be the domain of any one grade or year. All students should be provided with opportunities for experience in all areas.

Primary grades. Modern elementary school work is closely joined to pre-elementary work, particularly for pupils who enter first grade with some school experience in nursery school, kindergarten, or both. Although an increasing number of pupils have this orientation, the first school contact for many children comes in first grade. The so-called primary unit, an organization embracing kindergarten through grade 2 or 3, has provided a setting in which beginning elementary school experiences may be adjusted to remove or reduce failure.

The basic academic activity in the primary grades is reading. The nationwide Right to Read Program for the 1970s has stimulated great interest in reading, especially in elementary schools. The major types of reading stressed in the primary grades are (1) developmental, which is designed to initiate and improve reading skills, (2) functional, which is aimed at obtaining information, and (3) recreational, which is mainly for enjoyment and to develop tastes and appreciations. Obviously reading is not an isolated skill; social science, sciences, mathematics, and the creative arts all are integrated into the total process of reading, silent or oral. In certain areas reading is a bilingual activity. In many elementary schools the speaking and reading of a foreign language is begun in primary grades. Many disadvantaged 3- to 5-year-olds are enrolled in Head Start programs. These programs are reinforced by Follow Through programs for primary grades. As of 1974, only children from low-income families may be enrolled in Follow Through programs, with some exceptions. Half those enrolled must have a background of a year of Head Start or some other similar early-childhood program. According to some, Follow Through

never really got beyond the experimental stage. In 1976, $59 million was budgeted for Follow Through activities, but the program may be phased out. The federal government invested about $20 million for Stanford Research Institute to evaluate seven program models used in Follow Through classes. The educational approaches studied included the positive reinforcement theory, the cognitive developmental theory of Piaget, the open classroom modeled after the British infant school, and others. This study provides concrete evidence that correlates student achievement with classroom practices. Besides intensive instruction, Head Start and Follow Through youngsters receive medical and social services. Some psychologists and scientists now believe that children under age 7 are not ready for advanced intellectual tasks. They believe that pushing children into structured learning activities too soon not only has no lasting educational value but may cause permanent retardation. This is discussed further in Chapter 4.

Young learners develop not only mentally but also physically, socially, and emotionally. The primary school years constitute an interesting and significant division of education.

Intermediate grades. These are usually the fourth, fifth, and sixth grades. The most important curricular activity is still reading, but the emphasis is on extensive and enriched reading, rather than its mechanics, and on the skillful use of the basic tools acquired in primary grades. In some schools all subjects have been introduced by the time pupils reach fourth grade. These are then studied in more depth in intermediate grades. In conservative schools, some subjects, such as science and history, may begin in fourth grade. Programs of social importance introduced during these important intermediate years include drug-abuse education, sex education, consumer education, and career education.

Children of this age group have a vital interest in the world. This is the age level when many boys and girls develop a lasting interest in science. Topics taken from current affairs and social movements are included. Units on the history of civil rights and the protest movement might be taught. Many instructors use programmed instruction to help individualize the program. Greater creativity and freedom of learning are stressed. In some intermediate grades students help write their own textbooks and learning materials in such fields as environmental education. Some intermediate institutions, like many primary schools, do away with traditional report cards. As in many primary schools, the major emphases are on intellectual development and on development of desirable social skills, habits, and attitudes.

Middle school. The middle school is one of the major innovations in the last twenty years. Although the 6-3-3 plan is still most common, many districts now include middle schools. Five or six years of elementary education beyond kindergarten are followed by, most commonly, three-years of middle school. The middle school, sometimes called "intermediate school," includes students ordinarily enrolled in grades 5 to 8 or, more frequently, grades 6 to 8.

Children have begun to mature earlier. Ninth-graders today are more like high school students (adolescents) than like junior high school students (preadolescents). Sixth-graders today are frequently entering pubescence and are increasingly out of place in elementary school. In general, middle school is an attempt to provide an educational experience for this age group based on their special needs. Students of this age are in a transitory period of life, both in the change from elementary school to high school and in the change from childhood to adolescence. The school experience should provide opportunities that will make this transition smooth and meaningful.

Advocates of the middle school claim several advantages for it:

- It permits a four-year sequence of courses in high school.
- It avoids mixing 11- and 12-year-olds with adolescents.
- It groups together children passing through the awkward age of pubescence.
- It permits more gradual transition of students from the directed study of elementary school to the more independent study of high school.
- It encourages more flexibility of curriculum and more enrichment of instruction than the traditional arrangement.
- It permits teachers and administrators to specialize in developing educational programs uniquely designed for preadolescents.
- It relieves temporary enrollment bulges at either the elementary or the secondary level.

Those who have worked closely with middle schools see these factors as important characteristics of these schools: a nongraded organization; flexible teaching approaches, such as team teaching, flexible scheduling, individualized instruction, independent study, tutorial programs; interdisciplinary programs; an extensive guidance program, both group and individual; a faculty certified in both elementary and secondary, or some with each; social experiences based on needs; physical and intramural activities, stressing participation rather than watching; differentiated staffing, using paraprofessionals in addition to professional staff; open classrooms; innovative, creative teaching.

Educational programs in middle school most commonly include reading, English, literature, second languages, social studies, science, ecology, mathematics, home economics, industrial arts, health, physical education, and arts and crafts. Some include drug and alcohol programs and career education. Career education has been added in order to give students an awareness of the occupational world and various career opportunities. See Chapter 9 for further discussion of the curriculum.

Research is limited about whether the middle school is doing the job it was intended to do. Many feel that it is nothing more than another name for junior high school and, as such, is an imitation of high school rather than a unique institution adapted to the particular needs of preadolescents. In some cases they are right, but there is sincere effort by many to make the concept a working reality. And there is reason to believe they are succeeding.

New middle school state and regional organizations have sprung up, and much is being written about the movement. This increased communication is bound to be beneficial. More experience with and evaluation of the middle (or intermediate) school organization are needed before its advantages and limitations can be seen clearly. However, many authorities believe that such schools offer far more promise than junior high school as an institution for serving educational needs of preadolescents. On the basis of developmental theory, middle schools appear to be sound in principle. Currently there are more than 1,900 middle schools. Their destiny will be determined not by the realignment of grades but by how well these new institutions can develop curriculums, instruction, and service uniquely adapted to the needs of pupils between childhood and adolescence.[5]

CURRENT PRACTICES IN ELEMENTARY EDUCATION

Some current practices in elementary education are here presented in abbreviated form.

Organization and administration. The primary purpose of the pattern of an elementary school is to foster the maximum development of every child. There has been great emphasis in recent years on

[5]For additional reading about the middle school, see David Friesen, "The Middle School: An Institution in Search of an Identity," *Education Canada*, September 1974, pp. 5–9; Thomas E. Gatewood, "What Research Says about the Middle School," *Educational Leadership*, December 1973, pp. 221–224; and Michael F. Tobin, "Purpose and Function Precede Middle School Planning," *Educational Leadership*, December 1973, pp. 201–205.

humanizing our schools, and thus the thrust has been toward openness, freedom, and flexibility in school organization and in the classroom. A reduction in arbitrary divisions is effected through a reorganization of administrative units, as, for example, a unified six-year program in place of eight disparate grades. Grade classifications are made more flexible or are eliminated, especially in primary areas. Recent trends toward individually prescribed instruction, differentiated staffing, grouping by ability, and variable class size have already been noted. A reduction has been made in the number of grades, classes, and subjects. One-teacher schools, often epitomes of flexibility, are being reduced in number. Open education offers a free environment for children. It is based on the spontaneous development of interests and needs and is not bound by traditional schedules, subjects, or buildings.

Many humanized schools incorporate ideas of Dewey, Kilpatrick, and Piaget and adapt methods from Montessori and British infant schools. British

Open education offers a free environment for children based on spontaneous development of their interest.

infant schools have been the focus of real interest among many educators. These are ungraded schools for children aged 5 to 7. The curriculum centers around the children's own experiences. A wide variety of activities is provided in an open classroom setting. Individualized instruction is used extensively. Some American educators feel that this type of school should be a model for American schools.

More schooling is being provided for our youth. The school day has been lengthened in some communities to provide time for enrichment activities. The school week has been lengthened in some cities, such as Madison, Wisconsin, to include informal activities on Saturdays. Many systems elongate the educational year to provide recreational and educational programs during the summer. Rochester, Minnesota, has offered a full-time summer program for several decades. Some elementary schools operate a twelve-month program.

Buildings and facilities. Each elementary school building should be designed as a unique unit, planned to meet the educational needs of the community, to suit as well as possible the particular climate and site, and to house the specific educational program and learning activities of the school at a cost commensurate with the people's ability to pay. The ideal enrollment for most elementary schools is probably between four hundred and eight hundred. Modern elementary schools include large and well-equipped outdoor play areas and parking facilities on a well-landscaped site of 10 to 12 acres. Recent developments in land usage, including elementary school buildings, are educational parks. These parks are discussed further in Chapter 10.

More and more buildings for elementary schools are of the one-story type. They blend harmoniously with surrounding residential buildings and are homelike to young children. Many are small neighborhood schools.

School buildings and equipment have become more flexible and functional and are designed more creatively. In many elementary schools, a workroom is placed between two classrooms or is a part of the room, so that small groups can work on construction activities at any time during the day. Highly flexible equipment is installed. Running water and toilet facilities are within or ad-jacent to classrooms, especially for small children. Each classroom is provided with its own outside exit. Libraries are used extensively for enrichment. The elementary school library is a multimedia center and is spoken of as the "instructional-materials center." Modern elementary schools are equipped to handle television, programmed instruction, and other electronic and mechanical teaching media. Carpeting, bright fabrics, and bright furniture have added to the comfort and homelike atmosphere of many new elementary schools.

Elementary school enrollments are static or declining in most communities, forcing some school districts to close elementary school buildings. Another development in facilities is the use of trailers. For example, the Whisman School District of the San Francisco Bay area brings reading clinic facilities directly to pupils and teachers, with daily communication between clinic specialists and the classroom elementary teachers.

Curriculum practices. The curriculum is becoming more flexible. Some schools set up time allotments for major fields of learning in terms of weekly percentage ranges; minimum and maximum ranges of time are allotted weekly to each major division. There is an increase in programmed learning, that is, self-instruction by means of organized material built into computer-assisted instructional systems and programmed books.

Curricular materials are being reorganized into different relationships and with different purposes. The correlation, or fusion, of related materials and activities into broad fields such as language arts and social studies helps to integrate learning. Many teachers organize materials as teaching-learning units.

Many curricular materials are being shifted in the light of studies on maturation. There is a downward extension of several fields—such as social science, mathematics, and science—into lower grades. More work is expected of students. Perhaps the most significant trend has been the increased emphasis upon the humanization of the curriculum and greater relevance to students' needs.

New and neglected areas are being emphasized. Instruction in science is being extended and enriched. The Educational Development Center at Newton, Massachusetts, has produced a widely used program, Elementary Science Study (ESS)—a series of learning units that stresses investigation, placing students in the role of experimenting scientists. Minnemast (Minnesota Mathematics Science Teaching Project) coordinates science with mathematics in a program from kindergarten to ninth grade. In many elementary schools study of and practice in ecology are integral parts of the science program. One of the many special mathematics projects is Special Elementary Education for the Disadvantaged (SEED), used in several schools in California and elsewhere. The project is designed to help teach abstract math to disadvantaged students. Elementary schools in Oakland, California, are using computer-assisted arithmetic teaching programs for educationally disadvantaged students. The newly developed system Arithmetic Test Generation is designed to give the teacher precise identification of students' strengths and weaknesses in arithmetic.

Much more opportunity is given to elementary students to use more than one language in school. Bilingual programs extending through grade 6 have been developed by the Southwest Educational Development Laboratory (SEDL) for the Spanish-speaking children. First-grade students in selected Alaskan schools study arithmetic, language arts, and social studies in two Eskimo dialects.

Elementary school students manifest much interest in handicrafts, including pottery, metalwork, and woodworking. Language and the fine arts are used increasingly as a means of unleashing creative efforts. Manuscript writing, rather than cursive writing, is used in lower grades because of its similarity to printed words. United States history and the values and ideals of representative government are stressed. More emphasis is placed on helping children to learn about other peoples of the world and to develop sympathetic attitudes and understandings toward them—cultural empathy.

Learning in elementary schools is a cooperative enterprise. Classroom work is actively and realistically coordinated with other service departments. The guidance function is being strengthened. A greater effort is being made to identify potential school dropouts at the elementary school level and to alleviate their disenchantment with school and correct their educational disabilities before they reach the end of the compulsory school attendance age. The home is taken into partnership in many school experiences. Class mothers and teacher aides often assist in routine tasks. Elementary schools have extended their learning experiences into the community, especially through the "go-and-see" plan of education trips.

Television (both on closed-circuit and commercial channels), computer-assisted instruction, language laboratories, films, taped recordings, cassettes, and other audiovisual media are being used widely in elementary school instruction. Sometimes educational television programs are received in the classroom as part of the formal school program, and sometimes students are asked to view certain programs of educational importance at home. In metropolitan New York, several hours of educational programs are telecast daily over a radius of 100 miles. These programs range from English lessons for children of Puerto Rican descent to science lessons for teachers.

Outdoor education, including school camping, soil conservation, reforestation, wildlife study, farming, historical research, recreation, and therapy for handicapped children, has been introduced in various areas of the country, particularly Illinois and Michigan.

Many improved practices are becoming statewide or regional in scope. For example, elementary schools in North Dakota are becoming "informal classrooms with tested educational innovations." Many schools are using Individually Guided Education and the multiunit concept. Packaged materials have been developed to spread this program across the nation with the aid of the National Center for Educational Research and Development, a part of the U.S. Office of Education. Methods such as the British-originated Initial Teaching Alphabet (ITA) for reading and spelling are imported. Many other curricular developments in elementary schools are discussed in Chapter 9.

Elementary schools have been and are the experimental seed plots for many modern theories of learning and practices in teaching. For example, Individually Prescribed Instruction (IPI) was initially launched in elementary schools. There is much hope for reform. John Goodlad, a specialist in elementary education, sees a "humanistic curriculum" as one of the major developments of the 1970s. There is much stress today on behavioral objectives and outcomes.

Students and teachers. In good schools, students receive much individual attention. Opportunities to enhance further individualization are available because of the current surplus of elementary teachers and the increase in educational technology. Progress of students is evaluated more carefully, especially in view of the current criticism of elementary education. Teachers, especially in the primary unit, are often assigned for a period of two or three years to the same group of students. Special attention is being given to enriched programs of instruction for gifted students. Provisions for handicapped children are being improved and expanded. The mobility of the population causes many changes in class rolls.

Modern elementary schools should stress both cognitive and affective development and guidance. Several elementary schools have established child-guidance clinics. Cumulative records, including anecdotal reports, contribute to evaluation and guidance. Sociometric devices are more widely used.

In line with the modern accent on relevance in the curriculum, there is increased opportunity for students to do socially useful work. Student councils are used increasingly as a means of promoting democracy in the administration of elementary schools. A cooperative attack upon elementary school problems is made by pupils, teachers, school administrators, parents, and community leaders. The Carnegie Corporation supports various programs to promote the improvement of education. Among its programs are in-service activities to bring research findings about learning to teachers and to help teachers solve problems through interaction with other teachers. The National Society for School Evaluation, long active in the evaluation and accreditation of high schools and colleges, has recently developed guidelines and standards for evaluating elementary schools as well. As noted earlier, more extensive use is being made of team teaching, counseling, tutorial reading teams, and differentiated staffing.

One of the very significant developments in elementary education in the past quarter century has been the remarkable rise in the level of prepara-

Computer-assisted instruction increases the school's capability of individualizing instruction.

tion of elementary teachers. Since 1950, the proportion of elementary school teachers with four or more years of college-level preparation has increased from 50 to 99 percent, a truly remarkable rise when one considers the sharp increase in the demand for teachers and for workers in competing occupations during the same period. At no time in the past has the professional preparation of elementary school teachers been as good as it is at present.

Many elementary schools have added specialists. For example, a rather new position is instructional diagnostician, combining the functions of counseling, diagnosis, prescription, evaluation, and instruction. Child-development specialists are being added. More elementary schools are employing librarians, who are developing into multimedia specialists.

The future

Elementary education programs will be enriched through many new academic accents. Career education will be introduced in more elementary schools. Sex education and environmental studies will be started in the early years. Youth volunteer services will enlist many students and teachers. The study of ethnic groups will be expanded and will be presented in the social studies curriculum, rather than as a single offering.

Ungraded schools will be more prevalent. Differentiated instruction, various individualized instructional systems, and flexible grouping will become more common. Team teaching and flexible class size will become increasingly popular.

More use will be made of paraprofessionals to free teachers from unprofessional tasks. Many schools will undertake preparation programs for paraprofessionals. Greater use will be made of guidance counselors, psychologists, and social workers, and medical personnel will be more available to disadvantaged children.

Greater provisions will be made in regular classrooms for children with physical or emotional handicaps. More medical guidance personnel will be available to them.

The use of programmed instruction, television, and other instructional media will continue to increase. Classroom teachers will experiment more with teaching methods, materials, and procedures. Such experimentation in the actual teaching-learning environment could be more useful than that performed in artificial settings.

The middle school will continue to develop and take its firm place in the educational setting. As it does, certification programs for middle school teachers will be included in schools of education around the nation. However, this will not occur on a large scale in the near future.

In sum, the dilemmas that will confront elementary schools in the last quarter of the twentieth century will not be those of growth, which dominated recent decades, but those of enrichment and improvement of the educational experiences and services that are necessary for children's basic education.

Suggested activities

1. Visit an open classroom and state its advantages and disadvantages.
2. Visit a local elementary school and evaluate its use of individualized instruction.
3. Discuss the major objectives of elementary schools.
4. Visit an ungraded primary unit and describe how it differs from typical graded schools.
5. Visit a middle school; explain its philosophy and program, and tell how well it meets the unique needs of preadolescent pupils.
6. Contrast the methods of teaching and discipline in a typical elementary school of fifty years ago with those in use today.
7. Visit a nonpublic elementary school and indicate its strengths and weaknesses.
8. Describe the Right to Read Program proposed by former U.S. Commissioner of Education James E. Allen, Jr., and its effect on elementary schools.
9. Volunteer to teach reading on a one-to-one basis, tutoring a disadvantaged child.
10. Read John Dewey's *My Pedagogic Creed* and report on its appropriateness or inappropriateness in relation to modern needs for elementary education.
11. Interview an elementary school teacher about teaching in elementary school.

Bibliography

Collier, Calhoun C., W. Robert Houston, Robert R. Schmatz, and William J. Walsh: *Modern Elementary Education,* Macmillan, Riverside, N.J., 1976. Comprehensive textbook on curriculum, instruction, and learning in the elementary school.

Featherstone, Joseph: *Schools Where Children Learn,* Liveright, New York, 1971. Collection of essays describing British infant schools, child-centered, free environments for learning, and their implications for American schools.

Goldhammer, Keith, and others: *Elementary School Principals and Their Schools,* Center for Advanced Study of Educational Administration, University of Oregon, Eugene, Oregon, 1971. An interesting look at elementary schools—their problems and prospects—through the eyes of their principals.

Goodlad, John I., M. Frances Klein, and Associates: *Behind the Classroom Door,* Jones Publishing, Worthington, Ohio, 1970. Report on findings of visits to 150 classrooms, kindergarten through grade 3, in twenty-six school districts.

Goodlad, John I., and Harold G. Shane (eds.): *The Elementary School in the United States,* The Seventy-second Yearbook of the National Society for the Study of Education, part II, University of Chicago Press, Chicago, 1973. Collection of scholarly discussions of the impact elementary school has had on society and the forces and ideas that are molding it.

Holt, John: *How Children Fail,* Pitman, New York, 1964. Classic study of how children learn or fail to learn.

Jarolimek, John, and Clifford D. Foster: *Teaching and Learning in the Elementary School,* Macmillan, Riverside, N.J., 1976. Thorough description of the organization, educational program, and instruction in elementary schools.

Kimbrough, Ralph B.: *Administering Elementary Schools,* Macmillan, New York, 1968. Thorough treatment of all aspects of elementary school organization and operation.

Kozol, Jonathan: *Free Schools,* Houghton Mifflin, Boston, 1972. Discusses parent-operated ghetto schools that emphasize the 3 R's and are more environment-oriented than public schools.

McCarthy, Robert J.: *The Ungraded Middle School,* Parker Publishing, West Nyack, N.Y., 1972. Describes the middle school in a continuous progress plan, its potential and development.

Michaelis, John U., Ruth H. Grossman, and Lloyd F. Scott: *New Designs for Elementary Curriculum and Instruction,* 2d ed., McGraw-Hill, New York, 1975. Comprehensive presentation of curriculum developments; principles of analyzing, planning, and evaluating the curriculum; and challenges facing curriculum planners.

National Education Association: *Elementary Education Today,* Washington, 1971. Collection of articles from NEA publications dealing with elementary education and its impact on children.

National School Public Relations Association: *Reading: Issues and Actions,* Arlington, Va., 1974. In-depth report of current issues regarding reading instruction—methods, pupils' progress, the role of government, teacher training, and so on.

Overly, Donald E., Jon R. Kinghorn, and Richard L. Preston: *The Middle School: Humanizing Education for Youth,* Jones Publishing, Worthington, Ohio, 1972. Describes the concept of middle school and practical ideas for implementing personalized programs.

Ragan, William B., and Gene D. Shepherd: *Modern Elementary Curriculum,* 4th ed., Holt, New York, 1971. Textbook dealing with various aspects of the elementary school curriculum.

Rogers, Frederick A.: *Curriculum and Instruction in the Elementary School,* Macmillan, Riverside, N. J., 1975. Discussion of teaching methods and scope of learning in modern elementary schools.

Silberman, Charles E.: *Crisis in the Classroom,* Random House, New York, 1970. Carnegie Corporation report of a survey of American schools, with many examples from elementary grades.

Chapter 6
Secondary education

Foundations of secondary education

Adolescence is often a turbulent period in human development, and schools that serve adolescents are likewise in a period of turbulent change. More so than any other sector of education, our high schools are a microcosm of the larger problems of American culture. Secondary education's capability to respond to these problems is being tested, and substantial change is already evident.

We will sketch briefly the historical development of secondary schools, analyze their current ferment, and examine problems facing them. We will look at the purposes of secondary education, note the types of secondary schools—their organization, curriculums, and student bodies—and close with a forecast of their future.

HISTORICAL DEVELOPMENT

The history of secondary education in the United States is usually chronicled in four rather distinct periods, named after the institutions that characterized them: (1) the era of Latin grammar schools, (2) the era of tuition academies, (3) the era of free public high schools, and (4) the era of vertically extended or reorganized secondary schools. The significant events in the evolution of secondary education are listed in the historical calendar.

Latin grammar schools. The first step toward organizing Latin grammar schools in America was taken by Bostonians in 1635, in a town meeting, where it was voted to establish the first Latin grammar school. This marked the beginning of secondary education in the colonies, and by 1700 approx-

The Development of Secondary Education

1635	*First Latin grammar school founded in Boston*
1751	*Franklin Academy organized in Philadelphia*
1821	*First high school for boys organized in Boston*
1826	*First high school for girls initiated in Boston*
1856	*First coeducational high school established in Chicago*
1874	*Taxation for secondary schools upheld in the Kalamazoo case*
1884	*Manual training high school started in Baltimore*
1893	*Recommendations of the Committee of Ten published*
1904	*G. Stanley Hall's classic,* Adolescence, *published*
1910	*First public junior high schools opened*
1918	*Report of the Commission on Reorganization of Secondary Education published*
1933	*Reports of the National Survey of Secondary Education presented*
1933	*Cooperative Study of Secondary School Standards launched*
1938	*Classic study of youth,* Youth Tell Their Story, *published by American Youth Commission*
1941	*Eight-year Study by the Progressive Education Association published*

1944	*Report,* Education for All American Youth, *published by Educational Policies Commission*
1960	*Massive study of high school students' talents and achievements launched in Project Talent*
1960	*Conant's study* Recommendations for Education in the Junior High School *published*
1964	*Job Corps and work training programs for impoverished youth established by Economic Opportunity Act*
1965	*Elementary and Secondary Education Act passed by Congress, authorizing educational benefits directed mostly toward pupils from low-income families*
1967	*Conant's findings reported in* The American High School Today *updated in* The Comprehensive High School
1969	*Early prototypes of alternative high schools established in Philadelphia, Brooklyn, Chicago, and Portland (Oregon)*
1971	*Model secondary schools established to demonstrate pattern of secondary education for the future*
1973–1975	*Influential reports on secondary education published:* The Reform of Secondary Education; The Mood of American Youth; Youth: Transition to Adulthood; National Panel on High School and Adolescent Education; *and* Secondary Schools in a Changing Society
1976	*First decline in secondary school enrollment in a quarter of a century*
1977	*Number of alternative secondary schools doubling annually*

imately forty grammar schools had been founded in New England.

The main purpose of Latin grammar schools was to prepare students for college. Latin grammar schools, especially earlier ones, offered a limited curriculum. They were selective in character and sought to establish an aristocracy of educated intellectuals. Gradually these schools lost their popularity.

Tuition academies. Benjamin Franklin was primarily responsible for establishing the first academy. Its curriculum was broader than that of Latin grammar schools. Since it aimed to prepare for life as well as for the ministry, its students included those not intending to go to college as well as those who were college-bound.

The academies permitted young women to enter. They were supported in the main by tuition and donation, and so were semipublic in control. In their organization, administration, and program they were more democratic than the Latin grammar schools. Several private academies still exist in the United States as military academies or as special schools, but most older ones have either disappeared or have been transformed into public high schools.

Free public high schools. The third period in the history of American secondary education covers the rise and growth of free public high schools. This started with the establishment of the English Classical School in Boston in 1821. In 1827 Massachusetts passed a law requiring larger towns "to supply free, tax-supported instruction" in such high school subjects as surveying, logic, Latin, and Greek. A distinguished educational historian, Adolphe E. Meyer, thus evaluates this precedent-making though short-lived law:

Despite its ignoble fate, the law was of deep and vital importance. It not only mandated the public maintenance of free secondary education; it also became the model on which other states patterned themselves when the desire seized them to stake their children to something more than the usual lower learning.[1]

During the next half-century various types of high schools were organized. Among these were

the first coeducational high school, started in Chicago in 1856, and the first manual training school, founded in Baltimore in 1884. Many factors contributed to the steady development of these schools, particularly in the democratic West.

The Kalamazoo case decision of the Supreme Court of Michigan in 1874 became famous in school law because it lent legal sanction to the movement for the establishment of publicly supported high schools. Similar decisions followed in several other states, thus removing any question about the legality of having communities tax themselves to support public high schools. The Kalamazoo decision thus paved the way for a phenomenal growth in this new institution of democracy.

The search for identity and purpose. Thus the first century of this nation brought a struggle for the establishment of secondary education as an integral part of free public education. This achievement was to come in few other countries, and only many years later. The second century of our nation's history marked a search for identity and purpose within secondary education.

The Committee of Ten, appointed by the National Education Association in 1893, concluded that high school should not be limited to the preparation of youths for college; it nevertheless proceeded to recommend a curriculum that was largely college preparatory in nature and that tended to standardize academic offerings for many years.

In 1918 the Commission on the Reorganization of Secondary Education urged that secondary schools be reorganized to serve the needs of all youths and enunciated the famous Seven Cardinal Principles of Education: (1) health, (2) command of fundamental processes, (3) worthy home membership, (4) vocational efficiency, (5) civic participation, (6) worthy use of leisure time, and (7) ethical character.

The American Youth Commission in its influential report, *Youth Tell Their Story,* published in 1938, concluded that high schools were not meeting the needs of youths very well, particularly those from disadvantaged educational, cultural, and economic backgrounds. Its second report, *What the High Schools Ought to Teach,* urged greater emphasis on social studies, especially human relations and family life. It urged more humane and pleasant methods of teaching.

[1]Adolphe E. Meyer, *An Educational History of the Western World,* McGraw-Hill, New York, 1965, p. 399.

In 1941 the Progressive Education Association published *Eight-year Study,* a report of the results of applying progressive education theory in selected experimental secondary schools. These schools built their curriculums around youths' experiences and interests rather than around subject-matter formats designed for college preparation. The progressives, building on the educational theory of John Dewey, were more interested in the reconstruction of students' everyday experiences than in formal presentation of subject matter. The study concluded that success in liberal arts colleges did not depend upon formal study of subjects, because the youths in the experimental schools generally performed better in college than did graduates of more traditional schools. Much of the doctrine of progressive educators, although disparaged for two decades following the study, is being rediscovered and applied in contemporary schools.

The Educational Policies Commission published, in 1944, *Education for All American Youth,* in which it formulated policies for secondary education. This was supplemented by *A Further Look.* Schools should be dedicated, said the commission, to the proposition that every youth in the United States—regardless of sex, economic status, geographic location, or race—should experience a broad and balanced education.

The Commission on Life Adjustment Education for Youth was created by the U.S. Office of Education in 1947. Its report, published four years later, stressed the importance of "practical education," especially for youths who did not plan to attend college. Like the Progressive Education Association doctrine before it, this report was attacked vigorously by basic educationists who preferred hard academic discipline. Ironically, the essential doctrines of life-adjustment education and work-study programs were rediscovered in the mid-1960s and found expression in such programs as the Job Corps, the street academies, "action learning" (described later), career education programs, and other contemporary educational developments. One of the most ambitious studies of American secondary education, Project Talent, was mounted in 1960 under the direction of John Flanagan of the University of Pittsburgh. Flanagan and his associates concluded from their study that the full potential of a large portion of the nation's

young people is not being developed; that the number of young people who graduate from high school with vague and inadequate plans for the future should be reduced; and that the greatest reform necessary in secondary education was greater individualization of instruction to accommodate the great variation in knowledge, abilities, aptitudes, interests, and backgrounds of high school students. The study underscored the importance of assisting non-college-bound students develop appropriate educational and occupational goals and of providing educational opportunities to facilitate progress toward those goals. Project Talent provided insight through research into some of the reforms that were to be invoked by the popular critics of education in the late 1960s and 1970s.

Conant's two books, *The American High School Today* (1959) and *The Comprehensive High School* (1967), reinforced our faith in the soundness of comprehensive high schools, urged the elimination of small high schools through school district reorganization, and advocated strengthening of guidance in secondary schools. However, Conant's orientation was largely subject-centered rather than student-centered, and his recommendations in curriculum reform—more emphasis on mathematics and physical sciences, more concentrated attention on cognitive development, and more rigorous and stereotyped curriculum structure—were soon to become anachronistic and, indeed, contributed to the unrest in schools during the 1960s. This development prompted more emphasis on the social sciences and more attention to the affective development of youths.

Finally, the report in 1973 of the National Commission on the Reform of Secondary Education, *The Reform of Secondary Education,* along with other studies cited later, is presently helping to redirect contemporary secondary schools.[2]

Comprehensive high schools. By far the most common model of American secondary education is the comprehensive high school. It strives to meet the needs of practically all youths of secondary school age by means of its parallel curricu-

[2]National Commission on the Reform of Secondary Education, *The Reform of Secondary Education,* McGraw-Hill, New York, 1973.

lums—college preparatory, general, vocational, and commerical—all of which include some common courses in general education. Within each curriculum some flexibility is maintained through the use of electives. By bringing together under one "educational umbrella" students of varied backgrounds, interests, and abilities, it has, like the common school, played a vital role in the great melting pot of American society. It has harmonized the diversity of young people and helped to build strong national unity.

Secondary education for all. Many factors have contributed to quicken the realization of secondary education for all American youth, as portrayed in Figure 6-1. Young people are realizing that in an automated and cybernetic economy there is very little attractive employment without a high school education. The choice of whether to complete high school or to drop out and get a job is disappearing. State laws that raise the minimum age limit for beginning employment or lift the maximum compulsory school attendance age are factors in the great increase in secondary school enrollments. More than 95 percent of the population between 14 and 17 years of age (approximately high school age) is enrolled in schools in the United States. Figure 6-2 reveals total secondary school enrollments from 1900 to 1980. Note the decline in enrollments beginning with our bicentennial anniversary.

Secondary schools have increased their power to hold students until graduation, thus reducing the number of dropouts and "pushouts." The attrition rate has been and is being reduced to the point where now more than 80 percent of public school ninth-graders go on to be graduated from high schools. Indeed a major trend in American education in the first three-fourths of the twentieth century has been the marked increase in the number of people and the proportion of the total population attaining at least secondary school education.

Nowhere in the world is so large a percentage of young people attending high school as in America. In most European countries, less than one-fifth of the population of high school age is in school. The attainment of high school education by virtually all American youths is one of the truly great phenomena of American democracy and one of the greatest sources of its strength.

The comprehensive high school has helped harmonize the diversity of young people by bringing them together to share common interests.

Figure 6-1 Public and private high school graduates as percent of 17-year-olds. After a steady rise until 1970, the percentage appears to be leveling off at 78 percent. (U.S. Office of Education, *Progress of Public Education in the United States of America.*)

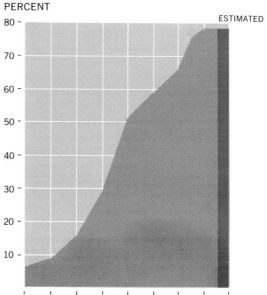

MILLIONS

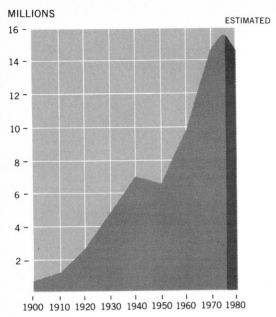

Figure 6-2 Total enrollment in public and private secondary schools, grades 9–12 (U.S. Office of Education, *Progress of Public Education in the United States of America;* and U.S. Office of Education, *Projections of Educational Statistics, 1983–1984.*)

CURRENT FERMENT IN SECONDARY EDUCATION

On the bicentennial of our nation we reached a noteworthy watershed in secondary education, the beginning of a decline in enrollments. For the previous quarter century, the preeminent problem had been that of building high schools, recruiting teachers, and raising money fast enough to meet the sharp rise in enrollments. These problems are now behind us. In most districts new buildings or teachers will be needed only for replacement. We are moving, then, from a period of growth to a period of invigoration and reform. We have an unprecedented opportunity to use surplus staff and space to enrich the educational experiences of all. However, state and local authorities are under great pressure from many taxpayers to reduce expenditures commensurate with declining enrollments. This strategy—alluring as it may be in times of unemployment, recession, or inflation—will deny us a superb opportunity to enrich educational experiences in directions suggested later in this chapter.

During the past dozen years particularly, American high schools, like all sectors of education, have been the target of vigorous criticism. Although critics do not always agree on either the nature of the faults or the means for correcting them, several problems are commonly underlined. One of the most inherent criticisms is that the high school curriculum is not relevant to the realities of life or the interests of students.

When high schools functioned primarily to prepare students for college and when students who could not meet the academic standards could drop out and find worthwhile employment, our society could perhaps afford the luxury of addressing secondary education primarily to the needs of academically talented students. However, within the last decade we have become persuaded that secondary education must meet the needs of all youths. The old academic model of secondary education with arbitrary academic standards was not appropriate for students who once dropped out. This poses the problem of redesigning secondary programs and practices to accomplish what neither this nation nor any other nation has previously attempted—namely, universal secondary education that is responsive to the needs and interests of all youths. This challenge poses problems of curriculum reform, teaching methods, school structure and organization, personnel practices, counseling, finance, and administration.

We believe that a great many of our high schools are responding to the needs and interests of youths. As evidence, we call attention to the very positive attitudes of most high school students toward their schools.[3] The growing respect for students' rights, the increasing protection of due process in the suspension and punishment of students, the great increase in alternative schools, additional options in programs of study, the enlarged capacity of schools to meet the needs of handicapped students, and the intensified concern for humanistic study and interpersonal relations are all salubrious movements.

Nevertheless, problems remain. The sharp rise in vandalism and crime by youths, both in and out of school, is alarming. At one high school in Los Angeles, for example, homecoming activities in-

[3]See National Association of Secondary School Principals, *The Mood of American Youth,* Reston, Va., 1974.

cluded the shooting of five youths, only one of sixty incidents involving guns in the Los Angeles school system. Marcus Foster, the fine superintendent of schools in Oakland, California, was assassinated. Physical attacks on both teachers and students are becoming frightfully common. The National Commission on the Reform of Secondary Education polled a national sample of high school students and learned that 41 percent were sometimes attacked and beaten up in rest rooms in their schools, and 35 percent were robbed there. The commission noted:

In many desegregated schools, both male and female students of both races are literally petrified at the thought of having to use the school's rest rooms. These facilities have become turfs where gangs of both majority and minority students concentrate, and waylay other students who come in. Crime is rampant in the washrooms. The problem is far more serious for girls than for boys. It is a very easy matter for a group to snatch a girl's pocketbook, block off the Kotex machine, threaten to burn her hair, or molest her in other ways.[4]

Large city high schools appear to be in the most difficulty. In some, absenteeism commonly exceeds 50 percent, and the school dropout rate is much higher than in other high schools. According to data provided by the National Assessment of Educational Progress, academic achievement in many urban high schools lags far behind that of high schools in general. These schools are too often the battleground for all the ills of urban living. Too often these schools are exploited for private or political gains. Principals become so preoccupied with hearings on teachers' grievances, disciplinary matters, and innumerable conferences that they have little time or energy for educational improvement. Francis Moseley, past president of the High School Principals Association in New York City and a principal for twenty years, describes high schools in that city as almost beyond repair.[5]

[4]National Commission on the Reform of Secondary Education, op. cit., p. 120. See also James R. Irwin, "Vandalism—Its Prevention and Control," *NASSP Bulletin,* May 1976, pp. 55–59.

[5]Francis S. Moseley, "The Urban Secondary School: Too Late for Mere Change," *Phi Delta Kappan,* May 1972, p. 564. For quite another view of the problems of urban high schools, see Robert J. Havighurst, Frank L. Smith, and David E. Wilder, *A Profile of the Large City High School,* National Association of Secondary School Principals, Reston, Va., 1970.

Surely many urban secondary schools have deteriorated badly. Many have failed to respond to a wide variety of proposed reforms.

Goals of secondary education

Largely as a result of the drive for accountability in education, the 1970s have been characterized by invigorated effort to assess the results of the educational enterprise. Results can be measured only in terms of explicit goals. Many states have mobilized committees of citizens, legislators, and educators to formulate educational goals. The National Commission on the Reform of Secondary Education analyzed the goal statements from thirty-seven individual states and derived a composite list from those most frequently stated. Using the Gallup international polling procedure, questionnaires were submitted to panels of superintendents, principals, teachers, parents, and students representing a mix of urban, suburban, and rural populations to substantiate the relevance of the stated goals for the national scene. The results revealed very little difference among the four groups of people relative to the desirability of the goals, the responsibility of the schools for achieving them, or the levels of success of recent graduates. These goals of secondary education, listed below, are divided into *content goals,* the general skills that students must acquire if they are to function at a level which is both personally and socially rewarding, and *process goals,* the individual abilities and attitudes that are influenced by the school procedures, environment, and activities.

CONTENT GOALS

- *Achievement of Communication Skills*—ensure that every student masters the basic skills of reading, writing, speaking, listening, and viewing... to a level of functional literacy
- *Achievement of Computational Skills*—ensure that all students master those computational and analytical skills necessary for the understanding of everyday problems... to a level sufficient for the management of household responsibilities
- *Attainment of Proficiency in Critical and Objective Thinking*—ensure that all learners develop, to the ex-

tent of their abilities, the skills of critical and objective thinking through research, analysis, and evaluation

- *Acquisition of Occupational Competence*—prepare students for a successful life of work through increasing their occupational options [and]... ensure that those students who wish to do so acquire job-entry skills before leaving high school
- *Clear Perception of Nature and Environment*—equip all students with an understanding of the wonders of nature, of the effects of man upon his environment, and of man's obligations to the viability of the planet
- *Development of Economic Understanding*—help students understand the American economy, its accomplishments, and its relationships to human rights and freedoms... [and] understand his role in the economy as both producer and consumer of goods and services
- *Acceptance of Responsibility for Citizenship*—help students understand the American system of government, and equip them with the knowledge and experiences necessary for dealing purposefully with the political process... [to] include respect for the opinions of others, the ability to conduct rational and informed discussions of controversial issues, respect for public and private property, and the acceptance of social duties

PROCESS GOALS

- *Knowledge of Self*—assist every learner in assessing his/her own mental, physical, and emotional capacities to the end that he/she has a positive self-image and can cope with problems of personal and family management... [and] help learners understand their own physical nature and the extent to which their subsequent potential may be affected by their habits of eating and drinking and use of leisure time
- *Appreciation of Others*—help each student develop an understanding of the differences and similarities and of the common humanity of members of different ethnic and religious groups
- *Ability to Adjust to Change*—endow students with the knowledge and attitudes necessary for survival in the twenty-first century and for coping with the unprecedented expansion of knowledge
- *Respect for Law and Authority*—develop within each student a respect for duly constituted authority and public laws as well as a knowledge of the strategy for changing both through the democratic process
- *Clarification of Values*—assist each learner in developing an increased awareness of himself and of his

relations with others and to the universe as he seeks to discover values and ethical standards which can promote growth toward his highest potential

- *Appreciation of the Achievements of Man*—help students understand and appreciate man's historical achievements in art, music, drama, literature, and the sciences so that they may acquire reverence for the heritage of mankind.[6]

The Commission emphasized that the responsibility for achieving these goals rests with teachers, administrators, school board members, parents, and, to a considerable degree, with the students themselves.

Types of secondary education

To meet the varied purposes of secondary education and the diverse needs of secondary school pupils, many types of schools have been developed. As indicated in Figure 6-3, some secondary schools are extended downward and upward. Some secondary institutions include students of junior high school age who are housed and programmed in the same building with those of senior high school age, thus producing a six-year secondary school. A few institutions include the lower division of higher education in the secondary school organization.

Two new public institutions have arisen to challenge any neat division of secondary education between elementary education and higher education: junior college and middle, or intermediate, school. Whether the middle school is more closely associated with secondary education than elementary education or whether it is indeed indigenous to neither is still a moot question. In any case, we choose to deal with the middle school for the most part in the chapter on elementary education (Chapter 5). The same dilemma exists with respect to the junior college, which in some districts is organized as an extension of secondary education but is more commonly regarded as a sector of higher education. We have chosen to deal with the junior college in the chapter on higher education (Chapter 7). The junior high school, on the other

[6]National Commission on the Reform of Secondary Education, op. cit., pp. 32–34.

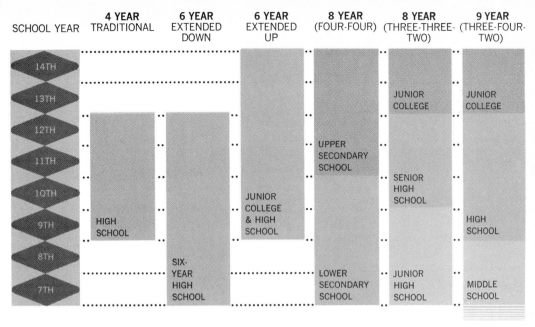

SCHOOL YEAR	4 YEAR TRADITIONAL	6 YEAR EXTENDED DOWN	6 YEAR EXTENDED UP	8 YEAR (FOUR-FOUR)	8 YEAR (THREE-THREE-TWO)	9 YEAR (THREE-FOUR-TWO)
14TH						
13TH					JUNIOR COLLEGE	JUNIOR COLLEGE
12TH				UPPER SECONDARY SCHOOL		
11TH			JUNIOR COLLEGE & HIGH SCHOOL		SENIOR HIGH SCHOOL	
10TH	HIGH SCHOOL					HIGH SCHOOL
9TH						
8TH		SIX-YEAR HIGH SCHOOL		LOWER SECONDARY SCHOOL	JUNIOR HIGH SCHOOL	MIDDLE SCHOOL
7TH						

Figure 6-3 Organizational patterns of secondary education. These are the more common patterns of secondary education, although many other variations and combinations of these patterns exist. In many districts, the middle, intermediate, school is often regarded as a division between elementary and secondary education and a part of neither. The middle school sometimes includes the sixth year.

hand, is traditionally regarded as a part of secondary education and is discussed in this chapter.

FOUR-YEAR HIGH SCHOOLS

General high school. During the heyday of the combination junior and senior high school the role of traditional, or general, four-year high schools declined. However, in many instances the four-year organization was never changed to the junior-senior combination. For example, in some states, such as California, Illinois, and New Jersey, many high schools have remained as separate school districts with their own boards of education, divorced legally from the elementary school district. The typical four-year high school, commencing with the ninth grade, has also remained a more practical arrangement for graduates from rural, small, eight-grade school districts. Long tradition has favored four-year schools. Today the rise in the number of new middle schools, for combinations such as grades 5 to 8, is also increasing the need for more four-year high schools, which are often

comprehensive secondary schools, described earlier.

Vocational and technical schools. Vocational and technical high schools constitute the most rapidly growing sector of secondary education from the standpoint of enrollment and expenditure. Enrollments in these schools have more than doubled during the past twenty years, and expenditures have increased approximately seven times during the same period. Some vocational and technical schools are post-secondary institutions. These post-secondary schools are described in Chapter 7.

Secondary-level vocational and technical schools have been developed to meet the nation's need for a technically trained labor force and to provide appropriate educational opportunity for employment in the trade and technical vocations for students uninterested in academic programs. Vandalism and absenteeism are often less frequent at these schools than at other types of high schools. Some programs of studies in these schools are terminal programs, while others offer preparatory study for advanced post-secondary technical education.

Curriculums of vocational and technical high schools vary widely and are usually well adapted to the particular labor needs of the regions they serve. Many prepare students for trades such as appliance repair, automobile mechanics, drafting, electrical construction, machine-shop operation, radio and television servicing, welding, refrigeration, heating, practical nursing, chemical technology, marketing, data processing, computer technology, nuclear technology, accounting, and secretarial and clerical work. Many schools also offer basic education in the physical sciences, social sciences, mathematics, and language arts, because these subjects are important for all broadly educated citizens and also because the physical sciences, particularly, constitute the academic basis for technical study. Some vocational and technical schools offer only technical education and permit students to attend comprehensive high schools for academic studies. Some enroll only juniors and seniors who have completed required basic education in comprehensive high schools during earlier years.

Most vocational and technical schools offer extensive tests of students' interests and aptitudes as well as vocational counseling services to help students make wise vocational choices. Many schools are open year-round and offer, in addition to the usual day classes, night classes for persons who must work during the day. Most also offer programs for adults. The graduates of these schools usually have little difficulty in finding employment.

Many schools are known as "area" vocational or technical high schools because they commonly are supported by various school districts in the county or area they serve, often under the jurisdiction of the county school or intermediate unit offices. Of course, many comprehensive high schools offer their own vocational education programs, but these are much less varied and extensive because of the great costs involved.[7]

The federal government has stimulated the development of vocational education through the Smith-Hughes Act of 1917, the National Defense Education Act of 1958, and the Vocational Education Act of 1963.

Specialized high schools. Although comprehensive high schools and general vocational-technical schools are the two basic types of secondary schools, there are quite a number of distinctive and excellent specialized schools, particularly in large cities. San Francisco's Apprenticeship and Journeyman School, New York's High School of Music and Art and its Maritime High School, Brooklyn's High School of Automotive Trades, the Interlochen Arts Academy, and Miami's Technical High School are examples of such specialized schools. Many states have instituted statewide systems of specialized trade and technical schools at the secondary level.

THREE-YEAR SENIOR HIGH SCHOOLS

While patterns vary, three-year high schools, with grades 10 to 12, are usually linked organizationally with junior high or middle schools, with grades 7 to 9. Often the size of the legal school district, the nature of the attendance units, the condition of the existing buildings, and the philosophy of the administrators and the board of education are factors affecting the type of secondary school organization. More orientation, wider experimentation, and greater latitude are possible for ninth-graders in the 6-3-3 organization, with a junior high followed by a senior high.

JUNIOR HIGH SCHOOLS AND MIDDLE SCHOOLS

Types. The most common form of junior high school organization is the three-year unit comprising grades 7 to 9 as part of a 6-3-3 system of organization. In this organization junior high school is regarded as a separate unit, with its own curriculum, schedule, and administration, though not always with its own building. However, this arrangement is being challenged increasingly by the middle school, which is composed commonly of grades 6 to 8 or 5 to 8.

Another form of organization is the 6-6 pattern, a plan in which grades 7 to 9 are combined with the upper three secondary years to form a six-year high school in a single unit. Several unified dis-

---

[7]For more information on these schools and their problems, see Thomas R. White, "The Area Vocational School: An Emerging Institution," *Phi Delta Kappan*, November 1971, pp. 189–191.

tricts operate two-year junior high schools, comprising grades 7 and 8 only, and include grade 9 in senior high school. A few school systems maintain other variations, but most of the remainder have 8-4 plans, with no junior high school. The larger the school district, the greater has been the frequency of separate junior high schools or middle schools. Most seventh- and eighth-grade students are now enrolled in some form of secondary school program. The particular pattern of the organization is of less consequence than its ability to fulfill the unique purposes proclaimed for prepubescent students.

Purposes. Junior high schools and middle schools were created to serve three distinct needs: to smooth the transition from childhood to adolescence, to ease the articulation between child-centered elementary schools and subject-centered high schools, and to permit students to explore various fields of study in preparation for later educational and vocational choices. Proponents believe that neither elementary schools nor traditional four-year high schools adequately serve the needs of early adolescents, who are significantly different from both prepubescent and late-adolescent youths. Early adolescence is a crucial period of development marked by physical, emotional, and social strains.

Programs. The junior high school curriculum continues the development of basic skills started in elementary school with emphasis on developmental and remedial reading. It emphasizes the tremendous changes taking place in the world and how adolescents can cope with these changes. It also stresses democratic values and ideals to guide students into socially acceptable and personally satisfying behavior.

Junior high school provides a variety of exploratory educational experiences in such fields as art, music, homemaking, and industrial arts, as well as in academic subjects. It helps students to elect courses more confidently in later years. It brings the more adequate guidance and other services of secondary school to bear upon problems of early adolescence. If the faculty is well prepared, it has the special understanding required to relate class instruction to students' unique needs. Unfortunately, many junior high schools are that in name only, failing to adapt their instruction, services,

and facilities to the functions they were designed to serve. Junior high schools are too often housed in cast-off senior high school buildings ill-suited to their needs. Junior high school teachers sometimes regard their positions as less prestigious than senior high school assignments. Middle schools were established in part to create a new image for this level of education without including the unfulfilled expectations commonly associated with junior high schools.

PRIVATE SECONDARY SCHOOLS

Private high schools, prep schools, academies, and other secondary educational institutions are numerous.[8] One in thirteen secondary school students is enrolled in a private school, including (1) parochial high schools, (2) independent schools, (3) private technical schools, and (4) street academies.

Parochial high schools. Parochial high schools, supported by various religious denominations, constitute by far the largest sector of private secondary schools, enrolling approximately 75 percent of the students attending nonpublic high schools. The largest number of parochial schools, more than two thousand, are supported by the Roman Catholic church. Their enrollment constitutes approximately 85 percent of students attending parochial schools. Lutheran and Jewish secondary schools are next in frequency, although they are much less numerous than Roman Catholic schools. Enrollments in Roman Catholic parochial schools began to decline in the mid-1960s, although the decline has been much less marked in secondary schools than in elementary schools. The rate of decline is now slowing down. Parochial high schools are maintained to provide greater emphasis upon spiritual growth and to propagate the faith of the church that supports them. Chapter 1 describes the educational philosophy that commonly shapes these schools. Some parochial high schools have worked out cooperative programs with public schools in which students' secular study is taken in public schools, while study in

[8]*Lovejoy's Prep School Guide,* published annually by Harper & Row, New York, lists approximately two thousand independent, private, nonpublic college preparatory schools in the United States.

sectarian subjects is offered by the parochial schools.

Independent high schools. Most of the remaining 25 percent of secondary students attend private day schools. A much smaller number attend private boarding schools. Private day schools vary widely in quality. Many of the better ones have sprung up in suburbs. Their curriculums are usually restricted to academic studies, since their function is largely college-preparatory. Many offer education of a fine quality within their limited purpose.

Within the last decade a great number of private day schools, sometimes called "segregation academies," have been thrown together hastily and inexpertly in the Southeastern states and in the Northeastern metropolitan areas as a haven for families who prefer that their children not attend desegregated school systems. Such schools often function without adequate faculties and facilities,

Nearly half of the private secondary schools are now coeducational and male and female students are increasingly comingled in many secondary schools, even in physical education classes.

although some are well supported. In 1976 the U.S. Supreme Court ruled that private, nonsectarian schools may not deny admission to blacks. But because of tuition costs the decision may have limited practical effect.[9]

The most famous independent schools are the old prestigious private boarding schools, such as Phillips, Groton, Andover, Exeter, Choate, and Lawrenceville. These are well-endowed institutions with faculties, campuses, and facilities that would rival those of many small colleges. Typical private boarding schools enroll 200 to 300 students with annual tuition fees equal to those of many private colleges. There are approximately 200 private boarding schools enrolling approximately 48,000 students. Here one can still find teen-agers reading Cicero in the original, going to bed at 10 p.m., and wearing coats and ties. Most of these schools are very old, and some date back to the seventeenth century. They are characterized by small classes, carefully chosen students, and college-preparatory curriculums, which give them the name "prep schools." Separate boarding schools formerly served either male or female students, but now nearly half of them are coeducational. Many are recruiting students from the ghettos and are subsidizing their education with scholarships. Some such as the Francis W. Parker School in Chicago, are progressive in educational philosophy, while others are conservative. Many of these schools, like small private colleges, are suffering financial strains.

Enrollment at prep schools has recently increased slightly. Some have two to three times as many applicants as can be admitted. There are several reasons for this growth. Some parents believe that teachers in prep school are more devoted to their work than are many teachers in public schools. The smaller class size in many private schools also appeals to some parents. Others fear the crime and racial disturbances that occur in some public schools. Then too, private schools are less constrained by state and federal regulations. Although not commonly admitted,

[9]For a distressing account of the rise of "segregation academies," see John C. Walden and Allen D. Cleveland, "The South's New Segregation Academies," *Phi Delta Kappan,* December, 1971, pp. 234–236, 238–239.

some parents prefer prep schools because they are more segregated with respect to race and social class.

Private technical high schools. Several thousand private vocational, technical, and special-ability schools on the secondary level teach trades to, and develop the talents of, teen-agers and adults who have not finished high school or who seek "retreading" in another trade or vocation. These secondary schools offer instruction in a wide variety of fields. The Interlochen (Michigan) Arts Academy, established in 1962, was America's first coeducational boarding school for talented arts students in grades 8 to 12. Countless cities have private schools of beauty culture, often bearing the lofty title of "college" or " university."

ALTERNATIVE SCHOOLS

Few educational developments have captured more interest recently than the remarkable proliferation of alternative schools, most of which are at the secondary level. The ideological roots of this movement had their origin in the works of Rousseau, Froebel, Pestalozzi, Montessori, Dewey, Kilpatrick, and others who spoke for the reconstruction of education in behalf of children. The unity among them was not in method or organization but in spirit and concern. A powerful prototype in this movement was the famed Summerhill school in England under the guiding genius of the late A.S. Neill.[10] During the late 1960s, a number of "free schools" were established. They tended to be short-lived, often because of their radical ideology, ambiguous structure and purpose, and "hippie" image, which did not attract a broad base of public support, especially financial support. However, 1969 was a banner year in the development of alternative schools, for the Parkway School in Philadelphia, the John Dewey High School in Brooklyn, the John Adams High School in Portland,[11] and Metro High School in Chicago—all im-

portant prototypes—opened their doors.[12] Two years earlier the California legislature passed legislation that gave legal sanction for the vast expansion of the "continuation high school" in that state. By 1972 more than 460 alternative schools were in existence, and by 1977 there were literally thousands of them in school districts across the land, with their number sometimes doubling in a single year.

Forces propelling alternative schools. What accounts for the rapid development of alternative schools? We have spoken of the inability of traditional inner-city high schools to meet the needs of the urban poor and of the high dropout rates that prevail in large city high schools. Alternative schools became the catch-all for an array of educational programs designed to return dropouts to school and to retain potential dropouts through educational experiences quite different from traditional secondary school programs. Alternative schools developed first in cities. Soon suburban and rural school districts discovered that the plan was compatible with child-centered educational doctrine and responsive to the needs of many students who were turned off by conventional school organization. Although some people regard the alternative school as the model for the reform of all secondary education, the prevailing view is that they are not appropriate for all students and should be considered only an alternative to traditional secondary schooling, not a substitute for it.

Purposes. Alternative schools are known variously as "street academies," "free schools," "continuation high schools," "learning centers," "second-chance schools," and "schools without walls."[13] There are distinctions among these types, and there is great variation among them both ideologically and operationally, which makes it difficult

---

[10]See A. S. Neill, *Summerhill: A Radical Approach to Child Rearing,* Hart Publishing, New York, 1960.

[11]A description of the John Adams High School appears in Robert B. Swartz et al., "Profile of a High School," *Phi Delta Kappan,* May 1971, pp. 513–530.

[12]For more on this important development, see Edward J. Weber, "The Dropouts Who Go to School," *Phi Delta Kappan,* May 1972, pp. 571–573; and Mary F. Crabtree, "Chicago's Metro High: Freedom, Choice, Responsibility," *Phi Delta Kappan,* May 1975, pp. 613–615.

[13]We do not include "open schools," discussed in Chapter 9, in this category because open schools are commonly new styles of classroom organization and instruction found in conventional elementary and secondary school units.

to describe them collectively. However, most of them tend to include certain common purposes:

● To encourage the return of dropouts and the retention of potential dropouts
● To provide more opportunity for students to plan and manage their own learning experiences
● To help students find new ways of learning
● To establish a proving ground for new educational ideas and practices
● To mobilize more attention upon the personal problems of students and on their affective development
● To stimulate flexible learning environments capable of meeting a wider range of learning needs and styles for many educational purposes

Whatever their names, these schools tend to have several common characteristics:

● Student enrollment is voluntary.
● Instruction is highly individualized to meet idiosyncratic learning needs, interests, and styles.
● Counseling pervades the entire educational effort, and every teacher is regarded as a counselor.
● Community resources are utilized intensively.
● A high degree of autonomy is granted.
● Wholesome relationships are emphasized between children and adults.
● The climate is flexible, informal, and relaxed.
● The concept of failure is renounced.
● Each student works at his or her own level and rate.
● Self-reliance and self-responsibility for learning are nurtured.

Obviously these schools require a special type of teacher and administrator, people who are comfortable and effective without the tighter structure of traditional schools, people who are understanding and respectful of atypical youth; people who are creative, eclectic, and flexible in their teaching styles; and people who are effective counselors.[14]

Prototypes. Let us briefly describe a few of these schools.

The Parkway School in Philadelphia functions not only without walls but also without marks, bells, authority figures, dropouts, attendance areas, and last names, and certainly without boredom. Its campus is the community, and its classrooms are the public institutions and businesses bordering the Benjamin Franklin Parkway, from which the school derives its name. Its headquarters are in an abandoned office building. Students go there for the only required part of their program, the tutorial groups, in which fifteen students and two teachers meet for two hours, four days a week. Here the students plan their outside activities, receive personal counseling, and satisfy their only two subject requirements—mathematics and English. The tutorial also helps handle the extensive written evaluations of both students' and teachers' work, which take the place of marks.

The remainder of the students' time might be spent studying zoology at the zoo; art at various museums, commercial art studios, or libraries; welding at a machine shop; automotive mechanics at a garage; law enforcement at city hall; or an array of about a hundred pursuits almost as varied as life itself. These activities are chosen according to students' interests. Many devote far more time to their work than would be required in more conventional schools. Although many students would be potential dropouts in conventional high schools, few drop out of Parkway. Except for the tutorials, attendance is voluntary; but interest is high because the emphasis upon community motivates students. Students are selected by lottery from long waiting lists, but teachers are carefully chosen because it takes special talents for such a sharp departure from conventional pedagogy. Parkway offers a four-year, full-time program satisfying state requirements, and it gives a diploma. Although student-teacher ratios are kept small to sustain close interpersonal relations, the costs per student at Parkway are the same as at other Philadelphia high schools. The major difference is that capital costs are much less because the modest facilities are leased and no large expensive school plant is needed. More than 60 percent of Parkway's graduates go to college, compared with about 40 percent for the Philadelphia school system as a whole.[15]

One of the most famous street academies is the

---

[14]For further discussion of the characteristics of faculty required for successful work in these schools, see Jonathan Kozol, "Free Schools: A Time for Candor," *Saturday Review,* Mar. 4, 1972, pp. 51–54.

[15]For more information on the Parkway School, see Donald W. Cox, *The City as Schoolhouse,* Judson Press, Valley Forge, Pa., 1972.

Harlem Preparatory School in New York, housed in an abandoned supermarket. Under the dynamic direction of its black headmaster, Edward Carpenter, Harlem Prep has been successful not only in rescuing dropouts but also in preparing many of them for successful admission to eminent colleges. Carpenter attributes Harlem Prep's success in reclaiming dropouts to the teachers' "unshakable faith that the students can make it." Sponsored originally by the New York Urban League, Manhattanville College, and private benefactors, Harlem Prep faced a financial crisis in 1973 and decided to close because of lack of funds. But —and this is some measure of its support —teachers and administrators voted to stay on the job without pay. A successful campaign persuaded the board of education to support Harlem Prep from public funds.[16]

Some of the street academies are financed by grants from private foundations, most notably the Ford Foundation and the Rockefeller Foundation. Many are "adopted" by private industries. They look upon these academies not simply as a charitable undertaking but also as a means of rehabilitating persons who may become employable in their industries. This benefaction by industry abrogates the charge that the capitalistic system is interested only in exploiting people.

As we have noted, some alternative schools are privately supported, while others are publicly supported, often as a part of the public school system. The latter arrangement appears to be taking root in many communities and is the solution to the financial problems that many private alternative schools face. It is hoped that these schools retain their vital idiosyncratic character, which contributes so much to their success, as they become integrated into public school systems.

How well are they doing? Although most alternative schools have not yet been evaluated sufficiently to justify firm conclusions, students' testimony is overwhelmingly positive. The fact that these students, who already rejected conventional schooling, are in school is important in itself. An astonishing number of them are going on to college. Perhaps the most persuasive evidence of the promise of alternative schools is the fantastic rate at which they are multiplying across the land. The National Consortium for Options in Public Education (NCOPE), as its name implies, is a national organization devoted to assisting their development.[17]

Despite their rapid growth, these "second-chance" schools are able to accommodate only a small percentage of youths who need help. It is hoped that these schools will demonstrate to the public schools that many youths who cannot make it in regimented traditional schools can nevertheless find success in schools which are willing to adapt to their needs, rather than the other way around.

OTHER TYPES OF SECONDARY SCHOOLS

While "summer school" is not a special type of school organizationally, it is a special program, covering an abbreviated period of six to eight weeks, rather than a semester or a year, and operating on a more concentrated schedule of double or multiple periods.

Various factors have stimulated the great growth of, and accelerated attendance at, summer schools for secondary school students. Many talented teen-agers use summer school work to hasten their graduation date or to accumulate extra credits. Some students take summer school classes to make up "flunks," to do remedial work, or to benefit from courses not generally available during the regular year.

The Economic Opportunity Act enables some high school juniors and seniors to attend summer sessions away from home on college and university campuses. For example, in the initial stages of project Upward Bound, some high school juniors and seniors complete two months of residence on a university campus and attend classes on the high school level. In their free time they are permitted to audit college classes. In addition to the academic programs, the students participate in recre-

[16]For a description of a quite different alternative school in the New York City school system, see "John Dewey: 'Free' School in the System," *American Teacher*, March 1972, pp. 16–17; or Sol Levine, "The John Dewey High School Adventure," *Phi Delta Kappan*, October 1971, pp. 108–110.

[17]For further discussion of alternative schools, see Mario D. Fantini, *Public Schools of Choice*, Simon & Schuster, New York, 1974; Jonathan Kozol, *Free Schools*, Houghton Mifflin, Boston, 1972; or Vernon H. Smith et al., "Alternative Schools: Analysis, Criticism, and Observations," *Phi Delta Kappan*, March 1973, pp. 434–476.

Upward Bound programs have been successful in helping more high school students find their way into higher education.

ational and musical activities. To broaden their fields of knowledge, they tour industries, cultural centers, and governmental offices in the college area. Counseling services continue after the close of the summer session.

Upward Bound programs have been remarkably successful. Their participants have been admitted to college at a higher rate (80 percent, compared with 65 percent of all high school graduates) and have attained approximately the same grade averages and retention in college as their peers. However, Upward Bound programs are still too few to accommodate more than a small fraction of students with potential who should be helped.

Practices in secondary education

Several characteristics of modern secondary education are presented here through brief descriptions of current practices in (1) organization and administration and (2) curriculum and instruction.

ORGANIZATION AND ADMINISTRATION

Generally, but with increasing exceptions, high schools are subject-centered, departmentalized, and graded. Recently there has been a trend toward longer school days and longer school years. As a result of the general increase in population and the reorganization of school districts, there has been a trend toward larger high schools.

One interesting innovation in secondary school organization has been the rise of the "school within a school" concept. This idea is manifested architecturally in the campus-style secondary school plant. A number of partially self-contained units, each housing a few hundred students, exist as satellites near but apart from a central service unit, which includes such common facilities as administrative offices, auditorium, cafeteria, library, and gymnasium. Also called the "little school" or "house plan," it is designed to recapture the intimacy and individual attention of small schools while retaining the greater efficiency and more extensive facilities of large schools.

Modern secondary schools are becoming larger. The urbanization of our society has resulted in higher densities of population in metropolitan areas and larger numbers of students in school attendance areas. The reorganization of school districts has resulted in the merger of many smaller school systems with small high schools into a single school district with a few large high schools. High schools with enrollments in excess of one thousand are common, and in metropolitan areas, high schools with student bodies in excess of two thousand are not uncommon. Although large size is no guarantee of quality, large high schools do permit broader educational programs and service at more reasonable costs per student.

The integrated, comprehensive secondary school—including a broad spectrum of vocational-technical-occupational programs—is envisioned in the concept of the "secondary education park."

Discussed in Chapter 10, the education park is designed to synthesize racial integration of schools and excellence in education. It is a large attendance unit with a broad spectrum of fine educational offerings that attract students from all races and all sectors of the school district.

In secondary schools, as in all education, pressure for accountability demands that evaluation receive rigorous attention. State-mandated accountability systems are generating more rigorous data germane to educational goals. Local districts frequently supplement state efforts with evaluation systems of their own, particularized not only for that district but commonly for individual high schools. These data are analyzed to derive insights into how to facilitate accomplishment of specific objectives. The National Study of School Evaluation has been engaged for many years in evaluating secondary schools through its regional affiliates. This body has developed standards for secondary schools which are used by local faculties to evaluate their schools. This is followed by evaluation by a visiting team of experts who cite the school's strengths and weaknesses with recommendations for improvement. The reports of these visiting teams of evaluators form the basis for accreditation of secondary schools.

CURRICULUM AND INSTRUCTION

Although the school curriculum is discussed at length in Chapter 9, we call attention here to some developments that are noteworthy and particular to secondary schools. Continuing explosions of knowledge and radical revolutions in technology are producing many changes in the curriculum and in the methods and materials of instruction in secondary schools.

New courses. The curriculum of comprehensive high schools is being broadened to include many new courses and much more substance. Among the newer course offerings are environmental education, education about drug abuse, sex education, world culture, international relations, economics, sociology, psychology, philosophy, education, electronics, computer training, astronomy, space science, earth science, public issues or problems, the Bible as literature, religious literature, and many languages rather new to high school curriculums, such as Italian, Japanese, Chinese, and Russian. International cleavages and competition have resulted in greater emphasis on the study of the values, ideals, and accomplishments of representative governments, often in comparison with other political and economic systems, notably communism.

Minicourses. The chairperson of the National Panel on High Schools and Adolescent Education has hailed "minicourses" and semester courses as "the single most promising and effective development in the history of secondary education." Although we think the claim is greatly exaggerated, nevertheless the movement is noteworthy. It is estimated that between 60 and 75 percent of the nation's high schools are now offering minicourses (usually six to nine weeks long) and semester courses (usually fifteen weeks long). This development is most evident in the fields of English, social studies, and science. These courses derive their value in permitting students a greater array of electives to choose from, thereby allowing more flexibility in programs of study as well as an opportunity to gain insight into a subject without being committed to its exploration in depth.

Career education. Former U.S. Commissioner of Education Sidney P. Marland expressed grave concern about the $2\frac{1}{2}$ million young people leaving formal education without a marketable skill or career goal. He believes that every student who leaves high school should be prepared either for entry into college or entry into the job market with marketable skills. Marland sees career education as an effort to inform students from elementary school through graduate school about the world of work and their opportunities in the labor force, to help them make the right career choices, and to develop their occupational skills.[18] This concept is discussed at greater length in Chapter 9. Here we shall describe and illustrate its applications to secondary schools.

The Chrysler Corporation, for example, "adopted" Detroit's predominantly black North-

---

[18]For an account of Marland's views, see "Marland on Career Education," *American Education,* November 1971, pp. 25–28.

western High School and renovated a wing to house a well-equipped training facility for auto mechanics, a placement office complete with testing and interviewing for jobs, and office and data-processing equipment. Some high schools are providing internship experiences for students who understudy newspaper reporters, commercial artists, city government officials, and a host of other occupations.

Combined work-study programs are not new, but they are taking on increased significance in career education. These programs combine academic and occupational studies within the school with salaried, part-time, supervised, on-the-job experience. These programs blend "hands on" job experience for those students who are eager to be employed with the academic and vocational skills they need to enter and remain in the work world. Both components, when skillfully blended, reinforce each other. By providing supplemental income, they tend to reduce dropouts. They also tend to reduce the discomfort which many youths feel because of the extension of forced dependency beyond the stage when they are ready for transition to earning their own living. According to a study by the U.S. Office of Education, these programs are as popular with employers as they are with youths.

The new Skyline High School in Dallas is a good illustration of the application of career education. This $21 million high school on an enormous

This class in aeronautics at Skyline High School in Dallas, Texas, is a good illustration of career education.

80-acre site is really three high schools in one. First, it is a comprehensive general-purpose high school for students who live in its attendance area. Second, it contains the Career Development Center, where students from other Dallas high schools come for three hours per day to work in one of its twenty-eight career clusters. Finally, it contains the Center for Community Service, where 3,000 night-school students—adults and dropouts—can take trade and apprenticeship courses as well as academic courses toward a high school diploma. But it is the Career Development Center that makes it different from most high schools. Here students may work in the school's own greenhouse or airplane hangar or actually construct houses all the way from drawing blueprints through doing carpentry, plumbing, wiring, air-conditioning, and landscaping to designing advertisements and brochures for the final sale. Students may also study in a wide variety of other occupations, many of which are planned and instructed cooperatively with local businesses. Skyline is a "magnet" school that attracts able students from all over the city and blends academic work with career education in a way that denies the second-class status commonly associated with vocational education.

Action-learning programs. We have spoken of the prolonged and artificial isolation of youths from the mainstream of society while in the custodial care of high schools. High school students often complain about the schools' lack of relevance. Probably youths would find anything irrelevant that interfered with their yearning for a more direct role in the real world outside school. "Action learning" is a concept of education that bridges the gap between schooling and society, but its method and purpose are somewhat different from those of work-study programs. Action learning satisfies youths' longing for significant group action in the real world—not for job training alone, but for development of self and for community service to others. It provides learning through real work in various community agencies: elementary schools, business offices, television studios, churches, homes for the elderly, mental health agencies, labor unions, retail outlets, animal hospitals, nursing homes, museums, and many others. The workers are usually paid but sometimes volunteer; their work fills genuine needs, provides challenges, offers reality-centered learning by doing, relates theory to practice, bridges the generation gap, and suggests possible careers. Action learning may or may not carry academic credit and may or may not be required for graduation, depending upon the policy of the school. Most schools with action-learning programs do allow credit for it but do not require it for graduation. Many action-learning programs use lay advisers in the various fields and utilize community advisory committees in planning and monitoring the programs. The National Association of Secondary School Principals, which advocates action-learning programs, suggests a number of projects to illustrate this innovation in secondary education in its publication *25 Action Learning Schools.*[19]

All three agencies that have studied secondary education and youths—the Panel on Youth of the President's Science Advisory Commission, the National Commission on the Reform of Secondary Education, and the National Panel on High Schools and Adolescent Education—favor the inclusion of action-learning experiences in secondary school programs.

Global education. The National Commission on the Reform of Secondary Education calls attention to the need for "basic international literacy" among our people. This need is quickened by the growing interdependence among nations, the shrinkage of our world into a "global village" by mass communication and fast transportation, the sense of humanity that should pervade us all, and the international cooperation essential to our survival. The commission recommended that global education must produce "an enhanced sense of the globe as the human environment, and instruction to this end must reflect not only the ancient characteristics of the world, but emerging knowledge of biological and social unity. All secondary students should receive a basic global education." The implications of global education upon school curriculums are explored at length in Chapters 9 and 15.

Advanced-placement courses. This country's growing concern for the maximum intellectual development of its gifted students prompted many innovations such as the downward extension of advanced subject matter in thirteen fields of college-level study, the enrichment of content, and the offering of advanced-placement courses. The latter, particularly, has been a remarkable and significant change in secondary schools. Under this plan, begun in 1956 by the College Entrance Examination Board, college-level courses are being offered to more than 70,000 bright high school students annually who, upon successful completion of examinations, receive advanced standing or actual college credit. Students from 3,500 high schools take the courses annually for credit in approximately a thousand cooperating colleges and universities. Some high school students are able to enter college as sophomores, saving perhaps $5,000 each in one less year of college study.

Students in secondary schools

Chapter 3 deals entirely with learners in our schools. At this point we shall merely call attention briefly to some aspects of student life in high schools. Following the intense student discontent and unrest of the 1960s, high school students are enjoying a period of relative tranquility, except for a minority of vandals and delinquents and their victims mentioned earlier in this chapter. A survey of a national sample of 2,000 high school students revealed that most praise their high school education and regard student-teacher interaction as good.[20]

There are sound explanations for this more positive mood among the majority of high school students. The recognition, explication, and protection of students' rights and responsibilities have done much to make high schools more humane. The Commission on the Reform of Secondary Education makes this recommendation:

Every high school should develop and adopt a code of student rights and obligations. This code should be published and distributed to every student. It should include all school rules, regulations, and procedures for

[19]National Association of Secondary Principals, *25 Action Learning Schools,* Reston, Va., 1974, pp. 3–4.

[20]National Association of Secondary School Principals, *The Mood of American Youth,* Reston, Va., 1974, pp. 12, 16.

suspension and expulsion with explanations of how students can defend themselves through established process.[21]

Student government is being reformed to respond more effectively and more powerfully to students' expectations. Students are being given more freedom in determining their programs of studies and the content of their courses. In many schools letter grades, hall passes, dress codes, censorship of student newspapers and assembly programs, searches of lockers, and other constraints and indignities are being eliminated. Grievance procedures and other equitable means for resolving disputes are being established. Ombudsmen are appearing in some schools to help students cut through red tape and misunderstanding. School administrators and teachers are struggling to create an open climate in which behavior can become more authentic and satisfying. And, as noted earlier, significant innovations in curriculum and instruction are making learning more germane to the outside community.

An interesting recent development has been the growth in the number of high school students who seek early graduation from high school, commonly after seven semesters of study. More than half the public high schools provide for early graduation through such means as summer schools, permission for talented students to carry extra courses, more extensive electives, work-study programs for credit, and credit for other types of educational experience outside the formal curriculum. The three reasons students give most frequently for seeking early graduation are the desire to begin college sooner, being bored with school, and the desire to get a job sooner. We think this trend will continue.

The future

In closing each chapter with a section about the future, it is sometimes difficult to distinguish between what the future is likely to be and what we wish it to be. Happily, the two are much the same for this chapter. We see many forces propelling secondary education into a rather easily perceived future. Consider society's commitment to equal opportunity to secondary education for all, regardless of sex, race, mental ability, learning handicaps, or socioeconomic status. Consider also the high schools' inability to provide satisfying and meaningful educational experiences for youths who drop out, either in actuality or in spirit. Much disenchantment among these dropouts, along with many who remain in school, results from their resentment of any institution that treats them too long like children or that keeps them from plunging into more adult life and labor. Compulsory education is illusory to a large degree—as many as half the young people of high school age in inner cities are not in school anyway, because of perennial truancy. These disenchanted students are responsible for most of the vandalism, violence, and crime in our schools. They fail because they see little relevance between what goes on in traditional schooling and the reality of the outside world, which they yearn to enter. We can no longer write them off and hope that they will find unskilled labor on the farms or in the factories. Without help they will become unemployable and become an unbearable burden on our welfare system or, worse yet, our penal or other custodial institutions. With welfare costs exceeding school costs in many cities, we can no longer afford the high costs of undereducation.

We think that one is forced to the conclusion that bold departures from conventional secondary schooling must be found. Unconventional alternatives—street academies, action-learning programs, work-study programs, schools without walls, and alternative schools of all types appear to be popular and effective with these young people. These alternatives are expanding rapidly.

Three blue-ribbon national commissions[22] studied youth and secondary education recently and reached these common findings:

[21]National Commission on the Reform of Secondary Education, *The Reform of Secondary Education*, McGraw-Hill, New York, 1973, p. 19.

[22]*Youth: Transition to Adulthood*, Report of the Panel on Youth of the President's Science Advisory Commission, University of Chicago Press, Chicago, 1973; National Commission on the Reform of Secondary Education, op. cit.; and *National Panel on High Schools and Adolescent Education*, U.S. Office of Education, Washington, 1974. For an excellent summary of these and other recent studies, see A. Harry Passow, "Reforming America's High Schools," *Phi Delta Kappan*, May 1975, pp. 587–590.

- Comprehensive high schools are not the sole source of an education; out-of-school learning is also highly significant.
- Greater recognition is needed for community-based learning activities.
- Students are too isolated from other age groups.
- Greater use of community resources should be made.
- The custodial and protective role of the schools is excessive; it inhibits students' responsibility and maturation.
- Keeping young people in school up to an arbitrary age apparently inhibits reforms.
- School structures, including excessive size, restrict the opportunity for reform.
- More diverse course offerings are needed.
- High schools are overburdened with ever-increasing demands from society.
- Youths are maturing physiologically and are being granted their legal majority at an earlier age today, a factor that few schools have sufficiently recognized.

Thus the rapid development of alternatives to compulsory attendance at traditional comprehensive high schools is inevitable. Although many variations will evolve at greatly different rates of diffusion across the land, the general shape of secondary education in the future is becoming more discernible. Harold Shane, an educator who has given serious attention to applying the science of futurism to education, speaks of future education as "lifelong learning" in a "seamless continuum." This "seamless continuum" would consist of the traditional curriculum (modified to accommodate improved educational technologies, more sophisticated programmed materials, and differentiated staffing) and the paracurriculum—"that body of out-of-school experiences that help to strengthen the intellectual ability, general background, and coping powers of the child or youth."[23] The secondary school of the future would make use of the paracurriculum. Students, as early as age 15, would engage in work experiences in the community arranged by the school. This paracurriculum would eliminate "pushouts," since one does not drop out of an educational continuum but rather moves without stigma into the paracurriculum with

"methodically planned lifelong exit and reentry privileges carefully coordinated through enlightened guidance practices." By abandoning graded structure and by making age ranges within the school more flexible and ephemeral, exit and reentry would become inconspicuous. The paracurriculum concept would extend throughout a learner's lifetime. It will help to accelerate the trend toward early graduation from high school.

This configuration is made up of components already familiar to the educational scene, such as "continuing education," "socially useful work," "action learning," and "paid internships." As Shane points out, with this seamless, lifelong, year-around educational continuum, we would not need alternatives to schools—just more imaginative alternatives within established educational programs.[24]

The Shane model suggests a proliferation of learning options that might serve not only students who drop out and reenter but also any learners who might find it desirable to move laterally throughout their lifetimes between the curriculum and the paracurriculum. Some students would still move directly through comprehensive high schools, but many students, perhaps most, would opt for "comprehensive education" rather than for comprehensive high schools. Supervised work-study programs, action-learning programs, external degree programs, internships, and alternative educational experiences would be further proliferated and available to regular students as well as educational reentrants. High schools would become more like colleges with open campuses, and students would be free to move at their own pace through substance of their own choice. The issue of compulsory attendance, at least beyond age 14, will become moot, and the regimen of secondary schools will become less essential and less rigorous. The concepts of failure and dropping out would become meaningless. Achievement would be measured in terms of mastery rather than by arbitrary grading. Time, space, and learning rate —rather than achievement against normative standards—would become the important vari-

---

[23]The paraphrasing in this paragraph and the next and the quotations included in them are taken from Harold G. Shane, *The Educational Significance of the Future*, Phi Delta Kappa, Bloomington, Ind. 1973, pp. 71–76.

[24]For a practical application of these concepts, see Stephen K. Bailey, Francis U. Macy, and Donn F. Vickers, *Alternative Paths to the High School Diploma*, National Association of Secondary School Principals, Reston, Va., 1973.

ables. Progress would be reported more descriptively than numerically. The adjective "open" would come to describe most aspects of education for youths: open education, open admissions, open space, open options, open exit and open reentry, open campus, open minds, and so on. Distinctions between academic and vocational education, between work and study—indeed, between school and community—will become obscure and meaningless as they all blend into Shane's seamless educational continuum.[25]

We will need creative, imaginative, and adaptable teachers and administrators. One of the greatest problems may be the constraints placed upon the organization and management of schools through collective bargaining between boards and teachers. Negotiated agreements are not distinguished by their toleration of flexibility in conditions of employment and other educational arrangements. But if we can overcome this problem, teaching should be more enjoyable and satisfying (albeit more difficult in many ways) for several reasons, not the least of which will be the absence of young people who don't want to be in school. If Coleman is right in his conclusion that students' success in learning is largely a function of their sense of control over learning experiences, then their education in the future should be successful.

As the nation enters its third century, the American dream of education for all youths will become no longer a stereotyped and somewhat unfulfilled legal mandate but rather an open, meaningful, and self-fulfilling opportunity for each young person according to his or her abilities and needs.

Suggested activities

1. Prepare a summary of the major findings and recommendations of one recent study listed in the bibliography.
2. Visit an independent school, parochial school, street academy, or "school without walls," if there is one near your campus, and evaluate its program in terms of the needs of its students and the applicability of its program for more conventional public high schools.
3. Compare the services of a small high school with those of a large, comprehensive school.
4. Examine the certification requirements for teachers of secondary schools in your state.
5. List the special qualifications and preparation you think secondary school teachers should have.
6. Interview a high school principal about the most significant changes in secondary education in the past decade.
7. Suggest how secondary schools can better prepare students for the institutions of higher learning, which are described in the next chapter.
8. Describe, preferably after a visit, the programs of a modern vocational-technical secondary school.
9. Prepare a list of characteristics that should distinguish a good middle school from a good junior high school.
10. Prepare a report on the Kalamazoo High School case, showing the effects of this court decision on the growth of high schools.

Bibliography

Bhaerman, Steve, and **Joel Denker:** *No Particular Place To Go,* Simon & Schuster, New York, 1972. Story of how the authors helped a group of middle-class students create a free high school and the successes and problems encountered.

Campbell, Roald F., Luverne L. Cunningham, Raphael O. Nystrand, and **Michael D. Usdan:** *The Organization and Control of American Schools,* 3d ed., Charles E. Merrill, Columbus, Ohio, 1975, chapter 18. History of, types of, characteristics of, and future of alternative schools.

Clark, Leonard H., and **Irving S. Carr:** *Secondary School Teaching Methods,* Macmillan, Riverside, N.J., 1976. Textbook treatment of modern instructional methods in secondary schools.

Coleman, James S.: *Youth: Transition to Adulthood,* University of Chicago Press, Chicago, 1974. Famous report by the Panel on Youth of the President's Science Advisory Committee dealing with the relationship between schooling and transition into adulthood.

Gross, Ronald, and **Paul Osterman** (eds.): *High School,* Simon & Schuster, New York, 1971. Collection of essays by radical reformers on what high schools are like and how they should be reformed.

Gruhn, William T., and **Harl R. Douglass:** *The Modern Junior High School,* Ronald, New York, 1972. Textbook approach to the function, program, organization, and

---

[25]For an interesting futuristic prototype of these reforms, see George Neil, "The Reform of Intermediate and Secondary Education in California," *Phi Delta Kappan,* February 1976, pp. 391–394.

trends in junior high schools.

National Association of Secondary School Principals: *American Youth in the Mid-Seventies,* Reston, Va., 1972. Report of a conference analyzing the nature of adolescents, their problems, needs, and attitudes toward education and life.

————: *The 80s: Where Will the Schools Be?* Reston, Va., 1974. Forecast of the nature of secondary education in the decade ahead.

————: *The Mood of American Youth,* Reston, Va., 1974. Report of a national survey of high school students' attitudes toward self, school, and society.

————: *Secondary Schools in a Changing Society: This We Believe,* Reston, Va., 1975. Report of a task force of high school principals with recommendations for improving secondary schools; primary focus is on the curriculum.

————: *Secondary Schools in a Changing Society,* Reston, Va., 1975. Secondary school principals' views on how secondary schools must adapt to changes in youth, society, and the economy in the years ahead.

————: *25 Action Learning Schools,* Reston, Va., 1974. Case descriptions of twenty-five secondary schools' action-learning programs.

National Task Force for High School Reform: *The Adolescents, Other Citizens, and Their High Schools,* McGraw-Hill, New York, 1975. Recommendations for reform of high schools emphasizing increased citizens' involvement, better programs of citizenship education, and alternative schools.

Romano, Louis G., Nicholas P. Georgiady, and **James E. Heald** (eds.): *The Middle School,* Nelson Hall, Chicago, 1973. Collection of readings on the needs of middle school students with generalizations about what middle schools should be.

Trump, J. Lloyd, and **Delma F. Miller:** *Secondary School Curriculum Improvement,* 2d ed., Allyn and Bacon, Boston, 1974. Textbook approach to the nature of secondary school curriculum and recommendations for its improvement.

Weinstock, Ruth: *The Greening of the High School,* Educational Facilities Laboratories, New York, 1973. Discusses needed improvements in secondary schools with particular emphasis upon facilities.

Chapter 7

Higher education

The evolution of higher education

The American university is unique because it is not government, business, social organization, welfare agency, or political party. Its purpose is not to rule; not to make a profit; not to please students or faculty or alumni; not to reform society; not to correct social injustice; not to influence political action. Although it may contribute at times to these ends, it could be destroyed by serving these ends.

Nor is a university a "community of scholars," although it is frequently described as such. All but the smaller institutions of higher education are far too fragmented and diverse to sustain any sense of community.

What then is a university? The university is a citadel of knowledge, which it creates, disseminates, and applies. This singular function of the university is threatened when intruded upon by any other function. To understand our institutions of higher education requires some historical perspective, which is sketched briefly here and summarized in the historical calendar.

Although it brought some of its early characteristics from abroad, the American university is distinctly indigenous to this country, reflecting the democracy, diversity, and dynamics of its people. The European university today differs markedly from the American in that European higher learning is characterized by more restricted admission of students, less highly organized student life, more specialized study, and less complex organization and administration.

EARLY AMERICAN COLLEGES

During the colonial period, nine colleges were founded in the United States. Harvard was the first in 1636. In connection with the last arose the histor-

The Development of Higher Education

1636	Harvard, first permanent university, founded		1918	American Council on Education formed, accenting higher education
1795	First state university opened in North Carolina		1947	Reports issued by the President's Commission on Higher Education
1803	First federal land granted for state "seminary of learning" in Ohio		1950	Federal loans for constructing college housing included in the Housing Act
1819	Dartmouth College decision rendered by the U.S. Supreme Court		1958	Report made by President's Committee on Education beyond High School
1836	Charter granted to Georgia Female College (Wesleyan College at Macon)		1963	Federal grants and loans authorized by the Higher Education Facilities Act
1837	Coeducation started at Oberlin College, founded in 1833		1965	Higher Education Act passed by Congress
1839	First state normal school organized in Massachusetts		1966	Funds to help meet the expenses of higher education for war veterans provided by permanent GI Bill
1854	First prototype of Negro university established at Lincoln, Pennsylvania		1968	First urban-oriented land-grant college, Federal City College, opened in District of Columbia
1862	Land-grant College Act passed by Congress		1972	Higher Education Act passed, increasing federal support for higher education
1876	First graduate work begun at Johns Hopkins University		1972	Education Amendments Act sought to provide federal financial assistance for all needy postsecondary students
1895	National Association of State Universities started		1974	Carnegie Commission's highly influential reports on higher education summarized in The Carnegie Commission on Higher Education
1900	Association of American Universities organized		1976	Target date set by Carnegie Commission on Higher Education for removal of all financial barriers to attending college
1902	First public junior college established at Joliet, Illinois		1978	Costs of higher education doubled in last two decades; many colleges in severe financial difficulty
1911	Division of Higher Education formed in the U.S. Office of Education			
1915	American Association of University Professors organized			

ic Dartmouth College case. This decision of the U.S. Supreme Court threw protection around higher education and stimulated the growth of colleges. All nine colonial colleges, with the exception of Benjamin Franklin's academy, were sectarian. By 1800 there were twenty-five colleges in the United States, but their enrollments were small. Most were supported financially by grants of land or money from legislatures, by donations of money or kind, and by miscellaneous means, such as lotteries. The small liberal arts college is indigenously American, designed originally for the education of a small socially and economically elite class.

State support was slow to develop. As late as 1860, only 17 of 264 institutions of higher learning were financed by the state.

THE DEMOCRATIZATION OF HIGHER EDUCATION

In 1862, during the darkest hours of the Civil War, President Lincoln signed the Morrill Act. This act made possible the development of a vast system of low-cost higher education that included ultimately sixty-nine institutions—many of them America's most distinguished universities. The act stimulated the democratization of higher education by opening its doors to many students of modest means, an undertaking never before attempted by any other people.

By the latter part of the nineteenth century, the great universities, as assemblies of colleges, began to emerge. The development of coeducation, pioneered in this country, marked a radical break from academic tradition. Coeducation on the college level began in 1837, when four women were admitted to Oberlin College. Wesleyan College at Macon, Georgia, claims to be the oldest chartered college for women, established as the Georgia Female College in 1836. But it was the Midwestern state universities—Iowa, Wisconsin, Michigan, and others—that threw their doors open widest to women. They needed students and lacked the conservatism of the private universities along the Eastern seaboard. Columbia, Harvard, Brown, and others refused to adopt coeducation and instead created affiliated women's colleges—Radcliffe, Barnard, Pembroke. Meanwhile, separate women's colleges (Mount Holyoke, Vassar, Smith, Wellesley, and Bryn Mawr) were opened.

THE BEGINNING OF NEGRO COLLEGES

Slowly the doors of higher education were opened to blacks, but not very wide. The first forerunner of a Negro university was established at Lincoln, Pennsylvania, in 1854, as an institute that later became Lincoln University. Shaw University, the first school of higher education for blacks, was opened in 1865. Many more Negro colleges were established in the Southern states following the emancipation of slaves. But with few exceptions, these colleges were severely handicapped, as they still are today, by meager resources. The story of their survival is often the legend of a determined band of persons, mostly blacks, who saw education as the prime means of escaping poverty and ignorance. Mary McLeod Bethune, for example, rose from picking cotton to become the founder of Bethune-Cookman College. This college arose from old crates, boxes, and odd rooms of old houses near Daytona's city dump. The rise of Tuskegee Institute is in large measure the story of its energetic administrator, Booker T. Washington. He insisted that the education of blacks, by increasing their purchasing power and social responsibility, would benefit all people.

THE RAPID EXPANSION OF HIGHER EDUCATION

One of the most powerful democratizing influences in American higher education in recent years has been the rise of junior colleges. Products of the twentieth century and indigenous to this country, their truly amazing growth constitutes one of the most significant developments on the twentieth-century educational scene. Since the first junior college was founded in Joliet, Illinois, in 1902, they have been established in all fifty states. Between 1890 and 1925 enrollment in institutions of higher education grew from four to seven times as fast as the population of the nation. But the greatest growth in higher education took place in the quarter-century following World War II. The GI Bill of 1944 and subsequent additions to it permitted millions of veterans to attend high school and college. This virtual tidal wave of students strained college facilities seriously, but fortunately it stretched the capacity of colleges and universities. It helped them accommodate more easily a second tidal wave of students two decades later—the

MILLIONS

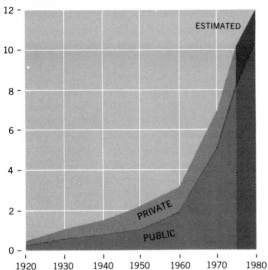

Figure 7-1 Enrollment in public and private colleges and universities. (1920–1970, U.S. Department of Commerce, *Statistical Abstract of the United States;* 1971–1975, U.S. Office of Education, *Projections of Educational Statistics;* and estimates by authors.)

Figure 7-2 College enrollments as a percentage of population 18 to 21 years of age.

PERCENT

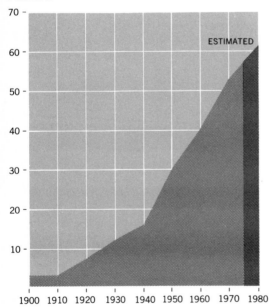

new generation of postwar students, many of them the children of veterans. Between these two tidal waves, the colleges survived a slump in enrollments and income. As shown in Figure 7-1, college enrollments have grown enormously since the close of the war. Moreover, as shown in Figure 7-2, a growing proportion of youths are going to college.

College was finally becoming a major force in upward social and economic mobility. Egalitarianism was replacing elitism as the hallmark of many colleges and universities. As noted later, curriculums, governance, student life, admission standards, and many other aspects of college life would never be the same again.

Largely because of their lower tuition, public institutions carried the major burden of expanding student enrollments. In California, for example, enrollment at private colleges rose by only two thousand students between 1948 and 1958, while enrollment in public institutions of higher education rose by fifty thousand.

HIGHER EDUCATION AND SOCIAL UNREST

The image of college as an ivory tower sanctuary of study and thought, isolated from the action of the marketplace, was shattered in the 1960s. Student activism exploded on campuses across the country. The violence of student protest had made a shambles of some campuses and sent many college presidents into premature retirement or into other careers. In 1969 the cost of campus riot damages reached $9 million, and insurance premiums became almost prohibitive for urban schools. By the early 1970s there was some hope that the wave of violent student activism on the college campuses had crested. Students learned that riotous actions, although effective at the moment, were self-defeating because they endangered the same individual freedoms they had sought to protect. Public opinion too had begun to harden against student violence.

NEW ISSUES EMERGE

By the 1970s new dilemmas began to emerge in higher education. The era of expansion was slowing, and the massive ingestion of public funds was ending with it, plunging many institutions into a state of depression. The antiegalitarianism of the Nixon administration and the deterioration of the nation's economy helped to quicken the financial malaise. Jobs for college graduates became scarcer, and the rate of return on investment in college education dropped off. The junior and community colleges were still growing and becoming the prime means of access to universal higher education. But the proportion of students in private institutions was declining rapidly, and the future of these private schools became uncertain. They were being eclipsed as higher education became more and more an enterprise of the state.

The crises in confidence, identity and role, and finance have been noted. Berman calls attention to the decline of discourse, objectivity, and freedom on campuses; the politicization of faculties; the decline of debate on campus; the hostility between colleges and legislatures; the loss of confidence in liberal education; the decline in academic rigor; and the condition of minority groups in higher education as critical contemporary problems. Most of these problems are discussed later in this chapter.[1] Certainly higher education is facing difficult new challenges—challenges that should be analyzed in terms of the purposes of higher education, which we will consider now.

Purposes of higher education

The various purposes of higher education are commonly classified into three major categories: instruction, research, and service. These might be spoken of as the dissemination, creation, and application of knowledge. The first two were inherited from European antecedents; the last is distinctly American. Much controversy about higher education is generated over conflict regarding the emphasis that should be given to each of these purposes in view of limited resources and latent conflicts of interest.

Some would argue that purposes and goals have never had much bearing on what happens on

campus and probably never will. However, the press for accountability in education is now forcing a new linkage between (1) mission, purposes, and goals and (2) policies, programs, budgets, and criteria for evaluation. Indeed many colleges that now face bankruptcy may have brought it on themselves because they were ambiguous about their priorities and uninterested in relating their resources to their purposes.

INSTRUCTION

The central and most evident purpose of higher education is the instruction of students. Institutions of higher learning have a long-standing allegiance to the task of enriching and passing along from one generation to another that liberal and humane learning which is humanity's finest heritage for the young. Universities have traditionally been regarded as both the generators and the repositories of knowledge. Although many other media of communication also serve to transmit the cultural heritage, colleges and universities have been the fountainhead of what George Peabody referred to as a "debt due from the present to future generations."

Sterling McMurrin, former U.S. Commissioner of Education and now a dean at the University of Utah, contends that the purpose of instruction has to do first with knowledge and reason and secondarily with sentiment and action. He sees instruction as being related to three subpurposes:

- Satisfaction of the intellectual interests of individuals
- Criticism and perpetuation of social institutions
- Renewal and strengthening of the culture[2]

RESEARCH AND OTHER SCHOLARLY WORK

Research is performed in industry, institutes, governmental agencies, and colleges and universities. In this country we place primary reliance upon institutions of higher education for the discovery of new knowledge—"pure research," as it is commonly called. Much of the most valuable research, although often unrelated at the time to practical

[1]Ronald Berman, "An Unquiet on Campus," *New York Times* magazine, Feb. 10, 1974, pp. 14, 17–26.

[2]Sterling M. McMurrin, "Purposes and Problems of Higher Education," *American Association of University Professors Bulletin*, Spring 1974, pp. 5–7.

Many great discoveries have emerged from university research, such as these archeological diggings into remains of early Indian habitations in western Pennsylvania.

application, is dependent upon the academic environment. The contribution of this university-based research and other scholarly work to our economy, security, and quality of life is incalculable. It is truly one of the great values returned from our tax dollars. Many great discoveries have emerged from university research laboratories. Dr. Selman Waksman won the Nobel Prize for his discovery of streptomycin and other antibotics after thirty years of research at Rutgers. Dr. Jonas Salk's discovery of a vaccine against polio at the University of Pittsburgh was a monumental advance in medical science. Professor Anne Sexton of Colgate University won the Pulitzer Prize for the book of verse *Live or Die*. Professor Richard Hofstadter of Columbia University won the Pulitzer Prize for the best book of nonfiction, *Anti-intellec-*

tualism in American Life. The list of distinguished research and scholarly work by college and university personnel goes on and on.

Another unique function of academic research, often unappreciated, is to generate detached, disinterested criticism of society under the protection of academic freedom. Institutions of higher education can perform this critical function only when they are free from partisan activities and positions, a circumstance that is vital to academic freedom. In modern pluralistic societies, the pressures on universities are so intense that their neutrality on great social and moral issues is seldom absolute. But if they deliberately and consciously stray from neutrality, they are in danger of forfeiting the protection that society affords them. This fundamental truth is often missed by professors, students, administrators, and legislators who are sometimes intent upon politicizing colleges and universities.

SERVICE

Perhaps the greatest controversy rages over the place of the service function in the university. This function is largely absent from most universities abroad. The public-service function probably had its greatest impetus in this country in the land-grant colleges. With their strong emphasis upon the improvement of agriculture and the mechanical arts, they set a contagious precedent of important but not necessarily scholarly public service. Most universities today find themselves engaged in a wide array of nonscholarly public services.

Robert Hutchins, former president of the University of Chicago and president of the Center for the Study of Democratic Institutions, notes that "in no other country in the world is the university the cannibal that it is in the United States." He points out that whatever the society wants, the university will do, provided it gets the money to pay for it. Hutchins believes that the greatest service the university can render, the one the nation needs most, the one that cannot be rendered by a service station, the one that only the university can provide, is intellectual leadership. While the university should be fashioning the mind of the age, the demands of the age are instead fashioning the mind, according to Hutchins. The fine line between appropriate and inappropriate public service is difficult to draw to the satisfaction of all. The decision is complicated when generous grants are available from government and industry, when great social issues are at stake, and when the destinies of the university and the society are so closely intertwined.

OTHER PURPOSES

An annual report of the Carnegie Corporation identifies these ancillary purposes of colleges and universities:

- To provide a "logistical base for a pool of specialized talent" of scholars available as moonlighting consultants to industry and government
- To become a kind of "academic aging vat" for youths during their transition from adolescence to adulthood
- To provide educational opportunity for adults
- To become a "purveyor of commercialized entertain-

ment," primarily through interscholastic athletic teams.[3]

Types of higher education

The range of higher education is served by a diverse array of institutions, much more diverse in the United States than in other countries. This diversity—the result of the freedom of higher education, its restlessness, its competition, its geography, and its tradition—is the genesis of much of the strength of American colleges and universities. Some observers believe that the diversity is gradually disappearing. Although many institutions of higher education defy classification because of their multiple nature, the more common types will be described.

COMMUNITY AND JUNIOR COLLEGES

The rapid rise of community colleges, junior colleges, and vocational and technical schools has been one of the most striking developments on the educational scene. Growing more rapidly than any other sector of higher education, enrollment in these institutions approximately tripled between 1960 and 1976. Beginning in 1969 more freshmen entered two-year colleges than four-year colleges and universities. Numbering about 1,250, these community and junior colleges now enroll approximately one-third of all college students. They are located in every state of the Union. If the present trend continues, by the year 2000 two-year colleges may have taken over the first two years of college almost completely. The sharp rise in community and junior college enrollment is shown in Figure 7-3. Projections indicate that enrollment is now leveling off or declining in many institutions.

In 1971 the Carnegie Commission on Higher Education recommended that each state have a plan for developing community colleges and that the goal of providing a community college within commuting distance of practically every potential student should be attained by 1976. It also recom-

[3]For further discussion of the purposes of higher education, see the Carnegie Commission on Higher Education, *The Purposes and Performance of Higher Education*, McGraw Hill, New York, 1973.

MILLIONS

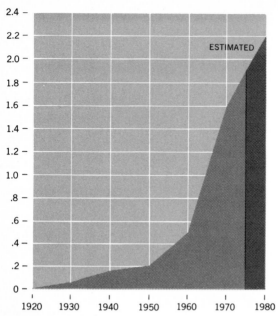

Figure 7-3 Total degree credit enrollment in public and private two-year institutions of higher education. (U.S. Office of Education, *Projections of Educational Statistics*.)

mended the elimination of all financial barriers to attending public community colleges.

Community colleges are distinctly an American creation. They offer large numbers of American youths an opportunity to extend their education at minimum cost, since tuition rates are nominal and many can live at home while attending. Certainly these institutions have reduced the alarming number of able high school graduates who formerly did not go on to college. It is clear that the universal availability of community colleges is as imperative today as the availability of high schools was a generation ago.

Two-year colleges serve four primary purposes: They provide (1) parallel programs for freshmen and sophomores planning to transfer to four-year institutions; (2) terminal programs of general education for students not planning to go on to four-year colleges; (3) technical and subprofessional studies, largely vocational in nature; and (4) continuing education studies in general, cultural, and vocational education for adults. Not all two-year institutions, of course, attempt all these functions.

The types of postsecondary institutions are as

varied as their nomenclature is confusing: junior colleges, community colleges, academies, extension centers, seminaries, technical institutes, trade schools, and others. Most offer two-year programs, although some offer only one-year, while others offer three- or four-year programs. Although the terms "community college" and "junior college" are often used interchangeably, the term "community college" sometimes distinguishes institutions that seek particularly to adapt their programs to the local community and as much as possible serve the educational needs of the community broadly.

These postsecondary institutions are generally of four basic types with respect to organization and support:

Local public community colleges or technical schools maintained and financed through local school districts

The two-year extension of a four-year college or university through off-campus centers

Regional institutions maintained by the state

Private institutions

The first type is common in California, where it arose as an extension of secondary education, largely financed and governed locally. The third type of institution is most common. New York State has followed this model with thirty-eight community colleges, second only to California in size. They offer higher education to any high school graduate who wishes to attend, and they ensure later admission to some public four-year college.

Most two-year postsecondary institutions are public and enroll 90 percent of the students. The public institutions charge little tuition, sometimes none, and the revenue for their support is commonly divided among the state, the community, and the student. Their admissions policies are often quite liberal. As a result, they enroll many high school graduates and adults who would not be admitted to most four-year colleges.

The disadvantages of these institutions may include the loss of the maturing experience of living away from home and the danger that academic standards will be less rigorous than in four-year colleges.

VOCATIONAL AND TECHNICAL SCHOOLS

One variety of the two-year college is the technical institute, institute of applied arts and sciences, or vocational and technical school. These schools are booming, too. Long the stepchild of our educational system, these schools now enroll over two million full-time students across the nation. The Vocational Education Act of 1963 had a great impact on the national program in vocational and technical education and has stimulated the growth of many county and area schools. Under this act, federal grants are given for construction of vocational-technical facilities in an amount up to 50 percent of the costs. The funds, allocated to states, are used to "improve, maintain, and extend" the facilities of existing vocational schools or to build new area vocational-technical schools in other geographic areas, such as a county or group of counties.

The term "area" describes schools that provide training for workers in the industries of a defined geographic area. The four types of area vocational-technical schools that are federally aided are

1. A specialized high school used exclusively or almost so to provide full-time vocational education in preparation for full-time work in industry
2. A department of a high school used exclusively or principally to provide training in at least five different occupational fields to those available for full-time study prior to entering the labor market
3. A technical or vocational school providing vocational education predominantly to persons who have completed or left school and who are able to study on a full-time basis before going to work
4. A department or division of a junior college, community college, or university providing vocational education in at least five different occupational fields, under the supervision of the state board, and leading to immediate employment but not toward a baccalaureate degree

PUBLIC COLLEGES AND UNIVERSITIES

A few public colleges and universities are municipally controlled and supported. Several, such as the service academies, are operated by the federal government. But most public colleges and universities are supported and controlled by state governments. Every state provides at least one state college or university. Most states provide several. Many state colleges originated as normal schools for the preparation of teachers and were extended later into four-year state teachers colleges and eventually into multipurpose colleges. A few have added graduate divisions and professional schools and have become universities. Many state universities and some state colleges originated as land-grant colleges, discussed later. State colleges and universities have experienced their least growth and influence in the Northeast—except for New York—where private colleges and universities were longer established, more outstanding academically, and more powerful politically.

Although there are great variations among them, approximately 40 percent of the operating revenues of state colleges and universities come from the state and the remainder from tuition, federal grants, and private contributions. Historically state colleges have been governed by their individual boards of trustees, which serve as buffers between the campus and the state capital and between political pressures and academic interests. Recently the authority and responsibility of these boards of trustees have been invaded increasingly by officials of governors' offices, state boards of higher education, state departments of education, and other bodies. This movement of power is viewed usually with alarm by most educators and with satisfaction by many state officials.[4]

In many states, state colleges and universities function largely as autonomous entities. In some states, such as California and New York, they function as integral parts of a unified state system of higher education. The State University of New York, for example, includes seventy-two state campuses housing thirty-eight community colleges, fourteen state colleges of arts and sciences, six agricultural and technical institutes, four health science centers, four university centers, and various professional schools—all coordinated by its own board of trustees. Its annual budget is approaching a billion dollars, and its enrollment is just under 400,000, making it the largest university in the world. This state university system has adopted the ambitious goal of offering some form of higher education to every high school student in the state who wants it.

Land-grant colleges and universities are those institutions, almost all of them public, which have been designated by the state legislature as quali-

---

[4]For further discussion of this trend and its consequences, see Allan W. Ostar, "Public Colleges in Jeopardy?" *Compact*, September/October 1973, pp. 27–28.

fied to receive the benefits of either or both of the Morrill funds. The term "land-grant college" originated from the wording of the first Morrill Act, adopted by Congress in 1862. The act provided instruction in "agriculture and the mechanic arts, without excluding other scientific and classical studies and including military tactics."

There are now sixty-nine land-grant colleges and universities. The latest, Federal City College in the District of Columbia, which opened in 1968, is unique because of its urban location and focus. Some land-grant institutions are state universities (as in Minnesota, Illinois, Arizona, Nebraska); some retain their agricultural and mechanical arts designations (such as Alabama Agricultural and Mechanical College); some bear the designation of state college, although they are sometimes truly universities (such as Virginia State College); and some function as part of private institutions (such as Cornell University).

Today land-grant colleges constitute less than 4 percent of American colleges and universities, but they educate 20 percent of the undergraduates and grant 40 percent of the doctor of philosophy degrees in the United States. More than half the living American Nobel Prize winners earned degrees at land-grant colleges. The land-grant college has been called democracy's college. It represented a liberalizing of the old classical college course, particularly in its emphasis on agriculture and home economics. The land-grant college helped to forge one of the great miracles of American technology—an astounding rise in agricultural production.

As the nation enters its third century, public institutions of higher education—state universities, state colleges, land-grant colleges, and community colleges—have clearly emerged as the largest and most significant sector of higher education.

PRIVATE COLLEGES AND UNIVERSITIES

The American landscape is dotted with approximately five hundred private liberal arts colleges, most of them small, and eight hundred private church-related institutions of higher education. In 1950 these private institutions enrolled approximately half the students in four-year colleges, as shown in Figure 7-1. By 1981 they will enroll less than one-fourth. With tuition at private schools running up to three thousand dollars per year higher than that of most public institutions, more students are opting for the latter. Then too, many students have completed a year or more of college-level work in high school and have outgrown much of the lower-division curriculum of these colleges.

A large number of small, independent colleges have closed or merged, and many others are in financial trouble. Some people advocate public subsidies for these institutions, as discussed later, to protect their survival. Others recommend extending the grant programs and increasing state scholarships to permit more students to attend these institutions. Many educators feel that, unless they are helped, we will witness the demise of these private colleges and universities, which provide much diversity in higher education—diversity in curriculums; instructional styles; intellectual, philosophic, or religious convictions; economic and political theories; and educational policies and practices. Without help, those that do remain will tend to become increasingly elitist and available only to the well-to-do. Others do not view the situation with such alarm, contending that those with the will and quality to survive will survive and become stronger in the process.

The highest concentration of these private schools and colleges is in the Eastern states. Their quality varies enormously. Approximately one-fifth of them are not regionally accredited.

The term "church-related" institution might mean that the college is owned outright by a religious denomination, that members of its board of trustees and perhaps its faculty must belong to the sponsoring church, that some financial support comes from a religious denomination, that its purposes reflect a religious orientation, or simply that it once had a religious affiliation that is now maintained only nominally. "Church-related" may mean any or none of these.

Approximately 350 church-related institutions of higher education are affiliated with the Roman Catholic Church, enrolling approximately 6 percent of all college students. There is an increasing trend toward more secularization in Catholic colleges and universities, notably in Boston College, Fordham University, and Webster College, among others.

Increasingly, the question is raised whether sectarian colleges are necessary or, more fundamentally, whether a college with religious affiliation is a contradiction in terms. When President Jacqueline

Grennan separated Webster College from the control of the Sisters of Loreto, she stated that "the very nature of higher education is opposed to juridical control by the church."

PROPRIETARY SCHOOLS

Proprietary schools are private schools run as a business for profit. Many of these are postsecondary institutions that commonly prepare people for careers in such fields as commercial and fine arts, computer technology, business administration, drafting, electronics, secretarial positions, and many others. Schools of this type are not new, but they appear to be growing in number and in prestige. In many states some of them are authorized to award associate degrees. Many of these schools are of fine quality, but some engage in misleading advertising and recruitment practices, abuse of federal assistance programs, fraudulent tuition refund policies, and huckstering cut-rate diplomas. Various proposals have been advanced to provide greater consumer protection, but it is difficult to separate the wheat from the chaff in the current context of innovation, openness, and nontraditional programs in higher education.[5]

[5]For further information about this problem, see George E. Arnstein, "Bad Apples in Academe," *Changing Education*, April 1975, pp. 1–3.

NONTRADITIONAL COLLEGES AND UNIVERSITIES

In the late 1960s, dissident students, after the fashion of medieval European university students, established "free universities," "counteruniversities," "experimental colleges," "protest counterinstitutions to the unfree universities"—their titles were both quaint and inexhaustible. Not really universities in any sense of the term, these enterprises were best known for their slogans, friendly ambience, youthful enthusiasm, bohemian quarters, and courses in magic, belly dancing, Celtic witchcraft, Volkswagen repair, and whatever was popular and available. Many of their leaders were more interested in political activism and the radicalization of society than they were in learning. Those that were free of tuition did not last very long.

In the 1970s, a new kind of model emerged—the "university without walls" or the "open university." The prototype university without walls, funded by a grant from the U.S. Office of Education, included a consortium of twenty colleges across the country. As its name implies, the university without walls seeks to escape the boundaries of the classroom or campus and provide learning from courses offered on any campus in the consortium—courses via television, radio, reading, independent study, travel, internships, and so on. Students construct their own study plans, often with the help of a men-

Informality has become the hallmark of many college courses which is epitomized in the "university without walls."

tor, often free from grades and credit requirements. The original university without walls has prompted a number of open colleges or universities in a number of states. These institutions seek to open the opportunity of higher education to students of all ages, including those who dropped out of conventional college programs, those who live in geographic isolation from conventional institutions, those who prefer to study at their own pace, those who lack financial resources, and those who wish to convert knowledge gained through life experience toward college degrees. The concept of the open university extends right up to professional degrees and doctoral programs. The University of Massachusetts in the 1970s developed an open approach to the professional education of teachers.

So far the open university and university without walls have triggered mixed views. On the positive side, they emphasize the progressive education doctrine of learning by doing, the meaningful linkage of academics with field experience, and the capability of permitting students to begin "where they are" rather than at "the beginning." Their common-market type of learning resources from a variety of educational agencies is alluring and productive when carefully planned and measured against respectable academic standards and criteria. Some programs, such as the State of New York's Regents External Degree program, are carefully evaluated.

But alas, this careful attention to the evaluation of out-of-classroom experiences is often lacking. Herbert London, Director of Experimental Programs at New York University, toured the nation for a first-hand view of nontraditional programs. He discovered a student who had earned a degree in beekeeping by helping his beekeeping father. Other students gained academic credits by waiting on tables, "hanging out with the guys," and teaching swimming. Another student received advanced standing in sociology for having lived in the ghetto all her life. No examination or paper reporting the experience was required. Although London concedes that such incidents may not be representative, he does regard the university without walls as a Pandora's box.[6]

Shapiro cautions that at the heart of all the experimental colleges is the classic anarchist's faith that if people were freed from all institutional constraints so that they might do their own thing, all would be well. He notes that the removal of structure and authority, inherent in most of these programs, offers as much hope of recreating Babel as it does of Eden.[7] Certainly there are some sound pedagogical principles inherent in many of these experimental programs. But we are skeptical of the dilettantism, romanticism, and fuzziness of design that characterize many of them.

The crudest form of nontraditional programs are the "degrees" offered by a number of diploma mills for a price. These agencies consist at worst of little more than a post office box and at best of a small resident staff, perhaps with part-time help, that delivers education primarily by mail or occasional lectures to hundreds of clients across the land. At the time of this writing, legislation is being drafted to regulate fraudulent diploma mills.

COLLEGES AND UNIVERSITIES FOR MINORITY GROUPS

There are approximately one hundred colleges and universities, most of them in the South, whose student bodies are predominantly black. Some of these—notably Howard, Fisk, Lincoln, Morehouse, and Tuskegee—rank among the best institutions of higher education in the country. Approximately 60 percent are private institutions, usually with religious affiliations. The remainder are state-supported institutions that enroll approximately 60 percent of the students attending predominantly Negro colleges. Approximately one-third of black undergraduate students attend these institutions. Stunted by financial blight, isolated from the mainstream of American society by segregation, and governed by predominantly white boards of trustees, these institutions have nevertheless provided the intellectual leadership for blacks that has been so essential during the struggle for equal rights. Their alumni are found in the ranks of leaders in government, business, education, and health throughout the nation and indeed the world. Although many of their faculties are integrated, their student bodies, with the exception of Lincoln and

[6]Herbert London, "Experimental Colleges: University Without Walls: Reform or Rip-off?" *Saturday Review World*, Sept. 16, 1972, p. 64. See also Raymond S. Moore, "Work-study: Education's Sleeper?" *Phi Delta Kappan*, January 1976, pp. 322–327.

[7]Harvey D. Shapiro, "Lights That Failed," *Change*, Summer 1974, pp. 57–58.

Howard and a few others, contain only a handful of white students.

The compelling need is to strengthen these institutions so that they may better fulfill their important role in higher education. Many of them are in severe difficulty, and their survival is in doubt. Some optimism springs from the fund-raising efforts of the United Negro College Fund, which was organized in 1944 to help independent colleges serving predominantly black students meet the spiraling costs of education. The Ford Foundation has allocated $50 million to strengthen some of these institutions. However, Earl McGrath, former U.S. Commissioner of Education who has studied the plight of these colleges, concludes that nothing less than $500 million of federal nonmatching funds will be required over the next five years to save them and bring them into the mainstream of higher education.

Howard University in Washington, D.C., seems to offer a model for the redevelopment of other predominantly Negro colleges. Fifteen percent of its students are white, and one student in seven is foreign. Students are attracted to Howard because of its reputation for excellence, its low tuition, and its image as a multiethnic and multiracial community of scholars. Here in microcosm may be both the model and the instrumentality for ethnic peace, an estimable service to the whole nation and indeed the world. Benjamin Mays, the eminent president of Morehouse College, has expressed this hope:

I believe that on the campuses of these colleges scholars of all faiths, cultures, and races will work together without a quota system. I believe that when the local climate is ready, students of other races will not hesitate to enroll wherever they can get a good education.[8]

There is a slight trend toward increased white enrollment in some black institutions. *The Black Public Colleges: Integration and Disintegration,* a report prepared by the Race Relations Information Center, concluded pessimistically that "wherever public black colleges exist, they are either facing the loss of black identity through integration or merger or the loss of quality through attrition and neglect. The only alternative they don't have—and

never have had—is to be black and equal." The controversial *Adams versus Richardson* case has mandated the desegregation of institutions of higher education, a decision that has grave consequences for Negro colleges.[9]

One of the few American institutions of higher education in the continental United States for minority ethnic groups other than blacks is the new Deganawidah-Quetzalcoatl University, a small institution at Davis, California, run by and serving American Indians and Chicanos.

PROFESSIONAL AND GRADUATE SCHOOLS

Since the middle of the eighteenth century, professional education has developed rapidly in American colleges and universities. Professional schools for engineering, medicine, dentistry, law, pharmacy, teaching, and other professional and technical fields have developed in approximately three hundred universities. These professional schools have been created to meet career needs that require advanced academic study and are indispensable to the public welfare. Not all professional schools are affiliated with universities. The George Peabody College for Teachers, the Brooklyn Law School, and the Moody Bible Institute are examples of some that are not.

Beyond the baccalaureate is the master's degree, which usually requires (1) at least a year of study beyond the bachelor's degree; (2) completion of a certain number of credits or courses totaling approximately 30 semester hours; (3) examinations, both preliminary and final comprehensives, both oral and written; and (4) completion of some research project—a thesis, its equivalent, or added course work.

An increasing number of institutions are offering an intermediate degree or diploma between the master's and the doctor's degrees. This award usually corresponds to two years of graduate study. Some graduate schools are awarding various certificates or degrees as substitutes for the doctorate, such as the Candidate in Philosophy or Master of Philosophy for those who have completed all requirements except the dissertation. Numerous doctors' degrees—such as doctors

---

[8]Benjamin E. Mays, "The Achievements of the Negro Colleges," *Atlantic,* February 1966, p. 92. Copyright © 1966 by the Atlantic Monthly Company, Boston, Mass. Reprinted with permission.

[9]For further discussion of the controversies and consequences of this decision, see John Egerton, "Can Separate Be Equal?" *Change,* Winter 1974/1975, pp. 29–36.

Graduate study is important in advancing the skills of people in the various professions, such as these special education teachers participating in a computer-assisted instructional program.

of medicine, dentistry, or education—are offered in professional fields; and the doctor of philosophy is commonly granted in academic fields of study by graduate schools or advanced professional schools. The usual requirements for this degree are 75 to 90 semester hours of graduate study, written and oral examinations, and a dissertation or its equivalent.

Various advisory bodies have recommended increased federal funding for graduate study through grants to both graduate students and institutions they attend. Federal support for graduate study is justified, according to a study by the National Science Board, because graduate schools constitute a critical national resource that produces knowledge of wide applicability and because knowledge and scholars are needed by government.

However by the mid-1970s, the market for doctorates in conventional fields such as teaching had become oversupplied, although there was an undersupply of individuals trained professionally to deal with problems of energy, environment, and urban living. The federal government reduced its financial support for graduate and professional education instead of increasing it, as practically all studies had recommended.[10]

Organization of higher education

ARTICULATION OF SECONDARY AND HIGHER EDUCATION

The gap between the completion of high school and the beginning of college was once so broad that many promising students—lacking money or motivation—failed to go to college. Since the nation could ill afford this, many stratagems have been undertaken to capitalize more fully on latent talent. Several are mentioned briefly below.

Upward Bound programs identify promising high school students from low-income families and offer them college-level experiences during the summers of their late high school years without cost. This experience has helped many students to develop enthusiasm and confidence about college and has eased their induction into college life. Intensive counseling services also help overcome problems that might discourage entry into higher education.

There has also been a striking growth of cooperative arrangements designed to bridge the gap between high school and college. Many colleges and universities now participate in the most significant manifestation of this trend, the Advanced Placement Program, conducted under the auspices of the College Entrance Examination Board. Although advanced-placement courses are available in only 15 percent of the nation's high schools, they have stimulated high schools and colleges to share responsibility for providing enriched and challenging academic programs for superior students. These programs improve articulation between secondary and higher education. Able students can take college-level courses while still in high school, and some enter college as sophomores, thereby saving a year of study.

Various other prototypes of better articulation of high school and college are appearing. Some include the feature of time-shortening by combin-

[10]For further discussion of the problems and needs in graduate education, see Charles V. Kidd, "Graduate Education: The New Debate," *Change,* May 1974, pp. 43–50.

ing and compressing the traditional four years of high school and four years of college into a six-year integrated program, such as the one at Seattle University. Perhaps the best-known model is Si-mon's Park, a residential "early college" in Massachusetts that begins its four-year college program for gifted students at age 16 by shortening both secondary and college work. Other institutions, such as State University of New York, reduce the four years of college to three years for some students by having students spend mornings at nearby high schools and afternoons at college during their upper years of secondary work.[11] These programs are rationalized on several bases:

● Youth mature earlier and are ready for college work.
● The programs eliminate the "seam" between high school and college, thus reducing dropouts.
● The 16-to-20 age group is a natural peer culture that should not be interrupted by terminal programs at age 18.
● The financial press of higher education demands bold new ways of attracting students by making education less expensive.

Many of these programs are being financed by the Carnegie Corporation and are being watched carefully by other high schools and colleges.

GOVERNANCE OF HIGHER EDUCATION

Colleges and universities are caught in a swirling vortex of conflicting demands from many sources. Taxpayers insist upon fiscal responsibility. State boards of education ask for cost-effectiveness results and occupational programs to meet manpower needs. Professors demand higher salaries, lighter teaching loads, and freedom to do their thing. Students resist rising tuition rates and demand better instruction. Local boards of trustees ask for peace on the campus. Somewhere in the middle of all this, stand—or cringe—college presidents. All these constituencies make up the governance structure, which is both diverse and ambiguous. Nevertheless, the following generalized statements apply to many campuses.

State boards. State authority over private institutions of higher education is commonly limited to a few prudential functions such as granting charters and approving programs for professional licensure. The governance of these private institutions rests largely with their own boards of trustees.

The role and structure of state governance over public institutions differ widely among the states but can be categorized roughly into two types: (1) the multicampus state university of a single system governed by a single statewide body, such as in North Carolina, Maine, Wisconsin, and Utah, among others; and (2) the statewide coordination of multiple and disparate institutions under coordinating state boards of higher education and local boards for each institution, such as in New Mexico, Oklahoma, Kentucky, and New Jersey, among others. Authorities tend to agree that these state boards of higher education should be separate from the more general state boards of education. Most educators agree that they should not engage in the management of colleges and universities. Nevertheless there is a sharp trend toward the escalation of state agencies' authority over public colleges and universities as education becomes increasingly important in the affairs of state, as the costs of education escalate, and as state leadership becomes more necessary to offset rivalry among institutions.[12] Most observers predict a continued rise in authority of state boards of education at the expense of local boards of trustees.

Local boards. Many public institutions and virtually all private institutions of higher learning are governed by their own boards of trustees. These boards of trustees are commonly self-perpetuating and meet infrequently, perhaps three or four times a year. They are often rather isolated from the mainstream of the campus. College trustees commonly fulfill ceremonial functions, establish general policies, approve operating and capital budgets, and appoint college presidents; and in private colleges particularly, they often play a major role in fund raising and as a vital link between campus and community. Boards of trustees do not commonly have much to do with curricular

[11]For further description of this program, see Jane B. Shaw, "Speeded-up, Souped-up and Skip-a-year Programs Get Kids into—and out of—College Sooner," *Nation's Schools and Colleges*, October 1974, pp. 35–42.

[12]For further discussion of state boards of education, see John D. Millett, *Strengthening Community in Higher Education*, Academy for Educational Development, New York, 1974, chap. 3.

and instructional matters, which are delegated to the president, deans, and department chairpersons, along with authority for operational matters. Unfortunately most colleges and universities have not articulated very well the role of their boards of trustees.

Positions on college boards of trustees are often honorific recognition of distinguished alumni, businesspeople, public officials, or professionals. Rodney Hartnett reported in his book *College and University Trustees* that members of college boards of trustees are predominantly male, over 50 years of age, moderate in political view, Protestant, white, and well-to-do; they are in business and the professions. He found that less than 1 percent of college trustees were artists, musicians, writers, or journalists. Some college boards of trustees have moved to include students, young alumni, women, and members of minority groups. However, the Carnegie Commission on Higher Education recommends that professors and students not serve on boards of trustees at their own institutions because of the inherent conflict of interest in these dual roles. The commission did not object to their service on boards of trustees on other campuses. The commission did recommend a better representation of occupational and ethnic backgrounds, as well as females, among boards of trustees.

Administrators. College presidents are named by the board of trustees. Their powers and responsibilities are often not well defined. Many college presidents find themselves being held fully accountable for circumstances on their campuses, but without being given commensurate authority. The general public and students often regard the college presidency as a powerful position, which in fact it is not on most campuses. Nevertheless, the president's office is often the point of collision among conflicting demands of students, trustees, alumni, faculty, deans, and legislators. The presidents of many leading universities find the demands upon their offices intolerable. The Reverend Theodore Hesburgh, president of Notre Dame, reports that he has only one-tenth the power he had when first appointed years ago. Although he regards the diffusion of power among faculty and students as generally desirable, he believes that some resolution must be found of the conflict between the dilution of presidents' power and their increase in accountability, or "no intelligent person will want to be a university administrator."[13]

The administrative staffs of many colleges and universities include an array of vice-presidents, administrative aides, planning and development officers, public-relations officers, government liaison officials, administrators of student services, ombudsmen, and deans. Where once "old president Smith" was attacked, now "the administration" or "the growing bureaucracy" is assailed by all as an omnipotent, impersonal, remote, unfeeling establishment.

Faculty. Patterns of faculty participation in governance is a tangled web on most campuses. Decisions on admissions, curriculums, degree requirements, and faculty appointments are commonly decentralized among various divisions, schools, and departments. On most campuses a faculty senate—along with an imposing array of faculty committees—provides faculty input into decisions, but more commonly in an advisory role than in a governance role. On some campuses student representatives serve on these senates. Senate meetings are not usually well attended unless matters threatening the security of the faculty are on the agenda.

Individual professors have considerable autonomy on most campuses—autonomy with respect to what they teach, how they teach, what research they undertake, and many other aspects of their work. Many professors feel more loyalty to their academic or professional fields than to their institutions. They turn out en masse when a dramatic issue arises but otherwise are content to leave the day-to-day business of university government to a small minority of their concerned colleagues who serve on the committees or senate with the administrative officers. As long as parking space and graduate student assistants are provided, such professors like to be free to do their own thing. Most professors have considerable authority, at least over their own domain, while assuming little responsibility or accountability for the general affairs of the institution. This arrangement is not accidental. It was so designed to sustain academic

[13]For interesting discussions of the kind of educational leadership demanded by the future, see M. D. Cohen and J. G. March, *Leadership and Ambiguity*, McGraw-Hill, New York, 1974.

freedom and scholarship; but a worse design for institutional response to emergency and upheaval could hardly be imagined.

College faculties flex their muscles through their organizations, particularly with respect to the conditions of their employment. The American Association of University Professors has historically served as a watchdog of academic freedom, tenure, salaries, and other conditions of employment on most campuses. On many campuses local affiliates of the American Federation of Teachers, the National Education Association, the American Association of University Professors, or state associations of higher education have been chosen by faculty elections to represent them at the bargaining table. All these organizations have mounted vigorous campaigns for elections regarding collective bargaining on campuses. So far their greatest gains have come from two-year community colleges, along with several public institutions and a few private ones. Their greatest thrust at the moment is toward large multicampus universities where the greatest potential membership lies. A poll of the nation's college faculty members on these matters revealed that only about one-third of the respondents believed that collective bargaining is the most effective way for faculty members to influence campus decisions. Only one-fifth felt that faculty members should become more militant in dealing with administration.[14] Notwithstanding these attitudes, there are forces that could change the picture rapidly: restraints in financing higher education and their depressing effect on faculty salaries, the impact of inflation on take-home pay, the cutback in numbers of faculty on campuses with declining enrollments and its effect on the job security even of tenured faculty members, the increasing invasion of decision making on campuses by state boards, and the passage of more state laws granting bargaining rights to public employees. It is still too early to forecast the impact of collective bargaining on the governance of colleges and universities, although opinion and rhetoric are not scarce.[15] Many educators yearn for a

model of faculty participation in governance more effective than the current faculty senate model. They prefer a model more particularly attuned to the delicate structure of university governance. In the minds of many, the industrial model of collective bargaining is inappropriate in higher education. Collective bargaining is discussed at greater length in Chapter 1.

Students. What should be the students' role in university government? Many experts believe that the participation of students in decision making relevant to student life is crucially important and justifiable. Many believe that students should serve on academic committees and that their counsel should be sought with respect to academic matters normally decided by faculty and administration. Students, however, though long on interest in the university, are short on accountability. They do not have responsibility for the future, for raising funds, or for holding the university together. For this reason, some educators believe that participation of students in the ritual of government usually controlled by the board of trustees would be unimportant and inappropriate. They point to the transient nature of the student population, the difficulties of identifying representative opinions from the largely amorphous mass of students on large campuses, academic immaturity of students, and other factors. Certainly it can be said that the power of students over university affairs is increasing and that this development is in general an essential ingredient in the educative process. It can be hoped that it will serve also to strengthen higher education and quicken its response to the great social issues of our times.[16]

Other groups. Other groups influence college and university governance. Both state and federal legislatures exercise profound influence over colleges and universities through financial appropriations and through other legislation regulating the affairs of higher education. Guidelines developed by the Department of Health, Education, and Welfare governing fair-employment practices along

[14]*Academic Politics, Morale, and Involvement,* Stanford University Project on Academic Governance, Stanford, Calif., 1973.

[15]Donald Bylsma, Jr., and Robert Blackburn, "Some Consequences of Collective Bargaining in Higher Education," *Phi Delta Kappan,* October 1972, p. 130.

[16]For a more thorough discussion of the expectations of trustees, presidents, faculties, and students in university governance, see William C. Stolk et al., "Who Runs the University?" *Saturday Review,* Jan. 10, 1970, pp. 53–82.

with other federal and state agencies also have impact on university governance. Alumni, particularly those who are major donors, often exercise influence directly through the conditions specified in their bequests or indirectly through trustees or administrators who are mindful of their largess and their interests. Foundations, businesses, and other benefactors also influence program development through the grants of money they provide to universities and colleges.

OPERATION

Faced with tighter budgets and the public's press for more fiscal responsibility, many institutions are implementing modern management systems to maximize their cost effectiveness and to move out of debt. This involves more careful definition of purpose or mission of the total university as well as its components. Priorities are established, and budgets, programs, and policies are linked more closely to purposes. This is done commonly through the program-planning-budgeting system (PPBS) described in Chapter 11. Computer-based management information systems are used to provide a better information base for management decisions. The National Center for Higher Education Management Systems has been established to help colleges and universities in this effort.

To accommodate rising enrollments and to make more effective use of time, space, and facilities, a growing number of institutions of higher education have instituted year-round schedules of three trimesters, four quarter-sessions, or other variations. Many students at universities with conventional two-semester schedules attend summer schools. On major university campuses, summer schools frequently have enrollments nearly half as large as regular enrollments during the academic year. Many colleges and universities are accelerating instruction in other ways. Some institutions have established semiautonomous small colleges or "clusters," each with its own faculty, student body, and minicampus but sharing expensive common facilities with the parent university. After the fashion of Oxford University, Pamona College became the first United States prototype of this sort in 1925.

As noted elsewhere, a number of colleges and universities, such as the University of Illinois, have compressed programs of studies into three-year degree programs, a recommendation advanced by an influential Carnegie Commission report *Less Time, More Options*. No agency has done more to illuminate the problems of higher education and to point the way toward their solution than has the Carnegie Corporation through its many influential studies and reports. Its report *Institutional Aid: Federal Support to Colleges and Universities* contained many recommendations that were incorporated in the Higher Education Act of 1972.[17]

Figure 7-1 charts the extraordinary increase in college enrollments resulting from two major factors: the arrival at college age of the postwar babies and the striking increase in the percentage of high school students attending college. College enrollments are expected to increase at a smaller rate in the immediate future. The job market for college graduates is tight, and the difference in income between college and noncollege graduates is narrowing.[18] College diplomas are more plentiful than high school diplomas were in 1945. Although the United States has only one-seventeenth the world's population, it has one-third the world's college students. This rise in numbers has been accompanied by increased diversity of the student body. College, once reserved for the privileged few, as it always has been in other countries, is now the opportunity of the masses. Far more money is expended for higher education in this country than in all the rest of the world combined. Figure 7-2 reveals the rise in the percentage of youths between 18 and 21 in this country who are in college. The proportion will probably approach 70 percent by 1980.

COOPERATIVE RELATIONSHIPS

Colleges and universities have developed a variety of cooperative relationships with other universities and various governmental agencies. Some-

---

[17]For a summary of Carnegie Commission on Higher Education reports, see Lewis B. Mayhew, "Jottings," *Change*, May 1973, pp. 61–63.

[18]For further discussion of these implications, see Richard Freeman and J. Herbert Holloman, "The Declining Value of Going to College," *Change*, September 1975, pp. 24–31, 62.

times these take the form of regional associations, such as the Southern Regional Education Board, to improve educational resources through political action, cooperative research, and planning. Sometimes the scarceness of facilities prompts cooperative enterprise among universities. Many universities join to provide research capabilities that would be too expensive to undertake individually.

Minnesota and Wisconsin have established a "common market" in higher education that permits students to cross state lines under a reciprocity agreement without paying higher nonresident tuition rates, thereby expanding students' options and saving them money. Other institutions are forming consortiums to conserve costs through reciprocity in enrollments, faculty exchanges or joint appointments, cooperative use of expensive resources, and other joint efforts toward common goals.

Many bilateral arrangements permit cooperation between pairs of institutions of higher education. This type of educational reciprocity benefits both partners through student and faculty exchanges, consultation on curriculum development, advisory conferences on administrative procedures, and joint participation in research and development enterprises.

ACCREDITATION

In most countries of the world, colleges and universities are approved by national ministries of education. Most states in this country have provisions, sometimes perfunctory, for the approval of colleges and universities. But the accrediting agency that designates those institutions which have met required standards of quality is unique to this country. The United States is covered by a network of six regional accrediting agencies, such as the Middle Atlantic States Association of Colleges and Secondary Schools, under the aegis of the parent national body, the National Society for School Evaluation. These agencies provide general accreditation of high schools, colleges, and universities. In addition to these general regional accrediting associations, there are a number of national professional accrediting agencies, such as the National Council for Accreditation of Teacher Education (NCATE), which accredits programs of pre-

paration for the teaching profession. The National Commission on Accrediting recognizes twenty-three professional accrediting agencies, including NCATE. These accrediting bodies, which began as cooperative self-policing agencies to ensure quality education, have no regulatory function or legal authority. However, accreditation by these bodies is often essential in qualifying for federal appropriations.

Curriculum and teaching in higher education

Many age-old questions continue to prompt curricular conflict in colleges and universities. One question centers on the choice between the free elective system and a body of compulsory general studies. The free elective system, once common throughout the country, was regarded as the essence of academic freedom, since it permitted students to study and specialize wherever they chose. Then in the 1930s a reform swept college curriculum toward required core courses in broad interdisciplinary areas of the social studies, physical sciences, and humanities to provide each student with a base of common knowledge deemed essential for the broadly educated person. Under the slogan of "relevance," the issue has arisen again. Students complain that the required courses are often poorly taught and irrelevant to their interests. Some demand the freedom to take courses they wish and reject others, and the trend is turning toward an elective system. Stanford University has attempted to find a middle ground without returning to the free elective system. Its model would permit every freshman to have an introduction to "the nature of scholarly inquiry" in a selected field through a small seminar with in-depth tutorial work with a professor.

Some institutions, such as Yale and Dartmouth, encourage students to take a year or a term off near midpoint in a five-year program to engage in nonacademic work—field work, travel, or service in a developing country. This interruption is designed to remind students that there is more to life than study and to invigorate them upon their return, when the college turf may look greener after a period in the "school of hard knocks."

An increasing number of small, struggling liberal arts colleges have reversed declining enrollments by adding an array of career-oriented courses in hotel management, cardiopulmonary technology, or whatever, in full- or part-time study by students of all ages to meet local or regional needs.

Many students come to college with high expectations for the expansion of their personalities. They seek deeper understanding of themselves and others, better emotional self-sufficiency, and refinement of their tastes and values. They seek both affective and cognitive development in institutions that have traditionally neglected the former.

In the 1970s many new electives began to appear with frequency: black and ethnic studies, environmental education, economics of the disadvantaged, and sexual identity, among many others.

The study of religion, so important in early American colleges, continues to occupy an important place in the curriculum. This is true not only in church-related schools but in independent colleges as well. Enrollment in elective courses in religion has soared at many institutions.

Increased use is being made of independent study and self-instructional technology in colleges generally. Multimedia material and closed-circuit television are used increasingly to expand the impact of teaching talent. Educational television programs are transmitted through commercial and educational channels to students outside the college campus. The popular television series "Sunrise Semester" and "Ascent of Man" have provided course credit to thousands of students and countless others on a noncredit basis.

Increased emphasis is being placed upon honors courses and independent study by students, freeing them, through proficiency examinations and assigned readings, from course credit requirements and compulsory class attendance.

While some institutions are dropping letter grades in favor of pass or fail designations at least in elective courses, there is evidence that where letter grades are still used, fewer low grades are given. Grade-point averages have increased over the last decade, although there is disagreement over the reason. Some contend that today's college students are brighter and better educated upon arrival and that they study harder and better, perhaps because of competition in the labor market. Others point to a simultaneous decline in scores on the Scholastic Aptitude Test and attribute higher grades to lower academic standards. Some critics regard this inflation in grades as a scandal that threatens credibility in measures of academic quality.

In sum, we are seeing a rapid expansion of efforts to revamp undergraduate education, to free students from academic monasticism, to link the campus "hothouse" with the fields and vineyards. This movement is prompted partly by economic necessity in a buyers' market, partly by the more heterogeneous student body, and partly by pedagogical theory. Some innovations are absurd, while some are beautiful. But who is wise enough to make the distinction in all cases? Some off-campus experiences are educative, some are noneducative, and some are miseducative. Some may be useful preparation for life but do not educate in the sense of expanding one's intellectual development. There are those who lament the elimination of required study in the liberal arts and who shudder at the thought of students' graduating from college without taking a course in English or history. Controversies over the traditional and the unconventional will continue, as they always have and probably should in a society as pluralistic as ours.

Students in higher education

Despite controversy over the possible shortcomings of higher education, one magnificent achievement is often overlooked. This nation provides higher education for a greater proportion of young people than any other country. C. P. Snow, the British author and scientist, spoke thus of his envy and admiration for American colleges:

You were the first people in the world to bring higher education to an enormous slice of an enormous country and to remove it from the privilege of a small elite . . . . I have no doubt whatever that college education over the whole width and breadth of America is one of the real achievements of this world . . . .

I am far from the only foreigner who thinks highly of your system of higher education.[19]

ADMISSION

Figure 7-2 shows the steady rise in the percentage of youths attending college. Nevertheless, children of high-income families are five times as likely to enter college as are children of low-income families. Clearly race, family income, geographical location, and additional factors other than academic ability are constraining the educational opportunity of young people. "Open admission" has become a battle cry among social reformers, while others see it as a plot to destroy the quality of higher education. Some put the question more adroitly: Could higher education be both universal and excellent?

Admission to college has traditionally been limited by academic ability and financial resources. Open admission removes the former restriction but not the latter, unless it is accompanied by free or low tuition or adequate financial aid for poor students. The concept of open admission to higher education is not new. Many state universities, particularly in the Midwest, have been open to any high school graduate in the past, although most less able students soon dropped out or flunked out in the "revolving door" stream, as it was called. In some institutions with open admission policies, such as the City University of New York, overall grade-point averages dropped substantially, and approximately half those admitted under open admission provisions have dropped out within a year. But, like the argument over whether the wine bottle is half full or half empty, half the new students now receiving a college education would have been denied one before open admission. Moreover, one-third of those who drop out return later to complete their studies. The irony is that the argument over open admission became moot on many campuses after 1975, when economic troubles forced many institutions to admit almost anyone who applied who had money for tuition.

We believe that there is no essential contradiction between the expansion of opportunity in higher education to all who wish to attend and the maintenance of excellence in our institutions as long as certain cautions are exercised. These include the exclusion of some institutions of extraordinary excellence from the open admission policy, counseling programs to help students choose institutions whose programs and admission policies are most compatible with their needs, substantial modification of curriculums and instructional methodology appropriate for students of modest academic ability, delay of admission to college for youths who need work or service in the community to acquire the maturity necessary for success in college, and the expansion of community colleges and technical schools to meet the needs of students who cannot succeed in four-year colleges.

FINANCIAL HELP

Loan funds, scholarship programs, and talent searches offer precious financial help to many students. A frightful statistic is the default by students of an astonishing 25 percent of the federally guaranteed student loans, a renege rate that would close the doors of most banks. The Woodrow Wilson National Fellowship Fund and the National Merit Scholarship program, along with countless other public and private scholarships, have contributed significant financial help for needy students.

Deferred-tuition plans help to spread the cost of college education over the entire year. Some colleges are forming cooperative arrangements with local banks and insurance companies to provide college financing on the installment plan. Many states have provided insured loan funds. Thus more students are studying now and paying later.

Under the Educational Amendments Act of 1972, the Congress approved aid for students in most public and private postsecondary institutions in the form of Basic Educational Opportunity Grants up to $1,400 annually, not to exceed half the total annual cost of college. This was the first time that the federal government attempted to provide a minimum level of assistance to every needy postsecondary student who wanted it.

In recent years a number of colleges and univer-

[19]C. P. Snow, "Higher Education in America," *NEA Journal,* April 1964, p. 11.

sities have increased scholarship funds on the basis of academic merit rather than on financial need. The practice is defended as a means of attracting more capable students from middle-income families who were feeling the pinch of escalating tuition. This is a means of improving the quality of the student body and, as some would contend, a sort of "academic clearance sale" to fill classrooms that would be partially empty otherwise. In many instances the amount of the scholarship is determined by the quality of the student's Scholastic Aptitude Test and high school class rank. Colleges discovered that with merit scholarships they could get more students for their money because larger stipends are needed to attract poor students. Some oppose merit scholarships because they reduce the number of poor students.

MINORITY GROUPS

Although the proportion of black students in college enrollment rose from 3 percent in the early 1960s to 9 percent in 1972, it has been declining slightly thereafter. The decline is attributed to economic pressures as well as to less intensive recruiting and decreased financial aid.

The desegregation of higher education remains a problem in many institutions, despite affirmative action programs. The suit in the *Adams versus Richardson* case accused the federal government of failing to enforce Title VI of the Civil Rights Act as it applied to the dual system of higher education in ten southeastern states. These states were ordered to file desegregation plans to comply with the act, but at the time of this writing, four years after the case, many states are still not in compliance. Throughout most of the remainder of the country many schools and colleges are still not racially balanced either in student bodies or in faculties. The greatest advances toward racial balance, still short of the mark in many cases, have been in public institutions in urban centers, where affirmative action plans are most feasible.[20] Even

in institutions with biracial student bodies, social integration of black and white students is often elusive. Students' life-styles tend to limit their interactions to others of their own race.

WOMEN

Segregation of students by sex in higher education is declining as former men's and women's schools admit students of the other sex or merge with coeducational institutions. Undoubtedly some men's and some women's schools will remain as such to serve students who prefer to study undistracted by the opposite sex. One study revealed that among women listed in *Who's Who of American Women,* graduates of women's colleges were more than twice as likely to have been cited for achievement than were women graduates of coeducational institutions.[21]

The women's liberation movement has sharpened our awareness of discrimination against women in society and particularly in higher education. Until recently, only one of four women capable of college work was in college, compared to one of two men. Women with baccalaureate degrees were only half as likely as men to earn graduate degrees. Women have been discriminated against in financial help and in quotas limiting their access to certain career programs. Counselors have discouraged women from entering predominantly male occupations. The contribution of women to our culture has been neglected in our curriculums. Reentry restrictions, limitations in the transfer of credit, limited child-care facilities, and a host of other arrangements have all discriminated against women—sometimes overtly, sometimes covertly. Happily, all this is changing, although some of society's more deep-rooted conventions and long-standing attitudes make progress slower than justice demands.[22] Anti-sex-discrimination guidelines formulated by federal and state agencies and by colleges and universities are helping

[20]For further discussion of the problems of desegregating higher education, see Reginald Stewart, "Public College Desegregation: We Didn't Have an Approach Before," *Compact,* September/October 1974, pp. 2–4.

[21]M. Elizabeth Tidball, "The Search for Talented Women," *Change,* May 1974, p. 51.

[22]For further discussion, see Audrey C. Cohen, "Women and Higher Education," *Phi Delta Kappan,* November 1971, pp. 164–167.

to accelerate improvement. The slowest progress is being made in employment and promotion opportunities for women on college faculties.

DROPOUTS

National surveys show that only 40 percent of all entering college freshmen get a degree within four years, but that 60 percent get it eventually within seven to ten years. The percentage of completions has been increasing with the spread of nontraditional programs and improved reentry privileges on some campuses. Dropout rates are slightly higher among men than women, although a higher percentage of men eventually complete their degrees. Some educators believe that for many students it is desirable to drop out of college for a while, and some institutions, as noted earlier, are encouraging this. The flood of veterans who entered college after military service demonstrated that students were more highly motivated toward better-defined goals after they had matured during noncollege experiences.

STUDENT LIFE

A revolution has occurred in the private lives of students on campus. The old doctrine of the college standing *in loco parentis* was swiftly discarded in the late 1960s and early 1970s. Parietal rules that once governed the lives of undergraduates were quickly swept away on most campuses. Rules governing dormitory hours were widely discarded, and housemothers and chaperons became an endangered species. Coed dormitories became common, and college men and women were free to visit each other's rooms on many campuses. It is no secret that these changes were demanded not by parents, deans, and presidents, but by students.

Fraternities and sororities, which fell on hard times during the period of student activism in the 1960s, are enjoying a resurgence. Membership is increasing. But fraternities and sororities are changing. Dangerous hazing is almost unknown. Less importance is attached to secret rituals, panty raids, and horseplay as Greek societies have taken a new seriousness of purpose and social con-

sciousness. More effort is devoted to study and to helping with worthwhile social causes. Students have rediscovered the value of brotherhood and sisterhood. A few have combined to become coeducational.

Various national organizations of college students compete in the struggle to represent students' interests on campus and in society. The National Students Association is the largest and the oldest and probably most representative of college students generally. It represents well over a million students on campuses across the country. It has been a moderately liberal force in quickening the social consciousness of college students. In 1970 a group of black students, impatient with the National Students Association's stance on civil rights, broke from NSA to form the National Association of Black Students. The Young Americans for Freedom is a conservative organization of college students, numbering approximately fifty thousand students on four hundred campuses. It strives to neutralize the efforts of the more radical groups to protect colleges from disruption and violence.

The women's liberation movement has reduced discrimination against women's entry into formerly masculine careers.

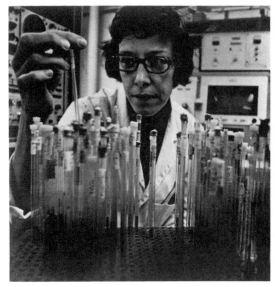

BILLIONS OF DOLLARS

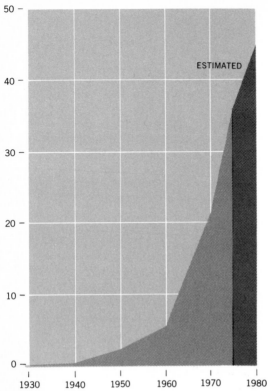

Figure 7-4 Total current expenditures for higher education. (1930–1970, U.S. Department of Commerce, *Statistical Abstracts of the United States;* 1971–1975, U.S. Office of Education, *Projections of Educational Statistics;* and estimates by authors.)

Financing higher education

The greatest problem facing colleges and universities now is money. As indicated in Figure 7-4, expenditures for higher education have risen sharply over the last several decades. Some campuses were overbuilt during the "baby boom" period, especially in terms of dormitories, which students are fleeing in great numbers. Despite their sharp rise, tuition costs have not kept pace with costs. High as tuition may seem to college students and their parents, tuition rates remain one of the greatest

bargains in the American economy because the typical college must receive three or four additional dollars from other sources for each one it receives in tuition.

Between 1966 and 1976, the average tuition charges for undergraduates rose by one-third in public institutions and by more than one-half in private colleges and universities. The sharpest increase in tuition fees has been applied to out-of-state students in public universities.

Many college officials fear that they are having to price themselves out of the market. Making students pay an increasing proportion of the costs of higher education will, if it continues, be disastrous to American society. As the Association of State Universities and Land-grant Colleges points out:

It is based on the false theory that higher education benefits only the individual and that he should therefore pay immediately and directly for its costs—through borrowing if necessary . . . . This is a false theory.

The Carnegie Commission on Higher Education and the Committee for Economic Development contend that tuition should be raised at public colleges and universities commensurate with rising costs to make them more competitive with private schools. These bodies recommend a kind of voucher plan in which students would be given scholarships and loans and would then go to private schools in greater numbers. As Lawrence Kempton noted while he was chancellor of the University of Chicago, "It is hard to market a product at a fair price when someone down the street is giving it away." Others argue that at the very least college tuition should be tax deductible, as it already is, in effect, for students attending public schools, where much of the cost comes from public funds. Figure 7-5 shows the various sources of income of public and private colleges and universities and reveals the greater reliance of private institutions upon tuition.

Private gifts to colleges and universities amounted to approximately $2½ billion in 1976. Alumni are contributing $560 million a year to their alma maters. Although exceptionally large gifts are becoming fewer, many more alumni are making

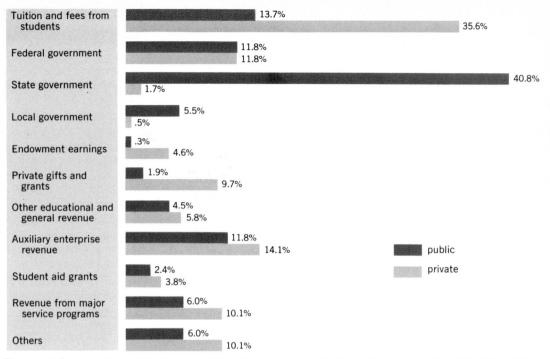

Figure 7-5 Sources of current fund revenue of public and private institutions of higher education. (U.S. Office of Education, *Digest of Educational Statistics*.)

small contributions. The business community realizes that the prosperity of American industry is closely dependent upon the vitality of higher education. Corporations large and small contribute about 14 percent of all voluntary support to higher education, amounting to over $350 million annually and rising steadily. Private foundations have made outright grants-in-aid as well as subsidies for experimentation and research. The Ford Foundation and the Carnegie Corporation particularly have made hundreds of millions of dollars available to hundreds of institutions. Billions of dollars are reaching colleges and universities through federally funded research projects, student loans, scholarships, the GI Bill, construction loans, and grants-in-aid. Chapter 14 documents some federal subsidies to higher education. Federal financial support constitutes over one-fourth of higher education's total budget. However, by the mid-1970s federal funding was being cut back.

State support for higher education more than doubled during the 1960s but is now leveling off at about 28 percent of the cost of public higher education. Further expansion of the state's share is difficult because the federal government has preempted many of the more productive sources of public revenue.

With the decline of large bequests, endowment income is becoming a shrinking proportion of total university income. Some colleges have had to eat into their endowment funds to cover rapidly increasing operating expenses.

Colleges and universities must also help themselves by effecting economies. The fiscal inefficiency of higher education is widely recognized. Needless duplication of programs and facilities by neighboring institutions must be reduced. More effective utilization of space and faculties is possible through better scheduling and year-round programming. Competition and duplication of service among public and private institutions should be displaced by cooperative and complementary arrangements.

Most colleges and universities are engaged in cost-trimming measures: increasing class size, hiring freezes, replacing departing or retiring professors with younger and lower-salaried instructors, reducing maintenance and janitorial services, and cutting back on travel expenses for professors. Some universities are requiring each professional school or division to generate enough income or cut costs sufficiently to make revenue and expenses balance. New York University, near bankruptcy in 1972, used many of these devices to barely escape what was described as "the largest and most spectacular collapse in the history of higher education." Some savings could be realized through greater use of instructional technology.

Effective as these measures may be, they are not the ultimate solution to the financial distress of higher education. More fundamentally this is a problem of our priorities. This nation can afford to spend what is needed to extend and enrich its system of higher education if we would but make the effort as we do for highways, welfare, national defense, and so many matters.[23]

The future

The Carnegie Commission on Higher Education identified six priorities for action in the future: advancement of social justice, clarification of the purposes of higher education, preservation of quality, constructive reform, strengthened governance, and assurance of adequate resources. These might be useful topics for the construct of our discussion of the future of higher education, but we prefer another. Here are the trends we see.

Two-year colleges will take over the first two years of higher education almost completely.

Private institutions, particularly small private liberal arts colleges, will find themselves practically priced out of the market unless they become universities, as some are doing, or unless public funds become more widely available to them. But the distinctions among types of institutions will fade. This trend is already underway. The line between public and private institutions is sometimes hard to draw. Liberal arts colleges are becoming more like universities, and professional schools are extending their general education components.

One of the most significant changes in higher education will be the clientele. Traditionally our campuses have been populated by youths between the ages of 18 and 22 (and beyond for graduate students). The economic realities will force colleges and universities in the future to do what they should have been doing all along—develop programs that are responsive to the needs of older adults including mothers, veterans, former dropouts, minority groups, and the handicapped. Many of these programs will focus on new career development and occupational rehabilitation. Liberal arts education, somewhat bypassed by the current generation of young people, will be rediscovered and more keenly appreciated as they grow older. Flexibility and convenience in packaging will be the hallmarks of these programs.

The governance of higher education will continue as chaotic, or more so, as it is now. National policy with respect to higher education will remain as ambiguous and as unstable as it always has been. The future direction of higher education will not be shaped so much by boards of trustees, administrators, legislators, governors, or presidents, who are sometimes confused and quixotic. Future direction will be shaped, as it has been, by the competition of the open market place.

Robert Nisbet, a distinguished Columbia University professor and an astute observer of the educational scene, predicts that we are on the verge of a decline in our homogenized "academic nationalism," that is, our past movement to nationalize our culture through higher education. He welcomes this decline. We will see instead, says Nisbet, a return to strong localism and regionalism deriving from a resurgence of racial and ethnic kinship and

---

[23]For further discussion of the financial problems of higher education, see Education Commission of the States, *Financing Postsecondary Education in the United States,* Denver, 1974.

our local and regional roots. He believes that our rediscovery of religion and the renaissance of ethnic identity will quicken this "mini-Reformation" in higher education. He notes that institutions of higher education have enjoyed their greatest flowering during periods of strong localism, regionalism, and pluralism.[24]

The most critical problem of higher education will be finance. The costs are already staggering. Increases in tuition, private philanthropy, and state aid will probably not keep pace with the need. The only possible solution, in our view, lies in increased federal support for higher education. Comprehensive and long-range state planning of systems of higher education, common now in only a handful of states, will be necessary in order to deploy limited resources to this expensive enterprise more effectively. New modes of instructional technology may change the delivery of instruction substantially.

The university of the future may become fairly indistinguishable from the community. It is already sometimes difficult to determine where the university ends and the rest of the world begins, as many students are taken into the community for more and more educative experiences in the community action projects, work-study programs, and internships in field agencies.

The boundaries of academic disciplines will become more obscure as they are breached by interdisciplinary inquiry into the great problems of humanity—energy shortages, environmental protection, the reduction of learning disabilities, among many others. We expect the trend toward more existential, less classical, study to continue. However, we predict greater emphasis upon quality of learning on many campuses. Those that cannot respond to the press for quality will go the way of the free universities in the 1960s. Economic pressures on students as they compete for scarce jobs or highly restricted admission to graduate schools may quicken the return of rigorous and more explicit grading. We are old enough to recall that curriculum development in education is cycli-

cal, and we do not deny the possibility of an eventual return to more classical study.

Clark Kerr, head of the Carnegie Commission on Higher Education, warns that other periods of student activism lie ahead. We hope so, because we regard responsible and nonviolent student activism as the best antidote to orthodoxy and a constructive force in any open and dynamic society. We do not expect this activism to be directed at the university, as it was in the 1960s.

The greatest alienation on the campus will be felt by the faculty, among whom intense pressures are already building. University faculties are almost adequate for the remainder of the century. After the 1980s very little new hiring will be done, even though our capacity for turning out doctorates has tripled. There will be tenured places for very few of them and no place on campus for most of them. Insecurity among young, nontenured faculty members is already extant. As financial resources decline and public demands for fiscal responsibility intensify, even tenured faculty members will be discharged on many campuses, as is happening already. Intense battles over tenure are shaping up. Competition, even hostility, between young and senior faculty members is growing. Demands for increased productivity and larger classes, more advisees, longer work days, salary cutbacks, greater use of educational technology, and earlier mandated retirement will all energize more faculty members toward collective bargaining.

The dilemmas are difficult, the hazards are fateful, and the future of higher education is by no means certain, as indeed it never has been. We think our colleges and universities will change but also survive and prosper reasonably well. The walls of academe are thick.

Suggested activities

1. Prepare an essay on "The Most Imperative Reforms Needed in Higher Education in America."
2. Select a book from the bibliography that interests you and prepare a critical review of it.
3. Prepare an essay on "Sexism in American Higher Education."
4. State the pros and cons relative to nontraditional colleges.

[24]Robert Nisbet, "The Decline of Academic Nationalism," *Change,* Summer 1974, pp. 26–31.

5. Prepare a description of the governance of the institution which you attend, including an analysis of powers held by the trustees, administrative staff, faculty, and students; also include your recommendations for reform.

6. Interview a major administrative officer in your college to determine the greatest changes that have taken place on your campus in recent years and the most difficult problems presently confronting it.

7. Prepare an essay on "Higher Education for blacks in America—Past, Present, and Future."

8. Arrange an interview with the admissions officer of a graduate school of education in a major university to discover (1) the fields of specialization available and the advanced study requirements, (2) the requirements for admission to graduate study, and (3) the opportunities for financial assistance during graduate study.

9. Interview at length someone who was an undergraduate prior to 1955 and note contrasts between collegiate life then and now.

10. Prepare an essay on "The Satisfactions and Frustrations of Teaching in College."

Bibliography

Astin, Alexander W., and Calvin B. T. Lee: *The Indivisible Colleges,* McGraw-Hill, New York, 1972. Describes small, private, four-year colleges and their problems.

Barber, Virginia, et al.: *Women on Campus: The Unfinished Liberation, Change* magazine, New York, 1974. Essays by twenty-one writers on women's struggle for a fairer share in academic life.

Bernhard, John T., et al.: *The Changing Role of the College Presidency,* American Association of State Colleges and Universities, Washington, 1974. Collection of essays on the nature of the college presidency and the governance of higher education.

Bowen, Howard R., and W. John Minter: *Private Higher Education,* Association of American Colleges, Washington, D.C., 1976. Survey of the precarious position of the nation's private colleges and universities.

Carr, Robert K., and Daniel K. Van Eyck: *Collective Bargaining Comes to the Campus,* American Council on Education, Washington, 1973. Describes the development and consequences of collective bargaining by college faculties.

College Entrance Examination Board; *The College Handbook,* Princeton, N.J., 1976. Contains pertinent information about each of the 2,000 institutions of higher learning.

Gallagher, Buell G.: *Campus in Crisis,* Harper & Row, New York, 1974. Discussion of higher education, our moral sensibilities, and our national life-style by a former college president.

Glenny, Lyman, and Thomas K. Dalglish: *Public Universities: State Agencies and the Law,* Center for Research and Development, University of California, Berkeley, 1975. Examines the increasingly controversial relationship between campus and state.

Gross, Patricia: *Beyond the Open Door,* Jossey-Bass, San Francisco, 1971. Significant study of the new college students resulting from open admission—their problems and prospects.

Kidd, Charles V.: *Graduate Education: The New Debate, Change* magazine, New York, 1976. Discussion of the problems and dilemmas inherent in graduate education.

Lichtman, Jane: *Bring Your Own Bag,* American Association for Higher Education, Washington, 1974. Discusses academic fare, teaching, learning styles, and clientele of free universities.

Livesey, Herbert: *The Professors: Who They Are, What They Do, What They Really Want, and What They Need,* Charterhouse, New York, 1975. Very readable book whose descriptive title makes annotation unnecessary.

McCluskey, Neil G. (ed.): *The Catholic University: A Modern Appraisal,* University of Notre Dame, Notre Dame, Ind., 1970. Essays by eminent educators on various aspects of Catholic colleges and universities.

Mayhew, Lewis B.: *The Carnegie Commission on Higher Education,* Jossey-Bass, San Francisco, 1974. Skillful summary and comment on the vast volume of influential studies and recommendations by the Carnegie Commission on Higher Education.

———— and Patrick J. Ford: *Reform in Graduate and Professional Education,* Jossey-Bass, San Francisco, 1974. Critical analysis of improvements needed in graduate and professional education.

Millett, John D.: *Strengthening Community in Higher Education,* Academy for Educational Development, Washington, 1974. Analyzes the governance of higher education and makes recommendations for reform.

Mood, Alexander M.: *The Future of Higher Education,* McGraw-Hill, New York, 1975. Recommendations for future reforms in higher education aimed toward equalizing opportunity and improving quality.

Nisbet, Robert: *The Degradation of Academic Dogma,* Basic Books, New York, 1972. Critical commentary on how American universities have betrayed their historic mission.

Trivett, David A.: *Proprietary Schools and Postsecondary Education,* American Association for Higher Education, Washington, 1974. Describes proprietary schools and their operation and the need for regulating abuse by some of them.

Wilson, Robert C., et al.: *College Professors and Their Impact on Students,* Wiley-Interscience, New York, 1975. Reports on study of professors' commitment to teaching and other scholarly endeavors, their interest in students, and students' opinions relative to effective college teachers.

Woodring, Paul: *Who Should Go to College?* Phi Delta Kappa, Bloomington, Ind., 1974. Discusses issues surrounding admission to college in relation to social mobility and economic and intellectual abilities.

Yarmolinsky, Adam, et al.: *On Learning and Change, Change* magazine, New York, 1973. Essays by fourteen writers on changes, politics, new social consciousness, and instruction pervading higher education.

Zwerling, L. Steven: *Second Best: The Crisis of the Community College,* McGraw-Hill, New York, 1976. Disturbing argument that community colleges prepare lower-middle-class youth for lower-middle-class jobs and actually retard upward mobility.

Chapter 8

Adult and continuing education

YOU WILL HAVE MASTERED THIS CHAPTER WHEN YOU CAN

Define

● **adult and continuing education**
● **lifelong learning**

Describe

● **the imperatives of adult education**
● **a representative sample of creative new adult education programs**
● **the probable changes and developments of adult education necessary for the future**

Analyze

● **your own potential and interests in a career in adult education**

Foundations of adult and continuing education

In earlier times, when society was less complex and living less arduous, it was perhaps reasonable to assume that learners could acquire, by the age of 18, most of the education they would need throughout life. But the fantastic tempo of social and scientific change has vastly complicated our existence and given unprecedented urgency to lifelong learning through adult education.

Indeed, the world has changed far more in the past ten years than it had in the previous two hundred. Moreover, it is evident that we are on the threshold of even more fantastic change. Human beings will explore the solar system, extract vast riches from the oceans, control the weather, and do other wondrous things. But the prospect of present and future change is not entirely pleasing. It will be accompanied by massive and compelling forces that have already begun to revolutionize personal and national life. The specter of runaway inflation

and disintegrating economic systems; the despoilation of our atmosphere and water; shortages of food, fuel, and other commodities; the threat of war and other disasters can only be avoided by civilizations wise enough to comprehend the problems and courageous enough to come to grips with them before it is too late. In this perilous and perplexing age no one's education can be considered complete. Adult and continuing education become increasingly imperative if, as H. G. Wells forecast, "Human history becomes more and more a race between education and catastrophe."

THE NATURE OF ADULT AND CONTINUING EDUCATION

Varied in character and widespread in its manifestation, adult education practically eludes precise definition. In its broadest sense, it embraces all informal and formal activities that induce learning and promote better living for people 18 or older. In a narrower sense, it is organized learning sponsored by a responsible educational agency for persons beyond compulsory school age who are not usually full-time students. The broader definition would include such pursuits as reading books, listening to music, visiting museums, and traveling. As indicated below, adult education has many purposes and varied programs. Linked with adult education is the newer concept of continuing learning.

A middle-aged housewife, her children grown, returns to college for refresher courses in education in order to resume her interrupted career in teaching. An airline pilot attends a company school to become proficient in the operation of the latest jet. A young career diplomat, preparing for a new assignment in Peru, learns Spanish at home with the help of phonograph records. A young mother learns the art of infant care at a Red Cross class. A retired attorney finally finds time for a neglected hobby and attends an evening class in oil painting at the local high school. A young married couple learns to rumba at a local dance studio. An enterprising business executive who had to leave school early catches up on her general education by joining a "great books" discussion group. Across America, adults of all ages are engaged in the quest for richer living through lifelong learning.

Thus adult education has become established as the fifth level of our educational system—the natural culmination of early-childhood, elementary, secondary, and higher education.

Continuing education has a somewhat different connotation from adult education. Peter Drucker, in his book *The Age of Discontinuity*, speaks of continuing education as "the frequent return of the experienced and accomplished adult to formal learning." Thus continuing education tends to be engaged in (1) frequently and (2) formally by persons who are (3) already educated and (4) seeking modernization of their professional knowledge. Adult education, on the other hand, need not necessarily satisfy these conditions. Obviously there is much overlap in adult education and continuing education, and the term "lifelong learning" is used to cover both. A report by the Center for Continuing Education of the University of Notre Dame states:

Terms like Continuing Education or Adult Education are

too conventional and administrative in meaning to encompass the comprehensive responses called for in attitudes and national policy. The Learning Society is based on the concept of lifelong learning and refers to a universe of purposeful learning opportunities found both within and outside the formal or "core" academic systems.[1]

Terrel Bell, former U.S. Commissioner of Education, regards lifelong learning as evidence of the conviction that life is fascinating, and that it grows more interesting the more one learns and experiences. So he would establish as the first objective of a plan for lifelong learning that it helps adults find meaning and fulfillment in their living. Second, it should provide them with the skills to be productive and independent. And third, it should increase their capacity to function as parents with love, hope, and guidance for their children.[2]

Education as a "developmental continuity" extends vertically and chronologically along all horizontal and sequential levels of learning from the cradle to the grave, from early childhood through adult learning. As indicated in Figure 8-1, continuing education has a temporal axis extending through all the years of living and all the formal levels of learning.

Continuing learning also has a "circumferential dimension," with the radii of enlarging circles embracing more and more education and living. An Oriental proverb poses this paradox: "The greater the diameter of light, the greater the circumference of darkness." The more we learn, the more we find to learn.

New imperatives and continuing education

We mentioned earlier that changes in life and labor are occurring at a rapidly accelerating rate. The forces underlying these changes and the need for lifelong learning are examined in some depth.

[1]Center for Continuing Education, University of Notre Dame, *The Learning Society*, Notre Dame, Ind., undated, p. 3.

[2]From an address by Commissioner Bell to an AFT consortium in Chicago on Apr. 26, 1975.

OUR FAILURE TO REACH OUR FULL POTENTIAL

The charts reproduced in Figure 8-1 reveal results yielded by a decade of research based upon observations of human physical and intellectual behavior. The upper lines reveal our potential for physical and mental growth; the lower lines reveal our more usual performance. The difference between the "success" curves and the "failure" curves represents a tremendous loss to society in productivity and human happiness. Joseph Still, who reported the data illustrated in these charts, asks:

Why do so many fail to achieve their physical and mental potentials? It seems pretty clear that it is not because of poor heredity but because they fail to discover that they are able, if they choose, to make more of their lives. How to prevent these failures constitutes one of the great unsolved questions facing our society today. As a starter, everyone should say: "If I want respect as a human being I have the obligation to respect and care for and develop my body and mind." This is the basic philosophy for successful living—and for a successful society.[3]

Clement Martin, in his book *How to Live to Be 100*, argues with cogency that our "natural" life expectancy would be 100 to 125 years, rather than the present 70 years, if we cared for ourselves as we now know we should. Dr. Martin believes that the secrets to increased life expectancy lie in (1) improved physical fitness through better diet, exercise, recreation, rest, and medical care and (2) improved mental activity. He notes:

In studying people who are ninety and more—successful agers—one common possession among them stands out. These individuals from various nations and all walks of life share a common mental outlook; an ability to apply, in life, the best thoughts of the ages.[4]

A new psychological school of thought, transpersonal psychology, emphasizes the development of a person's fullest sensory, psychic, and spiritual potential. Jean Houston, Director of the Foundation for Mind Research, reaches this conviction:

Ordinary people, given the opportunity and training, can come a long way toward attaining their unsuspected potential. Once they can emancipate themselves from a

---

[3]Joseph W. Still, "Man's Potential and His Performance," *New York Times* magazine, Nov. 24, 1957, p. 37.

[4]Clement G. Martin, *How to Live to Be 100*, Frederick Fell, New York, 1963, p. 179.

Figure 8-1 Human potential and performance. The upper lines indicate the physical and psychological potentials of normal people, with peak periods for various activities; the lower lines indicate how most people fail to measure up. (© 1957 by The New York Times Company. Reprinted by permission.)

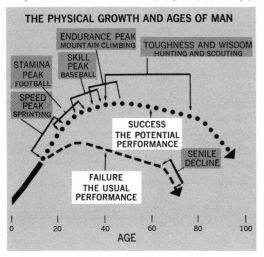
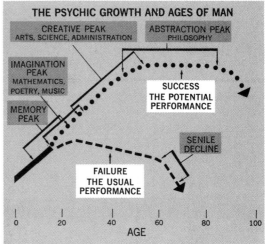

host of anxieties, fears, inhibitions, outmoded and unflattering images of themselves, they can quickly begin to think, feel, and know in genuinely new ways, and to aspire, within realistic limits, to a multidimensional awareness of their mind-bodies and the environmental context in which they are immersed.[5]

Adult education offers the opportunity for more adults to "apply, in life, the best thoughts of the ages." Imaginative, appealing, and inexpensive programs of adult education could help to keep alive a positive mental outlook, quicken adults' sense of purpose and meaning in life, and sustain the intellectual capital that permits us to live up to our full mental potential.

THE LACK OF BASIC EDUCATION

Illiteracy in the United States was cut in half during the 1960s, according to a survey conducted by the Bureau of the Census. Less than 1 percent of the

[5]Jean Houston, "Putting the First Man on Earth," *Saturday Review,* Feb. 22, 1975, p. 29.

adult population is now functionally illiterate, which is defined to mean "unable to read or write a simple message in English or another language." However, a recent study, *Adult Functional Competency,* under the auspices of the U.S. Office of Education, revealed that nearly one-fifth of our adults have difficulty filling out job applications; understanding written instructions on medicine bottles, home appliances, and recipes; filling out income tax forms; understanding labels on food containers and other critical tasks. Of the population over 25 years of age, 28 percent have had no education beyond the eighth grade, and 53 percent (53 million) have not completed high school. A great many of these adults are unemployed; without work, they have little sense of dignity or self-realization. They constitute a large sector of the welfare rolls. The President's National Advisory Council on Adult Education reported strong evidence that these people were "the generations left behind" who will find it increasingly difficult to cope with an industrialized economy. However, as shown in Figure 8-2, the educational level of our people is rising sharply.

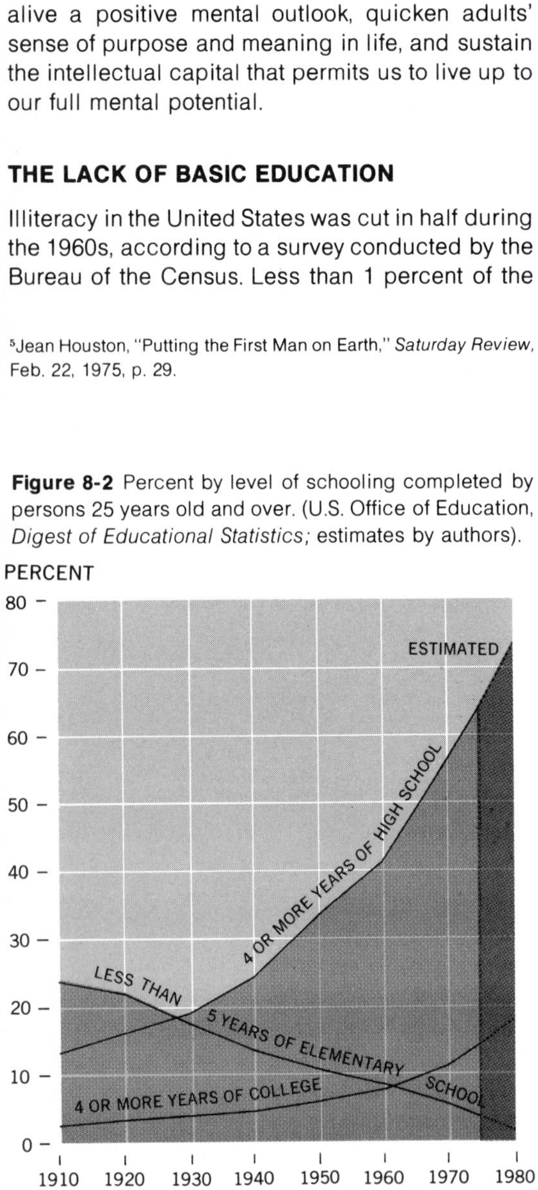

A recent study conducted under the auspices of the U.S. Office of Education revealed that adults engaged in basic education programs gained a full grade or more in reading over a four-month period, that their average earnings increased by 13 percent in one year, that the percentage of those working increased from 55 percent to 65 percent, and that the percentage of those on welfare declined from 25 to 21 percent. The study revealed, unfortunately, that migrant workers, members of minority groups, and people over 44 years of age were seriously underrepresented in the basic education programs financed by federal funds. The Economic Opportunity Act of 1964, supplemented by the Adult Education Act of 1966, enabled many adults from minority and low-income groups to enroll in public school adult education classes. The federally supported Right to Read Program, launched in 1970, was designed to wipe out illiteracy. Although it was not funded sufficiently well to accomplish this ambitious task, it has nevertheless made inroads. On-the-job literacy programs have been set up in industries. Literate employees are trained to tutor their illiterate coworkers. "Adult academies," modeled after the Peace Corps, have been set up in churches and libraries, and specially trained tutors, many of

Figure 8-2 Percent by level of schooling completed by persons 25 years old and over. (U.S. Office of Education, *Digest of Educational Statistics;* estimates by authors).

them retired, teach basic language skills to their neighbors.

THE PROLIFERATION OF KNOWLEDGE

It has been said that more new knowledge has been revealed within the lifetime of the present adult population than existed at the time of its birth. There are exciting new fields of learning scarcely identified a generation ago: transcendental meditation, cybernetics, astronautics, oceanography, atomic physics, aerology, and geriatrics—to mention a few. Books about science, as well as books in other fields, sometimes become obsolete almost as soon as they are published. Ninety percent of all the prescriptions written by physicians today could not have been filled twenty-five years ago. Ninety percent of all the scientists who have ever lived are alive today. Not only is knowledge increasing at a fantastic rate, but old knowledge becomes increasingly perishable; the person who depends upon it is not only obsolete but often dangerous. As Huxley noted, "If a little knowledge is dangerous, where is the man who has so much as to be out of danger?"

Across the nation, in all fields of human endeavor and interest, adult education programs are placing increasing emphasis upon keeping the learner's knowledge up to date. This extension and modernization of knowledge is the central aim of adult education. Adults are responding as never before to intellectual challenges. It is quite apparent that our thirst for knowledge is never quenched.

RECOGNIZING OUR CONTINUOUS CAPACITY TO LEARN

Adult education has been stimulated by the growing realization that you can indeed teach an old dog new tricks. Educational psychologists once believed that the mind was set like plaster at about 25 and that the later acquisition of new ideas was extremely difficult, if not impossible. Modern experimental psychology has exploded this myth. Edward Thorndike, Irving Lorge, and other psychologists have demonstrated that adults can continue to learn, in some respects even better and faster than children. Performance on tests of mental ability improves with age, even for those who scored high in youth. It is also clear that continuous practice in learning helps adults to retain their mental powers longer. Disuse, rather than age, is the chief cause of the loss of the ability to learn. Senility is less a consequence of aging than it is the aftermath of mental laziness.

Examples of keen mental capacity in advanced years are legion. Winston Churchill's wartime leadership was an inspiration not only to the British but to the entire free world as well. A decade later, when he was in his eighties, he emerged as a gifted and prolific writer. Voltaire at age 80 was an intellectual giant. Titian painted both the "Transfiguration" and the "Annunciation" when he was 88 and continued to accept commissions until he died, at 99.

Appreciation of this never-ending capacity to learn has stimulated countless millions of adults to engage in intellectual pursuits with new vigor and enthusiasm. A lively academic interest and persistent mental exercise are undoubtedly more powerful determinants of useful adulthood than chronological age.

THE IMPACT OF AUTOMATION AND TECHNOLOGY

The story of American industry is a chronicle of miraculous invention and discovery. In 1833 the head of the U.S. Patent Office offered to resign because he felt that the limit of human inventiveness had been reached. But our advancing technology has demonstrated the folly of his prediction. And now a second industrial revolution, spearheaded by automation, cybernation, and advanced technology, heralds far-reaching changes in human labor and leisure.

Machines have already taken over much of the brute work in industry. Unskilled laborers will all but disappear within a decade. School dropouts will become virtually unemployable, unless they acquire vocational skills through adult education. Many workers trained in the first three-quarters of this century are being technologically dislocated in the last quarter. Production workers in the next generation will have to be retrained occupationally four or five times in the course of their working life. Approximately one-fourth of the adults attending school are enrolled in job-training programs. A manufacturer of automation equipment has stated that automation is eliminating two million jobs a year, not only through direct displacement of workers, but also through the "silent firing" of workers who would have been employed had their jobs not been eliminated.

THE INCREASING COMPLEXITY OF SOCIETY

Our social, economic, and political life is becoming progressively more complicated. Bigness and complexity are the hallmarks of government, corporations, labor unions, mass media, political parties, and communities. Even school systems, as reported in Chapter 12, have become increasingly large and complex. Without adequate education, our ability to understand the issues and challenges of these institutions and to direct their destiny lessens.

The density of population arising from increased urbanization imperils human relationships, increases interdependence, generates tensions, accelerates crime, and strains social organization. As government expands, the number of elective offices increases and ballots become so long that even conscientious voters have difficulty knowing the candidates sufficiently well to vote intelligently. The preservation and strengthening of society require the best continuing education that we can muster.

PROTECTING AND STRENGTHENING HEALTH

The complexity of modern society adversely affects health, especially in the cities. Approximately three-fourths of our population live in cities and metropolitan areas. The air in countless cities is contaminated, to a critical degree at times. Congestion of population accelerates the spread of infectious diseases. Across the country water is in short supply, and numerous streams and lakes are polluted.

Especially as one grows older, ill health becomes a greater problem. However, half the chronically ill are under 45. An alarmingly large number of young men, supposedly in the prime of life, have had to be rejected for military service because of poor physical or mental health. Nearly half the hospital beds in the United States are occupied by the mentally ill. Much mental illness stems from anxieties generated by the increasing complexities of modern life and by the problems of aging. Yet, according to one authority, greater progress has been made by medical science in the past fifty years than in the previous five thousand. Ob-

viously, there is a great gap between medical knowledge and individual health practices.

PROTECTING OUR FREE SOCIETY

Today's world is deeply divided. We live in a world marked by rigorous rivalry between democratic and communist nations. This uneasy era of history is characterized by cleavages and competition, by a succession of dangerous crises, and by a continuous progression of awkward dilemmas and fateful choices.

Our people must understand that the conspicuous and unwise squandering of our riches at a time when half of humanity is hungry may threaten the peace of the world. How can we expect other peoples to cherish the ideal of universal suffrage when half our eligible voters fail to cast their ballots in an important election? Apathy about the quality of education, and about adult education in particular, may well deny our people the knowledge and insights they sorely need. The individual whose education is not continuous will become dangerous to society. Despite the great advances in adult education noted in this chapter, it still lags behind social need in a time of world crisis. Clearly the preeminent challenges to education in our time are those of preserving world peace and extending freedom and justice.

POPULATION CHANGES AND INCREASED LIFE EXPECTANCY

Several major changes in our population will have a profound impact upon the need for adult and continuing education.

Although the birth rate has been decreasing since 1957 in the United States, the population continues to increase because of the increase in the number of adults of child-bearing age, lower mortality rates at all ages, and an excess of immigrants over emigrants. The total population of our country by the year 2000 could be anywhere between 260 million and 322 million. The most important population statistic, from the standpoint of adult education, is the sharp rise in the number and proportion of adults in the total population. This phenomenon results in part from dramatically increased life expectancy. When today's grandparents were children, the average adult lived less than fifty years. A baby born in the 1970s in this

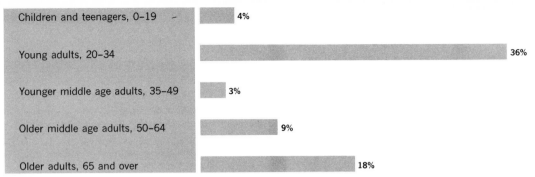

Children and teenagers, 0–19	4%
Young adults, 20–34	36%
Younger middle age adults, 35–49	3%
Older middle age adults, 50–64	9%
Older adults, 65 and over	18%

Figure 8-3 Percentage increase in population, by age groups, 1970–1980. (Estimates are based on data from the U.S. Census Bureau, 1970.)

country has a life expectancy of more than seventy years, and their offspring will probably have a life span of nearly a century, barring catastrophes such as war, food shortages, environmental decay, and other disasters. Figure 8-3 shows a bimodal distribution of population increase by age groups in this surging population growth. There are presently 32 million adults over 65 years of age, and the number will increase by another 8 million within a decade. At the other end, two of every three Americans added to the population during the 1970s will be young adults. By 1980 nearly one-third of the population will be in their twenties and thirties. Future adult education programs, although serving adults of all ages, must nevertheless be geared most intensively to young and to elderly adults.

The Retired Senior Volunteer Program (RSVP) is one program for the elderly that merits further discussion. Funded under the Domestic Volunteer Service Act of 1973, this program now operates in all fifty states. It numbers over 100,000 participants and is growing rapidly. These aging adults are trained for a wide variety of volunteer activities, such as tutoring students of all ages. The payoffs of this program are several. First, it provides valuable volunteer help for schools, libraries, hospitals, nursing homes, and countless other public enterprises. Second, the volunteers themselves benefit from their involvement in stimulating activity. It rescues them from the "disengagement syndrome" by which the elderly tend to degenerate because they no longer function in the mainstream of society. The science of geriatrics has revealed that when people lose interest in society and pur-

poseful interaction with others, a physiological atrophy sets in and mental disorders ranging from disorientation to severe depression may result. Third, the interaction between the volunteers and young people enriches the lives of both and reduces the generation gap. Some school districts, such as Hastings-on-Hudson, New York, have set up in their school buildings recreation rooms for older people to increase their interaction with youths. The Older Americans Act makes funds available to state and local agencies on aging to stimulate the development of a wide range of programs for older citizens.

Colleges too are striving to meet the needs of the elderly. Ohio State, for example, admits elderly people free of charge to regular classes when space remains after regular college students have registered. For adult students, high school diplomas, homework, exams, and college credit are not required. The range of their interests as well as their capabilities is wide. One man in his 80s was taking diving lessons along with students in their teens. No doubt he helped the teen-agers see how one can age gracefully and healthfully.

FAMILY-LIFE EDUCATION

Family-life education is one of the oldest forms of adult learning. Children learn from their parents and often teach them a thing or two. Many adult education programs recognize the advantages of having family members study together. Husbands and wives enroll together in courses in dancing, bridge, rapid reading, swimming, classical literature, and many other recreational and intellectual subjects. Parents and children take evening courses together in such subjects as nutrition, cooking, sewing, woodworking, automotive mechanics, radio repair, painting, and golf. Many parents have recaptured the great joy of sharing in the educational development of their children.

More and more, adult education programs are including instruction in managing the family income, investments, consumer education, interior decorating, landscaping, nutrition, safety education, personal hygiene, child care, home care of the sick, and so forth. Family-life education is becoming increasingly important as more and more families become multigenerational, with grandparents and great grandparents living at home or in private nursing homes.

THE INCREASE IN LEISURE TIME

Unions have been instrumental in gaining more leisure time for workers. Many unions are working toward the goal of a four-day, 32-hour week. Some companies now have four-day, 36- or 40-hour weeks. Reduced hours of labor give adults increased leisure time.

The earlier age at which retirement is permitted also gives millions of men and women more leisure time. Some labor-management contracts provide a bonus for employees who retire before

More and more adult courses are addressed to family-life education, such as this instruction in infant care for young parents.

the age of 65. The current trend is toward earlier retirement. Most persons receiving social security benefits today are under 65. Not only does retirement come a lot sooner than it did at one time, but increased longevity means that it lasts much longer, thus giving the individual worker a much greater lifetime accumulation of leisure time. Many middle-aged and older people, faced with early retirement and boredom, are seeking new skills and intellectual adventures. New York State's long-term continuing education plan states:

Persons of all ages are searching for self-renewal and cultural renewal. For adults, the search for cultural enrichment is heightened by the dimension of increasing leisure time. Ours has always been a work-oriented society. This condition is changing rapidly. The problem of how best to use our *free* time matches that of how we *work.*[6]

CONTINUING EDUCATION FOR WOMEN

In response to the women's liberation movement, many colleges and universities are proliferating programs for women. More mechanical servants in the home and more formal pre-elementary education for her children, which takes place outside the home for at least part of the day, give modern housewives and mothers more leisure time and more hours for academic work. Single employed women, with the shortened workday and workweek and through labor-saving equipment, also find more leisure to use for personal enrichment through an informal or a formal program.

THE PLIGHT OF DROPOUTS

Many adults dropped out of elementary school. Almost a million students leave high school each year without a diploma. Thousands of able students desert college classrooms prematurely.

Several federally supported programs, such as Upward Bound, are designed to reduce the number of dropouts from high school and college. After-school work activities help many remain in school. Experimental programs giving potential dropouts school credit for the on-the-job experience are being used by several state departments

---

[6] Regents of the University of the State of New York, *Continuing Education*, State Education Department, Albany, 1969, p. 8.

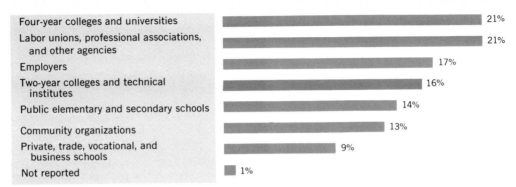

Figure 8-4 Percent of participation in adult education by source of instruction. (U.S. Office of Education, *Digest of Educational Statistics*). Totals do not equal 100 percent since some participate in several categories.

of education and the U.S. Office of Education. The federal government has reshaped its Neighborhood Youth Corps program for high school dropouts. The Job Corps, which came into existence in 1964 "to increase the employability of young men and women," has brought many dropouts to learning centers. If educaton is really lifelong, then young and old dropouts can—with guidance, help, encouragement, and motivation—continue to learn.

Organizations and programs

Adult and continuing education are being implemented in a wide variety of programs organized and administered with more diversity than any

other level of education. Figure 8-4 shows the number of adults participating in educational programs by sources of support. Figure 8-5 shows the general fields of study in which adults are most interested.

PUBLIC SCHOOLS

Education for youths and adult and continuing education are fundamentally a matter of public concern. As the National Association for Public School Adult Education pointed out:

The public schools are maintained by society, are convenient to all adults everywhere, and are the agencies best equipped to provide the coordinating administrative framework, some of the physical facilities, and much of the specialized personnel to implement adult education

Figure 8-5 What adults want to study. (Report of Commission on Nontraditional Study, Carnegie Corporation.)

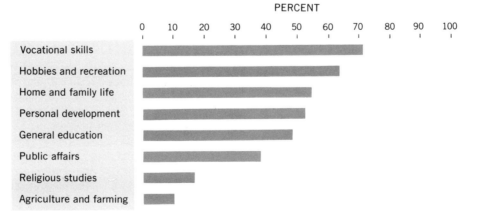

in each community, including the programs of voluntary groups. The education of adults, therefore, is an integral and necessary service of the public school system.[7]

Begun originally in the mid-nineteenth century in a few large eastern cities, public school adult programs at the outset centered largely upon Americanization classes for immigrants, helping millions of new Americans to familiarize themselves with the language and culture of their new homeland. As more communities opened their public schools to adults, attention was given also to the continuation of the education of adults who had dropped out of school early. Many of these programs, usually carried on in the evenings, became known as "continuation schools" or "evening schools." With the rapid rise of industrialization and the consequent demand for skilled labor, vocational courses were added. In more recent years, particularly since World War II, public school adult education programs have been conceived more broadly and include general and avocational education.

Enrollment in public school adult education programs has reached a total of nearly twenty million at a cost of more than $130 million. This increasing return of adults to school is manifest in communities of all sizes and types. Many public schools are learning centers for people of all ages. Many so-called "night schools" are becoming opportunity schools for youths and adults, with daytime sessions and Sunday afternoon forums as well as evening sessions.

The community school is an increasingly popular design for continuing education under public auspices. The concept originated in Flint, Michigan, in the 1930s and led to the integration of school and community facilities and educational and recreational services. The eight-hour schoolhouse became the eighteen-hour school and community center. Adult learners and youths were comingled. Stimulated by grants from the Mott Foundation, Flint's community school program contributed to reduced vandalism; erosion of the generation gap; more intensive use of school facilities by community organizations; reduction in the duplication of recreation, library, and other services by high school and community; and sharp increase in adult enrollments.

This concept has spread to approximately seven hundred school districts whose leaders are affiliated through the National Community School Educators Association. The John F. Kennedy School and Community Center in Atlanta (Georgia), the Thomas Jefferson Junior High School and Community Center in Arlington (Virginia), and the Whitmer Human Resources Center in Pontiac (Michigan) are some well-developed community-school centers. This exciting development could help us to escape from the archaic notions that (1) schools exist to educate only children and youths; (2) schools deliver their services only between 8 a.m. and 4 p.m.; (3) school and community are separate entities; and (4) schools and communities require separate libraries, gymnasiums, auditoriums, swimming pools, and other expensive facilities. The community school may become the vehicle for delivering lifelong learning in an articulated continuum in one facility. It also may help to integrate living and learning more fully.

The larger the school district's population, the more likely it is to offer an adult education program. Many public schools have joined their resources in an area organization for furnishing adult classes. For example, eleven school districts in the southern part of Kent County, Michigan, promote an areawide adult education program.

For the nation as a whole, about two-fifths of the total expense of public adult education programs is met with local tax revenues, one-fifth with student fees or tuition, one-fifth with general state aid, and one-fifth with federal and state funds for vocational education. But adult education received only about 1 percent of the total expenditure for public elementary and secondary education.

The majority of instructors are drawn from the public school faculty, although lay experts are commonly employed. In many school systems these programs are planned with the help of advisory groups of citizens, and sometimes they are administered by lay groups outside the regular public school program.

More and more, public school systems must recognize and accept responsibility for the education of adults as the logical and necessary extension of the public educational system. Only one-

[7]*Adult Education in the Public Schools,* National Association of Public School Adult Education, Washington, 1961, p. 1.

fifth of the states provide adequate aid for adult education, with the result that many districts have come to regard adult programs, like kindergartens, as a marginal part of the total program—nice, but not necessary, something that can be dispensed with at the first sign of financial difficulty. Teaching adult classes should be regarded as a professional specialty in its own right rather than as an extra, part-time job for weary day-school teachers. The administration of adult programs should be brought under the aegis of the regularly constituted local school authorities. Volunteer lay advisory committees, however dedicated and well-intentioned, are not adequate substitutes for well-trained, creative administrators. Finally, the curriculums of adult programs must be reconstructed to make available more academically respectable fare. Courses in the tango and fly casting are all right except when they exist at the expense of instruction in more substantive matters.

PRIVATE SCHOOLS

Many nonpublic institutions, including parochial elementary and secondary schools and colleges, offer local adult and continuing education courses. Many nationally known privately owned and operated schools offer instruction for adults. Besides the well-known Berlitz schools of language and the Arthur Murray and Fred Astaire dance studios, for example, schools of driver training, business education, technical education, fashion modeling, beauty culture, drama, and music are quite common.

COLLEGES AND UNIVERSITIES

Colleges and universities have long participated in programs of adult education. Approximately one hundred universities maintain a school of general studies or extension division that offers both credit and noncredit courses for adults. The noncredit courses are often informal, have no prerequisites other than interest, and require no examinations or grades.

The new "external" degree, bestowed by colleges upon persons who cannot or have not availed themselves of the regular college route, but who have acquired knowledge and skills through other sources, including on-the-job train-

ing and the ripening process of maturation, coupled with high motivation. Approximately one-fourth of the adults pursuing education are enrolled in college and university programs. College programs for adults were once limited to "night school," evening courses for credit and degrees taught by moonlighting instructors and serving weary students who could not afford the luxury of giving up jobs and attending day school full time. Now these college and university evening and extension programs have added a new look with an "open university" concept that permits students more flexibility in designing their own guided study program under the advisement of a faculty member. Credit may be earned through on-the-job experiences and independent study. The academic bill of fare has been broadened to include not only general education but professional education as well. Some courses are pursued off campus at locations nearer to the place of employment or residence of students; these sometimes are delivered by television, radio, or correspondence, which is why the term "external studies" is associated with many of them.[8]

The New School for Social Research in New York City over a decade ago started a unique do-it-yourself program for retired professionals who create their own educational and social community. All the courses are taught by volunteer members of the program—retired teachers, physicians, executives, and businesspeople.

Two pioneer prototypes of college degree programs designed especially for adults are the University of Oklahoma's Bachelor of Liberal Studies and the University of South Florida's Bachelor of Independent Studies Adult Degree Program. We briefly describe the latter because we think it illustrates a type upon which many college programs for adults will be modeled in coming years. The curriculum is interdisciplinary and is organized around four major areas of study: social sciences, humanities, physical sciences, and interarea studies. Most study is undertaken through directed reading of inexpensive paperbacks tailored to the

---

[8]For further description of higher education's response to the adult education movement, see Fred M. Hechinger and others, "Lifelong Learning: The Back to School Boom," *Saturday Review*, Sept. 20, 1975, pp. 14–29.

backgrounds and needs of individual learners. Each student is assigned to a university adviser who is available through conference, mail, phone, or tape to help plan the program of studies, to tutor, and to monitor and evaluate progress through examinations that may be taken at the nearest university or community college. Intensive three-week seminars are held on campus for each of the four components of the program. Adult students work at their own pace and complete their baccalaureate degrees in anywhere from six to twenty-four months. Adult students who succeed in the program—although diverse in age, sex, and occupational and educational backgrounds—have certain common characteristics that make them highly educable: high motivation, intellectual curiosity, self-discipline, willingness to learn, and the ability to assume for themselves much of the responsibility for their own learning.

Declining undergraduate enrollments and the financial pinch on many campuses have prompted some universities, particularly community colleges, to move boldly into the field of nontraditional adult education programs, which are becoming the "budget balancers" for many institutions of higher education. At New York University's expanding School of Continuing Education, studies range from "Administration of Office Operations" to "The Occult, Witchcraft, Magic, and Astrology."

In many colleges and universities, the enrollment of adults far exceeds the enrollment of young undergraduates.

Television has made it possible for universities to send both credit and noncredit courses into the homes of countless adults. Most universities conduct a wide variety of workshops, institutes, conferences, forums, and lecture series. Graduate divisions of the universities provide both preservice and in-service degree programs for advanced students in varied professional fields. In many colleges and universities, the enrollment of adults far exceeds the enrollment of undergraduates.

Through extensive research over many years, Cyril Houle and other leaders in adult education have found that the more formal education an adult has, the more likely one is to be active in continuing learning. However, this likelihood should not be left to chance, as a recent study of continuing education pointed out. It recommended that "a substantial part of the undergraduate curriculum in every subject matter area should be redesigned to help students learn how to carry out a program of self-education and lifelong learning."[9]

CONTINUING PROFESSIONAL EDUCATION

Spoken of variously as "in-service education" or "continuing professional development," this type of adult education is imperative for all professional persons, as well as for many subprofessionals who wish to escape occupational obsolescence. Few professions are more committed to continuing education than is the teaching profession. With the rapid advance in science and technology in all fields, professional men and women—not only at all levels of education but in many other fields such as medicine, research, psychology, industry, and banking—take courses, participate in seminars, observe in clinics, attend professional conferences here and abroad, subscribe to professional journals, and become academic addicts of lifetime learning.

The growing array of "summer camps" for businesspeople illustrates this growing field of continuing professional development. They combine recreation with rigorous intellectual pursuits ranging from Aristotle to the newest computer

[9]Center for Continuing Education, University of Notre Dame, *The Learning Society*, Notre Dame, Ind., undated, p. 3.

technologies. Some are directed toward sharpening management skills. Others are aimed at extending executives' general education, not so much to make them into better businesspeople but to make them into better human beings. Some are conducted at exotic resort areas; others are summer programs on college campuses; while others are within the educational divisions of large corporations.

A new dimension has been added to American education by the widespread growth of educational and cultural programs sponsored by business and industrial firms. A survey shows that 85 percent of the country's largest corporations have some kind of educational program in which knowledge or skills are taught according to some predetermined plan. Western Electric, for example, has a $5 million Corporate Education Center in Hopewell, New Jersey. This 190-acre campus, with its residences and educational buildings, is labeled an "in-company college."

Many programs are sponsored or supported by the federal and state governments through the Labor Department, the Office of Economic Opportunity, and the U.S. Office of Education. The National Alliance of Businessmen launched the Job Opportunities for the Business Sector (JOBS), which pays the costs of training the hard-core unemployed. The Labor Department has opened Residential Manpower Centers in major metropolitan areas, which are somewhat similar to the closed Job Corps Centers.

LABOR UNIONS

Trade unions have long been active in continuing education. There are two types of labor education: instruction in matters related to union welfare and instruction in skills related to jobs. The former focuses upon the improvement of labor union organization and leadership, the strengthening of techniques of negotiation with management, and general concern for domestic and international affairs. These programs are frequently offered on university campuses. Such institutes and courses embrace study in economics, political science, sociology, psychology, trade union history and philosophy, labor law, business organization and management, and civil liberties. Extension courses at land-grant colleges are often conducted to help

labor union officers provide more effective leadership. Labor union officials are the students at the National Labor Relations Studies Center, established in Washington, D.C., by the Executive Council of the AFL-CIO.

The second type of labor education consists of both apprenticeship programs for beginning workers and skill-improvement programs for established craftsmen. The apprenticeship programs are the oldest and perhaps the best known. They exist most commonly in the building, metal, and printing trades and are financed and administered jointly by employers and employees. Apprentices learn their skills by working side by side with experienced journeymen and attending school several nights a week, their pay increasing as they progress. The newest programs are designed to improve the skills of experienced craftsmen.

PRISON EDUCATION

Another program of informal and formal adult learning is the correctional education offered in prisons and reformatories. According to a survey conducted by the Federal Bureau of Prisons, typical inmates of a federal prison read from five to ten times as many books, usually nonfiction, as average citizens. Furthermore, many major penal institutions have academic programs from the first grade through high school graduation. Two-thirds of prison inmates have not completed high school, according to a survey by the Census Bureau. The Federal City College of Washington, D.C., conducts a freshman college program in the prison complex at nearby Lorton, Virginia. Many have functional vocational programs and guidance centers. High school and college correspondence courses are widely provided.

Penological studies show that currently more than half the persons released from prison eventually return there. On the other hand, research by the National Council on Crime and Delinquency indicates that with proper prerelease education and postrelease supervision, more than 80 percent of all convicted criminals can be trusted to remain in society as good citizens.

With more than one-quarter of a million persons in federal and state prisons, plus those in county and local jails, the numerical potential for rehabilitation is a great challenge to continuing education.

EDUCATION OF VETERANS

Certainly the GI Bill of Rights of 1944 and its various extensions, discussed in Chapter 14, would have to be regarded the most significant single effort by far in adult education in our history. The GI Bill made it possible for millions of veterans of the Armed Forces to continue their education and to make a powerful contribution to our prosperity as a nation and to their own well-being.

CHURCHES AND SYNAGOGUES

Most religions offer important programs in education for adults, as well as for young people. These commonly include not only Saturday and Sunday morning classes, but also informal forums and discussions often held on weekday evenings in the homes of church members. Churches of all denominations have broadened the scope of their educational enterprise to meet a wide range of religious, cultural, and social problems, with considerable emphasis upon home- and family-life education. Many churches have organized leadership training classes to strengthen the work of church offices and teacher-training courses to help church school faculties improve their teaching. Many denominations have come to realize that their programs must include a large measure of both religious and secular education for parishioners of all ages.

Much adult education is conducted informally by a wide variety of community organizations, such as this YMCA "class" in folk music.

CLUBS AND ORGANIZATIONS

The Adult Education Association classifies organizations active in adult education into the five general categories discussed below; we have added a sixth category.

Voluntary associations. Voluntary associations operate educational programs for adults through their local, state, and national units. Women's clubs—such as the League of Women Voters, the Junior League, business and professional women's clubs, the YWCA, and the American Association of University Women—attract women of all interests and ages to lectures, seminars, forums, and classes on an endless variety of topics of general interest. Men, too, find that a host of organizations—such as the Lions, Rotary, Kiwanis, and the YMCA—feature lectures and other programs which are focused upon contemporary problems and events of general interest.

Educational associations. Groups such as the Council on National Organizations for Adult Education, the American Association of Adult Education, the Adult Education Association of the U.S.A., the National Association for Public School Adult Education, the American Foundation of Continuous Education, and many others, are concerned primarily with the advancement of adult education.

Associations in related professions. National organizations such as the American Medical Association, the American Society of Newspaper Editors, the National Association of Manufacturers, and the American Management Association—as well as local associations of people in all the professions and major occupations—meet regularly and provide a vital channel for the continued education of their members along professional lines. They frequently undertake to provide information to the general public, hoping to influence opinion.

Specialized interest groups. Specialized interest groups exist in every area of public concern. Parent-teacher associations advance adult understanding of problems of education and child development. The National Safety Council's educational programs have the worthy purpose of reducing accidents. The Senior Citizens of America and Golden Age clubs have been formed to help older citizens adapt to the problems and challenges of advanced age. Chambers of commerce carry on studies, discussions, and other programs intended to increase business in their communities and to advance the general economic well-being of our society. Scores of other examples could be cited.

Special disability groups. Some groups of people help themselves by helping others similarly afflicted. Alcoholics Anonymous is an outstanding example. Neurotics Anonymous is modeled along similar lines. Many groups are organized to help drug addicts. Volunteers in Probation, Inc., is a national foundation, with state and local groups, promoting the rehabilitation of youths and others who are court cases. Our deceased coauthor, Chris DeYoung, was a founder of Volunteers in Probation.

Federal organizations and workers. This category includes specialists, field agents, and teachers in such organizations as the the Department of Agriculture, the U.S. Office of Education, and the Atomic Energy Commission. These workers often have common interests with workers in other groups mentioned above. Postal workers, police officers, FBI agents, Internal Revenue Service officers, diplomats, and a whole army of civilian employees of federal, state, and local agencies attend specialized classes supported by various branches of government.

The exact number of voluntary associations carrying on adult education programs is indeterminate. One authority estimates that there are 100,000 persons engaged as full-time teachers and directors of the education programs of these six categories of voluntary associations, in addition to 5 million part-time teachers and discussion-group leaders. Part-time teachers are an important component of these adult education programs, helping greatly through their voluntary efforts to reduce the financial burden of the programs. These informal, problem-centered adult education programs reach into every neighborhood and every public interest, constituting a vital element of society's progress in providing lifelong learning.

CORRESPONDENCE COURSES

One old and still important means of continuing one's education is the correspondence course. The International Correspondence Schools of Scranton, Pennsylvania, were founded in 1891. Thousands of business and industrial firms and the U.S. Armed Forces use the resources of correspondence schools to bring knowledge to approximately five million people who, for one reason or another, find it impractical to attend an institution of learning. These "learn by mail" courses, once restricted to printed media, now sometimes include tape cassettes or records, slides, and even films. The University of Nebraska, a pioneer in the development of correspondence courses, reports that over 10,000 high school students use its courses. Many of these students are in high schools too small to offer academic and vocational courses that they desire. Of the five hundred correspondence schools in operation, however, only about one hundred are admitted to membership in the National Home Study Council, organized in 1926 and approved by the U.S. Office of Education for the nationally accrediting correspondence schools. This council, which has its headquarters in Washington, D.C., is attempting to eliminate the racketeering and fraudulent "diploma mills" that have, unfortunately, characterized too many of these enterprises. According to the U.S. Postal Service, the number of fraudulent correspondence schools operating in this country has increased greatly. These "fly-by-night" schools usually run advertisements in want-ad columns using a job-opportunity approach as a come-on.

INDEPENDENT STUDY THROUGH READING

The term "independent study" in its broadest sense covers perhaps all cognitive activity in which initiative rests with the learner. In a more restricted and precise sense, independent study may be regarded as including all three basic elements of the instructional process: a learner, a teacher, and communication between the two. Unlike institutionalized instruction, the learner and the instructor are separated in space and time in independent study. This places an added burden on the learner's initiative and upon the communication mode, which in independent study must substitute for face-to-face teacher-learner contact in conventional instruction.

Under the broader definition, communication from the "instructor" (lecturer, book author, telecaster, or newspaper writer) is entirely one way and includes personal reading. In fact, the most universal medium of independent study is reading. It provides for everyone—through books, newspapers, and periodicals—ready and inexpensive access to wide realms of knowledge. The newspaper, a very old knowledge delivery system, has recently become a medium for widespread home study. The Extension Division of the University of California at San Diego in 1973 instituted the first national course by newspaper. It began with a series on "America and the Future of Man," which is presented to thousands of students through hundreds of newspapers in nearly all the states. Students interested in college credit can obtain it through 188 colleges and universities affiliated with the program. The newspapers each week carry 1,400-word lectures in the series prepared by some of the most eminent scholars in the land. Learning kits include reading materials and study guides for students who wish to delve more deeply into the topic. "Contact sessions" are arranged between students in a region and the local teacher or coordinator of the newspaper courses to provide dialogue that clarifies and expands the one-way written communication. In 1976 the program was expanded to include audio cassettes.

Magazines and other periodicals are used widely in adult education, both in organized study groups and in individual reading. No other nation enjoys such an abundance of periodicals.

Books are among the oldest and most effective media of adult learning. Paperback books have enjoyed a mercurial rise in sales. One million paperbacks are sold daily from the racks in bookstores, newsstands, drugstores, supermarkets, and department stores. Library book circulation is increasing three times as fast as our population. Book clubs have helped to extend the scope and raise the level of adult reading, as have a number of book-based discussion groups such as the Great Books Program, the World Politics Program of the American Foundation for Political Education, and the American Heritage Discussion Programs of the American Library Association.

However one may define it, independent study remains the most ubiquitous, most flexible, most inexpensive, and most widely used mode of continuing education.

LIBRARIES, MUSEUMS, AND OTHER CULTURAL CENTERS

The free public library movement, stimulated by the generous gifts of Andrew Carnegie, has made the community library almost as common as the public school in cities and villages of all sizes. Bookmobiles have brought libraries on wheels to villages and rural areas all over the nation.

Once regarded simply as a repository for books, modern community libraries have also become information centers replete with tape recordings, films, and other multisensory aids and equipped with reference, committee, lecture, radio, television, and periodical rooms. Many libraries conduct organized reading clubs, book-review circles, and discussion groups.

Larger communities support historical, scientific, industrial, and art museums that exhibit the arts and crafts and artifacts of virtually all facets of our culture. Formal classes, lectures, seminars, and guided tours frequently enhance the educational value of these institutions.

The facilities and programs of the libraries and museums, both public and private, are steadily being improved. New standards have been developed by the American Library Association.

Many cities maintain observatories, planetariums, aquariums, aviaries, arboretums, zoological and botanical gardens, and other centers for observation and for the study of the natural sciences.

MULTISENSORY MATERIALS AND MEDIA

Chapter 10 describes more fully the impact of films, television, radio, and other audiovisual means of education for adults as well as youngsters. In the last two decades television has become an important medium of education for learners of all ages. Commercial channels bring many programs into countless classrooms and homes. The Children's TV Workshop, creators of "Sesame Street," has developed a fine new television series on health for adult audiences in an interesting instructional format. These programs are supplemented by related printed materials. It is hoped that this series will help young parents particularly to improve the health and nutrition of their families and to gain better access to the nation's health system.

Nonprofit educational television channels help millions of adults to make up for what they missed in their earlier education by offering courses that range from elementary reading to college-level instruction. Adults find radio and recordings useful in their pursuit of education. The high portability of transistor radios has brought the world of sound to the farthest reaches of travel. Records and tapes, long recognized as valuable for the appreciation of music, now offer re-creations of great moments in history as well as instruction in foreign languages.

The telephone too has great potential for bringing education to adults who find school attendance inconvenient. For example, the Los Angeles school district uses the telephone to serve hundreds of learners, mostly patients in hospitals or convalescent or nursing homes, persons who are homebound because of family responsibilities or physical handicaps. These courses cover the standard high school curriculum and are supplemented by many special courses. Additional learning materials are sent to learners. However, the potential for learning by telephone is greatly underdeveloped.

TRAVEL

More Americans go more places more often than people of any other land. It is estimated that typical Americans travel more than 5,000 miles a year. Over $1\frac{1}{2}$ million Americans, young and old, go abroad yearly. Each year, 20,000 students and educators study and teach abroad. Seminars and conventions, tours and cruises, for business and pleasure, inexorably draw our people across mountains, plains, oceans, and continents and thus into closer communication with their neighbors around the world. "The world is a great book," said St. Augustine, "of which they who never stir from home read only a page." Pretravel seminars are increasing in popularity for those who contemplate trips here and abroad. Many universities arrange educational travel tours that go beyond the travel-beaten paths of yesterday's tours to "encounter" crucial world problems, especially the problems of developing countries, where the explosive issues of the future are being determined.

DISCUSSION

Discussion is certainly the oldest medium of adult education, dating back as far as human communication itself. Free discussion is so vital to democracy that it is guaranteed in the First Amendment to the Constitution. An excellent antidote for bias and dogmatism, discussion that brings together the ideas and experiences of different people helps individuals to find deeper meanings and gain wider perspectives. Discussion helps people to identify with one another and to unite for effective group action on common problems. Small wonder that human beings are so prolific in establishing discussion groups, small and large, organized and informal, addressed to almost every aspect of human experience.

The future

The continued expansion of adult education is inevitable. There are now more adults in this country involved in educational pursuits than the number of children in kindergarten through grade twelve. The adult sector of our population is large and growing and is better educated than past generations; it is therefore a more demanding market than ever before. These adults have an enormous appetite for learning. They have increased leisure time. The growing unemployability of undereducated people will stimulate their return to school. The compelling need for greater opportunity in adult learning is increasingly recognized by government, and increased financial support will be available (but probably far short of the need if the past is any indicator). The frenetic rush to build public school and college buildings and recruit teachers fast enough to accommodate the surging enrollments of the 1960s has subsided, at least for a while. Classroom and teacher surpluses can now serve adults while bolstering school and college revenues in a period of otherwise depressed income. New instructional technologies and improved information-delivery systems permit greater flexibility, and sometimes economy, in adult education.

Adult education in this country has been characterized by a spontaneity, informality, and diversity of sponsorship that have made it adaptable to a vast spectrum of needs. However, this circumstance has resulted in a patchwork pattern that lacks central purpose and overall planning. Carried on, as we have seen, by miscellaneous public agencies, industries, civic groups, churches, and labor unions, adult education has developed haphazardly along the route of its sponsors' self-interests. This disunity of purpose and program has been deplored by many thoughtful education leaders.

The future will see a change in the concept of adult education, as well as in its nature. The idea of lifelong learning will be transformed from a cliché to reality when we recognize that childhood and youth education are not terminal but rather preparation for continuous learning as a necessary condition for effective adult living. Continuous learning is prerequisite for survival, and we can no longer regard it as incidental and supplemental. This view of lifelong learning should permeate all levels of learning. It should impose upon young learners the conviction that they must strive for intellectual independence at the earliest possible age, transform themselves into self-teachers by learning how to learn for themselves, and assume greater initiative for their education throughout life.

This concept of lifelong learning will greatly modify the structure of educational institutions themselves. Professor Harold Shane, in his book *The Educational Significance of the Future*, speaks of the "seamless continuum" of lifelong opportunities for learning. High school and college programs will no longer be terminal points in learning but integral components of a continuous program of lifelong learning. Secondary and higher education will become easily available for persons of all ages, whether for credit or not. Infinite exit and reentry privileges will become available to ensure that no one of any age is deprived of secondary and postsecondary education from which they might profit, after the model of Britain's open university, as well as American models described in this chapter. Youths and adults will be comingled. Colleges will increasingly view their clientele as all adults eager to learn, rather than only as full-time students in their late teens or early twenties who are enrolled in full-time four-year programs. We will witness a flexibility in school and college programs and policies heretofore unprecedented. Shane emphasizes that this will require job security, imaginative financial provisions, and changes in employment and retirement policies to permit repeated reentry of adults into both full-time and part-time study. We will come to view as dropouts anyone of any age who stops learning.[10]

As Fred Hechinger, former education editor of the *New York Times,* suggests, we may witness by the year 2000 a national program of "Educare," modeled somewhat after our present Medicare program. In a frantic search for new clientele and revenue, colleges will turn attention to the adult population. Two-day workweeks and sabbatical leaves for workers in most enterprises may become commonplace. Boredom may become widespread unless this new leisure time is turned to one of our most compelling quests—the search for new knowledge. The government may come to realize that it cannot afford to undercapitalize our nation's most priceless resource, a highly educated citizenry. Society may come to recognize that the right to education at all ages, regardless of financial means, may be as imperative as the right to health-delivery systems now provided under Medicare. Educare could provide full cost of tuition for all "nonuseful" courses, while tuition for "useful" courses could be assessed at the rate by which study increases personal productivity and income. Hechinger sees the open university as the prime agency for serving Educare recipients. There will be computer terminals in most homes, subscribed to in much the same way as telephone service is now provided, along with two-way audiovisual communication provided by various sponsoring educational agencies. This revolutionary educational development could transform American society into a learning society and produce the golden age of American civilization; it could enrich life far beyond anything heretofore undertaken.[11]

We hope the future will provide more and better continuing education for those sectors of the adult population presently underserved—the poor, the undereducated, ethnic minorities, women, and the aged. This will lead to newer and better ways of teaching and learning, including self-instructional devices, improved audiovisual methods, simulation techniques, sociodrama, and other tools and techniques in educational technology.

Significant progress in adult education programs sponsored by the public schools cannot be

[10]Harold G. Shane, *The Educational Significance of the Future,* Phi Delta Kappa, Bloomington, Ind., 1973, pp. 76–79.
[11]Fred M. Hechinger, "The Case for Educare and the Open University," *Saturday Review World,* Aug. 24, 1974, pp. 74–75.

made without increased financial support. A study of the financing of adult education by the Adult Education Association concluded that few communities could sustain adequate programs through fees and tuition. Clearly, increased financial support from public funds—local, state, and national—is needed.

Certainly much that goes on in the name of adult education suffers from a lack of serious purpose. It is probable that in the future adult education will transcend our pedestrian and immediate human needs and come to grips with the more fateful social, economic, political, and cultural challenges of our time. Already there is a strong indication of this tendency.

Although public schools and colleges will continue to expand their role in lifelong learning, the importance of other agencies will continue to grow even more dramatically. The number of public school systems offering adult education programs will undoubtedly increase. Institutions of higher education will serve more adults, not only formally, through study programs on campus and at extension centers, but also informally, through such media as television, workshops, and conferences. Community colleges will play an increasingly important role and will make college-level adult education more widely available geographically.

Undoubtedly, adult education will become the fifth level of education. Then the teaching of those things needed only in adult life will no longer be the responsibility of the other four levels. Adult education will widen its scope through continuing education and will improve its performance through the pursuit of excellence, thus capitalizing on America's most priceless commodity—human resources, at all ages.

Suggested activities

1. Describe some important trends and future directions of adult education in our society.
2. Prepare a description of adult education programs offered by the college or university you are attending.
3. Summarize the important recommendations in the book *The Learning Society*, listed below.
4. What are some modern imperatives demanding continuing education?
5. Discuss the role of the public school in the education of adults.

6. List all agencies in your community that are directly or indirectly connected with adult education.
7. Write a brief history of some aspect of adult education, such as the labor colleges.
8. Describe one federally financed program in adult education.
9. Report on one scientific investigation of adults' learning ability.
10. What are some implications for education of the fact that the nation's population is growing older?
11. List desirable qualifications for a teacher of adults. Do you possess these qualifications?

Bibliography

Adult Education Association of the U.S.A.: *Handbook of Adult Education in the United States,* Macmillan, New York, 1970. Helpful resource volume for an overview of adult education programs.

American Association for Higher Education: *Lifelong Learners: A New Clientele for Higher Education,* Washington, 1974. Examines current social, political, and economic contexts of lifelong learning programs in higher education and the new clientele.

Grabowski, Stanley M., and **W. Dean Mason** (eds.): *Education for the Aging,* Capitol Publications, Washington, 1974. Describes the educational needs of the elderly and the reforms essential in our educational institutions to meet these needs.

Houle, Cyril O.: "Adult Education," in *Encyclopedia of Educational Research,* 4th ed., Collier-Macmillan, Toronto, Ontario, 1970, pp. 51–57. Review of research and leading thought on adult education.

Long, Huey B.: *Are They Too Old To Learn?* Prentice Hall, Englewood Cliffs, N.J., 1975. Summarizes what is known about the learning aptitudes, styles, and performance of adults.

Rauch, David B. (ed.): *Priorities in Adult Education,* Free Press, New York, 1972. Pleasantly readable discussion of the most important aspects of continuing education.

Snyder, Robert E.: *Guide to Teaching Techniques for Adult Classes,* Prentice Hall, Englewood Cliffs, N.J., 1974. Explains through case studies several sound approaches to teaching adults.

Thomson, Francis C. (ed.): *The New York Times Guide to Continuing Education in America,* Quadrangle, New York, 1975. Catalogue of the thousands of institutions offering adult education for credit, professional advancement, and pleasure.

University of Notre Dame, Center for Continuing Education: *The Learning Society,* University of Notre Dame Press, Notre Dame, Ind., 1973. Report of a study of adult and continuing education, including recommendations for changes.

Chapter 9

Curriculum

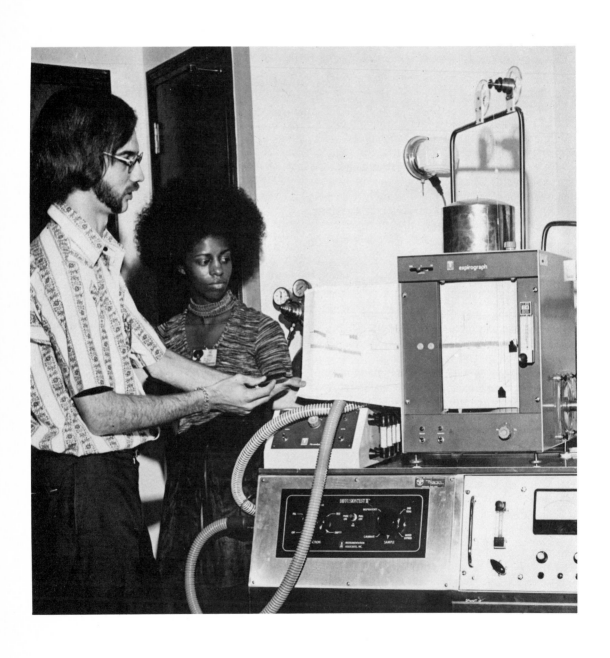

Foundations of curriculum development

Curriculum construction was a simple task in the primitive life of early American schools. Pre-elementary schools did not exist. The common schools stressed the four Rs—reading, 'riting, 'rithmetic, and religion. High schools emphasized the college preparatory curriculum, consisting largely of classical studies. College courses of study offered a combination of liberal and professional education suited to a relatively simple agrarian society and economy. Adult education, at least on an organized basis, was virtually unknown. In those days it was generally assumed that the curriculum of the schools at all levels was built upon separate academic subjects. These subjects were organized around the academic disciplines—English, other languages, mathematics, science, history, geography, and so forth. Courses of study included as much content of the subject field as could be taught to students. The function of schools was almost exclusively the transmission of organized knowledge.

Several forces have had important impact upon the development of the curriculum in recent years: discovery of new insights into the nature of learning; the compelling need for humanizing school experience; the growing capacity of the school for accommodating individual differences; and the increased capability of building coherence and continuity into the curriculum. We shall consider each of these briefly.

INSIGHTS INTO THE NATURE OF LEARNING

It is clear that we know little about human learning, notwithstanding the vigorous attention researchers have devoted to this task over the years. It is also clear that sound pedagogy and curriculum development must be rooted in learning theory. The curriculum reform of the 1950s and early 1960s focused upon subject matter in the academic fields. The academicians who led this undertaking soon discovered what curriculum specialists had long understood: that curriculum cannot be developed without reference to the developmental characteristics of learners. As John Holt explicates so clearly in his books *How Children Fail* and *How Children Learn,* the manner in which children think and learn must be regarded as organizing principles for the curriculum. Fortunately, intensive investigation is now being directed toward the science of human learning and development. Subject-oriented academicians have joined with behavioral scientists to bridge the objects of the verb "to teach"—the learner *and* the subject. This advance has been stimulated by the development of programmed instruction, which depends so heavily upon understanding modes of learning as well as upon the structure of knowledge. Instructional programmers have learned the hazards of ignoring either. Observation, research, and experimentation in human learning have been sustained by the work of many, such as Holt, Piaget, Pressey, Dewey, Gesell, Skinner, and Bruner; many organizations have also contributed, including regional educational laboratories, PACE, IDEA, and the NEA's National Foundation for the Improvement of Education. Harry Broudy and John Palmer's *Exemplars of Teaching Method,* John Holt's *How Children Fail* and *How Children Learn,* John Goodlad's *The Changing School Curriculum,* James Conant's several works on American high schools and junior high schools, and Jerome Bruner's *The Process of Education* were especially noteworthy contributions to the development of school curriculums during the 1950s and 1960s.

HUMANIZING THE SCHOOL EXPERIENCE

The hallmark of proposals for educational reform in the early 1970s has been the demand to humanize the schools. Post-Sputnik reformers were primarily interested in learners' cognitive development in defense-related subject fields. Some reforms were counterproductive with respect to the development of learners' affective development—tastes, values, and emotions. Curriculums were not relevant to the personal needs and interests of students and the sometimes harsh reality of their milieu. As John Goodlad noted, "The schools do not, in general, foster man's creative talents, nor grapple with his great ideas, nor relate these ideas and talents to the contemporary environment where man's dramas are continually re-enacted." By the early 1970s many books were calling for humanizing the schools by adopting a spirit of reverence for children and youth.[1]

Conant, Bestor, Koerner, Rickover, and other essentialist reformers, all but ignored in the new crusade for humanism in education, were replaced by a new breed of romantic reformers—Goodman, Friedenberg, Holt, Kozol, and Silberman, among others—who insisted that schools should accommodate to learners, rather than the other way around. The alienation of many students from school and society quickened interest in developing school programs and practices that were at least as concerned with the human spirit as they were with cognition. New understandings of how children learn and rekindled concern for individuals prompted a new openness in education. Virtually all major cities and large suburban school districts manifest evidence of openness through one or more of the following: open schools, open classrooms, free schools, alternative schools. The trend has had a strong impact on schools and their curriuclums. Its influence has touched thousands of classrooms and has helped to make even many traditional classrooms more relaxed and open.

Many schools are also opening their walls and enlarging their boundaries. The classroom is no

---

[1]See, for example, Charles E. Silberman, *Crisis in the Classroom,* Random House, New York, 1970; Ryland W. Crary, *Humanizing the School: Curriculum Development and Theory,* Knopf, New York, 1969; and Herbert R. Kohl, *The Open Classroom,* Vintage, Random House, New York, 1970.

longer confined to a stationary building but extends to the whole community. Many programs for students promote the use of community resources, such as work-experience and action-learning programs. In a broader sense, the schools are beginning to extend their resources to the community, providing opportunities for intellectual fulfillment for all members of society.

There is more openness in opportunity, too. Courses in such areas as vocational education and physical education are more open to both sexes. And ethnic studies are beginning to fill in gaps caused by years of neglect.[2]

INDIVIDUALIZED INSTRUCTION

There has been a new thrust toward individualized instruction in recent years. This trend is compatible with the humanization of education, because learning can hardly be humane if it is not attuned to the needs, interests, and abilities of individual students. Individualized instruction is sometimes spoken of as "adaptive education," because the environment should be adaptable to a wide variety of learning styles.

Individualized instruction consists of a plan that is tailored to each student's unique learning needs and individual learning style. The setting, materials, methods, and goals vary with each student, and a wide variety of approaches are used. Individualized instruction is often facilitated by the use of technical advances. Harvard professor B.F. Skinner's pioneering work in learning theory has established the basis for teaching machines and other devices for programmed learning. It has also cast important light upon the orderly, sequential presentation of content, which is basic not only to programmed learning but also to efficient and systematic ordering of all courses of study. It has forced teachers and researchers to raise fundamental questions about the objectives of teaching, the nature and order of materials to be learned, the function of evaluation and reward in learning, the adaptation of the curriculum to individual differences, and other important facets of the entire educative process.

Many schools are opening their walls to let students gain broader knowledge of community services and jobs.

The linkage of programmed instruction with computer-assisted instruction now makes individualized instruction technically possible. Computer-assisted instruction permits each student to carry on a sort of tutorial dialogue that is responsive to his or her particular capabilities and achievements.

It will be many years before it becomes financially feasible for most school systems to use differentiated staffing, a method of deploying teachers and students more effectively. This will also enhance individualized instruction. Independent study, minicourses, flexible grouping of students, and nongraded school organization will also be employed more commonly as stratagems for individualizing instruction.[3]

---

[2]For an interesting discussion of major changes in education, see John I. Goodlad, "An Emphasis on Change," *American Education,* January–February 1975, pp. 16–21, 24–25, 28.

[3]For an extensive discussion of the future of individualized instruction, see Harold E. Mitzel, "The Impending Instruction Revolution," *Phi Delta Kappan,* April 1970, pp. 434–439.

THE DEVELOPMENT OF CONTINUITY AND COHERENCE

Today there is greater capability for building continuity and coherence into the curriculum. Harold Shane defines this goal as "an unbroken chain of ventures and adventures in meaningful learning, beginning with early childhood education ... and extended through post-secondary education and on into later-life education."[4]

Many educators agree that the future requires far more fundamental consideration of the purposes of education, priorities of education stated as goals, better assessment of progress toward these goals, and more vigorous experimental comparison of alternative ways of achieving these goals. The application of systems theory and management to curriculum development may or may not succeed in bringing order, system, coherence, and continuity to the school curriculum.

The curriculum and educational objectives

One of the ageless educational questions, the one central to all others, is: "What is the purpose of education?" If this question could be answered to the satisfaction of all—as, of course, it never will or should be—practically all other educational issues could be resolved. Is it the purpose of education to transmit subject matter? To reform society? To encourage individual self-realization? To develop better citizens? To train more productive workers? To build better attitudes and values? To improve intergroup and international relations? Is it all of these, or none of these?

These various points of view reflect positions on a continuum ranging from essentialism to progressivism and life adjustment. Obviously the curriculum one finds most satisfactory depends heavily upon the philosophical position one takes in defining education.

A COMPOSITE SET OF EDUCATIONAL GOALS

Phi Delta Kappa, a national honorary fraternity in education, has formulated a set of eighteen educational goals along with kits of materials which have been widely used by citizens, students, and educators to arrange these goals by preference. The goals are eclectic in nature, drawing upon all the philosophical views mentioned above:

1. Develop skills in reading, writing, speaking, and listening.
2. Develop pride in work and a feeling of self-worth.
3. Develop good character and self-respect.
4. Develop a desire for learning now and in the future.
5. Learn to respect and get along with people with whom we work and live.
6. Learn how to examine and use information.
7. Gain a general education.
8. Learn how to be a good citizen.
9. Learn about and try to understand the changes that take place in the world.
10. Understand and practice democratic ideas and ideals.
11. Learn how to respect and get along with people who think, dress, and act differently.
12. Understand and practice the skills of family living.
13. Gain information needed to make job selections.
14. Learn how to be a good manager of money, property, and resources.
15. Practice and understand the ideas of health and safety.
16. Develop skills to enter a specific field of work.
17. Learn how to use leisure time.
18. Appreciate culture and beauty in the world.[5]

BEHAVIORAL OBJECTIVES

In recent years great emphasis has been placed upon the formulation of *behavioral objectives* for units of work. Behavior is overt and observable and measurable, even though the more generalized goals, such as those stated above, are the ultimate goal. The purpose of stating behavioral objectives is to clarify one's instructional intentions so that they can be more easily accomplished and more

---

[4]See Harold G. Shane, "A Curriculum Continuum: Possible Trends in the 70s," *Phi Delta Kappan,* March 1970, pp. 389–392, for an extension of this concept.

[5]Harold Spears, "Kappans Ponder the Goals of Education," *Phi Delta Kappan,* September 1973, pp. 29–32.

precisely measured. The use of behavioral objectives has been gaining impetus since the 1960s, although the concept is not new. The advent of programmed instruction has made behavioral objectives quite essential to programmers. And the specification of these behavioral objectives by classroom teachers is important, even though programmed materials are not in use. These two examples of behavioral objectives are illustrative:

Identifies and reads decimal fractions to hundredths.
Subtracts with no borrowing up to three digits.

The increased use of such objectives has also brought confusion and ambiguity. Misunderstandings arise from the word "behavior," which people tend to interpret in the strict psychological sense. Ralph Tyler, developer of behavioral objectives during the 1930s, feels that behavioral objectives should be stated in more general terms. Tyler feels that behavioral objectives which are too specific tend to make people confuse "knowing *answers* with being *educated*." Behavioral objectives are meant as tools to help accomplish an end. They are not ends in themselves. They are valuable only if they serve the greater goal of educating students.

Agencies and organizations that collect behavioral objectives and supply them to educators are becoming more and more common. The great demand for these materials indicates the increasing use of behavioral objectives.[6]

MASTERY LEARNING

Mastery learning, somewhat related to behavioral objectives, is also increasing in use. Mastery learning suggests that any student can master any learning task commensurate with his or her level of maturity, if given adequate help, time, and materials. Students are expected to master each concept no matter how long it takes; they then proceed to the next. Since successful mastery is expected of all students without severe learning disabilities, F grades become obsolete. Indeed all letter grades are commonly eliminated. Report cards are descriptive progress reports that state the minimum level of mastery required and the time span in which the student acquired mastery, and, for some, the level of mastery achieved beyond the minimum level. Tests are given periodically to diagnose needs and evaluate performance. Students are helped as much as necessary to succeed. The teacher must define what is meant by mastery, so that the level of mastery can be evaluated. Many alternative means are used, so that all students can be reached. Peer- and cross-age tutoring, a variety of textbooks, workbooks, programmed materials, and other devices are used. Research evidence is varied. Students seem to enjoy learning because of the built-in success factor, although too much emphasis on complete mastery may discourage students. Mastery learning is a feature of programmed learning and is also being used in some forms of individualized instruction. One disadvantage of mastery learning is that it is very time-consuming. Some criticize mastery learning on the basis that in order to measure whether students have mastered concepts, it is almost necessary to break each subject into behavioral objectives. They feel that this type of learning can be helpful in some areas of learning and for limited periods of time, but it can also be just as stifling and dehumanizing as many methods decried during the 1960s.[7]

Principles of curriculum development

A common practice in the initiation of programs for curriculum development is to prepare a list of basic principles or guiding assumptions. This ini-

---

[6]For more information on behavioral objectives, see the following: W. James Popham, "Objectives '72," *Phi Delta Kappan*, March 1972, p. 432; James B. Macdonald and Bernice J. Wolfson, "A Case against Behavioral Objectives," *The Elementary School Journal*, December 1970, 119; and June Grant Shane and Harold G. Shane (interviewers), "Ralph Tyler Discusses Behavioral Objectives," *Today's Education*, September–October 1973, p. 42.

[7]For more information on mastery learning, see James H. Block, "Teachers, Teaching, and Mastery Learning," *Today's Education*, November–December 1973, pp. 30–36. See also Patrick Groff, "Some Criticisms of Mastery Learning," *Today's Education*, December 1974, pp. 88–91.

tial attack provides a unified point of view and a basis for consistency of action among the educational workers as they develop curriculums. The National Education Association, in honor of the United States Bicentennial, has rewritten and expanded its *Cardinal Principles of Education* in order to make it more meaningful both now and in the future. The principles were developed with a global perspective, emphasizing interdependence of all peoples. The following sections reflect the authors' preferences with respect to (1) the nature of the curriculum and (2) the process of curriculum development.

THE NATURE OF THE CURRICULUM

The curriculum should be rooted in a philosophy of education. School systems and individual teachers must consider certain fundamental questions relative to the purposes of education, such as those stated in Chapter 1, and must specify rather clearly in terms of learners' behavior the educational objectives that should be accomplished through the curriculum and instruction if the school is to be effective. Without a philosophic rationale, important decisions may be made on spurious considerations, and the curriculum is less likely to be coherent and consistent. A well-defined philosophy of education will also help to establish priorities. Clearly this philosophy of education should be developed cooperatively by the faculty, administrators, board of education, and students. Figure 9-1 relates the characteristics of the curriculum and instruction with the basic philosophies of education described in Chapter 1.

The curriculum should accommodate a wide range of individual abilities and needs of students. The doctrine of individual differences among students is axiomatic, and it is important

Figure 9-1 Characteristics of curriculum and instruction related to educational philosophies. "Yes" indicates a commonly strong relationship between a characteristic and a philosophical view. The absence of "yes" indicates either no relationship or a relatively weak or uncommon relationship. In reality, these relationships are not as categorical as the figure indicates.

CHARACTERISTICS OF CURRICULUM AND INSTRUCTION	Progressivism	Existentialism	Reconstructionism	Life adjustment	Personal development	Essentialism	Supernaturalism	Individual and global survival
Curriculum structure is subject-centered						yes	yes	
Curriculum structure is learner-centered	yes	yes		yes	yes			
Curriculum structure is problem-centered			yes	yes	yes			yes
Curriculum structure is flexible	yes	yes	yes	yes	yes			
Curriculum structure is interdisciplinary	yes	yes	yes	yes	yes			yes
Instruction is individualized	yes	yes		yes	yes			
Instruction is standardized			yes			yes	yes	yes
Cognitive development (knowing) is emphasized	yes	yes	yes	yes	yes	yes	yes	yes
Affective development (feeling) is emphasized	yes	yes	yes	yes	yes			yes
Learning process or experience is critical	yes	yes	yes	yes	yes			

that the curriculum be sufficiently broad and flexible to provide meaningful educative experience for students with quite varied interests, abilities, and goals.

The curriculum should be life-centered, shaped by both present and future needs of individuals and society. Considerable debate has raged over the issue of whether the curriculum should simply transmit the cultural heritage of the past or address itself to the contemporary and future needs of the culture. There is also the issue of whether the curriculum should be subject-centered, child-centered, or community-centered. Fortunately, these are not mutually exclusive choices, despite contrary claims by many critics of the curriculum.

The curriculum should be well balanced. Various components of the curriculum are emphasized while others are neglected. Special-purpose federal aid, prompted by various crises and designed to stimulate curriculum development in certain subjects, has contributed to this situation. Ideally, in a sound curriculum the several subject fields are kept in reasonable balance in terms of time allotments, money spent for research and development, and prestige associated with them.

THE PROCESS OF CURRICULUM DEVELOPMENT

The past quarter-century has been characterized by a wondrous expansion of knowledge. This has forced educators to look for more compact means of organizing programs of study, to prune out the irrelevant and obsolete, and to focus upon content that is most conducive to continued independent learning. Certain principles should govern the development of the curriculum in a free society because the quality of the curriculum depends on the wisdom of the process that produces it.

Curriculum building should be a cooperative enterprise. In local, statewide, or national programs, cooperative effort is essential in curriculum work. One postulate of democracy is that citizens enjoy those things they have helped to build. This is doubly true in regard to the curriculum of the

school. Local school faculties should have the freedom and authority to make decisions about how to teach and what to teach, within the limits of state and local requirements. Effective curriculums are the fruit of collaborative work by teachers, curriculum specialists, academicians, consultants, and to a more limited degree, students and citizens. In the open classroom, curriculums are largely worked out by the teachers and students.[8]

Evaluation is essential for curriculum improvement. The results of student achievement, as well as other measures, are necessary to appraise the effectiveness of the curriculum and instruction. Although the measurement of cognitive development is a fairly well-refined science, the measurement of affective objectives is much more difficult. The novel National Assessment for Educational Progress, sponsored by the Education Commission of the States, is an ambitious effort to gather normative data from a national sample of students' achievement, which provides schools with data that permit comparison of the effectiveness of the curriculum and instruction with national norms. Begun in 1964, the purpose of the National Assessment is to provide data on knowledge, skills, concepts, understandings, and attitudes of American youths aged 9, 13, and 17, and of adults aged 26 to 35. About 100,000 persons respond to exercises in each of ten learning areas: art, career and occupational development, citizenship, literature, mathematics, music, reading, science, social studies, and writing. Each area is reassessed every four to six years and results are compared with previous results in respective learning areas. Many types of testing are used: objective, essay, performance, interviews, and others. Approximately five hundred exercises are used to assess each learning area. Educators, scholars, and laymen develop the exercises according to predetermined objectives.

By the 1974–1975 school year, all ten learning areas were assessed for the first time. The results reveal much about performance levels of persons in the inner city, rural areas, and in geographic areas, such as, Northeast, Southeast, Central, and

[8]For more insight into the process of curriculum development, see Edwin MacBeth, "Who Masterminds the Curriculum? Educators or Profit-makers?" *The American School Board Journal*, August 1974, pp. 22–26.

West. Persons from the inner city usually did the poorest; those from suburbs had the best results. Data show that the education of parents is directly related to their children's success. The assessment can show how well achievement levels are being maintained over a period of time.[9]

Some states also try to test the quality of education in the schools of the state. Pennsylvania's Educational Quality Assessment tests are taken anonymously by fifth-, eighth-, and eleventh-grade students. The test covers mathematics, verbal skills, and citizenship, as well as other areas. A third of the districts participate each year alternately and repeat every third year.

The educational program audit (EPA), done by an objective outsider, is a relatively new procedure employed to assess strengths and weaknesses in an educational program. It reviews the process that is used by a district to assess its programs.

Project TALENT, funded largely by the U.S. Office of Education, has released its findings at various points. Project TALENT studied a 5 percent sample of the United States high school population of grades 9 to 12 in 1960 attending 1,225 junior and senior high schools. Extensive testing, including personal and interest studies, was done. Follow-up studies were completed one, five, and eleven years after graduation. A thousand former ninth-graders were involved in the follow-up studies, which covered leisure, family life, intellectual development, interests, and activities. Some weaknesses revealed through these studies are the lack of individualized instruction provided by schools and the inability of many students to relate their abilities with careers.

Curriculum support systems should be adequate. Curriculum development is handicapped in many schools by the lack of adequate resources, placing too much responsibility upon classroom teachers who have little time for curriculum improvement. Fine school systems provide experts in curriculum theory and method on their own staffs, who are supplemented as needed with consultants from intermediate district offices, state departments, regional laboratories, and other or-

ganizations. Some teachers are employed on twelve-month contracts so that they will be available during the summer months for curriculum development work.

Various material resources are also important. More and more good schools provide curriculum materials centers that stock sample textbooks and other instructional materials and often produce their own materials when commercial materials are inadequate. Testing programs, counseling services, child-study centers, reading clinics, and many other ancillary services are needed to support the modern school program. Other material resources—such as planetariums, learning laboratories, television facilities, and science laboratories—are discussed in Chapter 10.

Curriculum development should be a systematic process. One hallmark of a fine school system is the deliberate, systematic, continuous attention that it devotes to developing the total educational program, as opposed to the sporadic, incidental, intuitive approach to program building that still characterizes too many schools. The application of systems theory is refining the process of curriculum development even better.

Organization of the curriculum

The organization of learning experiences in the curriculum is important because it affects the effectiveness of teaching and learning.

TYPES OF CURRICULUM ORGANIZATION

Curricular patterns range from the traditional type to extremely experimental types. Six curricular patterns, with alternative designations, are (1) subject, or traditional; (2) correlated, or fused; (3) broad fields, or areas; (4) core, or common learnings; (5) open education; and (6) fundamental schools. These types are not mutually exclusive and have numerous variations.

The subject curriculum. In a subject curriculum a large number of subjects are taught independently of one another. Most of the students' time is spent in learning about various subjects from books and other written and printed materials in which the ac-

[9]Complete results of the National Assessment for Educational Progress can be found in *National Assessment Achievements: Findings, Interpretations and Uses,* Education Commission of the States, Denver, Colo.

cumulated knowledge of experts has been recorded. The emphasis is upon learning subject matter that is selected long before students enter the classroom.

In such a curriculum, history, geography, and civics usually are isolated subjects. A modern variation of the subject curriculum began to emerge in the late 1950s. It is spoken of as the "subject-discipline curriculum" and emphasizes not the memorization of information but the perception of the structure of the subject field—its concepts, modes of inquiry, and organization of knowledge. It was prompted by the impossible load of the growing subject matter, the desire to give students a mode of inquiry that would permit them to study the subject on their own initiative after mastering its structure, and the goal of helping students gain a fresh and enriched view of the nature of general education. Its disadvantages include its failure to relate to real-life problems, such as pollution, which do not come wrapped up in a single subject field; its failure to integrate knowledge from several subject fields; and its difficulty to apply in fields outside the physical sciences in which knowledge cannot be organized readily.[10]

The correlated curriculum. Here the underlying ideas are those described for the subject curriculum, but they are modified somewhat. The starting point is the subject matter set out to be learned. The correlated curriculum can be carried out in numerous ways, which can be conveniently arranged on a scale. At the bottom would be located the casual and incidental efforts to make relationships between subjects. At the top of the scale would be located the conscious and definitely planned efforts to make effective relationships between subjects. Among the correlations may be those between subjects within a field, as social science, or between subjects within two or more fields, as English and history. Subjects may be fused so that boundaries disappear.

The broad fields curriculum. This is composed of a few fields rather than a large number of small subjects. In broad fields, under the subject philosophy, the learning area is restricted, although definitely broader than what would be expected as a summation of various subjects. In broad fields, under the experience philosophy, the learning area is greatly increased. Examples of these broad fields or areas are social science and the language arts.

The core curriculum. This includes subjects or a common body of experiences required of everyone, but with variability of content and activities to meet the needs of individuals. The term "core" is used to cover a wide range of types of curriculum practice. Part of the work in the senior high may be a basic core running through grades 10, 11, and 12 with variable time allotments. A certain portion of each day may be devoted to the core, or common learnings.[11]

Open education. Open education is compatible with progressive, reconstructionist, and existentialist philosophies of education. Open education is based on British infant schools, which have been highly successful in England for many years. It should not be confused with free school, in which children are permitted to do what they want, even nothing. Most open classrooms are structured. Space is usually divided into learning areas, such as science, art, mathematics, language. But the curriculum is flexible and usually interdisciplinary. Children move around freely. The open classroom often seems more like a workshop than a classroom, and a variety of activities are performed simultaneously. In addition to standard subjects, activities may include such varied topics as photography, pottery, typography, and cooking. Often the curriculum grows out of classroom experiences.

Teachers in open education are facilitators of learning, rather than lecturers. Classrooms are not permissive, despite their flurry of activity and additional noise. Teachers are in control. They must keep in touch with children's work, even though children may be working on independent projects. Teachers must assess progress, needs, and interests of students and provide opportunities for ap-

---

[10]For further discussion of the subject-discipline organization, see Arthur W. Foshay, "How Fare the Disciplines?" *Phi Delta Kappan,* March 1970, pp. 349–352.

[11]For an interesting account of the core curriculum in practical use, see Laurel N. Tanner and Daniel Tanner, "The Core Curriculum Is Being Reinvented," *Educational Leadership,* December 1973, pp. 281–282.

The open classroom often seems more like a workshop than a classroom, and a variety of activities go on simultaneously.

propriate learning experiences. Classrooms must be rich in learning materials and opportunities.

Children work in small groups with or without the teacher, or on independent studies or projects. The whole class may come together to share some experiences. Instruction is individualized, even personalized, making use of programmed instruction, flexible pupil grouping, team teaching, peer tutoring, cross-age tutoring, paraprofessionals, vertical grouping, flexible scheduling, and multiage grouping. Of course, there are all degrees of open classrooms. There is no blueprint; nor should there be, for open education programs should develop from within. The environment, though, is one of mutual respect and trust in an atmosphere of openness that motivates children to learn, think, and work independently.

Is open education succeeding? It is difficult to say how widespread it has become, since no survey has determined the number of open classrooms that exist throughout the country. There is great interest in open education among educators, as evidenced by the thousands of teachers who attend open-education centers, seminars, and workshops to learn about and to exchange ideas concerning open education. Interest is also shown by the number of publications available. Study

tours of open classrooms both here and in England are in great demand. In 1974 the Rockefeller Brothers Fund made available $975,000 to help form a network of open-education centers that provide information and training for teachers. The Ford Foundation, the Carnegie Corporation, the Education Development Center of Newton, Massachusetts, and the U.S. Office of Education also support efforts in open education.

The 1975 report of a two-year comparative evaluation of open education and traditional education showed no significant difference in achievement in basic skills. It did show that children in open classrooms had more positive self-concepts and more positive attitudes toward school.[12]

Fundamental schools. A number of so-called "fundamental schools" have appeared recently in the same school districts with open schools, thereby providing parents an option between these two contrasting institutions. Fundamental schools emphasize mastery of the basic skills, training in logical reasoning, knowledge of our culture and government, citizenship and patriotism, and intellectual rigor. Discipline in these schools tends to be more strict than in conventional schools. Dress codes are more rigorous for both students and teachers. Homework assignments are substantial. These schools are popular with parents and students who prefer the essentialist philosophy of education; such schools are, of course, viewed favorably by the Council for Basic Education, which has long supported this type of schooling.[13]

TYPES OF INSTRUCTIONAL SYSTEMS

The various types of instructional systems might be classified on the basis of the deployment of students in the system: (1) group instruction and

[12]For more information about open education, see Dan Reschly and Darrell Sabers, "Open Education: Have We Been There Before?" *Phi Delta Kappan,* June 1974, p. 675; Alan H. Wheeler, "Structuring for Open Education," *Educational Leadership,* December 1973, p. 250; Arthur E. Salz, "The Truly Open Classroom," *Phi Delta Kappan,* February 1974, p. 388; Mortimer Smith, "Before and After 'The Truly Open Classroom,'" *Phi Delta Kappan,* February 1974, p. 390; and Lyn S. Martin and Barbara N. Pavan, "Current Research on Open Space," *Phi Delta Kappan,* January 1976, pp. 310–315.

[13]For further description of these schools, see Philip G. Jones, "All about Those New 'Fundamental Public Schools,'" *The American School Board Journal,* February 1976, pp. 24–31.

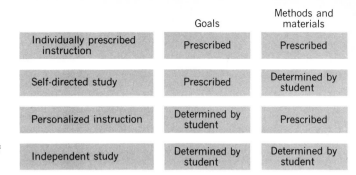

	Goals	Methods and materials
Individually prescribed instruction	Prescribed	Prescribed
Self-directed study	Prescribed	Determined by student
Personalized instruction	Determined by student	Prescribed
Independent study	Determined by student	Determined by student

Figure 9-2 Comparison of modes of individualized instruction.

(2) individualized instruction. They might be classified on the basis of the deployment of responsibility for directing the instruction: (1) teacher-mediated instruction, (2) computer-mediated instruction, and (3) student-mediated instruction, or self-instruction. These two sets of categories are overlapping. The categories rarely exist in pure form. We shall discuss both sets of categories.

Group instruction. We are all familiar with various types of group instruction that have prevailed almost entirely until recent years. Students are grouped in various sizes commonly, but not always, in grades on the basis of chronological age, reading ability, academic interests, intelligence, or various other criteria. The obvious advantage of group instruction is that it uses teachers' time more economically than individualized instruction. Its disadvantage is that it fails somewhat to accommodate individual differences in learners.

Individualized instruction. Four general approaches to individualized instruction are illustrated in Figure 9-2: individually prescribed instruction, self-directed study, personalized instruction, and independent study. Many schools use adaptations and combinations of all four categories.

The vertical organization of the curriculum should permit continuous progression of all learners, but at rates of progress differentiated according to their abilities. Ungraded and multigraded organizations are useful patterns for achieving this ideal. Programmed instruction offers a technological device by which instruction may be adapted more effectively and efficiently to the individual needs of learners. Figure 9-3 illustrates the sequence of a programmed instructional

Figure 9-3 Sequence of a task in programmed instruction. This figure illustrates the essential elements in a sequence of programmed instruction. When the feedback loop is present and offers remedial instruction, the program is "branched." Without this loop, the program is "linear." (Reprinted from American Association of School Administrators, *Instructional Technology and the School Administrator,* Washington, 1970, p. 40.)

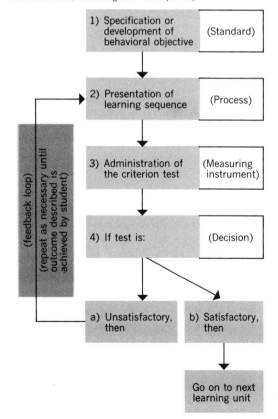

task. Individually Prescribed Instruction (IPI) was developed by the Learning Research and Development Center at the University of Pittsburgh and tested in the field in a number of schools beginning in 1964. IPI materials are available in elementary school language arts, mathematics, social studies, science, social education, and library and reference skills.

The essential procedures of an IPI instructional system accomplish the following:

Diagnose students' strengths and weaknesses with tests.

Prescribe instructional tasks built upon behavioral objectives and tailored to individuals' needs.

Analyze students' progress with the instructional task through tests.

Apply guidance or tutoring as needed to ensure mastery of the task.

Administer test to confirm mastery.

Repeat the cycle with the next set of learning tasks.

IPI is based upon the following instructional stratagems:

Help individual students proceed at their optimal rates in progress toward well-defined instructional tasks derived from specific educational objectives.

Involve each student actively in learning activities that are wholly or partially self-directed and self-selected.

Engage students in evaluating the quality and rapidity of their own progress toward mastery of instructional tasks.

Encounter various instructional modes and materials best adapted to students' particular needs and learning styles.

Assessments of the IPI program to date indicate that it yields generally higher achievement for students than is common in conventional instruction. IPI has been discussed at some length here because it is one of the most widely used and carefully developed programs of individualized instruction developed so far. Approximately four hundred schools provide IPI programs for 100,000 students. It promises much wider use in the years ahead and may one day be regarded as one of the most significant developments in instruction in our history.[14]

[14]For further description of IPI, see Diane Divoky, "Individually Prescribed Instruction," *The Nation's Schools*, November 1969, pp. 44–46.

Individually Guided Education (IGE) has increased in use since its development. It serves over two thousand schools in thirty-five states. IGE is used only in elementary schools at present. It is a form of individualized instruction involving multiunit organization. (See Figure 5-3 for an illustration of IGE organization.) A model of individualized programmed instruction and a model for evaluation are used. Curriculum materials are geared to behavioral objectives for each child based on his or her rate and style of learning, interests, and other knowledge. The staff selects materials to be used for each student. IGE materials are available commercially in reading, mathematics, and motivational procedures. The program constantly assesses and reassesses students' achievement and needs in order to specify individual objectives. IPI includes students in instructional decision-making, whereas IGE leaves most instructional decisions to teachers and the staff. IGE is also being planned for secondary schools. (See Chapter 5 for more information on IGE.)

Various other programs of individualized instruction are also noteworthy but can be mentioned only briefly here. Project PLAN, developed by the Westinghouse Learning Corporation, is a systematic specification of educational objectives tailored to meet each student's special aptitudes, interests, and patterns of learning. Unlike IPI and IGE, Project PLAN is a computer-managed system. A computer stores these data and presents "teaching-learning units" tailor-made for each student according to needs and achievement. The computer also monitors progress and feeds back evaluation of work. The function of the computer in Project PLAN—unlike some programs of computer-assisted instruction—is purely administrative. Students do not deal directly with the computer. Project PLAN can be used in elementary and secondary schools and has been widely tested in the field. It promises to have widespread impact on the whole development of computer-assisted instruction.

The open classroom is, of course, an excellent example of individualized instruction. It is a freer approach than most and does not require behavioral objectives.

Educational Systems for the Seventies (ES'70), initiated by the U.S. Office of Education, comprises a number of school systems across the country that are pioneering various instructional systems which are highly individualized and which are likely to become prototypes for the future. Many others are in various stages of development.

Individualized instruction is noteworthy generally for many reasons. It may eventually realize that age-old dream of adapting instruction rather precisely to the needs, interests, abilities, and learning styles of each individual. It may obviate conventional marking systems, which are usually so dysfunctional. It will prevent learners from falling hopelessly behind in their schoolwork and render obsolete the concept of failure and the practice of nonpromotion. Its chief disadvantage is that its costs will remain fairly prohibitive for most districts until the economies of mass production can be realized.

We will consider now the three basic types of instructional management systems: instructor-mediated, computer-mediated, and student-mediated instruction. We are dealing with each separately to distinguish them, but in modern classrooms it is not realistic to separate them this way. Although teacher-mediated instruction still predominates in most schools, one is more and more likely to see a combination of all types of instruction.[15]

Teacher-mediated instruction. Conventional instruction has been almost entirely teacher-mediated. The teacher selects the instructional materials and methods; the teacher dispenses the knowledge through lecture, discussion, and assigned readings; the teacher evaluates the results. In short, the teacher manages virtually all options within the parameters set by the school district.

Computer-mediated instruction. Computers are being used increasingly to store and analyze data concerning students' learning needs, problems, styles, and progress; to prescribe appropriate instructional tasks; to score and feed back the results of students' work; to monitor progress; and, in short, to handle many of the logistical instructional tasks formerly assumed by teachers. Many programmed instructional systems, such as Project PLAN, mentioned earlier, depend on computers. These systems are commonly spoken of as "computer-assisted instruction" (CAI). Computers eventually will make it financially feasible to handle the great burden of data processing that is generated by programmed instruction, which in turn provides individualized instruction. Cognitive and psychomotor skills are increasingly being taught through programmed materials and other self-managed systems. CAI is discussed at greater length in Chapter 10. Figure 9-3 illustrates a typical sequence of programmed learning.

Student-mediated instruction. Independent or self-study, which is not new, is common in many schools during part of the school day. Peer tutoring and cross-age tutoring are being used to help students learn.[16] Both parties benefit from such a system.

New and emerging curriculum areas

The school curriculum tends to reflect the times. It strives to keep relevant to the needs and interests of learners. Therefore, subject matter is ever changing. Areas that have commanded attention in recent years are black studies, ethnic studies, environmental education, education about drug and alcohol abuse, morality education, sex education, transcendental meditation, parenthood education, peace studies, death education, futurism, nutrition, and consumer education.

Some of these courses or topics do not fit into any one subject area neatly. They are either too broad and cross several disciplines, or they are too specific and may be taught as minicourses within other subjects or alone. Career education will be dealt with first because it holds a unique position in the educational program.

CAREER EDUCATION

Career education has been widely accepted as a worthwhile approach to preparing youths with skills that are marketable in their society. Career

---

[15]For comparative information on individualized instruction, see Ronald E. Hull, "Selecting an Approach to Individualized Education," *Phi Delta Kappan,* November 1973, pp. 169–173.

[16]For a closer look at peer-mediated instruction, see "Son of CAI," *Nation's Schools and Colleges,* September 1974, pp. 15–16.

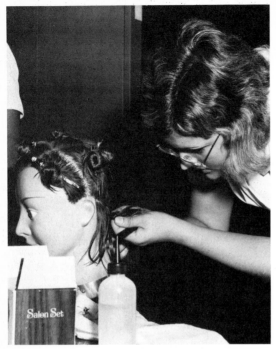

Career education provides skills, motivation, and opportunities for students to explore useful and fulfilling careers.

education is built around the assumption that the school's responsibility is to provide skills, motivation, and opportunities for students to explore, seek out, and find useful and fulfilling careers.

Career education is not a course, nor is it a new name for vocational education. It cuts across all subject areas. According to Hoyt, Evans, Mackin, and Mangum, the five basic components of career education are

1. The first component requires every classroom teacher in every course at every level to emphasize, where appropriate, the career implications of the substantive content taught.
2. The second component of career education is represented by vocational-skills training for successful entry (or reentry) into the occupational world.
3. The third component includes the provision of a comprehensive career development program involving active cooperation and participation of both school and nonschool personnel.
4. This component includes the provision of work obser-

vation, work experience, and work-study opportunities for students and for those who educate them in public school settings. It also provides consultative and advisory services to school officials regarding the nature and needs of the occupational society.
5. This component recognizes and capitalizes upon the interrelationships among the home, the family, the community, and the occupational society.[17]

Figure 9-4 shows the development of career education from childhood to adulthood.

Career education is growing rapidly. According to the U.S. Office of Education, forty-two states and territories have career education coordinators, one-third of the nation's schools have comprehensive career education programs, and about twenty institutions of higher education offer career education in teacher-training programs. A few even offer majors in career education.

Federal funds have been made available for career programs. The National Institute of Education (NIE) also contributes to career education. In 1975 it spent about $4 million on such programs. The U.S. Office of Education has established a Center for Career Education, which has developed instructional programs for fifteen "career clusters." These clusters are convenient ways of aggregating information about the 25,000 available occupations. The College Entrance Examination Board is studying career education at the state level with a grant from NIE. The group is analyzing state career education programs and developing models for coordinating career education. Councils for career education are being set up to coordinate the cooperative efforts of community representatives, educators, students, labor, and business. State councils will be headed by a national council.

Like any new educational development, career education is not without its problems and critics. Some contend that it places excessive emphasis upon utilitarian knowledge and poses a threat to liberal education. Others believe that in a recessive economy it accelerates frustration by raising youths' aspirations for occupations in which there is little employment or in occupations which may become obsolete. Some fear that it may force ca-

[17]Adapted from Kenneth B. Hoyt, Rupert N. Evans, Edward F. Mackin, and Garth L. Mangum, *Career Education: What It Is and How to Do It,* 2d ed., Olympus Publishing, Salt Lake City, 1974, pp. 25–30.

reer choices on youths too early. There are those who fear that it creates in students an egocentric view of schooling in terms of "what it can do for me" rather than an outward-directed view of what education can contribute to the building of a democratic, participatory social order. Some regard it as just another passing fad in the parade of educational reform. We think not, because it has so much promise in the reduction of some critical social, economic, and educational problems. More important, career education has great potential for youths' fulfillment. We think the time has come for this fateful concept. According to Gallup polls, our people place high value upon education that is attuned to helping students gain access to better career opportunities. The National Commission on the Reform of Secondary Education has recommended the expansion of secondary curriculums to include career education.[18]

NEW TOPICS

Death education. Death education, or thanatology, is one of the most unusual and most recent additions to the curriculum in secondary and higher education. Materials, including filmstrips and workbooks, are available from many reliable agencies. The purpose of the course is to help students become familiar with repercussions of death and to help prepare them to face the death of family members and friends, an inevitable part of life. Medical students and psychology students have shown an interest in the study of death, as have other students. Psychologists, sociologists, and educators are contributing ideas and research to this area of education. Where to place it in the curriculum and who will teach it are concerns yet to be resolved. Advocates of death education feel it should be approached early, even in nursery education or in kindergarten.[19]

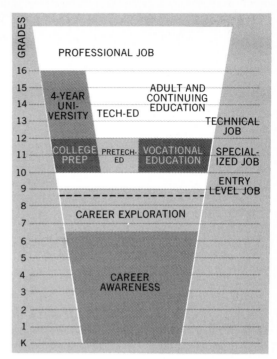

Figure 9-4 Graphic representation of U.S. Office of Education's model of career education shows a continuing focus from elementary school through adulthood.

[18]For further discussion of the dangers some people see in career education, see Robert J. Nash and Russell M. Agne, "A Case of Misplaced Relevance," *The Journal of Teacher Education,* Summer 1973, pp. 87–92. For more information on career education, see Ralph D. Berenger, "Career Education: How Big a Change?" *Compact,* June 1975, pp. 2–5.

[19]For a discussion of death education, see Joanne Zazzaro, "Death Be Not Distorted," *Nation's Schools,* May 1973, pp. 39–42.

Moral development. Some schools now include courses in moral development in their curriculum. Called "moral education" or "values clarification," the courses are used at various grade levels. Moral dilemmas are presented to students, and they decide which course of action should be taken. There are no "right" or "wrong" answers as such. Through discussion of these dilemmas and through practice at moral decision making, students can develop their ability to look at all sides of an issue and can improve their ability to make responsible moral and ethical decisions. The teacher remains neutral, stimulating discussion so that all sides or points of view are considered. Sidney Simon of the University of Massachusetts has designed techniques to help students in their moral judgments. Courses may last a semester or merely be a part of another course. Materials are being developed by a number of educational agencies. This type of course is gaining in popularity because of the feeling held by many that the country has experienced a moral breakdown and that we need to instill solid values in youths.[20]

Transcendental meditation. Recently transcendental meditation has become very popular as a mini-course in colleges and some high schools. It is discussed in Chapter 3.[21]

Futurism. Many areas in education, business, and science have become future oriented. Economists, environmentalists, and politicians try to predict the future. Career planning involves being able to predict what the job market will be like at a given time. Future-consciousness may be a special course, or its components may be placed in existing courses.[22] In Chapter 3, we call attention to the importance of future role orientation in the psychological development of students.

MULTIDISCIPLINARY STUDIES

Some multidisciplinary studies are included in areas of learning where they seem most appropriate. For example, environmental education, while multidisciplinary, is usually taught with science. Peace studies, while they transcend many subjects, are most often included as a part of the social science curriculum. We include here those areas of learning which do not fit neatly into other areas of the curriculum.

Ethnic studies. Black studies were begun in order to overcome the neglect of the Negro in the traditional curriculum. So black studies were prompted by the need to redress this injustice, to help black students gain a greater sense of awareness of their culture, and to help both black and white students gain deeper understanding of the problems of race and the means for their alleviation.

[20]For further reading on moral development, see Jack R. Fraenkel, "Strategies for Developing Values," *Today's Education,* November–December 1973, pp. 49–55; and Earl J. McGrath, "The Time Bomb of Technocratic Education," *Change,* September 1974, pp. 24–29.

[21]See Edd Doerr, "Transcendental Meditation Goes to School," *Church and State,* October 1974, pp. 3, 6.

[22]See Dennis Livingston, "For a Future with the Futurists," *Media and Methods,* March 1973, pp. 26–29, 70–71.

Inadequate funding and poor administration have contributed to the decline of some programs. Some enrollments have dropped. Others have risen, although the number of students majoring in the programs is small. Programs are generally better organized and defined than they were at first.

There is still disagreement over whether black studies can be considered an academic discipline. Some programs are limited in eduational value, and some courses tend to involve discussion exclusively and do not require academic-level work. Others are well conceived and sound academically; they fill a need and contribute to cross-cultural understanding.

Since black studies have come on the educational scene, other ethnic groups have begun to demand programs to study their own heritage. The federal government provided $2 1/2 million in 1974 under the Ethnic Heritage Studies Act for various ethnic programs. Grants were assigned to Polish-American, Italian-American, Mexican-American, and Chinese-American groups. The projects include the development of curriculum materials and their dissemination, as well as training personnel to use the materials. The Schweiker Bill, passed in 1972, was designed "to provide assistance to afford students opportunities to learn about the nature of their own cultural heritage, and to study the contributions of the cultural heritages of the other ethnic groups in the nation."

Elementary and secondary schools are also beginning to include ethnic studies in their programs. A survey of 715 school districts in the United States with student populations of 10,000 or more was conducted in 1974. Ethnic studies were reported in 288 of these districts. Figure 9-5 shows the variety of ethnic studies and how widely each is studied.

The concept of the melting pot is being modified. That our society is culturally pluralistic is now being emphasized. That people can feel proud of their ethnic backgrounds and still work for the common good of the United States is not a contradiction. Many believe, however, that emphasizing differences and moving away from the ideal of the melting pot will create polarization among many groups. An important feature of ethnic studies is realism, rather than the traditional superficial study of foods, customs, dances, and so on. The goal is

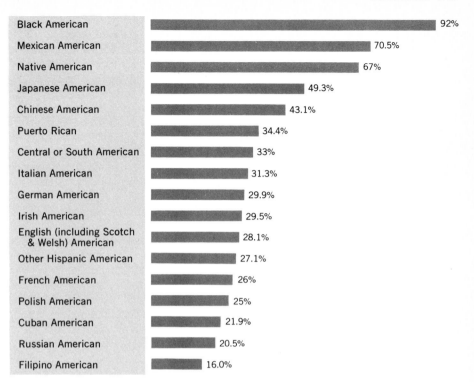

Black American — 92%
Mexican American — 70.5%
Native American — 67%
Japanese American — 49.3%
Chinese American — 43.1%
Puerto Rican — 34.4%
Central or South American — 33%
Italian American — 31.3%
German American — 29.9%
Irish American — 29.5%
English (including Scotch & Welsh) American — 28.1%
Other Hispanic American — 27.1%
French American — 26%
Polish American — 25%
Cuban American — 21.9%
Russian American — 20.5%
Filipino American — 16.0%

Figure 9-5 Percent of sample of 288 school districts studied reporting various cultural-group studies in curriculum. (David E. Washburn, "Ethnic Studies in the United States," *Educational Leadership,* March 1975, p. 411.)

not to foster ethnocentrism, but to help people acquire a respect for their own and for other ethnic groups. Ethnic studies can make an important contribution to cross-cultural understanding.[23]

Sex education. Sex education is another special field of education that cuts across various academic lines—social studies, biological sciences, and health education. Because of its multidisciplinary character, questions arise concerning the proper location of sex education in the curriculum. It may be offered as a separate subject, correlated with the subject areas mentioned above, or included in the health education curriculum. Many authorities prefer the latter.

Although some people still hold nineteenth-century attitudes regarding sex education, many others are agreed that it is vitally needed; that most homes and churches are not doing the job; and that school is the logical agency. The sharp rises in teen-age marriages, premarital pregnancies, venereal disease, and abortions have helped to quicken people's concern for sex education. More emphasis is being placed on cooperative efforts among school, parents, health officials, and other community agencies in providing education about venereal disease.[24]

Sex education is a delicate field of instruction that is frightening to many teachers and anathema to some citizens. It may be boring to students if it is not taught with intelligence, tact, and honesty. One

[23]For more information on ethnic studies, see Mark M. Krug, "White Ethnic Studies: Prospects and Pitfalls," *Phi Delta Kappan,* January 1972, pp. 322–324; and James A. Banks, "Evaluating and Selecting Ethnic Studies Materials," *Educational Leadership,* April 1974, pp. 593–596.

[24]For a picture of the status of such education, see Gloria Stashower, "VD Education: Efforts and Achievements," *School Management,* February 1974, pp. 20–23.

problem has been the unavailability of teachers who are adequately prepared for the task. Publishing companies are now preparing better instructional materials, and various professional organizations are attempting to provide training programs for teachers. The trend is to extend sex and family-life education into the elementary schools for young students who still have the frank and objective curiosity of children and have not yet developed all the emotional distractions that appear with puberty. The home economics curriculum, or "homemaking," as it is sometimes called, in most high schools commonly offers instruction in various aspects of family life including marital relations and sex education.

Drug-abuse education. Drug-abuse education is another multidisciplinary field of study that has assumed compelling importance because of the frightening spread of drug abuse. Many of these programs have been extended into the elementary schools, since the beginning of experimentation with drugs sometimes begins before adolescence. Many authorities believe that ninth grade may be the most effective time for concerted drug-abuse education, although the program should be continued throughout the high school and college years.

Programs provide scientific explanations of the physical and psychological effects of drugs on the human organism, information on sources available to assist students with problems relating to drugs, and information on the legal aspects of drug use. More and more help comes from outside resources —from pharmacists, physicians, lawyers, scientists, and, especially, rehabilitated former drug addicts. The last appear to be especially effective because they "have been there." Small informal group discussion helps to clear up many misconceptions that both students and teachers have about drugs. Sometimes student organizations are enlisted to sponsor the programs. For example, several Westchester (New York) school systems have programs in which high school seniors undertake projects to dissuade younger students from using drugs. These stratagems draw upon the concept that peers have more influence than adults on adolescent behavior and values.

Some drug-abuse programs involve community groups in helping with various aspects of the issues. Many programs consider tobacco and alcohol as well as narcotics and other drugs. Good films and other instructional materials are becoming increasingly available through the National Clearinghouse for Drug Abuse Information and the National Institute of Mental Health. The Education Commission of the States has begun to search for an effective means to prevent alcohol abuse.

The Drug Abuse Education Act, the National Institute of Mental Health, and the U.S. Office of Education, as well as many state governments, have provided funds for training teachers in the fundamentals of drug-abuse education.[25]

Consumer education. The consumer movement has brought renewed interest in consumer education and placed more emphasis on detailed knowledge of the economy and on regulatory agencies. The Institute for Responsive Education, sponsored by Yale University, is providing programs to train students in investigating the public interest. Consumer education fits into the educational program in different ways. Courses such as home economics, business, family living, economics, or vocational education can easily incorporate it into existing programs. Separate courses, or even an interdisciplinary approach, could also be effective.[26]

Changes and trends in traditional curriculum areas

This section provides an overview of the traditional curriculum areas—language arts, social studies, natural sciences, mathematics, foreign languages, the humanities, health and physical education, and vocational and technical education. The major trends and focuses of each curriculum area are presented, rather than a comprehensive, detailed picture of the curriculum, and the implications for each age level.

[25]For further discussion of drug-abuse education, see William C. Stoll, "Guidelines for Drug-abuse Education versus Actual Practice," *Phi Delta Kappan,* March 1974, pp. 489–490; and "Drugs and the Educational Antidote," *The Nation's Schools,* April 1970, pp. 49–52, 127.

[26]For a discussion of consumer education, see Roman Warmke, "Consumer Education: Goals and Realities, *Educational Leadership,* April, 1974, pp. 607–610.

LANGUAGE ARTS

Language skills, particularly reading, are basic to all other learning. It is estimated that a million students cannot read well enough to make full progress in school; that 1 million adults are functionally illiterate; and that 25 million jobholders are denied advancement because of reading difficulties. The National Assessment of Educational Progress revealed that reading is improving. A median test score of 70 was achieved. The Right-to-Read project was designed to help virtually all children learn to read. A new federally funded goals-oriented approach to reading instruction is the National Reading Improvement Program under Title VII of the Education Amendments of 1974. The U.S. Office of Education has selected—with the help of the American Institutes for Research—twelve outstanding reading programs to distribute to school districts. They are also distributing multimedia packages of Right-to-Read materials to big cities and state departments of education. In addition, their Program Information Packages (PIPS) provide orientation and research materials to teachers, board members, and parents in a usable form.

Controversy has raged for many years over the relative advantages of the phonic method of reading instruction (in which students associate spoken sounds of letters with printed symbols) versus the look-say method (in which students recognize whole words through association with pictures, clues from the context, or intuitive means).[27] A variety of approaches to reading are described briefly below.

Hay and Wingo's *Reading with Phonics* first teaches simpler phonetic sounds to provide a basic reading vocabulary, with more difficult sounds coming later. Caleb Gattegno has developed an ingenious simplification of reading instruction, *Words in Color,* in which various multiple sounds of the same letter are represented by distinctive colors. The Initial Teaching Alphabet (ITA), illustrated in Figure 9-6, was devised by Sir James Pitman, an English headmaster. ITA consists of forty-four symbols, each with a distinctive single sound, thereby conveying all the different sounds

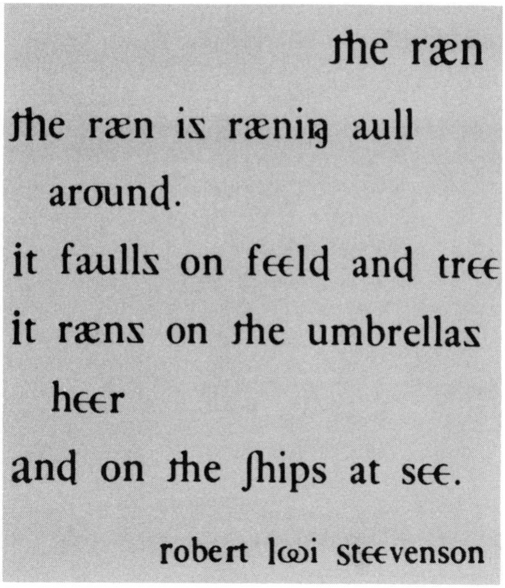

Figure 9-6 Example of the Initial Teaching Alphabet.

of the English language. This eliminates the confusion of multiple sounds for the same letter, phonetic inconsistencies, and different capital and lowercase symbols for the same letter. After gaining reading mastery with ITA, students appear to have little difficulty later in mastering the twenty-six conventional letters of the English language. Some reading systems attempt to combine the phonic system with the word recognition system. The Children's Television Workshop began a new series of programs in 1971 designed to help elementary school children learn to read by stressing "decoding strategies" that emphasize the relationship between printed and spoken words.

The major change in reading is individualization of reading instruction. The use of basal readers, once almost universal, has declined considerably and has been replaced by a variety of reading materials, audiovisual aids, and methods of assessing problem areas and achievement. Today reading systems are used, rather than placing total reliance on textbooks. The basal texts that are still in use have been adapted to make them more functional within new reading systems.

Research for better teaching methods continues. The National Institute of Education (NIE) is trying to learn how to help children gain skills necessary to function in school and society. The Institute has

---

[27]For further discussion of this controversy, see Patrick Groff, "Jeanne Chall Revisited," *Phi Delta Kappan,* November 1970, pp. 162–165.

spent millions of dollars to develop curriculum materials and teaching models.[28]

In many elementary schools the basic language skills—reading, handwriting, spelling, grammar, creative writing, and listening—are no longer taught as disparate subjects, but are fused into a language arts core curriculum.[29] This strategy offers many advantages. For example, the relationship between intonation in spoken sentences and punctuation of written sentences is more easily perceived when the two are taught together. Children can learn to develop their own creative writing skills by studying writing styles used in literature. Thus creative writing, study of literature, language games, and other devices are displacing the traditional abstract, dull, rote learning of grammar.

In high schools and colleges, the "new English" has triggered controversy between its proponents and traditionalists. Traditional instruction has emphasized explanation of correct usage of English through applying rules of grammar and parts of speech. Transformational grammar, characteristic of the new English, emphasizes construction of different kinds of sentences through the use of diagrams not unlike chemical formulas. This approach is compatible with the translation of languages by computers. Presumably the new English helps students read and write better. Its opponents claim that it is abstract, difficult, and frustrating for students.[30]

The science of linguistics is being applied to the teaching of all languages. Much of this work has been stimulated by the Center for Applied Linguistics of the Modern Language Association. Knowledge of linguistics helps students learn foreign languages more readily. The National Council of Teachers of English (NEA) is the major professional organization of English teachers.

[28]For more information on reading instruction, see Margaret Early, "Important Research in Reading and Writing," *Phi Delta Kappan,* January 1976, pp. 298–301; Edward A. Ide, "Programmed Instruction Can Teach Children to Read," *American School Board Journal,* February 1974, pp. 38–40; and Mary Horn, "They Help Me Read New Words," *D & R Report,* February–March, 1974, pp. 4–7.

[29]See Alvin Granowsky and Seena Granowsky, "Toward a New Direction for the Language Arts Program," *Phi Delta Kappan,* February 1974, pp. 421–423.

[30]See Edmund J. Farrell, "Perspectives on English in a Vortex of Change," *Phi Delta Kappan,* June 1974, pp. 670–674.

SOCIAL STUDIES

Curriculum improvement in social studies has been less deliberate than that in physical sciences in spite of the fact that our most compelling problems—peace, international understanding, race relations, urbanization, and social justice—look largely to social sciences rather than to physical sciences for solution. Changes are taking place however. Trends show a decrease in the study of history and an increase in the study of current issues. There is more emphasis on value analysis and on social problems. Global education and peace studies are often included in the social studies curriculum.

In geography the trend is away from physical aspects and toward human and economic ones. More recognition will be given to areas and peoples formerly neglected in the curriculum—non-Western civilization, blacks, and other ethnic groups.

Data released by the National Assessment of Educational Progress revealed that many students lack fundamental understanding of the essential obligations of good citizenship. This directs attention toward the need for improving the effectiveness and relevance of citizenship education. Toward this end, as well as to increase students' knowledge of the law, the Youth Education for Citizenship Project (YEFC), sponsored by the American Bar Association, has helped to get over 250 law-related projects into the schools. Joel F. Henning, director of YEFC, attributes today's interest in these projects to students' awareness of their rights, sex discrimination, and the Watergate scandal. He says, "Watergate is having a positive impact on law studies in the schools, much like Sputnik had on math and science education."[31]

The American Political Science Association, with funds from the National Science Foundation, is experimenting in twenty-five high schools to see whether political methodology, such as persuasive arts, can be learned effectively at the secondary level. The experiment is one of student participation. The curriculum developed from the study will be published after a three-year trial and evaluation period.

Ethnic studies, discussed earlier, have become

[31]See Richard Wynn, "What Ever Happened to Citizenship Education?" *The School Administrator,* September 1970, pp. 15–16.

a significant and sometimes controversial addition to high school and college curriculums.

Perhaps the most significant development in the social studies at the college level has been the increased trend toward interdisciplinary study in which social sciences are interrelated by experts in individual fields of specialization. Many undergraduate social science courses have been fused into broader core courses to reduce narrow compartmentalization. Much more work remains to be done in social studies curriculums at all levels before they will have been refined to a point adequate to our rapidly shrinking and anxious world.

Peace studies are an attempt to further world peace through the study of war and its causes. A combination of sociology, history, economics, political science, futurism, and other studies are used. The program, increasingly used in colleges, is also being included in secondary and elementary schools. Students plan designs for shaping world order and deal with issues of social importance. World-order education and global education are forms of peace studies. World-order education is discussed further in Chapter 15.[32] The National Council for the Social Studies (of the NEA) is the umbrella organization for social studies teachers, supplemented by other organizations of teachers in specific subjects, such as geography and history.

NATURAL SCIENCES

Some major strides were made in science education from the 1950s to the present time. Science education became more sophisticated; students were taught to approach their work in a scientific manner, as scientists would. Scientific processes were emphasized. Many of the early high school programs emerged under the impetus of the National Science Foundation, an agency of the federal government created in 1950 "to develop and encourage the pursuit of a national policy for the promotion of basic research and education in the sciences." National Science Foundation funds and grants from the National Defense Education Act have provided much more sophisticated science equipment for high schools across the nation.

Overarching concepts of science, the logical structure of scientific knowledge, and the unity and interrelationship of the branches of science were stressed. The science curriculums became more unified, better coordinated, and more sequential. Science was fused with other fields such as health and safety education. With respect to methodology, the shift was from reading and listening to problem solving, experimentation, and deduction. Advanced courses were created for gifted students, and more time was devoted to science in the schedule.

The curriculum of the senior high school influenced the curriculums of junior high schools and elementary schools. Programs had to be upgraded. Once restricted largely to nature study, elementary schools began to stress the identification and solution of simple scientific problems, exposure to the method of scientific inquiry, and the performance of simple experiments. Skills essential to learning science—such as observation, classification, inference, and prediction—were emphasized. These programs are still used widely in science programs. Some schools have tempered this intense science approach by using the programs with students who are interested in pursuing careers in science or who are academically oriented. Many people now feel that these programs do not meet the needs of all students.

According to the National Science Foundation, the new thrust in science is toward producing scientifically literate citizens. This involves giving students the skills and understanding they need to make everyday decisions and to live meaningfully with other people and with their environment. To fulfill this purpose, social aspects of science must be brought into the curriculum. This trend seems to contrast directly with test results revealed by the Scholastic Aptitude Test (SAT), that scores have been declining since 1962. The National Assessment of Educational Progress reported that students scored lower in science in 1973 than in 1970. There is disagreement over the trend. Some feel that standards are being lowered.

The pollution of air and water and the abuse of our natural resources have quickened the nation's interest in how we can preserve life through environmental education. This has been stimulated by the National Environmental Policy Act, and by the various organizations interested in conservation, wildlife, forestry, and health, with the support of

[32]See Gene Stanford and Barbara Stanford, "Teaching Students to Be Peacemakers," *Educational Leadership,* October 1974, pp. 46–50.

many industries and governmental agencies. The preservation and improvement of our environment has become a compelling crusade for many students at all levels of schooling. Environmental education is really multidisciplinary in nature, including the study of ecology, conservation, biology, geography, law, agriculture, forestry, political science, and even history. Economic, political, social, and cultural considerations are clearly involved. The trend is to weave study of environmental education into established courses and to stress learning through direct observation of the environment and student participation in action-oriented field projects. The emphasis on environmental education is manifested from elementary school through graduate school.[33]

MATHEMATICS

Mathematics programs once again are changing. What was hailed as the revolutionary "new math" in the 1960s is now about to give way to a less scientific, but more fundamental, approach.

The purpose of new math originally was to help students understand mathematical concepts and therefore to understand what they were doing. However, mathematical concepts became too abstract, and skills became obscured. Teachers and students grew disenchanted. Testing revealed lowered achievement. Parents were unable to help their children. Students were not learning the basic skills. Today classrooms using new math in its original sense are hard to find. In an attempt to salvage the situation, many teachers began teaching a combination of new and traditional materials.

New systems in mathematics are being devised to replace new math or adapt it to more usable programs. These programs are designed to relate to real situations. Nontechnical language is used, and the reading level is kept low so that students will not be held back by reading handicaps. The programs are designed to help students understand mathematics and gain computational ability. One program, designed by Science Research Associates, has had good feedback from users. Teachers say it is easy to use and brings results. Students like it. Standardized test results have been generally higher as a result of the system.

One constant controversy among mathematics teachers is whether students should be taught specific knowledge or the process of finding out. This controversy complicates the teaching of mathematics. Although there have been problems with new math, it is hoped that we do not slip back completely to where we were before it came on the scene. A wholesale rejection of programs every few years is unproductive. Creativity, flexibility, and practicality will be the bywords of mathematics, according to the National Council of Teachers of Mathematics. Some say the current trend is still "new math" but with more informality and simpler language.

Adoption of the metric system was delayed by the defeat in 1974 of a bill to change voluntarily to the metric system within ten years. Regardless of the delay, many schools are beginning to include the system in their curriculums. California and Maryland have taken the lead on a statewide basis to change over to the metric system. As of 1976, California is including units on the system in all mathematics and science textbooks. A consortium on metric education was begun by twenty-six states and territories with funds from the U.S. Office of Education. The consortium has made thirty-three recommendations concerning materials, in-service training, and other guidelines for implementing the metric system, one of which is that all schools in the country should be using the system by January 1, 1980.[34]

FOREIGN LANGUAGES

The teaching of foreign languages, so important in the school program in the 1960s, has been decreasing. The percentage of colleges requiring a

[33]For more information on science in the curriculum, see Jane S. Shaw, "Schools Engineer a Change in Science Courses," *Nation's Schools*, May 1974, pp. 29–32; Fred Blumenfeld, "Science: Yesterday, Today, and Tomorrow," *Today's Education*, September–October 1974, pp. 86–89; James Wheeler and Nobuo Shimahara, "Toward an Ecological Perspective in Education: Part I," *Phi Delta Kappan*, February 1974, pp. 393–396; and William H. Boyer, "Toward an Ecological Perspective in Education: Part II," *Phi Delta Kappan*, February 1974, pp. 397–399.

[34]See George L. Henderson, "Mathematics: Yesterday, Today, and Tomorrow," *Today's Education*, January–February 1975, pp. 44–47; Robert B. Davis, "New Math: Success/Failure?" *Instructor*, March 1974, pp. 53–55; Donald H. Firl, "The Move to Metrics: Some Considerations," *The Mathematics Teacher*, November 1974, pp. 581–584; and Vincent J. Glennon, "Mathematics: How Firm the Foundations," *Phi Delta Kappan*, January 1976, pp. 302–305.

Many schools are preparing students for the change to the metric system of measurement.

language for admission went from 37 percent in 1965 to 19 percent in 1974. Those requiring a language as a graduation requirement dropped from 89 percent to 56 percent. Thus high schools also lost incentive to continue language programs. Language programs have traditionally been for college-bound students and were labeled irrelevant by many. Foreign language study in elementary school, which also gained impetus during the mid-1960s, has declined steadily despite reason to believe that younger children learn to speak languages with less inhibition and more fluency than is possible later.

A practical approach to foreign languages is being used more and more, instead of a fundamental approach that would give students an understanding of language structure. The conversational approach, such as is used at Berlitz and other commercial language schools, is being used with much success.[35]

Bilingual education has become an important movement in United States education. The Bilingual Education Act (ESEA Title VII) was passed in 1968. This act provides for programs in which the cultures and languages of students become part of the school program. The original amount authorized for the bill was $400 million, to be spent over a six-year period. (As of November 1973, only $117 million had been spent.) By 1969 over three hundred federally funded bilingual programs

[35]See Joseph M. Vocolo, "What Went Wrong with Foreign Language Teaching in High School?" *Educational Leadership*, January 1974, pp. 294–297; Mary H. Jackson, "Foreign Languages: Yesterday, Today, and Tomorrow," *Today's Education*, November–December 1974, pp. 68–71.

served about 180,000 students in the United States and territories. By 1975 thirteen states had legislation relating to bicultural-bilingual education, and approximately one thousand federal, state, or local programs existed. The most effective programs use both languages fairly equally, as well as a bicultural and bilingual approach. Bilingual-bicultural education begins with a respect for students and their backgrounds. Ethnic studies, discussed earlier in this chapter, are related to bilingual education.

One big problem in implementing bilingual education is the shortage of qualified teachers. The American Association of Colleges for Teacher Education has endorsed the concept of multicultural education. Part of the endorsement reads: "To endorse cultural pluralism is to endorse the principle that there is no one model American. To endorse cultural pluralism is to understand and appreciate the differences that exist among the nation's citizens."[36] (See Chapters 1 and 14 for further discussion of bilingual education.)

THE HUMANITIES

The humanities are commonly regarded as "humane studies" that humanize us. Narrowly defined, they include language, literature, history, religion, art, music, and philosophy. Broadly defined, they include dance, drama, creative writing, photography, jurisprudence, archeology, and any other humanizing study. With the exceptions of literature and history, discussed earlier, the humanities have been badly neglected in most school curriculums until recently. The post-Sputnik hysteria prompted emphasis upon defense-related subjects, primarily physical sciences. However, the social unrest of the past decade—and students' resolute search for meaning, purpose, love, and beauty in life—excited interest in the humanities. Although most high schools offer courses in music and art, they are usually elective and are offered only one or two periods per week. Approximately 85 percent of high school students do not take art or music courses.

[36]For further information on bilingual education, see Francia M. Welker, "What Is Bilingual-Bicultural Education?" *Thrust*, January 1975, pp. 12–13; and Rene Cardenas and Lily Wong Fillmore, "Toward a Multicultural Society," *Today's Education*, September–October 1973, pp. 83–88.

Much instruction in the arts has been banal and rudimentary. The purpose of the arts in education has been widely misunderstood by both lay persons and educators. Until recently at least, many have regarded music, drama, dance, sculpture, poetry, painting, and many other humanities largely as entertainment—nice but not necessary. Yet the humanities offer the vehicle by which we can raise the aesthetic tone of our community and home, elevate our minds and spirits above the banality of our environment, and prevent ourselves from "growing up absurd," as Paul Goodman has phrased the plight of youths in a depersonalized society. The humanities are also superb media to nurture perception, communication, creativity, self-expression, and imagination, so highly prized by contemporary society. And many view the arts as intellectual disciplines in their own right.

Music education in high school has traditionally emphasized the production of student musicians and vocalists for school bands, orchestras, and choruses. Unless a student's musical talent is sufficient to promise a place in the marching band or the varsity chorus, it has all too often been neglected. In elementary school, too, music is taught as if it had no purpose other than entertainment and recreation, something to be done for relaxation after the study of more academic subjects. Music is taught too often in isolation from the sources of both high art and genuine folk art, and the relationship of music with other forms of art and literature is often missed.

The true purposes of music education must be more clearly understood. These include the development of musical competence—the ability to sing, to play instruments, and to read music; musical understanding—the ability to perceive musical structure, style, harmony, and rhythm; taste in discerning quality in musical performance and composition; and appreciation of music as both art and literature.

New methods of music instruction emphasize simplified technique, enabling students to play simple compositions early and avoiding, except for the serious performer, many of the tedious exercises that can discourage budding musicians almost before they begin to practice. Students are also encouraged to create simple musical compositions and find therein an avenue for creative expression and self-realization.

Fine arts education has also been popularized by emphasizing simpler techniques that permit beginning students to experience the pleasure of accomplishment early. The media have been broadened to include not only drawing and painting but sculpture, ceramics, plastics, woodcarving, linoleum-block printing, silk-screen printing, photography, and graphic arts. Facilities have been enhanced through better laboratories, studios, creative centers, and workshops. Creativity rather than perfection is stressed. Stereotyped methods of instruction are giving way to more permissive approaches in which children are encouraged to express themselves freely and imaginatively. Experimentation is encouraged in the studio of today. Many fear that this undisciplined sort of self-study has left students with an insufficient knowledge of fine art, undisciplined artistic techniques, and a low level of aesthetic taste. Certainly an effort should be made to develop greater understanding and appreciation of art, not only as a source of beauty but also as a form of communication and expression. The appreciation of art forms in everyday living is stressed, as in the design of furniture or buildings. A new curriculum in aesthetic education has been developed by CEMREL, the national educational laboratory at St. Louis. Aesthetic education is an attempt to help people enjoy their lives by sharpening their awareness of their experiences. Materials and learning centers for teachers are part of the program. A television project is used for team teaching and community involvement. Over two hundred school systems have tested these materials.

One promising development in arts education has been the trend toward fusing it with other humanities. High school students in many states may participate in new humanities courses that draw upon knowledge from English, social studies, art, and music to promote understanding of universal issues such as human beings' relation to God, truth, the natural world, beauty, society, and freedom.

Religion has found a place in the school curriculum, not in devotional Bible reading and prayer, which were banned by the Supreme Court, but in consideration of the Bible as literature and history. Religion and culture, the world religions, comparative religions, and the history of religious thought are being included increasingly in school and college curriculums. Educators hope that these studies will quicken the younger generation's interest and knowledge of religion as a humanizing force in the eternal quest for the good life. This development is somewhat handicapped by the lack of adequate instructional materials and teachers.

Interdisciplinary approaches to the arts are being used.[37] Resource personnel, art works, and other resources are brought to the classroom. Students go to the community for museums, art galleries, plays. Washington, D.C., has begun a special high school for the arts to meet the needs of talented students considering careers in the arts. Students in Duke Ellington High School of the Arts take an academic program as well.

The strengthening of curriculum development and instructional method in the arts and other humanities is being stimulated by several agencies. The creation of the arts and humanities branch of the U.S. Office of Education has helped to bring new vitality to education in these important areas. The Music Educators National Conference, the National Art Education Association, and affiliates of the NEA in other fields in the humanities are also active in improving curriculums and instruction.

HEALTH AND PHYSICAL EDUCATION

The importance of good health is readily apparent. Sound health practices tend to increase life expectancy, to deepen one's satisfaction with living, to reduce the financial burden of medical bills and loss of income during illness, and to improve physical appearance.

What is the scope of an adequate program of health and physical education? Clearly, a good program is multidisciplinary in nature. Its scope is broad and includes such diverse areas as the nature of disease; the awareness of environmental hazards; the prevention of accidents; health and medical care programs; first aid; intelligent selection of health products and services; driver education; community health services; recreation; physical exercise; motor skill development; sex education; understanding the hazards of alcohol, tobacco, drugs, and narcotics; and mental health.

[37]See Frances M. Carter, "Anatomy of a High School Humanities Course," *Today's Education,* January–February 1975, pp. 29–32.

There is considerable interest in a more organized approach to the teaching of nutrition in school, starting in elementary school and continuing throughout high school. The American School Food Service Association and the Association of School Business Officials, as well as other groups, are involved in developing these programs.

Today the focus of physical education is on helping students to develop habits that will help keep them in good physical condition throughout their lives. Elementary schools are being urged to provide more physical education, since attitudes learned early often influence habits in later life. Another major emphasis is on lifetime sports and leisure activities—helping students to develop recreational pursuits that will give them pleasure, as well as exercise, long after they are out of school. The President's Council on Physical Fitness and Sports reports that 45 percent of adult Americans do not participate in any form of physical exercise. Through activities such as dancing, golf, tennis, skiing, swimming, bowling, yoga, angling, and skish, in addition to traditional competitive team sports, the goal of engendering a lifetime interest in sports will be served.

Another goal of today's physical education program is to provide more equal opportunity and service to both girls and boys. Title IX of the Education Amendments of 1972 prohibits sex discrimination by schools and colleges. Through these amendments, coeducational gym classes are common.

Budget pressures often constrain the facilities, faculties, and time necessary for a well-balanced physical education program compatible with the needs and interests of individual students. When the costs of a new school building must be trimmed, the swimming pool is invariably the first facility to be sacrificed. More than one-fifth of elementary and secondary schools have cut back in athletic programs in recent years because of financial problems. About 45 percent of college athletic programs are in financial trouble as well.

The American Association for Health, Physical Education, and Recreation, an affiliate of the NEA, attempts to improve the scope and quality of health and physical education in the schools through conferences of teachers, research studies, and a wide variety of publications.[38]

VOCATIONAL AND TECHNICAL EDUCATION

Renewed interest in vocational and technical education has been generated by dramatic advances in technology, by the need for skilled workers created by automation, and by the plight of large numbers of underprivileged youths out of school and out of work. One-fourth of the young men and women who become 18 each year are not sufficiently educated to be employable. The new emphasis on career education has increased the importance of vocational education in the educational program. The objectives of vocational education have been defined to include imparting an understanding of industry and its place in our culture, the discovery and nurture of talent in technical fields and in applied sciences, the development of career consciousness and occupational orientation, the development of technical problem-solving skills, and the provision of a basic facility in the use of common tools and machines. The Smith-Hughes Act and subsequent enactments, such as the Vocational Education Act and the Manpower Development and Training Act, stimulated the growth of vocational education in many fields. Increased funding indicates the increased interest in career education.

The new emphasis on career education has stimulated career consciousness and occupational orientation.

[38]For information about new trends in physical education, see Leonard Ernst, "Revolution in Sports: The Sprint to Lifetime Sports," *Nation's Schools*, September 1973, pp. 39–46.

There is obviously no single best curriculum, because vocational education must be adapted to the needs of industry and to the resources of local school systems. Many districts are handicapped by their small size. Vocational education programs require expensive, highly specialized shops and laboratories. Further, the great proliferation of skilled jobs reduces high schools' ability to meet the needs in all fields. Schools cannot afford machinery and equipment for all possible jobs that students may be interested in. Therefore, greater use will be made of business, industry, and community resources to provide practical work experience for students. Action learning, used in many areas of the curriculum, provides opportunities for students to participate in community work or service programs (see Chapter 6). More use of minicourses and flexible scheduling will also result in better vocational programs. Cooperative work-study programs are very successful according to the U.S. Office of Education. They are practical and provide skills that are helpful in later job placement.[39] The U.S. Office of Education also reported that programs aimed at keeping students in school, such as the Neighborhood Youth Corps, do not provide any challenge for students and that career programs have not been highly successful in helping students choose careers.

Some goals and emphases for vocational education are

- An increase in adult and continuing education programs, particularly in distressed areas
- More opportunity for disadvantaged and handicapped students
- More marketable skills for non-college-bound students
- More secondary and postsecondary vocational-technical schools
- A wider variety of course offerings, including health services, fluid power, horticulture, aviation, data processing, and appliance repair

Many community colleges and technical institutes have helped to expand the nation's capacity for the preparation of technicians, which the age of automation demands in ever-increasing numbers. Vocational education at the adult level must also be expanded to accommodate workers whose jobs

are eliminated or whose skills must be updated as a result of automation.

There is controversy about whether vocational education should be provided in separate vocational high schools or included as part of the program of comprehensive high schools. Some believe it should be offered largely in postsecondary schools. In either case, the vocational curriculum too often suffers from the low prestige ascribed to both the students and the teachers engaged in it.

The American Vocational Association is the professional association for teachers of vocational education. Its conferences, meetings, research, and publications have helped give direction to improving education for the world of work.[40]

Cocurricular activities

Having discussed the academic sectors of the curriculum, we turn our attention now to that ancillary—but important—sector of the curriculum commonly spoken of as "cocurricular activities," "extraclass activities," or "student activities." In many schools cocurricular activities are assuming a prominence and function almost parallel with the curricular undertakings. These activities are increasingly included in the regular school day, making it difficult to distinguish between what is curricular and what is cocurricular.

GOALS

Cocurricular or extraclass activities serve a number of worthwhile educational goals, sometimes more effectively than the formal curriculum.

Satisfaction of unmet needs. Some cocurricular activities are initiated to satisfy certain drives among students not satisfied by the formal curriculum, which is usually controlled largely by school authorities.

---

[39]See Raymond S. Moore, "Work-Study: Education's Sleeper?" *Phi Delta Kappan*, January 1976, pp. 322–327.

[40]For more extended discussion of these trends, see Velma A. Adams, "Vocational Training: Still for Someone Else's Children?" *School Management*, September 1970, pp. 12–15. For a look at career education's effect on vocational education, see Carl E. Wells, "Will Vocational Education Survive?" *Phi Delta Kappan*, February 1973, pp. 369, 380.

Reinforcement of students' interest in school. Many students develop strong interests in extraclass activities that sustain their commitment to remain in school or to pursue their academic studies more vigorously. A common characteristic of school dropouts is their lack of participation in cocurricular activities.

Education for democratic living. Most cocurricular activities place upon students a major responsibility for their management. This experience requires students to practice group decision making, to consider the rights and responsibilities of others, to understand the necessity for order and justice, to assume the mantle of leadership or the discipline of followership, and, in general, practice good citizenship.

Enrichment of interpersonal relations. Cocurricular activities provide experience in group activities that very often depend for their success upon effective interpersonal relations. Cooperation, teamwork, racial understanding, poise, and social awareness are some possible benefits to be gained through working with others.

Exploration of vocational possibilities. Many vocational alternatives can be explored in cocurricular activities through experiences that are not provided commonly in the regular curriculum. Latent talent that might otherwise go undiscovered is often revealed through cocurricular activities.

Wiser use of leisure time. The squandering of leisure time in worthless or even harmful pursuits is tragic. Cocurricular activities can help young citizens develop hobbies or other recreational pursuits that can enrich their lives, improve their surroundings, and quicken their sense of well-being long after formal schooling is over. Many lifelong avocational interests have been discovered and enriched in cocurricular activities.

Development of sound character. Group activities force students to exercise their moral judgments, to set standards of behavior, and to reconcile individual aspirations with the welfare of the group. The opportunities for character development in a sound cocurricular program are even more abundant than those in the formal curriculum because students have more opportunity to make important decisions and take more responsibility for their actions.

In balance, we must recognize that cocurricular activities are sometimes miseducative. Fraternities, while extolling the high ideals of brotherhood, are commonly clannish and discriminate in their membership on the basis of race or creed or both, thereby reducing the opportunity for the improvement of racial and religious understanding. The pressure upon interscholastic athletic teams for victorious seasons sometimes prompts unethical practices and the exploitation of student athletes, thereby compromising the virtue of the institution. The coercion of administrative authorities of student activities, particularly the school newspaper, sometimes teaches unintended lessons in how special interests can constrain the freedom of the press in school and society. Many other examples could be cited. These are indictments, not of cocurricular activities per se, but of the frailties of the human beings who oversee these and other enterprises.

COCURRICULAR PROGRAMS

The numerous organizations and the complex interrelation of the various cocurricular activities make it difficult to group them, since many may be classified properly under several headings. Some schools' programs have changed little to meet the interests of today's students. Schools should be flexible in their cocurricular activities and aware of their students' needs.

Class organizations. An old and prevalent cocurricular activity is that of class or grade organizations. These groupings are found all the way from the kindergarten through higher education. The class usually elects a president, a vice-president, a secretary, a treasurer, representatives to the student council and other organizations, and a class sponsor or sponsors from the faculty. These class officers, along with various committees, assume responsibility for the social affairs of the class, participate in various ceremonial functions such as commencement, and represent their classmates in student government and often in advising school administration on various matters.

Student government. Student government offers great opportunity for the practice of democratic principles and the development of effective citizenship. Various forms of student government—student councils, student courts, student senates, interfraternity councils, student-faculty committees—exist in most high schools and colleges. Many elementary schools have also introduced limited forms of student government. Many student government organizations function well and realize the goals intended. However, some schools place so many restraints upon eligibility for membership that they fail to represent the entire spectrum of the student body. Some school administrators are reluctant to share any real authority with student government organizations, and some faculty sponsors supervise their affairs so closely that these organizations serve little function other than to delude students and create a facade of democratic school organization.

School clubs. Most cocurricular activities may be classified as clubs. Nowhere in school life is more freedom and variety displayed than in the names of clubs. Their vast variety testifies to the individualistic interests of youths as well as to their gregariousness. Through a wide variety of organizations, schools seek to interest each student in at least one meaningful cocurricular activity in which the desideratum is not mere membership but active and voluntary participation.

Journalistic activities. The most common student publication is the newspaper. Often in elementary and small secondary schools the students and teachers cooperate with the local newspaper in producing a school page. At least half the secondary schools have some form of news organ. The school newspaper today is an important agent in the transmission of ideas and school spirit. Through this medium many young people first learn the privileges and responsibilities involved in the freedom of the press in a democracy. Significantly, the principals of the schools usually rank the newspaper as the most important activity outside classes. The yearbook, once the only publication in most schools, is now being subordinated to the school newspaper, although its archival function will always give it a place in the program.

The current emphasis upon unleashing creative efforts and developing literary interests of students has focused attention upon school magazines and similar avenues for expression. These periodicals, issued in duplicated or printed format, constitute outlets not only for literary creativeness and insight, but also for expression through drawings, cartoons, and photographs.

Some student journalists in some high schools and many colleges have become sufficiently creative in their choice of language and vigorous in their criticism of the establishment to discomfort school administrators and school boards. In some cases these student journalists have been expelled from their offices or have had their writings censored, or school funds have been withdrawn—practices that generally are frowned upon by the courts. In some cases these enterprising journalists have gone underground and published "independent newspapers" which are distributed to students, posing a new dilemma for harried school administrators.[41] Although school authorities should not sanction libel and obscenity in school publications, most schools should be prudent in placing other restrictions upon student publications. Students can learn responsible journalism more effectively in an atmosphere of freedom than in an atmosphere of constraint.

Musical organizations and activities. Music is the center of many curricular and cocurricular activities. Singing is often combined with acting, as in operettas, and with instrumental accompaniment, as in cantatas. Music groups may include music appreciation classes, glee clubs or choruses, bands, orchestras, and other ensembles. The widespread popularity of rock music has spawned many small groups of student musicians who feature well-amplified guitars and uninhibited vocalists.

Speech activities. Generally school dramatics are handled either in regular classes or through cocurricular activities. Major productions or one-act plays may be promoted by a local drama club or by a chapter of National Thespians or by the junior or senior class. Usually the work is divided among various committees for costuming, lighting, scenery, and advertising. The drama coach may encourage more backward students to self-expres-

---

[41] For an interesting collection of articles taken from student underground newspapers, see Diane Divoky (ed.), *How Old Will You Be in 1984?* Avon, New York, 1969.

sion through acting. Many by-products accrue from drama, including the extensive reading of many plays and the practicing of clear enunciation. School drama helps students to see, hear, act, construct, and write their own plays.

Forensic activities include debates, poetry reading, extempore speaking, choral reading, telecasting, radio speaking, role playing, panel discussions, and forums. Writing original speeches appeals especially to students who possess creative literary talents and who hope thereby to inform, impress, or persuade the audience to thought or action. Debates constitute the chief activity in the field of public speaking. Debates help students to think logically, to organize materials carefully, to cultivate mental alertness, to analyze an argument critically, to promote reliance upon facts and research rather than prejudice, and to develop a lifelong interest in socioeconomic and governmental problems.

Play and athletic activities. Elementary schools are increasingly providing well-rounded physical education programs, rather than traditional games and free play. A well-balanced physical education program in secondary schools and colleges includes athletics, in addition to the regular programs for guidance and instruction in health and physical activities.

Athletics include intramural and interscholastic sports. Intramural sports programs may include several schools within a city. Intramurals, as distinguished from interscholastic sports, encourage maximum participation by local students. They seek to maintain many sports for the sake of all students rather than for the sake of a few athletic teams. They are directed toward developing lasting recreational interests and sport skills in people who must live in a highly industrialized civilization.

The effort to equalize opportunities for females in sports has increased. The Department of Health, Education, and Welfare's regulation, finalized in 1975, withholds federal funding from schools practicing discrimination. The ruling requires that schools and colleges provide coaches and equipment for all existing female teams. It does not, however, require that funding be equal to funding for male teams. Schools do not have to allow females in contact sports, but they must allow them in other sports or provide separate teams for them. The National Collegiate Athletic Association (NCAA) feels that these changes will end athletic programs as we have known them.

Critics find fault with huge football stadiums, large gate receipts, larger expenditures, postseason games, salaried athletes, athletic scholarships, lax scholastic requirements for athletes, long practice sessions, game schedules that take athletes away from their studies, and high-salaried and overzealous coaches whose tenure depends upon the production of winning teams. Great pressures, excessive competition, and financial problems are forcing many schools to close down or at least to curtail their programs. The NCAA reports that two-thirds of its athletic departments are losing operations. Forty-one colleges have dropped football since 1974.

Despite these accusations, interscholastic athletics continue to flourish. Conscientious efforts are being made to eliminate or reduce evils in the system. The American Council on Education, with funds from the Ford Foundation and the Carnegie Corporation, is studying the recruiting practices, scholastic requirements for athletes, and general ethics of athletic programs.

Social organizations and activities. A well-balanced educational program fosters the social development of students. This goal is achieved in large part through the cocurricular program. In elementary schools, parties and other simple social affairs are held during the school day. In high schools, social activities are usually an important part of virtually every extraclass organization. There are banquets for the athletic teams, musical groups, casts of plays, and other groups. Various classes sponsor dances, and schools sponsor mixers, parties, and picnics. These affairs help students to feel at home in a social environment and help them to acquire social skills.

There are many social organizations in colleges and universities, although fraternities and sororities are regarded as the major socializing institutions on most campuses.

Auxiliary organizations and activities. Ancillary to the curricular or cocurricular programs are the following: assemblies and programs, commencements, social activities, school lunch, camping and outdoor education, scouting, and miscellaneous activities far too numerous to mention.

ADVISEMENT OF COCURRICULAR ACTIVITIES

The success of many extraclass organizations may be traced in large part to faculty advisers or sponsors. Although sponsors should not assume a dominant role, they nevertheless should exert a real influence. Some general qualifications for faculty advisers are an understanding of youths and their interests and problems, the ability to win the confidence of both youths and parents, the capacity to lead and to follow, a willingness to be identified wholeheartedly with the organization, and a good sense of values in the expenditure of time, money, and talents. Besides these general requirements, directors of certain groups need specialized training, for example, those who advise journalistic, athletic, and music events.

How shall advisers be chosen? Usually the procedure involves selection by the principal, election by the students, or a combination of these. For example, students may choose an adviser from a recommended list. Often the advisers for activities that call for technical training are appointed to that task when employed by the board of education and superintendent of schools. Advisers and students should be happy and congenial in their cocurricular relations. Too often beginning teachers are "drafted" into sponsoring cocurricular activities.

PARTICIPATION OF STUDENTS

A goal in extraclass work is that of universality—having all students in the school participate in at least one cocurricular activity. This necessitates promotion and stimulation, preferably by the student body. A corollary is the principle that participation must be restricted. These are two parts of the same basic idea that cocurricular activities must be regulated in order to avert the danger that some students will move to the extreme of nonparticipation while others will overparticipate. Two methods of curtailing the ambitions of overzealous or talented individuals are a point system and a program of majors and minors. The former assigns to each activity a specified number of points and stipulates the maximum permitted each student. The latter divides activities or offices into majors and minors, restricting each student to a specified number.

The future

The thrust toward individualized instruction will continue to accelerate. However, it may be quite a while before it becomes financially feasible for all school systems to take advantage of all the technical advances. Programmed learning, computer-assisted instruction, multiunit organization, independent study, and many other factors will continue to be used for effective individualization of instruction.

The pendulum will continue to swing in the subject areas—from a hard-line, subject-oriented approach, to a humanized, concept-oriented approach, to a pragmatic, practical approach and back again. Some of this is to be expected. Times change and new trends come into fashion. It seems, though, that the vacillation is too often extreme. Can a school program be open to change and modification without completely abandoning one system for another every four or five years? It is hoped that in the future more gradual and thoughtful changes will take place and that educators will be guided by their own knowledge about how we learn and about what constitutes an effective curriculum, rather than being pushed one way or the other by outside voices less schooled but louder than their own.

There will be continued exploration of the more unorthodox additions to the curriculum, such as transcendental meditation and death education. Bilingual education, career education, and ethnic studies will continue to receive major emphasis in the immediate future. Practical approaches will be used for science, mathematics, and foreign languages. Vocational education will continue to expand its program. Athletic programs will change to emphasize participation by female students.

Much more learning will take place outside the schools through direct participation in the larger community. For students, the concept of failure will be replaced by the concept of varying rates of success in learning. Class schedules, regulations, courses of study, room assignments, school hours, examinations, and many other artifacts of the educational scene will be radically transformed and perhaps discarded in some cases.

The future will hold greater promise for the development of continuity and coherence in the curriculum. Although experts differ in their opinions about the ultimate effectiveness of applying systems theory and analysis to curriculum development, they agree that its application is still some years distant. In any case, school curriculums will be affected to a degree by prototype instructional systems such as Educational Systems for the 70s. Also, the National Assessment of Educational Progress will provide far better evaluative data to support the improvement of curriculums and instruction.

New curriculum development enterprises commonly recognize the importance of teachers in implementing new courses of study. Curriculum change, if it is to permeate the educative process, necessitates a change in teachers' performance. Thus increasing attention is given to institutes, workshops, and courses to instruct teachers in the design and use of new methods and materials. These in-service development activities have often invigorated teachers in new curriculums and higher standards of performance. Clearly the future will place greater burdens upon teachers to keep pace with accelerated change in curriculum and instruction.

There are some indications that the pendulum will again swing back to a hard emphasis on cognitive learning and the traditional classroom. Pressures toward dehumanization increase during periods of economic depression. When jobs are scarce, the emphasis usually shifts toward a knowledge of skills and how to do specific tasks. The public feels it cannot afford the luxury of openness. Also, cutbacks in money for education places more emphasis on a "no-frills" approach. Discontent over vandalism and discipline problems creates a cry for getting tough. As noted earlier, "fundamental schools," emphasizing basic education and stricter discipline, are growing in number. When both open schools and fundamental schools exist in the same school district, parents are given contrasting options. This may undercut the struggle between advocates of each, who want to convert all schools to their preference, and thereby foster the coexistence of each.

Some new research in neurosurgical and biochemical approaches to learning, discussed in Chapter 10, may have dramatic impact on the curriculum in the more distant future. It is clear that the curriculum is undergoing more careful scrutiny and more fundamental change than at any other time in our history. It is still too early to assess the value and impact of this change. The problem of building a curriculum adequate to the vast and complex needs of a rapidly changing world is difficult, frightening, and exciting; but the future promises more dramatic and far-reaching transformations in the school curriculum.

Suggested activities

1. After further reading on the topic, write an essay on "Open Education and the Needs of Youth and Society."
2. Discuss the relationship between the individualization of instruction and school organization.
3. Explain the controversies that surround black studies and establish your own position.
4. From your own experience with them, list the major advantages and disadvantages of cocurricular activities.
5. List the major current criticisms of the school curriculum and indicate your agreement or disagreement with each.
6. Prepare a comprehensive review of recent curriculum reforms and instructional innovations in your field of teaching.
7. Examine as many documents about curriculum development as you can and then formulate your own set of major purposes of education.
8. Prepare an essay on the progress and problems of curriculum development in your teaching field or at your grade level. Consult the bibliography.
9. Read the seven philosophical views of education in Chapter 1. Select the one that accommodates your views best and explain the reasons for your choice.
10. Make a critical examination of a given school's course of study in your field or at your grade level.
11. Describe some major curricular developments in your fields of study in college.
12. Study how one local school district is implementing career education in its school program.
13. State your ideas about how the Department of Health, Education, and Welfare's policy on female participation in sports will change school athletics.

Bibliography

Anderson, Robert H.: *Opting for Openness*, National Association of Elementary School Principals, Arlington, Va., 1973. Concise look at open education—history, description, and practices.

Banks, James A.: *Teaching Strategies for Ethnic Studies*, Allyn and Bacon, Boston, 1975. Introductory methods book, including history of major American ethnic groups.

Barth, Roland S.: *Open Education and the American*

School, Agathon, New York, 1972. Describes open education and its importance in the public school setting, including practical methods, the role of the principal, and the role of the teacher.

Block, James H. (ed.): *Schools, Society, and Mastery Learning,* Holt, New York, 1974. Collection of discussions about mastery learning and its place in public schools.

Boston, Robert E.: *How to Write and Use Performance Objectives to Individualize Instruction,* Educational Technology Publications, Englewood Cliffs, N.J., 1972. Four-book package designed to help teachers increase their skills with behavioral objectives.

Doll, Ronald C.: *Curriculum Improvement: Decision Making and Process,* 3d ed., Allyn and Bacon, Boston, 1974. Comprehensive introductory book on curriculum, including decision-making process and evaluation.

Dworkin, Martin S. (ed.): *Dewey on Education: Selections,* Teachers College Press, Teachers College, Columbia University, New York, 1959. Collection of John Dewey's writings related to the learner and the curriculum.

Eisner, Elliot W., and **Elizabeth Vallance** (eds.): *Conflicting Conceptions of Curriculum,* The National Society for the Study of Education, Chicago, 1974. Collection of essays dealing with the five different orientations to curriculum.

Ellena, William J. (ed.): *Curriculum Handbook for School Executives,* American Association of School Administrators, Arlington, Va., 1973. Collection of positions taken by sixteen organizations in their respective fields. Trends, description, and organization are included.

Goodlad, John, et al.: *The Conventional and the Alternative in Education,* McCutchan, Berkeley, Calif., 1975. Discusses the school program, past and present, and what is possible in alternative education.

Hicks, William V., et al.: *The New Elementary School Curriculum,* Van Nostrand Reinhold, New York, 1970. Describes curriculum theory, processes, and practices for elementary schools.

Hoyt, Kenneth B., Rupert N. Evans, Edward F. Mackin, and **Garth L. Mangum:** *Career Education: What It Is and How To Do It,* Olympus, Salt Lake City, 1972. Practical guide to career education, including need, philosophy, implementation, and potential.

Kline, Morris: *Why Johnny Can't Add: The Failure of the New Math,* St. Martin's, New York, 1973. Examines mathematics instruction in elementary and secondary schools.

Kozol, Jonathan: *Free Schools,* Houghton Mifflin, Boston, 1972. Evaluates the free school movement from firsthand experience.

Marland, Sidney P., Jr.: *Career Education: A Proposal for Reform,* McGraw-Hill, New York, 1974. Discusses the evolution of career education, including a definition of it and a description of several career education programs in operation.

Morley, Franklin P.: *A Modern Guide to Effective K-12*

Curriculum Planning, Parker, West Nyack, N.Y., 1973. Describes the failures of traditional values of curriculum planning, new instructional goals and principles, and the problems of motivation.

National School Public Relations Association: *Environment and the Schools,* Arlington, Va., 1971. Describes the best programs in environmental education and the views of expert authorities.

————: *Grading and Reporting,* Arlington, Va., 1972. Describes grading patterns and procedures and what critics say about them.

————: *IGE: Individually Guided Education and the Multiunit School,* Arlington, Va., 1972. Describes a relatively new form of school organization and the methods and strategies involved.

————: *Individualization in Schools: The Challenge and the Options,* Arlington, Va., 1971. Describes eight major types of individualized instruction and how they are working.

————: *Reading Crisis: The Problem and Suggested Solutions,* Arlington, Va., 1970. Summarizes the best discoveries and solutions to the problems of reading instruction.

Payne, David A. (ed.): *Curriculum Evaluation,* Heath, Lexington, Mass., 1974. Collection of articles dealing with evaluation of curriculum—purpose, planning, design, and studies.

Rubin, Lewis (ed.): *The Future of Education,* Allyn and Bacon, Boston, 1975. Collection of essays by eminent educators regarding the implications of the future upon schooling.

Salazar, Teresa: *Bilingual Education: A Bibliography,* Bureau of Research Services, Greeley, Colo., 1975. Influences in the development and promotion of bilingual education.

Saylor, J. Galen, and **William M. Alexander:** *Planning Curriculum for Schools,* Holt, New York, 1974. Treats various theories of curriculum development, the role of students and others in curriculum planning, and the use of externally developed materials in curriculum development.

Silberman, Charles E. (ed.): *The Open Classroom Reader,* Random House, New York, 1973. Anthology of seventy-seven readings for teachers and parents dealing with goals, methods, and guidelines for openness.

Trump, J. Lloyd, and **Delmas F. Miller:** *Secondary School Curriculum Improvement: Challenges, Humanism, Accountability,* 2d ed., Allyn and Bacon, Boston, 1974. Comprehensive look at the secondary school curriculum, its challenges, and its problems.

Van Til, William (ed.): *Curriculum: Quest for Relevance,* 2d ed., Houghton Mifflin, Boston, 1974. Collection of readings on curriculum, including criticisms, analyses, and predictions by leading educators.

Chapter 10
Technology and materiel

YOU WILL HAVE MASTERED THIS CHAPTER WHEN YOU CAN

Define

● **general systems applications to education**
● **instructional technology**

Describe

● **instructional materials center**
● **responsive environment**
● **computer-assisted instruction**
● **programmed learning**

Analyze

● **problems and issues inherent in the selection of instructional materials**
● **capabilities and limitations of various technological applications**
● **relationship between curriculum and physical environment of learning**

Foundations

This chapter considers the physical environment of learning—educational technology, the school building, its furnishings, and instructional and other materiel.

The term "technology" invokes an array of science-fiction inventions come true—satellite-borne television, computer-assisted instruction, talking typewriters, and perhaps even mind-expanding drugs. But technology is more than hardware (machines) and software (programs). The word "technology" comes from Greek words meaning "systematic treatment." More precisely, "technology" is the application of scientific method and knowledge to practical purposes. It is, then, a way of thinking. Machines may or may not be involved. Technology may be applied to instruction, school transportation systems, school management, or almost any aspect of organizational life. In this chapter we will be concerned primarily with instructional technology, which has been defined as

an effort with or without machines, available or utilized, to manipulate the environment of individuals in the hope of generating a change of behavior or other learning outcome. As such, technology is a means or a tool for accomplishing educational objectives.[1]

Although this chapter is confined to the physical environment of learning, we emphasize that technology relates as well to all the educational variables discussed in other chapters—including students, teachers, curriculum, finance, and governance.

[1]Stephen J. Knezevich and Glen G. Eye (eds.), *Instructional Technology and the School Administrator*, American Association of School Administrators, Washington, 1970, p. 16.

Although new inventions appear constantly, technology has been with us through many of them: the alphabet, the printing press, the measurement of intelligence, radio, television, and a host of others. Knezevich classifies instructional technology into several categories, related to photography; recording and reproduction of sound; long-distance electronic transmission of visual and audio images; electronic processing, storage, and retrieval of information; programmed instruction; systems approaches; and biochemical and pharmacological means.[2]

Unfortunately, technology generates an unusual amount of mythology, which impedes its utilization. There is the fear that technology—more particularly, machines—will conquer human beings by depriving us of our privacy and our powers of independent thought and action. Visions of George Orwell's *1984* become hauntingly poignant when agencies of government bug telephones and when credit agencies disseminate confidential information about people. The villain here is not technology but our misuse of it. Although automobiles cause thousands of highway deaths each year, we have little disposition to abandon them.

The opposite myth is that technology is a panacea for all our problems. During the 1950s and 1960s, for example, magazines repeatedly announced the coming revolution in education through television and other hardware, a revolution that still has not materialized. Who can forget the initial exuberance and overselling of the educational panaceas of yesterday—foreign languages in elementary school, teaching machines, voucher plans, performance contracting, closed-circuit television, to mention a few? These bandwagons have come and gone, their capabilities having been exaggerated by manufacturers, advertisers, vendors, and reformers who did not have to live with their consequences. Many school boards rejoice that they did not climb aboard every new bandwagon. When such "revolutionary" inventions fall short of their claims, disillusionment sets in, the technology is abandoned, and the popular press may not even note its demise. The science of technology becomes, as Torkelson views it, a struggle "between successful application of technology to human problems and growing disenchantment

with technological influence on human lives."[3] Like the automobile, other technology holds potential for either good or evil, for hope or disenchantment.

There is also the myth that technology will dehumanize people by programming their thought in a universal orthodoxy dictated by government. Any means of mass communication under government control poses that risk. Free societies avoid the risk through guarantees of academic freedom and freedom of the press, which currently is interpreted to include all mass media. Have students been dehumanized or humanized by textbooks, school buses, and intelligence tests? Will they become humanized or dehumanized by talking typewriters, satellite-borne television, computer-assisted instruction, or systems applications to education? Again, the problem of humanization or dehumanization, of good or evil, lies not with technology but with those who control it.

This chapter seeks to deepen our acquaintance with the essential elements of educational technology—its capabilities and limitations—and to speculate about our future alternatives for applying technology in education. Such an examination might help us shape educational technology toward desirable ends.

General systems applications to education

The application of general system theory to organizations is the essence of technology. Thorough understanding of systems theory and its application to education is more important to school administrators than to teachers. Consequently, a thorough discussion of systems applications to education is beyond the scope of this book.[4] However, an elementary understanding of systems applications is increasingly essential for all educators, because it is becoming more common and has impact upon the work of all educators.

A "system" is defined as a complex unity formed

---

[2]Stephen J. Knezevich, *Administration of Public Education*, 3d, ed., Harper & Row, New York, 1975, pp. 113–116.

[3]Gerald Torkelson, "Technology: Use and Abuse?" *Educational Leadership*, February 1974, p. 387.

[4]For a thorough discussion of systems applications to school administration, see Knezevich, *Administration of Public Education*, chap. 7.

of many diverse parts subject to a common plan or serving a common purpose. Knezevich offers this succinct description of the systems approach to school administration:

School administration based on the systems approach perceives the educational enterprise as a unified, systematic way of translating resources made available to it in the form of money, people with varying abilities, facilities, and processes, into outcomes, outputs, or benefits related to the educational goals of society. The school system is not viewed as a conglomeration of separate elements, but as a man-made system which experiences a dynamic interplay among its parts and with its environment.[5]

Knezevich identifies these component subsystems of a total educational system:

1. A goal and priorities setting subsystem
2. A resources subsystem
3. A control subsystem
4. A client service subsystem
5. An educational manpower subsystem
6. An environmental relations subsystem
7. A student manpower reentry and retraining subsystem[6]

Figure 10-1 is a simplified diagram of some relationships among several essential components of a subsystem applied to instruction. Although the components of this model cut across the content of other chapters of this book, the model is included here because it forms the crux of educational technology and because component 3 is directly related to this chapter.

Systems theory has been widely applied for many years in military science, industrial management, and public administration. Its application to school administration has developed primarily during the 1970s. We believe that systems theory will receive much wider application in education because of the following substantial capabilities:

1. It is the most feasible technology for responding to demands for accountability in education.
2. It is a highly rational and systematic approach to educational decision making, substituting science for intuition and political considerations.
3. It provides a management vehicle for coordinating

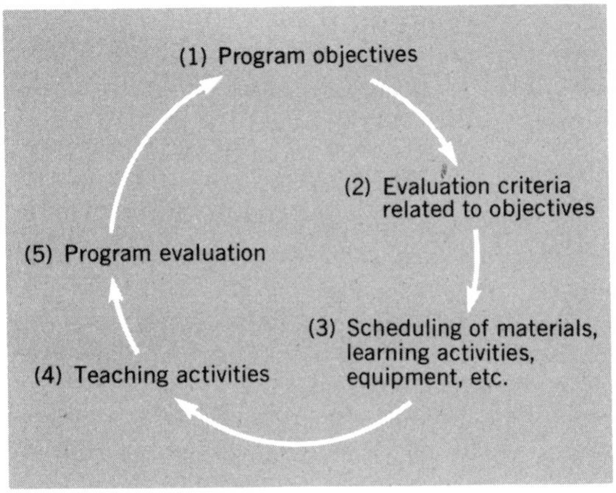

Figure 10-1 A simplified model of systems application to instruction. This model illustrates the sequential relationship of diverse parts serving a common purpose and reveals the circular relationship that is common in systems components. (American Association of School Administrators, *An Administrator's Handbook on Educational Accountability*, Washington, 1973, p. 50).

and harmonizing goals, resource allocation, manpower, instructional programs, and evaluation into a unified whole.
4. It emphasizes careful planning, programming, budgeting, and evaluation.
5. It forces more collaborative effort upon the growing array of specialists on the staff and quickens their understanding of other specialists' efforts.
6. It makes the school system more capable of dealing with change in a highly responsive and systematic way.
7. It accelerates understanding of administrative sciences and organizational behavior through the interaction of theory and practice.

Printed instructional materials

What is the greatest technology? Although answers will vary, for educators there is only one response: printing. Clarence Day, in a letter to a friend, said:

The world of books is the most remarkable creation of man. Nothing else that he builds ever lasts. Monuments fall, nations perish, civilizations grow old and die out and after an era of darkness new races build others. But in the world of books are volumes that have seen this happen

[5]Ibid., p. 167.
[6]Ibid.

again and again and yet live on, still young, still fresh as the day they were written, still telling men's hearts of the hearts of men centuries dead.

The history of education, at least until fairly modern times, can be witnessed in the evolution of printed instructional materials, primarily textbooks.[7]

TEXTBOOKS

Textbooks have always been the prime vehicle for learning. Noah Webster's famous old "blueback speller," for example, for forty years had the largest sale of any book except the Bible. *McGuffey's Reader,* another classic, with sales of 122 million, taught not only reading but moral and spiritual values. American school textbooks are better developed and more attractive than textbooks of other nations. Although other instructional media have assumed some of the burden of instruction, the ubiquitous textbook is still the primer.

Hillel Black, author of *The American School Textbook,* estimates that up to 75 percent of students' time in the classroom and 90 percent of their homework time is centered around books; by graduation from college, students study sixty-five or more books intensively. Annual expenditures for textbooks in elementary and secondary schools and colleges amount to approximately $9 million. Adult trade books, books for juveniles, professional books, and book clubs account for almost another $10 million.

But the biggest boom in the school book industry is the miraculous rise of paperbacks. Paperback books are less expensive than clothbound, permitting instructors to require more extensive reading, an important advantage in literature classes, for example. Their lower cost also permits students to mark them up and to retain possession of them, thus acquiring early the nucleus of a personal library. Paperbacks are fresh, clean, germ-free, and possibly more up to date than clothbound books that are passed along year after year. But their disadvantages are that they are less durable and often poorer in technical quality.

Educational publishers are influential in curriculum revision. Many publish materials generated by various agencies that develop curriculums. These publications are one major means of introducing and implementing instructional innovations in schools and colleges.

Supplementary aids. Educational publishing companies have also helped teachers and learners escape from reliance upon a single textbook as the exclusive mode. Correlated packages of printed and audiovisual materials are becoming increasingly common. Films and filmstrips, tapes and cassettes are developed by authors and publishers to combine printed text with sight and sound. These correlated packages sometimes accommodate greater individualization of instruction by permitting able students to use the time they saved to penetrate related and more advanced material. Multimedia packages also help students with reading difficulties to become less dependent upon the printed word.

Textbooks are often supplemented by workbooks, sometimes with material in programmed form, as described later. Some workbooks are designed to facilitate students' note taking and independent study. Some provide additional self-directed study for more able students. Although workbooks once developed a bad name when used as busy-work, good workbooks, properly used, can help individualize instruction beyond the capability of standard textbooks.

Criticism of textbooks. School textbooks have been criticized on a number of grounds. Some contend that they are bland and dull, that they lack opinion, controversy, and passion. Jacques Barzun, for example, in *The House of Intellect,* contends that

. . . the textbook writer must defend his words and views [against the classrooms where local prejudices and sacred illiteracies obtain] squaring his mind with those anonymous critics who are often his inferiors in learning and sense.

Others find some textbooks unacceptable because of material that they consider objectionable on the grounds of religion, subversion, eroticism, or obscenity. School auditoriums have rung with

[7]For an interesting historical account of the relationship between textbooks and education, see Edward E. Booher, "The Text for Today," *Change,* April 1975, pp. 44-47; and John C. Reynolds, "American Textbooks: The First 200 Years," *Educational Leadership,* January 1976, pp. 274–276.

debate over textbooks that contain four-letter words, praise of drugs, racial slurs, attacks on religious beliefs, criticism of government, sexual information, and a host of other objectionable material. In Kenawha County School District in West Virginia, for example, a controversy over textbooks raged for years and produced picketing, strikes, boycotts, dynamiting of school property, and even personal injury. Controversy over textbooks reflects the larger debate over the same issues in society, but it is intensified when young readers are involved. These issues have been carried as far as the U.S. Supreme Court without satisfactory resolution. The quarrel over textbooks is intensified by some adults' determination to protect the morals of young people. Although we have come far since the days of Socrates, the corruption of youths can still lead teachers, librarians, and school boards to the cup of hemlock.

The issue hinges on the dilemma between academic freedom and the possible corrupting influence of questionable literature. Schools should have well-reasoned policies, standards, and procedures for selecting the instructional materials. A publication by the American Association of School Administrators, *Censorship: The Challenge to Freedom in the School,* is helpful in delineating effective policies and procedures.

Another criticism of textbooks is that they reflect the sexism and racism that pervade our larger society. Although much racial and sexual bias may be unconscious or unintentional, it nonetheless endangers the equal protection of all people. For example, textbooks have traditionally stereotyped women as nurses and men as doctors, women as teachers and men as school administrators, and girls as meek and boys as courageous and aggressive. One study of illustrations in elementary school textbooks revealed that males outnumbered females in pictures about three to one.[8] Teachers should select books that show the least sex bias, and in their teaching they should counteract sex bias by creating a positive image of women.

[8]See Lenore J. Weitzman and Dianne Rizzo, "Sex Bias in Textbooks," *Today's Education,* January/February 1975, pp. 49, 52; Richard L. Simms, "Bias in Textbooks: Not Yet Conquered," *Phi Delta Kappan,* November 1975, pp. 201–202; and Ralph N. Fuller, "Textbook Selection: Burning Issue?" *Compact,* June 1975, pp. 6–8.

With respect to race, textbooks have commonly failed to do justice to the great contributions that minority groups and individuals have made to the advancement of our civilization. Teachers can help create a positive image of minority groups in our society. Race stereotyping, like sex stereotyping, has been far too common. Prejudice has an insidious effect on children; they pick up clues, however subtle or unintended, from the books they read, and so books have a powerful effect upon children's acculturation.

Authors and publishers are endeavoring to remove racism and sexism from instructional materials. The publisher of this book, for example, has developed an extensive guide for authors to call attention to sexist or racial overtones in textbooks. We have worked hard to eliminate prejudice in the language, ideas, and illustrations in this one.

Selection of textbooks. Nineteen states impose textbook selection upon local school districts. Fourteen states require local districts to select textbooks from a state-approved list. The remaining seventeen states permit local districts to exercise complete autonomy in selecting textbooks. Those who support statewide adoption of textbooks list these advantages: more uniform study across the state, especially for students who move among school districts, and reduced costs resulting from orders in larger quantity. The arguments against statewide adoption include the inability of teachers to choose professional tools for themselves; the imposition of uniformity, which fails to meet unique needs of local circumstances; and the long delay in adoption procedures, which tends to discriminate against more recent books. We find the arguments against statewide adoption more convincing than the arguments for it.

Virtually all public elementary and secondary schools of the nation now provide textbooks free to students. In some cases the cost is borne by local districts, in others by the state, and in a few by both. In a 1970 decision the Supreme Court of Michigan ruled that local school districts must furnish school pupils with free textbooks and certain supplies. The Elementary and Secondary Education Act passed in 1965 made textbooks and other printed and published materials available to public and private school students and teachers on a loan basis.

LIBRARIES, INSTRUCTIONAL MATERIALS CENTERS, AND LEARNING RESOURCES CENTERS

School libraries are the central repository of books, periodicals, encyclopedias, and other printed matter for students and teachers to use. In larger communities, school libraries often have a close relationship with community libraries, and interlibrary loans are possible. Sometimes the school library is operated as a branch of the city or county library. In rural areas where school and communities are too small for well-stocked libraries, bookmobiles provide an extension of the school's circulating library. A satisfactory book collection for a school library should meet the standards set by the American Library Association. The standards are based upon criteria such as the number of acquisitions per pupil, balanced distribution of titles, recency of publication, accessibility to students and teachers, and appropriate vocabulary and interest level for students served.

The federal government, particularly through the Library Services and Construction Act (1964) and the Elementary and Secondary Education Act (1965), provided grants for the improvement of libraries. New instructional technology has generated a host of nonprint instructional materials: films, models, mockups, cassettes, kinescopes, records, and others mentioned elsewhere in this chapter. In addition, collections of textbook series, other curriculum materials, and professional books for teachers are now commonly housed in the "professional library" or "curriculum materials center" within the school district's library. These added components include a wide variety of instructional printed and multimedia materials serving both students and teachers. They have brought many school districts the new nomenclature "instructional materials center" (IMC) or "learning resources center" (LRC). Technically speaking, the terms are not synonymous, but they are often used so. Here, in one place, students and teachers can find all kinds of instructional materials and equipment. They may find teletypewriter access to various information storage systems, or get instruction in the use of audiovisual equipment, or learn to handle futuristic learning technology that will be increasingly available to them in college and in life outside school. In addition, they may become oriented to computer and research laboratories.

One of the most fascinating developments in library technology is the miniaturization of recorded matter through photoreproduction processes onto microfilm or microfiche. It is now technically possible to store on one thin sheet of ultramicrofiche the entire contents of the book you are reading, though it must be magnified for use. This technology obviously saves library space, time, and money, and it is a much more durable medium than paper. So far, microfiche and microfilm have been restricted to library use, but someday they will be used in regular classroom instruction. Their use presently raises serious problems with copyrighted works. Thus the IMC and LRC make up the central nervous system, so to speak, of the entire array of recorded knowledge, putting it increasingly at the command of learners in any school system, college, or university.

Programmed instruction

Programmed instruction is one of the most remarkable new forms of pedagogy on the educational scene. The terms "programmed learning" and "programmed instruction" and their synonyms are used loosely to describe a wide variety of instructional methods. Some of the more primitive ones are not very different from the old-fashioned workbook. At the other extreme are entire courses of study and even curriculums.

In a common type of programmed instruction, a question appears, and students record their answers on paper or they punch a key to record them on tape. Students' answers can be scored and recorded permanently. After each question, students are presented immediately with the correct answer. This is not the case with most classroom tests and homework assignments. Thus learning is immediately reinforced. Subject matter is presented in a sequence of short units or "frames," which students must answer before moving ahead. Material is arranged in an orderly sequence of ideas, beginning with simple ideas and progressing gradually up to more complex concepts and their applications. Difficulty is introduced gradually, and clues or "prompts" are given to suggest correct responses. Students advance through the material at their own pace. Figure 10-2 illustrates a sequence of a programmed lesson.

Programmed instruction tends to be deliberately redundant, repeating the same thought in different language to reinforce learning. This systematic, cumulative sequence distinguishes programmed learning from old-fashioned drill of disjointed fragments of knowledge. Either a brief unit or an entire course can be programmed.

The programming of academic substance has become a highly refined art and represents one of the unique strengths of this medium. Programmed material should be thoroughly pretested and revised in the light of how children learn, rather than how teachers think material ought to be organized. This process yields valuable insights into the proper organization of substance for natural, orderly learning and promises to aid the overall improvement of teaching and curriculum construction. In some cases a "linear sequence" presents just one route of questions and answers for all students to follow. But some of the more sophisticated programs include a "branching" arrangement, which presents students who answer incorrectly some additional information that will help them discover the correct answer. One incorrect multiple-choice response would send a student along one branch; another incorrect answer, along another branch. This arrangement is obviously an effort to accommodate individual differences.

When programmed learning involves instructions and the presentation of materials on videotapes, filmstrips, or other media—perhaps in addition to printed matter—it may be referred to as "audiotutorial instruction." Various other nomenclature is used to refer to particular combinations of instructional media.

Programmed instruction is currently undergoing extensive development. A variety of models have been developed. Many textbook publishers have moved into the production of programmed texts. Much of this enterprise is stimulated by grants to schools from funds provided by the National Defense Education Act and the Elementary and Secondary Education Act. Several universities have set up centers for experimentation and research in programmed learning, such as the University of Pittsburgh's Learning Research and Development Center, which developed Individually Prescribed Instruction (IPI), described in Chapter 9.

The monthly periodical *Educational Technology* contains many articles on programming and de-

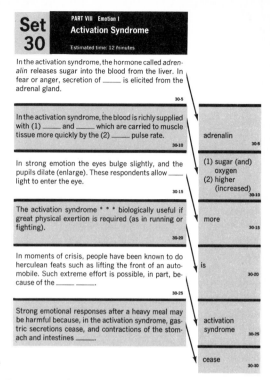

Figure 10-2 Sample sequence from a programmed lesson. In programmed lessons, the answer to a question at hand is not revealed to the learner until she or he has responded to the question and turned ahead to the next frame, at which time the answer to the completed question is revealed immediately, as indicated by the arrows. (From James G. Holland and B. F. Skinner, *The Analysis of Behavior: A Program for Self-instruction,* McGraw-Hill, New York, 1961, pp. 208–209.)

scribes numerous tools and techniques for facilitating the teaching and learning processes.

CAPABILITIES AND LIMITATIONS OF PROGRAMMED INSTRUCTION

What are the advantages and limitations of programmed instruction? Programmed instruction is quite adaptable to independent study. Students may use programmed material to gain mastery of courses not offered in small high schools or to make up work missed through absence. It helps students and adults to study independently at home. It relieves teachers from much of the drudgery of presenting routine information, correcting tests and homework, tutoring, and reviewing, thus freeing them for more creative aspects of teaching. It yields valuable understanding of how children learn by forcing attention upon the dynamic aspects of human understanding. This gives us insight into how courses and curriculums should be organized for most efficient mastery by students and will undoubtedly improve the organization of textbooks and other instructional media.

If instruction is programmed well, it permits students to move through the material at a pace compatible with their learning capability. Although advocates of programmed learning speak effusively of its ability to accommodate individual differences and often create fancy euphemisms for its nomenclature, most programs presently in use accommodate individual differences only with respect to the pace of learning. True, some programs are branched and do permit variation along alternate routes of remedial instruction, depending upon the nature of an individual student's difficulty with an item. Few, however, are programmed to handle much variability in students' interests, needs, or individual learning styles. Some enthusiasts have compared programmed instruction with a variation on what can be called the "tutorial method" of teaching. However, as Harry Broudy has pointed out so trenchantly, the two methods are exact opposites. Programmed instruction offers a canned and predigested dialogue of imposed response; any good tutorial method, on the other hand, offers genuine, open, inquiring dialogue.[9] Thus programmed instruction is, so far, individualized mostly with respect to the learner's pace of learning. It is certainly not *personalized*. We do not deny that programmed learning is capable of better accommodating total individual differences, particularly when linked with the computer's marvelous capacity for sorting and presenting material uniquely responsive to individual differences among students. The software for such an almost infinite combination of learning styles, interests, and needs has not yet been developed and will be expensive.

Certainly some kinds of learning—problem solving, discrimination, and convergent thinking—can be managed efficiently through programmed instruction. However, it is appropriate to ask for more

evidence that programmed instruction can manage appreciative learning or attitude formation as effectively as live teachers can.

Audio, visual, and multimedia materials

Modern education is delivered through a variety of visual, audio, and multimedia materials, the more important of which are discussed here.

TELEVISION

No discussion of education in our culture can be complete without considering the miracle of television. We are told that typical American students by age 18 will have spent more time (15,000 hours) watching television than in classrooms (11,000 hours), and more time watching television than anything else other than sleeping. Approximately 97 percent of American homes and one-third of our schools have television receivers. Clearly television is an incomparable means of delivering knowledge to nearly every home and to a great many classrooms in the nation. It therefore represents a powerfully educative—and at times powerfully miseducative—force in our culture. Ever since its inception in the late 1940s, television has been hailed by some as the vehicle for revolutionizing education. (Thomas Edison made the same claim for motion pictures in 1891.)

How well has television served our educational needs, and what is its promise for the future? Let us consider separately several types of television: commercial, public, cable, and satellite.

Commercial television. Commercial television brings news, documentaries, historical dramatizations, travelogues, musical presentations, and many other educational programs into our homes; it adds immeasurably to our understanding of the history of human experience and its contemporary setting. Some commercial network programs, such as "Sunrise Semester," are truly educational. Some carry academic credit under arrangement with local educational institutions. Commercial television has permitted us to experience vicariously man's first walk on the moon, the birth of a baby, transplants of human organs, congres-

[9]Harry S. Broudy, "Socrates and the Teaching Machine," *Phi Delta Kappan*, March 1963, p. 347.

sional hearings on the Watergate episode and impeachment, interviews with heads of state and other notable persons, great symphonies, political parties' national conventions, the lives of great Americans, and countless great moments in history. Some programs, such as Alistair Cooke's award-winning series "America," are beamed into schools during the day and repeated in the evening for adults, helping learners of all ages to witness Columbus's sailing to America, to feel the passions of the Civil War, and to relive the discovery of the West.

But commercial television also brings us gory spectacles of homicides and other violence in living color, a torrent of "words from our sponsor" that are frequently more mindless than informative, and a plethora of other fare that is often uneducative or miseducative. If commerical television is a window into our civilization, then one must have grave concerns about how well our civilization fares in its fateful race with catastrophe.[10]

Public television. Public educational television stations, such as WQED in Pittsburgh, the first community-owned educational television station, have grown to more than 125, placing four out of five of our people within viewing distance of these stations. This public broadcasting brings us some excellent viewing. "Masterpiece Theater" presents superb dramatizations of great moments in history and famous literary works. "Theater in America" brings us great theatrical productions. "Firing Line" presents provocative discussion of the issues of our times. For school-age children, "Mister Rogers' Neighborhood" is noteworthy for its attention to the affective development of young people, helping them understand and live with their anxieties and to become more humane persons. "Washington Week in Review" probes issues behind the current news. "Zoom" is the only program on television scripted and performed exclusively by children for children, helping them to reflect, laugh, communicate, and grow in their interpersonal relations. "Feeling Good" is a series on family health designed to help young adults

sustain better health habits through lifestyles aimed at the prevention of illness and its cure. The style of the series is both instructive and entertaining, capitalizing on music, dance, drama, and animation. Many other examples of good public television programming could be cited. A report, *Public Broadcasting and Education,* published by the Corporation for Public Broadcasting, recommended that television be used much more widely for the education of students of all ages and that "teacher centers of the air" be created to strengthen the in-service education of teachers.

The most noteworthy children's television program has been the much-acclaimed "Sesame Street," which is designed to help fill the void in good programming for young children, to assist early learning, and help disadvantaged children get off to a better start. It won the Peabody Award as the best children's show. It has demonstrated that television can be used effectively to help children learn to read. Five days a week, this program has over three hundred outlets on commercial and noncommercial stations. It is viewed by 9 million American preschoolers and millions more in fifty-seven other countries. It has been funded by both public and private agencies. Produced by Children's Television Workshop, it has a thoroughly integrated cast of children and adults plus a large cast of puppet characters.

Notwithstanding this success story, children's programs on public service stations do not escape criticism. Although hard evidence is sketchy, some contend that the enormous amount of time spent in television viewing prevents young children from socializing with their parents, siblings, and other young children. Children need to have stories read to them, to converse and play, to handle toys and develop psychomotor skills and body control, to fantasize and daydream, and to act out impulses. Some children come to school able to recite jingles heard on television but unable to carry on a conversation. Parents may depend too heavily upon television for their children's preschool development without realizing that it is very limited in helping young children to develop socially and emotionally.

Children's television is criticized on technical grounds as well. Some fear that the rapid shifts in scenes and the strident sight and sound produce sensory overkill that may increase tensions among children. Some people ask whether the identity

---

[10]For further discussion of the undesirable impact of public and commercial television on society, see Gary Wagoner, "The Trouble Is in Your TV Set: The TV as Homunculus," *Phi Delta Kappan,* November 1975, pp. 179–184; and Rose Mukerji, "TV's Impact on Children: A Checkerboard Scene," *Phi Delta Kappan,* January 1976, pp. 316–321.

Children's television programs help make early-childhood education more interesting and effective.

crisis suffered by the current generation of students—the first generation of young people exposed to television throughout their lives—their tendency to drop out of school and society, their misuse of drugs, and their proclivity toward violence may be the aftermath of overindulgence in television watching. Although these speculations are far from proved, they nevertheless cause concern and should be considered carefully by parents and educators.[11]

Although "Sesame Street" has been successful in demonstrating that well-programmed television can accelerate the educational development of millions of preschoolers, it is tragic that the commercial networks have not provided more fine educational programs for children. Gerald Lesser, educational director of the Children's Television

Workshop, describes poignantly the great problems of shoestring budgets and soul-searching ventures into the unknown world of children's programming that beset this enterprise.[12] Notwithstanding the contribution that television can make to the lives of children, the economic realities of commercial television do not hold much promise for the expansion of good children's programs on either commercial or educational wavelengths.

Public television has had severe financial problems. Although supported by private foundations, local school districts, community groups, private philanthropies, public fund drives, and the federal government, inadequate revenues have nevertheless seriously constrained the development of this powerful means of learning. Greater public support, largely from the federal government, will be required if educational television is to reach its potential. The Agency for Instructional Television

[11]For further discussion of these concerns, see Philip G. Jones, "The Educational TV in Your Schools May Be Anything but Educational," *The American School Board Journal*, March 1974, pp. 25–30.

[12]Gerald S. Lesser, *Children and Television: Lessons from "Sesame Street,"* Random House, New York, 1974.

(AIT) is a new national consortium, formed at the instigation of the Council of Chief State School Officers to stimulate cooperation among the states both in funding and programming. Other major organizations are attempting to encourage the government to provide sound long-term financing of public television free from political pressures.

Cable television. Cable television is potentially the most viable mode of television delivery. It permits two-way telecasts between school and home or school and school or wherever cable hookups exist. Educators are aware of the vast potential of cable television in providing instruction to ill or otherwise homebound students and in making classroom instruction from a school district available in any other classroom or any home in the district. Videotapes of any previously recorded program can also be made available. Cable television can expand greatly the variety of lessons and courses available to students. If linked with satellite telecommunications, discussed below, television receivers in one school or home could be linked by cable to ground centers linked in turn to the communications satellites. Ultimately this would mean that any lesson taught anywhere within reach of the satellite could be piped into any classroom or living room hooked up with cable television. Nevertheless the potential of cable television is far off because of the costs involved.

Satellite television. Satellite television is an exotic advance in telecommunications with exciting possibilities for education. Telstar, launched more than a decade ago, pioneered global communication by space satellite and was refined and extended by later satellites. The "teacher in the sky," Applications Technology Satellite (ATS-6), launched in 1974, marked the beginning of what may become the most complex application of technology to education ever attempted. Along with other satellites in orbit, this $180 million, $2\frac{1}{4}$-ton satellite—one of the most sophisticated ever launched—brings direct television reception to the homes of one-fifth of our population beyond the viewing range of television transmitters on the ground. It brings educational television to the Rocky Mountain states, Arizona, New Mexico, and Alaska. It marks the first widespread use of satellite-based telecommunications systems in direct educational application. It has the unusual

capability of providing two-way communication between students and programmers during periods of live broadcasting. Through its several audio channels it can also deliver simultaneous broadcasts in English, Spanish, American Indian, and Alaskan native languages. A bank of 300 videotapes may be drawn upon by receivers for instruction over a wide range of subjects—aging, health care, drug abuse, among many others.

At first this instruction from outer space focused upon career education, oral language development, health education, Alaskan culture, and in-service education for teachers in reading and career education. Programs for early-childhood education were also offered. This miraculous marvel of communication—"far out" both literally and figuratively—will eventually transform education, bringing knowledge that exists anywhere to learners anywhere. Unfortunately, the fate of this project beyond its experimental stage is uncertain.[13]

Television cassettes. Television programs in black and white or color can be recorded on low-

[13]For further discussion of ATS-6, see Walter B. Hendrickson, "Teacher in the Sky," *Phi Delta Kappan*, April 1975, pp. 539–542.

The Applications Technology Satellite, the "teacher in the sky," marked the beginning of one of the most complex and exciting applications of technology to education.

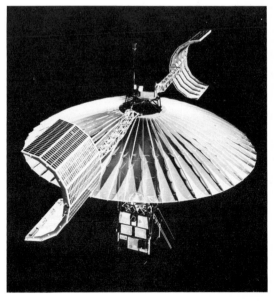

cost, $1/_2$-inch videotape cassettes and played at learners' convenience in school or at home by plugging a portable cassette player into a conventional television set. Older video equipment was costly, bulky, and confined to black-and-white transmission, often of marginal quality. Unlike live telecasts, cassette recordings can be interrupted, rerun over difficult passages, and reduced to slow motion. Another instrument, about the size of a shoe box, records programs in color onto cassettes so that students and teachers can make their own cassettes.

Capabilities and limitations. How well has educational television done the job? According to a review of approximately four hundred research studies, it is clear that students generally learn about as well with instructional television as they do in typical classrooms. The overall verdict in most studies has been "no significant difference," at least as far as standardized achievement tests are able to measure. Television teaching appears to be most successful in elementary school. At secondary and college levels, traditional classrooms appear to produce slightly better results. Although there is great variation in attitudes, elementary school pupils and teachers appear to like instructional television more than high school and college students and teachers, who favor it less and sometimes oppose it.

As evaluated by the Commission on Educational Technology, television does not get a high mark on its report card:

Instructional Television has made little impact on American education. Commitment to the use of television is generally lacking on the part of administrators and teachers. While individual systems can claim some success, the simple imposition of television on traditional administrative and educational structures is usually disappointing. The medium itself cannot be blamed, however; the major reforms necessary are much more basic than a single medium.[14]

It is somewhat surprising that educational television has failed to demonstrate more marked superiority over conventional classrooms, since the best teachers are usually chosen for the telecasts, and they are given generous time and help in lesson preparation as well as the best facilities and materials.[15]

TAPES: AUDIO AND AUDIOVISUAL

Audio and audiovisual tape recorders and players have been on the scene for some time, but for many years the recorders and players were heavy, cumbersome, and expensive. More recently, small, portable machines accept audio cassettes that snap easily into the machine and eliminate tangling of tape. They permit fast rewind and forward advances. The same machine handles both recording and playing. Solid-state technology has improved microphones and amplifiers, and thus the fidelity of reproduced sound. High-speed duplicators produce multiple copies of magnetic tape swiftly and inexpensively. Thus the audiotape recorder-player has become a versatile, inexpensive, and convenient machine that is probably more widely used in learning than any other electronic medium. Teachers and students can easily record information for themselves. One author of this book has recorded on audio cassettes all the lectures commonly delivered in his graduate class so that students may borrow the tapes and listen to them at their convenience, thus freeing class time for more individualized learning.

Various series of audiotapes on cassettes now exist for virtually all sectors of the curriculum through elementary and secondary education as well as certain fields in higher education. These cassettes are available for home use and provide a vital medium for adults' continuing education. For toddlers, cassettes offer nursery rhymes, songs, and other educational and entertaining material. Other series of tapes are available in professional fields, such as in the continued professional development of teachers. Cassettes are increasingly used as parts of instructional packages along with slides, study guides, worksheets, and other printed matter. Although cassettes have almost replaced larger reels with their wider tapes, the latter are still used in rooms where greater volume is required or where better fidelity is needed, for example, in the reproduction of music.

---

[14]Sidney G. Tickton (ed.), *To Improve Learning: An Evaluation of Instructional Technology*, vol. 1, Bowker, New York, 1970, p. 150.

[15]For further discussion of the advantages and limitations of technology applied to instruction, see American Association of School Administrators, *Instructional Technology and the School Administrator*, Washington, 1970.

Recent advances in videotape recorders have made them easier to handle, cheaper, capable of recording color pictures, and of better fidelity. Compatibility problems between recorders and projectors have been greatly reduced. Schools can tape their own programs produced locally or tape programs off their television receivers for later use. These videotapes can now be reproduced quickly and inexpensively. Their instant replay possibilities, familiar to all television sports watchers, provide great versatility in reexamining scenes for more careful study or review. Tapes offer the obvious advantage of overcoming reading handicaps or visual problems of partially sighted students. Tapes can also communicate music, drama, and other messages that don't lend themselves to printed communication. Clearly tape has become an essential and convenient learning medium in modern education.

Students can interact with computer-assisted instruction through the teletypewriter, thereby receiving more individualized instruction.

FILMS AND FILMSTRIPS

Under the stimulation of the National Defense Education Act, the number of educational film and filmstrip libraries has grown at an astonishing rate. They have made the pages of history come alive and have brought everything from great symphonies to space flights to the eyes and ears of schoolchildren. Slow-motion photography permits the examination of phenomena that happen too fast to be perceived by ordinary vision. Time-lapse photography speeds up the blooming of a flower or the growth of a plant so that an event that might take several hours or months to materialize can be seen in a few minutes. Many teachers prepare their own filmstrips.

COMPUTERS

A computer is an electronic device that stores, analyzes, and retrieves data. The processing of data by computers is miraculous. They can perform complex mathematical operations and sort and reclassify data at fantastic speeds, according to preset programs designed by human programmers. The final step is the printout of data in response to queries.

In the late 1960s, many were predicting that computers would soon revolutionize our educational systems. Although the trend has fallen short of a revolution so far, computers have become a

valuable asset in many aspects of school management: school business management, inventory control, scheduling, grade reporting, record systems, attendance accounting, and research. Computers provide instantaneous entry into a growing array of data banks that can provide students, teachers, and administrators access to vast information, thereby providing a broader and more reliable base for decisions. For example, Westfield (N.J.) High School, Rhode Island Junior College, and other institutions are developing fascinating computer-assisted guidance programs. Computers are used to provide instantaneous, complete, and current information about virtually all occupations, job openings, training programs, scholarships, and current jobs listed by the U.S. Employment Service; they even will tell students the kinds of jobs they are best suited for. The Uniform Migrant Student Record Transfer System with a computer bank at Little Rock, Arkansas, provides background information on any migrant child within twenty-four hours. These data help school and health officials to keep track of migrant children as they travel from state to state with their parents. The possibilities are almost limitless, and we shall surely see many more computer applications to education in the future.

However, the computer use that grabbed head-lines in the late 1960s was the revolution promised through computer-assisted instruction (CAI) in classrooms. Advocates of CAI claimed a number of appealing capabilities: individualized instruc-tion, immediate feedback of learning results, the ability to carry on dialogues with many individual students and instructors simultaneously, and the relief of teachers from handling routine drill activi-ties in the classroom. Figure 10-3 illustrates a model of computer-assisted instruction.

Notwithstanding the formidable potential of computers as a vehicle for delivering instruction, progress has not been as encouraging as one might hope. Much computer use has been limited to drill and practice routines. CAI is still very ex-pensive—more than most districts can af-ford—although costs per pupil may decline rapid-ly with more intensive use. Some tests of learning benefits are favorable, but the overall evidence is ambiguous. Many computer parts are fragile, and technical difficulties are common. When they occur, trained repair personnel are necessary.

One noteworthy prototype of CAI is the Wes-tinghouse Learning Corporation's Program for Learning in Accordance with Needs (PLAN), de-scribed in Chapter 9.

Despite the limitations of CAI, our long-range view of it is optimistic. CAI is still in its infancy. Its cost and technical problems will be overcome eventually.

CALCULATORS

Mechanical and electronic calculators come in all sizes for all tasks of mathematical computation. Large, multipurpose calculators are found in re-search and business offices of school systems and in research laboratories for students, thereby eliminating the tedium of mental data processing. But the biggest educational debate over this tech-nology has arisen over the abundance of low-cost pocket calculators available to students. These small calculators can save time and drudgery and let students concentrate on concepts rather than figures. However, some fear that calculators may become a crutch and that students may forget or perhaps fail to learn to add, subtract, multiply, and divide. It seems to us that students should be required to master basic computational skills in el-ementary school without calculators and then be permitted to use them in upper levels of schooling.

Occasional review of the mental processes would ensure that they are not forgotten.

TALKING TYPEWRITERS

Talking typewriters are an ingenious invention in which an electric typewriter is coupled with mag-netic tape recordings and a sound system. A student can type letters and words and immedi-ately see the printed characters and hear the let-ters and words pronounced by the machine. From a master console the teacher can program words and sentences. The keys on the typewriter are ren-dered inactive except for some that, when struck in proper sequence, print the programmed words or sentences and pronounce them for the student. A student's own spelling list can be programmed into the machine. Acronymed SLATE (Stimulated Learning by Automated Typewriter Environment), talking typewriters have received much attention because of their ability to teach very young children to read, spell, and typewrite. However, because of their high cost, relatively few schools have been able to use them.

TELEPHONES

Telephones, long used to instruct homebound students, are now being used to instruct small groups of students in different towns that are too small to justify a regular teacher in a specialized subject. Through a conference telephone arrange-ment, one teacher can conduct classes in several places simultaneously. Equipment is portable and inexpensive and includes built-in loudspeakers and microphones in each location for transmitting and receiving.

MAPS, GLOBES, AND PLANETARIUMS

In the early part of this century, the front wall of most school classrooms was sure to be adorned with pictures of Washington and Lincoln, the Amer-ican flag, and rolled maps of the United States and the world. Today, many modern maps are struck in bas relief and show the topography of the land as well as its other physical features and political divisions. Globes are also commonly found in classrooms, standing in simple symbolism of this shrinking world. Many modern high schools extend students' awareness into the universe through means of a planetarium, a room with a domed

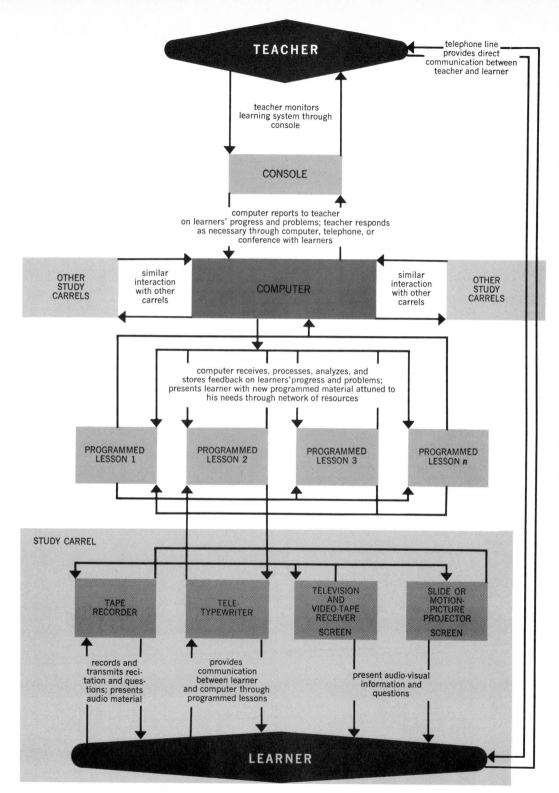

Figure 10-3 Model of a computer-based instructional system.

ceiling on which a multilensed instrument in the center projects the sun, moon, planets, and stars and displays their apparent motions in a realistic space environment. It is an astronomical aid in such related subjects as mathematics, science, aerospace education, and, of course, astronomy itself. The picture on page 262 shows a school planetarium. Many municipal and community planetariums are available for educational use.

RADIO

The Federal Communications Commission allocated numerous channels for noncommercial, educational FM (frequency modulation) service, with static-free, high-fidelity bands. Increasingly, lesson material is broadcast in audio correspondence courses. Through radio, many rural schools are losing their one-teacher status.

PHONOGRAPH AND RECORDS

Despite the growing popularity and use of modern teaching tools such as cassettes, the phonograph of yesteryear is still a good teaching machine. Long-playing, stereophonic, unbreakable, unscratchable records are easy for students and teachers to use. The repertory of records includes many high-quality educational and cultural programs. Records made by students or teachers can also enhance motivation and learning, especially for shut-ins.

CAMERAS

In some schools elementary students have been motivated to improve speaking and writing abilities by reporting on observations made with an inexpensive camera using black-and-white or color film and their own eyes and ears. Some movie cameras make possible low-cost sound-on-film recording, putting sound-film production within reach of most schools. Many schools and colleges now produce their own instructional films. Instant duplicating machines are used to produce copies of high fidelity and clarity for classroom use. Thermocopiers produce transparencies and master copies for dittoing from printed pages and from originals made by the teacher. Many schools sponsor camera clubs as cocurricular activities, academic subjects, or adult education noncredit courses.

OVERHEAD PROJECTORS

Versatile overhead projectors are being used increasingly in classrooms. They permit direct projection of charts, drawings, pictures, or printed materials from a book, without first transforming them into slides. They also project instructors' writing directly onto a screen as they solve a mathematics problem, correct an English theme, balance a chemical equation, or fill in a map, making it unnecessary for teachers to turn their backs to the class, as they must when using a chalkboard.

LEARNING LABORATORIES

Learning laboratories involve a special kind of programmed learning. They had their beginnings during World War II, when the Armed Forces wanted thousands of servicemen to acquire conversational command of other languages in a hurry. Their development has been stimulated by funds from the National Defense Education Act and other legislation, such as the Elementary and Secondary Education Act, which subsidizes such equipment.

Physically, learning laboratories consist of an eggcratelike pattern of private cubicles equipped with tape-recording and listening equipment tied into a central monitoring system through which students and teachers can communicate. The cubicles provide privacy, eliminate distractions, and reduce students' self-conciousness about reciting on tape. The method also permits individualization of instruction, since students may work on different subjects and at different levels. It permits a teacher to tune in on any student's work and to play back the student's recorded work. Learning laboratories can be used either for organized instruction of a class group or for independent, individualized study. Some laboratories contain a variety of embellishments such as a jukebox-type arrangement whereby students can dial tape recordings of more advanced difficulty or previous tapes for review, as they are ready for them.

RESPONSIVE ENVIRONMENTS

The provision of a large array of hardware and software in a classroom, controlled largely by students, is becoming common. Spoken of as the "responsive environment," "adaptive environment," or "saturated environment," this provides a setting in which students can assume greater initiative for their own learning and can have better access to a variety of hardware and software compatible with their needs or interests. Presumably, this quickens students' motivation and hence their learning rates. It permits the educational environment to react to individual learners, rather than forcing each to adapt to a more rigid and controlled school setting. Responsive environments emphasize learning rather than teaching and are compatible with open education.

Simulation and educational games

Simulation implies the creation of reality-centered instructional settings, with real-life problems to be solved.

While traditional childhood games provide little more than social experience, modern educational games are designs for specific practice in communications, problem-solving, scientific inquiry, information management, and decision making. As a tool in training, simulation has four crucial characteristics: it starts with an analogous situation; it provides for low risk input; it feeds back consequences symbolically; and it is replicable... providing an opportunity for iterative procedures in arriving at best solutions.[16]

Simulation, which proved to be a useful technique in placing human beings on the moon, is providing breakthroughs on the educational scene. While playing games and play environments have always markedly influenced the mental, physical, and social growth of children, now games, simulation techniques, and role playing are having a direct impact on their intellectual learning, academic attitudes, and social strategies. An illustration is the so-called "Life Career Game," in which teams of learners play the roles of hypothetical characters, make tentative life decisions for them, and then evaluate the success of the characters.

Other games teach ecology through gamelike competition between human beings and their environment; chemical formulas and equations; archeological and anthropological modes of discovery; economic principles of supply and demand, productivity and consumption, and prices and

[16]Isabel H. Beck and Bruce Monroe, "Some Dimensions of Simulation," *Educational Technology*, October 1969, pp. 45–46.

wages; competition in the struggle for equal rights; library research skills; computational skills; rules of logic; and even international relations, among many others. Games and other forms of simulation are highly motivating because they are grippingly realistic. They bridge the gap between concepts and real life, between theory and practice. Games offer the additional motivational factor of competition between teams of contestants and the coordination of effort and cooperation among members of the same team.

One elaborate simulation is finding its way into driver education classes. Students "drive" simulated cars while all the controls and instruments common to automobiles on "roadways" are projected onto a screen where the windshield would be. The driver encounters other traffic, traffic lights, pedestrians, and all the other realities of on-the-road driving. When situations on the film require a response from the driver, the computer automatically assesses the student's reactions and displays them on a monitor so that the instructor can apply remedial instruction as needed. Warning signals may appear on a display above each student's instrument panel to prompt corrective action. This simulator reduces the amount of time students must spend in on-the-road instruction and probably reduces the number of ulcers that driving instructors develop from hair-raising mistakes by their students on the road. Simulators are also used to train aircraft pilots.

Another form of simulation is the array of mockups of human bodies, body organs, machines, animals, plants, and other objects. These permit students to examine, disassemble, and assemble objects that otherwise could not be so handled.

Biochemical technology

Many persons have experimented with mind-expanding drugs, often with disastrous results. David Krech, an educational psychologist, along with others, has been engaged in research on the chemical, neurological, and anatomical factors related to memory. Their studies, confined so far to rats, suggest that it is possible to improve the memory of rats through biochemical intervention, by injecting new proteins and ribonucleic acids, and by inducing higher enzyme activity. Some experiments suggest that specific brain tissues taken from a rat that has mastered certain learning can be transferred to another rat, and the second rat immediately acquires the same knowledge without going through the learning process. What a panacea for indolent students if it were perfected on human subjects! But "smart pills" are still a long way off. (See Chapter 3 for a more complete discussion of biochemical intervention.)

The selection of educational technology

It is estimated that there are a quarter million textbooks, workbooks, films, filmstrips, transparencies series, audiotapes, videotapes, and programmed instructional systems available to schools and colleges. In 1967 the Educational Products Information Exchange Institute (EPIE), a kind of consumers' union for schools, was founded to help educators make wise selections among this vast and growing array of educational products. Kenneth Komoski, president of EPIE, warns that the "largest single group of unprotected consumers is the 50 million school children who are being required to learn from educational materials almost all of which have been inadequately developed and evaluated." He makes the shocking estimate that 99 percent of the materials used in schools have not been tested in the field. EPIE publishes *EPIEgram,* an educational consumer's newsletter, which analyzes and evaluates educational products. However, the magnitude of evaluating educational products outruns EPIE's capabilities and places a formidable burden upon educators, who often must make difficult choices without sufficient information.

In 1972 the National Center for Educational Technology was established within the U.S. Office of Education. Its purposes are to:

1. Administer all funds for the development, validation, and application of technology in education
2. Coordinate all federal activities in educational technology
3. Serve as a national focus for educational technology to define the issues and to help local districts make sensible applications according to their own needs and interests

Physical facilities

Physical facilities make up an indispensable part of the learning environment. Although studies have failed to establish significant correlation between the quality of school buildings and learning, physical facilities are nonetheless important. Learning is inseparable from its physical environment.

BUILDINGS

The quarter-century following World War II saw extraordinary growth in the nation's school buildings. An annual average of 70,000 classrooms were built during the 1960s. As the nation enters its third century, the rate of school construction is declining because enrollments are going down and costs are going up. In some districts some buildings are being closed because of declining enrollments. Yet, many school buildings are old and obsolete. A study by the National Education Association revealed that one teacher in eight is teaching in a building more than fifty years old. The average age of school buildings, according to the study, was about twenty-two years. Most buildings of that vintage do not meet the requirements of a modern educational program. A good school building must satisfy a number of criteria, described below.

Educational adequacy. A school building may be thought of as the space configuration of the curriculum. Since the instructional program finds its physical manifestation in the building, the specifications for the building should be derived from the educational program it is intended to house.[17] Teachers, administrators, and school boards should work together to delineate the educational specifications of the building before the architect approaches the drawing board. Better yet, educators should attempt to envision the educational program that the building will house for the next half-century, since that is the average life of most school buildings. An important aspect of educational adequacy, only recently recognized, is the building's ability to accommodate handicapped children. Newer buildings, for example, have treadle-actuated doors and ramps to permit chil-

---

[17]For an interesting historical account of school plant development and current trends, see Harold B. Gores, "The Habitats of Education," *American Education,* October 1974, pp. 16–23, 26.

dren in wheelchairs to get around in them safely and conveniently. Other modifications are being installed to accommodate students with a variety of physical handicaps.[18]

Health and safety. Although most schools are rather safe places, there is room for improvement. Most buildings of recent construction were built of fire resistant material and must meet the safety standards set by the states. Nevertheless, 75,000 teachers each year and an unknown number of students are injured seriously enough to require medical attention. The largest number of school accidents occur on stairways. Schools have recently come under the provisions of the U.S. Occupational Safety and Health Act (OSHA), which requires public and private agencies to observe prescribed health and safety standards, to keep accurate records of injuries, and to keep people informed of potential hazards in their work environment. Considerations include such matters as proper lighting, heating, ventilation, acoustics, and humidity control.

Comfort. Modern schools have become increasingly comfortable places for students and teachers. School furniture has been designed to reduce fatigue. Carpeting is common. Noise-free heating and ventilating systems contribute to sound control. More pleasing interior colors add to beauty and comfort. A growing number of schools are air-conditioned. And many classrooms and libraries provide the comforts of a living room.

Flexibility. The old lineup of boxlike classrooms along a corridor has given way to "open space," or "open planning," in school construction. Large areas of space house large numbers of students who can be grouped into instructional units of all sizes; these are separated within the large space not by walls but by movable furnishings. These open-space facilities permit infinitely more flexibility, not only in daily activities but also in long-range utilization of the building. Such flexibility is out of the question when classrooms are of uniform size and are separated by load-bearing walls that

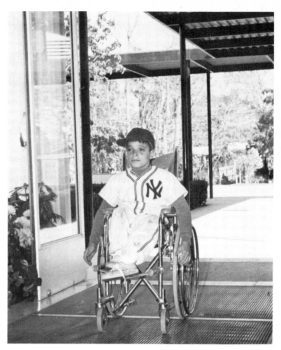

Modern school buildings accommodate handicapped children with devices such as treadle-actuated doors and ramps.

cannot be removed. Open-space construction retards the obsolescence of buildings because they can be adapted to future uses. It is also more compatible with open education, which requires flexibility in space to handle the greater variety of learning activities. Open space is also more compatible with new models of deploying teachers, such as differentiated staffing. Obviously, open-space construction requires intensive acoustical control.

Economy. Cost of school construction nearly doubled in the decade between 1965 and 1975. Many districts are searching for ways to reduce capital and maintenance costs of new buildings. These include minimizing noninstructional space, such as corridors; combining lunchrooms, gymnasiums, and auditoriums into multipurpose areas; choosing more economical shapes to reduce expensive exterior wall surfaces; making maximum use of standard sizes of windows; selecting materials that have low maintenance costs and that reduce insurance rates; and anticipating future in-

---

[18]For further discussion of building features helpful to handicapped students, see Larry Malloy, "The Handicapped Child in the Everyday Classroom," *Phi Delta Kappan,* January 1975, pp. 337–340.

stallations, such as cable television and air conditioning. In urban areas where land costs are high, some districts are incorporating schools within high-rise apartment buildings. This also produces savings in transportation costs.

The John F. Kennedy School and Community Center in Atlanta, Georgia, as its name implies, is a noteworthy example of how savings can be realized by combining the school building and community center. It has been described as a "shopping center of social services under one roof." It contains a middle school for 1,000 students, an adult education program, day-care services, job training and counseling for students and adults, public recreation facilities, welfare agencies, volunteer community services, and a distribution center for surplus foods. The community has free use of the facility throughout the entire day. Having all these services under one roof is both a convenience to the community and an economy, since joint financing by school and community is used, duplication of services is reduced, and the facilities permit more intense around-the-clock utilization. Joint community schools are becoming more common, as, for example, the Whitmer Human Resources Center in Pontiac, Michigan, and the Thomas Jefferson Junior High School and Community Center in Arlington, Virginia.

Many districts have explored the year-round use of school facilities through an "extended school year" design, in which children attend school over staggered spans of nine months. Although this does maximize the use of school buildings otherwise idle during the summer, it has not proved to be economical in other ways.

When new building costs are prohibitive, some districts have turned to renovating old school buildings or to converting other structures —homes, abandoned railroad stations, factories, barns, and even retired warships—to school use.

The rising costs of fuel and other services have accelerated the search for fuel-saving devices. With one, large solar cells containing aluminum plates are placed on the roof. They trap the sun's heat and use it to heat water that is stored and piped through classrooms. In Dorchester, Massachusetts, the Grover Cleveland Junior High School's solar heat system will probably save 15 to 25 percent in heating fuel. To conserve energy, a number of schools are installing computer-assisted, remote-control heating, cooling, ventilating, and lighting systems. Some remote-control maintenance systems not only conserve fuel but also spot latent equipment malfunctions before breakdowns, monitor controls, and inspect equipment electronically, thereby effecting savings in maintenance personnel.

Security. The costs to school districts of vandalism, arson, and thefts have been estimated at more than $1/2 billion annually. This tragic waste has generated a variety of school security measures. The Elk Grove (California) High School District initiated the first "vandal watch project," which is spreading to many other districts. It provides on each of its school grounds a rent-free site for a mobile home whose occupants keep a watch on school grounds. The project pays for itself by reducing vandalism as well as the cost of insurance.

Many schools have installed devices that detect intruders and notify local police when vandals tamper with doors or windows; closed-circuit television monitoring systems that permit a single guard at a master console to watch a number of buildings; automatic sprinkling systems or fire sensors that set off alarms in the nearest fire stations; and electronic devices that warn custodians when they leave the building if any doors remain unsecured.

Site. Important considerations of a school site include its size and dimensions; the character of the grounds; the location of the building with respect to population distribution; and the amount of space for parking, play, outdoor learning, and sports. The school site is viewed increasingly as an extension of the learning environment. School grounds are being used more intensively both for recreational purposes and for learning, particularly in nature study, biology, earth sciences, environmental education, and ecology.

Demographic factors affect the selection of a school site. The impact of the civil rights movement and the pressure for racial balance in schools have led many school districts to locate schools so that their attendance areas will include students of various races. Strategic location of buildings can help to minimize the cost of transporting students to school.

During periods of rising school enrollments, sites should be selected with consideration of possible future expansion. The location of buildings away from sources of air pollution, extreme noises, and other latent hazards is also critical.

Planning. In building schools, the importance of careful planning can hardly be overemphasized. Teachers, administrators, and school boards should all be included in planning stages. They can all help to delineate the educational philosophy of the district, the fundamental activities that will grow out of the curriculum, and the types of educational technology and teaching-learning procedures to be used. These all help to determine the educational specifications that must guide architects in rendering building specifications. Many states require districts to develop long-range plans for school construction according to guidelines established by the state. The Educational Facilities Laboratory, an independent, nonprofit organization, has been a wellspring of experimentation, research, and consultation in the improvement of school buildings.

Financing. As noted earlier, the costs of school construction have risen sharply in recent years. Fortunately, costs did not rise rapidly until after the great wave of school construction during the 1950s and 1960s. Most new school construction (approximately 67 percent) is financed through some form of borrowing, usually through the sale of bonds issued either by local school districts or by state authority. In many states local school districts have sole responsibility for the approval, issuance, and sale of bonds, but the state sets the debt limits. The great rise in interest rates during the early 1970s added to the cost of amortizing new school construction. When building costs are financed through borrowing, public approval through referenda must be secured in many states. Because of increasing costs, the number of such referenda defeated by the public reached frightful proportions in many parts of the country. Means of financing other than borrowing include pay-as-you-go plans, building reserve funds, and donations. Approximately 83 percent of the cost of new school construction has come from local sources in recent years, a burden that many districts find onerous.

Approximately 12 percent of the costs of new school construction on a nationwide basis comes from the states, although some states provide virtually nothing. In 1971 Maryland became the first state (except for the single-district state of Hawaii) to provide full state funding for all public school construction. This development is being watched carefully by some other states. When the state pays all the costs, it helps to equalize across the state both the burden of financing and the quality of school facilities for all students. It also brings better planning resources to bear and results in lower interest rates on bonds.

The federal government has also provided some subsidy for certain types of school construction for schools and colleges. The federal government's share, about 3 percent, is hardly noteworthy and is limited to special purposes, such as vocational schools.

Educational parks. Some school districts have consolidated attendance areas into a single campuslike configuration enrolling thousands of students. Sometimes this is accomplished by combining all or many elementary schools in the district. In other cases, elementary, middle, and secondary schools are combined to form "educational parks," as they have come to be called. These parks provide specialization, concentration of resources, and flexibility that would be obtainable in smaller school buildings only at exhorbitant cost. They make it possible, at a reasonable cost per student, to provide larger and better libraries, laboratories, and facilities for recreation, health care, and other services, as well as broader and more enriched curriculums. However, the more compelling reason for educational parks in most instances is the better opportunity they provide for racial integration, especially when they are located near boundaries of segregated housing patterns.

FURNISHINGS

Many interesting changes are taking place in school furnishings. Four-legged, conventional chairs and desks and bulky storage cabinets and laboratory units are giving way to more flexible and casual appointments. Beanbag-type lounge chairs and carpeted tiers are not uncommon seating facilities. Group-sized tables with chairs, often of the stacking variety, are replacing individual desk-chair units. Free-standing modular boxes that can be fitted together and easily reassembled into a variety of sizes and shapes enhance flexibility.

Light-weight plastics are replacing steel for some furnishings, making them more portable and therefore more flexible. Do-it-yourself materials, such as structural corrugated cardboard, provide inexpensive and flexible work and storage spaces. Display cases that house students' work in art or science add human interest to classrooms and corridor walls. Individual carrels, sometimes combined with locker space, provide private, convenient facilities for individual study in many schools. The new forms of classroom furnishings are designed for flexibility, durability, informality, and attractiveness. More and more elementary school furnishings are being pushed about like toys, which they often are.

School buses

Next to school buildings, the largest capital outlay in education goes for school transportation. The need for transportation is still growing for several reasons: reorganization of school districts, racial desegregation of schools, more educational field trips, increased hazards of walking to school, and the increasing number of states that mandate transportation of those students attending private schools. Nationally, about 4 percent of total current expenditures for education goes for school transportation. In a few states, most of the cost is borne by parents. Twelve states subsidize all operating costs. More than half the costs of transportation comes from local sources, with most of the remainder coming from the states. Two out of five students, approximately 20 million, ride to school on buses at an annual cost of almost $1 billion.

Although the safety record of this vast fleet of buses is better than that of other motor vehicles, improvement is necessary. In one recent year, 150 school-bus passengers were killed, and 5,600 were injured in 47,000 accidents. Ralph Nader and other consumer advocates have demanded federal legislation that would ensure greater structural integrity and crash-worthiness of buses, better emergency exits, reduced flammability, safer fuel and exhaust systems, better seat-belt provisions, and other protections for young riders.

Another interesting development is the combination of transportation and learning. A few districts have installed earphones in buses, permitting students to listen to recorded instruction during their ride to school. Whether this extension of the school day to include the bus ride will displace time-honored pastimes of hair pulling, punching, munching, or hugging remains to be seen.

The future

During the 1960s, many grandiose predictions were made of a coming technological revolution in education. Subsequent events ruled otherwise. The high costs of both hardware and software and the technical limitations of the hardware were underestimated. Nevertheless, two inexorable forces—accountability demands and tight money—have combined to press for greater efficiency in education. Schools are still highly labor-intensive, which is to say that education is still delivered largely through salaried employees, rather than through machines. Greater efficiency will be sought through electronic-mediated instruction, and the pressure for this will become increasingly intense. As noted earlier, technological advances are reducing costs and improving the effectiveness of electronic instruction.

Three recent technological advances now make telecommunications media more feasible: solid-state and integrated circuits, reduced power-consumption requirements, and miniaturized hardware and software. Although the problems are still formidable, we predict continued exciting advances in educational technology. But we think it will be more evolutionary than revolutionary. Our tremendous investment in facilities and personnel does not permit drastic transformation of our schools. Then, too, we are still uncertain about how all the elements of technology fit together in a total learning environment, because we still know too little about the learning process.

We forecast accelerated systems applications in education. School administrators are crowding into conferences on goal-setting systems, planning systems, management information systems, financing systems, instructional systems, and evaluation systems—the list goes on and on. A plethora of subsystems in school management are appearing. We regard this trend as beneficial. It tends to transform educational decision making from an art to a science and to reduce the influence of politics and intuition in school management. Perhaps the major contribution of systems applications has been its stimulation of new ways of thinking about education.

With respect to instructional materials, textbooks will remain the prime vehicle for instruction. Their convenience and mobility are considerable, despite rising costs of production. We think microfiche will not replace textbooks for most basic instruction—one can't underline microfiche or read it in bed. We will continue to see the development of a host of ancillary audio and audiovisual materials combined with textbooks in integrated instructional packages to augment the printed word with pictures and sounds. Regional instructional materials centers serving many schools, perhaps through intermediate units, will probably reduce but not replace local school libraries. Regional resources become increasingly feasible through electronic reproduction or display of printed matter from distant sites.

Programmed instruction will continue to displace conventional modes of instruction, but progress will be fairly slow and painstaking because of the substantial labor and costs involved in developing first-class software. As noted earlier, programmed instruction has the great advantage of individualizing instruction, the perennial dream of educators. Computer-assisted programmed instruction will become increasingly common and will reduce the enormous managerial effort required to support teacher-mediated individualized instruction. This development and refinement of programmed instruction will continue to deepen our insights into the phenomenon of learning and will make all instruction and learning more effective.

Steady advances will continue in audio, visual, and multimedia development. We are not optimistic about the future of commercial television with respect to instruction. The economic forces that determine commercial programming are not well attuned to sponsorship of good educational fare. We perceive satellite-based telecasting as a breakthrough in delivering low-cost television to schools and eventually to homes, making it feasible to share resource material from any library on a regional, national, or even international basis. Telelecture hookups will eventually bring to any classroom great teachers from anywhere in the world. Small schools will have equal access to specialized instruction that is now available only in larger districts. These satellites truly represent a quantum leap forward in communication, which is the backbone of learning and teaching. Schools should prepare now for this miracle by installing coaxial cables in all new construction and renovation and by training personnel to use videotape and videocassette equipment. When satellite-based telecasts are linked with cable television, every living room becomes a potential learning center.

Computer technology will continue to advance. The computer of the future will have the capacity to create and learn for itself, so to speak. It will learn from and correct its own mistakes, a capacity not always prevalent in human beings. But perhaps the most miraculous computer development of the future will be its capability to deal with spoken language in such a way that any of us will be able to communicate with it just as we do with people. This will eliminate the cumbersome interface of human beings and computers through punched cards and complex retrieval programs. Households will be able to subscribe to computer services as they now subscribe to cable television. The possible educational applications of computer technology boggle the mind. Its vast capability for handling information makes real individualization of instruction feasible when combined with programmed learning. We have only scratched the surface of computer applications to both instruction and school management.

The hologram is another marvel not yet in common use in schools. It projects a three-dimensional lifelike image that can be rotated 360 degrees. It presents an exact duplicate in fine detail and can be magnified with no loss of detail. Thus students can view rare objects such as a piece of Inca pottery in a museum in Peru or a painting that is too delicate to be hung on a museum wall.

Then there is the "neural efficiency analyzer," a computerized instrument designed to test brain waves. It produces a "neural efficiency score" that tells how well the brain is functioning. Still experimental, this invention may predict a child's potential to learn, and perhaps detect latent learning disabilities. Developed by psychologist John Ertl, the neural efficiency analyzer is not a substitute for intelligence tests nor a diagnostic tool, since it measures only the speed of information transfer in the brain. It is now being used experimentally in the Washington County, Maryland, schools. Surely countless other scientific marvels with fascinating educational possibilities lie ahead.

We expect that valuable new insights will be gained by biochemical, pharmacological, and neurological approaches to the study of how the human mind functions. Much later, the transplantation of brain tissues, drugs, enzymes, and who knows what else may become safe and effective interventions in extending learning capacity.

New developments in school facilities will include the use of mobile homes and trailers to transport highly specialized classrooms and equipment. In vocational education, for example, a variety of school sites can be served that otherwise could not afford them on a permanent basis. We expect a trend toward smaller school buildings that accommodate 500 or fewer students in an attempt to provide greater peace, intimacy, and peer interaction. Inflatable plastic bubbles will be used to house gymnasiums, swimming pools, temporary instructional facilities, and a variety of other services.

Learning will become less dependent upon traditional school plants, as it already has in alternative programs. As career education and work-study programs gain momentum and the worlds of learning and gainful employment become more integrated, other structures in the community will house learners for part of the school day or week. We predict continued expansion of joint-occupancy, multipurpose structures by schools and other community agencies.[19] Certainly the technology described in this chapter suggests that homes will be used increasingly as learning centers. One educator forecasts that typical students of the future will spend approximately one-third of their learning time in a "shopping center" type of school, one-third at a learning station at home, and one-third in work experiences in the community. Learners will probably become more nomadic, and our notions of the schoolhouse and the school day will be greatly modified. One futurist predicts that by the year 2000 any place can be a classroom and that we may have no school buildings at all. Others disagree.

Travers cautions that technological development sponsored by government is likely to be reactionary and far removed from the welfare of people because its development is used to "preserve the world of the establishment."[20] He stresses that much of our educational technology has been conservative in nature and has reflected the federal emphasis upon achieving the traditional goals of education at minimum cost. Educational technology, says Travers, need not be oriented toward maintenance of the status quo but is likely to be so when controlled by the governmental bureaucracy. According to him, "Any solution that seeks to solve social ills through the development of a uniform educational product by technological means is unlikely to produce the smoothly running social machine it is designed to produce, for it includes features that are highly abrasive to the spirit of man."[21] Travers believes that educational technology should allow human beings to escape from the tyranny of machines and should be capable of providing rich and interesting environments in which learners can make real decisions about what to explore. He thinks this is most likely to occur when scientists and developers of educational technology are in close intellectual proximity and free of government control.

Certainly the emerging new technology can go far toward accomplishing two of our most pervasive and heretofore unrealized educational dreams—the ultimate individualization of instruction and the equalization of educational opportunity even around the world. If this could be done without the horror of universal thought control, it might be regarded as the ultimate human triumph over machines—rather than the reverse—and the liberation of the educative process from the constraints of inequality, time, and space.

Suggested activities

1. Discuss the following statement: Modern technology is on the threshold of producing a revolution in education.

[19]See Richard J. Passantino, "Community-School Facilities: The Schoolhouse of the Future," *Phi Delta Kappan*, January 1975, pp. 306–308; and Harold B. Gores, "The Future File: Schoolhouse 2000," *Phi Delta Kappan*, January 1975, pp. 310–312.

[20]Robert M. W. Travers, "Educational Technology and Politics," in Robert M. W. Travers (ed.), *Second Handbook of Research on Teaching*, Rand McNally, Chicago, 1973, p. 983.

[21]Ibid., pp. 988–989.

2. What effects will programmed instruction have on teachers and learners?

3. Give the historical evolution of some aspects of educational materiel and technology, such as textbooks or educational television.

4. Contrast an old textbook with a modern one in the same field.

5. Visit a modern instructional materials center and describe how it differs from a traditional school library.

6. Prepare a bibliography of the best paperback books available as supplementary readings in your field of teaching.

7. Examine or prepare a scorecard for evaluating a textbook in your major field.

8. Write a report on "The Computer in Modern Education."

9. List some radio and television programs that have an educational emphasis.

10. List the changes in school building construction that have been prompted by new instructional methods such as ungraded classes, multiple grouping, television, team teaching, programmed instruction, and audiovisual aids.

Bibliography

Association for Supervision and Curriculum Development: *Open Schools for Children,* Washington, 1973. Describes opportunities and problems in designing space and curriculum structures for open education.

Boucher, Brian G., Merrill J. Gottlieb, and Martin L. Morganlander: *Handbook and Catalog for Instructional Media Selection,* Educational Technology Publications, Englewood Cliffs, N.J., 1975. Catalog of instructional media and devices available for use to meet specific learning objectives.

Council of Educational Facilities Planners: *Guide for Planning Educational Facilities,* Columbus, Ohio, 1969. Nontechnical treatment of current practices tracing the creation of schools from concept through design and use.

Issues in Children's Book Selection, Bowker Co., New York, 1973. Anthology of essays on philosophical and practical considerations in selecting library and classroom books for children.

Kapfer, Philip G., and Miriam B. Kapfer: *Learning Packages in American Education,* Educational Technology Publications, Englewoods Cliffs, N.J., 1974. Useful information for teachers about learning packages available in many subject fields for individualizing teaching.

Knezevich, Stephen J.: *Administrative Technology and the School Executive,* American Association of School Administrators, Washington, 1969, chap. 5. The implications of technology for educational staffing patterns and organizational arrangements.

_____ and Glen G. Eye: *Instructional Technology and the School Administrator,* American Association of School Administrators, Washington, 1970, chap. 1. Some basic perspectives on technology and instruction.

Leibert, Robert M., John M. Neale, and Emily S. Davidson: *The Early Window,* Pergamon, New York, 1973. Well-written compilation of social psychological research on children's television viewing and its effect upon them.

Lipsitz, Lawrence (ed.): *Technology and Education,* Educational Technology Publications, Englewood Cliffs, N.J., 1974. Interesting and readable introduction to the use of educational technology.

Melody, William: *Children's Television: The Economics of Exploitation,* Yale, New Haven, Conn., 1974. History, economics, and policy issues inherent in producing children's television.

Minor, Ed, and Harvey R. Frye: *Techniques for Producing Modern Visual Instructional Materials,* McGraw-Hill, New York, 1970. Methods and processes in producing audiovisual teaching aids.

National Academy of Sciences: *Issues and Public Policies in Educational Technology,* Heath, Lexington, Mass., 1974. Public policy, technical, and educational issues in adoption of educational technology with recommendations for its use.

Pearson, Neville P., and Lucius A. Butler: *Learning Resources Centers,* Burgess, Minneapolis, Minn., 1973. Describes purposes and characteristics of modern learning resource centers.

Pratt, David: *How to Find and Measure Bias in Textbooks,* Educational Technology Publications, Englewood Cliffs, N.J., 1974. Provides teachers and other educators with a handy means of determining whether the language of textbooks discriminates against or stereotypes members of minority groups.

Rubin, Louis, (ed.): *The Future of Education,* Allyn and Bacon, Boston, 1976, chaps. 6,7. Explores the learning environment and the technological possibilities of future schools.

Travers, Robert M. W.: "Educational Technology and Politics," in Robert M. W. Travers (ed.): *Second Handbook of Research on Teaching,* Rand McNally, Chicago, 1973, pp. 979–996. Exposes the dangers of governmental control of educational technology and describes reforms needed in its development.

Chapter 11
Educational finance

The trouble with a cheap education is that we never stop paying for it.

Consider the roots of poverty.

Half of the kids in the primary grades won't finish high school. In America today, one out of three high school students won't graduate.

If the dropouts don't wind up as delinquents or criminals (and their chances are ten times greater than average), they'll wind up with a family.

But with less chance to earn the money it takes to support a family.

The chances are two to one that a man with less than eighth-grade education will earn $3,000 or less. Too little to support a family.

So while we can skimp on dollars for education, we'll spend the money we save—and more—supporting the people who don't have the education they need.

Good schools with good teachers and good facilities can produce good citizens.

Which is why money spent on education represents the best investment we can make.

An investment that never stops paying.

Foundations of educational finance

As the public service advertisement on the opposite page tells us, "The trouble with a cheap education is that we never stop paying for it. . . . Money spent on education represents the best investment we can make." Let us begin our consideration of educational finance with an understanding of the current financial crisis in our schools and with some historical, economic, and political perspectives on the subject.

THE FINANCIAL CRISIS

Our educational systems are currently facing a severe financial crisis. In a little over a decade the costs of elementary and secondary education have leaped from 4 to 8 percent of the gross national product (GNP). The burdens of runaway inflation, a depressed economy, high costs of fuel, taxpayers' backlash against higher tax rates, and court-mandated reforms of inequitable school finance programs have collided simultaneously to produce near chaos in school financing. The consequences bode ill for education. Certainly the problem will get worse before it gets better.

Let us consider some of the causes and consequences of this financial crisis. In a number of states, such as Ohio, where school districts are forbidden by law to borrow money to operate, some school districts have been forced to close before the completion of the school year. Across the nation the percentage of school bond referenda approved by voters dropped from 75 to less than

50 in the last decade. These referenda on school budget and bond issues are about the only opportunity that voters have to express explicitly and directly their objection to higher taxes generally. Proposed amendments to state constitutions to achieve major property tax reforms have been overwhelmingly defeated in a number of states including California, Colorado, Michigan, and Oregon. Although there was little disagreement over the need for some kind of reform, negative coalitions of voters who objected to certain aspects of the proposed amendments combined to defeat them. The New Jersey legislature recently defied a court-ordered deadline for the reform of that state's school finance structure, a structure that violated the state constitution because of its overreliance on local property taxes. The New Jersey legislature could not agree on the new taxes required to accomplish the reform.

With educational costs constituting more than half of state revenues in many other states and with taxpayers' backlash against new tax proposals, the problem reached crisis proportions in other states as well. Various large cities—most notably New York—are on the verge of bankruptcy, unable to raise the revenue needed or even to borrow the money necessary to continue deficit financing.

Most school districts have been forced to adopt stringent economy measures. In some districts, replacements are not hired for teachers who resign or retire. In many cases where enrollment is declining, nontenured teachers are dismissed, and even tenured teachers are furloughed. Class sizes are increasing. Curricular programs are being cut back. Building construction, renovation, and maintenance are being curtailed. The quality of school lunches has declined in many districts, even while their price has increased. In colleges and universities, too, there are freezes on hiring, quotas set on the number of faculty members placed on tenure, and urgent demands for increased productivity.

An understanding of the causes of the current fiscal crisis in our schools, the malaise in our educational finance structure, and the fiscal reforms needed to revitalize our schools is important for all citizens and most especially to readers who are planning careers in education. Most of this chapter deals with public elementary and secondary school systems. The financial circumstances of higher education are discussed in Chapter 7.

THE EVOLUTION OF EDUCATIONAL FINANCE

To understand our current problems, we must know a bit about the history of school finance. Until the nineteenth century, education was regarded in all countries as a privilege for those able to afford it. In the early years of our nation's history, most schools were private and were financed largely through tuition fees that were sometimes paid in commodities rather than in money. Denominational schools were supported both by tuition and by grants from the churches to which they were related. A few pauper schools, supported largely by charity, existed for the poor. Thanks to the tireless efforts of Horace Mann and other determined advocates, "the general diffusion of knowledge" was increasingly regarded as essential to the survival of a free people and their democratic government. As Jefferson had warned, "If a nation expects to be free and ignorant, it expects that which never was and never will be." Through the early nineteenth century the principle of free public education came to be accepted, but only after great struggle. The more significant events in the emergence of our educational finance structure are set forth in the historical calendar accompanying this chapter. First, state legislatures granted permission to local communities to levy taxes for the support of schools upon those citizens who consented. Later, taxes on all property were mandated, regardless of consent and regardless of whether the property owners had children in school. The notion that one could be taxed to support the education of other people's children, although commonly accepted today, was a revolutionary doctrine at the time, both here and abroad. First elementary schools and later secondary schools were by law made free to all students. It was not until the twentieth century that the principle of free access was applied to higher education. Meanwhile compulsory school attendance laws became common. Education was increasingly recognized as a function of the state. State school funds were established to supplement revenues from local property taxes. Substantial federal support for elementary and secondary public schools did not appear until after World War I. The development of this federal funding of education is traced in Chapter 14.

State aid was at first distributed on a flat grant-per-pupil basis. As described later, by the early twentieth century many states had established

The courts have held that the quality of educational opportunity must not be a function of wealth; all students should have equal access to well-financed schools. (Note the inequality in these facilities.)

The Development of Educational Finance

1633	A town school established and a school tax levied by the Dutch in New York		1933	Emergency grants for education initiated by Congress during the Depression
1643	Earliest record found of rate bills or tuition fees for support of schools		1944	Original GI Bill, with federal subsidies for veterans' education, enacted
1693	Massachusetts towns given the legal power to levy school taxes		1946	National School Lunch Act passed by Congress on permanent basis (extended and expanded in Child Nutrition Act of 1966)
1785	Land set aside in the Northwest Territory by the Ordinance of 1785, beginning federal aid for education		1946	Financing of Fulbright program for international exchanges approved by Congress
1795	First state-supported university— University of North Carolina—opened		1953	Council for Financial Aid to Education established as nonprofit organization to encourage voluntary support of higher education
1795	First permanent public school fund established in Pennsylvania		1958	Epoch-making National Defense Education Act enacted by Congress
1819	Inviolability of charters of private colleges established by Dartmouth College decision		1963	Higher Education Facilities Act, including funds for undergraduate and graduate facilities, passed by Congress
1821	First free public high school organized in Boston		1964	Civil Rights Bill passed by Congress, containing a provision for the withdrawal of funds from any school district practicing discrimination
1834	Free elementary education first adopted by the state of Pennsylvania		1964	Economic Opportunity Act passed by Congress, with special provisions affecting education of the poor
1862	Morrill Act, creating federally supported land-grant colleges, signed by President Lincoln		1965	Elementary and Secondary Education Act passed, providing some services and loans for private schools
1869	First state law providing some financial aid for school busing approved by Massachusetts		1965	Higher Education Act passed by Congress
1874	Taxation for secondary schools upheld in Kalamazoo (Michigan) case		1967	Education Professions Development Act adopted by Congress
1902	First publicly supported junior college established at Joliet (Illinois)			
1917	Federal funds for vocational education provided through Smith-Hughes Act			

1969	A private educational firm awarded, for the first time, a "performance contract" by public schools (Texarkana, Arkansas) to provide academic instruction for its students		1971	Report of the National Educational Finance Project, most comprehensive study of school finance, published
1970	GI educational benefits substantially expanded and increased by Congress		1972	Report of Presidential Commission on School Finance published
1970	Supplemental federal funds provided by the President to help predominantly black colleges, their students, and staff		1972	State and Local Fiscal Assistance Act passed, providing federal aid for schools through revenue sharing
1970	Largest of all federal-aid-to-education grants ever appropriated approved by Congress in the passage and three-year extension of Elementary and Secondary Education Act and amendments		1974	Drive for accountability in school finance through PPBS and other means adopted by most states
1971	Direct public aid to private schools ruled unconstitutional by U.S. Supreme Court		1976	Target date proposed by Carnegie Commission on Higher Education for removal of all financial barriers to higher education
1971	Property tax as major factor in school support ruled unconstitutional by California Supreme Court		1977	Total cost of public and private elementary, secondary, and higher education reached $125 billion

"foundation programs" designed to guarantee that each child's education would be supported at a minimum, or foundation, level. Although the formulas by which these state funds were appropriated were often spoken of as "equalization formulas," they equalized the minimum base only, and great variations in expenditures per pupil continued to exist among districts. The courts, primarily state courts, began within the last decade to apply the equal rights protections of state constitutions to school finance plans. These decisions caused school finance structures to be reformed to reduce inequities in expenditures per pupil among districts within state boundaries. In essence, the courts held that the quality of educational opportunity must not be a function of wealth—either a family's wealth or a school district's wealth—but only the state's wealth. These judicial edicts prompted a veritable revolution in shool finance that has not yet run its course. The dilemmas and con-

sequences generated by this litigation are discussed in Chapter 1.

In 200 years, education has progressed through these significant stages:

- A privilege under private auspices for those who could afford it
- A privilege for all at public expense, regardless of ability to afford it
- A right for all that must be provided equally without discrimination based upon race, sex, intellectual ability, or wealth of school districts

The evolution of free and equal education for all is truly one of the great contributions of our society. Horace Mann regarded it as the greatest discovery in the course of human history. It is both the marvel and the envy of other lands. It is without doubt the most significant factor in our success and prosperity as a nation and one of the most significant chapters in our history.

POLITICAL FOUNDATIONS OF EDUCATIONAL FINANCE

It is important to review the political rationale for maintaining free and equal public education because the welfare of our government and the welfare of our schools are so powerfully and reciprocally related.

Free, universal education is essential to the preservation of popular government. Universal suffrage cannot long endure without universal education. When decisions are made by the people, the people must be knowledgeable in order to make enlightened decisions. This conviction has been expressed eloquently by Jefferson, Adams, Madison, Lowell, Mann, and other distinguished Americans.

Free, universal, and equal education is essential to the protection of equal opportunity. In Chapter 1, we explored the relationship between educational opportunity and social and economic opportunity. Where educational opportunity is unequal, there can be no equality in the individual pursuit of happiness and prosperity. Although equality of educational opportunity does not guarantee social or economic equality, it does make the quest more equal—the least that our Constitution requires. As Hubert Humphrey has warned:

Education is the keystone in the arch of democracy. Ignorance breeds only slavery. Enlightenment liberates the human mind and spirit. As a free people—as a democratic people—we must accept the moral obligation of providing the means whereby every American—regardless of race, color, age, religion, income, or educational achievement—has an equal opportunity for education and training limited only by his own capability and initiative.

Differentiation of educational programs and costs on the basis of different needs is both permissible and essential. Students vary widely in their abilities and their needs. Physically, emotionally, and intellectually handicapped students commonly require education that is often both difficult and costly. Most states in the past have excluded or otherwise discriminated against certain types of handicapped children under certain conditions. In a leading case in Pennsylvania, the forerunner of "right to education" edicts, the court

outlawed such practices and ruled that these children must be placed in a free, public program of education appropriate to their capacity. Special education, compensatory education, and vocational education are examples of higher-cost programs that are appropriate for certain students' needs. Mandates regarding equal educational opportunity and "fiscal neutrality" in the support of schools in no way deny either the right or the obligation of schools to spend more money per student for those with special handicaps or needs.

Education is a function of the states and its financing is a responsibility of the states. Although local, state, and federal levels of government all assume certain responsibilities for the advancement of education, and although all participate in its financial support, education is nevertheless a primary responsibility of the states, as explained in Chapter 13. Every state constitution requires the establishment of a state system of education. Although all states except Hawaii delegate some authority to local school districts, the states cannot abdicate the responsibility for maintaining "efficient, thorough, and uniform" educational systems, as it is often phrased in state constitutions. Although local control of schools is widely cherished and vigorously sought and desirable to a degree, ultimate responsibility and accountability rests with the state, as numerous court decisions have made clear. The state is the only level of government that is close enough to the educational scene and in sufficient control of revenue to determine appropriate educational needs and to allocate resources equitably.

Federal support of education is both appropriate and necessary. As described in Chapter 14, the federal government has had a long but ill-defined role in the support of education. This role finds legal justification in the general welfare clause of the Constitution. The federal government has had an interest in education through our two centuries as a nation and has participated in the financial support of those programs which are most critical to the national interest. Federal financial support has become most prominent during the last quarter-century, but it still amounts to only one dollar in thirteen of the expenditures for public elementary and secondary schools. In the absence of well-defined national policy with respect to the role of the federal government in education, much of its support has tended to be quixotic and fragmented. Perhaps the ultimate responsibility of the federal government, one that it so far has failed to acknowledge, is to provide without federal control sufficient fiscal support to equalize educational opportunity throughout the land.

Local interest, initiative, and influence are critical in the support of public schools. Local control of education is highly prized, with good reason. There is something persuasive about keeping control of schools close to the people. Local government is closest to the needs and interests of citizens and students and therefore more able to respond more swiftly and surely to educational problems arising from local concerns. Many good educational practices have developed from local inventiveness and initiative. Local control of education is perhaps the best guarantee that our schools will not become instruments of propaganda in the control of despotic government, as has happened in some countries. Until recently, more than half the cost of public schools was borne by local sources. This circumstance is changing rapidly as states move toward full funding of public schools. Many observers note that as state funding of schools increases, so does state control, at the expense of local control. Although some shift in control is probably inevitable, most authorities agree that local interest, initiative, and influence should be sustained as much as possible.

Another aspect of local control of education deserves mention. In many school districts, the board of education has full control of its budget and the power to levy the local taxes necessary to meet the costs of the school program as determined by the board. These districts are termed "fiscally independent districts," as opposed to "fiscally dependent districts," where the budget and tax rates must be approved by the city council or other county or municipal agency. As states assume more fiscal responsibility and more power of governance over local school districts, the fiscal and administrative dependence of the latter type of district becomes less necessary and more dysfunctional. Fiscally and administratively dependent districts find themselves subservient to two bosses—local municipal government and the state. By releasing these districts from the controls

of local government, the state can exercise its responsibility more effectively.

A real dilemma exists with respect to the future of local control and influence over education. It will generate even more debate and controversy in the future than it has in the past as local and state interests and power over schools increasingly collide. Some authorities contend that local control of education has become a myth anyway, particularly in those districts too poor to raise the revenue they need to exercise the options they seek. Others believe that local governance of education has been weak and generally ineffective and that the loss of local control is no great tragedy. Others believe that state funding can be increased greatly without significant loss of local control. Although it is still too early to reach confident conclusions on these matters, our prediction is that local influence and initiative in public education will recede rather rapidly. We would wish it otherwise, but we think the political and economic realities will require it.

Public funds cannot be used to support sectarian education. In recent years, the courts have tended to prescribe ever narrower limits upon the use of public funds in church-related schools. Public funds may still be used for certain restricted purposes where the benefit is primarily to students rather than to the church, but the scope and variety of these uses are increasingly circumscribed by judicial opinion. In some states, such as Pennsylvania and Rhode Island, there has been persistent determination to search for loopholes in the wall of separation of church and state, forcing the courts to inveigh against these attempts over and over again. This principle and the dilemmas it generates are discussed more fully in Chapter 1.

Public funds cannot be used to sustain racial segregation in schools. Some states and local school districts have sought to escape their legal and moral obligation to desegregate schools by diverting public funds either directly or indirectly to the support of private schools that discriminate against members of minority groups. This has commonly been attempted through state subsidies to parents for tuition payments for private schools. This, too, has generated considerable litigation, and the courts invariably hold such efforts unconstitutional. The 1964 Civil Rights Bill provided that

No person in the United States shall, on the ground of race, color, or national origin, be excluded from participation in, be denied the benefits of, or be subject to discrimination under any program of activity receiving Federal financial assistance.

The Internal Revenue Service in 1970 removed the tax-exempt status from all segregated private schools, whether they received federal financial assistance or not. The courts have increasingly less tolerance for subterfuge in avoiding school integration through devious schemes of financing private schools as a haven for students whose parents object to racial integration.

THE ECONOMIC FOUNDATIONS OF EDUCATIONAL FINANCE

A fundamental objective of every enlightened society is to provide the kind and quality of education that will meet the needs of its citizens both individually and collectively. But good education is expensive. Difficult choices have to be made among these expenditures for education and the costs of other services and materials also attractive to our people. There are, or course, limits to the amount of money that can be made available to schools in any state, or community, or home. There are also limits to the progress that any nation, state, community, or family can achieve without adequate provision for the education of citizens. We shall explore some critical economic realities that affect the financial support of education in our society.

Education is both the consumers' good and producers' good. Economists distinguish between consumers' goods (those which satisfy consumers' wants) and producers' goods (those which are used in the production of other goods). Education is both. It not only helps to bring satisfaction and prosperity to its individual beneficiaries but also contributes to the production of other goods and services required by society through educated engineers, physicians, business executives, artists, judges, and persons in virtually all occupations.

Education is a high-yield investment. Economists distinguish between consumptive expenditures and investments. The former include expenditures for either durable or nondurable goods

or services that are consumed over time and that are a drain upon consumers. They produce no wealth in their consumption. Investments result from the conversion of money into income-earning assets. Consumptive expenditures, however necessary, are a burden upon the economy. Investments are a contribution to the growth of the economy. However, as noted later in this chapter, we have tended to finance education as though it were a consumptive expenditure rather than an investment. Generally speaking, it is economically beneficial to minimize consumptive expenditures and maximize investments. One major indicator of both the level of civilization of a people and the health of their economy is the proportion of the productive capacity of the economy allocated to investments. Let us explore the investment nature of educational expenditures.

The GI Bill of Rights is one of the most dramatic and persuasive demonstrations of the investment power of educational costs. The increased tax collected from the income of these more highly educated and productive veterans has already paid the U.S. Treasury more than four times the $19 billion investment made in the education of World War II veterans, and most of these ex-GIs still have years of earning power remaining. The rate of return to individuals for investment in college education is conservatively calculated at 10 to 11 percent.[1]

Figure 11-1 shows the rise in the educational level of our labor force. The Conference Board describes this increase in the educational attainment of our workers as

an increase in human capital investment—investment in human productive potential—with benefits for employer and employee. As the knowledge and skills of workers are upgraded, the opportunities to improve labor productivity—more output from the same amount of labor input—are enhanced. Increasing the supply of goods and services produced from the same level of employment leads to a rise in the standard of living. In addition, a better educated population can more readily adapt to the increasingly complex and changing nature of our economy.[2]

[1]Roe L. Johns and Edgar L. Morphet, *The Economics of Financing Education,* Prentice-Hall, Englewood Cliffs, N.J., 1975, p. 96. See also K. Forbis Jordan and Carol E. Hanes, "Financing Education in an Era of Limits," *Phi Delta Kappan,* June 1976, pp. 677–678.

[2]The Conference Board, "Educational Attainment of the Work Force," *Road Maps of Industry,* March 1975, p. 1.

MILLIONS OF PERSONS

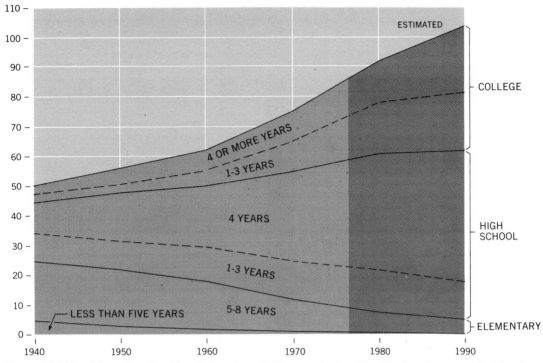

Figure 11-1 The rising educational level of workers. An increase in the educational attainment of the labor force means an increase in human capital investment—investment in human production potential—which benefits both employer and employee. As the knowledge and skills of workers are upgraded, the opportunities to improve labor productivity—more output from the same amount of labor input—are enhanced. Increasing the supply of goods and services produced from the same level of employment leads to a rise in the standard of living. (The Conference Board, *Educational Attainment of the Work Force*, March 1975.)

What can be said about the rate of return to society from investment in educational expenditures? In one noteworthy and careful study, economist Edward Denison reached the conclusion that education has been responsible for 23 percent of the annual rate of growth in our gross national product. Johns and Morphet have reviewed Denison's and others' studies and report that "all the economists who have seriously researched this matter have concluded that investment in education has a vital effect upon economic growth."[3]

Cheap education is expensive. This may sound like a paradox, and so explanation is in order. Let

[3]Johns and Morphet, op. cit., p. 97. For a good, nontechnical explanation of the relationship between educational finance and growth of the economy, see American Association of School Administrators, *Education is Good Business*, Arlington, Va., 1966.

us examine the cost of not educating people as they ought to be educated. As the caption for the photograph on the first page of this chapter points out, "The trouble with cheap education is that we never stop paying for it." The first major effort to place dollar values on the loss to our society through educational neglect was undertaken by Henry Levin, a Stanford University professor, for presentation to a U.S. Senate committee. Levin reached the following conclusions:

1. The failure to attain a minimum of high school completion among the population of males 25–34 years of age in 1969 was estimated to cost the nation:
   - $237 billion in income over the lifetime of these men.
   - $71 billion in foregone government revenues of

which about $47 billion would have been added to the federal treasury and $24 billion to the coffers of state and local governments.

2. In contrast, the probable costs of having provided a minimum of high school completion for this group of men was estimated to be about $40 billion.

● Thus, the sacrifice in national income from inadequate education among 25- to 34-year-old males was about $200 billion greater than the investment required to alleviate this condition.

● Each dollar of social investment for this purpose would have generated about $6 of national income over the lifetime of this group of men.

● The government revenues generated by this investment would have exceeded government expenditures by over $30 billion.

3. Welfare expenditures attributable to inadequate education are estimated to be about $3 billion each year and are probably increasing over time.

Levin notes that other costs of inadequate education, such as higher incidence of disease and reduced political participation, were not included because they are impossible to estimate.[4] From this evidence it is reasonable to conclude that it is no longer appropriate to ask whether we can afford to educate our people as they should be educated. We cannot afford poor education: it is too expensive.

The relationship between schooling and economic opportunity is disputed. For many years it was assumed that better education would reduce poverty and that equal educational opportunity would tend to equalize economic opportunity in our society. These complex issues are discussed at greater length in Chapter 1. Bane and Jencks, in their provocative book *Inequality: A Reassessment of the Effects of Family and Schooling in America,* concluded that making schools more equal will do little to equalize economic success. They were convinced that a school's output rate depends more heavily upon the characteristics of children entering school than upon the characteristics of the schools themselves. Coleman reached

similar conclusions in his classic study reported in *Equality of Educational Opportunity,* commonly spoken of as the Coleman Report.

James Guthrie and associates reached a contrary opinion, however, from their research. They concluded (1) that major inequalities do exist among school districts, (2) that the level of financial input into schools is directly related to the quality of educational services delivered, and (3) that the quality of these services is significantly linked to both the level of students' achievement and the economic status of students in adult life.[5]

Part of the controversy centers upon whether one thinks of educational equality in terms of equal access to well-financed schools (input) or equal performance on standardized achievement tests (output). The swiftest will still win the race toward achievement (output), but the principle of equal rights demands at least that we allow all to begin the race at the same place.

The financial burden of education should be equalized. There is little dispute that the financial burden of education, like the opportunity for fine education, is unequal across the land. In most states the range of market value of taxable property per student is as great as 10 to 1 among districts and ranges of even 50 to 1 can be found in some states. Tax rates vary more than 2 to 1. Great differences also exist at the state level. Public school revenue receipts as percentages of personal income range from 9 percent in Alaska to 4 percent in Nebraska. This unequal burden in the financing of education results from wide variations in both the ability and the effort of local districts and states. It results also from the methods used by the states to allocate revenues for school support. The principle of equal protection before the law dictates that both the burden of financing schools and the educational opportunity provided by the schools must be equalized. The task will be difficult. It is seldom easy to persuade citizens that much of the revenue from their taxes must be taken from their school districts or states for use in less affluent districts or states. Difficult though it may be, we must get on with it.

[4]Henry M. Levin, *The Effects of Dropping Out,* A report to the United States Senate Select Committee on Equal Educational Opportunity in the United States, U.S. Government Printing Office, 1972, p. xi.

[5]James Guthrie, George Kleindorfer, Henry Levin, and Robert Stout, *Schools and Inequality,* Massachusetts Institute of Technology, Cambridge, 1971.

The business management of schools must be prudent and efficient. Taxpayers have the right to expect that public money will be managed efficiently. This applies to school business management at all levels of government. Efficiency requires that fiscal affairs be handled by business managers professionally prepared to administer funds wisely through careful budgeting, purchasing, planning, accounting, investing, and property control. Prudence requires that everyone who handles school funds be impeccably honest and properly bonded.

School officials should be held accountable. The concept of accountability, although not new, has found intensive currency in recent times. It focuses attention not only upon fiscal stewardship but also upon objectives and accomplishments. This concept and its practical applications to school administration are explored later in this chapter.

Educational expenditures

On our nation's two-hundredth anniversary, the annual cost of public and private elementary and secondary education was approximately $70 billion, and for private and public postsecondary education the total cost was $50 billion. Figures 11-2 and 7-4 show the great rise in the cost of elementary and secondary education and the cost of higher education during the twentieth century. These data include annual operating expenses as well as capital expenditures, debt service, and all other school-related expenditures, such as transportation and food services.

Another way of viewing the cost of education is in relation to its proportion of the gross national product, which is the total monetary value of all goods and services produced in the nation. The total costs of our educational institutions has risen from 2 percent of the GNP at the close of World War II to 8 percent in recent years. This rapid growth in school costs can be attributed largely to four factors: (1) substantial growth in school enrollments, (2) greatly expanded scope and quality of educational programs and school services, (3) inflation, and (4) substantial increases in teachers' salaries.

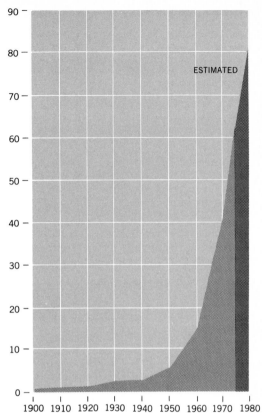

BILLIONS OF DOLLARS

ESTIMATED

Figure 11-2 Current expenditures for public and private elementary and secondary schools. (1900–1970, U.S. Department of Commerce, *Statistical Abstract of the United States;* 1971–1975, U.S. Office of Education, *Projections of Educational Statistics;* estimates by authors.)

For purposes of comparison among states, school districts, and schools, it is useful to consider costs in terms of current expenditures per student. This statistic excludes variations in the aggregate costs caused by enrollment increases. It includes only operating expenditures and omits capital costs and debt services, which are affected by fluctuations in school construction and borrowing. Figure 11-3 shows the increase in average expenditures per pupil in the nation during the twentieth century. The national average was approximately $1,300 per pupil in public schools in 1976. Expenditures per pupil vary widely, both

ANNUAL COST PER PUPIL

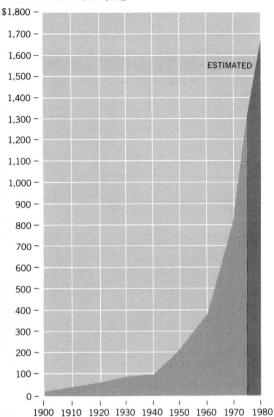

Figure 11-3 Current expenditure per pupil in public elementary and secondary schools. (1900—1970, U.S. Office of Education, *Digest of Educational Statistics;* estimates by authors.)

health and food services, capital outlay and debt services. Another analysis of school expenditures reveals that on the average 68 percent of the costs go for salaries of teachers, administrators, custodians, and all other employees. This is a point of great interest to cost analysts, who point out that with two of every three dollars being spent for salaries, education is still a labor-intensive enterprise. This is in sharp contrast to most production enterprises where, unlike schools, much more is spent on the material means of production than on human delivery systems. This has been a consequence of automation, and it gives rise to speculation that education might become more cost-effective if schools, like industries, were to invest more heavily in educational technology and if they were to deliver instruction through machine systems rather than through human-mediated instruction.[6] Others argue that the education enterprise is fundamentally a social service and is less amenable than production enterprises to machine delivery systems. Nevertheless, with the rapid expansion of instructional technology, there will be

[6]For further discussion of this proposition, see James G. Abert. "Wanted: Experiments in Reducing the Costs of Education," *Phi Delta Kappan,* March 1974, pp. 444–445.

among state averages and among districts in the same state. However, as discussed earlier, these wide variations will be reduced as school finance is restructured in compliance with court mandates for equalizing educational opportunity.

Yet another way of viewing school expenditures—a very meaningful mode for school boards and administrators—is by allocation of funds for various functions within school districts. Again, variations result from differences in programs and clientele. Figure 11-4 shows that, on the average, approximately two-thirds the total cost goes for instruction, and the remainder is divided among various supporting functions—administration, plant operation and maintenance, transportation,

Figure 11-4 Where the school dollar goes. ("Annual Cost of Education Index," *School Management,* January 1974, p. 19.)

FUNCTION	PERCENT OF TOTAL COST
Instruction	65%
Capital outlay and debt services	10
Plant operations	7
Fixed charges	7
Plant maintenance	3
Transportation	3
Administration	3
Health services	1
Other services	1

increasing pressure in the years ahead to reduce school expenditures, or at least to make them more cost-effective, through greater utilization of instructional technology.

School receipts

We shall consider school receipts from several perspectives: categories of receipts, nonrevenue receipts, sources of revenue by levels of government, revenues by sources of taxation, and private sources of receipts.

CATEGORIES OF RECEIPTS

The U.S. Office of Education recommends major accounting classifications for school receipts, including these:

Revenue receipts
  Revenue from local sources
  Taxation and appropriation
  Tuition from patrons
  Transportation fees
  Other revenue from local sources
  Revenue from intermediate sources
  Revenue from state sources
  Revenue from federal sources
Nonrevenue receipts
  Sale of bonds
  Loans
  Sale of school property and insurance adjustments
  Income transfer accounts

NONREVENUE RECEIPTS

Nonrevenue receipts do not constitute a genuine source of income, since they incur either the sale of property, or loans, or the sale of bonds or other obligations that must be met at a future date.

The prevalent ways of financing schools when cash is not available are long-term obligations or short-term obligations. Indebtedness by school districts is incurred most commonly to finance capital outlay for the construction, renovation, or furnishing of additional facilities or equipment. However, a number of school districts, notably large city districts, have had to incur indebtedness to meet current expenses in recent years, an inef-

ficient and devastating means of financing schools over the long term. Bonds may be issued and sold by local school districts or, in some states, by state government. The latter arrangement is more advantageous because state bonds can usually be sold with a lower interest rate. Many states place a limit, expressed as a percentage of local wealth, upon the amount of indebtedness that a local district can incur. The wisdom of this practice is questionable, since it presupposes that the local electorate cannot be trusted to manage school finances. Many states require that bond issues be approved by the electorate and sometimes require more than a majority vote for approval, another questionable practice. The requirement of a two-thirds vote for approval has thwarted the will of the majority in many communities and has been responsible for the defeat of many school bond issues. It has been tested in the courts but without reversal by the U.S. Supreme Court. As noted earlier, taxpayers in recent years have been rejecting school bond issues in increasing numbers, further aggravating the financial situation of schools in many communities.

SOURCES OF REVENUE BY LEVELS OF GOVERNMENT

For the first 150 years of our history, schools were supported almost entirely by local property tax revenues. For purposes of this discussion, county revenues, which are not substantial in most states, are included with local revenues. As shown in Figure 11-5, the share of local school support began to decline with the Great Depression of the 1930s. Meanwhile, the share of state contributions increased from 17 percent in 1930 to 40 percent in 1950, a level that held until the mid-1970s. The federal contribution gradually increased from a mere 1 percent before World War II to a high of 8 percent during the Great Society of the 1960s. The share of federal aid also varies greatly among the states, from a high of 28 percent in Mississippi to a low of 3 percent in Connecticut. The proportion of state and local support varies greatly as well. In 1976, state funds in Hawaii accounted for 89 percent of the receipts for public elementary and secondary schools, while in New Hampshire only 6 percent of the receipts came from state funds.

The last quarter of this century will see major strides toward fuller state funding of public school

PERCENT

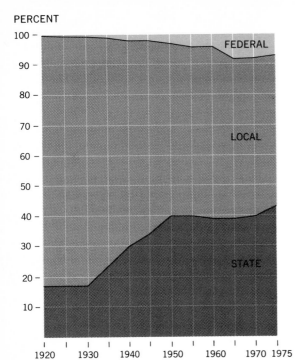

Figure 11-5 Percentage of public school revenue from federal, state, and local sources.

systems. The court decisions mentioned earlier, prohibiting gross inequalities in the level of school support among districts in a state, will inevitably force increases in the states' share as the only option for accomplishing this end. But the need for reform in school finance has been evident even apart from pressure. A number of state commissions studying school finance recommended full state funding. The President's Commission on School Finance agreed, saying: "The most practical system for fulfilling the requirements for reform would be one in which the revenue raising and the distribution of educational resources were centered at the state level." The commission believed that the local contribution to the costs of education should not exceed 10 percent of the state allotment. The National Educational Finance Project, probably the most comprehensive school finance study ever undertaken, concluded that the states should pay 55 to 60 percent of the cost of public elementary and secondary education. At the time of that report in 1972, only ten states were above the 55 percent level. The trend in that direc-

tion is now underway. North Dakota recently boosted its state share of per-pupil costs from 48 to 70 percent. Kansas went from 29 to 48 percent. At the time of this writing, Rhode Island, Florida, California, Maine, Texas, and Alaska have either drafted or enacted legislation that would increase their shares substantially.

However, the late 1970s were not an opportune time for increasing taxes at any level. Politicians know that levying higher taxes is a good way to lose reelection, especially in a depressed economy.

Greater federal financial support of education has been a matter of vigorous debate for decades and has been advocated on several grounds. First, equal educational opportunity is desirable, but it can never be achieved across state boundaries without federal equalization funds, because of the great disparities in wealth among the states (see Figure 11-14). Second, the tax collecting capacity of the federal government far exceeds that of the states and local districts. Figure 11-6 reveals a serious problem in school finance. Although the federal government collects 59 percent of the taxes, it provides only 10 percent of school revenues. Local school districts, which sustain nearly half the costs of education, collect less than one tax dollar in five. It is small wonder that many local school districts are impoverished and that communities are increasingly voting down higher local school tax rates. Third, the high costs of poor education—welfare, unemployment compensation, and crime—are already paid for in part by the federal government.

Figure 11-6 Comparison of percentages of total tax revenues and public expenditures for elementary and secondary schools by federal, state, and local governments, 1975. Tax revenues shown do not include social security taxes, which, if added, would increase the federal share to nearly two-thirds.

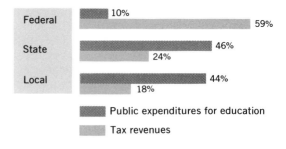

The National Educational Finance Project concluded that the federal share of public school costs should be 30 percent, a great jump from its current 10 percent. But the President's Commission on School Finance and the Advisory Council on Intergovernmental Relations felt that school finance should be primarily the responsibility of the states. It was evident that the 1970s were not propitious times for boosting the federal contribution to education. The unpopularity of additional public expenditures during periods of high unemployment, and the need to reduce federal taxes to slow inflation, were two factors. The disappointing results from federal grants enacted during the period of the Great Society and the decline in school enrollments also combined to defeat any substantial increase in federal funding of education for the immediate future. Controversy over school desegregation and aid to church-related schools have also impeded federal support for education.

The 1970s did, however, mark the enactment of a federal program of revenue sharing with the states. This was accomplished through the State and Local Fiscal Assistance Act of 1972, which provided $30 billion to state and local governments burdened with high taxes to use as they saw fit. Some states used all this revenue-shared money for schools, some with remarkable results. North Carolina, for example, was able to establish kindergartens statewide, to reduce the size of classes, and to improve the state's program for exceptional children. Other states used the money to offset the need for increased state and local taxes for education.

SCHOOL REVENUES BY SOURCES OF TAXES

Shifting the shares of school fiscal support from one level of government to another inevitably creates changes in the proportion of revenue generated by various types of taxes.

Property tax. Historically, about 98 percent of local tax revenues and 38 percent of all tax revenues in this country have come from taxes on property, which have been reserved largely to local communities. Property tax is fairly stable in its yield, and property can less easily escape taxation than most other taxable items. Beyond that, the property tax has little to recommend it. It is not well related to ability to pay, as farmers and elderly

home owners on fixed incomes can attest. Assessments are notoriously unequal and deflated in most communities. Property taxes commonly lag behind growth in national income. In urban communities, particularly, the local property tax, along with other local taxes, suffers from what is termed "municipal overburden." In these high-density population areas the costs of other municipal services—police and fire protection, environmental protection, highway maintenance, among others—are more costly than in nonurban communities, leaving a smaller proportion of tax revenue for educational purposes. Without doubt, the property tax is our most overburdened tax.

Since property tax values per pupil range as high as 50 to 1 among communities in the same state, unacceptable inequalities in educational opportunity are created if the property tax is a factor in levels of school fiscal support. This is commonly the case in states where the share of local support is more than 10 or 15 percent. It can be said that flaws in the local property tax are the most important reason for the revolution we are witnessing in the reform of educational finance. Among the literally hundreds of studies of school finance, few, if any, have failed to recommend less dependence upon local property tax as a source of school support.

Despite its many shortcomings, the property tax is not likely to be abandoned, although it is being relieved to varying degrees in many states. Some states are considering phasing out local property taxes and levying state property taxes to collect and distribute the revenue more equitably according to need. Most states will probably retain it as a local option at reduced rates to permit local districts some leeway in providing flexibility and enrichment in education beyond that provided by state funding. Wherever the property tax remains, it should be reformed to eliminate inequities in assessment and collection.

Sales tax. Although a number of large cities levy a sales tax, this is generally reserved for state use. Forty-five states levy sales taxes, usually at rates between 2 and 6 percent, by which they generate about one-third their total revenues. Sales tax is simple to collect, but its return is somewhat unpredictable since it varies with business conditions. The greatest disadvantage of sales tax is that it is regressive (it hits poor people disproportionately), unless such essentials as food, clothing, and medicine are exempt. Sales tax may also discourage commercial development, particularly if adjoining states are free of it.

Personal income tax. Personal income tax is the largest single source of income for the federal government, bringing in 44 percent of total federal tax revenues. Forty-one states levy personal income taxes at widely varying rates, but always well below the federal rate. Some cities do, too. In some states, local municipalities are permitted to levy local income taxes, usually at the rate of 1 percent. Income tax is easily collected, is directly related to ability to pay, and can be adjusted through exemptions or credits to take care of hardship factors. The chief disadvantages of personal income tax are that it declines during depressions and is more easily evaded than most other taxes.

Corporate income tax. Corporate income tax is levied by the federal government and generates 17 percent of federal tax revenues. It is used also by 44 states to generate 8 percent of all state tax revenues. Rates vary widely among the states. Corporate income tax is responsive to changing economic conditions and is easily collected. However, it may be disadvantageous to a state's economy if the rate is higher than in nearby states.

Other taxes. Although there is a great variety of other taxes, such as those on motor vehicles and fuel, they do not constitute important sources of school revenue.

Additional tax revenues. As noted elsewhere, additional tax sources must be generated to equalize education fiscally among communities. To meet the goal of quality education for the nation's increasing concern for learners, greater financial effort must be made by both the private and public sectors of American economy. Currently the United States is spending about 8 percent of its gross national product on education—public and nonpublic institutions at all educational levels. This can and should be increased soon to at least 10 percent. Since Russia, England, and many other nations spend between 5 and 10 percent of their national income for education, this is not an unreasonable expectation in the United States, the cradle of free public education.

A nation whose real per-capita income, after all taxes, has risen over 60 percent in the last twenty years can hardly be unable to provide better schools. Clearly the United States effort to educate its people is not equal to its ability or its needs.

PRIVATE SOURCES OF EDUCATIONAL FINANCE

We shall consider briefly some major sources of private funds for the support of education: tuition payments, subsidies from churches, private foundation support, contributions from corporations, and miscellaneous sources.

Private school support. Private schools have become an accepted and important part of our educational system. The total annual expenditures of nonpublic elementary and secondary schools is almost $6 billion. Most of this is supplied by tuition payments, which, in the case of church-related schools, are supplemented by grants from the churches. Today there are over a thousand private institutions of higher education, and they expend more than $12 billion annually. Their severe financial plight is discussed in Chapter 7.

Private foundation support. The Foundation Center estimates that there are over 22,000 foundations with resources of over $20 billion. In a single year all foundation gifts to educational, charitable, and religious organizations are approximately $12 billion. Throughout this book, we have mentioned the large number of educational enterprises supported fully or partly by such foundations, particularly by the Ford Foundation, the Carnegie Corporation, the W. K. Kellogg Foundation, the Rockefeller Foundation, the Kettering Foundation, and the Sloan Foundation.

Corporate support for education. Financial support of education, especially higher education, by business firms has increased greatly in the past decade. One major reason is the growth in the number of "matching gifts" programs sponsored by American businesses. Under the plan, when an employee of a participating company sends a gift to an accredited alma mater, or to a college of his choice, the company matches the gift to the institution. It is estimated that corporations contribute nearly $\$^1/_2$ billion annually to education, primarily to higher education.

Miscellaneous gifts to education. An indirect annual gift to private schools and universities, as well as public ones, is their tax-exempt status; they do not pay local, state, or federal taxes. Some school districts receive benefactions through the purchase, by private subdividers, of bonds to help build schools. Numerous other types of gifts, direct and indirect, are made to schools and colleges, both private and public.

Allocating revenues to education

The manner in which funds are allocated to educational institutions has great impact on the quality and equality of our schools. Earlier we called attention to the legal, political, and economic implications inherent in fiscal allocation patterns. Now we shall consider some technical aspects of these patterns and describe alternatives.

ALLOCATING FEDERAL FUNDS

Chapter 14 describes the great variety of federal special-purpose grants for education. These grants have been aimed at a number of enterprises of particular concern to the federal government: vocational education and manpower development, education of the handicapped and impoverished, and national defense, among others. A 1975 U.S. Office of Education publication listed 126 different categories of federal aid for various educational programs. There is a growing conviction that the federal government's subsidy of education through such a miscellany of special-purpose grants, or "categorical aid," as it is called, has not been beneficial in proportion to the cost. Moreover, these categorical grants have resulted in a tangle of red tape, since they are administered by many agencies of government. They have consumed a great deal of administrative time and effort, time that small or impoverished districts do not have. Then, too, much of this federal funding has been sporadic—here today, gone tomorrow, made up with too little lead time to plan properly; and too temporary to produce much result. Each new Congress has tended to become quixotic, aban-

doning last year's favorites and turning to crash programs to solve today's problems. Federal funds have tended to emphasize innovative programs disproportionately over time-proven programs. Federal grants have superimposed on state systems and local districts separate auditing and accounting procedures that are superfluous except in those few cases where state procedures are inadequate. Many federal grants have bypassed state educational agencies and gone directly to local districts, an arrangement designed to discourage state planning and coordination.

All this has created imbalance, confusion, and instability and has indirectly contributed to federal control of education, which almost everyone abhors. Most authorities recommend that this miscellany of categorical grants should be consolidated into a few large blocks. The National Education Finance Project recommends six blocks: vocational education, research and development, school food service, education for handicapped children, education for children of low-income families, and compensation to schools for federal-exempt property. Although progress is being made in this direction, much more should be accomplished.

Another reform is the need for substantial increase in federal sharing of general-purpose support for schools. This could be done through more revenue sharing, by directly returning to the states more of their share of federal tax revenues.[7]

ALLOCATING STATE FUNDS

Methods and models for the allocation of state funds for schools are varied and often complex. For our discussion, we shall illustrate in oversimplified form the more common possibilities and comment on the advantages and limitations of each. At least an elementary understanding of these allocation methods and models is essential for all educators and citizens who are concerned about reducing inequalities in educational opportunity that result from fiscal allocation patterns.

The flat grant model. The flat grant model is the oldest and most primitive model, especially if per-

[7]Readers interested in a description of alternative models for the distribution of federal funds for education are referred to National Education Finance Project, *Alternative Programs for Financing Education,* vol. 5, Gainesville, Fla., 1971, pp. 211–229.

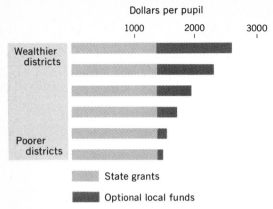

Figure 11-7 Flat grant model.

pupil amounts are unweighted. State allocations to districts are determined by a flat grant or a fixed amount that is multiplied by the number of pupils enrolled in the district. Local districts can supplement the state grants through revenue from local taxes. This model is still used in some states to distribute portions of state school subsidies, usually categorical or special-purpose grants.[8] As shown in Figure 11-7, wealthier districts with greater taxpaying ability can use the same tax rate to maintain greater expenditures per pupil than can poor districts. It is impossible to equalize educational opportunity in a state under the flat grant model.

The foundation model with substantial local leeway. This model has been widely used; by the mid-1960s, it was still predominant in about two-thirds of the states. Although commonly referred to as an "equalization model," we regard it as a foundation model because it does not equalize costs or opportunity. It does, however, guarantee an equal minimum or foundation, expressed in terms of unit costs, by providing whatever state aid is needed to supplement a minimum required local tax effort. The amount of a state's contribution is inversely related to local property tax wealth per student. The difficulty with this model has resulted from most states' unwillingness to commit sufficient funds to overcome gross inequities. As Figure 11-8 shows, wealthier districts can use surplus

yields from local taxes to finance their schools above the foundation level through what is known as "local leeway." As shown in the figure, some wealthy districts require little or no state aid to achieve the foundation level, but minimum dollar amounts have usually been written into the formulas to make this pattern more acceptable to legislators and citizens from wealthy districts. There are many variations and added complexities to this pattern, but the critical elements are (1) the degree of local tax effort required and (2) the amount of local leeway permitted. In Figure 11-8 there is no limit on local leeway. Local leeway has been the source of financial support for much innovation and invention in so-called "lighthouse" school districts, those which point the way toward improved educational practice for all districts. However, the privilege of local leeway is exactly the characteristic of the traditional foundation models that has perpetuated inequality and has prompted litigation to prohibit this model. Many experts believe that to remove local leeway—the fiscal source of creative educational practices—through full state funding would slow educational progress. The dilemma is the familiar one of educational quality versus equality, discussed in Chapter 1.

The foundation model with limited local leeway. Because of concerns about the elimination

Figure 11-8 Foundation model with substantial local leeway.

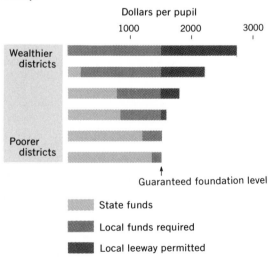

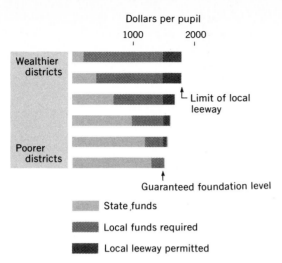

Figure 11-9 Foundation model with limited local leeway.

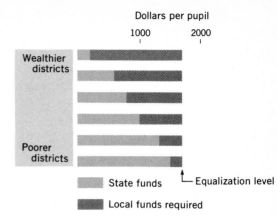

Figure 11-10 Equalization model with no local leeway.

of local leeway and its effect upon educational progress, the foundation model with limited local leeway, illustrated in Figure 11-9, has been proposed. Note that with the same tax rates, the guaranteed foundation level can be set higher when local leeway is limited. It is obviously a compromise on the quality-equality dilemma, reducing but not eliminating local leeway and raising the guaranteed level of quality without eliminating inequalities. Lindman contends that local property taxes should be retained to a degree to finance some locally initiated supplementary programs and thereby to preserve the fiscal basis for some local control. He believes that local districts should not be completely dependent upon state and federal funds or upon state and federal approval of programs. Lindman believes that educational progress would be slow if approval from state or local government were required for all local innovation.[9] The virtue of the discretionary funds is evident, but how much the courts will tolerate under the fiscal neutrality principle remains to be seen.

The equalization model with no local leeway. Figure 11-10 shows how state subsidies could be used to supplement the required local tax yield to equalize fully all school districts without

permitting local leeway. This model produces real equalization through the combination of local and state revenues. Figure 11-11 illustrates another equalization model, which is accomplished through full state funding. As noted earlier, a number of states are moving in the direction of these truly equalized models.

Equalized percentage grants, or "power equalization" models. A number of states (principally Colorado, Florida, Illinois, Kansas, Maine, Michigan, Montana, Utah, and Wisconsin) have sought to satisfy the principle of fiscal equality and at the same time to permit local option in applying greater fiscal effort through higher local tax rates so as to achieve higher levels of school financing and higher-quality education. In this model each

Figure 11-11 Equalization model with full state funding.

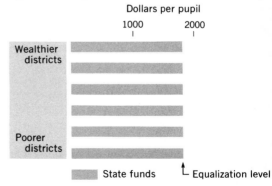

[9]Erick L. Lindman, *Dilemmas of School Finance,* Educational Research Service, Arlington, Va., 1975.

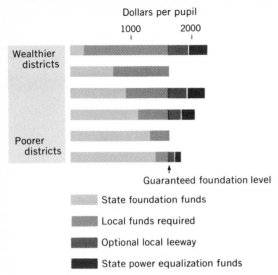

Dollars per pupil

Wealthier districts

Poorer districts

Guaranteed foundation level

State foundation funds

Local funds required

Optional local leeway

State power equalization funds

Figure 11-12 Model of power equalization or equalized percentage grants.

school district is permitted to choose its own level of expenditure—sometimes within limits set by the state—beyond the required minimum. This local choice of expenditure level simultaneously designates a local property tax rate. Districts choosing the same expenditure levels would automatically have identical property tax rates. Through this new model, the state guarantees equal levels of expenditure for equal tax effort, and in that sense the equal-protection clause of the Constitution may be satisfied. However, as seen in Figure 11-12, this model permits inequalities in expenditure levels. However, these inequalities arise from variations in local effort rather than from variations in local wealth. This model establishes an equal tax base per student and thus equalizes potential income per student. The state's contribution toward the foundation level is inversely related to local taxable wealth per student. The state adds funds proportionate to the local school district tax rate; hence the name "power equalizing." Because of this latter feature, the model is sometimes referred to as an "incentive grant" model. This model is desirable from the standpoint of stimulating local effort, initiative, and innovation.[10]

[10]Readers interested in further explanation of this model, see Lindman, op. cit., pp. 9–15.

Which model is best? The answer depends upon the values and goals of citizens and legislatures in the various states.

Budgeting and educational planning

In 1936 our deceased co-author, Chris De Young, in the first graduate textbook in school budgeting, presented a classic and widely used new concept of the school budget (see Figure 11-13). Traditional budgets had previously focused only upon balancing expenditures and receipts. De Young insisted that the budget should be tripartite:

The ideal school budget contains three parts: (1) the *work* plan, which is a definite statement of the educational policies and program; (2) the *spending* plan, which is a translation of the accepted policies into proposed expenditures; and (3) the *financing* plan, which proposes means for meeting the costs of the educational needs.[11]

The base of the budget triangle, as shown in Figure 11-13, is the educational program. De Young contended that expenditures should be derived from and be justified by the educational program they are intended to support. He introduced the essential new element of program planning to the budgetary process. This concept was the forerunner of the modern planning, programming, and budgeting systems (PPBS) applied to school financial management.

THE PLANNING, PROGRAMMING, AND BUDGETING SYSTEM (PPBS)

The glossary defines PPBS as "an application of systems analysis to the allocation of resources to various competing educational purposes and needs through systematic planning, programming, budgeting, and evaluation." This system was first developed by the Rand Corporation and was implemented in the Department of Defense. In 1965 President Johnson directed the adoption of this modern management system throughout the

[11]Chris A. De Young, *Budgeting in Public Schools*, Doubleday, Garden City, N.Y., 1936, p. 7.

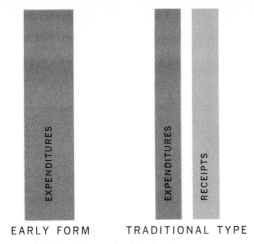

EARLY FORM   TRADITIONAL TYPE

Figure 11-13 Modern school budget.

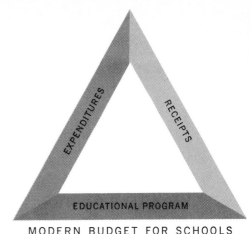

MODERN BUDGET FOR SCHOOLS

FIGURE 16-3   Evolution of the school budget.

executive branch of the federal government. The U.S. Office of Education, which had initiated a nationwide study of the possibilities of PPBS in educational reform, awarded in 1968 a three-year contract to the Research Corporation of the American Association of School Business Officials:

To provide an improved method for determining the quality and cost of the product of education as a means toward improved management of educational and fiscal resources.

While the Research Corporation developed the conceptual design for the integrated budgetary system, the public schools of Dade County, Florida, served as a demonstration of an operational system. The Research Corporation more aptly calls this sophisticated budgeting program "Educational Resources Management System." The guidelines aid in setting educational goals, identifying and allocating resources, developing programs, considering alternatives, using detailed methods of allocating and accounting, and evaluating results.

Stephen Knezevich added the evaluation component (PPB*ES*) by insisting that evaluation be related to both the plans and the objectives to be pursued and the costs involved in attempting them. This juxtaposition of costs and benefits led to another powerful concept called "cost-benefit analysis," which Knezevich defines as the

scientific examination of an alternative as determined by the economic value (advantages) of the alternative as related to its economic costs (disadvantages); an analytical approach to solving problems of choice where both costs and benefits are measured and analyzed in monetary terms. The outcome is expressed as an index score or ratio of benefits derived from costs.[12]

Cost-benefit analysis is related to "cost-effectiveness analysis," which Knezevich defines as the

systematic examination of an alternative in terms of its advantages as measured by a fixed level and quality of an outcome, and disadvantages, as measured by the economic cost. The measure of desirability (effectiveness) is not the same as the measure of costs. The index or ratio shows the costs of various alternatives that produce the same degree of effectiveness.[13]

These concepts have been invaluable in our quest for accountability in education because they provide a more rational basis for making decisions regarding more effective deployment of financial resources in relation to educational goals. They also help to marshal better evidence to justify the retention, modification, or abandonment of programs in light of their effectiveness. And they have

[12]Stephen J. Knezevich, *Program Budgeting (PPBS)*, McCutchan, Berkeley, Calif., 1973, p. 326.

[13]*Ibid.*, p. 326.

forced the development of more effective and relevant evaluation systems, thereby providing better evidence of the achievement of educational institutions. PPBES and cost-benefit or cost-effective analysis, which go hand in hand, are now used by many schools and colleges. Like any new technology, PPBES has experienced its successes and failures. A major difficulty is the great amount of time needed to make PPBES work.

At the time of this writing, several states have applied program budgeting, a more limited technology than PPBES, to their school districts. Program budgeting makes it possible—as De Young advocated—to break down all costs (including salaries, equipment, plant maintenance, and others) by specific programs, such as automotive shop course in a particular school or foreign language instruction in all schools in a district or even in a state. Program budgeting is primarily a cost-analysis system that is just one part of PPBES. But it does give legislators, administrators, and school boards better information about costs of specific programs.

THE SCHOOL PLANNING, EVALUATION, AND COMMUNICATIONS SYSTEM (SPECS)

The Center for Advanced Study of Educational Administration at the University of Oregon, under the direction of Jack Nagle, developed the first comprehensive accountability system designed specifically for school systems. This technology—the School Planning, Evaluation, and Communication System—is commonly referred to by its acronym, SPECS. This comprehensive system enables schools to apply various subsystems—needs assessment, goal definition, program planning, budgeting and accounting, and evaluation—into a highly integrated suprasystem. This involves a highly collaborative process including teachers, administrators, school boards, and citizens.

THE SCHOOL BUDGETING PROCESS

Budgeting in public education may be divided into four major steps: (1) preparation, (2) presentation and adoption, (3) administration, and (4) appraisal.

Preparation of the budget. Budget building is a continuous job. The starting point is the development of objectives—behavioral and academic

—and an implementing educational program that help make the budget a professional document rather than a statistical report. This educational emphasis in school business management is made possible through the cooperation of all staff members and the board of education. The preparation of the educational specifications is inextricably linked with the development of spending and financing plans for the budget, and with appropriate alternatives and their potential cost benefits and effectiveness.

Presentation and adoption of the budget. After the budget has been prepared in tentative form, it is usually presented to the board of education and to other legal and extralegal groups. Fiscal publicity is important in the broader program of public relations. Various techniques aid in interpreting the school budget to the board of education, the school personnel, and the general public. After the budget has been presented, it is legally ratified by the proper body or bodies, such as the board of education and, in fiscally dependent districts, by the city council, or by the people in some states.

Administration of the budget. After the estimated figures have been transferred to the school accounting books as initial entries, the budget is ready to be administered. It functions not as a dictator but as a definite guide for the economical and efficient conduct of the schools.

Appraisal of budgets and budgetary procedures. One means of appraising budgets and budgetary practices is the audit of expenditures and educational results. Then there is also the objective appraisal of the format and content of the document itself as an instrument for building public relations. But most important is the evaluation of the outputs in sound learnings and desirable changes in students.

In 1973, after six years of development, the U.S. Office of Education published its long-awaited *Revised Handbook II, Financial Accounting Classification and Standard Terminology for Local and State School Systems.* This document, with its awesome title, served two new and important functions. First, it provided a standard financial accounting system for schools, which facilitates comparison of school expenditures among all states that have adopted it. Second, its method of classifying expenditures makes it possible to relate costs to programs, a necessity for program budgeting.

LONG-TERM EDUCATIONAL BUDGETS

The annual budget has many items with long-term implications and obligations. Hence long-term budgeting is a necessity in education. A common impression is that long-term budgeting involves making a forecast for a period of five or ten years and then, at the end of that time, making an evaluation and preparing a new long-term budget. That is *periodic*, not *continuous*, long-term planning. Continuous long-term budgeting for education uses the correction technique of adjusting forecasts annually or periodically. This is budgeting constantly ahead in the light of recent developments, and always several years in advance of the annual budget. Large corporations—such as telephone companies, public utilities, and others—have long used the budget and related data in extending their projections a decade or more into the future.

Proposed reforms in educational finance

The bearish economic factors prevalent in contemporary society and the circumstances surrounding the end of the growth period in American education during the 1970s have all added urgency to a more prudent approach to the planning of educational finance and the management of school funds. We shall consider briefly some important reforms that have currency on the educational scene.

AN EMPHASIS ON ACCOUNTABILITY

The word "accountability," perhaps more than any other, became the watchword of school governance and administration in the 1970s. We have already spoken of cost-benefit analysis and cost-effectiveness analysis as tools for generating greater accountability in education. The broader issues of accountability are discussed in Chapter 1. We shall limit our discourse here to two proposals for improving accountability that are primarily financial in nature: educational vouchers and performance contracting.

Educational vouchers. Voucher plans give parents public funds or credit vouchers to cover the cost of educating their children at any school they choose. Voucher plans destroy the monopoly of public schools presumably making them better by forcing them to compete with alternative schools, primarily private schools. Opponents of voucher plans—which include most educators and the powerful National Education Association, the American Federation of Teachers, and the American Association of School Administrators—believe that vouchers would result in hucksterism, would foster segregation, would encourage the rise of marginal institutions, and eventually would weaken public schools.

At the time of this writing, support for voucher plans has lost most of its thrust. The future of voucher plans does not look bright.

Performance contracting. Various prototypes of performance contracting were underway in a number of school districts, notably in Norfolk (Virginia), Grand Rapids (Michigan), Gary (Indiana), and Texarkana (Arkansas). In performance contracting private firms contract with the district to provide instructional and sometimes other services; remuneration is based on a sliding scale in relation to the degree of success as measured by students' performance. This arrangement is regarded as an alternative to the alleged failure of the public schools to provide satisfactory education, particularly in ghetto schools.

In some school systems—including Mesa (Arizona), Dade County (Florida), and Stockton (California)—performance contracts are executed by teams of teachers within the school system; the teams receive bonuses calibrated to the degree of their success. Many proponents of performance contracting favor this internal model over external performance contracts awarded to private firms. So far, the evidence does not support the advantages claimed for external performance contracting, although more experimentation is needed before final conclusions can be drawn. An independent evaluation of performance contracting in five school systems produced disappointing results. Students' achievement was no better than under conventional instruction, and the costs of contracted instruction were as much or more. The AFT is opposed to performance contracting, regarding it as "an invasion of the responsibility of teachers."

The NEA appears to be unopposed to performance contracting with teachers. The Council of Chief State School Officers recommends an open mind with respect to this development. Federal legislation has been proposed to permit performance contracting on a much broader scale in ghetto schools.

Many accountability efforts break down because of difficulties in measuring results with any data other than scores based on cognitive development, as revealed by standardized achievement tests; such tests, of course, are limited measures.

ECONOMIES ARE IMPERATIVE

When the national economy is depressed, school authorities in most communities are forced to find ways of reducing school expenditures with as little loss in school achievement as possible. Some educators look upon economic crisis as an opportunity that forces schools to eliminate programs which cannot meet the cost-effectiveness test while preserving and strengthening proven programs. Two experts on school finance, Roe Johns and Edgar Morphet, have noted a number of proposals aimed toward improving the cost-effectiveness of schools:

- Reorganization of school districts and the consolidation of small schools... to enhance the efficiency of administrative and supervisory services
- Improvement of teacher productivity through improvements in knowledge of subject matter and of teaching methods
- Increasing the length of the school term
- Improvement of the functional planning of school buildings and equipment
- Improvement of the quality of books and other instructional materials
- The provision for special pupil personnel services of many types
- Extending upward and downward the age groups served
- Operating summer and night programs
- Extending the length of the school day
- Using many types of instructional media, including audio-visual aids, radio, television, computer-assisted instruction, and teaching machines
- Organizing schools on a nongraded basis
- Making more extensive use of the special competencies of teachers by team teaching and other methods

- Developing community schools and making school services and facilities available to the public
- Cooperation with other governmental agencies in providing certain services, such as health. recreation, library, part-time employment, etc.[14]

PREFERENTIAL FUNDING OF URBAN SCHOOLS

In Chapter 12 we discuss the unique and perplexing problems of trying to maintain quality education in city schools.These problems result from a number of factors. The proportion of impoverished, undereducated, aged, nonwhite, unemployed people in the cities is growing at the same time that the cities are losing commerce, industry, and middle- and upper-income families to the suburbs. Simultaneously, city property values and tax bases are deteriorating. On the average, city tax bases in the mid-1970s were increasing at the rate of only 1 percent annually, while school costs were rising at the rate of 15 percent.

The tax problem is exacerbated by the higher burden of other public services—police and fire protection, public transport systems, welfare, snow removal, and environmental protection, among others—in high-density population areas. This municipal overburden is illustrated by the fact that Boston schools get only 23 percent of the total local budget, while in the nearby suburb of Lexington, schools get 81 percent of the local budget. The cost of living is also higher in cities. City school districts must pay much higher prices for land for school buildings than do suburbs and rural regions. City school systems also have a much higher proportion of students whose proper education is more expensive. The obvious solution is through state and federal allocations weighted in favor of urban districts. Some federal allocations have been so weighted but are still insufficient. In states where the legislature is dominated by nonurban representation, it is difficult to enact state fiscal formulas that are preferential to cities. A few states, notably Florida and Illinois, have revised their state aid formulas to favor cities. However, in most states large city districts are in grave financial trouble; in some cases, they verge on bankruptcy.

[14]Roe L. Johns and Edgar L. Morphet, *The Economics of Financing Education*, Prentice-Hall, Englewood Cliffs, N.J., 1975, p.140. Reprinted by permission.

THE REORGANIZATION OF SCHOOL DISTRICTS

Most small school districts are not very cost effective. They have too few students to provide a wide breadth of educational experience, and their tax bases are too narrow to generate sufficient revenues in states that still rely heavily on local property taxes. Although much progress in reorganizing districts into larger and more efficient units has been made in many states, there are still far too many small, inefficient school districts. We are optimistic about this reform. As states are forced to assume the major share of the cost of education, legislatures will quickly become interested in gaining efficiency through school district reorganization. Legislatures have the power to force swift reorganization and will do just that out of economic necessity.

REFORMS IN TAX ADMINISTRATION

Local property taxes are overdue for reform in most states. Assessments are often inequitable and commonly are not based upon uniform standards. The wrong properties are often exempt from taxation. More property tax relief is needed for low-income and elderly home owners. The cost of property tax collection is higher than necessary because it is collected inefficiently in so many small jurisdictions. Transformation of the property tax from a local to a state basis, which may happen in many states, will help to solve these problems. State income taxes, like their federal counterpart, often contain unjustifiable loopholes, which, if closed, would produce more revenue. Regressive state and local taxes, particularly sales taxes, should be replaced by progressive taxes such as income tax.

INCREASED FEDERAL FINANCIAL SUPPORT FOR EDUCATION

By far the most imperative reform in school financing lies in substantially increasing the federal share of costs. We discuss this challenge in Chapter 14. Here we will simply call attention to one unique proposal for accomplishing more adequate federal participation in school financing. This proposal would help to reduce the great inequality in school expenditures among the states, as shown in Figure 11-14. Pennsylvania's Governor

Milton Shapp has proposed an eminently sensible means of reforming the financing of education. He urges the creation of a National Education Trust Fund (NETF) modeled after the Federal Highway Trust Fund, which has financed our interstate highway system. The highway fund has been repaid through a federal surtax on motor fuel paid for by the users of these roads. Arguing that education is an investment, Shapp insists that we stop trying to pay for it entirely out of current revenues and handle it in much the same way any private corporation would handle its investments. Shapp contends that corporations would go broke too if they tried to pay for capital investment through current operating revenues. With an initial investment of $5 billion to $8 billion, Shapp says the NETF could be established, after which it would operate on a revolving, self-liquidating basis. The share of money advanced by NETF to cover students' education would be repaid through a small surtax added to individuals' federal income taxes when they become wage earners. The surtax would be graduated on the basis of the number of years of education attained. The repayment plan rests on the assumption that the federal investment in the costs of students' education should be repaid by those who benefit from that education, namely, the students. Students are better able to pay it without any aggregate loss, since their earnings increase greatly as a result of the education. Shapp believes that approximately half the costs of students' education should come from the NETF, with 49 percent coming from state sources and 10 percent from local sources.[15]

Regardless of the mechanism, we must find some means of ensuring that the federal government assume approximately one-third the costs of public education. Otherwise our schools cannot be financed as they must be to ensure the continued well-being of our civilization.

The future

The financing of schools will continue to be our main problem in education for many years. "Chaos" and "revolution" may not be too strong a

[15]For further discussion of this unique idea, see Milton J. Shapp, "A Governor's Solution to Court-mandated Change," *Compact*, August 1972, pp. 23–26.

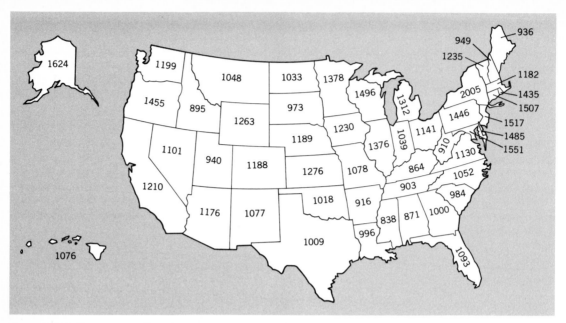

Figure 11-14 Current expenditure by each state in 1974–1975 for public elementary and secondary schools per pupil in average daily attendance. (National Education Association, Research Division, *Estimates of School Statistics,* 1974–1975. Copyright © by the National Education Association. All rights reserved.)

way to describe the immediate future of educational financing. Revolts by taxpayers will continue as long as inflation and unemployment are high. Bankruptcy of school districts—already evident in New York, Cleveland, and Newark—will become more commonplace. Bankruptcy will be barely avoided in other districts only through stringent retrenchment that will include shortening of school terms and school days, drastic cutbacks in faculties, larger class size, greater use of instructional technology, and elimination of experimental and high-cost programs. Teachers will strike not only because of concerns over salaries but increasingly because of concerns over job security. We expect increased funds to be made available to urban school districts on a preferential basis. Except for early-childhood education, vocational and career education, special education, and adult education, the educational enterprise will become increasingly bearish through the coming decade at least.

The decline of education as a growth industry will shift financing dilemmas from quantitative to qualitative terms. The critical question will no longer be: What is best? For the immediate future,

the critical question will be: What is cheapest? However, as systems management becomes more highly refined—and as cost-effectiveness, PPBES, and other programming-financing-evaluation systems become more widely applied—the critical question will become: What is most cost-effective? The pressure to reduce labor-intensiveness in education will increase, as will the pressure to displace teachers with instructional technology. The latter will probably remain less cost-effective than human delivery systems until 1985, after which new technology can be expected to grow rapidly.

The equality-quality dilemma in education will trigger considerable controversy and much litigation. States with well-established traditions in broad-based tax structure will move swiftly and almost effortlessly toward full state funding. Other states with long traditions of local school funding will move more slowly and agonizingly. We predict that the desire to level up will be strong, but the cost will be enormous. We look for state support on the average of around 75 percent, rather than 90 percent, as recommended by most authorities. There will still be considerable variations in allocation models and levels among states. We expect the control of education to shift substantially from the local to the state level of government. Most big money issues, such as teachers' salaries, will be bargained increasingly at the state level. This shift in funding will result in less dependence upon local property taxes. Some states will carry more of the burden of school costs through state income and sales taxes. Others will move toward state property taxes.

We expect, unfortunately, only slight expansion of the federal government's participation in financing education in the next decade. There is the possibility of much larger increases by the 1980s if the national economy is back in a growth pattern by then. However, we do not expect the federal share to reach 30 percent, as it should, unless some new scheme should emerge, such as a National Education Trust Fund. It will emerge only when this nation belatedly realizes that education is an investment and that it must be financed as such rather than as a consumptive expense.

We regret that our forecast is gloomy, and we have grave concerns about the impact of inadequate school financing upon so many critical factors of our society: our national productivity and prosperity, the relief of social injustices, individual prosperity and happiness, the reduction of poverty, and the improvement of race relations.

Suggested activities

1. Select one statement about the political or economic foundations of school finance stated in this chapter, study it further, and prepare an essay on it.
2. Prepare a graph showing a comparison of public expenditures for education with other public expenditures, such as national defense, housing, or welfare.
3. Prepare an analysis of public financing of education in your state showing (a) the proportion of local, state, and federal funding; (b) sources of tax revenues; and (c) the model, as described in this chapter, for allocating state funds for education.
4. Select the model for allocating state funds for schools described in this chapter that you prefer and prepare an argument for it.
5. Prepare an essay on the topic "The High Cost of Cheap Education."
6. Explain the relative importance to education of the following main sources of revenue: local, county, state, federal, and private.
7. Trace the historical development of financial support for education in the United States.

8. Give some of the important court decisions (of both state supreme courts and the U.S. Supreme Court) that have affected the financing of education.
9. Examine a school budget or an annual financial report and evaluate its contents and format.

Bibliography

Alexander, Kern, and K. Forbis Jordan: *Educational Need in the Public Economy,* University Presses of Florida, Gainesville, Fla., 1976. Discussion of economic benefits of education and reforms needed.

Benson, Charles S.: *Education Financing in the Coming Decade,* Phi Delta Kappa, Bloomington, Ind., 1975. Readable, nontechnical guide to future reforms in school financing.

————: *Equity in School Financing: Full State Funding,* Phi Delta Kappa, Bloomington, Ind., 1975. Excellent primer in school finance, with cogent arguments regarding full state funding of schools.

Guthrie, James W.: *Equity in School Financing: District Power Equalization,* Phi Delta Kappa, Bloomington, Ind., 1975. Good, brief exposition of one of the most viable approaches to reform in school finance.

Johns, Roe L., and Edgar L. Morphet: *The Economics and Financing of Education,* 3d ed., Prentice-Hall, Englewood Cliffs, N.J., 1975, chaps. 1–4, 7, 10. Classic textbook treatment of school finance through systems approach.

Knezevich, Stephen J.: *Program Budgeting, (PPBS),* McCutchan, Berkeley, Calif., 1973, chaps. 1–3. Introduction to program budgeting and PPBS—its meaning, history, and capabilities.

Lindman, Erick L.: *Dilemmas of School Finance,* Educational Research Service, Arlington, Va., 1975. Analyzes the issues and options in improving school finance.

National Education Finance Project: *Future Directions for School Financing,* Gainseville, Fla., 1971. Brief, easily read summary of one of the most thorough and excellent studies of school finance.

Phi Delta Kappa, *Financing the Public Schools,* Bloomington, Ind., 1973. Brief, nontechnical report of this fraternity's Commission on Alternative Designs for Funding Education, including recommendations.

Pincus, John (ed.): *School Finance in Transition,* Ballinger, Cambridge, Mass., 1974. Comprehensive treatment by educators and socioeconomic experts of the courts' decisions on school finance and their consequences.

President's Commission on School Finance: *Schools, People, and Money: The Need for Educational Reform,* U.S. Government Printing Office, 1972. Report of panel of experts commissioned to study the future revenue needs and resources of the nation's schools.

Chapter 12

Local school systems

YOU WILL HAVE MASTERED THIS CHAPTER WHEN YOU CAN

Define

● **the legal status of local school districts**

Describe

● **the types of local school systems**
● **the criteria of adequate school districts**
● **the characteristics of effective school boards**

Analyze

● **the problems of school district reorganization**
● **the promise and problems of decentralization of large districts**
● **the problems confronting private schools**
● **the forces that are changing local districts and their probable consequences**

Foundations of local educational systems

One of the most distinguishing characteristics of American education has been the high degree of control over schools exercised by local authorities. Although education is a legal function of the state, much of the operational responsibility for schools is delegated to local school districts.

THE DEVELOPMENT OF LOCAL DISTRICTS

The little villages of the colonies were the first school-unit prototypes in America, preceding by many years county, state, or national units of school organization. Local school districts had their beginning in a quaint law, known as the "Old Deluder Satan Law," enacted by the Massachusetts Bay Colony in 1647, nearly 150 years before the founding of the republic. This statute required every town of fifty families or more to appoint one of its people to teach reading and writing, since "one chief point of that old deluder, Satan, [is] to keep men from knowledge of the Scriptures."

Colonial America was largely rural. Wide-open spaces separated the little villages that dotted the land. Transportation and communication were difficult. It was natural to organize schools around local communities, since state and national government had not yet emerged. The founders of America, who had struggled for independence from oppressive centralized government, were not disposed to let the important function of education rest with the central government after it was established. These and other circumstances established firmly the tradition of strong local control of education in America. Because of America's great faith in education, the schools have been kept close to the people. This has also helped to keep the people close to the schools.

THE LEGAL STATUS OF LOCAL SCHOOL DISTRICTS

All states except Hawaii have delegated much of the responsibility for local school operation to subdivisions commonly known as "school districts" or, in some states, "school corporations." The breadth of responsibility delegated to local districts varies widely among the states. The scope of this responsibility is defined in the statutes enacted by state legislatures, and regulations are established by state educational agencies and, in a general way, by state constitutions.

Local school districts are legally analogous to corporations, and although their corporate status is not identical among the states, there are similarities. They have, for example, the right to buy and sell property, erect buildings, enter into contracts, levy and have collected school taxes, and conduct other necessary business under the laws of the state. The board of education represents the state and is the legal authority over local schools. Local board members are usually officers of the state, rather than local officers, although this is poorly understood even by many board members.

Types of local schools

The 16,000 or so school districts in the United States range in size from a few students—or none, in some cases—to the New York City school system, which enrolls over a million students in its public elementary and secondary schools, more students than are enrolled in each of thirty-nine of the states. Approximately 300 districts operate no schools at all, either because they have no students or because they send their few students to other districts. The median-sized district enrolls approximately one thousand students. Four-fifths of all districts enroll less than one-fourth of all students.

Figure 12-1 reveals the changes in public and private elementary and secondary school enrollments in this century. In 1971, for the first time in the century, elementary and secondary school enrollments declined slightly. The decline is expected to continue until 1982 when it is expected to level off. Thus the problems of most local districts are changing from the struggle to provide new buildings rapidly enough to keep up with enrollments in the 1950s and 1960s to, since 1971, the problems of disposing of unneeded buildings and furloughing teachers. Salt Lake City, for example, closed twenty buildings in recent years because of declining enrollments. The drop in school attendance is most pronounced in metropolitan school districts; many suburban school districts continue to grow.

School districts are frequently called "administrative units," to distinguish them from "attendance units," which are served by a single school building within a district. Let us now consider various types of local administrative units.

TYPES OF SCHOOL ADMINISTRATIVE UNITS

State districts. Even though both are state systems, the contrast between the Alaskan and the Hawaiian school organization is striking. Alaska School District One, the largest in the country, con-

Figure 12-1 Enrollment in public and private elementary and secondary schools. (U.S. Office of Education, *Projections of Educational Statistics.*)

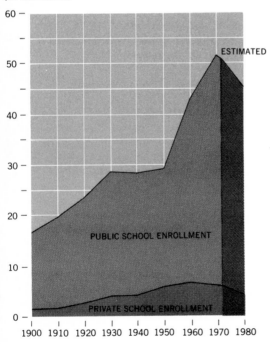

ENROLLMENT
(IN MILLIONS)

tains all the schools of the forty-ninth state except those of twenty-seven cities and villages. This enormous district, which spans four time zones and includes about 586,000 square miles, is almost one hundred times as large as Hawaii, and yet it is only one-third the size of Hawaii in terms of population. In the twenty-seven cities and villages of Alaska, where schools are operated autonomously, control of education is vested in local municipal governments—city councils and borough assemblies—since no local boards of education exist in Alaska. Hawaii, with only one school district, is the state district in its purest form. In all other states, a larger measure of responsibility for the operation of schools is delegated to many local units.

County and intermediate units. The county is the actual operating unit for all schools in Florida, West Virginia, and Nevada, which contain only county school units. Utah, Virginia, Kentucky, Nebraska, Texas, Wyoming, Indiana, Tennessee, Georgia, Alabama, North Carolina, South Carolina, Mississippi, Maryland, and Louisiana are also in the group generally organized on the county unit, except for a city or a few larger towns in each state, which are organized as separate districts.

In all the above states, with the exceptions noted, the schools are under elected or appointed county boards of education. School revenue is gathered largely through county taxes. Schools are administered by the county superintendent of schools, who is appointed by the county board in some states and elected by popular vote in others. In county units of organization, the county superintendent's functions are similar to those of a local superintendent. Where the county is the local or basic educational unit, the county superintendent directly administers elementary and secondary schools. No intermediate unit exists.

In most states the county's educational officer does not directly administer the independent school systems in the county. The county board of education coordinates and stimulates but does not control education. In most states this type of county unit is controlled by a county board of education, elected by the people or by the local boards of education within the county. The unit is administered by a county superintendent who is elected by the people in some states and appointed by the board in others. This position is now regarded as a pro-

fessional position. However, short terms of office, low salaries, inadequate finances, and the rigors of campaigning for the job—conditions that prevail in many states—detract from the attractiveness and the effectiveness of the position. The county superintendent serves as the executive or advisory officer for small towns, townships, or districts within the county that are too small to employ a full-time administrator.

There is a growing tendency toward regarding the intermediate unit as an entity not necessarily coterminous with the county. Counties are being combined in a number of states into substantially larger intermediate-unit areas. Consequently, the terms "county unit" and "intermediate unit" are not necessarily synonymous, although the county is the intermediate unit in most states. The situation will not remain so in years to come. The National Commission on School District Reorganization has defined the intermediate unit as

an area comprising the territory of two or more basic administrative units and having a board, or officer, or both responsible for performing stipulated services for the basic administrative units or for supervising their fiscal, administrative, or educational functions.

The intermediate units have various names among the states: intermediate school districts or units; educational service units or centers; boards of cooperative services; or regional educational service agencies, which is probably the most descriptive title. Presently about half the states have some type of intermediate-unit structure. These intermediate units amount to a reorganization of county units into multicounty units in most cases and in a redirection from state agencies of control to regional service agencies. Intermediate units in Pennsylvania, for example, render the following services to local districts: improvement of curriculum and instruction, research and planning, development of instructional media, continuing professional education for school employees, coordination or operation of special education programs, provision of special services for students, assistance in administration and business management, and liaison with state and federal agencies. These intermediate units permit greater equalization of educational opportunity for all students, the specialization of staffing necessary to deliver specialized educational services, more cost-effective educational benefits because of economies realized through cooperative services—conquering the limitations of small districts—and better educational planning. The emergence of intermediate units is a significant educational development in recent times.

Town and township units. The educational systems of the New England states, parts of Pennsylvania, and New Jersey, are organized on a town and township basis. Under the township system, many cities, incorporated villages, towns, and some consolidated schools are set apart as independent school districts. In some states, such as Illinois, high schools are organized on a township basis, but smaller districts within the township operate their own elementary schools.

New England towns, which usually comprise a cohesive combination of urban and rural territory, are natural geographic centers and form much more logical school units than do townships of most states, which took their form from early sur-

veys, Indian trails, or cow paths. In many instances, town school districts exist within township units.

Many town and township districts are too small to operate efficient school programs; in recent years they have been combined to some extent into larger units.

District units. In most Western states and in Michigan, Delaware, Ohio, and New York, the district is the local school unit. The majority of these districts are smaller than the other types of units described previously. Some still exist even though they operate no schools at all, sending their students to other school systems. In most instances, these districts were established by early surveys and have little relationship to natural community boundaries or to logical school organization. This type of organization is generally considered least efficient.

The reorganization of school districts into larger merged attendance units in many states has

Figure 12-2 Prevailing types of school-system organization by states. In some states various combinations of types exist.

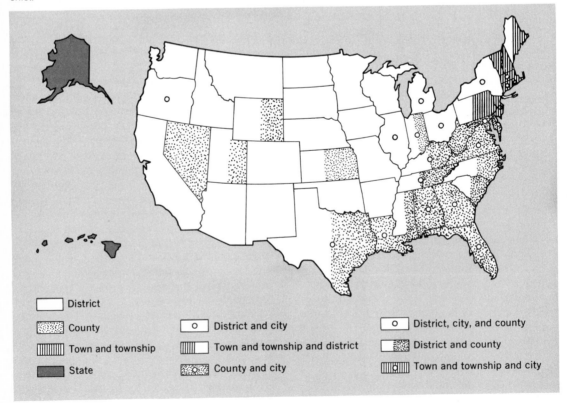

	District
	County
	Town and township
	State

	District and city
	Town and township and district
	County and city

	District, city, and county
	District and county
	Town and township and city

tended to blur these distinctions among types of local school units. Figure 12-2 shows the prevailing types of local school units among the various states.

Structural changes in district organization

The three major types of structural changes common in school district organization are (1) consolidation, (2) redistricting, and (3) decentralization.

CONSOLIDATION

"Consolidation" refers to the merging of small attendance areas within an administrative unit to create larger school-building units that can provide more comprehensive educational programs or better racial balance.

REORGANIZATION

"Reorganization"—or "redistricting," as it is sometimes called—of school administrative units involves the merger of administrative units or the rearrangement of district boundaries in order to construct larger, more efficient local units and to consolidate resources to provide more cost-effective education.

At the end of World War II there were about 103,000 school districts in the United States. Through reorganization, this number has been reduced to about 16,000 districts at the time of the nation's two-hundredth anniversary. The number of districts too small to operate their own schools has been reduced by more than two-thirds since the war. The number of one-teacher schools has been reduced by more than 99 per cent since 1930. This dramatic progress is revealed graphically in Figure 12-3. Nevertheless there is room for needed improvement. There are still approximately three hundred very small districts, mostly in the Great Plains states, which do not operate schools but pay neighboring districts to educate their children. Approximately one-fifth the nation's school districts enroll fewer than 150 students, and four-fifths enroll fewer than 3,000 students each, which is probably the minimum enrollment essential for an efficient and fairly comprehensive instructional

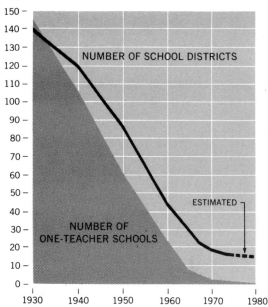

THOUSANDS

Figure 12-3 Decline in the number of school districts and one-teacher schools. (U.S. Office of Education, *Digest of Educational Statistics.*)

program. The National Educational Finance Project concluded that 80 percent of the districts in the land do not have sufficient enrollments to provide even minimally adequate programs and services without excessive costs. However, these districts enroll less than one-fourth of all students. Eventually, the total number of school districts should be reduced to approximately 5,000.

Advantages of reorganization. Reorganization of school districts into larger administrative units usually results in a number of advantages. Larger enrollments make it feasible to extend and enrich educational programs through the addition of new curriculums such as vocational and business education, new courses, advanced study in other courses, and remedial instruction. The curriculums of reorganized schools usually tend to combine the best from each district.

The wider area enlarges the educational clientele. Larger districts are better able to provide their own high schools, junior colleges, and adult education programs. The employment of additional specialized personnel—such as librarians, counselors, administrators, supervisors, and health personnel—becomes feasible. More specialized school facilities—such as laboratories, shops, health rooms, libraries, gymnasiums, and auditoriums—can be provided. The proportion of high school graduates in reorganized districts attending college is strikingly larger than the proportion in smaller districts. Larger districts also permit more efficient use of personnel and facilities. For example, more teachers teach in their fields of specialization. The pattern of services enlarges with the increase in the size of the districts. Thus reorganization of local school units results in a richer instructional program and supporting services as well as greater equalization of educational opportunity and financial burdens. In some regions, the creation of larger administrative units helps to reduce racial segregation in schools.

A commission of the American Association of School Administrators studying school organization concluded that "the real trouble is outmoded school district organization—school district organization that is now called upon to provide services, to perform functions, and to operate programs that were scarcely dreamed of when it was established."

Disadvantages of reorganization. Although advantages of reorganization generally far outweigh disadvantages, consolidation of school units may cause new problems. The close relationship of the schools to the people may be weakened as the locus of authority becomes further removed from local communities. Reorganization of districts is frequently inhibited by the persistence of the American tradition of home rule. Attempts to enlarge district boundaries are often viewed as threats to the homogeneity and autonomy of a community. Total school costs inevitably rise, although greater educational opportunity is provided at modest increases in costs per pupil.

Fleets of school buses are needed to transport pupils to consolidated schools. The lengthened day, caused by long bus rides, induces extra fatigue, especially for young children. The possibilities for parent-teacher conferences and for parental participation in the educational program decrease as the size of the district increases.

Criteria for an adequate school district. In general, it can be said that an adequate school district should satisfy four basic criteria. First, it should be large enough to be able to provide adequate basic educational opportunity at reasonable cost. Estimates of adequate size vary. The National Academy of Education recommends the following: "The number of school districts in the United States should be drastically reduced, and normally no school district should contain fewer than 5,000 nor more than 150,000 pupils. . . . We probably need no more than 5,000 such districts."[1] If a district implemented recommendations and instituted a sixteen-year program extending downward to include nursery schools and kindergartens and upward to embrace two-year junior colleges, then obviously the minimum numerical requirement for student enrollment should be raised, probably to the optimum figures just cited.

Second, a school district should be large enough to include sufficient wealth. Although small districts are not necessarily poor, nor large districts wealthy, per-pupil wealth tends to become more equalized as the size of the district increases. Again, there is no universal agreement on what level of wealth is adequate. One common rule of thumb suggests that there should be about $50,000 of true valuation per child of school age. A reasonable tax would yield from this base sufficient money for a fairly adequate program. Obviously, the amount of state aid would influence this consideration.

Third, a school district should include a natural geographic area. Ideally, a school district boundary should include people who are held together by common economic, social, and cultural ties and interests. School districts should encompass rather than bisect natural communities.

Fourth, a school district should encompass a racially balanced student body, a difficult specification in many urban and suburban areas because of the high concentration of minority groups in inner cities. Much of the initiative for the merger of urban and suburban districts is generated by this desire for better racial balance. In 1974 a federal judge ordered the merger of two Kentucky school districts, Louisville and Jefferson counties, to implement a metropolitan school desegregation plan. Another federal judge did the same with

---

[1] Committee on Educational Policy, *Policy Making for American Public Schools*, National Academy of Education, Washington, March 1969, p. 7.

Richmond and two surrounding suburban districts. In Detroit another federal judge, while not ordering the redrawing of school district boundaries, did order cross-district busing to link Detroit's largely black schools with the nearly all-white schools in the suburbs. But in both the Richmond and the Detroit cases, the U.S. Supreme Court by margins of only one vote failed to sustain the lower courts on the grounds that segregation in those cities had not been deliberately contrived. However, these decisions did not foreclose the possibility that in other circumstances the decision might have been different. Other cities had cases pending and many experts felt that the Supreme Court's ultimate decision on this issue had not yet been written. A few metropolitan areas, such as Nashville and Jacksonville, have voluntarily formed a single metropolitan-area school district including the inner city and surrounding suburbs to achieve better racial balance. This problem of reorganizing city and suburban districts into metropolitan units is discussed in the context of school desegregation in Chapter 1.

Methods of reorganization. Some states have accelerated reform by passing "K-12 laws," which require that every square mile of a state be covered by a school-district organization offering thirteen years of schooling, from kindergarten to twelfth grade. Some states, such as Nevada, have abolished all local school districts and have reorganized them into county units by legislative decree. Some state legislatures have decreed that all districts beneath a certain size must be reorganized into larger units.

Most states have attempted to accomplish reorganization through laws prescribing the procedures by which local citizens or officials might reorganize local districts on their own initiative. This may be done through merger, annexation, or transfer of territory. In this procedure, proposals for reorganization are initiated locally or by the county board and are sometimes presented to voters on referendum, which usually requires the approval of the state.

Many state legislatures are reluctant to compel reorganization but are disinclined to endure the slow progress that is made under local initiative. Thus an increasing number of state legislatures are enacting laws that will stimulate reorganization where needed but also retain some permissive

features. Such plans often provide for the development of a statewide plan for reorganization based upon studies of local needs and conditions. In many states, encouragement is generated through state-aid programs that provide financial advantages to reorganized districts.

A combination of three procedures is used increasingly; it involves passage of general legislation by the state's highest lawmaking body, adoption of a framework of a master plan by the state board of education, and consideration of locally recommended reorganization plans by the state superintendent of education.

DECENTRALIZATION AND COMMUNITY CONTROL

In the closing days of its 1969 session, the New York State Legislature was held captive in a grueling ten-day debate that continued through the last day without a break. The debate involved considerations of racism, ethnocentrism, unionism, bureaucracy, partisan politics, and poverty. At issue was a bill, eventually enacted, that dictated the division of the New York City school system, the nation's largest, into thirty semiautonomous districts, each with a locally elected board of education. Similar demands for decentralization and community control of schools have been advanced in virtually all cities and many have responded.

Reasons for decentralization. What are the reasons for this change in structure? Many people believe that schools have failed to meet the needs of students in inner cities, especially those who are poor or members of minority groups. Originally it was hoped that integration of urban school systems, compensatory education, and more effective school programs would correct the educational disadvantage of inner-city youths. In balance, these reforms have not really solved the problems in any fundamental manner. Although most liberals have not abandoned school desegregation as the ultimate long-range goal, it is nevertheless clear that racial imbalance is difficult to eliminate in most big-city schools, particularly in those where most students are black. Even in metropolitan school districts that are predominantly white, racial balance is often elusive because of segregated housing patterns. The objective of some parents from minority groups is therefore toward

Achieving racial balance in schools is an elusive goal in metropolitan areas.

control over the schools their children attend, rather than districtwide desegregation.

Stokely Carmichael and Charles Hamilton, in their influential book *Black Power,* contend that the black-white partnership in social reform is a myth. They urge blacks to seize control of schools in black neighborhoods away from whites, who bring white middle-class biases and instructional methods and means that are at best dysfunctional and at worst destructive to black children.[2] Barbara Sizemore, former superintendent of the District of Columbia schools, argues that blacks can overcome their powerlessness and oppression by gaining control of their schools. She contends that this should be done not so much for educational purposes but to maintain "solidarity against oppression, enhance the myths, rites, and rituals which preserve this solidarity. . .and produce ideologies that make liberation possible."[3] Thus some reformers see black control of black schools through decentralization and community control as

a struggle for educational reform and escape from oppression.

Apart from racial issues, highly centralized urban school systems, we are told, manifest the dysfunctions usually associated with bureaucratic organizations: unresponsiveness to needed reforms, unnecessary constraint of behavior and opportunity, inflexibility and inability to adapt to variations in educational need among different neighborhoods of the city, lack of accountability of school authorities to the wishes of the people, discrimination against minority groups, and a generally closed system.

Arguments against decentralization. Some people despair of ever integrating society if blacks insist upon separatism in schools. Some argue that decentralization of control will perpetuate balkanization of society. City boards of education and administrative authorities often view decentralization as invasion of their powers and point to the ward politics, corruption, and inefficiency that often result when city schools become decentralized. Some fear that lay persons will replace professionals in decision making, that valuable wisdom and experience will be unheeded, and that children's education will be weakened. The counterargument is that schools in inner cities are now failing their students anyway and that changes are worth trying.

In understanding the problem, it is essential to distinguish between decentralization and community control, which may or may not be related. Decentralization is understood to mean that important decision-making prerogatives and management authority are delegated to local schools or clusters of schools rather than residing in the board of education and central administrative offices. If delegation is made to the administrative officers and faculties of the schools, no factor of community control is introduced. If authority is delegated to lay citizens in large measure, then community control results. Thus it is possible in large cities to have decentralization of administrative control without community control, but the converse is not possible. Much difficulty arises over what kinds of decisions might better be made by lay citizens and what kinds by professionals. This delineation of prerogatives must be made carefully.

Some opponents of decentralization fear that it

[2]Stokely Carmichael and Charles V. Hamilton, *Black Power,* Random House, New York, 1967, p.166.

[3]Barbara A. Sizemore, "Is There a Case for Separate Schools?" *Phi Delta Kappan,* January 1972, p. 283.

will result in several dozen bureaucracies rather than one. In some cases local community control has resulted without much increase in the involvement of parents. Some insist that decentralization and community control will simply transfer to local boards the bankruptcy of funds and expertise which formerly rested in the central office. Some urban school authorities believe that decentralization and community control will raise citizens' expectations but eventually will fail unless the more compelling problems of poverty, which appears to be the primary cause of learning difficulties for ghetto children, are relieved.

How well is decentralization working? Kenneth Clark, an eminent psychologist and early advocate of decentralization, now concludes that "school decentralization has been a disastrous experience in which the basic issue, teaching children, has been substituted by selfish forces. . . . These forces include the radical politics of small local groups."[4] Where community control has been combined with school decentralization in large school systems such as Los Angeles and Philadelphia, reports have concluded that community control has the potential for more harm than good. They reason that policy making should remain in the hands of the central school board.[5]

Potential flaws of decentralization. Robert Havighurst, a noted sociologist, believes that the large urban educational system "best serves its varied clientele and performs its diverse functions if there is substantial power, wisely administered, at the local school level and if this is balanced with substantial power and authority, wisely administered, at a central place in the school system."[6] He sees two fatal flaws in most approaches to urban school decentralization. First, decentralization is usually too limited. creating subunits that are still too large, often the size of Omaha or Syracuse. These large subunits are still segregated and politically charged. The second flaw is the failure to find a satisfactory balance of power between the central office and local building units. Havighurst

believes that large and complex school organizations must endure some bureaucracy, laws, and controls over human behavior, irksome as they may be. He sees hope in increasing the options of parents and students through a variety of educational programs from which they may choose and in greater involvement of local community groups. Havighurst rejects the contention that centralized urban schools are unmitigated failures.

Perhaps too much has been expected of urban school decentralization and community control. Probably no organizational restructuring can overcome the deeper problems of underfinancing, poverty, housing blight, broken homes, crime, and underprivilege that characterize most inner cities. Clearly the solution to these more fundamental problems of urban education transcend school organization and require action beyond the cities themselves, much less their school systems. There is also the temptation to draw conclusions too hastily and from too few cases. The movement toward decentralization is but a decade old. It has been supported by statute only in New York City and Detroit. The New York City attempt at decentralization has been disappointing. Thousands of dollars of public funds have been misappropriated on political giveaways or otherwise wasted. Unlicensed teachers have been hired, while licensed applicants remain unhired. Salaries are paid to many persons who do not show up for work. Many district meetings have been disrupted, and school personnel have been attacked without reason. Personal rights have been flagrantly violated, and some decentralized schools are near chaos. The issue may boil down to whether cities must once again repeat the dreary history of ward political control of schools in the late nineteenth century or whether some cities—some way—may be able to make decentralization of control work.[7]

It is hoped that some form of increased participation of citizens in public education will give parents a better grasp on the destiny of their children; give teachers a more wholesome understanding with the community, and possibly new allies in the quest to improve education; and give children a school system that is more responsive

---

[4]Kenneth B. Clark, quoted in the *New York Times*, Dec. 3, 1972, p. 7.

[5]Allan C. Ornstein, "Administrative/Community Organization of Metropolitan Schools," *Phi Delta Kappan*, June 1973, p. 674.

[6]Robert J. Havighurst, "The Reorganization of Education in Metropolitan Areas," *Phi Delta Kappan*, February 1971, p. 354.

[7]For one success story, see Russell C. Doll, Barbara J. Love, and Daniel U. Levine, "Systems Renewal in a Big City School District: The Lessons of Louisville," *Phi Delta Kappan*, April 1973, pp. 524–534.

to their needs and more positive in its expectations of them.[8] John Dewey posed the challenge well: "What the best and wisest parent desires for his own child, that must the community want for all its children. Any other ideal is narrow and unlovely; acted upon, it will destroy democracy."

TRANSPORTATION OF STUDENTS

A quarter-million yellow school buses transport about 20 million students over 2.2 billion miles each school day. This large transportation fleet helps to equalize educational opportunity by bringing students to larger and usually more adequate schools than the one-room country schools that many of their parents attended.

The transportation of students is not a recent enterprise. It was begun in a Massachusetts district in 1840, and many students were hauled to school in horse-drawn wagons and carriages, boats, or trolley cars before the advent of buses. By 1919 pupil transportation at public expense was authorized by all states, and today it is mandatory for both public and private students who live beyond certain specified distances. Most states provide subsidies for students' transportation in order to encourage the reorganization of school districts and to help equalize educational opportunity; it is also done in some districts to help reduce racial segregation. Many states have established more rigid safety standards for school buses.

Types of school systems

School systems, or school districts, may be differentiated on the basis of their demographic setting—rural, town, suburban, and urban—which we will now consider.

RURAL SCHOOL SYSTEMS

The increase in and dispersion of the population in the United States are blurring or blotting out traditional distinctions between rural and city life. As a result, rural education, which once dominated the American landscape with its thousands of one-

[8]For further discussion of the issues and prospects of decentralization and community control, see Allan C. Ornstein, op. cit., pp. 668–673; Robert J. Havighurst, op. cit., pp. 354–358; and Kenneth B. Clark, *A Possible Reality*, Emerson Hall, New York, 1972.

room schoolhouses, is steadily losing ground. Teacher-education institutions, which once had special curriculums for rural teachers, have long since dropped this classification.

In spite of progress in the reorganization of school districts, many small systems remain, although they enroll a small fraction of the nation's students. These small schools, almost without exception, are unable to provide instruction of reasonable breadth and quality at reasonable cost. They typically offer narrow curriculums, send a relatively small proportion of their graduates to college, have difficulty hiring and keeping good teachers, and are unable to provide necessary supporting facilities and personnel such as guidance and health services. As this research points out, "rurality does impose certain conditions which exacerbate educational problems."

Although many rural schools have been consolidated into large systems that are modern and efficient, it is inevitable that sparsity of population and topographical conditions in some areas of the country will force the continued existence of many small districts and small schools.   .

TOWN SCHOOL SYSTEMS

During the early 1970s demographers reported that the movement of people back to towns and small cities had accelerated to a point where their rate of growth now exceeds that of metropolitan areas, one of the most dramatic shifts in population since the turn of the century. Some of this movement has been prompted by people's disenchantment with city living, including, no doubt, concern over the problems of schools in large cities.

Larger towns offer their own high school programs; smaller ones usually send secondary school students to nearby high schools on a tuition basis. Like rural schools, small-town schools are usually too small to offer a modern educational program at reasonable cost, and many have been consolidated with the districts of surrounding rural areas or other nearby communities.

SUBURBAN SCHOOL SYSTEMS

The nation's suburbs have become the largest sector of the population. For the first time in American history, the population of the suburbs exceeds that of the rest of the country.

What significance does this marked increase have for suburban living and education? The United States Civil Rights Commission has been concerned about suburban jurisdictions that remain all or largely white and are adjacent to cities with heavy concentrations of blacks.

The exodus of blacks and other minority groups from cities to suburbs is increasing rapidly. The departure of many blacks from congested central cities to suburban towns and adjacent areas is bringing more blacks and other minority groups into suburban schools, although the proportion is still small. In some areas black children are bused to predominantly white schools in the suburbs or environs. The number of teachers from minority groups is increasing in many suburban school districts.

One of the most interesting frontiers of American education has been the suburban school districts. Some of the best educational sysems in the country are to be found in affluent suburbs such as Bronxville, Scarsdale, Newton, Lower Merion, Shaker Heights, Grosse Point, Evanston, Webster Grove, Winnetka, Anaheim, Palo Alto, and Mount Lebanon. Strong impetus for educational innovation and improvement springs from well-financed suburban school districts, which are able to employ a sufficient number of teachers and administrators of quality to staff outstanding programs. The highest teacher salary schedules and the highest expenditures per pupil are typically found in suburban school districts.

However, the educational scene in the suburbs is not entirely rosy. Many suburban areas consist almost entirely of mushrooming low-cost housing developments that are long on children to be educated and short on industries to furnish a tax base.

These amorphous "bedroom communities," made up of highly mobile families whose breadwinners commute to nearby cities, often lack cohesion and stability. School and municipal governments designed to serve rural and village settings are overwhelmed by suburban growth. Natural community lines frequently do not exist and, if they do, often are not congruent with school-district boundaries. Reorganization of these districts is complicated by outmoded legislation, lack of common identity, competition for annexation of rich areas, and reluctance to join with less favored communities.

Suburban development will continue to pose complex problems. The difficulty of keeping schools attuned to this growing segment of American society is likely to increase in many areas before it decreases. It is predicted that the Atlantic seacoast from Boston to Washington, for example, will before long become one continuous complex of contiguous urban and suburban congestion, posing new problems in housing, transportation, water supply, and sanitation, as well as in education.

URBAN SCHOOL SYSTEMS

The population in many urban school systems has been declining sharply. Between 1970 and 1976 eight of the fifteen largest cities lost 1.7 million people. Nevertheless over 60 million people live in cities, and the fifty largest urban school systems enroll 17 percent of the nation's public elementary and secondary school students.

The changing urban milieu. Before World War II, many city schools were the aristocrats of American education. But the past three decades have brought a tragic decline in the quality of education in most large cities.

Several forces have contributed to this decline. During the two decades following World War II, the urban milieu changed drastically. Millions of middle-class families moved to suburbs and to smaller cities and villages, to be replaced in the central city by Southern blacks, Appalachian whites, Hispanics, and American Indians. Although it has now run its course, this influx of largely nonwhite people has engendered severe racial problems. Because they are often poor and are discriminated against in housing, many of these people live in ghettos and attend schools that are as segregated as their neighborhoods.

Many of these former rural families have difficulty adjusting to urban life and to a culture that is almost alien to them. Very often they and their families must live in blighted and overcrowded housing. Often the children and parents are not home at the same time, and in many cases parents are separated. Around their ghetto they see poverty, unemployment, crime, disease, alcoholism, and drug addiction. Small wonder that these children are easily disenchanted with school and drop out as soon as they can. They have little opportunity for gainful employment in an age of automation, in which there is little need for uneducated labor. Undereducated, they are unable to compete occupationally, and their segregation by economic class persists despite any gain made in racial desegregation. The only escape for the victim of this self-perpetuating cycle of such underprivilege is through education.

Economic and governmental problems. Urban schools are often hampered further by financial strictures. Formulas of state aid to school systems, designed years ago, before the era of urban crisis, sometimes discriminate against city districts in many states. The underrepresentation of city interests in state legislatures dominated by rural influence militated against the correction of the city's disadvantageous position in relation to state aid to schools. The problem is complicated further by blurred lines of responsibility among city school boards, municipal officers, and state education agencies. City schools are often hamstrung by municipal control of school finances, state control of the city's tax rates and debt limits, and political control of the board of education and even of professional staff appointments.

The bureaucratic nature of many urban school organizations handicaps schools by establishing a climate of inflexibility, depersonalization, conformity, close supervision, evasion of responsibility, and inertia. Under these conditions teachers develop feelings of frustration, servility, despair, and even fear. Attacks on students and teachers are becoming increasingly common.

The plight of urban schools is in microcosm the plight of cities themselves. The question of whether urban schools can be saved begs the larger question of whether cities can be saved. All urban governmental enterprises suffer from underfinancing, bureaucratic sluggishness in response to people, institutional overload, credibility gaps, and social lag.

Some positive forces. Without doubt, this is the most serious blight on our entire educational scene, but the picture is not hopeless. It must not be assumed from this discussion that all urban schools are poor. All metropolitan communities include some adequate schools. Many cities are taking imaginative steps to alleviate the problem. The Elementary and Secondary Education Act provided funds earmarked for the improvement of education in slum schools. Federally aided urbanrenewal projects offer some hope for an educational and cultural renaissance along with physical rehabilitation of our cities. Several states have revised their state-aid formulas and have not only discontinued financial discrimination against urban areas but also provided additional sums for what has become known as "compensatory education," that is, programs designed to compensate for cultural disadvantages among slum children.

In Louisville, Kentucky, the "systems approach" to change has been undertaken to reverse the decline in schools. Educational needs assessment, curriculum planning, in-service education for teachers, and administrative leadership have been interlocked into a massive effort to improve. "Neighborhood school boards" have been established to strengthen citizens' participation in the affairs of their school district. A strong administrative team has been mobilized to provide overall leadership.

Hopeful movements in other cities could be cited.[9] Many of them are built around efforts to reconnect schools with communities and thereby make them more responsive to people's needs and expectations. This is often accomplished by involving citizens more meaningfully in the critical process of decision making, often through modes of decentralization discussed earlier.

The school principal is a key figure in improving urban schools. The evidence is strong that the destiny of schools depends heavily on the vision, wisdom, commitment, and even daring of principals. The urban school crisis calls for principals with an intense sense of humanity, an unconquerable faith in the ability of all children to learn in the right school environment, a deep knowledge of pedagogy, a determination to change schools to serve children rather than the other way around, an ability to strengthen the bonds between school and home, and the charisma to motivate teachers toward the same behavior.[10] The quality of school

[9]Some of these movements are described in Joseph M. Cronin, *The Control of Urban Schools*, Free Press, New York, 1973.

[10]For an excellent statement of the characteristics of effective urban school principals, see William W. Wayson, "A New Kind of Principal," *The National Elementary Principal*, February 1971, pp. 9–19.

superintendents is also critical. Too many urban citizens and school boards, impatient for progress in schools, seek instant improvement by replacing the superintendent. Very often this action merely adds to the problem.

The University Council for Educational Administration, a confederation of fifty major universities has undertaken a cooperative program to prepare administrators better for the difficult tasks of city school administration. In addition, the unique problems of urban school leadership are getting greater attention in many university training programs for administrators, teachers, and other professional specialists.

These are some significant attempts to alleviate the vexing problems of urban education. But the problems of large metropolitan areas are complex and enormous, and the hour is late. Nothing short of our most vigorous effort can arrest the deterioration of large cities and their schools. Truly, this is the nation's gravest educational challenge.

NONPUBLIC EDUCATION

Among the many types of local schools are nonpublic pre-elementary, elementary, and secondary institutions, here classified for discussion purposes as (1) independent and (2) parochial schools connected with churches or synagogues.

Independent schools. Many independent or private schools have a long and noble tradition. Independent schools are supported by endowment and rapidly rising tuition; they do not offer instruction in the tenets of a particular religion and do not ordinarily restrict admission to students of a particular faith. Independent schools usually charge rather high tuition, and some of them are exceptionally fine schools, with small classes, select teachers, excellent facilities, and carefully screened students. Very often these schools, unhampered by the strictures of public education, pioneer in the development of progressive teaching methods and curriculums. Not all independent schools are good.

Some private schools have joined in consortiums as Independent School Councils to merge some of their business and academic efforts in order to reduce costs and increase efficiency. Most long-standing, high-quality schools are members of the National Association of Independent Schools.

A few states have provided fiscal assistance by awarding stipends to parents who choose to send their children to private schools. The U.S. Internal Revenue Service, which once granted tax-exempt status to such schools, has ruled against continuing their favored tax status if they practice racial discrimination.

Many Southern communities have opened private schools, "segregation academies," which are sometimes church-related and usually have high tuitions that make them unavailable to black students. This, of course, is an arrangement that appeals to affluent white families who prefer not to have their children attend desegregated schools. In some towns public school enrollment has declined by 25 percent. The same development is occurring in several Northern cities, particularly in New York, Washington, and Philadelphia. In Philadelphia, public school enrollment is 61 percent black, while the city's private and parochial schools are only 10 percent black. The authors view this development with dismay, fearing that influential people will resist, or at least withdraw their support from, public school improvement. There may be the danger in many Southern communities and some Northern cities that public schools will become "pauper schools," as they were in some communities in an earlier period of our history.

Parochial schools. The vast majority of private elementary and secondary schools are church-related. By far the greatest share of these are affiliated with the Roman Catholic Church. These 10,000 parochial schools have declined from 13,000 a decade ago. They enroll approximately $3\frac{1}{2}$ million elementary and secondary school students, about one-third the Catholic children and youths of school age in the country. Like other church-related schools, these parochial schools were established to provide instruction in church doctrine as well as education more spiritually oriented than public school education.

Studies of the entire Catholic school complex reveal that many Catholic schools are operated on a much lower per-pupil cost than typical public schools and employ teachers who have less academic preparation than public school teachers.

One study revealed that students in Catholic schools are superior to public school students both in academic achievement and in ability but that this advantage can be attributed largely to Catholic schools' selective admission of students.

One study reported that, contrary to popular belief, there is no evidence that Catholic schools are divisive or vehicles of prejudice. The study of Greeley and Rossi pondered the question of whether the continuation of this large Catholic school system is desirable; it concluded that Catholic schools are not necessary for the survival of American Catholicism. However, the writers reported that they did not expect this massive school system to be terminated.[11] With the increase in church and denominational mergers, with the movement of many Catholic families to the suburbs away from the parochial school buildings in the cities, and with the rising costs of financing both public and nonpublic schools, many of these small denominational schools face practical problems of enrichment and even survival. Enrollment in Catholic parochial schools dropped 20 percent from 1971 to 1975. According to a recent study the decline may be nearing its bottom and the future may be more hopeful.[12]

At one time, most teachers in local Catholic schools were priests, seminarian brothers, or nuns; but the proportion of lay teachers is increasing. Teachers in these schools are banded together in numerous religious educational organizations, such as the National Catholic Education Association and the Catholic Lay Teachers groups. Many Catholic schools have their own councils or school boards at the diocesan, area, and parish levels. Many members of these control or advisory boards of education are lay people.

The next largest number of church-affiliated schools are sponsored by the Lutheran church. Approximately 200,000 students attend Lutheran schools. Approximately 42 million students attended church-related elementary and secondary schools in 1976.

To continue with their present standards and proportion of total enrollments, these private schools will require a tremendous increase in income. Because of the financial pinch, many Catholic elementary and secondary schools have closed. Many Hebrew and Protestant day schools are also experiencing financial and recruiting problems.

The Jewish religion represents about 6 million people (about 3 percent of the national population), including 1 million children. The Jews have long cherished education. The first Hebrew day schools in this nation were established in the seventeenth century. Today Hebrew- or Yiddish-language day schools are supplemented by afternoon and Sabbath schools that primarily teach religion. 82,000 students attend Jewish schools.

These denominational schools represent a small but important minority in the educational enterprise. Their survival is threatened by rapidly rising costs, limited sources of income, constitutional constraints upon their access to public funding, and some diminution of their traditional emphasis upon spiritual education.

A new national federation of independent and church-related private schools, the Council for American Private Education, has been formed. It includes the National Association of Independent Schools and various other organizations representing Catholic, Lutheran, Seventh-Day Adventist, Christian, Episcopal, Hebrew, and Quaker schools. This new council is expected to promote cooperation among private schools and between them and public schools and federal agencies. A major aim of the council is to develop a unified position for seeking constitutionally acceptable federal aid for nonpublic schools.[13]

OTHER TYPES OF DISTRICTS AND SCHOOLS

Special-charter school districts. Some schools, usually city schools, have a special charter granted directly to the local district by the state. Al-

---

[11]Andrew M. Greeley and Peter H. Rossi, *The Education of American Catholics*, Aldine, Chicago, 1966.

[12]Andrew M. Greeley and William McCready, *Catholic Schools in a Declining Church*, University of Chicago, Chicago, 1976.

[13]For an excellent discussion of nonpublic schools, their progress, and their problems, see Otto F. Kraushaar, *American Nonpublic Schools: Patterns of Diversity*, Johns Hopkins, Baltimore, 1972.

though the majority of these districts were established in the early history of the states' educational development, some of them operate under a special charter of special laws because of the size of the district. The multiplication of specially chartered districts is likely to complicate school administration within the state; hence there is a trend toward bringing all school districts under the general school laws.

Laboratory schools. Many laboratory or experimental schools on the elementary and secondary levels are in reality public in that they are practice or training schools for state institutions that prepare teachers. Generally no tuition is required, and the pupils are admitted as they would be to a public school, although the limitation of facilities and the experimental nature of the work may restrict the enrollment.

Boards of education

Nearly every school district in the United States is governed by a group of lay people called the "selectmen," "board of education," "school board," "board of trustees," "school committee," "board of school commissioners," "board of school directors," "township board of education," or "county board of education." These board members are the direct representatives of the people in the school district. Local school boards are probably the purest form of representative government in the land.

The board of education plays a unique role in American life. Its work impinges on so many areas of public interest that it becomes interdependent with many groups. As elected representatives of the people, board members must be able to keep in contact with their constituents or at least to gauge their feelings. The importance of such connections is manifested in the increasing prevalence of committees on public relations, community relations, and human relations. Many boards encourage lay people, teachers, and students to attend their sessions. A number of states have enacted so-called "sunshine laws," which require public governmental bodies including school boards to hold their meetings open to the public and to permit public participation in those meetings, with certain exceptions.

THE DEVELOPMENT OF SCHOOL BOARDS

In colonial times the governance of local schools was usually handled in town meetings with all the interested persons in the community participating. Then developed the practice of appointing temporary committees. These temporary committees were replaced by permanent committees. There gradually developed the pattern of selecting boards of education, accountable to the people, who were given the responsibility for organizing and administering free schools. The autonomous school district, organized separately under an elected board of education, is essentially an American institution.

SIZE, TENURE, AND SELECTION OF SCHOOL BOARDS

There is little uniformity among the states with respect to the size, terms of office, and selection of board members. Terms of office range from one to six years. Authorities recommend that the term be at least four years and overlapping. The trend in recent years has been toward boards composed of not more than nine members.

In some states school board members are selected at general elections, usually on partisan tickets, while in other states they are elected at special school elections in which case their candidacy is commonly nonpartisan. Again, there are exceptions. In some larger cities board members are appointed by the mayor or by municipal bodies. The appointment of boards in cities is commonly defended on the grounds that minority groups are more likely to be represented by that mode. Election of board members is defended on the grounds that elected boards tend to be more responsive to the people. When boards are appointed, they are said to be politically dependent. In such circumstances they are commonly fiscally dependent as well, which means that school budgets and appropriations must be approved both by the school board and by the municipal governing body. Elected boards, on the other hand, are considered politically independent and are commonly fiscally independent, having full authority to enact budgets, set school tax rates, and expend funds without the approval of municipal government. Methods of nominating board members vary greatly. They may be nominated by petition, caucus, primary election, individual announcements, citizens' committees, or mass meetings.

It was once widely held that board members should be elected by nonpartisan ballots on the assumption that partisan political considerations have no place in school governance. However, there is a growing conviction among many people that it is unrealistic to believe that school governance can or should be free of politics. Several studies have indicated that politically oriented boards tend to be more responsive to the public, that the political arena provides a necessary forum for critical debate on school issues. and that political parties are endowed with a mantle of accountability for school governance that is essential for stability in times of crisis. Although many still regret the trend, school district governance is without doubt becoming increasingly political in many communities.

Studies of the composition of school board membership reveal that the percentage of women members has been increasing, although men still exceed women by about four to one. In urban school boards one member in five is nonwhite, a ratio far below that of the general population in the cities. About half the board members in the nation are college graduates. Professional persons, business owners, and officials predominate, while blue-collar workers are underrepresented.

A small but increasing number of boards are including nonvoting students who are elected by the student body. These student members have the right to place items on the board's agenda and to speak to the agenda. It is hoped that this practice will deepen understanding between the board and the student body. But it may raise the problem of whether the board is willing to grant similar privilege to other interest groups, such as teachers, PTA members, and secretaries.

Collectively, members of the board of education should reflect a variety of vocational experiences, economic levels, educational interests, and leadership abilities so as to represent the community broadly. School board members should be chosen from among the best men and women obtainable in the community and should be given adequate orientation and preservice training in school board service.

QUALIFICATIONS OF BOARD MEMBERS

The magnitude of education emphasizes the need for a very careful selection of board members. Among the qualifications usually specified by law are that the candidate be over twenty-one years of age, a legal voter, and a resident in the school district. Besides these legal stipulations, however, a member of a board of education should possess many other desirable qualities: an interest in schools, the willingness to subordinate self-interest, an open-minded and creative outlook, courage in facing criticism, willingness to give time to the office, skill in working with people, the respect of the community, a forward-looking attitude, a reasonably good education, friendliness and cooperativeness, an understanding of the community, and the ability to discuss school affairs. Of greatest benefit is intelligent cooperation among members of the board and among the board, teachers, and community.

A recent study of school boards noted a remarkable improvement in the caliber of board members in the nation, particularly in their knowlege of and concern for vital educational issues and in their effectiveness in dealing with those issues. It noted also a more rational and disciplined approach to school governance by boards.[14]

FUNCTIONS AND POWERS OF SCHOOL BOARDS

Boards are generally granted broad powers by the state and vested with much discretionary authority in the exercise of those powers so long as they do not violate statutes, regulations of state ed-

[14]L. Harmon Zeigler, M. Kent Jennings, and G. Wayne Peak, *Governing American Schools,* Duxbury, North Scituate, Mass., 1974.

ucational authorities, or the civil rights of students and employees. Boards of education should be primarily goal setting, policy making, and evaluating bodies. They are analogous to legislative bodies and they should not intrude upon the executive functions of the professional administrative staff. This line is sometimes difficult to distinguish. The least effective boards tend to be those which preempt the executive functions. Good boards are characterized by the care with which they formulate school district policy.

ORGANIZATION AND PROCEDURES OF SCHOOL BOARDS

Most school boards are organized with a president, who presides at the meetings, and a secretary or clerk, who may serve as the treasurer. Business is conducted usually in regular open meetings held in the school once or twice a month, in addition to special meetings held as the need arises.

Many boards use standing committees of board members to deal with such matters as finance, buildings, facilities, personnel, and community relations. However, experts in school administration do not regard this as a desirable practice, since standing committees can often preempt the responsibilities of the full board. Board members usually can render better service and be informed more thoroughly on all matters if the board functions as a committee of the whole. The major argument in favor of standing committees is they tend to reduce the time that would be required for the board to deal with all matters as a committee of the whole. In any case, there is nothing wrong with the creation of temporary special-purpose committees to study unusual or temporary problems or needs.

In many states the laws specify that the superintendent shall be an ex officio, nonvoting member of the board. Effective relationship between the board and the administrative staff is crucial to the successful governance of schools. Where this relationship is not mutually supportive, schools invariably suffer. The primary function of the board is to enact educational policy, and the function of the administrative staff is to execute that policy. When either the board or the administrative staff intrudes upon the prerogatives of the other, controversy results.

SCHOOL BOARDS AND THE ELECTORATE

Control of education lies ultimately with the people. "We, the people," elect representatives who, as a board of education, take the place of the unwieldy larger group, the electorate. Citizens should maintain active interest in their schools. This interest should be manifested in voting at school elections, visiting schools, attending board meetings, and participating in parent-teacher associations. Good schools tend to be found in communities where there is a high level of public understanding of, and interest in, education.

Never before in the nation's history has American education enjoyed such unprecedented public interest and criticism. Wise boards of education are seeking to capitalize on this surge of public interest to improve education.

Many school boards work closely with citizens' committees. In some districts, permanent general-purpose committees or councils of citizens advise school boards on a wide variety of matters. The preferred practice, however, is to create temporary special-purpose committees to deal with specific problems; these are disbanded when their task is completed. These committees may deal with such matters as defining educational needs or goals, establishing priorities, improving human relations, strengthening public information programs, planning, and many others. The involvement of citizens in defining the goals and priorities of school districts has become especially noteworthy in many communities. It is felt that the people are more likely to support additional school revenues when they have had an opportunity to assist in defining the mission of their school system. Increased public understanding of their schools and educational problems is a critical by-product of public involvement. Citizens' advisory committees have multiplied from a handful to many thousands over the past quarter-century. It is imperative that these committees be broadly representative of the community. They should serve in an advisory capacity only, rather than becoming superboards that preempt the legal prerogatives of the school board.

Many school boards work closely with citizens' committees on a wide range of problems.

SCHOOL BOARD ORGANIZATIONS

In most states school boards have formed county or regional associations, and all but one state have formed statewide associations. These state associations keep the interests of local boards before the governor and state legislature, conduct in-service programs for school board members, conduct research on problems of education—particularly problems of school governance—and inform the general public about educational needs and problems.

The state associations are linked with the National School Boards Association (NSBA), which is emerging as a potent force in American public ed-

ucation. The NSBA publishes *The American School Board Journal,* the nation's oldest educational journal, as well as *Washington Fastreport,* a fortnightly newsletter that keeps local board members abreast of news from the nation's capital which impinges upon local school interests. The NSBA's annual convention commonly attracts 18,000 board members, superintendents, and other educational leaders. This national body also conducts workshops for board members and produces materials, such as its excellent film *On Board,* designed to strengthen the skills of local board members. The NSBA's Educational Policies Service helps local districts develop and maintain effective policy documents. Its Division of Federal

Relations influences Congress in its consideration of legislation affecting education. The more important purposes of the organization are "to advance high quality education in the United States by preserving and strengthening local lay control of public education; to protect and advance the interests and needs of the nation's lay boards of education; and to provide needed services to these school boards, their members, and their state associations."

Parent-teacher associations

PTAs are still common in most school communities and usually are organized around local elementary schools. These organizations appear to be undergoing an identity crisis evident in macrocosm by the changing fortunes of their national parent body, the National Congress of Parents and Teachers. Membership in the national body has declined from a high of 12 million in 1966 to approximately 7 million, making it still by far the largest educational organization in the land. The excellent *PTA Magazine* once had a circulation of 350,000 but was discontinued in 1974. Financial resources of the national organization are also dwindling, causing a sharp reduction in staff and services.

The number of local PTA units has dropped from 46,000 to 35,000, and attendance at most PTA meetings has declined. What accounts for this? The reasons are many and varied. As elementary school enrollments have declined in recent years, the number of elementary school teachers and parents of elementary school children has declined, but not as rapidly as the number of local units or national membership. By charter, PTAs are committed to improve schools "without seeking to direct their administration or control their policies." Most PTAs have rigorously maintained this "hands-off" stature with respect to school boards and administrators. This has reduced the organization's appeal to aggressive citizens interested in forthright educational change in an era of activism. Teachers have found the collective bargaining table a more powerful arena than the PTA meeting for achieving their purposes. In many communities teachers' militant victories at the bargaining table

have prompted an adversary relationship with the community and upset the delicate partnership of parents and teachers. Thus the PTA is often regarded as a gentle, harmless, highly feminized body meeting over coffee and cookies to plan the next bake sale. It is upstaged by more aggressive groups of citizens or teachers who seek to accomplish more significant action through direct assault on specific problems and who have no compunctions about "directing the administration or controlling policies." Then, too, many federally funded programs have required citizens' participation in the funded programs and thereby have drawn off parents' energies into more purposeful activities than many PTAs can offer.

The root cause of the PTA's decline centers on the dilemma of whether it should continue its traditional "hands-off" stance or whether it should become, like competing community groups, a more forceful agent of educational change; whether it should confine itself to discussing school developments or enter the political arena in helping to shape those developments.

Although some local units have recruited student members and become PTSAs, the national body has so far resisted the movement to become a congress of parents, teachers *and students*. This, to our minds, is an anachronism in these times.

The PTA still has great potential for influencing education, if for no other reason than its size. One writer has referred to the PTA as a "sleeping but good giant." It will probably remain asleep as long as it resists activism in the highly political world of school governance. (And as long as its national dues are only twenty cents per member!) There is some indication that the national officers are beginning to promote the organization more vigorously in an effort to strengthen its services and improve its image.

The future

We foresee gradual but significant changes in the organization, governance, and administration of local school units. Although the tempo of change is likely to accelerate, it probably will be less rapid than social need would demand or than many futurists predict. Public schools have a history of resistance to rapid change that, for better or for worse, may well continue unless there is social and political revolution in the nation itself. Many changes are already evident from forces and trends underway.

We look for continued decline in the powers of local boards of education, particularly in policy making. Some forecasters would go further and predict the demise of local school boards and the transfer of their powers to state and federal agencies. Indeed, a few writers even recommend this development on the grounds that local school boards have not governed well and lack both the power and the will for their own salvation. We do not agree with this extreme position, although we do think significant changes in local boards' powers and functions will be prompted by a number of irreversible forces. First, local taxing capacity for the support of schools is overloaded and exhausted. The sharply rising costs of education will increasingly be met from federal and state revenues. This shift in funding will be followed in large measure by a shift in control. We know that some advocates of full state funding of education hope that state control will not follow, but we regard this as unrealistic. The public demand for accountability is powerful politically, and state legislators are not disposed to assume responsibility for increased taxes while leaving accountability with local school boards. A number of states have made it clear that control of educational policies does indeed follow control of the purse. These controls are manifested in statutes that limit local tax ceilings and school expenditures, that mandate accountability or quality control systems, and that impose state controls over collective bargaining. In times of rising costs and tight money, concern for efficiency in expenditures will outrun concern for the preservation of local control.

The growing concern for equalizing educational opportunity throughout the state (and, we think, eventually throughout the nation) is another powerful force toward increased state control over school financing. Local districts alone are powerless to accomplish equalization, and legislatures, courts, and human rights organizations all press toward moving this challenge of the state (and eventually federal) level of government. However,

equalization of educational opportunity is not necessarily the same as equalizing educational experiences. We hope that local boards retain critical influence in developing programs that are responsive to their unique needs, but only after poorer districts have been protected against discrimination by constitutional safeguards. Thus it is possible, and we think highly desirable, that the states will assume increased responsibility for removing fiscal disadvantage, while local boards will retain responsibility for differentiating educational programs that substantively accommodate local needs and interests. However, this distinction is subtle and delicate, and the struggle to recognize it may be lost in some states.

State and federal courts are also prompting the movement of vital educational policy making from the local level to the state and federal levels. Executive agencies at state and federal levels will also continue to intrude upon the powers of local boards. The Department of Health, Education, and Welfare, for example, generates an increasing volume of "guidelines" that local districts must adhere to if they want to receive federal monies. These guidelines deal with such matters as protection of equal rights, due process, equal employment opportunity, health and safety, and a host of other legitimate safeguards. State executive agencies—such as state boards of education, human relations commissions, public employment relations board, professional rights and responsibilities commissions, and others—issue rulings that require local boards to eliminate sexism and racism in schools, enforce balance of power and due process in public employee-employer relations, and enunciate students' bills of rights, among others.

At the local level various forces will act to constrain school boards' and school administrators' freedom in the governance of schools. Receipt of federal funds is often contingent upon public participation in the planning and evaluation of enterprises to be funded. Citizens' groups are demanding and receiving increased opportunity to influence board decisions under the banner of participatory democracy. As competition for scarce resources continues, local boards will find it increasingly necessary to cooperate more effectively with other local bodies—juvenile courts, recreation commissions, youth centers, community action programs, and welfare agencies, among many others. Each of these new cooperative enterprises will further restrict school board options. Some board members and administrators will agonize and resist this reduction in the board's unilateral powers. Then, too, teachers' organizations have rapidly gained power through collective bargaining, stronger lobbying, and political action designed to elect their supporters to public offices. Harland Cleveland, in his book *The Future Executive,* predicts that the governance of all public and private enterprise will become increasingly pluralistic and ambiguous. He does not regard this as a disaster but a challenge. We also view this trend optimistically. Although multilateral approaches to decision making and problem solving are always more difficult and agonizing than unilateral modes, the advantages that accrue are worth it: deeper understanding and better decisions. We think that school boards will not be stripped of their powers but rather will be forced to exercise them more responsibly, carefully, and openly.

As school enrollments continue to decline or plateau, we think that local school government will be increasingly liberated from problems of *quantity* (the numbers of students, teachers, and buildings) to problems of *quality*. The shortages of buildings and teachers that occupied our attention during the previous decades are now behind us.

The problem of school desegregation will, we fear, remain unsolved for the immediate future and become even more distressing in many urban communities, as noted in Chapter 1. The future of urban education will remain depressing for some time to come. The problem has many interlocking facets: the underfinancing of city schools; family poverty and the disaffection of the urban poor among all races; and the alienation of urban students from school and society as manifested by dropout rates, absenteeism, vandalism, drug abuse, assaults on students and teachers, and crime. The intensity of these problems threatens the existence of some city schools. The rapid turnover of school superintendents and board members in cities is symptomatic of the real difficulties endemic to educational leadership in urban areas. There are some hopeful indicators, such as alternative schools, but we do not see any

disposition on the part of society to provide them in the quantity and quality commensurate with need.

We believe that the reorganization of school districts into larger and more effective units will continue at an accelerated pace. In times of rising costs and tight money, small districts become a luxury that we cannot afford. Permissive legislation will be replaced by mandatory legislation as states that have fallen behind in this movement struggle to catch up. We forecast a decline in the number of school districts from 16,000 in 1976 to 10,000 by 1986.

The outlook for nonpublic schools is not bright. The financial crisis of most of these schools is critical, and we will not find the constitutional means to make funds available for them. We see their numbers declining further and, eventually, the partial merger of many of them with public schools; religious instruction will be handled privately on a part-time and separate basis.

In sum, the problems of local school organization, governance, and administration will become increasingly complex and ambiguous. The transcending problems will be those of reallocating responsibilities more effectively among the three

A number of local, state, and federal agencies are intruding upon the powers of local school boards.

levels of government, finding new and viable ways of making local school governance more responsive to students and society, discovering means of revitalizing our urban schools, equalizing educational opportunity without the loss of local control, continuing to search for the golden mean between the protection of human rights and freedom while retaining enough administrative control to permit schools to survive, and reviving public confidence in local schools. Our short-term view is pessimistic, but our long-term view is cautiously optimistic.

Suggested activities

1. State the advantages and disadvantages of decentralizing administrative responsibility in school districts.
2. Prepare an essay on "The Unique Problems of Urban School Systems."
3. Visit a parochial school and describe the major differences between it and typical public schools.
4. Attend a school board meeting and prepare a critical analysis of it based upon the criteria of effectiveness discussed in this chapter.
5. Discuss the pros and cons of electing board members on partisan as opposed to nonpartisan tickets.
6. Differentiate between the proper functions of the school board and the school superintendent.
7. Interview a superintendent of schools to discover the major responsibilities and problems of this office.
8. Visit a county school office or intermediate unit office and report on its major services.

Bibliography

Campbell, Roald F., et al.: *The Organization and Control of American Schools*, 3d ed., Merrill, Columbus, Ohio, 1975, chaps. 4, 5, 6, 8, 9. Textbook treatment of local school districts, intermediate units, school attendance areas, school boards, and the superintendency.

Cistone, Peter J., (ed.): *Understanding School Boards*, Lexington Books, Lexington, Mass., 1975. Good explanation of the role and problems of local school boards.

Cronin, Joseph M.: *The Control of Urban Schools*, Free Press, New York, 1973. Analyzes the problems and prospects of urban school governance.

Hummel, Raymond C., and John M. Nagel: *Urban Education in America*, Oxford, New York, 1973. Discusses the students, people, milieu, economics, governance, and organization of urban schools, along with trends, probable outcomes, and needed reforms.

Iannaccone, Laurence, and Frank W. Lutz: *Politics, Power, and Policy: The Governing of Local School Districts*, Merrill, Columbus, Ohio, 1970. Case-description approach to the politics and governance of local school districts.

Kimbrough, Ralph B., and Michael Y. Nunnery: *Educational Administration*, Macmillan, New York, 1976, chaps. 9, 11, 12. Discussion of local school districts; impact of urbanization, technology, and interest groups.

Knezevich, Stephen J.: *Administration of Public Education*, 3d ed., Harper & Row, New York, 1975, chaps. 9, 10, 14, 15, 16. Discusses local school districts, intermediate units, school boards and other local educational agencies, the superintendency, and the school principalship.

Kraushaar, Otto F.: *American Nonpublic Schools: Patterns of Diversity*, Johns Hopkins, Baltimore, 1972. Describes nonpublic schools—their unique functions, programs, purposes, problems, and prospects.

La Noue, George, and Bruce L. R. Smith: *The Politics of School Decentralization*, Heath, Lexington, Mass., 1973. An account of how local school decentralization has affected education and agencies of municipal government.

Morphet, Edgar L., Roe L. Johns, and Theodore L. Reller: *Educational Administration and Organization*, 3d ed., Prentice-Hall, Englewood Cliffs, N.J., 1974, chaps. 7, 10, 11, 12, 13. Discusses the local environment of schools, local school districts, area service agencies, school boards, organization and administration of schools in metropolitan areas, and internal school organization and management.

National School Public Relations Association: *Citizens Advisory Committees*, Arlington, Va., 1973. Discusses current trends and policies regarding citizens' advisory committees—how they should be selected, how their roles should be defined, and how to avoid pitfalls.

Ornstein, Allan C.: *Race and Politics in School Community Organizations*, Goodyear, Pacific Palisades, Calif., 1974. Humorous but hard-hitting attack on the mythology of education for the poor, with attention to decentralization and community control, federal funding of antipoverty programs, compensatory programs, rise of white ethnocentricity, and affirmative action programs.

Rash, Julie, and Patricia M. Markun (eds.): *New Views of School and Community*, National Association of Elementary School Principals, Arlington, Va., 1973. Collection of essays dealing with interaction of schools and community, stressing the importance of making the schoolhouse an integral part of the community.

Saxe, Richard W.: *School-Community Interaction*, Mc-

Cutchan, Berkeley, Calif., 1975. Textbook approach to school-community relations, local district organization, pressure groups, power structure, decentralization and community control, and citizens' participation.

Zeigler, L. Harmon, M. Kent Jennings, and G. Wayne Peak: *Governing American Schools,* Duxbury, N. Scituate, Mass., 1974. Startling look at American school boards and who really runs our schools.

Chapter 13

State systems of education

YOU WILL HAVE MASTERED THIS CHAPTER WHEN YOU CAN

Define

● the states' authority over education

Describe

● various state government agencies with jurisdiction over education
● some common reforms in state government essential to the improvement of education
● the major hallmarks of effective state programs of education

Analyze

● the forces that are changing the future of state governance of education

Foundations of state educational systems

Most people tend to think of public schools as local enterprises. Although much of the operational responsibility for schools is delegated to local school districts, education in the United States is a legal function of the states, which have plenary power over public school systems. This is not the case in most other countries, where jurisdiction over schools tends to be centralized at the national level.

The Tenth Amendment to the Constitution of the United States specifies that "the powers not delegated to the United States by the Constitution, nor prohibited by it to the States, are reserved to the States respectively, or to the people." Since education is nowhere mentioned in the Constitution, it is reserved to the states. Let us reflect on how this came to pass.

THE DEVELOPMENT OF STATE CONTROL AND LEADERSHIP

The early colonists hewed the logs to build first their cabins, then their churches, and then their schools. The records of colonial legislatures, town meetings, and county courts contain frequent mention of education. As early as 1642, the Massachusetts General Court enacted a law requiring parents to provide education for children and levying fines for those who failed to do so. This was the first instance in which colonial public authority required compulsory education for children. The laws expressed the political aspiration that children be educated properly for the sake of the commonwealth. Apparently recognizing that this law could not be enforced unless there were schools for children to attend, the Massachusetts General Court five years later passed the famous act of 1647, requiring the towns to provide schools. This act established the principle that colonial government had the authority to control education. It was a principle of profound importance, for it set the precedent in this new society that later permitted the states to promote education as a public and civil enterprise. The Massachusetts example was followed in other New England colonies. There were four important principles in this pattern of development in New England: (1) the state could require children to be educated; (2) the state could require towns to establish schools; (3) the civil government could supervise and control schools by direct management of public officials; and (4) public funds could be used to support public schools.

Many schools of colonial America were essentially private in terms of both control and support, and many of the colonies lagged behind Massachusetts and other New England colonies in establishing civil authority over schools. Nevertheless, when the federal Constitution was drafted in 1787, the tradition of local and state control of schools was so well accepted that there was little disposition to make education a responsibility of the new federal government.

The first 100 years following 1779 witnessed the development of the great state school systems. This development was not easily achieved, because there were many who felt that education was properly a matter of local concern. Others felt that education should be left to the private domain. But under the vigorous leadership of Horace Mann, the first secretary of the Massachusetts State Board of Education; Henry Barnard, chairman of the State Board of Education in Connecticut; Calvin Wiley, the state superintendent of schools in North Carolina; and Samuel Lewis, the state superintendent of schools in Ohio, the struggle for state control of public education was gradually won. Thus the young republic forged what Horace Mann regarded as America's most revolutionary and significant contribution to civilization—its state-controlled public school systems.

EDUCATION PRIMARILY A STATE FUNCTION

Thus education has become a legal function of the states, and fifty different state school systems have emerged. All states make constitutional or statutory provision for the organization and coordination of educational efforts. The Constitution of Hawaii, which has a strong centralized state system, makes this stipulation:

The State shall provide for the establishment, support and control of a statewide system of public schools free from sectarian control, a state university, public libraries and such other educational institutions as may be deemed desirable, including physical facilities therefor. There shall be no segregation in public educational institutions because of race, religion or ancestry; nor shall public funds be appropriated for the support or benefit of any sectarian or private educational institution.

Of course, the federal government may "promote the general welfare" and may contract with the states. It may, indeed, establish and support schools or offer contributions in aid of education; but its legal status seems to be that of an outside party contracting with the state. The federal government has exercised indirect control over various aspects of education through the granting of funds and conditions for the use of funds. And, of course, the federal government exerts control through the decisions of the U.S. Supreme Court. The Elementary and Secondary Education Act of 1965 provides a significant illustration of the federal government's interest in strengthening state leadership in educational development. Under the provisions of this act, Congress appropriated money to be used for the improvement of the basic administration of state education agencies, for experimental projects and research in education carried on under state auspices, and for the strengthening of state departments of education.

Since education is a responsibility of the various states, its control is said to be decentralized. Obviously, the absence of a strong centralizing agency does not promote uniformity or equality among the states, and certainly not within the states. Although the power to enact laws may be centered in the state government, the administration of such laws may be decentralized in that they are enforced by scores of county and local superintendents and boards of education. Dissimilarity, a striking characteristic of state school systems, naturally produces marked inequalities, which are discussed in Chapters 1 and 11.

THE RELATION OF EDUCATION TO STATE GOVERNMENTS

It is difficult to generalize about the fifty state school systems because they vary so much in their organization and operation. Figure 13-1 portrays one model of a state system of organization for education, which is fairly typical for many states.

State legislatures. As indicated in Figure 13-1, state legislatures, which represent the people, enact broad educational policy through statutes. The legislature is the most important and influential agency for educational policy making in a state. It establishes the general organization for education, determines the scope of education, establishes the means for the financial support for schools, appropriates money for state aid to education, charters institutions of higher learning, and approves or denies plans to extend or alter the educational system in any major way. In a few states, the legislature may also appoint members to the state board of education. As the Supreme Court of Indiana observed,

The authority over schools and school affairs ... is a central power, residing in the legislature of the state. It is for the law-making power to determine whether the authority shall be exercised by a state board of education, or distributed to county, township, or city organizations throughout the state.

Thus the legislature is regarded as the ultimate source of authority over public education within the provisions of the state and federal constitutions. In recent years there has been a distinct trend in most states toward a sharp increase in legislative power over education through the enactment of more and more specific prescriptions for the educational program and the management of schools. Some state legislatures enact laws that prescribe certain curriculum content; some states have created state textbook authorities that approve or select textbooks for use in all state schools; some governors have insisted upon firing certain teachers in public institutions because they held unpopular beliefs; some states have mandated the reorganization of school districts; some exercise very close control over

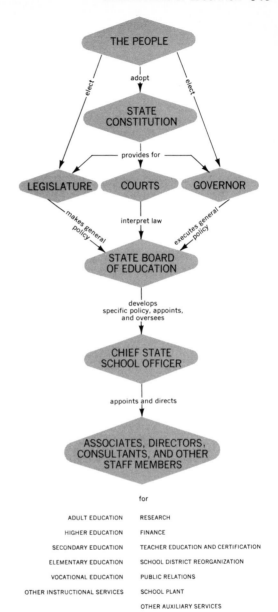

Figure 13-1 Organization of a typical state system of education.

budgets, tax rates, and debt limits in local school districts.

Are state governments preempting too much control over education from local districts? Since the states clearly have plenary legal power over education, the issue is more a matter of sound policy than of legal authority. The question is impossible to answer in the abstract. One must first ask: What decisions can be made more effectively and wisely at the state level than at the local level? What decisions are of such importance to the state that local determination cannot be tolerated? Should the state mandate only general educational goals, or specific goals as well? How much uniformity in educational policy and practice is desirable across a state? Are states justified in assuming a degree of control over local schools commensurate with the proportion of revenue for education which the states supply? For example, if the major portion of school revenue comes from state funds, are the states justified in limiting the levels of salaries that local boards of education negotiate with teachers, as some states have done? Generally speaking, the legislature should establish the general framework for the organization and governance of school systems and establish the general goals and policies that guide educational development. It should delegate to state and local boards of education the responsibility for setting more specific objectives, policies, and standards.

State governors. State governors are elected by the people and have important powers over education. They have authority, with their legislature's approval, to develop the state budget, which finances the work of the department of education as well as that of the other agencies of government. They exercise influence over legislation. A few governors serve as ex officio members of state boards and commissions that develop educational policies and programs. A few governors appoint the chief state school officer, and in most states they appoint members of the state board of education. Aside from formal powers, governors exercise considerable influence through their leadership of the body politic.

State judiciaries. State judiciaries have considerable influence over educational practice and policy. Courts are frequently called upon to protect the legal rights of individuals and organizations, to clarify the legal prerogatives of schools, and to interpret the law. The proper safeguard against unwise educational policy is at the polls. However, relief from illegal or unconstitutional educational practice is properly sought through the courts. It is commonly accepted in America that the law is what the courts say it is. Thus judicial decisions have the effect of law until the law in controversy is changed by the legislature. Many important decisions by state courts have greatly altered the course of education.

Most of the states' responsibility for the actual administration of public school systems rests with their state educational agencies, which consist of (1) the state board of education, which is the policy-making body; (2) the state superintendent of education, who is the chief executive of the board; and (3) the state department of education with its staff members, who carry out the policies of the board of education under the immediate direction of the superintendent. Together, these three forces are responsible for developing a state program of education. The relationships of these bodies are illustrated in Figure 13-1.

State boards of education

In order to develop a broad program of education, each state had to create an agency through which it could act. Just as a local community has a board of education to determine policies to be carried out by its chief executive officer, so too the state has a central body to plan for education.

THE EVOLUTION OF STATE BOARDS

The earliest foundation for a state school board was the Board of Regents for New York, organized in 1784. Other boards were started later in various states for special purposes. Not until Massachusetts established its State Board of Education in 1837 were many powers and duties assigned to any of them. From the perspective of nearly a century and a half, it is easy to see that the pioneering efforts of the inspired and indefatigable Horace Mann as secretary of the State Board of Education in Massachusetts rightfully earned him the title "father of public school education." Other leaders, such as Henry Barnard, DeWitt Clinton, Thaddeus Stevens, Caleb Mills, and John Swett, also helped to develop American public education through their harmonious and productive relationships with state agencies.

Only three states have a single board, such as the Board of Regents in New York, which has jurisdiction over all public education in the state —elementary and secondary schools, vocational and technical schools, community colleges, state colleges and universities. This structure strengthens cooperation and coordination throughout the educational enterprise, maximizes efficiency and economy by reducing duplication of effort and competition for resources, and permits comprehensive and balanced planning. A single comprehensive board might be disadvantaged by an inability to (1) cope with such breadth of responsibility, (2) relate effectively to the unique needs of many diverse educational institutions, and (3) avoid creating a huge bureaucracy that is unresponsive to needs.

Most states have one state board that is responsible for public elementary and secondary education, along with one or more boards that are responsible for higher education or vocational education or other components of the educational system. Some have separate boards for each institution of higher education. The advantages and disadvantages of the multiple-board structure are the reverse of the advantages and disadvantages of the single-board structure. We think the greater advantage generally lies with the single, comprehensive board, but special-interest groups tend to discourage movement in that direction.

The effectiveness of state educational agencies must be judged ultimately in terms of the quality of educational experience which the state provides for children and youth.

THE SELECTION AND QUALIFICATIONS OF STATE BOARD MEMBERS

Members of state boards of education are selected by the governor in approximately two-thirds of the states; they are elected by the people in approximately one-fourth of the states; and in the few remaining states they serve ex officio or are elected by the legislature or by local school boards.

Many authorities, including the National Council of Chief State School Officers, recommend that state school board members be elected by the people. However, Sroufe concludes from his study of state boards that the *mode* of selecting state board members is much less critical than the *criteria* by which they are selected. He contends that regardless of how they are selected, they should be political activists, able to represent particular segments of the population, and desirous of providing vigorous leadership for education.[1]

The question of professional qualifications of state board members is controversial. Some states insist that the board be composed entirely of lay people. A few states require that some of the members be educators. Although most states omit any specific reference to professional qualifications, approximately 40 percent of state board members are certified for work in the schools.

A qualifying clause in a few states where members are appointed is that "different parts of the state shall be represented." Wyoming adds the important general qualifications, which should be applied everywhere, that the members "shall be appointed solely because of their character and fitness. All members of the board shall be persons of mature years, known for integrity, culture, public spirit, business ability, and interest in public education." State board members tend to be predominantly white, male, older, middle-class, nonurban citizens. The National Council of Chief State School Officers recommends that "the non-partisan lay state board be composed of 7 to 12 able citizens, broadly representative of the general public and unselfishly interested in public education."

The size of state boards ranges from three to twenty-three members; the median size is nine.

Members' terms of office range from two to thirteen years, with six-year terms being most common.

IMPROVING THE EFFECTIVENESS OF STATE BOARDS

State boards of education vary widely in their effectiveness. Some appear to suffer from role ambiguity. Many state board members see their roles as exclusively involving policy making. They view themselves as above politics and in a collegial role with their state superintendents of education. Sroufe, on the other hand, believes that they should also be effective advocates of education and should be highly influential in state government. He concludes that most state board members are inexperienced politically, are uninvolved in the politics of education, have no clear channels for the exercise of legal authority, and have little influence or power over critical decisions in education, particularly financial decisions. He contends that state board members do not represent the public effectively and that the general public is not sufficiently aware of state boards of education and their role.

If the effectiveness of state boards is a function of political activity, it would follow that they could be strengthened by the selection of more persons who are experienced in state government.[2] Some believe that state board meetings are too infrequent and that the meetings are dominated by the state superintendent of education. Some authorities advocate that board members serve full-time, salaried positions.

State boards of education could profit from a careful examination that aims toward redirecting their role and function. The more important functions of the state boards should include:

- Appointing the chief state school officer and personnel of the state department of education
- Determining the areas of service of the state department of education
- Adopting policies and standards for the administration and supervision of the state's public school system
- Representing the state in the determination of policies

---

[1]Gerald E. Sroufe, "State School Board Members and Educational Policy," *Administrator's Notebook*, October 1970, p. 4.

[2]Ibid., p. 2.

on all matters pertaining to education that involve other state agencies and agencies of the federal government

- Conducting or authorizing studies to be conducted of means of improving the organization, administration, and operation of schools in the state and generating appropriate recommendations to the governor and legislature
- Adopting and administering a budget for the operation of public schools
- Keeping the public informed regarding the educational needs of the state

OTHER STATE BOARDS

Many states have established other boards or commissions with jurisdiction over special functions relating to education. We have mentioned the practice of having special boards to oversee higher education and vocational and technical education. Some states have separate textbook commissions that select or approve textbooks for use in schools. Most states have special retirement boards that supervise retirement programs for teachers and other public employees in the state. Some states have special boards that oversee collective bargaining as it relates to teachers or other public employees. A number of states have human relations commissions that serve as watchdogs in protecting human rights, fair employment, and equal employment opportunities prescribed by law. The list could go on and on.[3]

Chief state school officers

All states provide for a chief state school officer known variously as the "commissioner of education," "state superintendent of education," "state superintendent of public instruction," or "secretary of education." This official is usually the executive officer of the state board of education and head of the state department of education. He or she should be the most important educational leader in the state, although this is not true in all states.

Sometimes the salary is too low to attract highly competent persons. In some instances there are no professional qualifications for the position. And in some states the relationship of the chief state school officer with the state board of education is ambiguous.

THE EVOLUTION OF THE OFFICE

In 1812 New York became the first state to establish the position of chief state school officer. The Massachusetts State Board of Education in 1837 engaged the energetic Horace Mann as its secretary of education. Mann became an early exemplar of distinguished leadership in this position and perhaps more than any other person demonstrated the great potential of this office in advancing the cause of education. By 1913 all states had provided for this position.

In many states the potential of this position was slow to develop. The functions of the office were restricted largely to ministerial and regulatory duties. As the role of the state increased in importance, the responsibilities and influence of the chief state school officer did likewise. The Council of Chief State School Officers welded these officials into a national association, providing the leadership and understanding essential to the professionalization of this office.[4]

THE SELECTION OF CHIEF STATE SCHOOL OFFICERS

The chief educational officer of the state is appointed by the state board in twenty-six states, elected by popular vote in nineteen states, and appointed by the governor in five states. Each method has its advocates and advantages and disadvantages, although the strong trend in recent years has been toward appointment by the state board. This method permits the board to select an administrator whose style, values, and capabilities are most compatible with the board's expectations. This tends to reinforce a smooth working relationship between the board and its executive officer. It may also reduce the influence of spurious

---

[3]For a discussion of improvements needed in state departments of education, see Michael J. Bakalis, "The Curious Consistency of State Education Agencies," *Compact,* November/December 1974, pp. 2–4.

[4]For an analysis of recent trends in this office, see "The New Breed of Chief State School Officer," *Compact,* June 1975, pp. 9–12.

considerations such as political affiliations, willingness to campaign for the office, or patronage by gubernatorial appointment.

Election by the people, though expensive and time consuming, does give the chief state school officer a constituency as well as a sense of the people's will. Wilson Riles, a state superintendent of public instruction elected by the people in California, argues for this method. He says, "When I talk to the governor, it's as a peer. I got 54 percent of the vote, just as he did, and he understands that. . . . And when I'm talking to legislators or appearing before legislative committees, they understand where I'm coming from." Riles believes that the election should be on a nonpartisan yet political basis; as he reasons, the chief state school officer must be a political activist in order to influence the course of education through state government. However, election by the people, particularly in partisan elections, may not attract the most able candidates, who may be unwilling to undergo the rigors of campaigning for office. Riles, who appears as the speaker in the picture at the beginning of this chapter, exemplifies a brilliant and effective chief state school officer.

Appointment by the governor also serves to strengthen the relationship between the governor and the state department of education and to provide better coordination of educational interests with the broader realm of state government. On the other hand, this arrangement may weaken the stance of the state board and introduce partisan political interests in educational matters. Effective and ineffective chief state school officers have come into office through each of these methods, and more critical considerations may be the criteria for selection by any method and the qualifications of office.

QUALIFICATIONS AND TERM OF OFFICE

The school laws of Maryland indicate the general tenor of requirements for chief state school officers. The laws require that the state superintendent "shall be an experienced and competent educator; a graduate of a standard college, have not less than two years of specific academic and professional graduate preparation in a standard university, and not less than seven years' experience in teaching and administration." Most legal definitions of qualifications are general, and rightly

so; however, they should be specific enough to provide a pattern by which the electors, or the group or person selecting the superintendent, may be guided in the quest for the most competent person. Usually a master's degree is the minimum and a doctorate the optimum academic preparation. Some states permit the selection of a lay person to this professional office, usually with results that are not exemplary. The median legal term of office for the superintendent or commissioner is between three and four years. Tenure is longer when he or she is appointed by the state board than when elected or appointed gubernatorially. Sound educational administration suggests that the term of office be many years, subject to the best judgment of the state board, in order to ensure continuity in policy and staff personnel. Furthermore, the salary must be commensurate with the importance and labors of the office. Some cities pay their local superintendents more than the state gives its chief educational official. Naturally this does not draw the best talent into the state office.

DUTIES OF CHIEF STATE SCHOOL OFFICERS

Most duties of state superintendents and their staffs fall into a few major categories:

Leadership
   Drawing public attention to the state's educational needs and encouraging public action
Trusteeship
   Reporting to the public on educational accomplishments; compiling data on school enrollments, expenditures, school construction, measures of academic progress, and so forth
Advisory
   Giving counsel to local boards of education and administrators; interpreting school law to administrative officials; offering testimony on proposed legislation and regulations to state legislatures and other governmental bodies
Planning
   Preparing required state plans for federally financed programs, such as vocational education, and planning intrastate programs
Experimenting
   Innovating and implementing various pilot projects
Judicial
   Resolving controversies within local school systems; hearing appeals in much the same manner as an appellate court

Ministerial

Regulating public and private elementary schools, secondary schools, colleges, and universities; distributing state and some federal moneys; certifying teachers; approving school buildings; managing such diverse enterprises as museums, libraries, and historical sites

Coordinating

Attending meetings of various state boards and coalescing the various state educational efforts

Appointive

Filling vacancies in the state department of education, in county superintendencies, and in other positions

Evaluating

Participating in state and national assessment programs

RELATIONSHIP WITH STATE GOVERNMENT

As noted earlier, the chief state school officer typically serves as the professional head of the state department of education. In some states, as the executive officer of the state board of education, he or she serves also as the chairperson or secretary of the board. In a few states, the chief state school officer is the chief administrator for all state educational enterprises and a member of the governor's cabinet. This highly centralized and powerful arrangement permits the administrator to have access to the political power of the governor's office and facilitates better coordination and efficiency among various state educational enterprises. Arguments against this arrangement are that the state secretary of education then lacks an independent power base, the secretary's relationship with the state board is weakened, education becomes too highly politicized, and there is danger of a top-heavy centralization of power that may result in the weakening of representative decision-making processes.

State departments of education

THE EVOLUTION OF STATE DEPARTMENTS

When Gideon Hawley was the state superintendent of schools in New York and Horace Mann was the secretary of the State Board of Education in Massachusetts, each was the only member of his state's department of education. But as the concept of the states' function in education broad-

ened, no single official, even in a small commonwealth, could handle all the work; gradually there was an increase in staff personnel.

After 1917 rapid growth in department personnel resulted from four major causes: the new duties devolving upon the department as a result of the passage of the Smith-Hughes vocational education law; the startling revelations from physical, mental, and literacy tests administered during World War I; the growing appreciation of the need for a strong state program of education to meet present-day needs; and the task of administering the greatly expanded programs in education supported by federal funds, many of which are administered through state departments of education.

The Elementary and Secondary Education Act of 1965 helped to double state education agency budgets between 1965 and 1970 by adding funds intended to increase the planning capability of state departments and help them rethink priorities. The states profited from these funds in several ways. New Jersey, for example, established a statewide program of needs assessment and testing. Oregon developed a management information system to help local school administrators. Rhode Island established a teacher center to accelerate the dissemination of exemplary teaching practices.

State departments still vary widely in their effectiveness. The more effective ones have focused on long-range educational planning, accountability systems, and leadership in the improvement of educational practice. Today more than 30,000 persons are employed in the fifty state departments of education.

THE ORGANIZATION OF STATE DEPARTMENTS

At the head of the state department is the state superintendent or commissioner of education. Next in line are the assistant or associate superintendents or commissioners, other assistants, supervisors, and staff members.

Figure 13-1 shows the organization of a typical state system of education, the divisions of the state department, and the relationships between the state department, superintendent, state board, governor, legislature, and courts.

The personnel of the department should be

employed by the state board of education upon nomination by the chief state school officer. All appointments should be made on the basis of merit and fitness for the work. The state department should be adequately staffed to provide all needed services.

FUNCTIONS OF STATE DEPARTMENTS

The many specific functions of state departments of education are commonly classified into four general categories:

1. Regulatory

These embrace the so-called "police powers" of the state—developing minimum standards, rules, and regulations; observing and inspecting practices to identify cases of noncompliance; and instigating, where necessary, procedures to enforce compliance.

2. Operational

These include enterprises actually administered by the state, such as the operation of schools for the blind, the licensing of teachers, and the maintenance of state educational television networks, among others.

3. Financial

These include program budgeting, educational and fiscal auditing, authorizing funds for state and federal-state approved projects, plus recommending appropriate sources of revenue for education in state and local units of administration.

4. Leadership

These include the determination of educational purposes and goals for the state; planning, research, and development activities; coordination of various state educational programs; evaluation of the state system of education; and public relations activities.

The trend in recent years in the more effective state departments is to place greater emphasis upon leadership functions.

State educational programs

Each state is faced with the direct responsibility of organizing an effective system of public education that should extend from kindergarten through college and adult life. In developing this program,

certain elements seem essential, as described below.

EFFECTIVE EDUCATIONAL POLICY MAKING

State school systems can be no better than the policies that govern their operation. As pointed out earlier, general educational policies should be enacted by the legislature, and more specific and comprehensive policies should be established by the state board of education. In some states, legislatures cannot resist dealing with specific educational policies, often bypassing their own state boards of education. Legislators have neither the time nor the knowledge needed for detailed policy making. They are often subject to the pressures of special-interest groups that lobby for preferential treatment. This can result in policies that are not in the best interests of the total society. Moreover, when detailed educational policy exists in statute form, it is too difficult and time-consuming to amend it to satisfy changing circumstances. Yet many state legislatures preempt the legitimate prerogatives of state boards of education and chief state school officers, with the result that political considerations overrun educational considerations in policy making.

THE DEVELOPMENT OF EDUCATIONAL GOALS

Every state is engaged in some sort of needs assessment, which is necessary to qualify for federal funds available through the Elementary and Secondary Education Act of 1965. This determination of the state's educational needs is often accomplished through wide participation of both citizens and educators, and in some instances by students as well. It is an essential prerequisite to the delineation of educational goals. The central question in most matters of educational program and policy making is: Education for what? Until educational goals and priorities are set, much of the debate over programs, policies, and expenditures is meaningless. Goal definition is essential also for accountability and evaluation systems. Educators must know for what they are held accountable, and evaluation hinges on some criterion for judging what is good or bad. For example, the Pennsylvania State Board of Education was directed by the state legislature to develop procedures and standards for measuring educational quality in the schools of the commonwealth. The board took the sound position that evaluation of schools could not be undertaken confidently until the purposes of education had been made explicit. Thus steps were taken to involve a large number of educators and lay people in the development of a statement of educational goals as a basis for evaluation.

ESTABLISHING ASSESSMENT AND ACCOUNTABILITY SYSTEMS

As both the cost and criticism of schools have risen, the public has demanded that school systems be held more accountable for their results. Within a few years every state has initiated or plans to initiate statewide assessment systems for their schools. The states have various expectations of this assessment: measurement of educational progress, identification and remediation of weak areas, redirection of educational expenditures into more productive programs, improved education for disadvantaged children or children in poor school districts, and the provision of information necessary for planning at both state and local levels.

Assessment, once limited to testing in the three R's, has been expanded to cover more of the curriculum and to include measurement of attitudes, tastes, feelings, and values.

Accountability systems, although defensible in principle, pose a number of feasibility problems: the crash basis upon which many of them are implemented with insufficient testing of the instruments; enormous costs; technical problems including the reliability, validity, and cultural bias of tests; and the possibility of misusing results, such as rewarding or punishing teachers or school districts for results not entirely under their control. Some would add to this list the grave probability of increased state control over schools. These issues and problems are discussed at greater length in Chapter 1. Many teachers' associations are vigorously opposed to state accountability systems, some of which are too primitive to inspire much confidence.[5]

[5]For a brief review of state assessment and accountability systems, see Jane Earle, "The Compulsion to Know," *Compact,* May–June 1973, pp. 48–49 and John W. Porter, "The Virtues of a State Assessment Program," *Phi Delta Kappan,* June 1976, pp. 667–668.

HARMONIZING VARIOUS INTEREST GROUPS

In every state there are many groups vitally interested in schools. There are associations of teachers, school board members, administrators, parents, taxpayers, and many others. Frequently there is disagreement among these groups, and often within a particular group, on educational policies. Teachers' associations, school board associations, and administrators' associations are commonly in disagreement. This internecine conflict within the education profession permits legislators to "divide and conquer," playing off one lobby against another and thereby stalemating policy making that could improve education.

In some states these groups have developed extralegal coalitions to harmonize their interests as much as possible. Since these groups exist in most of the states that have made the greatest progress in education, many observers believe that they play a vital role in developing state educational policy. In any case, there should be machinery for integrating the many diverse interests in education so that all may have a voice in educational policy making and have an opportunity to reach the greatest possible accord on important issues.

EDUCATIONAL RESEARCH AND DEVELOPMENT

Goal setting and program development have been handicapped in many states by the paucity of data relevant to the problem at hand. Necessary information is often lacking, without which good decisions are seldom reached. Although most state departments have had for years a director of research, this office has traditionally been preoccupied with the gathering of the most rudimentary kind of data on enrollment, attendance, and costs. Sophisticated studies of important and complex problems—such as what practices are most successful in reducing dropouts or what kind of vocational education is needed for out-of-school youths—were often neglected. The increase of federal funds under the Elementary and Secondary Education Act for the strengthening of state departments of education has enabled most states to expand their research and fact-finding facilities. Some states have accelerated educational development by requiring local districts as well as the state educational agency to undertake long-range planning.

HIGH-QUALITY PROFESSIONAL LEADERSHIP

The better state school systems—such as New York, California, and Maryland, among others— tend to be those with fine leadership exercised by state superintendents, state boards, and governors, probably in that order of importance. This leadership is essential to assess the state's educational needs, to evaluate educational progress, to establish priorities, and to interpret these needs and priorities to the people and the legislature. Educational leadership is also essential in planning the policies, revenue programs, curriculums, and legislation necessary to accomplish the goals. A high order of diplomacy is also needed to coordinate the educational activities of a growing array of educational institutions and other agencies from early-childhood education through universities.

Strong leadership is critical in harmonizing relationships among local, state, and federal agencies that impact upon the schools.

SOUND FINANCIAL SUPPORT

A state educational system can be no better than its financial support. Figure 13-2 reveals that the percentage of revenue for public elementary and secondary schools from state sources ranges from a low of 7 percent in New Hampshire to a high of 89 percent in Hawaii. The clear trend in most states has been toward an increase in the state's share of school financing, and many authorities advocate full state funding of public elementary and secondary schools. Nevertheless, few states have attained a desirable level of financial support for their schools. The New Jersey Supreme Court in 1973 struck down that state's school finance system on the grounds that it failed to satisfy a constitutional mandate in New Jersey that guarantees a

Figure 13-2 Percent of revenue for public elementary and secondary schools from state governments.

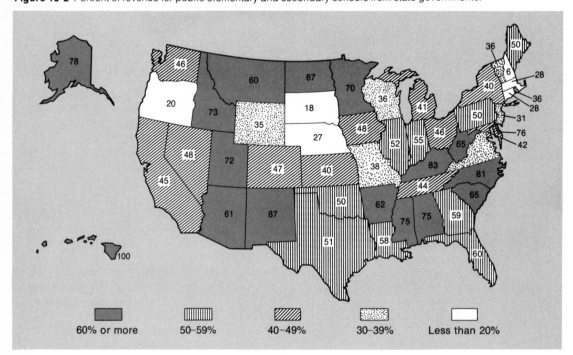

"thorough and efficient" education to every pupil in the state.

Many states have sought to equalize educational opportunity among school districts within their borders through equalization plans described in Chapter 11. However, great inequalities still remain and generate lawsuits in some states. In 1971 the California Supreme Court electrified the public by ruling that school funding in that state violated the equal rights provisions of that state because of the manner in which money was distributed to the districts. These cases triggered vigorous study of inequities in state financing programs, and reform is underway in some states. But reform is slow, and much progress remains to be accomplished.

Thus two prime criteria are critical in measuring the soundness of state school financing: (1) sufficient support to provide a thorough and efficient education for all and (2) the distribution of monies in a manner that wipes out inequality among districts.

COORDINATED RELATIONS WITH THE FEDERAL GOVERNMENT AND LOCAL DISTRICTS

With the growth of federal participation in the financial support of education, the state educational agency has become an increasingly important intermediary between the federal government and local school systems. Working relations exist between the state and federal levels of government that were unheard of a few years ago.

One by-product of federal-state cooperation is reported by the Advisory Council on State Departments of Education, which found "marked progress by state education agencies in strengthening their leadership roles, largely attributable to federal funds granted under Title V of the Elementary and Secondary Education Act."

The relationship between state and local school administrators is also becoming more difficult and complex. Many examples of strained relations at all levels of government are evident, as is natural perhaps with the growing interdependence at all levels. It is clear that the future demands even greater coordination of local-state-federal rela-

tions in education, as well as the best leadership that can be mustered.

The Education Commission of the States

In 1966 a national coalition of state governors, legislators, chief state school officers, and other educators and lay people was formed to coordinate and guide state goal setting, planning, and policy making in education. This coalition, the Education Commission of the States, was suggested by James Conant and was spearheaded by former Governor of North Carolina Terry Sanford, a vigorous advocate of strong state leadership in education.

The Education Commission of the States now brings together educational leaders who represent the forty-five member states. It plays a vital role in the exchange of educational thought through its meetings and its publication, *Compact*. Sanford phrased the mission of ECS in these words:

The key is to make "state initiative" our constant keynote. States must make the choice right now to assume their rightful responsibility. If they hesitate, there may be no choice. We know we must replace local sources as our primary funders of education, and the federal government, as always, is standing ready to contend state neglect and move in and take over this vital function. It is absolutely fundamental that we avoid federal predominance in public education. And the only way we can do that is for states to seize the initiative, now. That is the chief reason there is an Education Commission of the States.[6]

The future

The states' role in education has always been important and will become increasingly so as the influence over education continues its inevitable

---

[6]Terry Sanford, "State Initiative and Education," Education Commission of the States, *Compact*, August 1972, p. 19.

shift from local to state levels of government. This shift is accelerated by local districts' increasing difficulty in coping with such problems as school desegregation, aggressive bargaining by teachers, the estrangement of citizens from local decision making, and the burden of meeting the rising costs of education from limited local tax sources. Most states will continue to assume an ever-increasing share of the costs of education, which will encourage more educational decision making and planning in state capitals. During the 1970s the influence of the federal government on education declined, resulting in further concentration of power at the state level. Also, once-powerful coalitions of state educational associations, such as the Educational Conference Board in New York, have been weakened or dissolved by the growing polarization among their constituent bodies of school boards, administrators, and teachers. This creates a vacuum of leadership that attracts the state boards of education, chief state school officers, governors, and legislatures.

Then, too, as our nation enters its third century, education itself has taken on increased importance in human affairs. In many states education committees of the legislature have been elevated in prestige to a position second only to finance committees. In many states as much as half the major legislation enacted in recent years relates to education. Educational issues are increasingly critical in state political campaigns.

In many states fierce competition rather than cooperation exists among the governor, legislature, state board, state department, and chief state school officer in matters of education. In New York, for example, former Governor Rockefeller deplored the fact that so much power over education was vested in the state Board of Regents and the Commissioner of Education, while the legislature was expanding its appropriations to schools to meet the sharply increasing costs of education. The Governor felt that policy making and fiscal responsibility should be located more congruently, and he called for more power over education in the legislature and in his office. He recommended the appointment of an inspector general to serve as a watchdog over the state board and state department of education. This set off a bruising conflict between the Governor and the Board of Regents. The latter warned of the dangers of politicizing the $5 billion-a-year educational enterprise in New York if the powers of the state board were shifted to the governor and legislature.

We urgently need revitalization in state government if it is to capture the initiative in educational development adequate for these times. Viable relationships among the governor, the legislature, the state board, the chief state school officer, and the state department are needed in every state. Otherwise vital energies will be spent in in-fighting, rather than in leadership. Reform and invigoration of all these agencies is critical and long overdue in most states. In recent years state education authorities have been preoccupied largely with the day-to-day crises of trying to keep up with skyrocketing school enrollments. But if the birthrate remains stable, it would seem that the worst of these growth problems may be over, and state leadership may now address itself to more long-range priorities and to problems of improvement rather than growth.

Most authorities agree that our greatest educational problem in the remainder of this century will be the task of financing schools properly in order to make them a vital force in our nation's social, economic, and political renewal. Demands for full state funding of schools will require additional state taxation, which is always unpopular. The public is demanding, with increased intensity, evidence of a fair return for increased school expenditures. Legislatures have expressed these intentions in cost-benefit measures, which they are applying more rigorously to school operations. Many educators fear that this will increase state control over schools. Others regard legislatures' concern for productivity as a necessary and prudent consideration. The dilemma then becomes one of maximizing state responsibility for adequate financing of education while retaining sufficient local initiative and control of schools to make them responsive to the communities they serve.

As noted earlier, the states also face the challenge of repairing inequities in the distribution of funds so that students in poor communities, whose educational needs are typically greatest, are not further disadvantaged by receiving less state financial support than students in well-to do communities. Tax reform is also essential in virtually all states if the burden of supporting schools is to be distributed equitably among citizens according to their ability to pay. These issues are discussed in more detail in Chapter 11.

The public's concern that the quality of education keep pace with rising costs will continue to be met through state-mandated accountability systems. These systems require the linkage of rigorous measures of educational progress with distribution patterns of state aid so that resources become incentive for school improvement. These accountability systems will continue to create great controversy between professional educators and lay people, particularly as the former resist constraints on resource allocations while the latter insist that quality accompany increased expenditures. Although present accountability systems are still rather primitive, we expect to see rapid refinement of this essential technology in years ahead.

School desegregation will continue to be an explosive problem in many sectors of the land. No fundamental solution will be found without more aggressive state leadership in reorganizing metropolitan school districts to break down the concentration of minority groups that are surrounded by predominantly white suburbs. New York State's Fleischmann Commission, established to point the way for educational development in that state in the future, reported in 1973:

Our schools exist in an atmosphere of racial and ethnic isolation, imbalance and strife. It is our view that these barriers to social cohesion are becoming steadily higher. . . . We favor racial integration not only because it makes for better education but also because it helps students come to grips with the world in which they will live as adults.

The commission cited this problem as a major fear and one of the most compelling challenges to state education authorities. It is imperative for state leaders in years ahead to face courageously all the problems of urbanization that impinge upon city schools, which are usually large and unwieldy, underfinanced, and socially isolated.

Another major concern in years ahead will be better education for all kinds of handicapped

A major concern will be better education for all handicapped children and youths, whether their disabilities be mental, physical, social, emotional, or economic.

children and youths, whether their disabilities be mental, physical, social, emotional, or economic. Not infrequently state courts have recently held that their rights to educational opportunity are undiminished by their handicaps. As a result of this judicial prodding, most states will move rapidly to provide massive reforms for these students, reforms that are usually beyond the reach of local districts.

As noted earlier in this chapter, much remains to be accomplished in the extension and better coordination of educational services from early-childhood education through university and adult education. Early-childhood education, although critically important, is seriously neglected in most states. Higher education, on the other hand, is overdeveloped in some states, where too many institutions compete for scarce resources, resulting in redundant and overlapping services that generate inefficiency and waste. The several boards of higher education that exist in many states should be replaced by a single board, which could coordinate the efforts of these institutions and reduce unnecessary duplication of effort. State government must be revitalized to permit the orderly development of a lifelong continuum of education, rather than the piecemeal and unarticulated education segments that have developed in most states.

The general reorganization of small school districts into larger and more efficient administrative units is still overdue in many states. Some authorities estimate that we have approximately three times as many school districts in the nation as we should have. But small districts have a history of resisting reorganization; it can be brought about only through vigorous leadership at the state level.

While not disparaging the importance of the federal or local levels of government as forces in educational progress, we nevertheless believe that the state level of government is the most critical for reaching our educational goals. That is where the great bulk of legal authority rests. That is where most future school revenues will be generated. That is where the great social, political, and economic forces impact upon education most seriously. There are signs that a number of states are beginning to respond to these challenges, but progress is often tragically slow. The stakes are high, and the hour is late.

Suggested activities

1. Prepare a biography of Horace Mann emphasizing his pioneering work as the first chief state school officer in Massachusetts.
2. From the many principles of organization and operation of state educational agencies suggested in this chapter, evaluate your own state's governance of education and the quality of its educational program.
3. Draw an organizational chart for your state, showing the relationships among the governor, legislature, chief state school officer, state boards of education, state department of education, state courts, and other important bodies having jurisdiction over education.

4. Prepare a report on some of the more important decisions of courts in your state relating to education.
5. From the last annual report of your state superintendent, list the most critical problems your state faces in education.
6. Review the historical development of education in your state.

Bibliography

Campbell, Roald F., et al.: *The Organization and Control of American Schools,* 3d ed., Merrill, Columbus, Ohio, 1975, chap. 3. Historical development, emerging role, current organizational arrangements, and principles of state government of education.

————, and Tim L. Mazzoni, Jr.: *State Policy Making for the Public Schools,* McCutchan, Berkeley, Calif., 1976, chaps. 2, 3, 4, 6. Policy making at the state level as influenced by state boards, state superintendents, governors, and legislatures.

Harris, Sam P.: *State Departments of Education, State Boards of Education, and Chief State School Officers,* HEW publication OE 73-07400, U.S. Government Printing Office, 1973. Descriptive data from each of the fifty states relative to state educational agencies.

Johns, Roe L., and Edgar Morphet: *The Economics and Financing of Education,* 3d ed., Prentice-Hall, Englewood Cliffs, N.J., 1975, chap. 8. Theories of state financial support of education, evaluation of present state finance programs, and problems and issues.

Kimbrough, Ralph B., and Michael Y. Nunnery: *Educational Administration,* Macmillan, New York, 1976, chap. 8. Discussion of state agencies and their influence upon schools—courts, governors, legislatures, state boards and departments of education.

Kirst, Michael W. (ed): *The Politics of Education at the Local, State, and Federal Levels,* McCutchan, Berkeley, Calif., 1970, part 2. Discusses the politics of educational governance at the state level.

Knezevich, Stephen J.: *Administration of Public Education,* 3d ed., Harper & Row, New York, 1975, chap. 11. Analyzes the functions and problems of state legislatures, state boards, chief state school officers, and state departments with respect to governance of schools.

Morphet, Edgar L., Roe L. Johns, and Theodore L. Reller: *Educational Organization and Administration,* 3d ed., Prentice-Hall, Englewood Cliffs, N.J., 1974, chap. 9. Evolution, legal provisions, structures, and responsibilities relative to state educational agencies.

Murphy, Jerome T.: *Grease the Squeaky Wheel,* Center

for Educational Policy Research, Harvard University, Cambridge, Mass., 1973. Report of a study of nine state educational agencies, documenting their weaknesses and their progress.

Stoops, Emery, Max Rafferty, and **Russell E. Johnson:** *Handbook of Educational Administration,* Allyn and Bacon, Boston, 1975, chap. 3. Structures, functions, problems, and trends in state educational agencies.

Chapter 14
National program of education

Foundations of the national educational enterprise

"The whole people," according to John Adams, "must take upon themselves the education of the whole people and must be willing to bear the expense of it." This was radical doctrine in Adams' time because there was not then any precedent in any other nation for this ambitious aspiration of educating all the people. The development of our universal, free, compulsory educational system is one of the most significant chronicles in our history. It accounts for much of the remarkable growth and prosperity of our country.

Despite the firm commitment of our founding fathers to universal education, there is no reference to education in the United States Constitution. This was not an oversight. Many of the colonists had come to the New World to escape the tyranny of autocratic central governments abroad, and they were not about to risk having the control of something as important as education in the hands of the federal government. Even today this fear of control of education by Washington remains quite strong.

Although the Constitution left control of education to the states, the federal government has participated in the support and development of education throughout our history under the authorization of the clause of the Constitution that deals with the promotion of the general welfare. From that time forward, as revealed by the historical calendar in this chapter, federal participation has significantly shaped the destiny of our educational system.

An important distinction must be made between the terms "national" and "federal," which are often confused in common lexicon. Throughout this discussion, we shall use the term "federal" when speaking of the role of the federal government in education and the word "national" to describe the total educational enterprise in the country—federal, state, and local public and private school and non-school agencies.

Our system of free, universal schools is one of the unique and significant characteristics of our society. It is unique because free public education for all is a bold and visionary ideal without precedent in human history. It is significant because the story of our national strength and prosperity is, in large measure, the story of our schools. Truly the development of our educational system is one of the noblest and most distinguishing expressions of American civilization.

Americans have always had great faith in the power of education. Alexis de Tocqueville, the brilliant French scholar who visited the young republic shortly after its founding, observed that "the universal and sincere faith that they profess here in the efficaciousness of education seems to me to be one of the most remarkable features of America."

In this chapter we shall examine the relationship between each of the branches of federal government and the evolution of our unique educational system. We will describe several important private enterprises in education that are national in scope. We then will review some principles and proposals that have been advanced to improve our national effort in education. Finally, we will have something to say about its future.

Education and the executive branch

The great educational reformer Henry Barnard went to Washington in 1838 in search of facts about the nation's schools. When he found none, he undertook the task of establishing a federal educational agency. Over the next thirty years he was joined in this effort by many educators and organizations that recognized the need for a federal office of education. This eventually was established in 1867 as the forerunner of the present U.S. Office of Education.

THE DEPARTMENT OF HEALTH, EDUCATION, AND WELFARE (HEW)

In 1953 the Office of Education became a component of the newly created Department of Health, Education, and Welfare, which has a secretary in the President's Cabinet. In 1972 there was created in the Department a new Division of Education, consisting of the Office of Education and the newly created National Institute of Education as separate, coequal units. An Assistant Secretary of Education presides over the Division of Education. In 1976 the Senate proposed the elimination of this post and elevation of the U.S. Commissioner of Education's position.

The U.S. Office of Education (USOE). It was fitting that Henry Barnard, the crusader for a federal education agency, should become the first U.S. Commissioner of Education, the chief executive position in the Office. Many distinguished educators have held the position. The Commissioner is appointed by the President with the consent of the Senate and serves an indefinite term.

One major function of the Office of Education is to administer federal legislation and the flow of funds that accompanies many acts of Congress. The Office was greatly expanded in size in the 1960s and early 1970s to keep abreast of the sharp rise in federal funding of education.

Until the mid-1970s, the Office of Education served as the chief bookkeeper of the nation's educational effort, collecting, interpreting, and disseminating a mass of statistical data on schools. However, this function was transferred to the National Center for Educational Statistics, another component of HEW.

The Office of Education renders a wide variety of services to local, state, and international agencies. It conducts surveys and offers consultative help to local and state school systems; it calls conferences on various educational problems; it provides technical training for foreign educators in America and helps to provide educational specialists for service abroad; it provides an information center and library on all aspects of American education; and it conducts an extensive publications service through the Superintendent of Documents of the Government Printing Office. Its best-known publication is the widely read journal *American Education*.

Until recently the Office of Education conducted a number of research studies and administered federal grants for research in education and disseminated the results of these studies. However, this function has been transferred to the National Institute of Education.

The future of the U.S. Office of Education is ambiguous, to say the least. Here is an executive agency that grew rapidly during the halcyon days of the Great Society, when it was called upon to administer a vast array of federally funded projects funded at billions of dollars. It had to develop guidelines and regulations to administer the laws passed by Congress and to interpret the intent of Congress, which is often ambiguous. Almost any interpretation or guideline—particularly in the sensitive area of school desegregation—was certain to discomfort some legislators, citizens, and educators.[1] Then too, both Congress and citizens are more quixotic than patient about the federal effort in education. They commonly expect instant cures for the ills of education. But these ills do not emerge overnight, and neither will their cures.

Sometimes the Office of Education has had difficulty monitoring the enormous volume of legislation and the hundreds of programs and activities that the legislation generated. If the Office established controls over funding, many viewed the action as bureaucratic red tape. If it did not, the likelihood increased that funds would be misused. Sometimes problems have arisen from the spasmodic nature of the legislation, which funded activities over periods of time too short to produce lasting results. Often the targets of the legislation were narrowly conceived and funded inadequately. Moreover, the evaluation process in education is extremely difficult, and Congress grew impatient over the lack of hard evidence of educational progress. Sometimes the fault lay with the changing expectations and fleeting support of the White House. Then, too, some local and state educational agencies failed to cooperate with federal agencies and in some cases even misused federal funds.

With all these difficulties it is small wonder that

hard evidence of accomplishment was hard to come by. Without it, confidence waned in the Office of Education and in many federally funded programs. Sharp political differences arose over such issues as busing to relieve school desegregation, the enforcement of federal guidelines on school desegregation and affirmative action, the decentralization of the Office of Education through a number of regional offices, and the impoundment by President Nixon of funds appropriated by Congress, among others. Disenchantment with the Office of Education arose. Many people in Washington and elsewhere argued that federal funding might be better directed toward educational research and development and toward revenue sharing, rather than toward massive federal support of operating programs. To many observers, the National Institute of Education was created to by-pass the Office of Education, which symbolized so much of the frustration that had arisen.

The National Institute of Education (NIE). If the Office of Education had difficulties in fulfilling its mission, the National Institute of Education was soon even more beleaguered. Launched in 1972 with grandiose expectations in the Department of Health, Education, and Welfare, NIE has its own director, who is a presidential appointee working under the guidance of the National Council on Educational Research. NIE was expected to do for education what the National Institute of Health has done for health and what the National Aeronautics and Space Administration has done for space exploration. It was to bring together in a national center the efforts of some of the nation's most distinguished educational researchers from many academic disciplines for a fundamental attack on the problems of learning and instruction at all levels of schooling. NIE was hailed at the outset as "the most important addition to the federal government's education efforts of this century." Its mission included:

1. Providing technical resources to help teachers, administrators, and policy makers to interpret and apply research
2. Strengthening instruction in basic skills
3. Developing exemplary local educational practices, such as voucher plans
4. Sustaining various enterprises inherited from USOE,

---

[1] For further discussion of the causes and problems of federal regulations, see Samuel Halperin, "Federal Takeover, State Default, or a Family Problem?" *Phi Delta Kappan*, June 1976, pp. 696–697.

such as the regional laboratories and the research and development centers

5. Assisting state and local educational agencies in providing technical assistance, training, and demonstration in implementing promising educational programs

6. Improving the Educational Resources Information Center (ERIC), a national clearinghouse for reporting on educational research.

Unfortunately, NIE has so far failed to live up to its grandiose billing. Its own fumbling performance, political in-fighting in Congress, and atrocious relations between its first director and congressional appropriations committees all combined to produce cutbacks in its appropriations in the early 1970s. Its 1974 budget request was almost halved, and NIE had barely enough money to support the miscellany of research efforts it had inherited from USOE, many of which probably should have been abolished. Then, too, early directors of NIE had little or no experience in public education and lacked the support of the educational establishment, which might have been helpful in lobbying for more adequate financial support. Experiments with voucher plans and performance contracting—never popular in the educational establishment—were strong favorites of the NIE staff. Moreover, the NIE staff had a preference for long-term basic research on teaching and learning processes, as opposed to Congress' preference for research on immediate educational problems to yield immediate solutions— an unrealistic expectation. There were also long delays in the appointment of the National Council on Educational Research, which might have guided NIE's destiny more effectively during those turbulent years.

After its long period of drift, NIE has shifted its focus to these priorities: reading and mathematics, vocational education, educational technology, equal educational opportunity, and strengthening local school systems' administrative capabilities. One of NIE's new strategies will be to use "educational extension agents" modeled after agricultural extension agents who were so successful in disseminating agricultural research into practice in an earlier age. These agents are up to date on research findings and work directly with local practitioners to help them apply research in their work.

At this writing, the outlook for this splendidly conceived agency is grim indeed, a tragic consequence of its fumbling and arrogance in dealing with Congress, its lack of support from the educational establishment, and congressional politics. Thus we now have two, not one, executive agencies at the federal level with less distinguished records of accomplishment than our educational enterprise deserves. Many people believe, as noted later, that the federal government will never accomplish its mission in education effectively until we have worked out a clear federal policy with respect to education and have established a separate department of education with a secretary who holds Cabinet status.

EDUCATION IN SPECIAL FEDERAL JURISDICTIONS

The federal government administers educational programs in the special school district of Washington, D.C., the federal reservations, and outlying areas, such as the Virgin Islands, Puerto Rico, the Panama Canal Zone, American Samoa, Guam, Wake Island, and the trust territories in the Pacific.

EDUCATIONAL PROGRAMS SPONSORED BY OTHER FEDERAL AGENCIES

More than half the total federal expenditures for education are administered by dozens of agencies other than the Office of Education. The full account of these far-flung enterprises would fill chapters. A recent publication by the U.S. Office of Education listed 126 different federal programs of support for various aspects of education. Several are selected here for illustrative purposes.

In 1950 Congress created the National Science Foundation "to develop and encourage the pursuit of a national policy for the promotion of basic research and education in the sciences." Its chief functions are to support basic research, education, and training in the physical sciences and to disseminate scientific information. Its specific goals are focused on the following basic areas: (1) supplementing the learning of teachers of science, mathematics, and engineering; (2) improving subject matter in these areas; (3) identifying and motivating high-caliber students for these fields; and (4) granting funds for further education of graduate students and advanced scholars in these areas.

More recently, the National Science Foundation is emphasizing the production of scientifically literate students at all levels.

The National Foundation on the Arts and Humanities, created in 1965, maintains a similar but less ambitious program for those fields.

The National Aeronautics and Space Administration performs several educational services to deepen our understanding of the educational, social, economic, and political implications of peaceful exploration of space. In cooperation with universities, it sponsors research and training programs essential to understanding the universe.

The massive educational undertakings of the Department of Defense include the service academies, schools on military installations, and schools for dependents of military service personnel almost wherever they are stationed around the world.

In Chapter 15 we describe the educational enterprise in the international realm conducted by the Peace Corps, the U.S. Information Agency, the Agency for International Development in the Department of State, and other federal agencies.

The education of inmates in federal correctional institutions is administered by the Department of Justice. The Neighborhood Youth Corps is a responsibility of the Department of Labor. The Department of Housing and Urban Affairs administers various educational activities related to its mission. The Veterans Administration has domain over the educational benefits provided by the GI Bill. Many other illustrations of educational activities administered by various departments of government could be cited.

In addition, various federal agencies furnish educational services, as shown by expenditures in Table 14-1.

PRESIDENTIAL COMMISSIONS

Over the last half-century, United States presidents have appointed nearly fifty special commissions, committees, and conferences to study various aspects of American education and to advise chief executives accordingly. The reports of these groups have yielded some of the most insightful views of the nation's educational needs and the resources required to meet them.

The White House Conferences on Education, held approximately every ten years, have crystallized citizens' expectations of educational enter-

Table 14-1 Federal funds for education and related activities by agencies, 1975 (estimated)

Agency	Millions of dollars
Department of Health, Education, and Welfare	7,981
Veterans Administration	2,792
Department of Labor	2,079
Department of Agriculture	2,052
Department of Defense	1,435
Department of Interior	304
National Center for Educational Statistics	80
Library of Congress	74
Appalachian Regional Development Commission	68
Department of Justice	63
Smithsonian Institution	51
National Foundation of the Arts and Humanities	42
Department of State	40
Department of Housing and Urban Development	33
National Science Foundation	30
Corporation for Public Broadcasting	27
Other agencies	3,213

Adapted from National Center for Educational Statistics, *Digest of Educational Statistics,* U.S. Government Printing Office, Washington, 1975, p. 125.

prise and have resulted in many excellent recommendations for strengthening schools, including massive increase in the federal financial effort. The 1970–1971 White House Conferences focused their attention on the problems and needs of children, youths, and adults.

Throughout this book frequent reference is made to recommendations of these various presidential commissions. The great tragedy is that although these commissions have engaged in careful and sometimes brilliant studies and have formulated many excellent recommendations, only a few recommendations are ever put into practice. One problem is that a commission appointed by one president might not complete its report until another president has taken office. The new administration and legislature may see little political advantage in acting on the recommendations of a commission created by a previous administration.

The Development of Federal Relations to Education

1785	Land appropriated by Continental Congress in Northwest Territory to endow a common school system
1791	Education reserved to the states by the passage of the Tenth Amendment to the Constitution
1802	First federal institution of higher education established as the U.S. Military Academy at West Point
1818	First money for education granted to the states by the federal government
1862	Land-grant colleges established by the first Morrill Act, supplemented later
1867	National Department of Education, forerunner of U.S. Office of Education, established
1917	Federal assistance for vocational education provided by Smith-Hughes Act
1920	Federal-state cooperation in vocational rehabilitation initiated through Smith-Bankhead Act
1933	Emergency educational grants initiated during the Depression
1940	Aid authorized to schools in federally impacted areas by Lanham Act
1944	GI Bill for veterans' education passed by Congress and expanded in subsequent years
1953	U.S. Office of Education made part of Department of Health, Education, and Welfare, with Cabinet Secretary
1954	Segregation in public schools ruled unconstitutional by U.S. Supreme Court

1958	National Defense Education Act enacted to strengthen education in science, mathematics, and languages
1962	Retraining of nation's labor force accelerated by passage of Manpower Development and Training Act
1962	Use by schools of a prayer approved by the New York State Board of Regents ruled unconstitutional by U.S. Supreme Court
1963	Bible reading in public schools declared unconstitutional by U.S. Supreme Court
1963	Higher Education Facilities Act passed, providing loans and grants for construction of classrooms, libraries, and laboratories
1964	Civil Rights Bill passed by Congress, containing a provision for the withdrawal of federal support from any community or school district in which discrimination is practiced
1964	Economic Opportunity Act (war on poverty) passed by Congress, with several provisions affecting education, such as Job Corps, work training programs, Volunteers in Service to America, and literacy education
1965	New post of Assistant Secretary for Education created in Department of Health, Education, and Welfare
1965	Elementary and Secondary Education Act approved by Congress, authorizing benefits to pupils in elementary and secondary schools, including some services to private school pupils
1965	Higher Education Act of 1965 approved, providing for the first time for scholarships for needy college students, plus funds for institutions

1965	*National Foundation on the Arts and Humanities authorized by Congress*
1966	*Initial funds authorized by Congress for the National Teacher Corps, enabling teachers to serve in poverty-stricken areas*
1967	*Education Professions Development Act enacted to improve quality of teachers and meet educational manpower needs*
1968	*Bilingual Education Act funded special programs for non-English-speaking students*
1969	*Immediate end to racial segregation in schools demanded by U.S. Supreme Court*
1971	*Busing of students as a means of integration upheld by U.S. Supreme Court*
1971	*Attempts by several states to give direct financial aid to church-related schools ruled unconstitutional by U.S. Supreme Court.*

1972	*Reforms in the federal government's participation in the educational enterprise recommended by President's Commission on School Finance*
1972	*Revenue sharing begun, with some funds from federal income taxes returned to state and local governments*
1972	*National Institute of Education established in Department of Health, Education, and Welfare*
1972	*Education Amendments Act amended, consolidated, and extended earlier federal grants*
1975	*U.S. Supreme Court affirmed constitutional rights of students in guaranteeing due process for students suspended from school*
1975	*Education of All Handicapped Children Act ensured "free and appropriate" public education for all handicapped children ages 3 to 21 and provided for massive federal funding*
1977	*White House Conferences on Education held across the land*

Education and the legislative branch

The historical calendar in this chapter lists significant events in the evolution of federal interest in education. Events involving the federal government directly in the advancement of education are described below.

BASIC FEDERAL LEGISLATION

Although education is not mentioned in the United States Constitution, indirect justification for federal participation in our educational effort may be found in several of its provisions, the "general welfare" clause, and the Preamble.

That the central government is not to control education is evident from the Tenth Amendment to the Constitution, which by implication definitely leaves the governance of school systems to individual states: "The powers not delegated to the United States by the Constitution, nor prohibited by it to the states, are reserved to the states respectively, or to the people." The implied prohibition against the establishment of a centralized system markedly influenced the direction and scope of federal participation in education.

LAND GRANTS FOR SCHOOLS

During the first century of its existence, the federal government's support of education was manifested largely by grants of land to the states for the development of schools and colleges. The Continental Congress adopted in 1785 an ordinance that reserved one lot in every township for the maintenance of public schools. This provision, granting federal lands for school use, was the first enactment of federal support for education, antedating the ratification of the Constitution itself.

In the year 1787 the famous Northwest Ordinance stated that the following important principle should be applied to states to be carved from the territory: "Religion, morality, and knowledge being necessary to good government and the happiness of mankind, schools and the means of education shall be forever encouraged."

In 1803, the federal government actually inaugurated the epoch-making practice of giving the 1-mile-square section of each township for general educational purposes. The total of these land grants is estimated at 90 million acres, or an area larger than the combined territory of Ohio, Indiana, and Illinois. The funds derived from the sale and lease of these original school lands form the major part of permanent school funds of several states. Although some funds were poorly managed, these federal gifts to education have been extremely significant.

The first Morrill Act of 1862 provided 6 million acres of federal lands to the states for the support of colleges for instruction in "agriculture and the mechanic arts, without excluding other scientific and classical studies and including military tactics." This act established sixty-eight land-grant colleges, some of the best institutions of higher education in the nation. The act was conceived by a Vermont blacksmith's son, Senator Justin Morrill, who wanted to provide for other poor youths the low-cost college education he never had. The land-grant colleges did help to democratize higher education and throw open the doors of opportunity to a great many more youths, particularly in the fields of agriculture, engineering, and home economics. The original act was supplemented by other grants in the second Morrill Act of 1890, which at that early date prohibited discrimination by race in institutions receiving funds.

VOCATIONAL EDUCATION AND MANPOWER DEVELOPMENT

One of the most pervasive interests of the federal government in education over the past hundred years has been the development of our greatest national resource, educated manpower. This interest has been especially quickened during periods of national emergency—such as wars and depressions, when shortages of trained manpower threaten the security or prosperity of the nation. The thrust of much of this effort by the federal government is in the form of money grants to schools and colleges for vocational and professional education and, in some instances, direct grants to students. This federal support of manpower development has had a salubrious effect upon our national productivity and prosperity and explains in great part the miraculous growth of the American economy in the twentieth century.

Agricultural education. After the passage of the Morrill Act during the Civil War, there was little new support of education by the federal government for the next half-century until World War I, except for the Hatch Act of 1887, which provided small annual sums to state agricultural colleges to stimulate the development of agricultural science. Many years later, in 1914, the Congress passed the Smith-Lever Act, or Agricultural Extension Act, to stimulate farm families to make better use of the emerging new sciences of agriculture and home economics. Through the use of agricultural agents, conferences, classes, and demonstrations, the agricultural industry was greatly strengthened. The miracle of American agricultural production that followed these acts is well known.

Vocational education. The early twentieth century brought a call for increased emphasis on vocational education. In 1917 President Wilson signed the Smith-Hughes Act, which provided annual federal funds for distribution to the states for vocational education in the public schools of less than college grade. The act supported the training and employment of teachers and supervisors of agriculture, home economics, and trade and industrial subjects, and also research in vocational education. The Smith-Hughes Act marked the first massive federal money grants for education.

The scope of federal interest in vocational education was broadened in 1937 by the George-Deen Act, which more than doubled the amount of money previously available for vocational education. The George-Barden Act of 1945 further increased the federal funds available for vocational education. Amendments made such funds available for counseling, training vocational counselors, and research in guidance and placement. The National Defense Education Act of 1958 supported for the first time a new type of vocational education, namely, area vocational schools or centers.

The Vocational Education Acts of 1963 and 1968 opened a new era in federal governmental support. These acts strengthened existing programs of vocational education in the secondary schools and broadened their scope to reach youths who had completed high school or dropped out of school or were sufficiently handicapped academically or socially to profit from regular vocational education programs. New emphasis was placed upon work-study programs with part-time employment of young people to supplement their classroom vocational training. Provisions were made for the construction of area vocational centers and for such ancillary services as teacher education, supervision, evaluation, and demonstration of promising practices in vocational education, as well as for the development of new instructional materials and state leadership in these fields. This important legislation with subsequent renewals and revisions is producing many changes in traditional programs and is quickening the vitality of vocational education in a period when new technologies are creating a demand for educated personnel in new occupations.

Vocational rehabilitation and unemployment. Several federal bills are targeted specifically upon the occupational rehabilitation of persons who are handicapped in one way or another. The Vocational Rehabilitation Act of 1920 appropriated money to the states for the training of handicapped persons so that they could, whenever possible, become self-supporting. The Manpower Training and Development Act of 1962, later consolidated into the Comprehensive Employment and Training Act (CETA) of 1973, attacked the problem of retraining the hard core of unemployed

persons, both the unskilled and those whose occupational skills need updating through programs of vocational rehabilitation. Prime target groups for CETA are American Indians, migrants, and disadvantaged youths. Approximately $1 billion have been made available to create summer employment for youths and public service jobs, approximately one-fifth of which have been in local school districts. CETA has a strong record of growth, bringing unemployed people into the mainstream of productive life.

Some provisions of the GI Bill, discussed later, also were directed toward the rehabilitation of veterans of military service who, through injury in the defense of their country, would otherwise have found gainful employment difficult.

Manpower for defense. From the days of the earliest settlements through the modern age of nuclear weaponry, human beings have been interested in defense. In 1802, soon after the founding of the young republic, the U.S. Military Academy was established at West Point, New York, to train officers for the Army. The U.S. Naval Academy was established in Annapolis, Maryland, in 1845; the Coast Guard Academy in New London, Connecticut, in 1876; the Merchant Marine Academy in Kings Point, New York, in 1938; and the Air Force Academy in Colorado Springs, Colorado, in 1955. These institutions of higher education are administered under the auspices of the Department of Defense. The entrance requirements and academ-

The federal government has a long history of financial support for vocational education and manpower development.

ic standards of the service academies are high, and their graduates have won distinction not only in military service but also in civilian pursuits. The several branches of the services cooperate in the operation of the Reserve Officers Training Corps (ROTC) installations on the campuses of many high schools, colleges, and universities.

The educational programs of the Armed Forces extend from the first grade through the university level. The U.S. Armed Forces Institute at times enrolls thousands of students pursuing both military and general education. Thousands of soldiers have learned to read and write and have acquired other basic educational skills in the army. Thousands of other service personnel have acquired their high school diplomas or equivalency certificates after study in the armed forces and successful completion of the General Education Development Tests. It has been said that in every working day of the year, 10 to 15 percent of the personnel in the U.S. Armed Forces can be found in classrooms. During periods of national emergency, the educational establishment of the military is often the largest educational enterprise in the nation.

The National Defense Education Act (NDEA) of 1958 was largely a response to the Soviet Union's precedence in the exploration of outer space and to our national near-hysteria over the quality of an educational system that was presumably responsible for such embarrassment. Since its enactment the National Defense Education Act has provided billions of dollars to improve teaching in fields deemed crucial to space exploration and national defense.

Under the provisions of the act, millions of students have borrowed from the NDEA Student Loan Program, and thousands of graduate students have been awarded graduate fellowships. Preference has been given to students preparing for college teaching.

More than $500 million in NDEA funds have been granted on a matching basis for new laboratories and other equipment for teaching mathematics, physical sciences, and modern languages in public elementary and secondary schools.

Subsequent extensions of the act broadened its scope to include the teaching of English, reading, history, civics, geography, economics, and industrial arts and to educate teachers of disadvantaged youths, school library personnel, and educational media specialists. With NDEA funds, state educa-

tion departments have increased the number of their specialists in science, mathematics, and foreign languages. Under the program for language development, elementary and secondary school teachers have gone back to summer school to become familiar with new methods and materials. In addition to these institutes, nearly a hundred language and area centers have been developed in colleges and universities for the study of both the languages and cultures of other countries. Research in language instruction has also been supported by NDEA funds.

A major objective of the National Defense Education Act has been the improvement and extension of guidance, counseling, and testing programs. The number of full-time guidance personnel employed by the public schools has increased as a direct consequence of the act. Thousands of specialists attended over a hundred guidance and counseling institutes established on college and university campuses to deepen their competency in counseling, guidance, and testing.

This act, smuggled into legislation originally as an instrument of national defense, has had a powerful impact upon the strength of general education at all levels.

The education of veterans. In 1944 Congress enacted, without a dissenting vote, the historic GI Bill of Rights, which included educational benefits for the military men and women who served in World War II. Subsequently the educational benefits and others were extended to include veterans of the Korean conflict and the war in Vietnam. The provisions were further liberalized in 1967 and again in 1970, when additions were included to promote the education of disadvantaged veterans by providing funds for remedial courses, tutoring grants, equal-opportunity programs, and open admission policies in the institutions of higher education enrolling the veterans. These provisions were enacted to increase the percentage of veterans benefiting from the bill, a percentage that had slipped from 50 percent after World War II to 27 percent in 1970.

The impact of the GI Bill and its supplementary extensions has been tremendous. Approximately 15 million veterans of military service have extended their education in countless occupations and professions, thereby raising tremendously the nation's supply of educated manpower and strengthening both its economic prosperity and its national security. The original $30-billion cost of educational provisions of the GI bills has been repaid to the nation, and the return still increases yearly. Even more important has been the reduction of socioeconomic stratification of our people. Robert Hutchins, then president of the Center for the Study of Democratic Institutions, wrote:

The GI Bill of Rights is a historic enactment because it makes it possible for the veteran to go to college even if his parents have no money. It thus removes, for a large class of our citizens, the greatest, the most unjust, and the most unwise limitation on higher education.

The education of teachers. During the last two decades various acts have supported the education of teachers of the deaf, the partially sighted, and other physically handicapped students as well as mentally retarded and emotionally disturbed students. The Civil Rights Act of 1964 provided funds to help teachers deal more effectively with problems resulting from the desegregation of schools. Other legislation provided for the education of teachers of adults, preschool children, and non-English-speaking students. The National Science Foundation and the National Foundation on the Arts and Humanities assisted teacher-education programs in these fields. Many other federal acts discussed in this chapter contain provisions for the preparation and in-service development of teachers related to the thrust of the various statutes; it is increasingly recognized that new educational programs have little chance of success until teachers are prepared to deal with them.

One attack upon the education of poor children was the National Teacher Corps, which instituted a program of graduate fellowships to prepare elementary and secondary school teachers, and provided grants and contracts to improve teacher-education programs. The Teacher Corps was an effort to improve education at its weakest point, slum schools. It brought together dedicated teachers committed to use education to defeat poverty in the ghettos of the cities as well as in dilapidated rural areas. In typical Teacher Corps programs, teams of undergraduate or graduate student interns and a master teacher from a local school system worked together in a school in a poverty area. The student interns worked part-time in the schools while continuing their professional study during evenings, weekends, and summers. At the end of two years they earned their college degrees and teacher certification, along with two years of on-the-job experience. The success of the Teacher Corps is manifested in part by the fact that 86 percent of those who completed the program remain in teaching, most of them in schools in poverty areas. Every Teacher Corps program was a local program, planned and administerd jointly by a school system and nearby university and with the counsel of various community groups. More and more characteristics of Teacher Corps programs are being incorporated into the regular training programs of teachers.

The Education Professions Development Act (EPDA) of 1967 was enacted as a series of amendments to the Higher Education Act and the National Defense Education Act. EPDA brings together under one jurisdiction virtually all federally supported programs for the development of professional persons in education and expands the nation's grasp of the manpower problems in education. EPDA embraces five major purposes:

1. To obtain accurate information on education's manpower needs
2. To provide high-quality preparation and retraining opportunities
3. To attract more qualified persons into teaching
4. To encourage persons who can "stimulate creativity in the arts and other skills" to accept short-term or long-term assignments
5. To make preparation programs more responsive to the needs of schools and colleges

EPDA represents a transition away from former piecemeal programs of teacher education by emphasizing the education of the child—particularly disadvantaged, handicapped, and non-English-speaking children—rather than the training of the teacher as an end in itself; by focusing on areas of most severe personnel shortages in education, namely, early-childhood education, vocational-technical education, special education, and student personnel services; by shifting from short-term, college-based programs of teacher education to long-term projects built upon the cooperation of colleges and local school systems; and by encouraging change in the total preparation programs of teachers to make them more responsive to the elimination of racial, financial, physical, and mental disadvantages.

Some persons regard EPDA as the most significant federal legislation in the field of education in the 1960s. Certainly its impact is impressive on the basis of sheer numbers. Clearly this concentrated federal effort helped to end the period of personnel shortages in education while raising materially the quality of persons in educational endeavor.

SCHOOL CONSTRUCTION AND FACILITIES

During the Great Depression of the 1930s the federal government assisted in the construction of various educational facilities through the Public Works Administration and the Works Progress Administration. The Lanham Act of 1940 provided federal funds for schools in localities where school enrollments were swelled by students of families attracted by defense installations. The act was extended in 1950 to provide aid for school construction. The College Housing Program, begun in 1951, provided long-term, low-interest loans to colleges for certain facilities such as dormitories and cafeterias. The Higher Education Act of 1963 provided as much as $400 million annually for construction of facilities in colleges and universities and public community colleges and technical institutes. In 1965 the Appalachian Regional Development Act provided funds for the construction of vocational education facilities in the Appalachian area. The Library Services and Construction Act of 1956, which provided funds for books and bookmobiles to improve library service for rural Americans, was expanded in 1964 to include funds for both services and construction assistance to urban and rural libraries. The National Defense Education Act in the first decade of its existence provided $40 million for the use of various educational media including television, motion pictures, radio, and computers. The Educational Television Broadcasting Facilities Act of 1962 with subsequent additions supported both operating and construction costs and brought educational television within reach of more than two-thirds of the nation's students and a total viewing audience of more than 150 million people. Subventions are available under the act to public school systems, colleges and universities, state educational-television agencies, and to nonprofit foundations engaged in educational telecasting.

THE EDUCATION OF UNDERPRIVILEGED AND HANDICAPPED STUDENTS

The education of underprivileged students. Beginning mainly with the Great Depression of the 1930s, the federal government has sought to reduce inequality in opportunity by making special funds available for the education of disadvantaged children and youths. During the Depression, the National Youth Administration provided stipends to permit needy youths to remain in school, while the Civilian Conservation Corps and other acts provided modest wages to permit out-of-school youths to engage in productive work and learning. The Social Security Act, enacted originally in 1935 and broadened substantially through many later revisions, has provided through its welfare provisions financial assistance to poor families. In hundreds of thousands of homes across the nation this welfare has made it possible for youths to stay in school rather than drop out to search for employment—employment often so menial for undereducated youths that they are locked in hardship for life.

The greatest impetus in helping poor people educationally came with the enactment of the "war-on-poverty" legislation, or the Economic Opportunity Act (EOA), in 1964, which provided as much as $300 million annually for part-time employment and insured loans and "equal opportunity grants" for students from low-income families. The act helped to support college work-study programs to permit needy youths to earn some of the money needed to remain in college. In addition to its direct aid to students, this act established certain new educational programs designed to help relieve the tragic cycle of poverty, undereducation, unemployment, and disenchantment with the American promise of prosperity and the pursuit of happiness for all. These provisions included Head Start, Follow Through, VISTA, Teacher Corps, and the Adult Literacy Program. Head Start provided early-childhood education experience for children from low-income families. Follow Through programs, initiated a few years later, were designed to reinforce and extend into the early elementary years the special programs that were begun in Head Start. The Volunteers in Service to America (VISTA) program established a sort of domestic Peace Corps in which volunteers worked with poor people in the eroded hills of Appalachia, the dilapidated slums of the city ghettos, drug rehabilitation programs, centers for senior citizens, modest sun-baked hogans of American Indians, and the shanties of migrant families to help break the dreary legacy of poverty. The Adult Literacy Program of EOA was later subsumed in the Adult Education Act of 1966 to provide basic education for adults who had dropped out of school. Several of these volunteer programs, such as VISTA and Teacher Corps, have been merged into a new federal agency called ACTION.

One of the most controversial provisions of EOA was the Job Corps. Prompted by the earlier prototype of the Civilian Conservation Corps, Job Corps sought to salvage youths who had dropped out of school and languished unemployed in slum communities; it placed them in camps across the country to give them the vocational and general education that would permit them to assume a constructive role in society. However, the costs of the program were high, prompting the transfer of this program from the Office of Economic Opportunity into the Department of Labor's other manpower-training projects in an attempt to make the enterprise more efficient and productive. In recent years Job Corps boasts a 93 percent placement rate for those who finish the program, but unfortunately half of each year's enrollees drop out.

The Basic Educational Opportunity Grants (BEOG), part of the Education Amendments Act of 1972 (see Chapter 7), provided grants of money for poor postsecondary students. It established a national intent that all capable students have the right to higher education regardless of financial ability. It has opened the doors of higher education to thousands of students from low-income families.

Beginning in 1935 surplus foods purchased by the federal government to bolster farm prices were distributed to schools for lunches for students. This distribution of surplus foods is being phased out because the worldwide agricultural situation denies the federal government access to surplus foods at bargain prices.

The Elementary and Secondary Education Act of 1965 and its later amendments provide the largest program of federal aid specifically to elementary and secondary education. It is called Education of Disadvantaged Children. Since 1967 it has provided more than $1 billion annually to local districts to meet the educational deficiencies of poor people through remedial reading programs and special counseling programs. Funds are distributed to school districts on the basis of the number of children from low-income families enrolled in the schools. Additional special grants are given to both urban and rural districts that have an unusually high concentration of children from poor families, migratory farm workers, and delinquent and neglected children in special state or local schools. Other moneys are made available for bonuses to supplement the salaries of teachers assigned to schools with high concentrations of educationally deprived children and to encourage programs designed to reduce school dropouts. The act also provides funds for the education of American Indian children and other non-English-speaking children. These provisions of ESEA have been sharply debated in Congress and elsewhere on the allegation that much of the money is wasted and diverted from poor people because of shoddy local accounting for the funds, lax supervision of expenditures by some states, and the misuse of funds in some cases to replace rather than supplement local school revenues.

The education of physically, mentally, and emotionally handicapped students. The federal government has enacted a number of laws which provide financial support for the education of students who are mentally retarded, hard of hearing, or deaf; whose speech is impaired; who are visually handicapped, emotionally disturbed, or crippled; or whose health is otherwise impaired and who therefore require special attention in school. These young people constitute approximately one-tenth of the school population. The federal Rehabilitation Act of 1973 forbids discrimination on the basis of mental or physical handicaps by schools that receive federal funds. A number of piecemeal attacks on the special education of these children have now been coalesced under Education of the Handicapped, Title VI of the Elementary and Secondary Education Act.

By far the most massive attack on the education of handicapped students resulted from the Education of All Handicapped Children Act of 1975. In one of the largest federal aid-to-education acts in our history, this bill—with a potential annual price tag of $8 billion by 1982—promises free and appropriate education for the nation's 8 million handicapped children aged 3 to 21, whether they can attend regular schools or not. The act establishes for the first time a direct working relationship between the federal government and the nation's 16,000 school districts. It promises to be the final conquest in our aspiration to provide educational opportunity for all young people.

Chapter 3 provides a more extensive discussion of the problems of handicapped students and the nature of school programs designed to reduce those problems. It is hoped that this formidable assault on the education of handicapped learners will hasten the time when more victims of disease, birth defects, and accidents can find dignified and productive places in society.

The federal government has provided funds and guidelines for the desegregation of schools and for improvement of the education of all people.

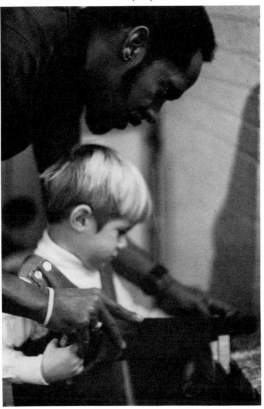

THE EDUCATION OF MINORITY GROUPS AND WOMEN

In Chapter 1 we spoke of the problems and issues related to the education of racial and ethnic groups and women in our multicultural society. As detailed later in this chapter, the federal courts have finally made it clear that the equal-protection clause of the Constitution applies to people of both sexes and all races, although much more litigation is inevitable before sexism and racism are extinct in our schools. Armed with the mandates of the Civil Rights Act of 1964, the Office of Education formulated guidelines for the desegregation of schools. The enforcement of these guidelines has been a matter of sharp debate and great difficulty in many communities.

The Elementary and Secondary Education Act provided funds to local school districts to support special educational programs for children of minority groups. By 1976 the Emergency School Assistance Act (ESAA) of 1972 provided $242 million to local districts (1) to meet special problems growing out of school desegregation, (2) to encourage voluntary integration, and (3) to help overcome the educational disadvantages of minority-group isolation in society. Activities eligible for funding include new curriculums related to instruction in multiracial classrooms, remedial instruction, guidance and community services to improve race relations in schools, and other supporting services. ESAA has had a rocky record because of court orders withholding federal funds from segregated schools. Evidently the paradox of withholding funds labeled for desegregation assistance from districts that have not been desegregated enough has escaped the courts.

Some ethnic groups are further handicapped in their education by coming to school without sufficient command of the English language. The Bilingual Education Act of 1968 provides approximately $1 billion annually for school districts to establish bilingual programs in English and the native languages of non-English-speaking students as well as to strengthen pride and knowledge of their ancestral cultures. The second language may be Spanish, French, Chinese, Yupik (Eskimo), Navajo, Cherokee, or other Indian languages. It is estimated that 5 million school-aged children (one in ten) come from non-English-speaking families,

80 percent of which speak Spanish. Although these programs are still inadequately funded, it is hoped that they mark a significant beginning in helping students of minority groups to acquire a sense of personal identification and self-respect and that they eventually will open doors of equal opportunity for all children in America. The curricular facets of bilingual education are discussed in Chapter 9.

The legal basis for the protection of equal opportunity for women in education was established in the Education Amendments Act of 1972 and further supported by guidelines developed by the Office of Education. Discrimination against women in education is discussed in Chapter 1. The enforcement of affirmative action plans is now relieving sex discrimination, although it may be years before all vestiges of sexism are removed from education. Until we have righted the wrongs done to women in our society, the promise of American democracy will remain unfulfilled.

CURRICULUM AND INSTRUCTION

Many of the acts mentioned earlier have direct impact on curriculum and instruction, but several other provisions merit special mention. One provision of the Education Amendments Act of 1972 established the Right-to-Read program, which aims to eliminate illiteracy in the land by 1980. It is estimated that one child in four has a serious reading disability; in 1975 1 percent of the population beyond 14 years of age was illiterate. Approximately $14 million of federal funds were budgeted in 1976 to support this program, which was conceived originally by the late James Allen, then U.S. Commissioner of Education. Although still badly underfunded, the Right-to-Read program has produced measurable results. It encourages, coordinates, and facilitates efforts by federal, state, and local educational authorities, foundations, public interest groups, and educational associations to improve reading instruction at all age levels. Nationally known athletes have been enlisted to motivate youngsters to want to read, to work with reading centers, and to mobilize the private sector of society behind the program.

Other federal funds support career education, drug-abuse education, vocational education, and many other sectors of the curriculum. Table 14-2 shows federal funding for major educational and related activities in 1975.

THE ERA OF NATIONAL FEDERALISM IN EDUCATION

The period since the Elementary and Secondary Education Act may be recorded by historians as the era of national federalism in education. This was an era in which the federal government increased substantially its expenditures for schooling, as shown in Figure 14-1. It was also an era in which the federal government, as one commentator put it, plunged "smack into the middle of the total educational enterprise—public and pri-

Table 14-2 Federal funds for major educational and related enterprises for Fiscal Year 1976. Many smaller enterprises are not included.

Expenditure	Millions of dollars
Department of Health, Education, and Welfare (USOE, NIE, etc.)	6,860
Higher education	2,440
Education of the disadvantaged	2,050
School assistance in federally affected areas	680
Vocational education	510
Emergency school aid (support to districts involved in desegregation programs)	242
Education of the handicapped	236
Support and innovative grants (health and nutrition, dropout prevention, libraries, etc.)	173
Bilingual education	98
Adult education	72
Follow Through programs	59
Teacher Corps	38
Early-childhood education	22
Right-to-Read programs	17
Educational broadcasting facilities	13
Women's educational equality	6
Community school programs	4
Consumer education	3
Environmental education	3
Education of the gifted and talented	3
Drug-abuse education	2
Metric education	2

Adapted from U.S. Budget, Fiscal Year 1976.

(IN MILLIONS OF DOLLARS)

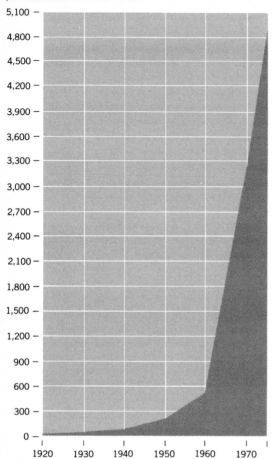

Figure 14-1 Federal expenditures for elementary and secondary schools, 1920–1975. (U.S. Office of Education, *Digest of Educational Statistics.*)

vate" instead of playing the role of "passive and distant financial patron." Heretofore, federal aid had been piecemeal, limited to a few specific targets. Although massive federal support for education had been sought ever since the Great Depression, three great issues had stood in the way: religion, race, and the principle of local control. The public school establishment had generally opposed federal grants for private schools, and the Catholic school establishment opposed any aid that did not include its schools. Many Southern legislators feared that federal aid would be used to force the integration of schools. Others held that increased federal support would threaten local control.

But several forces converged in the 1960s and 1970s to prompt more generous financial support for education. The civil rights movement called attention dramatically to the tragedy of racial discrimination and poverty and their impact upon social and economic inequality among people. Advancing technology quickened the need of the economy for better-educated manpower. Domestic and international tensions continued to press for better-educated citizens. Schools were seen as our best hope for improving the human condition. As Jimmy Carter noted:

America's commitment to education has facilitated equality of opportunity, yet we still do not provide all citizens with the education necessary to develop their natural potential and participate meaningfully in the decisions of their government.

A landmark act. These and other forces ensured the passage of the Elementary and Secondary Education Act in 1965. President Johnson, who had been a teacher, wished his administration to be remembered for its encouragement of education, and he adroitly handled the design and promotion of the bill. This remarkable bill is singled out for discussion here because it was perhaps so prototypic of the emerging new national federalism in education. First the bill required local schools to write their own plans for the use of the funds. This emphasis on local thinking, planning, and judgment was in sharp contrast with most earlier federal aid to education. It permitted the funds to serve a variety of uniquely local needs, whether it be the establishment of nongraded elementary school organization in Cleveland or classes in English for Navajo-speaking children in Kayenta, Arizona. Second, ESEA represented a high in federal financial support for education at that time, providing for the first time more than $1 billion under a single enactment. Although ESEA did not provide funds for the general support of education, it was an omnibus bill that was far more comprehensive in its impact on education than any previous legislation. It was also the first bill for federal aid to education that made substantial sums available to private elementary and secondary schools.

The bill consisted of seven sections or titles. Title I, the largest single source of federal funds for education to that time by far, was addressed to the development of children from low-income families.

The provisions of this section were discussed earlier in this chapter. Title II supported three types of educational materials: school library resources, textbooks, and other instructional materials. Title III supported various supplementary educational centers, sometimes called Projects to Advance Creativity in Education (PACE). Title IV provided for research and related activities in education. Title V was addressed to the education of the handicapped. Title VI provided funds for bilingual education for students whose native language was not English. Title VII supported programs designed to prevent school dropouts. Title VIII, adopted later, provided for health and nutrition education. Clearly ESEA reached a far greater number of young citizens more profoundly than any other federal financial support of education at that time. Truly it marked a watershed in the flow of federal funds for education and ushered in a new era in federal support of schools.

During the 1960s and 1970s more and more educationally oriented programs of the federal government were transferred to the jurisdiction of the U.S. Office of Education in the Department of Health, Education, and Welfare, although many other branches of the federal government still maintain important educational programs described elsewhere in this chapter.

In too many instances federal funds had been channeled directly to local school districts, bypassing state educational agencies that should have been involved in the coordination of federal, state, and local efforts. This was partially corrected by the Education Amendments Act (EAA) of 1972, which amended, extended, and consolidated parts of ESEA and NDEA. This act partially reversed the proliferation of special-purpose or categorical-aid grants, with their indigenous federal controls, in favor of more state and local responsibility for the use of federal dollars. EAA was delayed in passage for years because of bitter debate over (1) an inclusion of a prohibition against busing students beyond the school "next nearest" their homes for purposes of racial balance and (2) a formula for the distribution of funds to districts based on the number of students from low-income families. Many contended that poor states and city school districts were not getting a fair deal in the distribution formulas. Nevertheless, EAA was another milestone in the direction of national federalism in education.

Revenue sharing. Perhaps the greatest landmark in the development of national federalism in education was the passage in 1972 of the State and Local Fiscal Assistance Act, commonly called "revenue sharing." Although not strictly an education measure, in 1976 this act returned to state and local governments over $6 billion obtained from federal income taxes. Two-thirds of this goes to local governments, which may not use it for education; the remainder goes to state governments, which so far have used approximately two-thirds of the money for schools. The intent of the act was to give state and local governments a larger share of federal tax revenues. It had the effect of reducing approximately thirty piecemeal special-purpose grants to education into one package and giving state governments more leeway in determining how funds for schools should be spent. The intent of the act is salubrious and very much in the direction of national federalism. The act has been criticized on the grounds that it has not so far resulted in any large increase in federal funding for education, only a repackaging of existing categorical aid. Federal revenue sharing, along with other issues in federal financial support of education, is discussed more fully in Chapter 11.

A national authority on school finance, R.L. Johns, speaks of the concept of "creative federalism" this way:

The concept of creative federalism is based on the assumption that the power to deal with educational problems is not a fixed quantity but that it is expanding very rapidly. The increase in the power of one level of government to deal with a particular educational problem does not reduce the power of another level of government to deal with the problem. ... The increase in the educational power of the federal government to deal with social and economic deprivation actually increased the power of the state and local school districts to deal with the same problem. ... It is a concept of partnership in which the federal, state, and local school districts operate as equals, each assuming the responsibility to perform the educational functions that can be most appropriately dealt with at that level.[2]

[2]R. L. Johns, "State Organization and Responsibilities for Education," in Edgar L. Morphet and Charles O. Ryan (eds.), *Designing Education for the Future*, no. 2, Citation, New York, 1967, p. 263.

Education and the judiciary branch

The U.S. Supreme Court, other federal courts in the judiciary system, and the U.S. Attorney General have had profound impact upon education. Through hundreds of decisions bearing upon the governance and management of schools the Supreme Court has shaped educational policies and practices across the nation. This high tribunal does not legislate educational policy directly and has never challenged the principle that education is a state function. For many years the courts did not adjudicate educational policies unless policies contravened provisions of the United States Constitution. But within recent decades the scope of the courts' review of educational practices has been expanded greatly. Federal courts are still reluctant to intervene in matters involving the judgment or discretion of local school boards, but they nevertheless do so in clear cases of infringement upon constitutional rights or of abuses of power. Another reason for the courts' expanding review is the rapid buildup of constitutional questions that went unchallenged in the past, as well as the broadened interpretation of constitutional rights.

EDUCATION AND CHURCH-STATE RELATIONS

The First Amendment to the Constitution states in part that "Congress shall make no law respecting an establishment of religion, or prohibiting the free exercise thereof." Thus this provision of the Bill of Rights is commonly referred to as "separation of church and state." This principle has been the constitutional basis for many important Supreme Court decisions. In 1930 the Court ruled that a Louisiana statute which provided free textbooks to students attending church-related schools did not violate the Constitution. In 1947 it ruled similarly in a case in which New Jersey law provided transportation at public expense to children attending church-related schools. These cases helped to establish the "child-benefit theory," which dictates that subsidies for privileges granted to the child cannot be regarded as establishment of religion by the government. However, in 1971 the Court ruled unconstitutional the statutes in Rhode Island and Pennsylvania that allocated public subsidies for teachers' salaries in private schools.

In 1972 the Supreme Court banned a law in Ohio that provided indirect aid to parochial schools in the form of state reimbursement for students attending nonpublic schools. It also struck down laws in New York, Pennsylvania, and New Jersey that would have provided tax credits or reimbursements for parents of children attending nonpublic elementary and secondary schools. The Court held in the Ohio case that "what may not be done directly may not be done indirectly lest the Establishment Clause become a mockery." In a landmark case in Pennsylvania in 1975 the Supreme Court further narrowed the boundaries of permissible aid to nonpublic elementary and secondary schools by banning reimbursement from public funds for counseling, testing, and psychological services; speech and hearing therapy; special remedial instruction; and instructional materials other than textbooks. At present, the child-benefit theory appears to permit public reimbursement for little other than textbooks, school lunches, and school transportation. In the Pennsylvania case, the Court established these three tests of the constitutionality of public funds for nonpublic schools:

- Is the purpose of the act primarily to aid religion?
- Does the effect of the act substantially advance religion?
- Would the aid result in excessive government entanglement with religion?

Needless to say, these constitutional provisions have had a serious impact on the financing of parochial schools and have been bitterly criticized by them.

Religious instruction in the schools was held unconstitutional by the Court in 1948 in a case arising in Champaign, Illinois. However, in the *Zorach* case arising in New York State the Supreme Court held in 1952 that religious instruction on released time from school was not unconstitutional if it was held off school grounds and with no compulsion upon the student to attend. In 1962 the Court ruled that the recommendation by the New York Board of Regents of a prayer for use in the schools was an abrogation of the Constitution. Similarly, a year later, the Court held that state statutes requiring the reading of the Bible or the recitation of the Lord's Prayer contravened the Constitution. In a case in 1943 the Court ruled that students could not be compelled to salute the flag in school when such activity violated their religious beliefs.

EDUCATION AND EQUAL PROTECTION

The Fourteenth Amendment to the Constitution states in part that "no state shall make or enforce any law which shall abridge the privileges and immunities of citizens. . . nor deny any person. . . the equal protection of the laws." Many cases have been adjudicated on the basis of this amendment. Protection was given to private elementary and secondary schools in 1925 when the high tribunal ruled that an Oregon statute that inhibited private schools by compelling students to attend public schools violated the Fourteenth Amendment.

The rights of students. A Nebraska law that prohibited the teaching of German in public or private schools was held unconstitutional by the Supreme Court in 1919 on the grounds that it violated the liberty of parents to have their children educated as they see fit. The Court held in 1969 in the important *Tinker* case that schools could not prohibit students from wearing armbands or engaging in nondisruptive protest, that students have the same constitutional guarantees of freedom of speech and expression that are granted to all persons. Similar decisions have protected students' rights in matters of dress and hair style.

In the famous *Lau* case, the Supreme Court ruled that Chinese-speaking students in San Francisco were being denied equal educational opportunity and therefore equal protection of the laws because they were being taught in the English language, which they did not understand. This decision triggered a major review of practices in hundreds of school districts by HEW's Office of Civil Rights to ensure bilingual instruction in all schools that enrolled non-English-speaking students.

In another famous case, i.e. *Goss v. Lopez,* the Supreme Court struck down an Ohio law that allowed school officials under certain conditions to suspend students who were troublemakers. The Court held that such suspension is unconstitutional when it is done without giving students advance notice of the charges and a hearing with the opportunity to defend themselves. Otherwise, the Court reasoned, students are denied the right to an education under the protection of the Constitution.

This case had far-reaching consequences because virtually all states had similar laws. The Court faces the delicate task of protecting essential due-process considerations for students while at the same time giving school authorities the power they need to protect the school from disruptive students who sometimes constitute a threat to its well-being.

However, the Supreme Court in the *Rodriguez* case in 1971 ruled in a 5-4 decision that public schooling is not a fundamental right under the protection of the Constitution. However, a number of state courts find it to be a fundamental right under their state constitutions. The *Rodriguez* case involved unequal financial support among local school districts that resulted from variations in wealth among the districts.

The rights of teachers. The Supreme Court has also been attentive to the rights of teachers. In 1952 the Court declared that a loyalty oath for teachers, which was prescribed by law in Oklahoma, was an unconstitutional violation of freedom of thought, speech, and action as guaranteed by the First and Fourteenth Amendments. But in the same year, the Supreme Court upheld the Feinberg Law in New York, in which members of organizations deemed to be subversive were disqualified as teachers. In this instance, the Court held that the right to protect society from subversive doctrine took precedence over teachers' freedom of expression. The Court has also held unconstitutional the practice of requiring pregnant teachers to go on mandatory maternity leaves for an arbitrarily specified period of time before and after childbirth. The Court reasoned that this "unduly penalizes a female teacher for deciding to have a child" and is a violation of the equal rights protection of the Fourteenth Amendment. The Court ruled that maternity leaves must be considered on the same terms as other temporary disabilities.

Racial discrimination. The Supreme Court has reviewed many cases dealing with discrimination by race in the public schools. In 1896 the Court ruled that the segregation of students by race in schools was not in violation of the Constitution so long as the separate facilities were equal. In 1954 the Court reversed this position in *Brown v. Board of Education of Topeka,* which precipitated great controversy and affected educational policy and practice most profoundly. In this litigation, the Court maintained that separate school systems were inherently unequal and deprived black children of rights guaranteed them under the Fourteenth Amendment. The Court later ruled that segregation by race in schools must be terminated "with all deliberate speed." But many states and local school districts found adroit stratagems for violating the spirit and sometimes the letter of the 1954 decision, and litigation over the many implications of the decision, was contested bitterly in the courts thereafter. Its patience exhausted, the Supreme Court ruled in 1969—fifteen years later —that the deadline for deliberate speed had been exhausted and ordered an immediate end to delay in desegregation of schools. In 1971 the Supreme Court upheld the constitutionality of busing of students to reduce segregation.

Federal courts have also ruled that state aid in the form of textbooks and other services to racially segregated private schools is unconstitutional and that the refusal of independent schools to admit nonwhite students, even when the schools are totally supported from private funds, is a violation of the Civil Rights Act of 1964.

In a series of highly controversial cases, the Supreme Court has examined the possibility of racial discrimination that results from school-district boundaries in metropolitan areas. These boundaries often isolate predominantly black schools that cannot be integrated effectively without redrawing district boundaries to include predominantly white suburbs. Although we have certainly not had the last judicial ruling on this issue, the position of the Supreme Court presently is that local school-district boundaries need not be redrawn to accomplish integration unless it can be shown that interdistrict segregation results from racially discriminatory acts by the state or local school districts.

POWERS OF SCHOOL AUTHORITIES

A number of Supreme Court decisions have dealt with educational conflicts among federal, state, and local powers. One must not assume that the Supreme Court, in its devotion to enforce the Constitution, is unmindful of the virtues of local control of education. In a decision regarding a dispute over redrawing local district boundaries to desegregate schools, the Court declared:

No single tradition in public education is more deeply rooted than local control over the operation of schools; local autonomy has long been thought essential both to the maintenance of community concern and support for public schools and to the quality of the educational process.

The Court has also persistently recognized that education is a legal function of the state and has upheld the principle of states' rights in education except when the Constitution is violated or gross injustices otherwise occur.

In an important recent case, the Supreme Court ruled that board members may be held personally vulnerable in liability suits if they knowingly and maliciously violate students' constitutional rights. In the case that triggered this decision, three Arkansas high school girls who ineffectively "spiked" the punch at a school affair were suspended from school. The board members were held liable for violating the girls' rights of due process. This case has aroused anxiety that qualified people may not want to volunteer for service on school boards. Some have predicted that it will be necessary for attorneys of school districts to sit with boards constantly to make sure that no decision violates constitutional rights, which are often so vague that even experts on constitutional law disagree about them.

As is readily seen, the federal courts—as well as state and local courts—are extending their jurisdiction over educational practices, and many more cases are going to litigation. Moreover, court decisions promulgated yesterday can be no sure guide tomorrow in a society where educational practices and social outlook change so swiftly. Some educators denigrate the courts' expanding review of educational practices on the grounds that courts are taking over decision-making prerogatives of local boards and state agencies. Many more difficult decisions will face the courts in their struggle to protect the rights of teachers and young citizens and at the same time to protect the powers of administrators and lay board members who make decisions affecting the common welfare of our schools.

Private education programs

The national program of education in the United States is not a federal system. All the educational agencies of this country—federal, state, county, and local; governmental and nongovernmental; public, private, and parochial—constitute the national program of education. The educational activities of the federal government are only a part of the national program. Public—meaning tax-supported—education, though very important, is only a portion of the national effort in education. Private education, including parochial schools, colleges, and seminaries, has been and will continue to be an important component of our national program of education.

The earliest schools and colleges were parochial. Education in the early years was supported primarily by churches and synagogues. Many children do not go to public schools, and it is not compulsory for them to do so. In the parochial field, schools supported by the Roman Catholic Church enroll 83 percent of the nonpublic school students. Schools supported by the Lutheran church are second, enrolling 4 percent. Private, independent, non-church-related schools enroll 7 percent. In higher education, many colleges and universities are private.

Numerous nongovernmental professional organizations wield much power in education. The largest professional organizations are the National Education Association (NEA) and the American Federation of Teachers (AFT), described in Chapter 2. The largest parochial professional group is the National Catholic Education Association, organized in 1904. Professional organizations such as the American Council on Education and the national and regional accrediting associations affect secondary and higher education more than the federal government per se does.

Various private foundations have had great impact on our national program of education. Educational grants from numerous nongovernmental foundations (Carnegie, Ford, Duke, Mott, Rockefeller, Kellogg, and countless others) have been very influential in terms of both money and innovation.

The National Assessment for Educational Progress is an important enterprise financed in

Private education, such as this Catholic parochial school, has been an important component of our national program of education.

part by the Carnegie Corporation, the Fund for the Advancement of Education, and the Office of Education. This program functions under the aegis of the Education Commission of the States and under the direction of the Committee on Assessing Progress of Education (CAPE). This first massive effort to measure the educational attainment of young Americans by subject fields gives the nation very useful bench marks of progress and helps schools allocate resources and select programs and practices of instruction more effectively.[3]

[3]For more information on this topic, see Roy H. Forbes, "National Assessment: One Tool in the Educational Toolbox," *NASSP Bulletin*, May 1976, pp. 66–70.

Various other national testing programs have also had great indirect impact upon our schools. The College Entrance Examination Board, begun in 1901, is supported by the resources of the Educational Testing Service, the Carnegie Foundation for the Advancement of Teaching, and the American Council on Education. These national testing programs, used by many colleges and universities to help determine which applicants should be admitted to college, have shaped instruction in secondary schools because the results of the tests are viewed as a measure of the effectiveness of high schools.

Private corporations producing educational materials—textbooks, reference works, tests, and audiovisual materials of instruction—have also influenced the development of instruction in our schools. Within the last decade a score or more of large industrial corporations have purchased publishing houses to link the hardware of the former with the software of the latter, both in design and distribution. In some cases the federal government has contracted with these firms to stimulate the research and development necessary for new instructional technology.

The Council for Basic Education is one of many national, private, nonprofit groups that attempt through study and discussion to shape the future of educational practices and policies in the direction of their interests. The Council presses for more rigorous academic standards and more concentrated attention upon the academic subjects in the curriculum.

The National Committee for Citizens in Education, discussed in Chapter 1, is a private, nonprofit organization financed initially by a grant from the Ford Foundation. It was organized to find out who controls education and who should control it. This organization contends that the public is being pushed into the courts to establish its voice in education, which is otherwise being lost through the rising power of teachers' organizations and the increasing red tape and controls of state and local governments.

The Legislative Conference of National Organizations is an example of a coalition of national professional organizations that lobby together in the nation's capital for more effective federal legislation and funding of education. It attempts to speak for its member organizations with one voice in advancing educational interests. Known popularly as the "big six," this coalition consists of the American Association of School Administrators, the Council of Chief State School Officers, the National Association of State Boards of Education, the National Congress of Parents and Teachers, the National Education Association, and the National School Boards Association.

Many illustrations throughout this book depict governmental and nongovernmental educational activities that are *national* in scope and significance but that are not *federal* in the strict sense of the word. Diversity in support, purposes, program, and organization is indeed a vital characteristic of the American national program in education, as it should be in a dynamic democracy.

Principles and proposals for improvement

Without doubt the federal government's support of our educational effort has added considerably to the quality of our education. However, we still fall far short of realizing the federal government's full potential for educational improvement. There are many reasons for this; at the risk of oversimplification, we shall call attention to some important reasons and to some principles and proposals for improvement.

THE LACK OF NATIONAL POLICY

As a nation we have never faced very realistically the question of what we expect our educational system to accomplish. We have frequently imposed upon the schools, often through federal grants, responsibility for achieving certain national objectives that were not uniquely educational goals. A good example is the National Defense Education Act, which sought to strengthen our defense posture through education, thereby corrupting the purposes of education and unbalancing the curriculum. Without definition of the national purpose in education, there can be no definition of national policy. A well-defined national policy on education is long overdue. Spasmodic, crisis-oriented federal legislation, with its often unanticipated and sometimes unfortunate dislocations of federal-state-local relations, must be supplanted by a coherent, rational, long-range plan for the general improvement of the nation's schools.

The lack of a well-defined national policy on education can be explained but not excused by a number of factors. Changes in the White House, rapid turnover of U.S. Commissioners of Education, intrusion of partisan political considerations, the fragmentation of special educational interest groups lobbying in Washington, Congresses that enact significant educational legislation and then refuse to appropriate sufficient funds to implement the legislation—these and other circumstances all contribute to federal programs that are too often ill-conceived, hastily implemented, and at cross purposes with state and local aspirations. Moreover, responsibility for educational decision making is badly fragmented among many federal agencies of government: the U.S. Office of Education; the Office of Management and Budget; the Department of Health, Education, and Welfare; the President; the various education committees in both houses; and the Congress itself.

THE NEED FOR A DEPARTMENT OF EDUCATION

Repeated proposals have been advanced that the federal interest in education is so important that a separate department of education should be established headed by a secretary with Cabinet status. Bills providing for this have been introduced in almost every recent session of Congress, and it appears closer to passage. Such a department could be instrumental in better sensing national needs and goals related to education and in formulating a unified national policy in education. It has also been proposed that a national advisory commission on education composed of outstanding citizens be appointed to advise the department of education and Congress, functioning as a sort of supernational school board. Jimmy Carter has advocated the creation of a department of education to present a "stronger voice for education at the federal level" and to preside over the consolidation of presently scattered grant programs.

BETTER MANAGEMENT OF FEDERAL ACTIVITIES IN EDUCATION

One might assume that all federal programs in education are neatly headquartered in the Division of Education in the Department of Health, Education, and Welfare. This is not the case. Some duplication of effort exists between the Office of Education and the National Institute of Education. Job Corps is administered by the Department of Labor, the GI Bill by the Veterans Administration, the school lunch program by the Department of Agriculture—the list goes on and on. Moreover, some federal appropriations have not been prudently managed. For example, six civil rights groups examined the use of $75 million appropriated by Congress to assist desegregation in the South. They concluded that the consequences were a "fraud upon the Congress." They reported discovery of funds going to several programs which were "racist in conception and which were leading to the resegregation of schools." Then, too, federally funded programs are often not well attuned to needs. The phenomenon of inertia tends to perpetuate some programs beyond necessity, while others lag behind need. The reorganization of responsibility for the management of most federal activities of education into a single department of education could help to reduce proliferation and duplication of effort. Clearer distinction must also be drawn between the jurisdiction of the Office of Education and the National Institute of Education.

THE EXTENSION OF CREATIVE FEDERALISM

The concept of creative federalism should guide the federal government's participation in the educational enterprise. It could arrest the current unprecedented thrust toward control of education by the federal government and bring about an expanded partnership of the three levels of government in better-coordinated planning, programming, and budgeting. It would permit the federal government to participate more generously in the financial support of education while remaining a junior partner in its control. It would permit the federal government to limit its actions to financial assistance for educational needs that are critical to the nation or for activities that it can handle more effectively than state and local systems. Thus the federal government could exercise leadership that is stimulating but noncoercive.

The future

To our disappointment, we expect continued fragmentation in the federal effort in education. The ambiguity in the division of responsibility between the National Institute of Education and the Office of Education is not likely to recede. The scattering of administrative responsibility among various executive agencies is also likely to persist, but probably to a lesser degree than at present. Eventually, we predict, a separate department of education with Cabinet status will be established and, in time, bring greater coordination of effort. But progress will be slow because of established vested interests.

Unfortunately, we see no substantial increase in federal funding of education. The depressed state of the national economy, partisan preferences that split Congress, and the lack of effective advocacy of educational interests in the executive and legislative branches of government depress the outlook for federal funding. We do expect an increase in federal revenue sharing, but with the continuation of many categorical grants and an impressive array of federal controls.[4] These categorical grants will be directed primarily toward eliminating disparities in the education of the poor and toward strengthening further the education of students with learning disabilities. Other money will be targeted toward school reform, but not enough on long-range fundamental research on teaching and learning. This kind of research has the maximum potential payoff, but its results strain the patience of a quixotic Congress. We are sure that emphasis upon program evaluation and demonstration of benefits commensurate with costs will intensify.

We expect continued proliferation of Supreme Court decisions that impact upon education. Citi-

zens are increasingly inclined to take their educational problems to the courts, and the courts draw tighter protections around the constitutional rights of students. We believe that the Supreme Court will eventually rule that education is a right implicit in the Constitution, a step which they did not take in the *Rodriguez* case. We think the Court will not reverse its position on the use of public funds for church-related schools and will continue to protect the separation of church and state.

We see a rising influence of national professional organizations in education and greater intensity—but not necessarily greater effectiveness—in their lobbying efforts. We predict a decline in the spending and influence of private foundations in the support of education.

Our surest predictions are that the role of the federal government in education will continue to be a matter of sharp debate and that federal interests and states' rights will continue to collide.

Suggested activities

1. Choose a book of interest listed in the bibliography and prepare a critical review of it.
2. Visit a local school system to observe the kinds of programs that have been made possible through federal aid and report your observations and conclusions.
3. Investigate special programs for the preparation of educators that might be of interest to you in planning your own career, such as the National Teacher Corps and the provisions of the Education Professions Development Act.
4. Review the Coleman Report and derive from it the major changes in educational organization and practice that would seem to have the most promise for improving educational opportunity for black Americans.
5. Give the pros and cons of federal aid to education and state your own conclusions.
6. Review all the Supreme Court decisions dealing with a topic of interest to you—such as civil liberties of students and teachers, church and state relations in education, or racial discrimination in the schools—and summarize the Court's pronouncements.
7. Study the literature dealing with categorical versus general federal support for education, listing the advantages and disadvantages of each, and state your own convictions.
8. Summarize the major federal provisions for improving the education of disadvantaged students.

---

[4]For a discussion of how federal control has outrun federal financial support, see Joseph M. Cronin, "The Federal Takeover: Should the Junior Partner Run the Firm?" *Phi Delta Kappan*, April 1976, pp. 499–501.

9. Describe the nationwide educational program of some nongovernmental, private organizations, such as the Ford Foundation.

10. Prepare an anthology of the most important statements on education made by the early leaders of our nation, such as Washington, Adams, Jefferson, Madison, Monroe, and Franklin.

Bibliography

Campbell, Roald F., et al.: *The Organization and Control of American Schools,* 3d ed., Merrill, Columbus, Ohio, 1975, chaps. 2, 7. Discusses the role of the courts and the federal government in our developing educational system, emphasizing the political dynamics.

Carnegie Council on Policy Studies in Higher Education: *The Federal Role in Postsecondary Education: Unfinished Business, 1975–1980,* Jossey-Bass, San Francisco, 1975. Analyzes existing programs of federal support for postsecondary education with recommendations and priorities for the future.

Fuchs, Estelle, and **Robert J. Havighurst:** *To Live on This Earth,* Doubleday, New York, 1972. Examines the educational problems and needs of minority groups with particular emphasis upon American Indians.

Kimbrough, Ralph B. and **Michael Y. Nunnery:** *Educational Administration,* Macmillan, New York, 1976, chap. 7. Impact of Constitution, courts, Congress, and Office of Education on development of education.

Knezevich, Stephen J.: *Administration of Public Education,* 3d ed., Harper & Row, New York, 1975, chap. 12. Historical and contemporary description of the federal involvement in education—legislation, court decisions, and governmental structure.

Lapati, Americo D.: *Education and the Federal Government: A Historical Record,* Mason-Charter, New York, 1975. Easily read historical account of the background and circumstances that shape federal laws and regulations on education.

Levitan, Sara (ed.): *The Federal Social Dollar in Its Own Backyard,* Bureau of National Affairs, Washington, 1973. Examines the federal government's grants-in-aid programs in education and other fields.

Morphet, Edgar L., Roe L. Johns, and **Theodore L. Reller:** *Educational Organization and Administration,* 3d. ed., Prentice-Hall, Englewood Cliffs, N.J., 1974, chap. 8. Impact of federal courts, Congress, and executive agencies of government on education with emphasis on problems and issues.

National School Public Relations Association: *Desegregation,* Arlington, Va., 1973. Federal programs and guidelines for school desegregation plans and prospects for the future.

Shaw, Russell, and **Richard J. Hurley,** (eds.): *Trends and Issues in Catholic Education,* Citation, New York, 1970. Papers by leading Catholic educators on timely topics and forces shaping the future of Catholic schools.

Summerfield, Harry L.: *Power and Process,* McCutchan, Berkeley, Calif., 1974. Rare and accurate description of how power works in Washington with respect to the formulation of educational policies and federal aid to education.

U.S. Commission on Civil Rights: *Toward Quality Education for Mexican Americans,* Washington, 1975. Analyzes the needs of Mexican Americans to achieve full educational opportunity and makes recommendations.

Chapter 15

International education

Foundations of international education

Throughout our existence on this planet, we have been beleaguered by our inability to live in peace with each other. Recently we have been forced to question whether we will continue to dominate this planet. We are becoming persuaded that we cannot long survive in a world of ethnocentrism and chauvinism. We are reminded of Sir James Barrie's play "The Admirable Crichton," which depicted how shipwrecked persons isolated on a desolate island quickly learned how trivial and senseless were their class and ethnic differences in comparison with their relentless need to cooperate for survival.

A half-century ago, H. G. Wells warned that

human history becomes more and more a race between education and catastrophe. Many people have for centuries viewed education as our best hope for improving the human condition. The particular kind of education most related to this task is commonly referred to as "international education." This term embraces many meanings and many different types of activities. It includes "the study of educational, social, political, and economic forces in international relations, with special emphasis on . . . educational forces." It also includes international programs that "further mutual understanding by means of exchange of instructional materials, techniques, students, teachers, and technicians." "Comparative education" deals with studying and comparing various educational theories and practices in different countries in order to deepen un-

385

derstandings of other nations and their problems, and sometimes to look at and perhaps solve one country's problems in terms of methods that have worked for another.[1] "International development education," a relative newcomer to the realm of international programs in education, deals with processes involved in the national development of countries, making use of economics, political science, and other social sciences. These terms are not always used consistently. Sometimes they are used interchangeably, and they may overlap a great deal. Nevertheless, they can all make important contributions to the betterment of world conditions.

Although education is not the remedy for all of the cares of the world, it is unquestionably one of our most potent assets. But the hour is late, and the task is great; nothing short of a maximum effort will relieve what is rapidly becoming a world educational crisis.[2] Although educational systems have been expanding greatly in most countries since the early 1950s, too often the demand has outrun the resources. The frightening dimension of the problem can be seen from several sets of statistics. About two-fifths of the world's children between the ages of 5 and 14 find no schooling available. In a number of Arab nations, almost two-thirds of school-aged young people are unable to attend school. In Asia the percentage of those unable to attend school is close to the international average of 40 percent. Many countries are striving to achieve universal primary education by the late 1970s, but progress so far has been disappointing.

The number of illiterate adults in the world is increasing. UNESCO reports that their number increased from 700 million in 1950 to 783 million in 1970. (Although the total increased, there was a decrease in percentage, from 44.3 to 34.2, because population increased during this period.) Almost three-fourths of the adults in Africa are illiterate, and almost one-fifth of the adults in Latin America are illiterate. In the United States and Canada less than 1 percent are illiterate. Some experts in national development believe that it is

hardly possible for a country to sustain substantial industrial growth when more than 40 percent of its adults are illiterate. Figure 15-1 shows the correspondence between the literacy of nations and their economic prosperity.[3]

The crisis in education is abetted more by lack of resources than by lack of effort. In Africa, for example, most countries spend at least 20 percent of their total public expenditures for education; many spend 35 percent, and some spend as much as 40 percent. In many African countries the annual rate of increase in educational expenditures exceeds the rate of growth in national income. These countries, like many countries on other continents, are plagued by a shortage of funds, teachers, classrooms, and materials—shortages of everything except students. A report to the United Nations by Secretary-General Kurt Waldheim states that many physicians, engineers, scientists, and other educated persons move from their native countries to developed nations for various reasons, among them higher incomes, thus thwarting social and economic progress in needy, disadvantaged areas. In 1972 alone, 7,000 physicians migrated to the United States from developing nations. Many of these highly skilled persons may be forced to leave their native countries because of lack of opportunity. Money they send home helps, of course, but the result is still a loss of talent, which could make valuable contributions in improving conditions. Although the nature of the educational crisis varies among countries in form and magnitude, no nation is spared; the exigency exists in the rich and the poor, the large and the small, the old and the new, the industrial and the agrarian.

Even more serious perhaps than the crisis in education is the crisis in hunger. Some experts estimate that close to a billion people in the world suffer from malnutrition. According to data compiled by the United Nations and its Food and Agriculture Organization, the average daily caloric intake per person is less than the recommended minimum of 2,300 in more than a score of countries. The chief of the Food and Agriculture Organization states that it is not possible for the poorest and hungriest nations to achieve self-sufficiency in

[1] All above definitions have been taken, directly or indirectly, from Carter V. Good, (ed.), *Dictionary of Education,* 3d ed., McGraw-Hill, New York, 1973.
[2] For a fuller discussion of the impending world educational crisis, see Philip H. Coombs, *The World Educational Crisis,* Oxford, New York, 1968.

[3] For additional information on illiteracy, see Antony Brock, "The Battle against Illiteracy: A Unesco Survey," *School and Society,* March 1970, pp. 181, 189. See also U Thant, "Toward World Literacy," *School and Society,* Summer 1971, pp. 282–83.

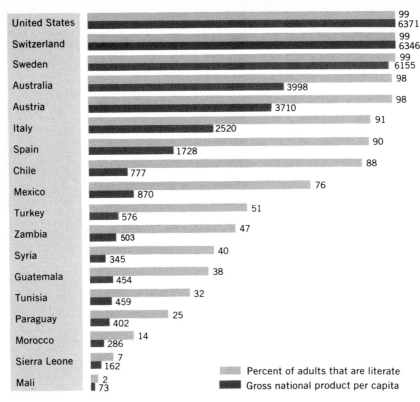

United States — 99 / 6371
Switzerland — 99 / 6346
Sweden — 99 / 6155
Australia — 98 / 3998
Austria — 98 / 3710
Italy — 91 / 2520
Spain — 90 / 1728
Chile — 88 / 777
Mexico — 76 / 870
Turkey — 51 / 576
Zambia — 47 / 503
Syria — 40 / 345
Guatemala — 38 / 454
Tunisia — 32 / 459
Paraguay — 25 / 402
Morocco — 14 / 286
Sierra Leone — 7 / 162
Mali — 2 / 73

Percent of adults that are literate
Gross national product per capita

Figure 15-1 Percent of adults who are literate and gross national product per capita in selected countries. (Data on literacy from UNESCO *Statistical Yearbook;* GNP per capita data compiled by Agency for International Development.)

food production within a decade. The problem is aggravated in some countries by crop failures and high prices of grain, fertilizer, and petroleum. One authority, Raymond Ewell, a chemical economist, has presented a timetable of what he calls "the greatest catastrophe in history." He warns that the serious famine already evident in India, Pakistan, and China may spread to other nations in Asia, Africa, and South America by the 1980s unless present trends are reversed.

Other forecasters are more optimistic. Herman Kahn of the Hudson Institute, which studies the probabilities of the future, believes that growth in food production will exceed population growth, although he concedes that widespread starvation will continue in some countries.[4] The National

Academy of Sciences, in its report *Population and Food,* states that the actual magnitude of the food problem is not known. Experts testifying at the General Assembly of the World Future Society in 1975 agreed that the world will feed its people only if a major effort is made to slow the growth of population and to increase food production in developing countries—two problems that seem to depend somewhat upon education addressed to family planning and agricultural development.[5]

Clearly the people of the world recognize as never before the need for strengthening education as one important response to these critical problems. The demand for education by the common people of all nations has never been so clear or so compelling.

[4]For further discussion of optimistic and pessimistic views of the world's food problem, see Herman Kahn and William Brown, "A World Turning Point—And a Better Prospect for the Future," *The Futurist,* December 1975, pp. 284–292.

[5]See Jean Mayer and others, "Feeding the World in the Year 2000," *The Futurist,* December 1975, pp. 293–306; and Harold G. Shane, "The Coming Global Famine," *Phi Delta Kappan,* September 1974, pp. 34–38.

THE HISTORICAL DEVELOPMENT OF INTERNATIONAL EDUCATION

The historical calendar for this chapter reveals important events related to the development of international education, which we now consider briefly.

The universities of ancient Greece, where students and teachers from many lands gathered to exchange knowledge, have been regarded as the earliest progenitors of cross-cultural learning. During the Middle Ages, informal intercultural exchanges took place in the great centers of learning in Europe and Asia. Great universities, particularly those at Prague, Bologna, and Oxford, attracted many foreign students.

The Moravian educator Johann Amos Comenius might be regarded as the father of modern concepts of international education. Comenius sought to end the political and religious wars that beleaguered his times. In the middle of the seventeenth century, Comenius proposed a "College of Light," which would serve as an international academy and office of education to see that "no one nation rises against another, and that no man dare to stand up and teach men to fight or to make weapons." Comenius believed that universal schools, universal books, and a universal language would be essential to this panharmony through which the whole world would be enlightened. In the centuries that followed Comenius' work, Montaigne, Rousseau, Kant, Fichte, and others insisted that international educational cooperation was essential to world peace.

Beginnings of international educational cooperation. The late nineteenth century marked the beginning of organized international conferences on education. In 1851 representatives from Germany, England, France, and the United States met in London to exchange knowledge about education.

The twentieth century ushered in a new phase of international educational cooperation in education. Previously activity had been confined mostly to international conferences and exchanges of educational materials. The new period quickened the exchange of educators and students and put international teams of educators to work strengthening schools in backward countries.

Cecil Rhodes, an Englishman, established in 1899 a new approach to cross-cultural education by providing scholarships at Oxford University for students from other lands. Many distinguished Americans, including Supreme Court Justice Byron White, were beneficiaries of this largess and thereby helped to deepen human understanding. By the middle of the century the United States was providing scholarships for students from other lands through the provisions of the Fulbright and Smith-Mundt Acts. Some other nations have made similar contributions.

In 1901 a wonderful but unheralded event ushered in an important new development in international cooperation in education. Six hundred American schoolteachers sailed across the Pacific to become volunteer teachers in the Philippines. Followed eventually by thousands more, they lived in Filipino homes, helped to construct the schools in which they would teach, and assumed many responsibilities in building the nation that took them far beyond the classrooms. This mass exportation of American teachers, a forerunner of the modern Peace Corps, was surely one of the most remarkable efforts ever undertaken in the realm of international cooperation in educational development.

In 1922 the Committee on Intellectual Cooperation was established under the leadership of such famous scholars as Eve Curie and Albert Einstein. Among other enterprises, the Committee in 1931 marshaled resources from several cooperating nations to aid in the reconstruction of China's educational system, thereby establishing the precedent of multilateral cooperation in improving educational opportunity in underdeveloped countries.

In the early decades of this century, the United States cooperated with other nations of the Western Hemisphere in many multilateral educational endeavors. This nation participated actively in the affairs of the Pan American Union, established in Washington in 1902. The Union, now the Organization of American States, has been active in educational and cultural exchanges among the nations of this hemisphere.

Private organizations joined in the effort to mobilize American know-how in the improvement of educational systems around the world and to deepen international understanding. The Institute of International Education was established in 1919 to supply information, counsel, and direct help to universities and to exchange students, both those going abroad and those coming to this country. Four years later, the International Institute was established at Teachers College, Columbia University, a mecca for thousands of students and teachers from overseas. Many other private and public organizations have undertaken various kinds of educational programs designed to promote literacy, health, and other manifestations of the good life around the world.

The era of accelerated technical assistance. During and following World War II, millions of American service personnel, government officials, and business people were thrust, for the first time in their lives, into foreign cultures and were forced to come to grips with the task of building postwar understandings and relationships that would repair the ravages of war and strengthen world peace. These Americans abroad had relatively little knowledge of the non-Western world.

By 1945 the United States was thrust into a role of international leadership at a time characterized by cold-war cleavages between the bloc of communist nations and the democracies of the West. Education was seen by the United States at that time as an instrument of foreign policy in strengthening democracy in its fateful struggle with communism. During the cold war much of the United States' educational activity abroad consisted of technical assistance programs and scholarly exchange programs as instruments of foreign policy.

The inauguration of the Marshall Plan in 1948 provided economic aid and technical assistance for the rebuilding of war-ravaged nations and their school systems. The Point Four program, begun in 1950, continued technical assistance for many purposes, including education, and was later embraced in 1961 by the Agency for International Development (AID), described in more detail later.

Some observers have characterized this period as an age of "cultural imperialism" in which the prime motivation was that of ensuring that other governments might be fit to survive by making allies of them through education for democracy. Many exchanges of students, teachers, and materials, however, were genuinely altruistic in character, motivated largely by a spirit of global understanding which became a more propulsive purpose of international education in the 1960s and 1970s.

The era of global civilization. Slowly but inexorably during the 1960s we were coming to realize that the most compelling characteristic of the modern world is not its great unrest, although that was most visible, but the increasing interpenetration of the destinies of peoples and nations throughout this shrinking globe.

The proliferation of nations with nuclear power capability, along with the fantastic development of weapon-carrying missiles and satellites, helped us realize that without international cooperation we were capable of destroying life on this planet. The great problems of the world—poverty, malnutrition, apartheid, population explosion, and illiteracy, among others—were seen increasingly as urgent challenges to all humanity rather than as Soviet-American issues.

We have spoken of these forces because they may augur an era in history which, it can be hoped, will forge a nobler view and destiny for international education.[6] The new argument for international education is based upon reaching common understanding among cultures and upon narrowing the gap between the have and the have-not nations—not for purposes of imperialism but rather as a means of bringing greater vitality, happiness, and freedom to all people. It is far too early to forecast the success of this spirit in international education but not too early to proclaim an avid hope that it will contribute to the United Nations' goal of "promoting social progress and better standards of life in larger freedom."

Purposes of international education

For several compelling reasons, it is easy to make a case for increased emphasis upon and improved quality of American education in its international context. The reasons are related to three broad purposes:

- Survival
- Improvement of the human condition in less favored communities
- Cultural enrichment

[6]For a discussion of this new era and its impact upon international education, see Harold Taylor, *The World and the American Teacher,* American Association of Colleges for Teacher Education, Washington, 1968, pp. 15–16.

Historical Calendar

The Development of International Education

1643	Establishment of a College of Light to serve as international office of education and universal academy urged by Moravian educator and churchman Comenius
1816	Training begun for officers from foreign countries at the U.S. Military Academy at West Point
1840	Library of Congress program initiated for exchanges with foreign countries
1849	Educational exchange service begun by Smithsonian Institution with similar agencies abroad
1854	Observations on overseas schools published by Henry Barnard in his National Education in Europe
1899	New approach to cross-cultural education established by Englishman Cecil Rhodes through scholarships to Oxford for students from abroad
1901	Mass exportation of teachers started when the first six hundred of thousands of American teachers arrived in Philippines to begin heroic service
1902	Pan American Union established to strengthen cross-cultural exchange among Western-hemisphere nations
1908	First world center for the exchange of educational information established in Ostend by Belgian educator Edward Peeters
1910	Carnegie Endowment for International Peace formed, with primary accent on international education
1919	Institute of International Education established privately, accenting international exchanges
1922	International conference of scholars and first major international organization to aid educational development in backward countries sponsored by Committee on Intellectual Cooperation
1923	World Federation of Education Associations formed with aid of National Education Association
1925	International Bureau of Education established in Geneva to publish studies of comparative education, teacher education, and school organization
1938	Division of Cultural Relations established in the Department of State
1941	Division of Inter-American Educational Relations formed in the U.S. Office of Education
1946	United States membership in, and funds for, UNESCO approved
1946	Fulbright program for international exchanges approved by Congress
1946	United Nations International Children's Emergency Fund (UNICEF) established to provide help for children in war-ravaged countries
1946	World Organization of the Teaching Profession (WOTP) organized with active participation of American educators (WCOTP in 1952)
1946	Division of International Education, U.S. Office of Education, established
1947	Program launched by the National Education Association to send food, clothing, and books to devastated countries and to bring teachers to the United States for visits

1948	Smith-Mundt law for global program in "information and educational exchange" approved by Congress
1949	Point Four program of technical assistance to other nations proclaimed by President Truman
1953	International Council on Education for Teaching started by educators of teachers
1956	Comparative Education Society, to study education around the world, organized in the United States
1958	Soviet-American Cultural Exchange Agreement, to promote cultural and educational reciprocity, signed
1960	East-West Center established with federal aid at the University of Hawaii, to promote "mutual understanding among the countries of Asia, the Pacific area, and the United States"
1961	Agency for International Development (AID), designed to unify and shape aid to other nations, created by Congress
1961	Peace Corps launched by the United States for sending Americans to work abroad in education and other fields
1961	Previous legislation consolidated by passage of Mutual Educational and Cultural Exchange Act (Fulbright-Hays Act)
1962	Education and World Affairs established by grants from Ford Foundation and Carnegie Corporation to strengthen performance of American colleges in world affairs
1962	Bureau of International Education in U.S. Office of Education created
1963	International Institute of Educational Planning established by UNESCO to "create workable plans for developing educational systems" around the world
1965	White House Conference on International Cooperation, including educational exchanges, held as part of worldwide observance of International Cooperation Year
1966	International Education Act approved by Congress, but its fiscal implementation postponed
1968	Institute of International Studies established by U.S. Office of Education to serve as central clearinghouse for work in intercultural education
1970	Four-year polycultural international liberal arts college named after the late Dag Hammarskjold opened at Columbia, Maryland
1970	International Education Year observed by the United Nations to emphasize educational planning and improvement in developing nations
1970	International Peace Corps Secretariat established to help other nations establish Peace Corps
1972	Permanent home for the United Nations International School opened in New York for youths from eighty nations
1972	Proclaimed by UNESCO as International Book Year
1974	United Nations University world headquarters opened in Tokyo
1977	World cultures and other forms of international and intercultural education common in most American schools and universities

Indeed, one might argue that these three reasons are reciprocal and inseparable. Nevertheless, for purposes of discussion we shall deal with each separately.

SURVIVAL

A new concept of world understanding is emerging as the world problems become more complex and more inexorable. We are facing crisis after crisis—problems of such scope and enormity that one feels they are too great to cope with or too far in the future to worry about. It is becoming clearer that the world problems cannot be dealt with simply by giving financial aid or distributing books and food. It is possible that we could destroy each other through a nuclear war; we could exhaust the world's supply of energy and other resources; we could continue to overpopulate the earth so that the food supply would give out and famine would eventually overtake us; we could rob ourselves and future generations of air and water, and thus of life itself.

The concept of international education is thought by many to be obsolete in terms of today's and tomorrow's needs. They feel it implies a descriptive approach to studying and understanding present problems and cultures instead of a long-range, future-oriented approach. It becomes more and more important for us to become aware of our interdependence. We need to rethink our values and goals as citizens of the world rather than as citizens of disparate nations. We need a plan to sustain our world, its resources, and its peoples. In his book *Education for a Global Society,* James Becker speaks of the world as a developing country. This helps to put things in perspective.[7]

World order education, a form of peace studies, is a solution-oriented concept to bring about social and cultural change. Its commitment is to peace and to the betterment of the human condition. World order education focuses on planning to create conditions in the world to serve human needs. William Boyer, director of the Alternative Futures Program and teacher of world order education at the University of Hawaii, says:

We are beginning to understand how it is often easier to solve a number of social and ecological problems simultaneously rather than one at a time. We are also discovering that sensible short-range planning disconnected from long-range planning can often assure that the wrong thing will be done in the long run. Also, rational plans to serve a local community, developed in isolation from the larger society, often assure results contradictory to the larger public interest.[8]

Richard N. Gardner, professor of Law and International Organization at Columbia University, believes that we should strike a world survival agreement, placing rights and limitations on both developing and developed countries for the mutual protection of the countries involved. He states:

We need to strike a great world "survival bargain" in which access to energy and other raw materials which industrialized countries need, is traded for other kinds of access that developing countries need—access to markets at stable and remunerative prices, access to technology, management skills and investment capital, and access to a fairer share of decision-making in international institutions.

Gardner also discusses the merits of establishing a World Food Board and appointing an energy commissioner to the United Nations.[9]

IMPROVEMENT OF THE HUMAN CONDITION

Although a long-range survival plan is the ultimate goal, we must still undertake some projects that show more immediate results. We have long been motivated by altruism in our international endeavor, even though not all our overseas enterprise has been altruistic. For centuries men and women have left their homelands to teach and to minister in other ways to less privileged persons abroad, in an effort to reduce ignorance, poverty, illness, and hatred. This purpose is certainly one of the oldest

---

[7]James Becker, *Education for a Global Society,* Phi Delta Kappa, Bloomington, Ind., 1973, p. 13.

[8]William Boyer, "World Order Education: What Is It?", *Phi Delta Kappan,* April 1975, p. 526.

[9]For highlights of Richard N. Gardner's major address, see "A World 'Survival Bargain,'" *Center Report,* February 1975, pp. 23–24.

in the history of international education. This reason alone would be sufficient to justify vast effort abroad.

Thousands of overseas missionaries from America and other lands of many denominations and faiths are assigned to educational work around the world. These dedicated teachers toil long hours at low salaries in all types of educational work from nursery through higher and adult education. Young nations, many of which are underdeveloped, view education as the key to unlock their natural resources, raise their economic productivity, and ensure their political stability. More and more they turn to this country for educational know-how. People who are ill-fed, poorly-housed, and undereducated are unable to enjoy the blessings of economic prosperity and social equality. Disadvantaged and disenchanted, they understandably turn to violence at times as their only means of attaining the necessities of life. Wherever we can roll back the darkness of ignorance, despair, poverty, and disease, we not only extend the prosperity and freedom of other people but buttress our own freedom and security as well.

CULTURAL ENRICHMENT

One fringe benefit that is derived through helping other nations is cultural enrichment. Consider how barren our own culture would be without the heritage of other civilizations—the works of Shakespeare, the artistry of Michelangelo, the educational thought of Pestalozzi, the inheritance of Roman and English law, the philosophy of Confucius, the social-action concepts of Gandhi, the art forms of Africa, the healing genius of Pasteur, the astronomy of Copernicus, the psychological insights of Freud, and the religious teachings of Jesus of Nazareth. Much progress in the exploration of space is attributable to the genius of scientists from abroad. No field of knowledge is indigenous to America, and few if any fields of knowledge are untouched by the scholarship of all nations. Education may be the only asset that can be exported while enriching rather than depleting a nation's resources. Thus we may regard international educational exchange as a modern-day example of the Biblical parable about casting bread upon the water and getting it back a hundredfold.

Programs of international origin

The United States participates in numerous international education programs at home and abroad. We shall consider first some of the more important programs which are of international origin and which are sustained by multilateral support and organization.

UNITED NATIONS AND RELATED PROGRAMS

In 1945 the United States, along with fifty other nations, signed the Charter of the United Nations. The Charter is a document of such vision that every prospective and practicing teacher may wish to study it. The Preamble opens thus:

We the Peoples of the United Nations Determined

To save succeeding generations from the scourge of war, which twice in our lifetime has brought untold sorrow to mankind, and

To reaffirm faith in fundamental rights, in the dignity and worth of the human person, in the equal rights of men and women and of the nations large and small, and

To establish conditions under which justice and respect for the obligations arising from treaties and other sources of international law can be maintained, and

To promote social progress and better standards of life in larger freedom . . . .

Today the United States is linked with 140 other nations in implementing the Charter of this organization, dedicated to peace.

UNESCO. The main vehicle of the UN for advancing knowledge in science and human understanding is the United Nations Educational, Scientific, and Cultural Organization (UNESCO), founded in 1945. UNESCO is one of the specialized agencies provided in the UN Charter and affiliated with the Economic and Social Council. UNESCO's mission is expressed in the following statement from the Preamble of its Constitution:

The Governments of the States Parties to This Constitution, on Behalf of Their Peoples, Declare

that since wars begin in the minds of men, it is in the minds of men that the defenses of peace must be constructed . . .

that the wide diffusion of culture, and the education of humanity for justice and liberty and peace are indispensable to the dignity of man and constitute a sacred duty which all the nations must fulfill in a spirit of mutual assistance and concern.

The statement reads almost like a passage from Comenius.

Official approval by the United States came in July, 1946, when both houses of Congress passed a joint resolution providing for the membership and participation of the United States in UNESCO and authorizing an appropriation. In signing the joint resolution, President Harry S. Truman said:

The government of the United States will work with and through UNESCO to the end that the minds of all people may be freed from ignorance, prejudice, suspicion, and fear and that men may be educated for justice, liberty, and peace.

Technical and financial aid continues to large-scale regional programs in Asia, Africa, and Latin America. These activities are financed by the United Nations Development Program. Among the many projects receiving the special attention of educators and others are those involving the creation of new teachers colleges and technical schools in underdeveloped countries and the strengthening of existing ones; the preparation of world-history textbooks; the reduction of worldwide illiteracy; the promotion of East-West cultural appreciation; the improvement of libraries, museums, and information centers; and the improvement of Latin-American education.

A significant UNESCO development was the establishment in 1963 of the International Institute of Educational Planning, located in Paris. Created with financial aid from the Ford Foundation, the Institute "helps member states of UNESCO create sound, workable plans for developing their educational systems." Two of the major activities center around the development of research and the training of teachers in international education.

The International Bureau of Education, formed by an international group of educators at Geneva in 1925, is now part of UNESCO. The Bureau has published studies of comparative education, organization of national programs of education, the preparation of teachers, and various other aspects of education.

The UN General Assembly designated 1970, the three-hundredth anniversary of Comenius' death, as International Education Year. During the International Education Year, nations were encouraged, through UNESCO, to take stock of their educational needs, undertake studies related to the improvement of education, strive to improve the financial support of education, strive for the elimination of all forms of discrimination and inequality of treatment in their schools, and heighten international awareness of students. The Associated Schools Project seeks to promote understanding through giving students in participating schools information and knowledge of other cultures.

For more effective results, UNESCO sometimes works in conjunction with other agencies, such as UNICEF, the World Health Organization (WHO), the International Labor Organization, and others. The United Nations Development Program finances many of UNESCO's projects that provide technical assistance to nations requesting it.

UNESCO activities are reported in its various publications. The best known of these is the *UNESCO Courier,* which reaches $1\frac{1}{2}$ million persons in more than 120 countries. A third of its subscribers are teachers.[10]

United Nations International School. One of the interesting and significant facets of the educational program of the UN is its International School (UNIS) in New York City for the children of UN personnel. This school, in which many tongues are spoken, occupied a new $10 million building in 1972, made possible largely through the philanthropy of the Ford Foundation. Former UN Secretary-General U Thant regarded UNIS as an "experiment in cultural understanding."

UNICEF. The United Nations Children's Fund was organized originally in 1946 as the United Nations International Children's Emergency Fund (UNICEF) to furnish food, clothing, and medical supplies to children in war-ravaged countries. Supported entirely by voluntary contributions from governments and individuals (almost 40 percent from the United States), UNICEF is currently helping children in more than a hundred countries, mainly in the developing areas of the world. UNICEF projects now include maternal- and child-welfare services and training, child nutrition, and

---

[10]For further discussion of UNESCO programs, see also *What Is UNESCO?* UNESCO, Paris, 1970.

control of disease. The United States Committee for UNICEF, a private, nonprofit organization set up to promote knowledge and support for UNICEF, has provided a wide variety of materials for teaching both adults and children about international cooperation.

In addition to cooperating in special schools and in UNESCO programs, the United States participates in many other educational or semieducational activities through the UN.

The World Bank. The International Bank for Reconstruction and Development, which is commonly known as the "World Bank" and is located in Washington, is a specialized agency of the United Nations. It has a membership of more than eighty nations and exerts support to education, agriculture, and family planning—the tasks which are most directly antidotal to the major world problems. In recent years the World Bank has become an increasingly important agency in the realm of international education. It has lent about $2 billion for education from 1960 to 1975, and about $250 million each succeeding year. The World Bank is contemplating changing its emphasis from secondary and higher education to primary and adult education in order to serve more adequately the needs of people in developing nations. A report from the World Bank says that these countries must choose between serving 30 to 40 percent of the children and a system that gives some kind of education to all children. Increased lending is also to be used for training nurses, medical aides, and agricultural technicians.

United Nations University. In 1973 the UN General Assembly voted to create a world university, which will be independent of national ties and be responsible only to the betterment of humanity. The university will differ from traditional universities in that it will grant no degrees and have no students. This is an attempt to study and solve problems on a global scale through an organized use of teams of scholars in various fields. Scholars will serve two- or three-year terms and work on specific research or training activities. They then will return to their home universities. Programs will deal with human problems and needs, such as issues in ecology, war and peace, dissemination of knowledge, human rights, the management of natural resources, and the general improvement of the

The United Nations International School is a multiracial and multinational school with a truly international curriculum which prepares children of families of the UN delegates and Secretariat, as well as local community students, to become well-informed citizens of their own countries and of the world.

quality of life. Although there will be no students or formal courses, younger scholars will learn from experienced scholars through working with them. There will also be workshops, seminars, and other learning situations.

Twenty-four scholars and educators appointed by the UN Secretary-General and the Director General of UNESCO will form the policy-making body. The world headquarters opened in Tokyo in December 1974 to coordinate affiliated groups, organizations, and regional centers in various parts of the world.

UN University will be financed through voluntary contributions from member governments, foundations, organizations. and individuals. A $400 million central endowment fund for general purposes and a $40 million annual budget would cover operation of the entire world headquarters, coordination of the world program, four or five regional centers, and other aspects of the program. Although the amount of money involved is quite small and the promise of such a university is great, the interest among member nations is not strong so far. The United States does not oppose the university but has given little encouragement or support to it. However, many groups in the nation greatly favor the idea. The Soviet Union is opposed and abstained in the voting. Several Eastern European countries support it. Japan showed its confidence, or at least its hope, in the world university by contributing $100 million to the endowment, in addition to all capital costs for the headquarters and an Asian research institute in Japan. Japan will also pay half the operating expenses of the institute.

How nations will respond once research is begun and whether the promise will be fulfilled will not be known for a long time. With the economies of most countries being very tight, and since the UN itself is having a hard time financially, support will probably be slow to come unless results are meaningful for world survival.[11]

THE INTERNATIONAL PEACE CORPS SECRETARIAT

The Peace Corps, established by the United States in 1961, assumed international dimension a year later with the inauguration of the International

[11]For a description of UN University, see Harold Taylor, "A University for the World," *Phi Delta Kappan,* September 1974, pp. 39–41.

Education is enriched through cross-cultural centers, such as this one at the University of Geneva where Vinh Bang, A Vietnamese psychologist, works on intelligence tests for young children based on the research of Swiss psychologist, Jean Piaget, who looks on with approval.

Peace Corps Secretariat. Since its beginning, the International Peace Corps Secretariat has helped more than a dozen nations in beginning their own Peace Corps programs for service abroad. In 1970, without a dissenting vote, the UN Economic and Social Council recommended the establishment of a world Peace Corps under the jurisdiction of the UN.

THE INSTITUTE OF INTERNATIONAL EDUCATION

The Institute of International Education, a private, nonprofit organization founded in 1919, develops and administers programs of educational exchange for students, teachers, and educational specialists among the United States and more than eighty other countries. It acts as a clearinghouse for all aspects of international education, working closely with governments, foundations, universities, corporations, private organizations, and individuals. It publishes the *Handbook on International Study for Foreign Nationals* and the *Handbook on International Study for U.S. Nationals,* which contain useful information on opportunities for foreign study, grants available, regulations, and other information of use to students abroad. Its Project City Streets arranged for students from abroad to work in community or antipoverty programs in this country, and for students from minority groups in America to work in similar activities abroad. Its annual report, *Open Doors,* provides statistics on international educational exchange activities. Its headquarters building at UN Plaza in New York has been a mecca for thousands of arriving and departing educators from many lands.

INTERNATIONAL CENTERS

A number of international centers have been established at various locations around the globe to bring persons together for the advancement of specified sectors of education. Among them is the University of Geneva International Center for Genetic Epistemology, which provides facilities where interdisciplinary teams can work together for protracted periods of time on specific problems of mental development of children under the guidance of the Swiss child psychologist Jean Piaget.

Many other centers for international study, such as the East-West Center at the University of Hawaii, are located on the campuses of major universities and colleges throughout the world. They serve students and teachers from many lands interested in acquiring the specialized knowledge accumulated in these centers.

INTERNATIONAL PROFESSIONAL ORGANIZATIONS AND CONFERENCES

The number of international professional organizations and conferences on education are legion. By far the largest is the World Confederation of Organizations of the Teaching Profession, which numbers 124 constituent teacher organizations from 78 countries, with a total membership representation of approximately five million teachers around the world. Its annual Assembly of Delegates brings together approximately five hundred leaders of teachers' organizations to come to grips with an agenda that covers a wide range of educational problems.[12] Phi Delta Kappa International, an honorary fraternity, has members on all continents. Many international organizations of teachers exist in several subject fields and teaching specializations, such as the International Reading Association, the International Graphic Arts Education Association, the International Childhood Education Association, and the International Council on Education for Teaching (ICET).

Many international conferences on education are held annually dealing with a wide variety of topics, as suggested by the following sample list: International Conference on the World Crisis in Education, International Conference on Human Skills, International Education and Teacher Education Conference, and International Moral Education Conference.

United States programs

We turn our attention now to the wide variety of undertakings in intercultural education that have arisen under the aegis of the United States in cooperation with other countries. These programs

may be categorized as those supported by (1) federal, state, and local governments; (2) private organizations; (3) schools and colleges; and (4) individuals. Some important undertakings in each of these categories are described below.

FEDERAL, STATE, AND LOCAL GOVERNMENT PROGRAMS

U.S. Office of Education programs. The Office of Education of the Department of Health, Education, and Welfare considers international education an integral part of its mission of strengthening American education at all levels. One of its best-known, oldest, and most extensive enterprises is the exchange program. Conceived by Senator William Fulbright in 1946 and modified in 1961 by the Mutual Educational and Cultural Exchange Act (popularly known as the "Fulbright-Hays Act") and subsequent legislation, this program supports three major types of enterprises: university lecturing and research abroad by American nationals, undergraduate and graduate study and research abroad by American nationals, and exchanges of American and foreign elementary and secondary school teachers. More than 150,000 American teachers and students have received grants to teach and study abroad, usually in non-Western countries, to gather materials that will be useful in curriculum development at home in such fields as foreign languages, world cultures, political science, international relations, anthropology, and sociology. They return with deeper knowledge and understanding of the language, geography, history, and culture of the country visited, which permits them to broaden and enrich their teaching at home. In many cases their positions at home are filled during their absence by teachers whom they replace abroad. Exchange teachers are chosen for posts abroad through national competition.

The Office of Education also helps develop curriculum materials about foreign countries for all school levels, helps other federal government and state government agencies internationalize their staffs for more effective service, sponsors comparative studies of educational systems in foreign countries, provides direct services to American educators and to educators from abroad who are studying in the United States, and serves as a general resource for American academic, civic, and business enterprises.

---

[12]For further discussion of WCOTP, see John M. Thompson, "Chauvinism and Realism in a Global Community," *Today's Education,* January/February 1976, pp. 22–25.

The Peace Corps. One of the most interesting and effective international programs of the United States is the Peace Corps, which was established by Congress at the request of President Kennedy in 1961. In signing the measure giving the Peace Corps permanent status, President Kennedy said it would "assist other nations toward their legitimate goals of freedom and opportunity." The purpose of the organization, as indicated by its name, is to advance peace through a corps of United States citizens who serve as volunteers overseas. In 1971 the Peace Corps was merged with other federal volunteer programs into a new agency, ACTION.

The Peace Corps is a modern governmental application of the old ideals of service and sacrifice overseas, which have been promoted by nongovernmental missionary organizations and other volunteer groups since the founding of the United States as a new nation. The sixty foreign countries to which Peace Corps members are sent are primarily newly independent nations.

More than half the volunteers have served in the Peace Corps as teachers, and half of these had had no previous teaching experience. Among the thousands of members currently serving overseas, the largest single profession represented is teaching. The Peace Corps has done much to quicken the quest for the good life in many countries and has deepened American understanding of other cultures.

Perhaps the greatest testimony to the success of the Peace Corps has been the dissemination of the idea in other countries, as noted earlier. Some of these countries are participating in the Volunteers to America program by sending their corps personnel to the United States as teachers, social workers, community development aides, and a variety of other occupations. These volunteers from other lands, like their American counterparts, are ambassadors of goodwill and understanding, demonstrating again the reciprocity which is endemic in most efforts of intercultural enterprise.

Other federal activities. Many other branches of federal government are also active in intercultural development. The Agency for International Development (AID) in the Department of State administers many activities that relate to educational development including the provision of model textbook depository libraries in other countries, the sharing of educational materials abroad, technical assistance in the improvement of national school systems, and various seminars, workshops, conferences, and other means of intellectual exchange. The Alliance for Progress was inaugurated in 1961 to accelerate AID's work in Latin American countries. The Book Brigade—formed by the National Academy of Sciences and United States book publishers—supplies millions of books for learners overseas.

The United States Information Agency provides publications, films, broadcasts, telecasts, and other media of education in many stations abroad to help other people learn more about our culture. The United States Travel Service in the Department of Commerce provides many visitors from abroad with the information about this country which they need to plan their visits. The Smithsonian Institution and the Library of Congress exchange educational materials with other nations. Many other activities of the national government in intercultural education could be cited.

State and local government programs. Several state and local educational agencies have undertaken programs in intercultural education. For example, the New York State Department of Education established the Educational Resources Center in India's capital city of New Delhi to develop better human and material resources for studying about India in American schools, as well as to strengthen channels of intellectual and cultural communication between India and the United States. The Center makes curricular materials on Indian life available to American schools, provides a convenient depository for research material for use by foreign and domestic scholars of Indian culture, and holds workshops and seminars for educators interested in deepening their knowledge of India.

Many local intercultural programs exist on college and university campuses. Some local public school systems are also strengthening their international interest through the School-to-School Program sponsored jointly by the American Association of School Administrators and the U.S. Office of Overseas Schools. In this program, American and foreign school systems are paired so that they may share curriculum materials and establish exchanges of students and teachers.

PRIVATE ORGANIZATIONS

Professional organizations. The Committee on International Relations of the National Education Association publishes instructional materials related to intercultural understanding, plans tours and provides hospitality for foreign educators visiting the United States, provides a clearinghouse service for teachers requesting information on international education, services requests on educational matters from various embassies in Washington, and compiles information on teaching positions abroad for United States teachers. It also distributes teaching materials in connection with UN Day, Refugee Year, and other events of international significance.

The NEA's Overseas Teacher Corporation, also operated by the Committee on International Relations, recruits many unpaid volunteers who conduct classes, workshops, and seminars abroad each year. The American Council on Education, a higher education organization, has been a major force in promoting exchange programs. Its Commission on International Education helps organizations, the government, and institutions of higher education to develop international education programs, providing liaison and advisory services.

Many local citizens' groups, such as the International Group of Memphis and the Pittsburgh Council for International Visitors, provide hospitality, plan tours, tutor visitors in English, and plan programs for foreign visitors to their cities. The National Catholic Education Association, the National Council for the Social Studies, the American Association of Colleges for Teacher Education, Phi Delta Kappa, and other national professional organizations maintain active committees on international education.[13]

Private foundations. Many American foundations have long been active in the support and encouragement of intercultural education. The Carnegie Corporation of New York, founded in 1911 as an educational foundation, has provided funds for several noteworthy enterprises, such as the Insti-

[13]For a more detailed account of the international activities of various professional associations, see H. Kenneth Barker, "International Education and the Professional Associations," *Phi Delta Kappan,* January 1970, pp. 244–246.

tute of International Education, the Russian Research Center at Harvard, the Commonwealth Studies Center at Duke University, and the Afro-Anglo-American Program to Train Teachers for Africa.

The Ford Foundation, founded in 1936 by Henry Ford, has provided grants for: international studies programs at Harvard University, Columbia University, Duke University, Northwestern University, Notre Dame University, University of Denver, and other institutions; the retraining of faculty members in world affairs in more than a hundred colleges; the support of the Center for Applied Linguistics, which has become a major force in language teaching; the Salzburg Seminar in American Studies; the strengthening of American studies through the American Council of Learned Societies; libraries in countries abroad; scholarships for foreign study for Americans as well as persons from abroad; the construction of the United Nations International School; and many other enterprises in intercultural education.

Numerous other foundations, such as Kellogg, Guggenheim, Kettering, and Pearl S. Buck, have contributed financial support to various programs in international education.

Other private organizations. Volumes might be required to record fully the good works of all private organizations in the United States that contribute to educational development abroad. We can consider here only a few illustrative ones.

The Franklin Books Program—composed of public-spirited American educators, businesspeople, librarians, and publishers—strengthens book-publishing capacity, book-distribution systems, and libraries in the developing nations of Asia, Africa, and South America. Foster Parents Plan channels financial support and gifts from individual Americans to needy families abroad and permits many children to remain in school who would otherwise have to go to work to help support their families. The English-speaking Union, upon learning that the inability to buy school books prevented 77 percent of the primary school pupils in Pakistan from continuing their education, provided thousands of basic secondary school textbooks for Pakistan and subsequently other countries.

Many local civic organizations, such as Kiwanis,

Rotary, and Lions, have sent educational materials abroad and have sponsored a great many of the thousands of people who participate annually in the Experiment in International Living. This enterprise was begun in 1932 by a small group who sought to bring people from many countries together in each other's communities and homes as a means of strengthening intercultural understanding. This paraeducational organization arranges home stays for approximately 4,500 people annually from more than forty-five countries on six continents.

International House near Columbia University in New York City has housed over 50,000 students from 130 nations for over fifty years. One-third of the 500 yearly residents are Americans, so that both American and foreign students can benefit through mutual relationships. International House was built with a grant from John D. Rockefeller, Jr. Most of the students attend Columbia, although about one-third attend other schools in the area.

The International Council for Educational Development studies various aspects of higher education, adult education, and nonformal education programs in several countries.

SCHOOLS AND COLLEGES

International schools and colleges. As we have seen, the dream of a truly international college dates back at least to the time of Comenius. Although multicultural schools and colleges have existed for some time in many places, the truly prototypical international college did not emerge until the last decade. After a successful experimental summer program in 1963, with a student body drawn from twenty-two United Nations countries, the Friends World College was inaugurated at Huntington, New York, in 1965. The Friends World College was conceived and pioneered largely through the efforts of its first president, Harold Taylor. The college is designed to have seven campuses in seven countries. Students begin their studies at their home campuses and spend a semester on each of the other campuses, returning to the home campus to consolidate and evaluate in a thesis the experiences of the four years. The curriculum of the Friends World College emerges from the creative talent of students and faculty from around the world. It is international in the sense that it uses the ideas and points of view of every nation represented to come to grips with the problems of world society.

Other international colleges outside the United States include Tagore's Santiniketan, Moscow's Friendship University, and the Experimental College at Copenhagen.

Exchange programs. The Foreign Study League and the American Institute for Foreign Study have offered summer programs since 1964. Each summer the FSL and the AIFS send about 20,000 students to study programs abroad. They offer courses in ecology, oceanography, comparative government, history, archeology, music, and art. These two organizations are private educational institutions. Their clientele are generally young people between the ages of 15 and 19. Since the mid-1960s junior high school students are also increasingly engaging in summer study abroad.

The Council on International Educational Exchange is a nonprofit organization that arranges transportation for educational groups sponsored by member organizations, as well as for students and teachers traveling on their own. Courses lasting from four to six weeks are offered by the Council at European universities. Members of the Council include over 160 North American educational, religious, and national institutions.

International programs in American higher education. Volumes have been written describing the wide range of college and university effort in international education. We shall describe them briefly here and cite a few varied examples.

Virtually every major American university and many colleges offer programs in comparative education, conduct research on various cultures of the globe, establish special programs for students from other lands as well as programs of study abroad for their own students, and conduct service projects abroad. Africa and Latin America are attracting more students. The City University of New York sponsors courses in West Africa at the University of Liberia and the University of Ghana. Eastern Michigan University sponsors a workshop in Kenya and Somalia. Stanford University offers several area-studies programs—East Asia, Latin America, Africa, and Western Europe—through which the cultures of these areas of the world are researched intensively and taught to graduate and undergraduate students interested in majoring in

Student exchange programs benefit both the foreign students and the host institutions which they attend. Education may be the only asset that can be exported while enriching rather than depleting our own resources.

these fields. The University of Wisconsin's Office of International Studies and Programs regards its campus as the world, hardly an idle boast on a campus that houses Ibero-American, Brazilian, Latin-American, African, Russian, Indian, East Asian, Scandinavian, Hebrew, Arabic, and other area studies programs. Michigan State University engages in an ambitious program of service, teaching, and research around the world. The East-West Center at the University of Hawaii capitalizes upon its strategic position, bridging Oriental and Occidental cultures both ethnically and geographically, to deepen the interaction and understanding of peoples from the Eastern and Western worlds.

A number of centers connected with schools of education specialize in international development. They perform research and conduct training programs. Many foreign students are included in such programs as the Stanford International Development Education Center (Stanford), the Center for Comparative Education (Chicago), and the Inter-

national and Development Education Program (University of Pittsburgh).

Over one-fifth of the institutes of higher education have programs to send American students and teachers abroad and to bring foreign students here. Over six hundred such programs are operated by United States colleges and universities. About two-thirds of the programs involve European countries, and one-third involve other countries. Most United States institutions sending students to study abroad provide and manage their own programs there, although most foreign students coming here study in United States institutions.

American universities have for a number of years provided technical assistance overseas. The Agency for International Development has over forty contracts with about thirty universities to provide technical services to other countries.

The Afro-Anglo-American Program in Teacher Education was begun in 1960 under the joint enterprise of Teachers College, Columbia University, and the Institute of Education of the University of London, with financial support from the Carnegie Corporation, for the purpose of preparing educators to teach in African secondary schools and teacher-training institutions. Within its first decade of existence, the project had recruited and trained nearly a thousand teachers and had helped to train an additional 1,400 Peace Corps teachers for service in nine African countries. The program's long-term goal is to strengthen African countries' teacher-training capability to meet their own needs. Toward this end, the Carnegie Corporation has made several million dollars available to African institutes of education. Recently members of this program formed a new organization, the Association for Teacher Education in Africa (ATEA), which will be headquartered in Africa.

This international thrust by our colleges and universities is not entirely new, but since World War II it has greatly expanded in volume and broadened in purpose. Higher education has long been interested in studying other people but until recently only as a matter of academic curiosity. Now the land-grant college concept of providing teaching, research, and service to the local or state community has been expanded to include the world community. In the entire educational enterprise, few sectors have expanded as significantly as the international dimension of our colleges and universities.[14]

Overseas schools. The United States maintains approximately 130 overseas schools in eighty countries abroad. About half their enrollment consists of children of American military and civilian families living abroad; the other half consists of native students from the host countries and their neighbors. Administered through the Office of Overseas Schools in the Department of State, these schools are staffed by both American and foreign educators. Local citizens serve with Americans on more than half the schools' governing boards. Most schools offer courses of study in local language and culture. As demonstration centers for American educational practice, these schools are visited frequently by native educators.

[14]For a discussion of the problems of the international enterprise of higher education, see Edward W. Weidner, "U.S. Institutional Programs in International Education," *Phi Delta Kappan*, January 1970, pp. 239–243.

The American College in Paris is the only four-year accredited United States college in Europe. It is licensed to give degrees through the District of Columbia.

Two interesting examples of overseas schools are located in the Lebanese capital city of Beirut. The century-old American University of Beirut is a mecca for students from the Middle East and other countries who are interested in the American model of higher education. Its sister institution, International College, founded in 1881, expanded in 1971 with the creation of a $4 million community college on a site commanding a magnificent view of the Mediterranean. The community college was conceived and funded through ten years of campaigning by International College's American president, Thomas Schuller. It serves many Lebanese students who are more interested in practical studies related to the everyday problems of Lebanese life than in the narrow, classical curriculums of the French models, which prevail in other colleges of Lebanon.

One United States ambassador observed that "the United States is doing more good, generating more goodwill, for less money, through the programs of these schools than through any other program I know of." These overseas schools offer a splendid but largely untapped resource for extending our international education for larger numbers of American teachers. A plan for achieving this goal has been developed by the Office of Overseas Schools, the Kettering Foundation, and the State University of New York.

American church boards help to staff and finance, for missionary children and others, many schools such as the Woodstock School in India and Robert College in Turkey. The United States cooperates in establishing American schools in such international centers as Brussels, Copenhagen, Geneva, Rome, and Vienna. These schools provide education for children of many nationalities. Through associations such as the International Schools Service, the administrators, teachers, and parents share ideas and techniques for increasing the effectiveness of this instrument of international education. The International Schools Association consists of more than one hundred independent schools that provide education for about 70,000 students annually. Thirty-two countries have such schools, offering a curriculum of American and British Commonwealth courses.

Some schools offer an International Baccalaureate degree, which is accepted for college entrance in some universities. A syndicate has been formed by the International Schools of Geneva, Switzerland, and the International Schools Association, which represents schools on four continents and which has official status with UNESCO. As more Americans travel and live abroad, these overseas schools attended by American children and others will increase their cooperative efforts, their numbers, and their prestige.

Curriculums in American schools. The role of American education in today's world is determined, in large measure, by the curriculums of its institutions. The discussion here will be confined to a few major aspects of the curriculum most closely related to international education.

Although nearly all academic disciplines provide latent opportunity for deepening students' understanding of other people, social studies, the humanities, and foreign languages can be most rewarding if they are well taught and addressed particularly to the goal of cross-cultural understanding. This international emphasis should pervade the learning experiences of students from early-childhood education through graduate school. The late Ralph Bunche, once American Undersecretary for the United Nations, grandson of a slave, and holder of the Nobel Peace Prize, stated:

We are today in an international age in which understanding and cooperation among states are the only roads to survival .... Our education, I think, should be geared much more to the world, to the future, than it is and with much broader perspective than it now knows.

As Harold Taylor points out in *The World and the American Teacher,* American schools suffer severely from an ethnocentric curriculum largely because teachers themselves are not well educated in the international realm. Until recently at least, relatively little instructional material has been drawn from other cultures with the exceptions of history, geography, foreign languages, literature, art, and music. Even in these fields the emphasis has been upon Western civilization almost to the exclusion of other cultures. The study of social, economic, and political geography merits at least as much attention as physical geography, which has predominated in the schools. More attention should be devoted to cultural anthropology, social

psychology, and intergroup relations, particularly at secondary and collegiate levels. Instruction in history and other social science courses should develop an appreciation for the great values inherent in the heritage of the democratic way of life and should also face forthrightly the tragic shortcomings of the nation in extending its goals to all people. The narrow focus of social studies upon Western cultures is being redressed in high schools and colleges with the introduction of African and other ethnic studies. Offerings in Asian and African languages are being increased. Schools are belatedly helping students realize that not all great literature, lovely art, splendid music, or scholarly thought has been produced by Western cultures.

Secondary school curriculums are offering more subjects prefaced by the word and concept of "world"—world history, world geography, world economics, world affairs, world religions, world "isms," world cultures, and world literature.

Colleges, too, are being challenged by worldwide concerns. Many institutions of higher learning have broadened their curriculums to strengthen students' understanding of the world through courses in communication, foreign languages, anthropology, and international relations and through comparative courses in fields such as law, political systems, cultures, and education. Many provide opportunities for overseas study and service. Peace studies, including world order education, are increasingly being included in college and high school curriculums. This type of education, if extended to more and more schools, may have great impact in reforming international education programs and, through such programs, in producing better world citizens who may help reform world values.

Comparative education, long one of the lacunae in teacher education in the United States, has been prominent in recent years. A group of educators organized the Comparative Education Society in 1956 in order to focus attention on this important facet of international understanding. Many universities now offer courses in this field; some have overseas travel seminars that permit administrators, teachers, and students to observe at first hand the educational programs of other lands, and to study these programs directly.

The Ogontz Plan for Mutual International Education has been in effect since 1961. Sponsored by the International House of Philadelphia, the plan provides for foreign representatives to go into schools and classrooms to interact with students about their cultures. Foreign visitors also gain insights into American education and culture through interaction with schools, communities, and homes. This and similar plans facilitate intercultural understandings and stimulate interest in other countries and peoples.

Many authorities believe that American schools are not fulfilling the needs of students and helping them to take their place among world citizens. Intercultural education, beginning with the study of minority groups and ethnic groups in our own country, will be a step toward understanding other nationalities and cultures throughout the world. Oliver J. Caldwell, in speaking of intercultural education in our universities, feels that humanities and social sciences must make major changes in their programs to meet the needs of the world society. He says:

No one should believe that any change or innovation in the educational process is sure to prevent man from exterminating himself. However, education is probably the only social tool capable of instilling in man a new awareness of his mutual obligations to his neighbors. . . .

The death of the International Education Act makes it possible to promote in Washington the passage of a new Intercultural Education Act. Such an act would focus first on intercultural problems within our own borders, then through our own minorities to the whole of

humanity. By studying ourselves, we will be better able to study humanity.[15]

INDIVIDUAL ENTERPRISE

Notwithstanding the many organized programs in the realm of international education, the scope and importance of individual initiative in extending cross-cultural education should not be overlooked. Perhaps the most important manifestation of individual enterprise is found in the exchange of students and teachers. Over 120,000 foreign students study in the United States each year. One-fourth of the world's students studying outside their own countries are enrolled in the United States. (Perhaps this indicates that American education is not as bad as some critics contend.) Approximately half these students come to American schools and colleges on their own resources without benefit of fellowships or other grants. About 25,000 American students are in full-time study programs abroad each year. Figure 15-2 shows the percentages of foreign students enrolled in fields of study. The data include only individuals who are engaged in regular academic work at institutions of higher learning. They do not include thousands of teachers and students who go abroad each year to attend summer programs or study tours.

This two-way educational traffic between the United States and many countries of the world is a phenomenon that has arisen largely since World War II. The interchange is prompted by several forces: the desire of individual students and teachers to enrich their understanding of other civilizations; the need of developing countries to look to other countries to train their teachers, businesspeople, physicians, engineers, scientists, lawyers, and other professionals; and the need of both American and foreign institutions to seek intellectual breadth and cultural enrichment for their own benefit.

The Junior Year Abroad (JYA) has become a tradition at a number of American universities. Yale has initiated a program in which juniors spend a year abroad, not for academic study but to live and

Figure 15-2 What foreign students study in the United States. (Institute of International Education, *Open Doors,* 1974.)

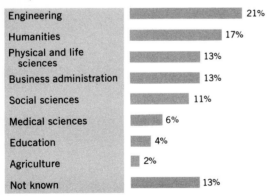

Engineering	21%
Humanities	17%
Physical and life sciences	13%
Business administration	13%
Social sciences	11%
Medical sciences	6%
Education	4%
Agriculture	2%
Not known	13%

[15]Oliver J. Caldwell, "The Need for Intercultural Education In our Universities," *Phi Delta Kappan,* May 1971, p. 545.

work in unfamiliar cultures in African, Asian, or Latin-American countries. Stanford has established its own campuses in France, Italy, Germany, Japan, and Taiwan for its students' use abroad.

High school students also engage in study abroad. The first and largest program of exchange of high school students is sponsored by the American Field Service, which arranges for nearly three thousand exchanges annually. There is good reason to believe that exchanges have a salubrious effect not only upon exchange students but also upon host schools.

In addition to the thousands of students, research scholars, teachers, professors, and lay leaders in education, thousands of other Americans go abroad annually. International travel is good per se, especially for students and teachers, but travel accompanied by serious study is better. However, the best teaching-learning situation is found by those Americans who implement cultural empathy by working directly with their overseas peers to promote the commonwealth of humanity.[16]

Another tangible type of exchange is that involving material. This includes one-way, two-way, and multilateral exchanges of equipment and/or information in its various forms. In addition to the more costly reciprocal exchange of personnel is the less expensive and more voluminous program of interchanging apparatus, publications, periodicals, letters, postage stamps, and coins.

Books are a common medium of educational exchange. Millions of books have been donated by Americans to overseas schools, colleges, and communities. In some war-devastated countries, the intellectual sustenance of books has replaced CARE packages of food. Orientation kits have often been sent overseas for visitors coming to these

shores, and many more packages are needed for those not coming to this country. Students and teachers in the United States need overseas books, especially those concerning art, music, social studies, and languages.

Problems of international education

International education, not unlike other forms of education, is beleaguered by many problems, some of which pose serious ideological issues.

THE CONFLICT BETWEEN NATIONALISM AND INTERNATIONALISM

Perhaps the prime ideological deterrent to strong effort in international education is the fierce sense of national pride and loyalty that prompts wariness in some people against any internationalization of public institutions, particularly of schools, which deal with young citizens, whom we often overprotect.

Many proponents of international education believe that the conflict between nationalism and internationalism is spurious, that these loyalties to both the nation and the world are additive rather than antagonistic. They hold that the national interest is inextricably related to the world interest and that ethnocentric education is neither in the national interest nor in the world interest. Nevertheless, the conflict continues.

INTERCULTURAL DIFFERENCES

International education development is handicapped by great cultural and language differences among nations. Different countries in various stages of development require different priorities in educational development. Different mores require different styles of pedagogy. It is not uncommon to find young students in Africa studying from English or French or Belgian books that have little relevance and meaning to their own cultures. In some cases, these young nations have inherited colonial school systems based upon an elitist educational system modeled after the former colonial power. This type of system has little

[16]Readers interested in gaining further information about study programs abroad are referred to *Handbook on International Study: For U.S. Nationals,* Institute of International Education, New York, 1972; John A. Garraty, Walter Adams, and Cyril J. H. Taylor, *A New Guide to Study Abroad,* Harper & Row, New York, 1969; *Students Abroad: Summer Study, Travel and Work Programs* and *Students Abroad: High School Student Programs,* Council on International Educational Exchange, New York; *Summer Study Abroad,* Institute of International Education, New York; *The Student Traveler: Work, Study, Travel Abroad,* U.S. National Student Travel Association, New York; and *Study Abroad,* UNESCO Publications Center, New York.

meaning in a country trying to raise itself by its bootstraps. In some countries the first priority should be the extension of basic literacy; in others, fairly sophisticated vocational and technical education attuned to an industrial society should be a more immediate priority. Educational consultants from abroad, Peace Corps personnel, and exchange teachers sometimes have difficulty sorting out the educational aims, values, and traditions that are unworkable in different countries. Many transplanted educational practices that were successful at home have failed abroad because cultural differences have not been considered. Much more research and experience is needed before we can master the task of sharing and modifying our educational know-how effectively in other cultures.

INERTIA IN EDUCATIONAL CHANGE

Many scholars have called attention to the slow tempo of change in human social enterprises, particularly schools. This reluctance to change educational practice is common to both new and old, rich and poor nations. Many developing countries are in a great hurry to improve the human condition but must reckon with school systems inherited from former colonial powers. Very often they face a serious disparity between their educational output and their developmental needs. Frequently their colleges produce an abundance of arts graduates and lawyers but a serious undersupply of teachers, scientists, engineers, and other technically trained persons. Many curriculums place too much emphasis upon classical education and too little upon the practical needs of everyday life. In some cases great expansion has taken place in primary and higher education, while secondary education has been neglected. A recent UNESCO study concluded that rigid graded organization, unsound promotion practices, poor teaching, and irrelevant curriculum content resulted in excessive waste in schools. Then, too, the goals of the educational system are often out of phase with the goals of economic and social development.

However, the picture is not entirely bleak. Much more careful educational planning is now taking place in many individual countries, quickened in part by UNESCO and particularly by the International Institute for Educational Planning. Also, the tempo of change is accelerated by the interchange of students and teachers, which is expanding.

UNDERFINANCING

International education, like all facets of education in most countries, suffers from inadequate financing. Not only are most national school systems underfinanced, but most international education programs also suffer from lack of sufficient funds. A tragic example of this is the United States' inexcusable delay in financing promptly and adequately the International Education Act of 1966. Brilliant and unselfish in concept, this act was never fully implemented with financial resources. This false economy was matched in the early 1970s by Congress' cutback in appropriations even for such well-established international programs as the Fulbright Act and the National Defense Education Act.

The benefits of international education are not very evident to average citizens, and when aroused over domestic problems, they are disposed to retreat into national and academic isolationism.[17] As the International Conference on the World Crisis in Education pointed out, there is a real crisis in education's ability to match performance with expectations. The conference noted a worldwide disparity between the hopes of individuals and the needs of society, on the one hand, and the capabilities of the educational systems, on the other. Cruel financial constraints have forced both developed and developing countries to turn inward and become preoccupied with internal priorities. Each country of the world has periodically experienced a shortage of buildings, teachers, and instructional materials. Most countries need more money, and, except for the most affluent, an increase in funds will be hard to obtain because education has in many countries already acquired a preemptive share of national income. The only solution for many nations lies in increased financial help from more prosperous countries.

Education alone does not seem to be the answer, nor does financial aid alone. Aid to these na-

[17]For further discussion of this tragic circumstance, see James M. Davis, "The U.S. Government and International Education: A Doomed Program?" *Phi Delta Kappan*, January 1970, pp. 235–238.

tions will probably diminish, since even "affluent" nations have become enmeshed in serious financial trouble. Gunnar Myrdal, one of the world's foremost economists, says that instead of decreasing aid to developing countries, we should increase it and insist that the countries strive to reform their societies.[18]

UNREALISTIC EXPECTATIONS

Finally there is the problem of unrealistic expectations. Without disparaging the tremendous potential of education for improving the human condition, it is nevertheless clear that education alone is not the cure, just as it is not the cause, of many great problems in the world. Even if it were, current resources cannot accommodate the greatly accelerated burden of education. As noted earlier, the hopes of people around the world for a better life, particularly a better life for their children, have been quickened extraordinarily within the past decade. Most people see better education as the prime vehicle in this journey toward a better life. When hopes outrun reality, disillusion and disenchantment may follow. Although we must continue to pin our hopes on the desirable rather than the feasible, the disparity between the two must be accepted with a sense of resignation but not complacency. That so much attention is being directed to education in the midst of world crisis indicates that better schools may indeed be our final hope for survival. Historian Arnold Toynbee has spoken of ours as "the first generation since the dawn of history in which man dares to believe it practical to make the benefits of civilization available to the whole human race."

The future

It is apparent that the scope of international education will be broadened and its tempo increased. The volume of exchange of students, faculty, and materials will continue to increase. This exchange will include communist-bloc nations and will

[18]For an interesting discussion on economic aid, see Gunnar Myrdal, "On Reforming Economic Aid," *Center Report,* February 1975, pp. 3–5.

Ours is "the first generation since the dawn of history in which man dares to believe it practical to make the benefits of civilization available to the whole human race." (*Arnold Toynbee*)

usually be sustained even during periods of tension in international relations. It will be sustained by international organizations such as UNESCO as well as by bilateral agreements between individual nations.

Development education—promulgated toward strengthening of social, political, and economic well-being of nations—will become increasingly widespread, especially among have-not nations. The yield of this effort will be enhanced through better planning by national and international agencies. Despite this thrust, the need for education will outgrow the capacity of educational systems unless the population explosion can be arrested. The outlook for money and personnel to sustain educational development will remain pessimistic for many countries. Since the population is expected to increase to 6 billion in the next twenty-five years, educational programs could be adversely affected unless plans and adjustments are made to allow for this growth. The major emphasis will be on primary education. More financial aid will be available in this area, and more effort will be made to provide primary education for all, instead of for only half. Efforts to curb the high dropout rates in most developing nations will also be of prime concern.

Rapid development of educational technology may eventually bring a breakthrough in international education. Consider the communications satellite's capability of instantaneous around-the-world telecasting, television's capability of reaching mass audiences, the laser's capability of handling great numbers of long-distance messages simultaneously, programmed instruction's capability of tailoring education to the unique levels and learning styles of any individual, and the computer's capability of managing the interfaces of all these complex telecommunications components. These and other possible advances can help to raise educational standards and living standards throughout the world.

The World Food Authority will become an important force in planning and coordinating food programs and in forewarning of food shortages. More agricultural assistance, such as land-reform methods and ways to increase crop yield and protein content, will be given to developing nations. Technological assistance will also help to diminish unemployment.

We hope that the promise of the United Nations University will flourish and that solutions to some of our problems will begin to take shape. Global education and other peace studies will continue to increase understanding of other cultures, to put world problems and national problems in better perspective, and to contribute to the betterment of the world. Some shift in emphasis from national to world values will occur, but unfortunately such change will be slow in coming. Many people and organizations will continue to work toward this end. Education will more and more be accepted as an important and necessary means to the improvement of world conditions, rather than as a separate and inferior sector of society.

Eventually we must come to realize that vastly increased expenditures on education are indeed essential to our survival. Much of this increased expenditure must come from the more affluent nations. It must come in a spirit of altruism rather than imperialism. As Philip Coombs warns in the closing sentences of his report *The World Educational Crisis,* "Whatever shape your educational system may be in, if others which must serve the vast majority of this planet's citizens are in a serious state of crisis, then no nation, however rich, can be exempt from the consequences. The educational crisis is everybody's business."[19]

Suggested activities

1. Investigate the current status of the United Nations University.
2. Select a dozen or more heterogeneous countries from all the continents and compare them with respect to various measures of educational need and accomplishment, such as percentage of total population that is of school age, percentage of school-age population attending school, percentage of population that is illiterate, expenditure per pupil for education, and percentage of national income spent for education. (Various UNESCO publications and *The World Crisis in Education* will supply these data.)
3. Examine an annual report of the Ford Foundation or the Carnegie Corporation and annotate briefly each major international effort it supports.
4. Sketch the major differences between foreign aid programs for education that are prompted by "cultural imperialism" and those which are prompted by "international cooperation and understanding."
5. Summarize the major undertakings of UNESCO in a recent year.
6. Make an inventory and describe briefly each major undertaking in international education under the aegis of your college or university.
7. Prepare an essay on "Nationalism and Internationalism in Education: Allies or Adversaries?"
8. Evaluate high school and college curriculums that you have completed in terms of their scope and effectiveness in deepening understanding of other cultures and international relations.
9. Interview a returned educational missionary, exchange student, member of the Peace Corps, or teacher in regard to education in another country.
10. Study the educational system of some other country and compare it with that of the United States.
11. Describe a college program that includes a year or a summer abroad.
12. Investigate the requirements for obtaining an over-

[19]Philip H. Coombs, *The World Educational Crisis: A Systems Analysis,* Oxford, New York, 1968, p. 173. For a look at major problems confronting us and possible approaches to their solution, see *Saturday Review,* Dec. 14, 1974, entire issue.

seas assignment in education, such as a Fulbright scholarship, a Peace Corps membership, or a short-term or long-term educational missionary position.

Bibliography

Beck, Carlton E. (ed.): *Perspectives on World Education,* Brown, Dubuque, Iowa, 1970. Series of articles by a worldwide writing team dealing with the historical development, current practices, and sociocultural factors that may influence the future of education in over forty countries.

Becker, James: *Education for a Global Society,* Phi Delta Kappa, Bloomington, Ind., 1973. Discusses how we can achieve a world-oriented system of education.

Bereday, George Z. F. (ed.): *Essays on World Education: The Crisis of Supply and Demand.* Oxford, New York, 1969. Eighteen essays by a distinguished group of international educators on various aspects of the growing crisis in world education and possible solutions to many problems.

Brown, Lester R.: *In the Human Interest,* Norton, New York, 1974. Discusses world problems, especially overpopulation and superaffluence, and what must be done to solve them; written by an economist with the Overseas Development Council.

Buxbaum, Edith: *Troubled Children in a Troubled World,* International Universities, New York, 1970. Report of the anxieties and needs of children throughout the world.

Coombs, Philip H.: *The World Educational Crisis: A Systems Analysis,* Oxford, New York, 1968. Overview of the situation in world education, analysis of major problems, and suggestions for priorities and solutions.

Curie, Adam: *Education for Liberation,* Wiley-Interscience, New York, 1973. Discusses education's purpose and place as an instrument of peace.

Henderson, George (ed.): *Education for Peace: Focus on Mankind,* 1973 Yearbook, Association for Supervision and Curriculum Development, Washington, 1973. Nine contributors describe various aspects of peace studies—the curriculum, cross-cultural understanding, causes of violence, and so on.

Shane, Harold (ed.): *The United States and International Education,* Sixty-eighth Yearbook, National Society for the Study of Education, University of Chicago, 1969, part I. Discussion by fifteen outstanding scholars of the scope of American involvement in international education and the relation of foreign experiences to the growth of education in the United States.

Taylor, Harold: *The World and the American Teacher,* American Association of Colleges for Teacher Education, Washington, 1968. Plea for stronger preparation and experience of American teachers in the international realm with examples of good practices and recommendations for general improvement.

U.S. Office of Education: *American Students and Teachers Abroad,* Government Printing Office, 1974. Excellent guide for educators planning to work or study abroad, including information on international exchange programs and assistance for students.

Glossary [1]

Ability grouping: the organization of pupils into homogeneous sections according to intellectual ability for purposes of instruction.

Academic freedom: the opportunity for the teacher to teach, and for the teacher and the student to study, without coercion, censorship, or other restrictive interference.

Academy: an independent secondary school not under public control.

Accelerated program: the more rapid advancement of superior students through school by early completion of advanced work.

Accountability: the responsibility of an educational agency or educator to be held answerable to the public for performance.

Accreditation: the type of recognition given to an educational institution that has met accepted standards applied to it by a competent agency or official association.

Action learning: a program that bridges the gap between schooling and the work world, providing students with learning experiences through real work in community businesses and agencies.

Activity curriculum: a curriculum design in which the interests and purposes of children determine the educative program; selection and planning of activities are undertaken cooperatively by teacher and pupils.

Administrative unit: usually synonymous with *school district*.

Advanced placement: programs provided by high schools in cooperation with community colleges or universities in which qualifying students take college level courses.

Affective learning: the acquisition of feelings, tastes, emotions, will, and other aspects of social and psychological development gained through feeling rather than through intellectualization.

Affirmative action: a plan requiring goals for personnel policies and hiring practices that remove discrimination in the employment of women and members of minority groups.

Alternative education: unconventional educational experiences for students not adequately served through regular classes; such alternatives include schools without walls, street academies, free schools, and second-chance schools.

Articulation: the relationship existing between the different elements of the educational program—the different curricular offerings, the school's program and out-of-school educational activities—and the successive levels of the educational system.

Attendance area: an administrative unit, or subdivision of a unit, consisting of the territory from which children may legally attend a given school building.

Atypical pupil: a loose term used in referring to a pupil who differs in a marked degree from others of a given class or category—physically, mentally, socially, or emotionally.

Audiovisual material: any device by means of which the learning process may be encouraged or carried on through the sense of hearing and/or the sense of sight.

Behavior modification: changing behavior toward more desirable directions through the use of rewards or other reinforcement.

Behavioral objective: precise statement of what the learner must do to demonstrate mastery at the end of a prescribed learning task.

Bilingual education: educational programs in which both English-speaking and non-English-speaking students participate in a bicultural curriculum using both languages.

Career education: the totality of educational experience through which one learns about occupational opportunities and about work—both the basic human need for accomplishment and the broader societal need for accomplishment.

Categorical aid: financial aid to local school districts from state or federal agencies for specific, limited purposes only; synonomous with *special-purpose aid*.

Certification: the act, on the part of a state department of education, of granting official authorization to a person to

---

[1]This glossary contains definitions of the more important and more common terms used in the book. Many other terms are defined or described in the text itself. Readers are referred to the index for definitions of terms not found in the glossary. Many of the definitions are taken from or adapted from Carter V. Good (ed.), *Dictionary of Education,* 3d ed., McGraw-Hill, New York, 1973.

accept employment in keeping with the provisions of the credential.

Cognitive learning: the acquisition by the learner of facts, concepts, and principles through intellectualization.

Collective bargaining: a procedure, usually specified by written agreement, for resolving disagreements on salaries, hours, and conditions of employment between employers and employees through negotiations.

Community school: a school that is intimately connected with the life of the community and that tries to provide for the educational needs of all in the locality. It utilizes neighborhood resources in improving the educational program and sometimes serves as a center for many civic and cultural activities.

Compensatory education: enriched or extended educational experiences or services made available to children of low-income families to compensate for handicaps they suffer as a result of their disadvantaged backgrounds.

Competency-based education: learning based upon highly specialized concepts, skills, and attitudes related directly to some endeavor.

Computer-assisted instruction (CAI): direct two-way teaching-learning communication between a student and programmed instructional material stored in a computer.

Consolidation: the act of forming an enlarged school by uniting smaller schools in order to provide better school facilities and increased educational opportunities.

Consortium: a confederation of persons or agencies joined to undertake an enterprise too large or too complicated to be undertaken efficiently by a single constituent.

Continuing education: an extension of opportunities for study and training following completion or withdrawal from full-time school and college programs.

Core curriculum: a curriculum design in which one subject or group of subjects becomes a center or core to which all the other subjects are subordinated.

Correlation: the process of bringing together the elements of two or more different subject-matter fields that bear on the same large problem or area of human experience.

Cost-benefit analysis: a means of comparing the costs of a particular undertaking with the benefits it is expected to yield.

Cost-effectiveness analysis: a means of analyzing the extent to which an undertaking accomplishes its objectives in relation to its cost in comparison with alternative undertakings.

Creative federalism: a partnership whereby federal, state, and local government perform those activities which they can best fulfill, without diminishing the power of the other levels.

Cultural pluralism: the peaceful coexistence of sub-groups having different culture patterns within one social-economic-political group.

Custodial student: a student so limited in mental, social, physical, or emotional development as to require institutional care or constant supervision at home.

Day-care center: a center where young preschool children can be cared for, usually with little or no educational program.

Decentralization: a process whereby some higher central source of responsibility and authority assigns certain responsibility and authority to subordinate position.

De facto **segregation**: separation of pupils by race for circumstantial reasons, such as housing patterns, rather than for reasons of school policies or practices.

De jure **segregation**: separation of pupils by race on the basis of school policies or practices designed specifically to accomplish such separation.

Desegregation: the repair, usually through legal remedy, of previous unconstitutional wrong of *de jure* segregation of students in school on the basis of race. (See also *Integration.*)

Development education: education designed specifically to improve the economic, political, and social development of a nation or community.

Developmental task: a task that arises at or about a certain time in an individual's life, the successful achievement of which leads to his or her happiness and success with later tasks.

Differentiated staffing: educational personnel, selected, educated, and deployed so as to make optimum use of abilities, interests, preparation, and commitments and to give greater opportunity and autonomy in guiding their own professional growth and use.

Dual progress plan: a plan for grouping pupils for instruction in which they are brought together homogeneously during part of the school day for instruction in basic subjects and heterogeneously for the remainder of the day for instruction in other subjects.

Dyslexia: a neurological impairment that causes a learner to reverse letters, words, and numbers.

Early-childhood education: learning undertaken by young children in the home, in nursery schools, and in kindergartens.

Educable child: a child of borderline or moderately severe mental retardation who is capable of achieving only a limited degree of proficiency in basic learnings and who usually must be instructed in a special class.

Educare: a proposed national program for providing low-cost education for adults, organized in a manner similar to Medicare.

Education audit: the evaluation, usually by an outsider, of what happens in an educational setting in a given time span.

Educational park: a large campuslike school plant containing several units with a variety of facilities, often including many grade levels and varied programs, and often surrounded by a variety of cultural resources.

Educational technology: scientific application of knowledge to educational institutions for purposes of instruction or institutional management. (See also *Instructional technology*.)

Educational television (ETV): educational programs in the broadest sense—cultural, informative, and instructive—that are telecast usually by stations outside the school system and are received on standard television sets by the general public.

Equalization: the act of equalizing or making more nearly equal the support of public education among the subordinate units within a governmental unit.

Essentialism: the doctrine that there is an indispensable, common core of culture (knowledge, skills, attitudes, ideals, etc.) that should be taught systematically to all, with rigorous standards of achievement.

Exceptional learner: one who deviates from the normal intellectually, physically, socially, or emotionally in growth and development so markedly that he or she cannot receive maximum benefit without modification of the regular school program.

Existentialism: a philosophic view that holds that the problems of human existence and values are paramount and that an individual's morality is achieved through positive social participation.

External studies: a program by which students obtain degrees after competency examinations without being in residence in the institutions.

Fiscal neutrality: school finance programs that create no inequality in educational opportunity.

Flexible scheduling: a technique for organizing time more effectively to meet the needs of instruction by dividing the school day into uniform time modules which can be combined to fit the task.

Foundation program: program for distribution of financial support designed to guarantee a specified minimum level of educational opportunity for each child.

Group dynamics: a branch of social psychology concerned with the interaction and psychological relationships of members of a group, particularly with relation to the development of common perceptions through the sharing of emotions and experiences.

Handicapped learner: one who is mentally retarded, hard of hearing, deaf, speech-impaired, visually handicapped, seriously disturbed emotionally, crippled, or otherwise health-impaired.

Head Start programs: pre-elementary school programs designed to provide enriched learning opportunity usually for disadvantaged children so that their educational disadvantage in later years is reduced.

Heterogeneous grouping: the classification of pupils by age or grade for the purpose of instruction without regard to similarity in other criteria.

Homogeneous grouping: the classification of pupils for the purpose of forming instructional groups having a relatively high degree of similarity in regard to certain factors that affect learning.

House plan: an arrangement by which attendance units are divided into component "houses" to retain a climate of homogeneity, flexibility, or semiautonomy within each of the houses.

Humanism: a philosophical view that emphasizes the dignity and interests of human beings and the importance of man in relation to the cosmic world.

Idealism: a doctrine holding that all knowledge is derived from ideas and emphasizing moral and spiritual reality as a preeminent source of explanation.

Independent school: a nonpublic school unaffiliated with any church or other agency.

Individualized instruction: instruction that is particularized to the interests, needs, and achievements of individual learners.

Individually guided education (IGE): a system to raise achievement levels of children through individualized instruction in a multiunit school.

Individually prescribed instruction (IPI): individualized instruction in a systematic, step-by-step program based on carefully selected sequences and detailed listing of behaviorally stated instructional objectives.

In-service education: efforts of administrative and supervisory officials to promote the professional growth and development of educational workers through such means as curriculum study, supervisory assistance, and workshops.

Instructional materials center (IMC): an area where students can withdraw books, newspapers, pamphlets, and magazines and have access to sound tapes, slides, and films; spaces are usually provided for the learner to use these materials.

Instructional technology: the application of scientific method and knowledge to teaching and learning either with or without machines but commonly responsive to the learning needs of individual students.

Instructional television (ITV): lessons telecast specifically for educational institutions and received usually only by special arrangements and on special equipment.

Integration: the process of mixing students of different races in schools to overcome *de facto* segregation. (See also *Desegregation*.)

Intelligence quotient (IQ): the most commonly used device for expressing level of mental development in relation to chronological age, obtained by dividing the mental age (as measured by a general intelligence test) by the chronological age and multiplying by 100.

Intercultural education: modifications in attitudes and conduct designed to bring people to accept others for what they are, or can become, and to value the rich and varied contributions of all cultures in the totality of a world community.

Intermediate school: used synonymously with *middle school.*

Intermediate unit: (1) a division of the elementary school comprising grades 4, 5, and 6; (2) a level of school organization between the state and the local district, often but not necessarily coterminous with the county.

International education: the study of educational, social, political, and economic forces in international relations with special emphasis on the role and potentialities of educational forces; also includes programs to further the development of nations.

Internship: paid service in preparation for a position as teacher or educational specialist, usually under the joint supervision of a university and an experienced teacher or specialist in the field, and correlated with graduate study.

Laboratory school: a school that is under the control of, or closely associated with, a teacher-preparation institution, whose facilities may be used for demonstration, experimentation, and practice teaching.

Land-grant college: a college maintained to carry out the purposes of the first Morrill Act of 1862 and supplementary legislation granting public lands to states for the establishment of colleges that provide practical education, such as agriculture and mechanic arts.

Learning disability: an educationally significant discrepancy between a child's apparent capacity for language behavior and his or her actual level of language functioning.

Learning resources center: a specially designed space containing a wide range of supplies and equipment for the use of individual students and small groups pursuing independent study.

Liberal arts college: an institution of higher learning with a four-year curriculum emphasizing broad, general education rather than technical or vocational training.

Life-adjustment education: learning designed to equip youths to live democratically with satisfaction to themselves and profit to society as homemakers, workers, and citizens; having special but not exclusive importance for pupils uninterested in academic or college preparatory curriculums.

Mainstreaming: a plan by which exceptional children receive special education in the regular classroom as much of the time as possible.

Mastery learning: an educational practice in which an individual masters one task before moving to the next.

Mental retardation: below-average intellectual functioning.

Mentally handicapped student: a student whose mental powers lack maturity or are deficient in such measure as to be a hindrance to normal achievement.

Merit rating: an evaluation of the effectiveness of a teacher or other educator based upon a scale of criteria and frequently used for determining salary differentials.

Microteaching: a type of teacher training in which a small group, consisting of teachers, students, and a supervisor, evaluates a brief, discrete teaching task, usually with the help of videotape, to improve teaching method.

Middle school: a type of two- to four-year school organization containing various combinations of the middle grades, commonly grades 5 to 8, and serving as an intermediate unit between the elementary school and the high school.

Minicourse: a short, self-contained instructional sequence.

Modular scheduling: arrangement of class periods in units of 15, 20, 30, or 40 minutes to permit greater flexibility, sometimes spoken of as *flexible scheduling.*

Multiunit school: a form of ungraded organization used to implement Individually Guided Education.

National assessment: a massive national testing program which helps ascertain the effectiveness of American education and how well it is retained.

Naturalism: a philosophic view that the whole of reality is natural rather than supernatural, emphasizing educational adaptation to the natural developmental stages of the individual.

Neurologically impaired learner: a person with an impairment of the central nervous system.

Nongraded school: a type of school organization in which grade lines are eliminated for a sequence of two or more years.

Nursery school: a school that offers valuable supervised educational experiences for prekindergarten children, giving them opportunities to express themselves and develop relationships within their peer groups.

Ombudsman: a personnel officer who helps students, faculty, and other employees to resolve grievances, cut through red tape, detect patterns of complaints, and recommend desirable changes.

Open admission: a policy of some colleges and universities of accepting any candidate who presents a high school diploma or equivalency certificate; nonselective admission instituted in some cases to make higher education more accessible to students of minority groups.

Open education: a learning environment where exploration of and learning about oneself and the world are emphasized through self-directed and small-group activities, with the teacher serving as resource person and facilitator of learning.

Open enrollment: the practice of allowing students to attend the school of their choice within their school district.

Open university: a university or college from which students of all ages may attain a degree by completing work at home, by correspondence, by television, by attending classes, and then by appearing for examinations in areas of knowledge when they are ready.

Orthopedic student: a student crippled or otherwise affected by disease or malformation of the bones, joints, or muscles.

Paracurriculum: the part of an education made up of out-of-school experiences.

Paraprofessional: a lay person who assists the teacher with limited, quasi-professional tasks, such as correcting papers and tutoring; the term is sometimes also used to include teacher aides.

Parochiaid: public funds granted to aid parents of students attending parochial schools.

Parochial school: a school conducted by a church or religious group, usually without direct tax support.

Performance-based education: learning designed to produce actual accomplishment as distinguished from knowing.

Performance contract: an agreement between schools and commercial educational agencies or teachers which guarantees to produce specified educational results.

Planning-Programming-Budgeting System (PPBS): an application of systems analysis to the allocation of resources to various competing educational purposes and needs through systematic planning, programming, budgeting, and evaluation.

Pragmatism: a philosophic view according to which the value and truth of ideas are tested by their practical consequences.

Primary unit: ungraded primary school or a building housing the primary grades.

Professional education: the total formal preparation that a person completes in a professional school, usually including the aggregate of his or her professional experience.

Professional school: an institution of higher learning or a division of a university that educates persons for the practice of a profession.

Programmed instruction (also *programmed learning*): subject matter arranged in carefully planned sequences or frames using cues or prompts to elicit responses and providing immediate confirmation of validity or error of the response.

Progressive education: an educational movement emphasizing democracy, the importance of purposeful and creative activity, the real-life needs of students, and closer relationship between school and community.

Proprietary education: programs conducted for profit and serving the educational needs of business and industry, professional training, or social and cultural needs.

Psychomotor learning: the acquisition of muscular development directly related to mental processes.

Reconstructionism: a philosophic view which holds that the primary function of education is the reconstruction of civilization through active participation of the school in the improvement of society.

Reorganization, school district: the act of legally changing the designation of a school district; changing the geographical areas of a school district or incorporating a part or all of a school district with an adjoining district.

Responsive environment: a learning center, usually well supported by educational technology, which permits learners to explore freely, to receive immediate feedback in response to inquiries, and to discover knowledge on their own initiative and at their own pace.

Revenue sharing: distribution of federal money to state and local governments to use as they wish.

School without walls: a type of alternative education that stresses the total community as a learning environment.

Segregation academy: a type of private school that functions primarily to educate students whose parents object to desegregation in public schools.

Self-contained classroom: a form of classroom organization in which the same teacher conducts all or nearly all the instruction in all or most subjects in the same classroom for all or most of the school day.

Self-instructional device: a term used to include instructional materials that can be used by the student to induce learning without necessarily requiring additional human instructional assistance, including computers, programmed textbooks, and other devices.

Shared time: a cooperative arrangement among public and nonpublic schools in which the former offer instruction in non-value-oriented subjects to all pupils and the latter offer instruction in value-oriented subjects to their own pupils.

Simulation: a rather elaborate kind of role playing in which students take part in recreated real-life situations.

Socially handicapped pupil: one whose personality disturbances are severe enough to interfere seriously with one's interpersonal relations.

Special education: the instruction of students who deviate so far physically, mentally, emotionally, or socially from so-called "normal students" that the standard curriculum and school environment are not suitable for their needs.

Special-purpose aid: synonymous with *categorical aid.*

Street academies: makeshift educational centers, usually operated by industries or neighborhood agencies, outside of regular school buildings to provide open education for students who reject more formal schooling.

Subject-discipline curriculum: an organization of learning activities and content around the intellectual disciplines of the subjects—their essential themes, principles, structures, concepts, and modes of inquiry.

Subject-field education: that part of the teacher education program in which students are provided instruction in the subjects that they plan to teach.

Subject-matter curriculum: a curriculum organization in which learning activities and content are planned around subject fields of knowledge, such as history and science.

Supernaturalism: a doctrine which holds that there is a divine source of truth that transcends nature; when applied to education, this doctrine holds that it is the essential function of the school to teach divinely revealed truth.

Systems analysis: a rational and systematic approach to education, which analyzes objectives, then decides which resources and methods will achieve those objectives most efficiently; each step is carefully measured, tested, and controlled to make sure it moves toward the next objective.

Talking typewriter: a typewriter programmed with sound to teach children the elements of reading and writing.

Teacher aide: a lay person who assists teachers with clerical work, library duties, housekeeping duties, noninstructional supervision, and other nonprofessional tasks.

Teacher center: combination library, workshop, and laboratory with rich resources to help teachers solve problems and grow professionally.

Teacher Corps: a federally funded program that gives teachers and student teachers opportunities to work with disadvantaged children in their homes and communities while attending courses and seminars on the special problems they encounter.

Teaching center: a school district selected as one of a few by a school of teacher education as a training site for student teachers and for trying out new educational techniques.

Teaching unit: the plan developed with respect to an individual classroom by a teacher to guide the instruction of a unit of work to be carried out by a particular group of learners.

Team teaching: a term applied loosely to a wide variety of collaborative activity in teaching, involving a group of teachers who are jointly responsible for planning, carrying out, and evaluating an educational program for a group of children.

Tenure: a system of school employment in which educators, having served a probationary period, retain their positions indefinitely unless dismissed for legally specified reasons through clearly established procedures.

Terminal education: a level of education not usually followed by a higher one.

Trainable pupil: one who is incapable of achieving significant proficiency in academic skills but who may be trained to attain a limited degree of social acceptance and ability to care for oneself, and perhaps even some measure of self-sufficiency.

Ungraded school: synonymous with *nongraded school*.

Unit of learning: a series of organized ideas and activities planned to provide worthwhile experiences for an individual or group and expected to result in a desired outcome.

Voucher plan: a means of financing schooling whereby funds are allocated to students' parents who then purchase education for their children in any public or private school.

Work-study program: program that combines part-time classroom study with gainful employment in industry or in the community.

Appendix

American Federation of Teachers

Bill of Rights

THE TEACHER IS ENTITLED TO A LIFE OF DIGNITY EQUAL TO THE HIGH STANDARD OF SERVICE THAT IS JUSTLY DEMANDED OF THAT PROFESSION. THEREFORE, WE HOLD THESE TRUTHS TO BE SELF-EVIDENT:

I
Teachers have the right to think freely and to express themselves openly and without fear. This includes the right to hold these views contrary to the majority.

II
They shall be entitled to the free exercise of their religion. No restraint shall be put upon them in the manner, time or place of their worship.

III
They shall have the right to take part in social, civil, and political affairs. They shall have the right, outside the classroom, to participate in political campaigns and to hold office. They may assemble peaceably and may petition any government agency, including their employers, for a redress of grievances. They shall have the same freedom in all things as other citizens.

IV
The right of teachers to live in places of their own choosing, to be free of restraints in their mode of living and the use of their leisure time shall not be abridged.

V
Teaching is a profession, the right to practice which is not subject to the surrender of other human rights. No one shall be deprived of professional status, or the right to practice it, or the practice thereof in any particular position, without due process of law.

VI
The right of teachers to be secure in their jobs, free from political influence or public clamor, shall be established by law. The right to teach after qualification in the manner prescribed by law, is a property right, based upon the inalienable rights to life, liberty, and the pursuit of happiness.

VII
In all cases affecting the teacher's employment or professional status a full hearing by an impartial tribunal shall be afforded with the right to full judicial review. No teacher shall be deprived of employment or professional status but for specific causes established by law having a clear relation to the competence or qualification to teach, proved by the weight of the evidence. In all such cases the teacher shall enjoy the right to a speedy and public trial, to be informed of the nature and cause of the accusation; to be confronted with the accusing witnesses, to subpoena witnesses and papers, and to the assistance of counsel. No teacher shall be called upon to answer any charge affecting his employment or professional status but upon probable cause, supported by oath or affirmation.

VIII
It shall be the duty of the employer to provide culturally adequate salaries, security in illness and adequate retirement income. The teacher has the right to such a salary as will: a) Afford a family standard of living comparable to that enjoyed by other professional people in the community; b) To make possible freely chosen professional study; c) Afford the opportunity for leisure and recreation common to our heritage.

IX
Teachers shall not be required under penalty or reduction of salary to pursue studies beyond those required to obtain professional status. After serving a reasonable probationary period a teacher shall be entitled to permanent tenure terminable only for just cause. They shall be free as in other professions in the use of their own time. They shall not be required to perform extracurricular work against their will or without added compensation.

X
To equip people for modern life requires the most advanced educational methods. Therefore, the teacher is entitled to good classrooms, adequate teaching materials, teachable class size and administrative protection and assistance in maintaining discipline.

XI
These rights are based upon the proposition that the culture of a people can rise only as its teachers improve. A teaching force accorded the highest possible professional dignity is the surest guarantee that blessings of liberty will be preserved. Therefore, the possession of these rights impose the challenge to be worthy of their enjoyment.

XII
Since teachers must be free in order to teach freedom, the right to be members of organizations of their own choosing must be guaranteed. In all matters pertaining to their salaries and working conditions they shall be entitled to bargain collectively through representatives of their own choosing. They are entitled to have the schools administered by superintendents, boards or committees which function in a democratic manner.

Code of Ethics of the Education Profession

Preamble

The educator, believing in the worth and dignity of each human being, recognizes the supreme importance of the pursuit of truth, devotion to excellence, and the nurture of democratic principles. Essential to these goals is the protection of freedom to learn and to teach and the guarantee of equal educational opportunity for all. The educator accepts the responsibility to adhere to the highest ethical standards.

The educator recognizes the magnitude of the responsibility inherent in the teaching process. The desire for the respect and confidence of one's colleagues, of students, of parents and of the members of the community provides the incentive to attain and maintain the highest possible degree of ethical conduct. The Code of Ethics of the Education Profession indicates the aspiration of all educators and provides standards by which to judge conduct.

The remedies specified by the NEA and/or its affiliates for the violation of any provision of this Code shall be exclusive, and no such provision shall be enforceable in any form other than one specifically designated by the NEA or its affiliates.

Principle I
Commitment to the Student

The educator strives to help each student realize his or her potential as a worthy and effective member of society. The educator therefore works to stimulate the spirit of inquiry, the acquisition of knowledge and understanding, and the thoughtful formulation of worthy goals.

In fulfillment of the obligation to the student, the educator—

1. Shall not unreasonably restrain the student from independent action in the pursuit of learning.
2. Shall not unreasonably deny the student access to varying points of view.
3. Shall not deliberately suppress or distort subject matter relevant to the student's progress.

4. Shall make reasonable effort to protect the student from conditions harmful to learning or to health and safety.
5. Shall not intentionally expose the student to embarrassment or disparagement.
6. Shall not on the basis of race, color, creed, sex, national origin, marital status, political or religious beliefs, family, social or cultural background, or sexual orientation unfairly:
a. Exclude any student from participation in any program;
b. Deny benefits to any student;
c. Grant any advantage to any student.
7. Shall not use professional relationships with students for private advantage.
8. Shall not disclose information about students obtained in the course of professional service, unless disclosure serves a compelling professional purpose or is required by law.

Principle II
Commitment to the Profession

The education profession is vested by the public with a trust and responsibility requiring the highest ideals of professional service.

In the belief that the quality of the services of the education profession directly influences the nation and its citizens, the educator shall exert every effort to raise professional standards, to promote a climate that encourages the exercise of professional judgment, to achieve conditions which attract persons worthy of the trust to careers in education, and to assist in preventing the practice of the profession by unqualified persons.

In fulfillment of the obligation to the profession, the educator—

1. Shall not in an application for a professional position deliberately make a false statement or fail to disclose a material fact related to competency and qualifications.
2. Shall not misrepresent his/her professional qualifications.
3. Shall not assist entry into the profession of a

Adopted by the National Education Association Representative Assembly, July 1975. Reprinted by permission of the National Education Association.

person known to be unqualified in respect to character, education, or other relevant attribute.

4. Shall not knowingly make a false statement concerning the qualifications of a candidate for a professional position.

5. Shall not assist a non-educator in the unauthorized practice of teaching.

6. Shall not disclose information about colleagues obtained in the course of professional service unless disclosure serves a compelling professional purpose or is required by law.

7. Shall not knowingly make false or malicious statements about a colleague.

8. Shall not accept any gratuity, gift, or favor that might impair or appear to influence professional decisions or actions.

Index

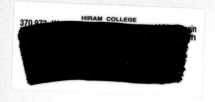